The Law in Context Series

Editors: William Twining (University College London) and Christopher McCrudden (Lincoln College, Oxford)

Since 1970 the Law in Context series has been in the forefront of the movement to broaden the study of law. It has been a vehicle for the publication of innovative scholarly books that treat law and legal phenomena critically in their social, political and economic contexts from a variety of perspectives. The series particularly aims to publish scholarly legal writing that brings fresh perspectives to bear on new and existing areas of law taught in universities. A contextual approach involves treating legal subjects broadly, using materials from other social sciences, and from any other discipline that helps to explain the operation in practice of the subject under discussion. It is hoped that this orientation is at once more stimulating and more realistic than the bare exposition of legal rules. The series includes original books that have a different emphasis from traditional legal textbooks, while maintaining the same high standards of scholarship. They are written primarily for undergraduate and graduate students of law and of other disciplines, but most also appeal to a wider readership. In the past, most books in the series have focused on English law, but recent publications include books on European law, globalisation, transnational legal processes, and comparative law.

Books in the Series

Anderson, Schum & Twining: *Analysis of Evidence*
Ashworth: *Sentencing and Criminal Justice*
Barton & Douglas: *Law and Parenthood*
Bell: *French Legal Cultures*
Bercusson: *European Labour Law*
Birkinshaw: *European Public Law*
Birkinshaw: *Freedom of Information: The Law, the Practice and the Ideal*
Cane: *Atiyah's Accidents, Compensation and the Law*
Clarke & Kohler: *Property Law: Commentary and Materials*
Collins: *The Law of Contract*
Davies: *Perspectives on Labour Law*
de Sousa Santos: *Toward a New Legal Common Sense*
Diduck: *Law's Families and Others: Nationality and Immigration Law*
Elworthy & Holder: *Environmental Protection: Text and Materials*
Fortin: *Children's Rights and the Developing Law*
Glover Thomas: *Reconstructing Mental Health Law and Policy*
Gobert & Punch: *Rethinking Corporate Crime*
Harlow & Rawlings: *Law and Administration: Text and Materials*
Harris: *An Introduction to Law*
Harris: *Remedies, Contract and Tort*
Harvey: *Seeking Asylum in the UK: Problems and Prospects*
Hervey & McHale: *Health Law and the European Union*
Lacey & Wells: *Reconstructing Criminal Law*
Lewis: *Choice and the Legal Order: Rising above Politics*
Likosky: *Transnational Legal Processes*
Maughan & Webb: *Lawyering Skills and the Legal Process*
Moffat: *Trusts Law: Text and Materials*
Norrie: *Crime, Reason and History*
O'Dair: *Legal Ethics*
Oliver: *Common Values and the Public-Private Divide*
Oliver & Drewry: *The Law and Parliament*
Picciotto: *International Business Taxation*
Reed: *Internet Law: Text and Materials*

Dispute Proces
ADR and the Pri

ONE WEEK LOAN

Th   –
neg   s-
cou   :h
cor   n,
are   )-
luti   is
mu   nt
and

                                                           1g
wit   a
sele   s-
pul   of
har   )-
tiat   al
to   es
and   of
pro

Sir   1d
Pol   1e
em

Mi   at
the   er
of l

Dispute Processes

ADR and the Primary Forms of Decision-Making

Second Edition

Simon Roberts & Michael Palmer

CAMBRIDGE UNIVERSITY PRESS
Cambridge, New York, Melbourne, Madrid, Cape Town, Singapore, São Paulo, Delhi

Cambridge University Press
The Edinburgh Building, Cambridge CB2 8RU, UK

Published in the United States of America by Cambridge University Press, New York

www.cambridge.org
Information on this title: www.cambridge.org/9780521676014

First published 2005
Reprinted 2008

A catalogue record for this publication is available from the British Library

ISBN 978-0-521-67601-4 paperback

Transferred to digital printing 2009

For Marian and Mingwo

Contents

Preface

This book has grown out of more than a decade of teaching Alternative Dispute Resolution (ADR) for postgraduate students in law at the University of London, as well as many years of research and writing in this field by both of us. The approach taken in assembling the text and materials is intentionally wide-ranging and comparative – indeed, more so than in the first edition – so that it can be read not only in its own right but also as a broader, contextualising companion to more conventional and jurisdiction-specific ADR texts. The present study is also informed by the view that adversarial litigation can no longer be seen as the paradigmatic process of decision-making in our civil justice system. Looking first at the sources of ADR ideas and the debates which have surrounded the rise of alternative approaches to dispute resolution, we then move on to examine the primary forms of decision-making: negotiation, mediation and umpiring. This is followed by an exploration of the emergence in contemporary Anglo-American practice of the fusions of the foundational modes of decision-making that are generally referred to as hybrid or mixed processes.

In putting together this book, we have been given generous help by others. First, we would like to acknowledge the inspiration we have derived from Hilary Astor and Christine Chinkin's pioneering book *Dispute Resolution in Australia* (1992; 2nd edn, 2002). Beyond that, William Twining persuaded us to write it in the first place, and has throughout remained a source of wise counsel. Marian Roberts, has helped not only by teaching family disputes for our students but also by providing consistent support and excellent advice. Kiran Kothari has been a most helpful and efficient research assistant. Last, but by no means least, there are the many students who gave enthusiastic and critical responses to our first edition, and whose observations have helped to make the second edition a better book.

Simon Roberts and Michael Palmer
London
April 2005

Acknowledgements

The authors wish to express their thanks to the following authors, periodicals and publishers for permission to use the relevant materials from their publications.

Every effort has been made to trace all the copyright holders, but if any have been inadvertently overlooked we will be pleased to make the necessary arrangement at the first opportunity.

J S Auerbach: *Justice Without Law? Resolving Disputes Without Lawyers* (1983) Oxford University Press, Oxford, pp 19–21, 96–97, 57–59, 131–135. Reprinted by permission of Oxford University Press.

D Bok: 'A Flawed System of Law and Practice Training' (1983) 33 *Journal of Legal Education* 570, pp 582–583. Reprinted with permission.

W Brazil: 'Special Masters in Complex Cases: Extending the Judiciary or Reshaping Adjudication?' (1990) 53 *University of Chicago Law Review* 394, pp 407–409.

R J Broderick: 'Court-annexed Compulsory Arbitration: It Works' (1989) 72 *Judicature* 4, 217, pp 219–222. Reprinted with permission.

R A B Bush: 'Efficiency and Protection, or Empowerment and Recognition?: The Mediator's Role and Ethical Standards in Mediation' (1989) 41 *Florida Law Review* 253, pp 266–270, 281–282.

R A B Bush and J P Folger: *The Promise of Mediation: Responding to Conflict Through Empowerment and Recognition* (1994) Jossey-Bass, San Francisco, pp 81–85.

M Cappelletti and B G Garth: *Access to Justice, Volume 1: A World Survey* (1978) Sijthoff & Noordhoff, Milan, pp 6–9.

G Chornenki: 'Mediating Commercial Disputes: Exchanging "Power Over" for "Power With" ', in J Macfarlane (ed) *Rethinking Disputes: The Mediation Alternative* (1997) Cavendish Publishing, London, 159, pp 163–168.

Sanford D Cole: 'English Borough Courts' (1902) 18 *Law Quarterly Review* 376, pp 380–382.

T Colosi: 'Negotiation in the Public and Private Sectors' (1983) 27 (2) *American Behavioural Scientist* 229, pp 229–230, 241–243.

J L Comaroff and S Roberts: *Rules and Processes* (1981) University of Chicago Press, Chicago, pp 108–110.

M R Damaska: *The Faces of Justice and State Authority* (1986) Yale University Press, New Haven and London, pp 32–38, 48–50, 58–60.

Boaventura De Sousa Santos: 'Law and Democracy: (Mis)trusting the Global Reform of Courts', in Jane Jenson and Boaventura De Sousa Santos (eds) *Globalizing Institutions: Case Studies in Regulation and Innovation* (2000) Aldershot, Ashgate, pp 253–255, 279–280. © Ashgate. Reprinted with permission.

Y Dezalay and B Garth: *Dealing in Virtue: International Commercial Arbitration and the Construction of a Transnational Legal Order* (1996) University of Chicago Press, Chicago and London, pp 311–317.

C Dickens: *Bleak House* (1994, originally 1852–1853) Harmondsworth, Middlesex, Penguin Books, pp 2–3.

Leigh-wai Doo: 'Dispute Settlement in Chinese-American Communities' (1973) 21 *American Journal of Comparative Law* 627, at pp 652–654.

G T Eisele: 'The Case Against Court-annexed ADR Programs' (1991) 75 *Judicature* 1, 34, pp 35–37. Reprinted with permission.

D C Elliot: 'Med/arb: Fraught with Danger or Ripe with Opportunity' (1996) 62 *Arbitration* 3, 175, pp 175–177.

W L F Felstiner: 'Influences of Social Organization on Dispute Processing' (1974–1975) 9 *Law and Society Review* 63, pp 79–80.

W Felstiner, R Abel and A Sarat: 'The Emergence and Transformation of Disputes: Naming, Blaming, Claiming . . .' (1980–1981) 15 *Law and Society Review* 631, pp 634–637.

O M Fiss: 'Against Settlement' (1984) 93 *Yale Law Journal* 1073, pp 1085–1086.

O M Fiss: 'Out of Eden' (1985) 94 *Yale Law Journal*, p 1669.

L Fuller: 'Collective Bargaining and the Arbitrator' (1963) 18 *Wisconsin Law Review* 3, pp 3–6, 39–42.

M Galanter: 'The Emergence of the Judge as a Mediator in Civil Cases' (1986) 69 *Judicature* 5, 257, pp 257, 261–262. Reprinted with permission.

M Galanter: ' " . . . A Settlement Judge is not a Trial Judge": Judicial Mediation in the United States' (1985) 12 *Journal of Law and Society* 1, 1, pp 12–15.

D Gifford: 'A Context-Based Theory of Selection Strategy in Legal Negotiations' (1985) 46 *Ohio State Law Journal* 41, pp 54–58.

S B Goldberg: 'The Mediation of Grievances Under a Collective Bargaining Contract: An Alternative to Arbitration' (1982) 77 *Northwestern University Law Review* 270, pp 281–284.

S B Goldberg, F E A Sander and N H Rodgers (eds) *Dispute Resolution: Negotiation, Mediation and Other Processes*, 2nd edn (1992) Little, Brown & Co, Boston, Toronto and London, pp 225–226.

L E Graham: 'Implementing Custody Mediation in Family Courts: Some Comments on the Jefferson County Family Court Experience' (1992–1993) 81 *Kentucky Law Journal* 1107, pp 1112–1116, 1120–1124.

Carol J Greenhouse: *Praying for Justice: Faith, Order, and Community in an American Town* (1986) Cornell University Press, Ithaca, New York, pp 108, 109, 110, 115,

116, 117 and 118. Used by permission of the publisher, Cornell University Press.

T Grillo: 'The Mediation Alternative – Process Dangers for Woman' (1991) 100 *Yale Law Journal* 1545, pp 1605–1610.

C Harlow and R Rawlings: *Law and Administration*, 2nd edn (1997) Butterworths, London, pp 401–404.

J M Haynes: 'Mediation and Therapy: An Alternative View' (1992) 10 *Mediation Quarterly* 21, pp 22–24.

J M Kelly: *Roman Litigation* (1966) Clarendon Press, Oxford, pp 21–23, 132, 147, 148, and 150. Reprinted by permission of Oxford University Press.

J B Kelly and M A Duyree: 'Women's and Men's Views of Mediation in Voluntary and Mandatory Mediation Settings' (1995) 30 *Family and Conciliation Courts Review* 1, 35, pp 37, 41–42, 45.

A S Kim: 'Rent-a-Judge and the Cost of Selling Justice' (1994) 44 *Duke Law Journal* 166, pp 166–167, 189–195, 199.

Kimberlee K Kovach and Lela P Love: 'Mapping Mediation: The Risks of Riskin's Grid' (1998) 3 *Harvard Negotiation Law Review* 71, at 71–75.

Herbert Kritzer: 'Adjudication to Settlement: Shading in the Grey' (1986) 70 (3) *Judicature* 161, pp 161–165. Reprinted with permission.

T D Lambros: 'The Summary Trial: An Effective Aid to Settlement' (1993) 77 *Judicature* 1, 6, pp 6–8. Reprinted with permission.

J K Lieberman and J F Henry: 'Lessons from the Alternative Dispute Resolution Movement' (1986) 53 *University of Chicago Law Review* 424, pp 427–428.

G T Lowenthal: 'A General Theory of Negotiation Process, Strategy, and Behaviour' (1982–1983) 31 *Kansas Law Review* 69, pp 74–75, 112–114.

S Lubman: 'Judicial Work in T'aihang' (1973) 6 *Chinese Law and Government* 3, 7, at pp 12–17. English translation copyright © 1973, by M E Sharpe, Inc. Reprinted with permission.

S Lubman: 'Mao and Mediation: Politics and Dispute Resolution in Communist China' (1967) 55 *California Law Review* 1284–1359, pp 1285–1286, 1287, 1358.

C A McEwen and R J Maiman: 'Small Claims Mediation in Maine: An Empirical Assessment' (1981) 33 *Maine Law Review* 237, pp 260–264.

A W McThenia and T L Shaffer: 'For Reconciliation' (1985) 94 *Yale Law Journal* 1660, pp 1662–1665.

C Menkel-Meadow: 'Is Mediation the Practice of Law?' (1996) 14 *Alternatives to the High Costs of Litigation* 5, 57, pp 57, 60–61.

S E Merry and N Milner (eds) *The Possibility of Popular Justice: A Case Study of Community Mediation in the United States* (1993) University of Michigan Press, Ann Arbor, pp 10–15.

C Morris: 'The Trusted Mediator: Ethics and Interaction in Mediation' in Julie Macfarlane (ed) *Rethinking Disputes: The Mediation Alternative* (1997) Cavendish Publishing, London, 301, pp 307–308.

P Newman: 'Mediation-Arbitration (MedArb): Can it Work Legally?' (1994) 60 *Arbitration* 3, 173, pp 174–176.

M Palmer: 'The Revival of Mediation in the People's Republic of China: (1) Extra-judicial mediation', in W E Butler (ed) *Yearbook on Socialist Legal Systems 1987*, Transnational Books, New York, Dobbs Ferry, pp 244–252, 265–271. Reprinted with permission.

R Posner: 'The Summary Jury Trial and Other Methods of Alternative Dispute Resolution: Some Cautionary Observations' (1986) 53 *University of Chicago Law Review* 366, pp 387–389.

R A Rappaport: *Pigs for the Ancestors: Ritual in the Ecology of a New Guinea People* (1967) Yale University Press, New Haven and London, pp 119, 121–123, 138–139.

L L Riskin: 'Mediator Orientations, Strategies and Techniques' (1994) 12 (9) *Alternatives* 111, pp 111–113.

M Roberts: *Mediation in Family Disputes: Principles of Practice*, 2nd edn (1997) Ashgate, Aldershot, pp 133–135. © Ashgate. Reprinted with permission.

Marian Roberts: 'Family Mediation: The Development of the Regulatory Framework in the United Kingdom' (2005) 22 *Conflict Resolution Quarterly* 4.

Marian Roberts: 'Systems or Selves: Some Ethical Issues in Family Mediation' (1992) 10 *Mediation Quarterly* 3, pp 4–10.

S Roberts: 'Mediation in Family Disputes' (1983) 46 *Modern Law Review* 537, pp 555–556.

J D Rosenberg and H J Folberg: 'Alternative Dispute Resolution: An Empirical Analysis' (1994) 46 *Stanford Law Review* 1487, pp 1495–1496.

A Sachs: 'Changing the Terms of the Debate: A Visit to a Popular Tribunal in Mozambique' (1984) 28 *Journal of African Law* 99, pp 101–104.

F E A Sander: 'Alternative Dispute Resolution in the United States: An Overview', in American Bar Association (ed) *Justice for a Generation* (1985) West Publishing Company, St Paul, Minnesota, pp 260–261.

F E A Sander: 'Alternative Methods of Dispute Resolution: An Overview' (1985) 37 *University of Florida Law Review* 1, pp 11–13.

F E A Sander: 'Varieties of Dispute Processing' (1976) 70 *Federal Rules Decisions* 79, pp 126–127, 130–132.

Jeremy Sarkin: 'The Tension Between Justice and Reconciliation in Rwanda: Politics, Human Rights, Due Process and the role of the Gacaca Courts in Dealing with Genocide' (2001) 45 *Journal of African Law* 2, 143, pp 157–159.

Sonia Nourin Shah-Kazemi: 'Cross-cultural Mediation: A Critical View of the Dynamics of Culture in Family Disputes' (2000) 14 *International Journal of Law, Policy and the Family*, pp 302–325.

M Shapiro: *Courts: A Comparative and Political Analysis* (1981) University of Chicago Press, Chicago and London, pp 8–11, 20, 22–24, 49–52, 54.

L Silberman: 'Judicial Adjuncts Revisited: The Proliferation of Ad Hoc Procedure' (1989) 137 *University of Pennsylvania Law Review* 2131, pp 2134–2137, 2143–2145, 2158–2161.

G Simmel: *The Sociology of Georg Simmel*, edited by K Wolff (1950, originally 1908) Free Press, Glencoe, Illinois, pp 146–151.

J M Spencer and J P Zammit: 'Mediation-Arbitration: A Proposal for Private Resolution of Disputes between Divorced or Separated Parents' (1976) *Duke Law Journal* 911, pp 932–938.

B E Stedman: 'Multi-option Justice at the Middlesex Multi-Door Courthouse', in R Smith (ed) *Achieving Civil Justice: Appropriate Dispute Resolution for the 1990s* (1996) Legal Action Group, London, pp 119–127, 133–135, 137–140. Reprinted with permission.

R C Van Caenegem: *The Birth of the English Common Law* (1988) Cambridge University Press, Cambridge, pp 18–23.

Sybille Van der Sprenkel: *Legal Institutions in Manchu China* (1962) Athlone Press, London, pp 92–94.

Katherine Van Wezel Stone: 'Dispute Resolution in the Boundaryless Workplace' (2000–2001) 16 *Ohio State Journal of Dispute Resolution* 467, at pp 468–471.

P R Verkuil: 'The Ombudsman and the Limits of the Adversary System' (1975) 75 *Columbia Law Review* 845, pp 847, 851–856.

J J White: 'Machiavelli and the Ethical Limitations on Lying in Negotiation' (1980) *American Bar Foundation Research Journal* 926, pp 928–931.

S A Wiegand: 'A Just and Lasting Peace: Supplanting Mediation with the Ombuds Model' (1996) 12 *Ohio State Journal on Dispute Resolution* 1, 95, pp 100–102, 120–122.

Lord Woolf: *Access to Justice: Final Report to the Lord Chancellor on the Civil Justice System of England and Wales* (1996) HMSO, London, Ch 1, paras 1–17.

Lord Woolf: *Access to Justice: Interim Report to the Lord Chancellor on the Civil Justice System of England and Wales* (1995) HMSO, London, Ch 3, paras 3–11, 30–39; Ch 4, paras 1–4, 7–12; Ch 5, paras 2–6, 16–17; Ch 18, paras 1–4.

CHAPTER ONE

Introduction

'. . . impressed with command, we see little else.'

C Geertz *Negara* (1982: 121)

'. . . there probably exists no social unit in which convergent and divergent currents among its members are not inseparably interwoven.'

G Simmel *Der Streit* (1908: trs 1955: 15)

Prologue

Across the world, there are disagreements between neighbours, family members, affines, colleagues and others. The manner in which quarrel situations are characterised, and the ways in which the particular modes of response are regarded, varies from society to society – indeed, also from group to group within any given society. The nature of disputes, the appropriate responses to disputing situations, and the remedies considered proper are inevitably informed by fundamental social values and even cultural identity. This is the starting point for the examination of dispute processes provided in this book below, which also locates current enthusiasms for 'alternative' modes of resolving disputes – especially those found in the United Sates and other parts of the Anglo-American common law world – in a wider comparative framework.

A: Shifting Ground in the Common Law World

Thirty years ago we could have said with reasonable confidence, in the common law world, what the principal institutions of public disputing 'were'. Over a long period, judges and lawyers had progressively become central, well-defined agents of public dispute management. The former held out the beautiful promise of an authoritative third-party decision; the latter, as both advisers and champions, presented themselves as essential companions along the arduous route of litigation.[1] With

---

1 Max Weber was perhaps not the first to recognise an extraordinary degree of reliance upon the legal profession for everyday matters in the common law world, when he noted the English layman's propensity to make his peace with the law 'by retaining once and for all a solicitor as his legal father confessor for all contingencies of life'. (Weber [1917] 1978: 891).

the increasing dominance of courts in an evolving public sphere as the nation state solidified, and the parallel emergence of lawyers as a specialised service profession, other institutionalised forms of disputing had receded in importance. For example, ordeals and duelling had ceased to be a recognised part of disputing cultures in the West. Mediation too had been elbowed aside and hidden in the background,[2] even if it was always 'there' as an irreducible element of any context in which more than two agents are involved.[3]

We should none the less be cautious as to how we present this picture of 'formal justice'. First, it is easy to exaggerate the extent to which a discrete 'public' sphere, characterised by a distinctive rationality and actively shaping a subordinate 'private' sphere, had ever historically evolved.[4] In this respect, we need to recall that the relationship of the courts to government in common law jurisdictions has always been a distinctive and ambivalent one. In England, for example, there is not now, and never has been, a career judiciary. In recent times, the higher ranks of the judges have been recruited exclusively from the legal profession, with appointment representing the ultimate career stage of the successful lawyer. While elaborate ritual, including the conferment of knighthood in the case of the higher judiciary, marks the transition from barrister to judge, and some formal distance is subsequently maintained between judges and former colleagues, judges remain socially very much part of the professional group from which they emerge. They will be 'Benchers' of their Inns and remain part of long-established networks of information exchange and support, including those centred on the chambers in which they formerly practised as advocates. These networks cross generations, beginning in the great 'public' schools, continuing in the older universities and subsequently in the London clubs (of which the Inns of Court are today in some senses a variant).[5] So the courts are perhaps just as accurately seen as the apex of the legal profession as a specialised branch of government.

A second caution must concern the manner in which civil courts have historically been employed, notably the use made of their procedural arena by lawyers. Until the 1970s the courts on the whole conceived their role quite narrowly, as one of providing trial and judgment. Pre-trial interventions were largely devoted to making sure the landscape did not change too much before trial, otherwise leaving the parties to proceed at their own pace. But while this narrow approach that common law judges traditionally took to their role may appear to draw a clear line between solutions achieved through negotiated agreement and authoritative third-party

---

2 For the way this transformation progressed in early modern France, see Castan (1983).

3 See the seminal discussion of the 'triad' in Simmel ([1908] 1950), especially p 138 et seq.

4 This point can perhaps be made particularly strongly in relation to Habermas' 'system'/'lifeworld' opposition (Habermas, 1981).

5 The pattern of 'network' recruitment also gives rise to problems of gender and ethnic underrepresentation in both the judiciary and the bar. The most sustained efforts to broaden access are to be found in the decision to allow solicitors to represent clients as advocates in the High Court, and perhaps to serve as judges. See Griffith (1997) for an exploration of the social provenance of the judiciary.

determination, this concealed something that had for generations gone on beneath the surface. Lawyers, conceptualising virtually their entire role in dispute manage-ment as 'litigation', had long used the framework provided by civil procedure as the primary arena for their attempts to 'settle'.[6] It is a common place that in English and other common law civil jurisdictions only a tiny proportion of proceedings com-menced ever reach trial, let alone judgment. So, through this clandestine use of civil process as an arena for negotiations, two apparently different modes of decision-making had long shared a single procedural route (one historically devised for the safe achievement of judgment).

Some elements of this picture were closely attended to in legal scholarship. The principal form of research in the growing number of university law schools consisted of commentary upon the decisions of superior courts.[7] Other areas, including the greater part of lawyers' contentious work – the out-of-court management of dispute processes, were virtually uncharted.[8]

At the beginning of the second half of the twentieth century this distinctive cul-ture of public disputing, under which courts treated their role as the delivery of judgment while a dominant legal profession used litigation as a vehicle for strate-gies of late settlement, appeared securely entrenched. Indeed, the growing state provision of welfare and a steady increase in rights consciousness further encour-aged reliance on litigation and the courts. But during the last three decades, the certainties represented in this apparently well-established universe were swept away right across the common law world. Over that relatively brief period, the known identities of the 'court' and the 'lawyer' were placed in question and the 'mediator' re-emerged as a major if ill-defined figure. Central strands of this transformation to an overt 'culture of settlement' have been advanced under the fugitive leitmotiv of Alternative Dispute Resolution (with its universal acronym, 'ADR').[9]

Characterising this new world and identifying the forces that have shaped it is not altogether straightforward even if at the heart of it lies a burgeoning culture and ideology of 'settlement' across the whole spectrum of dispute institutions.[10] It could almost be said that, in ideological terms, there has been a reversal of priorities as between two foundational processes, 'judgment' and 'agreement'. Of these two, the first – linked to the potent symbol of the Blind Goddess – long represented the *beau idéal* of public justice. The second, although represented in the powerful and

---

6 See Galanter (1984).   7 See Murphy and Roberts (1987).

8 Note some important exceptions: Johnstone (1967); Abel-Smith and Stevens (1967).

9 The phrase 'alternative dispute resolution' creeps into general use in the North American literature in the years around 1980, having perhaps been used first by Sander (1976).

10 'Settlement' is used here in the general sense of the search for negotiated, consensual agreement as opposed to resort to a third-party decision. The approach to settlement seeking found in practice may bear little relation to the foundational idea of consensual decision-making through a bilateral exchange. While the rhetoric of voluntary agreement is retained, settlement in the lawyer's sense can well be, perhaps is typically, the culmination of a bruising process, characterised by secrecy and suspicion, in which one party's representatives have successfully wasted the other to the point at which the latter decides reluctantly, perhaps facing the inevitable, that she or he has got to give up.

beautiful image of the handshake, never enjoyed ideological parity and was seldom even articulated as an objective of public justice.

In England, official recognition that the sponsorship of settlement was an explicit, official objective of the public justice system came only in the 1990s. Statements of this aspiration appear in the Heilbron/Hodge Report of 1993[11] and then in the Interim version of the 'Woolf' Report.[12] In the latter, judicial 'case management' is prescribed and its overall purpose identified as 'to encourage settlement of disputes at the earliest appropriate stage; and, where trial is unavoidable, to ensure that cases proceed as quickly as possible to a final hearing which is itself of strictly limited duration'.[13] Here 'settlement' is presented as the primary objective of the courts, with adjudication relegated to an auxiliary, fallback position. So 'settlement' itself becomes the preferred route to justice – an astonishing reversal.

This shifting balance between the ideologies of 'command' and 'joint decision-making' has been reflected in institutional terms through three closely linked developments. The first of these can be loosely described as the arrival of the 'new professionals' in dispute resolution. In most common law jurisdictions, specialist groups have emerged over the last two decades, in both the not-for-profit and the private sectors, offering facilitatory help with joint decision-making. The members of these groups, who generally identify themselves as 'mediators', thus provide services that compete only indirectly with lawyers.

A second strand of these developments has been represented in parallel, more or less contemporaneous initiatives within the courts to move beyond adjudicative roles to sponsorship of settlement. These initiatives, visible earliest in North America, have been driven by contradictory imperatives: both the attribution of a primary value to party decision-making and a more general ambition towards 'case management'.

Yet a third strand has subsequently become visible in responsive, defensive movements of recovery on the part of the lawyers. The arrival of the new professionals in dispute resolution, and the growing readiness of the courts to become involved in settlement processes, combined to encourage lawyers to re-examine their own practices. This process of re-examination has led lawyers both to move beyond advisory and representative roles towards non-aligned interventions, and to develop new specialist techniques in aid of their settlement strategies.

While the new professionals initially promoted mediation as promising a 'third way' between external, hierarchically imposed decision and representation by legal specialists, clear boundaries between these three strands of development did not last long. The boundaries were blurred, first, through the new professionals being drawn into association with public justice through court-sponsored mediation schemes

---

11 *Civil Justice on Trial: The Case for Change* (London: Justice, 1993).
12 *Interim Report to the Lord Chancellor on the Civil Justice System in England and Wales* (London: Lord Chancellor's Department, 1995).
13 Ibid.

and, second, through the incorporation of 'mediation' in the evolving practice of lawyers.

The heterogeneous nature of these practice developments has not prevented each of these strands laying claim to, and coming to be associated with, the shared label of 'Alternative Dispute Resolution' (ADR). As noted above, this term seems to have been used first by Professor Frank Sander in a paper to the Pound Conference in 1976 (Sander, 1976), a meeting largely attended by lawyers and judges, explicitly concerned with renovating court processes. So ADR cannot be seen as a label only associated with the movement of escape and resistance from lawyers and the courts. ADR in a narrow sense originated very much as something lawyers decided to do and judges to participate in and encourage.

The complex, interwoven nature of these developments is clearly reflected in contemporary scholarship around dispute processes. The considerable body of writing now found under the label of 'alternative dispute resolution' has been largely produced by lawyers. So this writing must by no means be read as a literature 'just' about alternatives to lawyers and courts. Indeed, it would not be an exaggeration to say that the literature of ADR has come to reside to a substantial extent within the discourse of law.[14] This literature conveys sharply the bitter struggle of different professionals to associate themselves with an emergent image supposedly attractive to client groups.

B: The Comparative Scene

These transformations in the practice of public dispute management coincided with a moment when legal scholarship was becoming much more sensitive to the social sciences and taking on a broader comparative view. This growing sensitivity was signalled in the language through which some academic lawyers, and a few legal practitioners, began to talk about conflict. In the course of self-conscious attempts by lawyers to theorise disputes, the terms of conversation shift from 'cases', 'litigation' and 'judges', to 'disputes', 'dispute processes' and 'interveners' (see Abel, 1973). This shift at the same time involved a growing familiarity with the ethnography of dispute processes to which leading Anglo-American social anthropologists contributed in the years following the Second World War (Gluckman, 1955; Bohannan, 1957; Turner, 1957; Gibbs, 1963; Gulliver, 1963, 1971). This exposure of lawyers to other cultures led sometimes to explicit 'borrowing' in the formulation of projects of domestic reform (Danzig, 1973), but more generally growing comparative awareness prompted expansive reflection on 'complementary' and 'alternative'

---

14 See, for example, these texts from both sides of the Atlantic: Goldberg, Green and Sander (1985) – now in its fourth edition as Goldberg, Sander, Rogers and Cole (2003); Murray, Rau and Sherman (1989; 1996; 2002); Riskin and Westbrook (1987; 1997); Mackie (1991; 2002); Bevan (1992); Brown and Marriott (1992; 1999); and Smith (1996).

arrangements at home (see Sander, 1976). Central to this growing concern was a return of attention to the primary processes of negotiation and mediation.

C: Civilian Parallels

When we turn to civilian jurisdictions, the major themes of processual transformation that we have noted here are all present: the re-emergence of institutionalised mediation, procedural reform of public justice systems and consequent accommodations within the legal professions. But the emergent picture is very different, for two linked reasons. First, in continental jurisdictions the common law culture of using civil process as an arena for strategies of late settlement was never replicated. Second, the late twentieth-century shift in the common law courts towards a managerial approach did not need to take place.

The continental judicial apparatus, inherently more bureaucratic and hierarchical than that found in common law systems, has traditionally given judges a much more active role to play in litigation so that, for example, 'delegation of any procedural step to outsiders is inappropriate or even repugnant. Private procedural enterprise is . . . almost an oxymoron in the lexicon of hierarchical authority' (Damaska, 1986: 56). In preparatory proceedings, judges of lower standing are charged with collecting factual material and preparing it as written evidence for their superiors. The evidence thus gathered and presented forms the basis for the written case file that is developed through a series of stages that culminates in the final public proceeding, the trial. The central position of the judge – or, better, the hierarchy of judges – dealing with a civil case gives civil litigation a different processual shape (Markesinis, 1990), one which has not generated the same pressure for reform experienced in common law jurisdictions.

Nevertheless, the judiciary in civilian systems has not necessarily been expected to give priority to adjudication in its handling of a civil case. For example, the courts in Germany have for some time been bound by the Code of Civil Procedure to 'promote at every stage of the legal procedure a consensual settlement', are encouraged by practice-related writings to adopt a 'peace-making function' and are pressured by heavy case loads to engage in settlement activities (Röhl, 1983: 2–3). Moreover, since the early 1960s there have been developments in Germany to promote informalism in some of the areas of social life that in common law jurisdictions have also been considered appropriate for ADR mechanisms. In particular, there have been operating for some forty years extra-judicial 'conciliation boards', designed to process disputes between consumers and producers, professionals and their clients, and so on (Eidemann and Plett, 1991). In France, too, efforts have been made to adopt ADR mechanisms to enhance the machinery of civil justice. Indeed, as long ago as the French Revolution the use of a *juge de paix* as a mediator was made obligatory for many kinds of civil disputes, and although this was not felt to be a particularly helpful device, it was not abandoned until 1975. For the resolution of certain kinds of administrative disputes, the French introduced in 1973 the *Mediateur de la Republique*, an ombudsperson system designed to deal with complaints raised by citizens against public bodies. In addition, in some areas of France, the mayor appoints a 'district mediator' in order better to deal with complaints against local administration. Moreover, Articles 21, 768 and 840 of the New Code of Civil Procedure encourage judicial mediation of civil disputes. Labour and family disputes appear to be the most commonly mediated types of disagreement, with the resolution of the latter type of conflict by mediation being encouraged in particular by the *Comité National de Service de Mediation Familiale.*

D: Legal Reform Initiatives and the Role of ADR

These developments in the civilian world have largely taken place in part as a result of inspiration from the ADR movement in the Anglo-American common law world. Elsewhere, too, ADR is slowly being incorporated into international legal reform projects – especially for developing countries. But the extent of this incorporation has been limited by conventional approaches to legal development. International legal assistance programmes continue to focus primarily on improving courts and introducing legal codes in the recipient countries – an enthusiasm for building up formal legal institutions that rests uncomfortably with the benefits that ADR is perceived to bring in the donor states themselves. So, while in the legal systems of North America and Europe complaints and reforms have focused on the problems generated by a perceived flood of litigation, the social divisiveness of litigation and court proceedings, and the rapacious activities of self-interested lawyers – the predators and parasites of modern society, as Galanter (1994) has suggested the public view them – the foundations of these elements are concurrently promoted in legal development programmes. At the same time, there is a certain irony – indeed an incongruity – in teaching contemporary forms of ADR to the very societies whose own traditions of community-based, extra-judicial dispute resolution have served as a key inspiration for the development of alternatives to conventional civil process in the Anglo-American common law world.

E: The Scope of this Book

These various developments within and surrounding civil justice reveal a range of contradictory, but entangled, agendas and projects. So where to go, when 'ADR' itself turns out to be a fugitive label, attached to a disparate group of evolving practices? It seems to us that the place to begin is with a fresh look at three primary processes – negotiation, mediation and umpiring. A sociologically informed understanding of these processes appears indispensable to forming a clearer view of the complex, culturally specific developments in different jurisdictions. Chapters Five, Six and Seven, built around these foundational processes, form the core of this book. The approach here thus takes us away from an exclusive concern with what lawyers and judges do in and around the trial, and from the analysis of legal doctrine – subjects which have traditionally preoccupied law schools in the common law world.

To prepare for this considerable shift in focus, Chapter Two sketches in the cultural and historical background to contemporary institutional change. Chapter Three then introduces the debates around 'informal justice' and the critiques of 'settlement' that have accompanied the ADR movement. Here a notable feature of the landscape we are examining has been the quality and intensity of the critiques that some seemingly common-sense prescriptions and practice initiatives have evoked. Chapter Four looks at the nature of disputes and draws in the typology of dispute processes that informs the subsequent shape of the book.

In Chapters Five and Six we turn to the primary processes of negotiation and mediation. Bringing these to the centre of the stage, we are deliberately concerned to redress some of the imbalances in the way we think about disputes inherent in the law school's historic preoccupation with what judges and lawyers do at and around the trial. That focus has inevitably marginalised the activities of the parties themselves – most notably, those predominantly bilateral processes through which decisions are typically reached at stages before resort to legal specialists. Beginning with negotiation underlines the fact that this mode of decision-making is common to everyday life and to the instance of dispute, providing the site of transition between them. At the same time, concentration on roles involving authoritative determination, on the one hand, and partisan advisory and representative activity, on the other, has left little room for a serious examination of the impartial, facilitatory interventions of the mediator.[15]

With Chapter Seven, on umpiring processes, we are inevitably brought back to the familiar terrain of superior court litigation and its formal goal of judicial determination. But we are concerned to locate these in a wider context of third-party decision-making as a whole. Chapter Eight, the last substantive chapter, is concerned with the very extensive hybridisation of processes that has accompanied contemporary procedural change. We conclude, in Chapter Nine, with a tentative look at the possible trajectory of alternative dispute resolution and speculate on its implications for our established conception of 'public justice'.

---

15 For English law students – and for many of those elsewhere in the common law and civilian worlds – this approach involves a radical break from the universe of understanding within which dispute processes have been traditionally located. Our own students have repeatedly drawn our attention to the need for a different approach. The case for a change in emphasis in North American legal education was forcefully expressed by Derek Bok in his seminal essay, 'A Flawed System of Law and Practice Training' (1983). See also Menkel-Meadow's examination of the main arguments in favour of changing understandings in her recent robust and insightful analysis of the development of ADR (2003).

CHAPTER TWO

Cultures of Decision-making: Precursors to the Emergence of ADR

A: Introduction

In this chapter we begin by marking out, in broad schematic terms, the larger background to the emergence of ADR in the latter part of the twentieth century. This apparently abrupt shift towards what we have loosely identified as a 'culture of settlement' came at the end of a long period during which the lawyer and the judge had emerged as central figures in disputing. The entrenchment of institutions of formal justice, closely associated with the maturity of the nation state, resulted in other foundational institutional forms being marginalised and lost sight of. But these institutional forms, and the values associated with them, were always somewhere in the picture; and as Auerbach (1983), Abel (1982a, 1982b) and Nader (1986) have suggested, a panoramic view would show something of an episodic alternation between values of 'formalism' and 'informalism'. Some sense of this larger picture, inevitably casting doubt upon contemporary claims to radical innovation, provides a necessary context for understanding the contemporary transformation of disputing under the *leitmotiv* of Alternative Dispute Resolution.

While, as we shall see in Chapter Three, self-conscious efforts to 'find a better way' (Burger, 1982) of dealing with civil disputes have in part shaped the ADR movement, co-option by government, large business interests and expansive professional agendas are also important in the movement's emergence and growth. The largely unchallenged critiques of 'informal justice' appearing at the beginning of the 1980s deserve careful examination today.

Two other related themes, articulated across a range of societies, inform the ADR movement. The first holds that there is a necessary tension between formal law and justice. The second claims that disputing institutions are there to secure outcomes that go beyond providing remedies for the parties themselves. So, these institutions are there: to maintain social order; to avoid conflict; to restore harmony; to achieve equality; and to express communal identity. As Auerbach has emphasised, the rejection of legal processes as an appropriate mode of decision-making in the context of disputes is often part of an attempt to develop or retain a sense of community: 'how to resolve conflict, inversely stated, is how (or whether) to preserve community' (1983: 4). We argue here that this impulse may manifest itself in a variety of specific contexts – religious, political, territorial, ethnic and occupational seem to be the most important of these. These values often constitute a counter-tradition to legalism or what Santos has labelled the 'neoclassical model' of law (1982: 256).

B: Ideals of Informal Justice

A 'model' of informal justice invariably contains a number of identifiable core elements that are seen as superior to orthodox, formal justice. These include the development of processes and associated institutions that are:

- non-bureaucratic in structure and relatively undifferentiated from society, relying on small, local fora which – unlike large legal bureaucracies – can get to grips with the social relationships of the parties;
- local in nature and, for example, rely on local rather than professional or official language;
- accessible to ordinary people, and not dependent on the services of ('expensive') professionals;
- reliant on lay people as third-party interveners, perhaps with some – but not a great deal – of training, and who are preferably unpaid;
- outside the immediate scope of official law, and reliant instead on local standards of conduct and common-sense thinking;
- based on substantive and procedural 'rules' that are vague, unwritten, flexible and good common sense – so that 'the law' does not stand in the way of achieving substantive justice in the 'instant' case; and
- intent on promoting harmony between the parties and within local communities, in part because they get to the 'real' underlying cause of the problem(s), in part because they search outcomes mutually acceptable to the parties rather than the strict application of legal rules and in part because they carry an ethic of treatment.

We would argue that there is in *every* legal system some line of thinking which manifests these principles of informalism to a certain extent. Even within our current legal practice, professional jokes may reflect such values, albeit in a negative manner – for example, 'any lawyer can achieve justice; it really takes a good litigator to achieve an injustice'.

In contrast, in centralised legal systems a dominant ideological strand typically stresses perceived values of formal justice, for dispute resolution through law and legal institutions. The values or elements that are, to a greater or lesser degree, given emphasis include:

- Specialised bureaucratic mechanisms that are differentiated from society so that such mechanisms are able to make good, independent and technically correct decisions.
- Professionals with relevant expert knowledge and the capacity to articulate and to enforce the law.

- An impartial, publicly available official law (typically, that of the state) that may be imposed on the parties, and which is interpreted in terms of the bounded discourses of law.
- Clear, fair procedures, and as concerned with procedural justice as with substantive justice, because due process is a key element in the rule of law.
- The authority of the state, with court able to compel the parties to accept that authority.

But, argue proponents of informalism, these ideals of formal justice may well come to act as a barrier to the provision of substantive justice. For example, with reference to adversarial proceedings:

> the effect of our exaggerated contentious procedure is to give the whole community a false notion of the purpose and end of law. If law is a mere game, neither the players who take part in it nor the public who witness it can be expected to yield to its spirit when their interests are served by eroding it. The courts, instituted to administer justice according to the law, are made agents or abettors of lawlessness (Pound, 1906: 406).

Thus, the growth of the modern ADR 'movement' by no means exhausts the history of the search for alternatives, and this growth is itself understood better in a broader historical context. If the time scale is expanded sufficiently then even in the common law world we may see that it is state-organised adjudication that is the real novelty – in England, for example, the Royal Courts only began functioning in the twelfth century. Moreover, any historical understanding should surely also encompass the experiences of dispute resolution mechanisms of more than northern Europe and North America.

C: The Establishment of Formal Justice

Since the arrival of political authority in the form of the state, the provision of dispute resolution mechanisms has been bound up with the ambition of those in power to govern. By and large, the preference of the state has been to provide processes and institutions that we would want to characterise as formal, with litigation and adjudication central to the state-sponsored system of civil justice. But, even as these formal systems of justice were being created, there were those who argued against them or who sought to modify their full rigour, or who simply looked for other ways to solve their differences.

In pre-imperial China, for example, there was by the third century BC, if not before, already an important ideology of legal formalism and strong state power. This ideology, known as 'Legalism' (Fajia), arose in part as a reaction to Confucian thinking on disputes and their treatment – thinking which emphasised the importance of harmony, moral leadership, education and self-sacrifice. The emergence of Legalism thus resulted in a marked dichotomy in Chinese legal philosophy between

'Legalist' and 'Confucian' schools. This dichotomy has persisted, in modified form, through to the present day. The Legalists have persistently advocated a strong centralised state, operating with a comprehensive set of law codes, and a rigorously administered hierarchical system of courts designed to enforce the rules of imperial statutory law. These rules should be unambiguous and comprehensible, and applicable with equal force to all subjects regardless of their social status. Those who break the law should be given appropriately stern punishment. Equipped with this philosophy, as well as a large and efficient army, the State of Qin unified China in 221 BC and installed itself as China's first dynasty. But the reign of the Qin was extremely authoritarian in nature and therefore short-lived, and Legalism abandoned as the official state philosophy by the succeeding dynasty, the Han (206 BC–220 AD), in favour of Confucianism. This alternative body of thought remained the prevailing creed in Chinese society until the toppling of the Qing dynasty in the early years of the twentieth century.

The Confucianist approach to law and morality has been resolutely to maintain that a formal 'law-based' approach encourages parties to be adversarial, strategically pursuing their rights at the expense of substantive justice. Much better, therefore, for the state to ensure order and continuity in social life by means of a ruler whose personal conduct is so superior that his subjects would be inspired to emulate his virtuous example. Ordinary people would have no need for law, and when involved in a dispute the good subject would not stand on his or her rights but, rather, 'yield' so that lawsuits could be avoided. This avoidance of state-administered justice was also perceived by ordinary people to be appropriate for other reasons, and a distrust of litigation was expressed in a wide range of popular aphorisms: for example, 'let householders avoid litigation, for once you go to law there is nothing but trouble', or 'win your lawsuit, lose your money', or 'even an upright magistrate has difficulty in deciding family disputes', or 'nine [disputes] out of ten are settled by mediation' (van der Sprenkel, 1962: 135–136).

The origin of formal justice in the Roman polity is not fully documented (Stein, 1999: 3), but a measured view is that 'in very early times . . . it is likely that the Romans had recourse to ordeals or battle or oath taking as a means of settling disputes' (Stein, 1984: 27). Initially, the Roman state was a theocracy in which legal matters were put in the hands of a college of pontifs serving as a judicial council, and where 'from the first a clear distinction was drawn between the procedure meant to secure the adjustment of private claims and the process by which penal pronouncements were made' (Greenidge, 1971: 8). Following the establishment of a Republic in the late sixth century BC, the Roman community showed considerable concern with maintaining social order and resolving disputes. The Law of the Twelve Tables reflected these concerns and attempted to demarcate the boundaries of self-help and other forms of unilateral force, and to stipulate the procedural requirements that a party had to meet in order to secure assistance from the state institutions for dispute settlement:

in particular, the Twelve Tables dealt with the details of legal procedure, what a citizen could do to help himself without invoking a court and what he had to do to start court proceedings. In the early republic there were few state officials to help an aggrieved person get redress for injuries which he claimed to have suffered and he had to do a lot for himself to activate the legal machinery. In certain cases self-help was tolerated, since the community was not yet strong enough to eliminate it. The Twelve Tables show, however, a determination to institutionalise such cases and keep them within strict limits (Stein, 1999: 4).

The development of a state-controlled civil process continued, although it seems that up to the mid-second century AD if not beyond: 'the average Roman lawsuit . . . was [still] one in which the plaintiff either commanded physical superiority over the defendant, or was at least a good match for him' (Kelly, 1966: 20).

In other important respects, too, the slowly emerging system of state justice did not fully displace 'alternative' forms. Instead, processes originating in pre-existing Italian society persisted; these included, in particular, the use of communal humiliation of an offending party by a stratagem known as *flagitatio*. Moreover, in the system of civil litigation that did develop, very considerable scope was still allowed for a 'culture' of settlement. (See Extract 2:1.)

In England, the process of state-building began well in advance of the Norman conquest of 1066, and the new Anglo-Norman rulers continued to build up the authority of the English monarchy, a process leading, inter alia, to the establishment under Henry II in the second half of the twelfth century of a system of national courts with broad powers of original jurisdiction and operated in a bureaucratic manner by justices appointed by the king. The various kinds of royal court were administered in a unified style:

Each court was run and its judgments made by a relatively small number of justices. It held daily sessions, often during specific periods of the year (terms). The Common Bench and the King's Bench held daily sessions during the four law terms each year. The General Eyre held continuous daily sessions in the counties it visited but did not divide its work up by terms until the reign of Edward I and then only in the largest counties it visited. Assize justices held sessions only at three specified times of the year under legislation of 1285. Each court kept a written record of the business it transacted. The court normally only heard such civil litigation as it had been specifically authorised to hear, and the authorisation normally took the form of a royal writ (an 'original writ') addressed to the local sheriff, instructing him to summon the defendant to answer a specific plea in a specific court on a specific date . . . and to 'return' the writ to the court where the plea was to be heard. Quasi-bureaucratic royal courts of this type were an innovation of the reign of Henry II and differ markedly from the type of court which had previously been the norm in England. In the older type of court judgements were normally made by a relatively large group of suitors whose obligation to perform this function was derived not from appointment by the king but from tenure of land in the area where the court exercised jurisdiction. Such courts normally only held sessions lasting for a day or less at more or less regular intervals. They did not keep any written record of their proceedings nor did they require any written authorization from the king for hearing litigation (Brandt, 1997: 112).

Nevertheless, the bulk of civil litigation continued to be carried out in lower courts and 'most litigation initiated in these various lower courts was none the less determined there or settled out of court' (Brandt, 1997: 110).

Moreover, for some types of civil dispute, pre-existing institutions continued to flourish as the preferred specialised forum for settling differences between the parties. For example, the boroughs possessed their own courts in which the burgesses, the citizens of the borough, were able to bring suit. These courts did not exercise criminal jurisdiction, which was a matter for the king's authority, but they did become important sites for laws governing trade and commerce, for the boroughs were themselves centres of trading and commercial activity. The royal law dealt with such matters as real estate, as this was an area of regulation that concerned the landed aristocracy. In contrast, the borough law more firmly reflected the interests of the merchant, and its courts dealt with many disputes between merchants and artisans. As a result, borough courts were partly responsible for the development of commercial law, and their utility was such that they were able to resist the intrusions of the royal tribunals for many centuries. (See Extract 2:2.) Indeed, the borough courts, which also helped to lay the foundations for the subsequent development of equitable procedures and remedies (Murray, 1959–1961), were not the whole story, for in addition there were ad hoc disputing mechanisms in the great fairs that the boroughs often hosted. During these events it was customary for the borough court to be entirely or at least partly suspended in favour of the so-called 'Piepowder' Courts:

> In these great fairs disputes would arise in the course of bargaining that would have to be settled before the wayfaring traders went their several ways, and temporary courts for this purpose have existed in England from the earliest times. In cases where the ordinary borough courts were not held during fair time, their place would be taken by these tribunals. . . . The fair courts have always been known in England as Courts of Piepowder (Cole, 1902: 377).

So, even a cursory examination of the emergence of the Royal Courts of Justice reveals a world in which many litigants, preferring the local knowledge and expertise of local dispute settlement institutions, relied on these local institutions rather than the royal courts to handle their grievances, and even when invoking the system of royal justice to pursue their grievance, the parties were inclined to settle when they perceived settlement to be in their best interests.

A broadly similar pattern of pluralist socio-legal ordering emerged with the spread of European economic power and political authority in the nineteenth and early twentieth centuries, resulting in many parts of Africa and Asia in the subordination of local society to colonial rule and its new forms of government, economic relations and systems of law. A common pattern was for the colonial state not only to monopolise criminal prosecutions but also to introduce 'Western-style' civil justice for more important and larger disputes, and in which colonial settlers, traders, missionaries and others might have an interest. The focus here was on adjudication. For less significant civil disputes, and especially those involving the indigenous population and that raised issues of 'customary' law – itself a product of local social ordering and colonial ideology – the colonial state allowed issues to be dealt with by more traditional-based dispute resolution processes, which often emphasised negotiation and mediation. And in the post-colonial situation, efforts to restore pre-colonial law and institutions have in many places been made not only in order to assist in the elimination of alien laws and processes introduced by the former colonial rulers but more recently also to try to deal with serious issues arising out of the collapse of political authority and the formal legal system in failed states such as Afghanistan and Rwanda. (See Extract 2:3.)

Extract 2:1
J M Kelly: *Roman Litigation* (1966) Clarendon Press, Oxford, pp 21–23, 132, 147, 148 and 150

> The ancient Italian custom of 'popular justice' . . . seems to have been known and practised at least up to the end of the Republic, and very likely well into the Empire. . . . In primitive Italian society the gaps [in the normal processes of law] were filled by the popular condemnation of a wrongdoer, which may originally have taken the form of mob justice and the forcible expulsion by flogging of the culprit from the community; later the forcible expulsion was replaced by a communal disgracing of the offender [known as *flagitatio*]. This communal disgracing took the form of an organized shouting of insulting words in the offender's presence . . . with a view to compelling him to make good or compensate for some disgraceful act (most often the non-payment of a debt) . . . Not altogether removed from this field of thought and behaviour is the permission accorded by the XII Tables to a person whose witness has failed to appear in court to go to the witness's house and shout . . . in front of it . . .
>
> The literary evidence seems to show that it was a living custom into the Empire. There is no doubt that it must reflect a state of affairs in which the processes of law were inadequate to ensure the righting of all wrongs; and because of its popular character it may be assumed that it tended typically to be employed against individuals who were more powerful than the wronged instigators of *flagitatio*. This evidence bears a certain relation to the Digest passages on *iniuria* cited above; wrongful insinuations against innocent parties are actionable, but we are left to infer that circumstances might sometimes justify public insinuations if no other course were open to an injured party, and indeed one Digest passage may well be read as expressly authorizing this . . . In the system of classical Roman law, as in that of our own, the rules relating to the settlement or compromise of actions do not form a separate chapter. In both systems the subject, despite its enormous practical importance, lies more or less concealed within

a structure of more general notions; in English law, the doctrine of consideration; in Roman, the rules about formless pacts and stipulations. The words *transactio, transigere*, &c., with the meaning of settlement of an action, occur frequently in the writings of classical jurists, but it does not appear that the concept of *transactio* enjoyed any special treatment before the publication of Justinian's *Codex* and *Digest*, wherein respectively imperial constitutions and a number of juristic texts from the most miscellaneous sources are gathered into separate titles under the rubric *De transactionibus* . . .

A question which requires some attention is that of the stages at which *transactio* was possible. It is clear, in the first place, that there was no obstacle to the conclusion of a settlement before the beginning of proceedings; . . .

Even after the proceedings had been begun by the summoning of the defendant by the plaintiff (*in ius vocatio*) a settlement must still have been possible; . . . it is certain that a settlement reached by the parties in the course of the proceedings before the praetor was valid, and indeed the praetor actively encouraged such a solution; it was to some extent his duty to induce the parties to compose their differences . . .

Finally, in this connexion there is the question whether *transactio* was possible after a decision had been given by a *iudex* . . . and there can be no doubt that the occasion to make such settlements arose commonly in the Roman world, as it does in our own.

Extract 2:2
Sanford D Cole: 'English Borough Courts' (1902) 18 *Law Quarterly Review* 376, pp 380–382

We proceed to look at one or two individual examples of towns and their courts. Some places are more typical than others, and in choosing a community where the influence of the commercial element has been exemplified we could probably take no better instance than Bristol, which has been remarkable for the number of local jurisdictions exercised within it, and is an example of a town that has owed all its eminence to trade, having been for centuries the greatest purely trading town in the country . . . [There were] . . . two courts, and . . . the first . . . [bore a] distinctive name – the Tolzey Court – . . . [and] . . . afterwards absorbed most of its companions . . . Tolls, we know, played a very important part in early trading, being often exacted in kind, and the Tolzey, or place where they were collected, was a gathering place of merchants. This was therefore a commercial court. Several leases of the town had been obtained, but Edward IV granted the town to the mayor and commonalty for ever (1461), and the Tolzey court then became annexed to the corporate jurisdiction. Both before and after this a contest for jurisdiction was carried on between the Mayor's and the Tolzey court. There was also a court of the Staple, but both it and the Mayor's court became quite disused . . . Under Henry VII the offices of sheriff and bailiff became united, and the court continued under the authority of the sheriff, being sometimes referred to as the Sheriff's court, but an official called assessor, who had long been attached to the court, came to be known as steward, and to preside as judge until, in 1835, the judgeships of borough courts were transferred to recorders.

Mention must be made of still another court whose business was absorbed by the Tolzey court. This was a Pie Poudre court . . . At all events the connexion between the two is very ancient, and for the last two hundred years at least they appear to have been practically one court. The ancient great fair of Bristol was held in July, but in the eighteenth century the time was altered to September. Latterly, the Pie Poudre court was held during a fair of fourteen days, commencing in September in a thoroughfare known as the Old Market. For this period the Tolzey court was suspended. This custom looks like a survival from the days when everything outside a fair came to a standstill till it was over. The Pie Poudre court was actually held till 1870 in a covered walk in front of the Stag and Hounds, but adherence to ancient ceremony involved the consumption of undue quantities of liquor, and the affair was suppressed. The court has since existed only as a name forming part of the full title of the Tolzey court.

The Tolzey court thus became the sole local tribunal . . . and it still exists as an active institution disposing of a fair amount of business. It is one of the very few local courts to which the modern procedure under the Judicature Acts has been applied, and this has a great deal to do with its survival. The practice is similar to that of the High Court, but actions for any amount, large or small, can be entertained, and a peculiar feature is that there is no appeal from the judge's decision.

Extract 2:3

Jeremy Sarkin: 'The Tension Between Justice and Reconciliation in Rwanda: Politics, Human Rights, Due Process and the Role of the Gacaca Courts in Dealing with Genocide' (2001) 45 *Journal of African Law* 2, p 143 at pp 157–159

While the criminal justice system has improved dramatically since 1994, it is still weak and the judiciary is still overwhelmed. The courts lack infrastructure, qualified personnel and funding. Due process rights have often been absent – in violation of both international standards and international law . . .

Trials did not begin in Rwanda until December 1996. The manner in which the trials have been conducted has raised questions about their fairness . . . [and paucity] . . . Part of the reason why so few trials have been held is because of the small number of trained judges in Rwanda. Many judges were killed during the genocide . . .

The use of the traditional *gacaca* has been adopted by the Rwandan government as a mechanism to ease the burden on the normal courts and to apply justice by assisting the legal system to deal with those in detention awaiting trial . . .

Traditionally, the *gacaca* had a dispute resolution focus. The name is derived from the word for 'lawn', referring to the fact that members of the *gacaca* sit on the grass when listening to and considering matters before them. The process involves the community in dispute resolution, making it community-based. It acts as a local healing and dispute resolution mechanism that is cheap and accessible. In general, where these structures operate, people have some degree of confidence in the system as they see respected community figures serving on the *gacaca* and are able to observe the proceedings in close proximity to where they live. The *gacaca*, similar to nearly all systems of traditional law, is part of the culture. It is established upon principles of morality and reverence of life.

D: The Religious Impulse Towards Informalism

The impulse to provide forms of dispute resolution that operate outside or along-side the legal system of the state is further manifested in a number of quite specific contexts in which emphasis is placed on the importance of dealing with trouble sit-uations within the community, thereby avoiding the state and its legal institutions. Here the emphasis is typically placed on decision-making processes other than adju-dication with its claims of certainty, legal rights and independence. One such context is the religious community, most obvious in the case of sectarian organisations that seek to establish and maintain a distinctive religious community that offers a moral order and social formation outside ordinary society, which is perceived to be deeply flawed and even corrupt. These alternative, often 'utopian', communities may be created by religious impulse alone, or encouraged by the experiences of migration and attendant ethnic discrimination. The alternative systems of dispute handling offered to members are thus one part of a more general withdrawal or separation from ordinary society. Community rules may even bar members from recourse to state courts, as in the case of Chinese lineages or clans – which existed, inter alia, as mechanisms for the perpetuation of the memory of the founding ancestor and the performance of ancestor worship: 'one who takes the case into court without submitting it to the clan organisation, even if justice is on his side, should also be penalized for having forgotten that the other party who has wronged him is a fellow clan member and a descendant from the same origin' (Wang Liu, 1959: 157).

Examples abound, but some of the most persistent strains of informalism can be found in the Protestant sectarian tradition. In North America, for example, Auerbach has demonstrated that during the colonial period formal legal institu-tions played a relatively minor role in dispute settlement because the colonists were hostile to any external interference that challenged the religious and social values of the local communities. (See Extract 2:4.) Courts and commercial arbitration[1] then came to play an increasing role in handling disputes as a result of increases in trade and commerce during the first part of the eighteenth century. But a fresh impetus towards alternatives was provided by the development of utopian communities in the first half of the nineteenth century – again, often inspired by religious ideals as in the case of the Shakers, the Mormons and so on. Auerbach argues that the 'counter tradition to legalism', in particular mediation, was, however, impossible to sustain in the face of the ever-growing pressures of greater economic and social inte-gration, increasing immigration and secularisation (in particular, declining church membership).

But amongst some communities of believers, the religious impulse to informal-ism has persisted right through to the present day. In her important study of the Baptists of 'Hopewell', a county situated close to Atlanta, Georgia in the southern

---

1 We view arbitration not as an alternative but, rather, as a private form of umpiring and therefore processually very similar to adjudication. See Chapter Seven.

United States, Carol Greenhouse provides an insightful account of the continuing impact of religious belief on disputing behaviour in the mid-1980s in Extract 2:5 below.

Extract 2:4

J S Auerbach: *Justice Without Law? Resolving Disputes Without Lawyers* (1983) Oxford University Press, Oxford, pp 19–21

> The first generation of New England colonists comprised a religious people whose covenants with God (and with each other) bound them together in congregational communities where Christian precepts of brotherly love were taken seriously. Tolerance was not a virtue in these communities. Puritans were orthodox Christians for whom the word of God was clear, and clearly stated in the Bible. They left England to escape what they perceived as individual greed, social disintegration, and an impure Anglican Church. Their New World 'city upon a hill' was designed to serve as a model for others to emulate. It was a communal prescription, not a geographical description. Society was an organism; its members were part of a social unit dedicated to serving God's will on earth, not an aggregation of individuals. As John Winthrop declared in his sermon on board the Arbella, before the Puritans landed in Massachusetts Bay, 'We must entertain each other in brotherly affection. We must delight in each other, make others' condition our own, rejoice together, mourn together, labor and suffer together.' It is not the fine points of the Puritans' theology, but the tenacity of their perfectionist communal vision, that is illuminating. Their fundamental principle of association, expressed in one typical town covenant, was 'everlasting love.' It required, paradoxically, exclusion of the 'contrary minded'; any 'differences' must be mediated by members, not consigned to lawyers. For Zion to survive in the wilderness according to Puritan design, the dispute-settlement framework, like the holy experiment itself, must be communal, not individual. Its spirit was religious, not secular; the style was consensual, not adversarial.

Extract 2:5

Carol J Greenhouse: *Praying for Justice: Faith, Order, and Community in an American Town* (1986) Cornell University Press, Ithaca, New York, pp 108, 109, 110, 115, 116, 117 and 118

> Baptists believe that Christ's saving power is available to all people, regardless of their previous sins or lack of faith, their wealth, or their race[2] . . . [and] . . . a consequence of [this] egalitarianism is that conflict cannot be overtly expressed for several reasons. First, because Jesus is presumed to have everyone's interests in mind in his plan, untoward events should not be questioned but should be taken as objects of reflection and thresholds of spiritual development. Second, since Jesus has everyone in mind, pressing

---

2 Although, as Greenhouse also emphasises, segregation between black and white congregations persisted in Hopewell, apparently on the basis of the white view that while blacks were 'authentic Christians' they were not 'Christians capable of a deep understanding of faith' (1986: 108).

one's own interests in the from of a claim or an expression of anger is superfluous. These two reasons constitute important checks on individuals' much-felt impulses to express themselves in conflict situations, and the verse from Romans, 'Avenge not yourselves . . . I will repay, saith the Lord (13:19),' is perhaps quoted more often than any other. It is important to note that Hopewell's Baptists have not eradicated their feelings of anger or overt conflict but that a fundamental aspect of their experience with their faith in Jesus is to refuse to act on those feelings. To accept Jesus is to accept the logic of the ideology that makes conflict among humans unnecessary in an absolute sense . . .

[Nevertheless] Baptists do find themselves in overt conflict situations and with inner feelings of conflict, and they draw on a number of effective . . . responses. Baptists' remedies are verbal: narratives and gossip, joking, duelling with scripture, and prayer . . . The verbal strategies current among insiders have the potential to reduce conflict and for anticipating conflict that would not apply across the boundary between Baptists and nonbelievers, since nonbelievers do not do not share the same ideological concerns. Narratives, or duelling with passages from the scripture, are ineffective between parties who do not share the same understanding of their capacity to transmit messages.

On the other hand, although Baptists can control the appearance of anger, they cannot control external events, such as when they feel cheated in a transaction, or when other drivers damage their cars, or when they are otherwise put in a position of being victims. Even in justiciable cases, conflict across this line simply dissolves. Auto accidents, incidents of violence, and debt are explained as simply being an example of 'God's will.' The rationalizations of nonaction are also explained by Baptists in terms of the wider ideological reference point of the group. By refusing to engage in open dispute, church members reaffirm the power of their own faith and simultaneously believe they are witnessing to the potential defendant . . .

This group of Baptists places high value on harmonious relationships and, like other groups, develops strategies for resolving conflicts that are effective in certain sociocultural contexts and within the particular limitations of their beliefs. The manipulation of verbal exchanges allows local Baptists to obviate what would be a fundamental contradiction to their perception of the secular and religious order in which they participate. The crucial element is adversarial conflict. The temptation to pursue one's own ends is continual – indeed, a premise – in modern society. If Baptists preclude disputes, it is not because they cannot conceive of self-interested remedial action but because they *can*, all too well. The effort of refraining from adversarial conflict forms the reservoir that feeds the transformation of meaning so crucial to their social relationships. In other terms, their refusal to dispute makes Christianity both important and possible for believers . . .

It is not only conflict resolution that is redefined by Hopewell's Baptists; conflict itself is redefined and relocated. The very possibility of conflict within the church community is moot in its own terms, since the order of the church reflects God's plan and so contains no contradictions. Even among the saved, then, offensive behavior is presumed to derive from spiritual defect and is tolerated only within limits, for example, if the offender is responsive to narratives and seems anxious to remain close to the group. Others are selectively avoided . . . All conflict is said to flow from the self-interest of non-Baptists; thus the two important experiences associated with belief – absence of conflict and resistance to materialism – become linked. Since all conflict is said to come from non-Baptists, . . . non-Baptists are said to be avoided partly because one can expect trouble from them. Furthermore, it is known that non-Baptists have none of the spiritual faith that would prevent them from going to great lengths in their own interest. Because non-Baptists do not belong to the community of God, Baptists believe them to be dangerous and corrupting . . .

The consequences of this system of belief is that Baptists do not conceptualize or discuss conflict in terms of cases and rules but in terms of salvation. Cases and the adversary model are entirely extraneous to this idea. The difference between harmony and conflict is not one between the sanctity and violation of rules and their lapse, or even the Bible's exhortations, but simply the difference between salvation and damnation. Any mode of processing a dispute that involved a remedy – and none of the techniques discussed above does – would be beside the point. The only valid remedy, in the Baptists' eyes, is salvation; the only valid sanction, damnation.

E: The Political Impulse Towards Informalism

The close association between the state and formal justice, and the tendency to domination of the system of formal justice by ruling classes, encourages those who reject the prevailing social order, and who wish to create a more just political community either by withdrawal in whole or part from mainstream institutional life or by popular revolution, to create alternatives for the handling of disputes.

There is, for example, the well-documented Philadelphian working-class organisation that developed in the late 1860s under the title 'Knights of Labour'. This was a kind of general trade union that aimed to move the American value system away from materialism in the direction of greater moral worth, as well as to improve the pay and conditions of its members. In the eyes of the leaders and many of the members of this organisation, the conventional court structure seemed weighted against working people, dealing out overly severe punishment in criminal cases and proving inaccessible in civil cases in which a working-class person was the plaintiff. An 'alternative' system of dispute resolution was established for members, but one that, as the movement became more firmly institutionalised, came to model itself on the official court system so that it both lost the advantages of informalism and incurred the wrath of the authorities who viewed it as a threat to state power. Nevertheless, at the high point of its development the Knights' court system consisted of some 8,000 tribunals dealing with problems in more than 3,000 communities, and it apparently proved very popular as a result of its good work in settling disagreements between working people. As a result, it clearly stands out as a precursor for later attempts at developing 'alternatives' (Garlock, 1982).

More generally, the development of socialism in the twentieth century encouraged ideals of informalism, with attempts being made in a wide variety of societies to create a new system for resolving disputes that would no longer serve the interests of the bourgeoisie but, instead, incorporate the will of the masses and assist in the construction of a socialist society. Writing in the early 1980s, but with the experience of the Portuguese revolution of 1974 in mind, Santos characterised this search for informal or 'popular' justice in the following terms:

> Historical analysis of the most important revolutionary crises in modern times leads us to a concept of popular justice in which the following elements tend to be present. It is class justice; that is, it appears as justice exercised by the popular classes parallel to or in confrontation with the state administration of justice. It embodies alternative criteria of substantive legality or at least alternative criteria for the interpretation and enforcement of pre-existing legality. It is based on a concrete notion of popular sovereignty (as opposed to the bourgeois theory of sovereignty) and thus on the idea of direct government by the people. Consequently, it requires that judges be democratically selected by the relevant communities and act as representative members of the masses, who are autonomously exercising social power. It operates at a minimum level of institutionalisation and bureaucratisation (a non-professional justice with very little division of legal labour and immune to systematic rationality). Rhetoric tends to dominate the structure of the discourse mobilised in the processing and settlement of conflicts. Formal coercive power may or may not exist, but when it does it tends to be used in interclass conflicts for the punishment of class enemies, whereas educative measures tend to be favoured in intraclass conflicts. In sum, popular justice in a revolutionary crisis is a form of 'revolutionary law in action', the embryo of a new power structure, though popular justice is less comprehensive than revolutionary legality since it is restricted to revolutionary actions that directly confront the judicial decision-making apparatus of the state (Santos, 1982: 253–254).

These observations help us to understand, for example, the extraordinary experiments in civil (and indeed criminal) justice undertaken by the Chinese Communist Party ('CCP') in areas of China 'liberated' by the revolutionaries prior to the creation of a People's Republic throughout China in 1949. Essentially, the comrades carrying out 'legal work' in the pre-1949 'Liberated Areas' sought to create a system of justice that was socialist in nature but not necessarily in the image of that developed in the Soviet Union. Instead, it had to be adapted to local Chinese conditions. On the basis of traditional values and practices of dispute resolution, the CCP thus experimented with ways of incorporating traditional approaches into its emerging system of popular justice. This approach was called, after the judge who played the most role in its development, the 'Ma Xiwu Judicial Style' (Ma Xiwu Shenpan Fangshi). Among the most distinctive features of this system were on-the-spot trials and circuit tribunals – so that the courts could have direct contact with the masses, gather evidence themselves, draw in local people to assist in the processes of settling disputes and educate the masses through their participation in the trial proceedings. In addition, a system for appointing 'people's assessors' was created in which lay members of the community were invited onto the bench by the invitation of the court, or by election by local organisations, or by nomination by appropriate body (for example, nomination by a trades union in employment dispute cases, or the women's association in divorce cases). In this way, the court could benefit from the lay but sometimes specialised knowledge of the assessor, the assessor could supervise judicial work in the name of 'the people' and increase the possibility of publicity for laws and policies. Furthermore, the importance of both extra-judicial and judicial mediation was stressed as this would 'strengthen the unity of the people', reduce litigation and enhance production. One of the key features of informal justice that was not in this system was, however, disassociation from state power – this was a very hands-on system, with the CCP authorities in firm control, running a system in parallel with the state legal system of the Nationalist Government:

Extract 2:6
S Lubman: 'Judicial Work in T'aihang' (1973) 6 *Chinese Law and Government* 3, p 7 at pp 12–17

> I. Proposal to Mediate Civil Actions, Its Situation and Results
> Before 1942 civil cases were generally very few. Moreover, because of the war environment, most people had the viewpoint of emphasizing criminal cases and neglecting civil cases. After 1942 civil cases gradually increased in the old Liberated Areas. Beginning in 1944 the rate of civil cases became equal to that of criminal cases. At this time, after the cadres had gone through the Great Rectification Movement, their thought underwent a great change, and their concept of serving the masses began to be even more explicitly established. At the same time, in the actual work, there were some problems which proved to be unsolvable purely by judicial decision. For example, while the laws and decrees did not permit divorce judgments, the wife stubbornly refused to be reconciled with her husband or to return home, creating serious cases of troubled families and miserable husbands. In cases combining these conditions, some places began to try methods of mediation, which resulted in proper solutions in many civil disputes and truly gave the people a thorough solution to the difficulties of their disputes. Under these circumstances, in the spring of 1945 the Border Region Government and the High Court issued regulations on mediation of civil and criminal cases with a view to further concretizing, clarifying, and systematizing mediation work. Hence mediation work developed further . . .
>
> Mediation work was usually carried out in two forms: mediation in the court and mediation outside of the court. Generally speaking, judicial mediation would do in simple cases where the facts were agreed and could be understood in one session. But in complicated cases or ones which involved historical disputes, where the circumstances could not be quickly understood, we would utilize the out-of-court form of mediation. For instance, in such disputes as those between family members, or husband and wife, that were difficult to solve, we would usually go to the village and organize a family meeting to solve them or combine with the masses to carry out mediation. In some places, under our leadership and influence, many mediating organizations (such as village mediation meetings) of a mass nature were established, and they performed an important function.

II. Legal Basis for Promoting Mediation . . .

The special characteristic of our law in the Liberated Areas is that it does not protect only one specific class while oppressing another class, as most laws do. Our law protects the interests of all classes which support anti-Japanese democracy. Therefore, if disputes arise among the anti-Japanese democratic classes, especially among the broad masses, we must develop the unifying function of our law. Mediation is the best method we have found for improving unity among men and between classes.

Moreover, we advocate mediation in civil cases because civil disputes concern only matters of interest to individuals and do not endanger society. Therefore, if only the parties agree to compromise, mediation should be proposed. Article 377 of the Code of Civil Procedure provides:

> Regardless of the state of the proceedings reached, the court, if it considers that there is hope of establishing a compromise, may at the time of oral argument attempt to bring the parties to a compromise or cause a commissioned judge or a requested judge to do the same.

As for minor criminal cases we have provided that they too may be compromised. This might appear to be unsuitable on the surface, because criminal cases are those which can injure society and ought not to be compromised. (For instance, in cases of scuffling and fighting we have the aggressor apologize to the person whom he hit, and we have thieves return the property with an apology.) But according to the principle of economy, which is a legislative guideline in the Criminal Code, Article 61 of the Criminal Code provides, 'When the circumstances of a case are not serious and obviously can be forgiven, if [the court] concludes that even if the punishment were reduced under the provisions of Criminal Code Article 59 it would still be excessively heavy, [the court] must dispense with the punishment.' This implementation of compromise between the parties in minor criminal cases in which the punishment must be dispensed with is in accord with legislative guidelines.

III. Two Problems Which Must First Be Solved in Carrying Out Dispute Mediation

There are two basic problems in carrying out dispute mediation, and they must be solved first. The first is the problem of standpoint. That is to say, what is the standpoint from which we proceed to work? Is it to serve the people? Or is it something else? Several years of experience have proved that if one does not have a complete spirit of serving the people one can not carry out compromise, for mediation is much more difficult than conducting a trial. In a trial, all one has to do is to get clear what is true and what is false, and then one can pass judgment and wind up the case. But when it comes to whether the parties are in agreement or disagreement, that does not concern one. Mediation is not like that. In mediation both parties, or even several parties, must be in agreement, and only then can the case be concluded. Sometimes, therefore, when we use the trial method of dealing with a case we hold a couple of court sessions, and in three to five days the case is concluded. But with mediation we might have many court sessions, and it might be a month or two before we are able to bring the parties around to the correct attitude and get them to agree with each other. This is not an easy affair, and if one does not have a complete spirit of serving the people it will be impossible for one to overcome the difficulties and make a success of the mediation.

The second problem is that of work style. If one is not able to overcome bureaucrats and to put down the bureaucratic style of a legal officer, one will never be able to accomplish a compromise . . . Legal scholars and legal personnel of the past also have advocated mediation and have said that mediation could resolve disputes and calm the parties down. But they were only able to write this down on paper, so that it could only become a magnificent fantasy, and the reason for this was simply that they had not solved the problems of standpoint and work style.

F: The Ethnic Impulse Towards Informalism

Although often overlapping with religious communities, ethnic minority communities too have sometimes felt the strong need to close out the outside world and to enjoy a degree of local sovereignty or control over their own affairs. Indeed, where a distinctive ethnic group has been created by the process of migration, and is therefore perceived by other local people as something of a body of outsiders, its members (and especially its leaders) may feel the strong need to withdraw from mainstream society in order to avoid prejudiced attitudes and discriminatory conduct. In the case of the Chinese diaspora, such withdrawal often took the form of retreat into Chinatowns, urban enclaves within which they developed a tightly knit community, and where leadership was provided by office holders in the major voluntary associations that the Chinese migrants had established, with this leadership settling disputes, controlling deviant conduct, and providing assistance for the less well-off. In the United States, Chinese migrated in steadily increasing numbers until 1882, when federal law introduced new barriers to such immigration in response to white hostility that included mob violence. It was not until many decades after, that the Chinese-Americans felt able to integrate more firmly with mainstream society. In the extract which follows, the system of dispute resolution, and the impact of change on that system, are discussed with primary reference to the Chinese communities of New York and Boston:

Extract 2:7
DOO Leigh-wai: 'Dispute Settlement in Chinese-American Communities' (1973) 21 *American Journal of Comparative Law*, p 627 at pp 652–654

Chinese-American dispute settlement is person-directed rather than act-directed. Its progress has been from past didactic mediation, sometimes called arbitration, to voluntary mediation . . .

Didactic mediation is predominantly authoritarian and characterized by a background of coercion while being persuasive, educational, and instructive as to what is required of disputants. In the distant past, the Chinatown social context allowed didactic mediation by social enforcement of the decision of the Association's board or elders. Enforcement was by ostracism, economic boycott, or the weightiness of imposed moral righteousness. These forms of enforcement, to be effective, require wholehearted community support which exists only in a society where mutual dependence is strong. This was initially the case in Chinatown because of the hostility of the larger American environment, the lack of occupational options, and the resultant need for internal social cohesion. With no practical alternative, a disputant was subject to the decision of the mediating association or to the greater bargaining power of a wealthier, more established or better respected opponent.

Hence didactic mediation required heavy dependence of the disputants on the enforcing authorities. Prior philosophic and pragmatic roots in Ch'ing [Qing] China helped to determine the direction and distinctive forms of dispute settlement. 'Saving face' was a subsidiary issue resulting from the pragmatic factor of having to live in an interdependent community, rather than the basis on which the decisions were enforced . . .

Chinatown's stability and stagnation are due in large measure to its control by elderly, conservative, non-American-educated association officers whose Confucian values emphasize status differences in a hierarchically organized society. In fulfilling their social duty, the officers stressed community harmony and hence favored the more established disputants, and discouraged unconventional behavior. As harmony entails the least amount of disruption, if the more established disputant is disrupted, there is greater disruption of community harmony. Moreover, mediation involves bargaining and compromise. By requiring mediation rather than the winner-takes all effect of a court suit, didactic mediation compromises otherwise valid claims. The traditional Ch'ing social duty of the officers also caused them unconsciously to serve their own class interests (though their services were free), since officers were generally selected from among the influential and economically successful. Because the mediators had both the power to persuade and to invoke sanctions, didactic mediation was always on the side of authority, serving the dominant elements in the community.

But all dispute settlement could not have been didactic. As the public effect of the dispute decreased, so also should the social pressure to resolve the dispute and the degree of coercion involved in enforcing a decision. Hence in a dispute affecting only the immediate parties, the mediator would be neutral, perhaps even passive, while the disputants freely specified their own resolutions and established their own sanctions.

As discrimination against the Chinese decreased, their method of dispute settlement changed. Voluntary mediation gradually replaced didactic mediation as court remedies became feasible and opportunities increased in employment, residence and assimilation. Like didactic mediation, voluntary mediation . . . takes place in a structured society between disputants subject to the same legal order, but differs in having an available judicial remedy.

No longer feeling a strong internal pull toward community cohesion, disputants are now more free to discontinue mediation or go directly to court. The bargaining position of a non-establishment disputant against a more established opponent and against a disagreeable decision by association officers is thus increased. There are still many who are psychologically dependent on Chinatown and others who, unable to speak English, remain dependent on Chinatown institutions. Nevertheless, for the great majority, dispute settlement in Chinatown associations is now merely an option, to be used or avoided at will and without stigma. Most associations have adapted to acting as neutral buffers, educators and patient persuaders, even in important disputes involving the community. Adjudication is increasingly favored, while mediation has become, for most, only a favored custom. If they are to survive, the associations must accept their changed role.

G: The Occupational Impulse Towards Informalism

Within various kinds of economic institutions, too, there is often a feeling that certain kinds of economic activity give rise to particular kinds of problem, and also a preference for self-governance that tends to encourage specialised modes of dispute resolution. Some indication of this was given above in our discussion of fairs and borough courts in England. But such tendencies are found across a whole range of societies, and one institution in which they were prominently located was the urban guild which, from Europe to imperial China, often dominated the urban social landscape. The guild was an association in which members engaged in the same line of commerce or craft joined together in order to protect members' businesses from outside competition and control their conditions of business in such matters as standard of product, methods of sale and employment relations. Guilds were often religious brotherhoods, dedicated to specific saints, with their regulations urging members to follow a strict religious way of life, and their rules (including those relating to economic activities) might well be expressed in religious terms. The guilds were by and large self-regulating, especially when their rules had been approved by the state authorities. An assembly of guild leaders would consider alleged violations of rules and impose penalties. The ultimate punishment was expulsion from the guild. Only criminal offences were excluded from the jurisdiction of the guild. Various kinds of pressure encouraged the handling of disputes – both between guild members and between members and their workers – within the guild. Disputes impeded business or production, and therefore needed to be dealt with quickly. Taking a dispute to court often meant delay, and as important, possible revelation of trade secrets and other matters best kept from the eyes of outsiders. Commercial and employment relationships were important, sometimes complex, and often more significant than assertion of legal rights. In such circumstances, mediation and arbitration within the guild were almost everywhere the preferred processes for handling disputes.

Although the power of guilds in Europe declined from the fifteenth century onwards as a result of the growth of the state, improvements in communications, expanding trade and, subsequently, the industrial revolution, the commercial preference for arbitration, mediation and other extra-judicial modes of dispute handling continued. In the United States, the transition from colonial to modern society involved the decline of 'geographical, religious and ideological boundaries of community' and their replacement by commercial bonds which generated their own communitarian values including a stress on commercial arbitration. The ending of slavery and the need to create new kinds of economic relations in the south was an additional significant complication. In Europe, too, there was a persisting preference amongst merchants for commercial arbitration and self-regulation. Later, with the development of labour unrest towards the end of the nineteenth century and the maturing of the industrial revolution, in both the United States and Europe special approaches were also needed for the resolution of employment disputes. These included industrial arbitration. And with the development of organised labour, arbitration and mediation came to serve as important mechanisms for collective bargaining. Here, the technical issues that are often involved, the fact that the parties are well-informed and practised opponents, and the large constituencies that the negotiating parties often have behind them, make mediation and arbitration especially suitable processes.

Extract 2:8

Sybille Van der Sprenkel: *Legal Institutions in Manchu China* (1962) Athlone Press, London, pp 92–94

Every guild had its regulations printed on red paper and hung in stores and workshops. These covered such matters as hours of work . . . conditions of apprenticeship . . . quality of product. seasonal adjustment of prices . . . fair weight . . . measures to maintain members' existing shares in the trade . . . [and] required members to submit their disputes to the guild before going to the official courts . . .

[In some cases] members were expressly forbidden to appeal to the magistrate without first giving the guild court the chance to adjudicate. The reason for this may have been the desire of the stronger members to keep control in their own hands without unwelcome publicity or the unpredictable interference of the [magistrate's court]; or it may have been the need to maintain internal cohesion and prevent, if possible, the bitterness that would arise if members were ranged opposite one another in a court action; or fear of endangering the good name and future influence of the whole guild by an irresponsible action against an outsider; or it may have been a combination of these motives.

It is agreed that members having disputes about money matters with each other shall submit their cases to arbitration at a meeting of the guild where the utmost will be done to arrive at a satisfactory settlement of the dispute. If it be impossible to arrive at an understanding, appeal may be made to the authorities; but if the complainant have recourse to the official direct, without first referring to the guild, he shall be subjected to a public reprimand and any future case he may present for the opinion of the guild will be dismissed without a hearing.

So reads the rule of one guild. Another was the following:

It is impossible to say that disputes may not arise . . . If anything of the sort occurs, the guild shall settle the difficulty in the manner most advantageous to all. Justice shall be observed and the facts of the case brought to light, and the matter be decided according to what is right. No concealment must be employed that justice may be manifested.

The guilds had other sanctions at their disposal to enforce obedience on their members. One which they frequently used was to fine an offender the cost of a feast or a theatrical performance for the entertainment of the membership. This penalized the guilty party but allowed him to regain dignity by playing the part of host and so re-establish himself in the affections of his fellows. If on the other hand the guild were set at defiance by a recalcitrant member, they could expel him, which would mean that he would lose the benefits of membership and would have instead to face the hostility of the guild – that is, his organised competitors. This would probably make it impossible for him to continue in business in that place.

Extract 2:9
J S Auerbach: *Justice Without Law? Resolving Disputes Without Lawyers* (1983) Oxford University Press, Oxford, pp 57–59

In the history of American efforts to escape from formal legal institutions, antebellum utopian communities marked the end of the beginning. The Civil War was the watershed: beyond it, amid the turbulence of race and labor relations, alternative dispute settlement was reshaped. The older pattern of indigenous community initiatives survived, but in attenuated form. Occasionally it flourished, especially in ethnic communities whose members clung to their own familiar cultural institutions amid the turmoil of resettlement in an alien environment. But in the second half of the nineteenth century, the purpose (if not the forms) of alternative dispute settlement were redefined. Fears of racial discord and class warfare injected arbitration as a remedy for the congestive breakdown of the court system and as an externally imposed deterrent to social conflict. Until the Civil War alternative dispute settlement expressed an ideology of community justice. Thereafter, as it collapsed into an argument for judicial efficiency, it became an external instrument of social control. That momentous shift still pervades the use of alternative dispute settlement more than a century later.

The first attempts to provide justice for freed slaves after the Civil War give the earliest hint of the new approach. The end of chattel slavery promised a new era of labor relations, based on contract rather than servitude, between white landowners and black field workers. But there were serious difficulties from the outset. A drastic imbalance in power relations between the races quickly converted the new labor contracts, which in theory expressed the will of freely consenting individuals, into another compulsory labor system. The Freedmen's Bureau, a government agency established to supervise and support the transition from slavery to freedom, unexpectedly confronted a huge volume of civil disputes – perhaps as many as 100,000 annually – generated by suspicion and antagonism between former masters and their newly freed slaves.

General O O Howard, Commissioner of the Freedmen's Bureau, stumbled upon a solution . . . Spontaneously, according to his autobiographical account, Howard proposed three-man arbitration tribunals for labor-contract disputes involving less than two hundred dollars. A Bureau agent would represent the government; planters and freedmen would each choose one representative. 'In nine cases out of ten,' Howard blithely predicted, 'the freedmen will choose an intelligent white man who always seemed to be their friend. Thus in our court so constituted, every interest will be fairly represented'.

This proposal expressed a paternalistic concept of fairness that rested upon continued planter domination. Howard offered arbitration to induce planters to comply with a contract labor system which already reflected and reinforced their superior bargaining position. Indeed, he seemed genuinely surprised to learn from his agents in South Carolina that freedmen there intended to choose one of their own to sit on an arbitration tribunal. When planters strenuously objected to the appointment of freedmen, Howard used his power to force their replacement. If the planters were mollified, he insisted, they would treat their black workers kindly.

The internal contradictions of Howard's approach were rooted in the logic of white supremacy. Howard, like other Reconstruction reformers, believed in a blend of formal equality and paternalistic justice. Although his stated goal was equality 'by law and justice,' he elevated the forms of equality above its actual substance, relying upon the principle of contractual freedom despite the enormous disparity in bargaining power between whites and blacks. In this context, any substantive effectiveness of arbitration as an alternative to adjudication was undercut. Planters tolerated arbitration tribunals as long as planters controlled them. Consequently the diversion of disputes from the formal court system (where blacks, palpably disadvantaged, had no right to testify until 1866) to arbitration had few discernible benefits for the freedmen. Informality, in a social setting of disparate power relations, inevitably served the interests of the dominant group.

Extract 2:10

Katherine Van Wezel Stone: 'Dispute Resolution in the Boundaryless Workplace' (2000–2001) 16 *Ohio State Journal of Dispute Resolution*, p 467 at pp 468–471

At present there are three different conceptions of the role of arbitration in the workplace. Each of these views embodies a distinctive notion of how arbitration systems should be designed and how much the courts should intervene.

The first conception is the *technique view of arbitration*, in which arbitration is valued as a method for resolving conflict that is faster and cheaper than litigation. In this view, arbitration is not a priori superior to other methods; rather, its goal is to avoid conflict, and its value depends upon the degree to which it accomplishes that goal . . .

A second conception of arbitration is a *public policy view*, in which arbitration is seen as a better method for implementing the public policies that are embodied in statutory employment law. In this view, a court should be supportive of arbitration only so long as arbitrators resolve the dispute in a manner that approximates what a court would do in the same case . . .

A third view of arbitration is that it is not a mirror image of litigation but rather a method for applying norms and resolving nonjusticiable disputes that arise within a self-regulating normative community. In the *self-regulation view*, the distinctive value of arbitration is not that it can enforce laws, but that it can enforce fairness norms that were not presently embodied in law. This view is based on the insight that face-to-face communities generate their own fairness norms for certain types of situations, and that community elders know and can apply these norms better than a court can.

Traditionally, arbitration has been designed to permit arbitrators to blend internal fairness norms with the norms of the larger community in order to reach results that are neither compelled by the law nor inconsistent with it, but fair in the context of the particular dispute. Arbitration originated as a form of dispute resolution for use within craft and merchant guilds to resolve disputes between members. These trade groups set their own norms of conduct and business standards, and established their own dispute resolution procedures to resolve disputes that might arise. Disputes that arose often blended allegations of breach of contract with allegations of violation of customary norms. Arbitrators were expected to resolve them by applying both the parties' own contracts and informal customary norms of the trade. The self-regulation view of arbitration counsels courts to support this aspect of arbitration, when arbitration constitutes and enhances the normative life of the workplace community.

H: Territorial Identity and the Impulse Towards Informalism

An additional and important context within which strong impulses for informalism may emerge is the local community. Of course, these may well be overlapping with other forms of community or social organisation, religious, ethnic, political and so on. But a recurrent and sometime distinguishing feature of such impulses is a concern to create or restore a sense of identity between the individual and the local community or neighbourhood, and an 'empowerment' of local people.

Indeed, contemporary moves are visible across a wide range of jurisdictions both to develop community justice, especially neighbourhood mediation, and to link it with the public justice system. These developments, however, must recall the powerful, and largely unchallenged, critiques of informal justice that were developed at the beginning of the 1980s (Abel, 1982b; Auerbach, 1983; Freeman, 1984) and which are dealt with in some detail in Chapter Three. Suffice it to state here that those analyses argued that informality of process and the diversion of disputes towards alternatives to adjudication seldom improved the position of the disadvantaged, but tended rather to entrench inequality and increase opportunities for coercion and manipulation. They revealed the limitations of innovatory dispute institutions as empowering schemes and as means of reconstituting community or social solidarity. They also underline the potential complexity of agendas for the recovery or transplanting of 'traditional' modes of dispute resolution.

Here in Britain, the much later emergence of interest in 'alternatives' on the part of those responsible for running the public justice system has enabled them to consider the North American experience in developing their plans. While attention is paid to ADR in Lord Woolf's 1995 and 1996 proposals for the renovation of the civil justice system as a whole, it is notable that he comes out strongly against using ADR as a channel of deflection to reduce court loads and against mandatory mediation. Nevertheless, the past decade has seen a flourishing growth in community mediation programmes in the United Kingdom, as both voluntary associations and local government have followed the United States example and increasingly committed themselves to providing such schemes in order to address problems of neighbour disputes, family quarrels, homelessness and juvenile misconduct.[3]

We look here at three texts: the relatively positive examination by Merry and Milner of the potential of the San Francisco Community Boards, one of the most significant North American attempts to develop community mediation; Lubman's examination of the transformation of extra-judicial, community-based mediation by China's leaders in the 1950s in pursuit of political mobilisation; and finally Auerbach's somewhat pessimistic evaluation of North American community justice schemes.

Extract 2:11

S E Merry and N Milner (eds): *The Possibility of Popular Justice: A Case Study of Community Mediation in the United States* (1993) University of Michigan Press, Ann Arbor, pp 10–15

A form of popular justice labeled community mediation mushroomed in the United States in the 1970s and 1980s. It aspired to build a justice system under the authority and normative order of the community rather than that of the state. Demands for community mediation grew out of community organizing and legal-reform efforts in the early 1970s and crystallized into community-mediation programs by the late 1970s and early 1980s. Community-mediation programs often sprang from neighborhood policing and neighborhood watch efforts and from criminal-justice reform movements such as bail reform and prisoner self-governance. At the core of this movement was the hope that handling local problems in community-run forums independent of the legal system would strengthen local self-governance and rejuvenate the self-reliant communities of the past. Community-run forums promised to empower ordinary people by giving them control over their own conflicts. Community mediation hoped to replace the dominance of the legal profession and the courts in the lives of ordinary citizens with the control of neighbors and peers. At the same time, the community-mediation movement aspired to create a system free from what it identified as major flaws in the legal system. Advocates of community mediation characterized the law as adversarial and suffused with win or lose outcomes artificially imposed by judges. Community mediation was the opposite: informal, participatory, nonprofessional, and reflective of the norms of local communities. Instead of the violence of imposed, coerced settlements, it followed consensual, conciliatory, and compromise-oriented procedures. Agreements required mutual consent.

Interest in community mediation also reflected growing disappointment with the inability of rights-oriented law-reform strategies to eliminate racial and economic

---

3 See, for example, 'Mediation Projects in London', at www.onwebsite.co.uk/on.Medn.html.

inequality and to improve the quality of community life. For many, the loss of community became a more fundamental social problem than inequality. Law, with its adversarial, coercive characteristics, was reinterpreted as a problem rather than a means of reform. Replacing the state legal system with community legal processes and building the capacity of communities to manage conflicts promised to restore this sense of community.

But exactly what community meant remained elusive. For some, community was defined by a mythic construction of a harmonious society in which local groups settled their problems without the intrusion of state law. This was the vision most extensively mobilized by advocates of community mediation in the 1970s. Leading anthropologists were called upon to present accounts of small-scale societies in which conflict was handled consensually, and conferences were held to discuss the possibilities of transplanting these approaches to the United States. Such conferences typically brought together academics, legal elites, and highly placed government officials.

The San Francisco Community Board was one of the most prominent examples of a form of community mediation deeply rooted in community life. Its ideology focused on the capacity of popular justice to embody community power and to express community values. This vision captured the attention of idealistic program developers, foundations, government policymakers, and countless eager volunteers. It has inspired numerous programs and training models. SFCB continues to stand for a grass-roots vision of mediation when other wings of the field are becoming more technocratic, more closely annexed to courts, and more involved with large-scale, routinized processing of cases. It still espouses neighborhood organization, empowerment, and self-government, although it also has shifted to a greater emphasis on service delivery. Its ideology is powerful, its founder charismatic.

SFCB is similar to most community-mediation programs in that it endeavors to apply conciliatory procedures to a range of family and neighborhood problems as an alternative to the courts. Unlike most other mediation programs, however, it has historically eschewed all contact with the legal system and endeavored to be a self-standing entity rooted in local communities. It claims that the creation of local judicial forums under the management of the community frees individuals from dependence on the state and its alienating, disruptive, and adversarial legal system. Most other community-mediation programs in the United States claim to deliver a better judicial service, to reduce court congestion, or to help people understand themselves better; SFCB, along with closely related programs, attempts to strengthen and rebuild community as well.

Since its inception in 1977, the program has spawned a large number of derivatives, attracted a great deal of private-foundation funding, created a nationwide center for policy and training, and developed a nationwide organization, the National Association for Community Justice, dedicated to spreading its version of community mediation. The program operated until the mid-1980s entirely on foundation funding, sustaining a budget of almost five hundred thousand dollars a year. For a program in a poorly funded field, this represented an enormous pool of resources.

SFCB has had a profound ideological impact on the subsequent development of the alternative dispute-resolution movement. The SFCB ideology provided legitimacy for a community focus during the early years of the alternative dispute-resolution movement. Long after many other community-mediation programs in the United States down-played aspirations toward broader social change, SFCB continued to claim that it provided better conflict-resolution services as well as contributing to a regeneration of civil responsibility and neighborly helpfulness in American community life, although, as Thomson and DuBow show, the current SFCB mood has shifted to service delivery. SFCB also offers a distinctive vision of mediation, one that encourages the expression of feelings. It is founded on a paradigm of communication in which problems of interest or right are transformed into issues of feelings and relationships.

Provocative and inspirational, California-hot-tub in its feel, grass-roots as well as empire-building in style, self-governing and autocratic, ideologically charged yet apolitical, SFCB is an institution full of paradoxes. It offers a vision of neighborhood, community, and helping, yet it alienates many of those most dedicated to those ideals as they become frustrated with its centralized control and with the lack of social change achieved through mediation. Sometimes the process provides cathartic breakthroughs, but at other times it is manipulative and formalistic. Despite the widespread appeal of its offer to handle problems through talking and neighborhood care, it draws few cases away from the courts. Promising to concentrate on the problems of people involved in ongoing relationships, it more often deals with problems between strangers. Rather than restoring and repairing relations, it often helps to sever them. Yet, through its massive training programs and neighborhood outreach, it has promoted and implemented a fundamentally different and potentially transformative style of thinking about conflict, where communication and the expression of feelings replace force and violence.

American cities are not mosaics of small, self-governing neighborhoods, nor have they probably ever been. Is a form of popular justice rooted in the power of local communities possible here? Are people willing to submit their problems to their neighbors for consideration? Is there a community system of values by which these problems can be managed? Can a program of community mediation continue to function outside the legal system, separate from its coercive power? SFCB attracts volunteers in an era when volunteerism seems to be on the wane; it appeals to people who are single, recently arrived in the city, and more often than not, women. Why do they join, and what does the vision of community that SFCB constructs mean to them?

Many of the recurrent debates within the community-mediation field stem from these contradictions of popular justice. How much legal pressure should be exerted to bring plaintiffs and defendants to the table? Should mediation be a specialized mechanism for handling certain kinds of cases referred by the court or a new form of authority outside the court altogether. Should mediators define the authority they exercise as derived from the court through, for example, 'oaths of confidentiality' administered by a judge or as derived from a self-governing community? Some forms of community mediation incorporate the discourse and symbols of law, while others endeavor to rely on that of the community, or therapy, or of relationships. SFCB is important in this debate because it has in the past deliberately resisted any contact with state law.

Extract 2:12

S Lubman: 'Mao and Mediation: Politics and Dispute Resolution in Communist China' (1967) 55 *California Law Review* 1284–1359, pp 1285–1286, 1287, 1358

There is undeniably much mediation within the new collectivities for residence and work which the Communists have fashioned in reordering Chinese society. . . .

[But] the Communists have set themselves against the Confucian emphasis on compromise and the traditional Chinese avoidance of encounters with the government. They have infused into mediation absolute criteria of right and wrong rather than allowing mediation, as it once did, to seek a compromise that would not disrupt a delicate network of personal relationships within a narrow social context. The political functions of mediation are so pervasive that they frequently overshadow the settlement function by directing the mediators' perceptions of disputes and the standards used to resolve them. Political involvement has replaced passivity. In short, the Communists have incorporated mediation into their effort to reorder Chinese society and mobilize mass support to implement Party policies.

Contemporary Chinese dispute resolution seems to owe more to Communist ideology, experience, and practice than it does to Confucian tradition. While there may be 'resonances' between traditional and Communist dispute resolution, the mediational devices used by the Communists seem more directly traceable to their own development as Communists than to the tradition they so resolutely oppose. The Communist Party has had considerable success in altering the nature of courts, unifying judicial and extrajudicial methods of resolving disputes politicizing the mediation process, and, in general, changing and redistributing the functions of mediation . . . Both the purposes which the Communists have assigned to mediation and the mediators and the style they are expected to use in resolving disputes contrast sharply with traditional resolution.

Extract 2:13

J Auerbach: *Justice without Law? Resolving Disputes without Lawyers* (1983) Oxford University Press, Oxford, pp 131–135

The new neighborhood justice centers, a response to Pound Conference proposals, opened in Atlanta, Kansas City, and Los Angeles during 1978. They were sponsored by the Department of Justice and securely located within the judicial system. The Atlanta and Kansas City centers functioned in the shadow of the local courts. Most referrals came from judges and prosecutors; relations with court officials were 'carefully cultivated.' These relationships determined the identity of disputants and the nature of their disputes, for the cases consigned to mediation were those that the courts wished to divert. The disputants were disproportionately female, black or Hispanic, and poor; their disputes were with each other (involving domestic disagreements and neighborly nuisances), not with organizations or businesses. Only the Los Angeles project, sponsored by the local bar association, achieved a measure of independence from the courts. But, located amid a transient population in a multi-ethnic neighborhood 'without common goals and values,' it rested on a precarious community base. Whether the new justice centers turned toward, or away from, the courts, they faced the impossible task of combining community autonomy with judicial control.

Wherever new dispute-settlement institutions sprouted in the seventies, lawyers were conspicuous and local residents were conspicuously silent. 'Trial by lawyer,' not trial by jury, was becoming the pervasive mode. Small-claims arbitration was conducted before three-lawyer panels in Pennsylvania. Arbitration by lawyers constituted part of a court reorganization plan in New York, where private law offices served as small-claims court-rooms. In Florida, a 'citizen dispute settlement' mediation program referred disputes to panels of volunteer attorneys. In California, the most prominent feature of a small-claims court in a largely Mexican-American neighborhood of San Jose was the presence of lawyers, nominated by the local bar association and appointed by the courts as mediators and arbitrators. Bench and bar were appropriately supportive. Judges were delighted with the prospect of reduced caseloads; lawyers complimented each other for promoting 'good public relations' at a time of low professional esteem after Watergate. A streamlined judiciary, supplemented by efficient dispute-settlement procedures outside the courtroom (but not too far from the courthouse), pleased the Chief Justice, the Attorney General, and the bar associations and judicial conferences that enthusiastically endorsed the new reform. If the key to any reform is what it provides to the reformers who propose it, bench and bar clearly had the most to gain from alternative dispute settlement.

There were, as always, unanticipated consequences of the reformers' good intentions. Perhaps the most illuminating (and historically poignant) example was Dorchester, the largest neighborhood in metropolitan Boston. It contained the standard urban volatile mix of established middle-class whites, hostile to a massive influx of impoverished black and Hispanic newcomers. In Dorchester, by the late sixties, these 'striking and undoubtedly provocative disparities' had erupted into overt hostility that threatened to engulf the judiciary, whose tasks of dispute settlement were compounded by the most rapidly accelerating crime rate of any neighborhood in metropolitan Boston. Dorchester was located not far from Dedham and Sudbury, its seventeenth-century forebears in the development of non-legal dispute settlement, but there was little to connect their respective experiments. A new urban court mediation program – an alternative to criminal prosecution for family and neighborhood disputes – was designed for Dorchester. If it could build 'a human connection' between defendant, victim, and community, it might change 'a busy and mechanical urban court into an institution that would provide justice in human terms, as a healing and reconciling experience.' One enthusiastic preliminary assessment suggested that 'there may be in the rich, "participatory" symbolism of community mediation the seeds for the growth of a new ethos of cultural values,' an ethos rooted in harmony and consensus rather than in disruptive conflict.

According to early evaluations, the Dorchester program successfully resolved varied interpersonal conflicts that involved minor assaults and harassment between neighbors, friends, and family members. Disputants responded positively; they attributed substantial improvement in their situations to mediation, expressing considerable satisfaction with the mediators, who were all Dorchester residents, for their empathetic listening and support. As more evidence accumulated, however, it suggested that the new urban court, ostensibly designed as an alternative to adjudication, actually functioned as a lesser adjunct of the local district court, from which it received nearly all of its referrals. Indeed, the two courts represented competing interests in Dorchester. The law reformers who founded the urban court were committed to active community participation in dispute-settlement processes that would heal and reconcile, not isolate and punish. But the presiding judge of the district court, expressing strong reservations about involving lay citizens in dispute settlement, preferred mediation to serve the efficiency needs of his own tribunal. By controlling the diversion of cases to mediation, and deterring self-generated cases, district court personnel deprived the mediation tribunal of an independent existence. 'Community' mediation was absorbed by adjudication. Despite high neighborhood visibility, approval, and cost-free services, Dorchester residents only four times in two years sought mediation on their own initiative. The most striking feature of the new mediation process (in neighborhood justice centers as in Dorchester) was its inability to attract disputes independent of referrals from the judicial system. With the presiding district court judge apprehensive lest judicial control be compromised by deflections from his own court, mediation slipped into the institutional cracks between the 'community' proclaimed by reformers and the adjudicatory power of the local judge.

The fragility of the Dorchester community empowered the local district court and undercut mediation as an alternative. In an atomistic social environment, only the court possessed sufficient coercive power to secure the compliance of disputing parties. Mediation was an unfamiliar process in Dorchester. Mediators, although local residents, were 'strangers with known values.' Above all, mediation required a social context of intimacy, reciprocity, and permanence that was conspicuously missing in Dorchester, as in other American urban neighborhoods. The choice of forum, in Dorchester as elsewhere, reflected the degree of neighborhood cohesion. In a Boston inner-city neighborhood near Dorchester, for example, black and white residents, lacking a sustaining network of community supports, readily took their disputes to court; while their Chinese neighbors, who depended upon community relationships for employment and social interaction, went to court with considerable reluctance. Dorchester and Dedham were only miles apart, but the possibilities for communal dispute settlement without law, so evident in the seventeenth century, were all but obliterated in the twentieth. Alternative dispute settlement served as a tenacious metaphor for missing elements of community in American cities, but there was little in urban life to sustain it as a functioning process. All signs pointed to the same conclusion about urban justice: 'Life rather than logic makes self-referred mediation as unpalatable to Americans as it is attractive to the peoples of other cultures.'

The new urban mediation alternatives contradicted virtually every prerequisite for informal justice that comparative anthropology and American history provided. Communities played no role in their design or implementation. The site-selection process suggested that community fragmentation, not community cohesion, was the primary criterion. Rochester, Dorchester, and Harlem, to cite three early recipients of mediation programs, all had recently experienced acute tension and overt conflict – and, significantly, signs of incipient political activism among community residents, which government officials and legal professionals preferred to stifle, through formal or informal means. Legal institutions hovered over the new mediation programs; virtually every project, by design, received the overwhelming preponderance of its referrals from criminal justice agencies. With legal coercion permeating the mediation process, few neighbors brought their disputes to neighborhood justice centers. An indigenous community practice had come to serve the interests of the state legal system in promoting the efficient processing of criminal complaints.

I: Movements for Legal Reform and Informalism

In the United States, the growing dissatisfaction with the formal justice system at the end of the nineteenth century resulted in a number of significant attempts made during the period 1900–1930 to develop alternative dispute settlement mechanisms. These were given jurisprudential inspiration by Roscoe Pound in his firm condemnation of the 'sporting theory of justice' (Pound, 1906). In Pound's view the adversarial approach to justice found in common law systems promotes an excessively instrumental attitude to law, and discouraged disputants from making concessions on the basis of shared values. Auerbach traces subsequent North American moves to informalism in the early years of this century. (See Extract 2:14.) But in addition to the development of conciliation centres described by Auerbach, efforts were made to reform courts by making them more efficient through the application of scientific management principles, and socially responsive by the introduction of specialised chambers for dealing with particular kinds of case – domestic relations, juveniles, small claims and so on – often relying on mediation as the principal process for decision-making. (See Extract 2:15.) That process of reform continued beyond the Second World War, and was given particular impetus by the emergence of the 'access to justice' movement described in Chapter Three.

Extract 2:14

J S Auerbach: *Justice Without Law? Resolving Disputes Without Lawyers* (1983) Oxford University Press, Oxford, pp 96–97

> As dissatisfaction with legal institutions increased during the early decades of the twentieth century, there was renewed interest in alternatives to litigation, especially conciliation and arbitration. Both were touted as speedy, inexpensive procedures to dispense with lawyers and reduce the acrimonious, costly delays that suffused litigation. But they originated in separate constituencies to serve divergent interests. Conciliation was a reform offered by the legal community to a marginal clientele; it was designed to resolve the claims of poor people who could not afford counsel, and who were especially victimized by court congestion and delay. Arbitration, by contrast, expressed the preference of commercial interests, especially in New York, for self-regulation untrammeled by the intrusion of law and lawyers. Consistent with these differences of origin and purpose, conciliation limped along in a state of neglect, while arbitration flourished

to become a national institution – deeply enmeshed, ironically, in the legal system. Their respective histories illuminate the first modern attempts to divert disputes from a legal system that was perceived as too expensive, contentious, and inefficient to resolve them satisfactorily.

Conciliation was part of a package of reforms designed to alleviate procedural injustices that bore down most heavily upon the urban poor. Along with legal aid, small-claims courts, and public defenders, it was intended to undercut the claim that justice was available only in proportion to the ability to pay for it. The modern conciliation movement began in 1913 in Cleveland, where a conciliation branch of the municipal court was authorized to assist litigants who were unable to obtain lawyers to settle their small claims. All claims for thirty-five dollars or less were entered on the conciliation docket; parties were encouraged to appear before a municipal judge without lawyers; in the absence of formal legal procedure, the judge, relying upon an 'appeal to common sense' to resolve the disagreement, tried to arouse amicable feelings and suppress fighting instincts. Conciliation procedure was voluntary and formless, intended to encourage disputants to compromise their differences. Judgments rested entirely upon the consent of the parties; if conciliation failed, the dispute went to trial.

The conciliation idea spread slowly during the next decade. The Cleveland plan provided a model for Chicago, where a similar program was implemented two years later. In New York, the state bar association endorsed conciliation as an alternative to what one member described as 'the hell of litigation.' In Philadelphia, the Municipal Court established a special division for conciliation, small claims, and legal aid. And in Iowa, controversies involving less than one hundred dollars were consigned to conciliation at the discretion of the judge. The presence of lawyers was discouraged; the object was 'to get the parties themselves to meet and talk over their differences.'

The rhetoric of conciliation emphasized harmony and amity as alternatives to conflict, which litigation encouraged even as it provided legal forms and procedures for containing disputes. 'Disputes run all too easily into class, religious, and racial animosities and prejudices,' warned law reformer Reginald Heber Smith. Litigation tended only 'to inflame and perpetuate quarrels'; conciliation, however, offered 'moderation, forebearance, mutual adjustment and honourable compromise,' thereby avoiding the bitterness of a contested trial. It was, according to an editorial written in praise of the Cleveland experiment, 'a movement toward justice in spite of lawyers.'

Extract 2:15
Christine B Harrington: 'Delegalisation Reform Movements: A Historical Analysis' (1992) in Richard Abel (ed) *The Politics of Informal Justice, Volume 1: the American Experience*, Academic Press, New York, pp 48–63

A brief overview of the management concepts and procedural reforms associated with the early unification [of courts] helps to reveal the relationship between court reorganisation and the implementation of informal procedures. The most significant development was the centralisation of management through the creation of a presiding judge in the municipal court. This established a single judicial officer empowered to supervise record keeping, control caseload, and 'clerical subordinates'. The introduction of a unified calendar regulating caseload enhanced the administrative power of the presiding judge . . .

The calendar system of caseload management also introduced specialization . . . dockets were specialized to maximise the efficiency of each judge. Specialized tribunals – small claims, domestic relations – were also developed as branches of the municipal court . . . Each branch was headed by a presiding judge who performed management tasks similar to those of the judge . . .

On the one hand, this expansion of judicial autonomy legitimated the exercise of discretion by lower court judges, who could now establish specialized tribunals and adopt informal procedures through judicial rule-making. On the other hand, the rise of court management stratified judicial personnel, creating management posts and dividing work into specialized calendars and tribunals . . .

The domestic relations, small claims and conciliation court were called 'socialized courts' in the sense that their 'procedures and remedies focused on diagnosis, prevention, cure, education' . . .

[In addition] the use of 'unofficial' dockets in juvenile courts reflected the belief that children could be treated more effectively through informal dispositions . . .

Domestic relations courts . . . represent the institutionalization of informal dispute processing . . . [and] adopted the juvenile court philosophy of social justice and applied it to cases of wife abandonment, illegitimacy, failure to support, offenses against minors and custody disputes . . .

Criticisms of the socialised courts after 1940 focuses on the fact that they were appendages of traditional judicial institutions rather than genuine alternatives to the adversarial process . . . [and that] the socialized courts did not complement a unified lower court but rather increased the organizational complexity of the judicial structure.

Unification continued to be the dominant management strategy . . . Court unification between the 1940s and 1960s was aimed . . . at greater centralization and control of the judicial work process.

The unified model has recently been challenged by court reformers who argue that the management and organisation of courts must be decentralised to integrate them within the local environment and utilize local resources more effectively . . .

Yet within the decentralised management model, minor disputes are channelled into appended tribunals that emphasise therapeutic intervention by trained lay citizens. Individuals, assisted by mediators, seek to reach an agreement on how to restructure their future behaviour to avoid or prevent conflict. Disputes such as violence against women, neighbourhood quarrels, and landlord-tenant problems are reduced to individual problems. The origins of these disputes are depolitized or ignored, and the resolutions are internalized by the individualized form of participation. Conflict in this setting is absorbed into a rehabilitative model of minor dispute resolution . . .

Discretion once exercised by court officials and police officers is formally exercised by mediators and arbitrators in a therapeutic setting. Delegalization in this context serves to rationalise the adjudication process. The form of judicial intervention in specialized tribunals such as the neighbourhood justice center expands the scope of dispute processing by the state.

J: Temporal Dimensions

The identification of informal values and processes across a range of cultural contexts is complicated by the changes that may occur over the course of time. Although there is seemingly a perpetual movement between informal principles and those of 'formal' justice, the process of development is often much more complex than a simple 'oscillating' model would allow for.

The experience of China's system of people's mediation also shows clearly the manner in which changes in political climate radically affect of the nature of that system. The scheme for community mediation that has been resurrected in post-Mao China does, in both form and substance, bear the imprint of the system that was replaced in the 1960s by the highly radical and politicised style of 'mediation' pursued during the Cultural Revolution. Nevertheless, this revivification is not a simple replication of the 1950s. The revived system is more decentralised, more professional, and is placed in a much more firmly subordinate position in relation to the state courts than its 1950s predecessor. (See Extract 2:16.)

Even within particular political and economic contexts there are pressures of institutionalisation at work that may result in changes that fundamentally transform the meaning of the institution, often with a tendency for it to become incorporated in the state system or at least to become juridified (Flood and Caiger, 1993)[4] so that 'despite its formal opposition to state law, popular justice often replicates and strengthens its language and cultural forms' (Merry 1993: 60). An important factor here is the close connections that often exist between formal and informal justice (Abel, 1982b; Harrington, 1985). In addition, in an important commentary on 'popular justice' Peter Fitzpatrick argues further that the ideals of informal justice are rarely capable of being sustained, in large part because they are put into effect in a process which mirrors the ideology and practice of formal justice, so that the ambitions of informalism – expressed in its 'origin myth' – are only achieved with great difficulty (1993).

Extract 2:16

M Palmer: 'The Revival of Mediation in the People's Republic of China: (1) Extra-judicial mediation' (1988) in W E Butler (ed) *Yearbook on Socialist Legal Systems 1987*, Transnational Books, New York, Dobbs Ferry, pp 265–270

> The role of the people's mediator is being modified in directions that closely reflect the Chinese leadership's concern to foster a more systematic, professional, and comprehensive approach in extra-judicial mediation work. As a result of these modifications, the characteristics of the post-Mao mediator differ in several important respects from those of the type of mediator who operated before the Cultural Revolution. Typically, the mediator in these earlier periods was a housewife – more specifically, an unpaid,

---

4 Menkel-Meadow's work powerfully explores some of the crucial ethical issues that such processes raise (2001). See also Chapter Seven below.

elderly, poorly-educated and female city dweller. She often lacked the authority and status necessary to operate effectively as a dispute settler unless aided by persons from other institutions, such as the local residents' committee, public security, or the police. Nevertheless, mediators were expected closely to identify with the Party and its political goals: 'the Party has tried to select politically "progressive" activists as urban street mediators'; and 'mediators, being activists or cadres, belong to the State and Party apparatus whose most important goal is to maintain and strengthen Party control. The closeness of activist mediators to both urban police and the Party has been stressed frequently by the Chinese press and corroborated by emigres.'

There continues to be some reliance on this type of mediator, especially in urban neighborhoods, primarily because it is the elderly housewife who is most willing to undertake the often thankless task of people's mediator. Over 80% of the mediators in Beijing today are women. In addition, however, it should be noted that there are important rationalizations in the Chinese legal press for using women as mediators: life histories of model mediators generally characterize women as particularly insightful and patient in handling inter-personal relations, especially within the family.

The effectiveness of mediation work is considered to be undermined by the dilatory style of some mediators. To a certain extent the problem of sloth is attributed to the adverse impact of the Cultural Revolution. The harsh treatment that they were afforded has left many of the older mediators – the 'mainstays' (*gugan*) of mediation – reluctant to involve themselves in other people's problems: they no longer identify strongly with the goals of mediation, being content merely to carry out their duties in a perfunctory manner . . . The problem is exacerbated by the low educational standards of many mediators whose grasp of mediation regulations and principles is correspondingly 'inadequate.'

In order to reduce reliance on these types of mediator and to improve the scope and effectiveness of mediation, a series of important reforms have been introduced in recent years. The current leadership is determined to improve the standards of mediation work, raise the status of mediators, and expand the number of mediators . . . For example, mediators are no longer expected to serve on a purely voluntary basis. Efforts are being made to introduce systems of payment for mediators. One report indicates that in urban areas they now receive the same stipend as workers in civil affairs neighborhood offices. Another report informs us that in rural areas they now receive an annual payment of between 180 and 350 yuan. Since September 1985 the Ministry of Justice has given State funds to mediation committees for the purchase of stationery and other materials, the payment of subsidies to those mediators who have had to absent themselves from their full-time employment in order to carry out mediation work, the production of publicity materials, and the provision of short-term training for mediators.

In addition, the leadership is attempting to make mediation 'more learned' by greatly improving the educational background and so on of persons who typically serve as mediator. The goal is to achieve significant changes in the social identity of mediators by attracting retired teachers, workers, cadres, and other persons with significant levels of education and experience of work outside the home. Younger persons are being recruited: in one county in Shandong it is reported that 75% of the mediators are under the age of forty-five years. Not surprisingly, many of the newly-recruited mediators are either Party members or cadres. In some rural areas a substantial proportion of the persons now serving as mediators are reportedly men who come from wealthy households, enjoy a stable family life, and are respected and trusted by local people. By encouraging this latter development the leadership is supporting the policy of allowing greater inequalities of wealth in order to promote the rural economy and opposing the malign influence of 'leftism.' In addition, in a number of districts the election of mediators by local residents is being promoted, and this too is intended to have a favorable impact on the social identity of the person that typically becomes a mediator. Another important development in this context is the increasing use of lawyers as extra-judicial mediators. Lawyers now not only have the right to represent disputants in extra-judicial mediation but also in some districts operate legal advisory offices in which out-of-court mediation is an important legal service offered to local people.

Another important feature of these reforms in the functioning of mediators is a concern to upgrade 'the quality of professional work' (*yewu suzhi*) and 'mediation abilities' (*tiaojie nengli*) of mediators by the introduction of a variety of systems of education and training. These are considered to be important not only in view of the low standards of many mediators but also because in rural areas especially there has been an increasing number of serious disputes arising out of the introduction of rural economic reforms. Although the programs are in many respects superficial, they do reflect the PRC leadership's commitment to building a structure of people's mediation that strengthens the work and status of the people's courts, and we have noted that the Ministry of Justice provides mediation committees with special funding to be used for mediators' training. One recent example of the type of training involved is provided by the case of the large city of Lanzhou in northwestern China where:

> The local Department of Justice conducts monthly professional work meetings [*yewu huiyi*] for those persons holding positions of responsibility on mediation committees. The meetings enable mediators to broaden their knowledge of the law. The Department also regularly organizes visits to court for mediators in order that they may observe and learn from the proceedings. This improves their understanding of policy and law as well as the quality of their professional work.

Other reports indicate that similar systems are being promoted in other parts of China. In some cases the training takes place more directly under the supervision of the basic-level people's courts. In most situations the Party appears to be in ultimate control of these schemes.

K: Conclusions

The various contexts within which informal principles of justice have often been found reveal a widespread and persistent tendency to create alternatives to adjudication, or at least modified forms of adjudication, for handling disputes. Despite considerable cultural diversity and variations over time, we can often see a strong impulse to create institutions that rely on modes of decision-making other than adjudication for handling disputes. A general aversion to state-based formal justice, or religious, political, ethnic or territorial forces, or a felt need to refurbish courts and other agencies of formal justice are perhaps the most common contexts – sometime enclaves – within which ideologies and practices of informal justice have most readily taken hold. The contemporary ADR movement is thus backed by quite firm historical credentials, and given this experience it is perhaps surprising that current efforts across a range of jurisdictions – but especially in the Anglo-American common law world – to encourage greater attention to the value of the key processes of informal justice, namely negotiation and mediation, have met stiff and sometimes fierce resistance. In Chapter Three we attempt to identify and explain the main strands of this criticism.

CHAPTER THREE

The Debates Around Civil Justice and the Movement Towards Procedural Innovation

A: Introduction

Across common law jurisdictions generally, the decades since 1960 have seen native institutions of civil disputing subject to more or less continuous re-examination and renovation. This process has taken place against the background of a particular jural inheritance, of which three foundational elements stand out. First is the historical dominance of state-sponsored adjudication, and hence of litigation, in the theory and practice of civil justice in the common law world. Second is the extent to which, as litigation has acquired a privileged status as the approved mode of dispute resolution, lawyers have through its practice achieved over generations a near monopoly over dispute management. The nature of this monopoly is only fully revealed when it is remembered that judicial appointment represents the ultimate career stage for the successful lawyer. Third is the manner in which lawyers have utilised civil procedure as the vehicle for their negotiation strategies, bringing about the profound entanglement of 'settlement' and 'litigation'. Behind an ideology under which settlement remains virtually invisible and submerged, it is in practice pursued through use of the procedural framework prescribed for bringing a dispute to trial and judgment.

Disenchantment with this distinctive culture of disputing has generated some complex, overlapping conversations, for the most part recognisable earliest in the United States. These conversations have varied in pace and direction from one jurisdiction to another and are not readily subjected to generalisation. But, at the risk of over-simplification, they can at first be reduced to three broad discussions: one about the conditions of availability of 'judgment'; another about the corresponding merits of 'settlement'; and a third around the search for 'alternative' forms.

The first of these conversations could probably be traced back to the very emergence of adjudication, to a time when the earliest kings and other rulers were struggling to establish a steering role. But for our purposes we can locate its recent origins in the 1960s and the 1970s. It was then articulated as an 'access to justice' movement. It represented the contemporary expression of primordial concerns about the costs, delays and general inaccessibility of adjudication, and called for quicker, cheaper, more readily available judgment with procedural informality as its hallmark. This was thus a conversation directed towards the renovation of adjudication. (See Extract 3:1.)

The second conversation, emerging during the 1970s, problematised adjudication itself, pointing to the advantages of 'settlement' (Burger, 1976; Bok, 1983). In a fierce critique of existing arrangements, Derek Bok analysed the factors which in his view underlie 'the blunt, inexcusable fact that [the United States], which prides itself on efficiency and justice, has developed a legal system that is the most expensive in the world, yet cannot manage to protect the rights of most [of its] citizens' (1983: 574). He concluded:

> Over the next generation, I predict, society's greatest opportunities will lie in tapping human inclinations toward collaboration and compromise rather than stirring our proclivities for competition and rivalry. If lawyers are not leaders in marshaling cooperation and designing mechanisms that allow it to flourish, they will not be at the center of the most creative social experiments of our time (1983: 583). (See Extract 3:2.)

In the mid-1970s a third conversation began to develop which looked beyond the renovation of adjudication and arguments about the merit of settlement through lawyer negotiations to the possibilities of 'complementary' and 'alternative' forms. Auerbach identifies the 1976 National Conference on the Causes of Popular Dissatisfaction with the Administration of Justice (the Pound Conference) as 'the decisive moment in the legalization of informal alternatives' (1983: 123), and that Conference seems also to have been the first occasion on which Frank Sander used the term 'alternative dispute resolution' (1976). We have already noted in Chapter One how this shift was signalled in a fundamental change in the way academic lawyers, and to some extent practitioners, began to talk about conflict. We saw there how new ways of thinking about disputes were linked to a growing sensitivity on the part of lawyers to the social sciences, and in particular to anthropological studies of dispute.

This exposure of lawyers to other cultures sometimes led to explicit 'borrowing' in the formulation of projects of reform (Danzig, 1973), but more generally growing comparative awareness prompted expansive reflection on 'complementary' and 'alternative' arrangements at home (see Sander, 1976). It is notable that in much of this conversation the court still remains the pivot around which discussion proceeds, as it is in Sander's seminal proposal of the 'Multi-Door Courthouse'. (See Extract 3:3.)

Extract 3:1

M Cappelletti and B G Garth: *Access to Justice, Volume 1: A World Survey* (1978) Sijthoff & Noordhoff, Milan, pp 6–9

> The concept of access to justice has been undergoing an important transformation, corresponding to a comparable change in civil procedural scholarship and teaching. In the liberal, 'bourgeois' states of the late eighteenth and nineteenth centuries, the procedures for civil litigation reflected the essentially individualistic philosophy of

rights then prevailing. A right of access to judicial protection meant essentially the aggrieved individual's formal right to litigate or defend a claim. The theory was that, while access to justice may have been a 'natural right', natural rights did not require affirmative state action for their protection. These rights were considered prior to the state; their preservation required only that the state did not allow them to be infringed by others. The state thus remained passive with respect to such problems as the ability, in practice, of a party to recognize his legal rights and to prosecute or defend them adequately.

Relieving 'legal poverty' – the incapacity of many people to make full use of the law and its institutions – was not the concern of the state. Justice, like other commodities in the laissez-faire system, could be purchased only by those who could afford its costs, and those who could not were considered the only ones responsible for their fate. Formal, not effective, access to justice – formal, not effective, equality – was all that was sought.

Until recent years, with rare exceptions legal scholarship was similarly unconcerned with the realities of the judicial system: 'Such factors as differences among potential litigants in practical access to the system or in the availability of litigating resources were not even perceived as problems.' Scholarship was typically formalistic, dogmatic, and aloof from the real problems of civil justice. Its concern was frequently one of mere exegesis or abstract system-building; even when it went beyond this concern, its method was to judge the rules of procedure on the basis of historical validity and their operation in hypothetical situations. Reforms were suggested on the basis of this theory of procedure, rather than on actual experience. Scholarship, like the court system itself, was removed from the real concerns of most people.

As the laissez-faire societies grew in size and complexity, the concept of human rights began to undergo a radical transformation. Since actions and relationships increasingly assumed a collective rather than an individual character, modern societies necessarily moved beyond the individualistic, laissez-faire view of rights reflected in eighteenth and nineteenth century bills of rights. The movement has been toward recognizing the social rights and duties of governments, communities, associations, and individuals. These new human rights, exemplified by the Preamble of the French Constitution of 1946, are above all those necessary to make effective, ie, actually accessible to all, the rights proclaimed earlier. Among such rights typically affirmed in modern constitutions are the rights to work, to health, to material security, and to education. It has become commonplace to observe that affirmative action by the state is necessary to ensure the enjoyment by all of these basic social rights. It is therefore not surprising that the right of effective access to justice has gained particular attention as recent 'welfare state' reforms have increasingly sought to arm individuals with new substantive rights in their capacities as consumers, tenants, employees, and even citizens. Indeed, the right of effective access is increasingly recognized as being of paramount importance among the new individual and social rights, since the possession of rights is meaningless without mechanisms for their effective vindication. Effective access to justice can thus be seen as the most basic requirement – the most basic 'human right' – of a modern, egalitarian legal system which purports to guarantee, and not merely proclaim, the legal rights of all.

Extract 3:2

D Bok: 'A Flawed System of Law and Practice Training' (1983) 33 *Journal of Legal Education* 570, pp 582–583

If law schools are to do their share in attacking the basic problems of our legal system, they will need to adapt their teaching as well as their research. The hallmark of the curriculum continues to be its emphasis on training students to define the issues carefully and to marshal all of the arguments and counter arguments on either side. Law schools celebrate this effort by constantly telling students that they are being taught 'to think like a lawyer.' But one can admire the virtues of careful analysis and still believe that the times cry out for more than these traditional skills. As I have tried to point out, the capacity to think like a lawyer has produced many triumphs, but it has also helped to produce a legal system that is among the most expensive and least efficient in the world.

One example of this problem is the familiar tilt in the law curriculum toward preparing students for legal combat. Look at a typical catalogue. The bias is evident in the required first-year course in civil procedure, which is typically devoted entirely to the rules of federal courts with no suggestion of other methods for resolving disputes. Looking further, one can discover many courses in the intricacies of trial practice, appellate advocacy, litigation strategy, and the like – but few devoted to methods of mediation and negotiation. Throughout the curriculum, professors spend vast amounts of time examining the decisions of appellate courts, but make little effort to explore new voluntary mechanisms that might enable parties to resolve various types of disputes without going to court in the first place.

Many people have debated whether lawyers exacerbate controversy or help to prevent it from arising. Doubtless, they do some of each. But everyone must agree that law schools train their students more for conflict than for the gentler arts of reconciliation and accommodation. This emphasis is likely to serve the profession poorly. In fact, lawyers devote more time to negotiating conflicts than they spend in the library or the courtroom, and studies show that their bargaining efforts accomplish more for their clients. Over the next generation, I predict, society's greatest opportunities will lie in tapping human inclinations toward collaboration and compromise rather than stirring our proclivities for competition and rivalry. If lawyers are not leaders in marshaling cooperation and designing mechanisms that allow it to flourish, they will not be at the center of the most creative social experiments of our time.

Another glaring deficiency is the lack of attention given to the very problems of the legal system that I have been discussing. This neglect is particularly striking when one hears the repeated claims of established law schools that they are not training lawyers but preparing 'leaders of the bar.' If this assertion is to be taken seriously, one would suppose that students in these schools would be studying ways of creating simpler rules, less costly legal proceedings, and greater legal protection for the poor and middle class. Yet even a cursory glance at the law school catalogue will serve to destroy this illusion. I can scarcely recall a single class, let alone an entire course, devoted to these issues during my three years of law study. Although the situation has improved since then, courses on the problems of the legal system are almost always relegated to elective slots where only a handful of students typically attend.

Leadership also calls for more than merely preparing leaders of the bar. Law schools will need to take the initiative in educating for a broader range of legal needs in our society. An efficient system of extending access to legal services throughout the society will demand the imaginative use of paralegal personnel. An effective system for extending legal protection to the poor must involve greater efforts to educate the disadvantaged about their rights, so that they can defend their interests without being exploited or having to go to court. A serious attempt to provide cheaper methods of resolving disputes will require skilled mediators and judges, who are trained to play a much more active part in guiding proceedings toward a fair solution. In short, a just and effective legal system will not merely call for a revised curriculum; it will entail the education of new categories of people. It is time that our law schools began to take the lead in helping devise such training.

Extract 3:3
F E A Sander: 'Varieties of Dispute Processing' (1976) 70 *Federal Rules Decisions* 79, pp 126–127, 130–132

At one time perhaps the courts were the principal public dispute processors. But that time is long gone. With the development of administrative law, the delegation of certain problems to specialized bodies for initial resolution has become a common-place. Within the judicial sphere, too, we have developed specialized courts to handle family problems and tax problems, among others.

These were essentially *substantive* diversions, that is, resort to agencies having substantive expertise. Perhaps the time is now ripe for greater resort to an alternate primary *process*. As I have indicated earlier, such a step would be particularly appropriate in situations involving disputing individuals who are engaged in a long-term relationship. The process ought to consist initially of a mediational phase, and then, if necessary, of an adjudicative one. Problems that would appear to be particularly amenable to such a two-stage process are disputes between neighbors, family members, supplier and distributor, landlord and tenant. Where there is an authority relationship between the parties (such as exists between prisoner and warden or school and student) special problems may be presented, but, as indicated earlier, such relationships, too, are, with some adjustments, amenable to a sequential mediation–adjudication solution ... What I am thus advocating is a flexible and diverse panoply of dispute resolution processes, with particular types of cases being assigned to differing processes (or combinations of processes), according to some of the criteria previously mentioned. Conceivably such allocation might be accomplished for a particular class of cases at the outset by the legislature; that in effect is what was done by the Massachusetts legislature for malpractice cases. Alternatively one might envision by the year 2000 not simply a court house but a Dispute Resolution Center, where the grievant would first be channelled through a screening clerk who would then direct him to the process (or sequence of processes) most appropriate to his type of case. The room directory in the lobby of such a Center might look as follows:

Screening Clerk	Room 1
Mediation	Room 2
Arbitration	Room 3
Fact Finding	Room 4
Malpractice Screening Panel	Room 5
Superior Court	Room 6
Ombudsman	Room 7

Of one thing we can be certain: once such an eclectic method of dispute resolution is accepted there will be ample opportunity for everyone to play a part. Thus a court might decide of its own to refer a certain type of problem to a more suitable tribunal. Or a legislature might, in framing certain substantive rights, build in an appropriate dispute resolution process. Institutions such as prisons, schools, or mental hospitals also could get into the act by establishing indigenous dispute resolution processes. Here the grievance mechanism contained in the typical collective bargaining agreement stands as an enduring example of a successful model. Finally, once these patterns begin to take hold, the law schools, too, should shift from their preoccupation with the judicial process and begin to expose students to the broad range of dispute resolution processes.

B: The Debates of the 1980s

A notable feature of these three 'movements' – towards the renovation of civil justice, the sponsorship of consensual decision-making and a search for 'alternatives' – was the nature and power of the critiques which they evoked. These critiques, though delivered from a range of very different positions in ideological terms, shared a common starting point in identifying what was seen as the beginning of a major shift in the wider socio-political landscape within which dispute processes were located. Over a long period, culminating after the middle of the twentieth century, government had become progressively differentiated, creating 'public' and 'private' spheres, each characterised by distinctive processes and rationalities. The most powerful institutions had evolved as formal institutions in the public sphere. Among these powerful institutions were the courts; with the consolidation of government's involvement in the management of disputes had come a conception of 'public justice', presented as the delivery of authoritative third-party determinations. In the late 1970s, the process showed signs of going into reverse, breaking down the hitherto apparently clear distinction between the 'public' and the 'private'. One early commentator, Richard Abel, presented this shift as an expansion of state power under which the mode changes from open coercion to covert manipulation, from 'command' to 'inducement' (Abel, 1980). Correspondingly, this shift was reflected in dispute institutions in a growing emphasis upon state sponsorship of 'settlement'.

Working on an even larger canvas, Boaventura de Sousa Santos argued that the state was now 'expanding in the form of civil society' and, predicted that this would take place through a 'dislocation of power from formal institutions to informal networks' (Santos, 1980: 391, 392). In the area of dispute institutions, this general transformation would be reflected in an expansion of state power as, through informalisation, the state sought to co-opt the private sphere and 'to integrate the sanctioning power of ongoing social relationships' (Santos, 1980: 391). Santos summed up his analysis, with its echoes of Althusser and Foucault, with the forecast that state and non-state would come 'to look more and more alike and it is not absurd to predict the development of a face-to-face state' (Santos, 1980: 391). (See Extract 3:4.)

In contrast with these forecasts informed by Marxist and Post-Modern perspectives is the contemporary account of this forthcoming transformation by Gunther Teubner from within the paradigm of neo-systems theory (Teubner, 1983). Starting from Luhmann's assumption of 'functionally differentiated society', Teubner appears to leave 'government' right out of the picture. Developing a conception of 'reflexive law', he forecast a new evolutionary stage in which law becomes 'a system for the co-ordination of action within and between semi-autonomous social subsystems'. With this integrative function of 'furthering reflexive processes in other social subsystems', attempting 'the control of self-regulatory processes' (1983: 281), Teubner predicted that 'reflexive law, now just an element in a complicated mixture of legal orientations, may emerge as the dominant form of post-modern law' (1983: 246). So, while the story is told in terms of self-generating systems of communication rather than of state power, the emergent transformation is in many ways strikingly close to that envisaged by Abel and de Sousa Santos.

Extract 3:4

B de Sousa Santos: 'Law and Community: The Changing Nature of State Power in Late Capitalism' in R L Abel (ed) *The Politics of Informal Justice, Volume 1: The American Experience* (1982) Academic Press, New York, pp 261–263

> Bourgeois society is based on a dualistic power conception – two basic modes or forms of power that, though complementary, have been kept separate and even treated as mutually exclusive. I call them cosmic and chaosmic power. The first is centralized, 'physically' located in formal institutions, and hierarchically organized. This is the traditional conception of juridical power. It is a macropower that, since the seventeenth century, has found its most complete embodiment in state power. The second is the power emerging wherever social relations and interactions are unequal, in the family, at school, on the street, etc. It is a micropower. It is eccentric, atomized, multiple, without specific location, mobile – in sum, chaotic.
>
> Liberal political theory is based on a militant refusal to recognize this dualistic power structure by reducing it to a unity, namely, state or juridical power. And this, of course, is the source of the distinction between state and civil society. The state is the realm of power and violence, whereas civil society is the realm of freedom and equality.

The present, deep crisis of this theory is the result of two changed perceptions that have been stimulated by transformations in the accumulation process. First, there are two forms of power corresponding to the two basic forms of inequality: macro (or class) and micro (or interactional). Second, these forms of power, though structurally very different, are complementary – each is made tolerable (and is reproduced) by the other.

The proliferation of informalization and community justice reforms (which have counterparts in many other areas of social life) may signify changes in the nature of state (cosmic) power and its relation to the chaosmic power inherent in the social relations of civil society. To the extent that the state tries to coopt the sanctioning power inherent in ongoing social relationships, it is explicitly connecting its cosmic power to the chaosmic power, which until now had been outside its reach. Insofar as the state thereby manages to control actions and social relations that cannot be directly regulated by formal law, and insofar as the entire social environment of the dispute is integrated in its processing, to that extent the state is indeed expanding. And it is expanding through a process that, on the surface, appears to be a process of retraction. What appears as delegalization is actually relegalization. In other words, the state is expanding in the form of civil society, and that is why the dichotomy of state and civil society is no longer theoretically useful, if ever it was. And because the state expands in the form of civil society, social control may be exercised in the form of social participation, violence in the form of consensus, class domination in the form of community action. In other words, state power expands through a kind of indirect rule.

'Native' processes, interactions, atmospheres, and environments are overintegrated in the global strategy of capitalist political domination. On the surface such overintegration is negated (hidden) by the undercodification made possible by the extensive use of legal rhetoric (which mobilizes commonsense knowledge and ordinary language). This transformation of political domination is also relevant for an understanding of the significance of the fiscal crisis and the crisis of legitimacy. As already mentioned, under conditions of stagnating accumulation the bond between the capitalist state and the working classes runs the risk of collapsing. But the state may repair its legitimacy not only through material expansion (by delivering goods and services) but also through the production of symbols and deals that make a radically different social life appear either impossible or irrelevant. By appealing to transcendental values, the reforms under analysis will contribute to this shift in the strategy of legitimation. If these reforms signal a general trend, the state under the late capitalism of the 1980s and 1990s will probably survive and expand more through the production of symbols than through the production of goods and services.

The state is therefore reaching far beyond its present formal apparatus; in the process it may become more informal and less organized. State and nonstate may look more and more alike. Indeed, it is not absurd to predict the development of a face-to-face state. The formal institutions that, as Foucault has shown, have always been the 'physical' locus of state power recently have been criticized and even undermined. This movement has its material base in state participation in reproduction of labor power (a process that has become more prolonged and costly and has led to unprecedented institutional growth) under conditions of increasing structural unemployment. The resultant anti-institutional movements may indeed help to relieve the fiscal crisis, provided that the state develops alternative methods for the production and reproduction of power. I would even speculate that the relations between cosmic and chaosmic power will change in the future, as the latter progressively displaces the former, with a resultant transformation in the relations between core and periphery areas, leading to an acentric domination that has no periphery. In this case there will be a transfer of power from formal institutions to informal networks. Social networks will then become the dominant unit for the production and reproduction of power – a source of power that is diffuse and interstitial, and therefore is as familiar as it is remote.

Early Critiques of 'Informalism'

Against this background of a perceived, apparently large-scale, shift in the nature and reach of state power and law, two broad critiques of corresponding changes in the nature and direction of dispute institutions emerged. One critique, exemplified in Richard Abel's *The Politics of Informal Justice* (1982b, 1982d), identified a range of linked problems associated with moves towards 'informalism'. The second, formulated by Owen Fiss in a terse but powerful polemic, 'Against Settlement' (1984), opposed any further move to deflect disputes away from adjudication.

The Politics of Informal Justice

Richard Abel begins by arguing that the growth of informal institutions generally constitutes an expansion, rather than a contraction, of state power; so that what may appear at first sight as a reduction in state activity is in reality likely to represent covert expansion. State sponsorship of a neighbourhood justice scheme, for example, exposes more behaviour to review, increases governmental expenditure and co-opts a voluntary sector initiative. There is simply a change in the mode of state domination as the overtly coercive agency of the court is replaced by covert, ideological penetration through community mediation schemes, with 'the state co-opting the sanctioning power of on-going social relationships'.

Abel goes on to argue that beneath the rhetoric of consensus, informal, settlement-directed approaches to the management of disputes simply massaged, neutralised and suppressed conflict. As a result, the disadvantaged are left worse off, getting less than they would under adversarial, adjudicatory processes. (See Extract 3:6.)

Other problems come with the relaxation of the procedural safeguards associated with formal adjudication that generally occurred with the move to informalism. Intervening third parties were left free to engage in coercive and manipulative action. At the same time, the removal or relaxation of procedural safeguards typically operates in the interest of stronger, institutional litigants rather than the disadvantaged. The latter find themselves left with poorer substitutes for adjudication.(See Extract 3:7.)

Overall, Abel argues that the position of disadvantaged litigants is seldom improved, and typically worsened, where state-sponsored informal procedures are substituted for formal adjudication. There is a certain irony in the fact that this work, lying at the heart of the critical legal studies movement, has in the last resort to be read as an heroic rescue, if not quite a celebration, of judgment.

Contemporary critiques of these embryonic transformations did not forecast an entirely unrelenting story of domination. The corresponding potential for oppositional strategies of resistance is emphasised in Jurgen Habermas' discussion in *Theorie des kommunikativen Handelns* (1981), where he points to the potential of the shift to secure the communicative and decision-making procedures of the 'lifeworld', as against those of 'system' (trs. 1987: 371):

> The place of law as a medium is to be taken by procedures for settling conflicts that are appropriate to the structures of action oriented by mutual understanding – discursive processes of will-formation and consensus-oriented procedures of negotiation and decision-making. . . . From the perspective of social theory, the present controversy . . . can be understood as a fight for or against the colonization of the lifeworld.

Extract 3:5
R L Abel: 'The Contradictions of Informal Justice', in R L Abel (ed) *The Politics of Informal Justice, Volume 1: The American Experience* (1982) Academic Press, New York, pp 270–271, 275

> Informal justice can extend the ambit of state control. Here I am talking only about those institutions that are somehow implicated in the state apparatus (although the boundaries are often amorphous). Informalism permits this expansion, in the first instance, by reducing or disguising the coercion that both stimulates resistance and justifies the demand for the protection of formal due process. Coercion is indeed relaxed: parties are often 'referred' to informal institutions rather than arrested; the police are involved briefly, if at all; the symbols of state authority that so dominate the courtroom – a male judge, in black robes, on a raised dais, supported by security personnel – are all banished from the mediation center; and that epitome of force, the prison, is almost never threatened. Even more important, coercion is disguised: In place of prosecution we find the forms of civil litigation, arbitration, or mediation; staff go to great lengths to make participants feel comfortable; the mediator is often female, dressed like the parties, and seated with them round a table; even the language is different, stressing help rather than threats, speaking about a respondent rather than an accused – the velvet glove has largely hidden the iron fist. Penalties are far milder: restitution rather than fines, the promise of behavioral change rather than imprisonment. Because coercion is less extreme and less visible the state can seek to control more behavior: deviance that was too trivial to interest officials (police, prosecutors), justify cumbersome formal procedures, or warrant severe sanctions. Informal justice purports to devolve state authority on nonstate institutions, to delegate social control to businesses, neighborhoods, and other private entities. But in fact informalism expands the grasp of the state at the expense of other sources of authority that appear to be potential competitors. Whether

or not 'law [always] varies inversely with other social control', the capitalist state actively seeks to undermine, displace, and coopt other forms of social control. Because the state is the only legitimate source of authority, other forms of social control must either be its creation or exist at its sufferance. The establishment or recognition of informal institutions by the capitalist state bears a striking resemblance to the strategy of indirect rule employed by the imperialist state in the nineteenth and early twentieth centuries. Indirect rule claimed to respect and strengthen indigenous authority, but its actual effect was to subordinate and undermine countervailing power. Indeed a precondition for the survival of informal justice in civil society appears to be the inaccessibility of competing state institutions. When the official state legal system, formal and informal, is highly remote and inhospitable, then true informal justice thrives outside it. Reforms that increase access to state control – of which informalism is an example – draw clients away from nonstate institutions and distort the processes of the latter.

Extract 3:6

R L Abel: 'The Contradictions of Informal Justice' in R L Abel (ed) *The Politics of Informal Justice, Volume 1: The American Experience* (1982) Academic Press, New York, pp 280–281

Informal legal institutions neutralize conflict that could threaten state or capital. Of course, formal legal institutions do this too, but informalism has its own distinctive strengths and weaknesses. Although neutralizing conflict and extending state control may appear to be inconsistent processes, they actually overlap and complement each other in ways I will consider later. Here it is sufficient to observe that whereas informal state control connotes active intervention to suppress or modify specific behavior, informal institutions neutralize conflict by responding to grievances in ways that inhibit their transformation into serious challenges to the domination of state and capital.

Both state and capital create informal institutions so that they can retain control over the handling of those grievances that escape the purview of formal institutions and can continue to influence: which complaints get aired, by whom, to whom, in what form and forum, how they are processed, and what remedy is granted. All these institutions are created and controlled by respondents, never by the grievants themselves. Frequently, state intervention is unnecessary. The larger capitalists (manufacturers, retailers, service industries) and those that are well organized in trade associations have established numerous, often highly elaborate complaint procedures. Sometimes the state explicitly authorizes or requires them to do so (Magnuson-Moss Warranty Act 15 U.S.C. §§2301–2312, Supp. V 1975) and even delegates to capital the responsibility for establishing the substantive standards of conduct the grievance mechanism will apply. But it is neither efficient nor feasible for every enterprise to construct its own complaint procedure, and those in the competitive sector may be strongly motivated not to do so (just as smaller entrepreneurs have consistently resisted reductions in work hours and improvements in worker health and safety, whereas larger enterprises, especially those in the monopoly sector, more readily accommodated such demands and then turned to the state to impose them uniformly). Therefore the state assumes this function, performing its traditional role of correcting market failure. Indeed, grievance mechanisms may be seen as the latest service of a constantly expanding welfare state, which thereby socializes another of the costs of reproducing capitalism. In addition, the state must develop mechanisms for responding to grievances directed against itself – and as the state grows, these grievances will multiply.

Enterprises (public as well as private) already control the voicing of grievances by their employees, in which process informal institutions like labor arbitration play a central role. But advanced capitalism requires the planning of consumption as well as production; the present economic crisis is in large part a crisis of consumption. Consumer grievances must be satisfied so that consumers continue buying. Consumers must also be kept passive – consumerism has the potential to generate organizations, and even cooperatives, that actively negotiate price and quality. For these reasons it is necessary to generalize to relations of consumption those mechanisms that have been developed to control relations of production. Such mechanisms take a number of forms. A producer or seller may establish a procedure through which consumers can voice grievances. Yet this may create even more discontent if grievances are not satisfied. Some, therefore, take the further step of announcing a policy of unconditional returns of unsatisfactory merchandise. The cost of such a practice is both predictable and small relative to total sales. It therefore becomes just another cost of doing business, a cost that is often amply repaid by the enhanced reputation. Maurice Rosenberg has proposed that the state implement such a policy with respect to all private enterprise: that it reimburse all aggrieved consumers in token amounts and then assume the task of seeking redress from the offending businesses. This would enormously extend the state expropriation of citizen grievances that was begun by the state prosecution of crimes.

Extract 3:7
R L Abel: 'The Contradictions of Informal Justice' in R L Abel (ed) *The Politics of Informal Justice, Volume 1: The American Experience* (1982) Academic Press, New York, pp 295–296, 297–298

Some institutions that are represented as 'informal' actually increase the capacity of those who are already advantaged (socially and legally) to enforce their rights. The most notable are small claims courts and, more recently, landlord-tenant courts. The notion that these are intended to benefit individuals or tenants is a contemporary post factum legitimation; small claims courts were explicitly established to facilitate debt collection by merchants. The enormous expansion of consumer credit has made them an essential element of the retailing process. Similarly, landlord-tenant courts are an integral part of residential leasing, without which it could not function. 'Informal' alternatives to criminal prosecution are now becoming a significant weapon in the arsenal of sellers. Contemporary retailing mandates open displays and few sales personnel, thereby presenting a substantial temptation to shoplift. Formal prosecution is rarely attempted because it is too expensive and the store stands to gain little. But in Canada, a mediation diversion program has been substituted that requires fewer resources and helps the store to secure restitution. In each situation it is argued that the creditor cannot be denied a remedy (it is ethically wrong, illegal, and economically undesirable) and will secure it in a formal court if no alternative is offered. This assumption (empirically very questionable) lays the foundation for justifying informal processes on the ground that they are less costly and threatening to the defendant. This is a variant of the widespread mystification that legal rights and remedies cannot alter economic relationships – the landlord will simply raise the rent, the merchant will deny credit or increase the price of the product – a form of economic determinism that these same liberal skeptics attribute, disparagingly, to Marxist analysis. The consequence of accepting this argument is a constant increase in the jurisdiction of small claims courts and their like. If informalism grants additional offensive weapons to those already endowed with disproportionate legal resources while depriving the legally disadvantaged of the protection of formal defenses, it also denies the latter the sword of formality while assuring the former that they can continue to invoke formality as a shield. For the disadvantaged, informal institutions are a substitute, not a supplement. To use Galanter's concepts: informal institutions tend to be an arena in which one-shot plaintiffs make claims against repeat players, or against other one-shot defendants (whereas repeat players prefer formal institutions when they act offensively). Thus arbitration is often substituted for adjudication when insured are claiming against insurers, consumers against sellers, students against teachers, tenants against landlords, welfare recipients against the government, patients against physicians or health plans, prisoners against prison administrators, and employees against employers. This is not because the legally disadvantaged prefer informal institutions; they would like the leverage of state coercion. Informalism is not a grass roots movement; rather, informal institutions are imposed from the top down, typically by the state or by capital. Small claims court litigants rated neighborhood justice very low when asked to rank a number of proposed reforms of those courts. What individual grievants want is an authority with adequate resources. They are particularly aware of the need for coercion when confronting a more powerful adversary; even the mediators recognize their own inadequacy and seek to avoid such disputes between unequals.

Informal institutions do not satisfy this need for coercive authority for several reasons. First, they often cannot obtain jurisdiction: Sellers and producers refuse to submit to arbitration when consumers complain; more than a third of the respondents failed to appear in one mediation program. Second, they deny legal representation: Some specifically exclude lawyers on the ground that the institution is informal and the grievant has a right to a formal rehearing, others simply fail to provide lawyers. Although the unrepresented plaintiff does better in arbitration than in adjudication, in neither situation does he do as well as the litigant who is represented in court. Individuals are more disadvantaged by being denied representation than are businesses. And the claimants themselves sense this: They affirm their need for representation in small claims court; of all the referrals by neighborhood justice centers, they found referrals to lawyers most helpful. Third, individual grievants confronting more powerful adversaries want an authority that is sympathetic, predisposed toward their plight – eg, an administrative agency or jury – mediators and arbitrators do not help to right the scales. Fourth, informal institutions deprive grievants of substantive rights. They are antinormative and urge the parties to compromise; although this appears evenhanded, it works to the detriment of the party who is advancing a claim – typically the individual grievant. Informalism may ensure that more claimants get some redress, but the relief is almost always less adequate – that is certainly the history of workers' compensation, no-fault divorce, and no-fault compensation for automobile accidents. Laws designed to protect and benefit the disadvantaged, such as those protecting the consumer, are ignored in informal tribunals.

Against Settlement

The response to proposals, such as those of Derek Bok, that more disputes should be deflected from the court in the direction of settlement, was just as vigorous. Here the attack comes from those who see a paramount beauty in adjudication. The classic statement appears in Fiss's article 'Against Settlement' (1984). One plank of the Fiss argument echoes the critique of informalism in pointing to the propensity of 'settlement' to underline disparities of power between disputants. Imbalances of power shape the processes of grievance construction, the perception and progress of a dispute, and understandings of the likely outcomes. Fiss worries about settlement, inter alia, because of the impact of imbalances of power on the processes involved:

> By viewing the lawsuit as a quarrel between two neighbours, the dispute resolution story that underlies ADR implicitly asks us to assume a rough equality between the two parties. It treats settlement as the anticipation of the outcome of trial and assumes that the terms of the settlement are simply a product of the parties' prediction of that outcome. In truth, however, settlement is also a function of the resources available to each party to finance the litigation, and these resources are frequently distributed unequally. Many disputes do not involve a property dispute between two neighbours but rather concern a struggle between a member of a racial minority and a municipal police department over alleged brutality, or a claim by a worker against a large corporation over work-related injuries. In these cases the distribution of financial resources, or the ability of one party to pass along its costs, will inevitably 'infect' the bargaining process and settlement will be at odds with a conception of justice that seeks to make the wealth of the parties irrelevant (1984: 1076).

Fiss highlights three major ways in which disparities in resources – that is, power differentials – can influence the process of settlement. First, the financially less well-off litigant may be less capable than his or her opponent of gathering and analysing the information necessary in order to gain a reasonably accurate picture of the probable outcome of the litigation. Second, the poorer party may need the damages he or she seeks and, as a result, be induced to settle in order to accelerate payment. Third, the poorer disputant may be forced to settle precisely because he or she lacks the resources to finance litigation. The better-resourced party is able to anticipate the poorer party's costs as if the case were to be tried fully, and decrease his or her offer by that amount, so that 'the indigent plaintiff is a victim of the costs of litigation even if he settles' (1984: 1076).

Overshadowing Fiss's concern with the impact of power imbalances on individual litigants, his central objection to settlement lay in the assertion that a move away from the court would compromise key legal and political values. In a fundamental apology for adjudication, Fiss presents the role of judges in resolving disputes as secondary to their function of restating important public values. The centrality of adjudication is reasserted by presenting judgment as the means through which the core repertoire of norms in society is publicised and refurbished. With the substitution of settlement, the opportunity for the courts to articulate central values is lost, and as these values fall from public attention the stability of the polity is compromised. (See Extract 3:8.)

Fiss met with a vigorous response. Thus McThenia and Shaffer counter in the following terms: 'Fiss's argument rests on the faith that justice – and he uses the word – is usually something people get from the government. He comes close to arguing that the branch of government that resolves disputes, the courts, is the principal source of justice in fragmented modern American society' (1985: 1660). Follow the exchanges between them in the extracts that follow:

Extract 3:8
O M Fiss: 'Against Settlement' (1984) 93 *Yale Law Journal* 1073, pp 1085–1086

The dispute-resolution story makes settlement appear as a perfect substitute for judgment, as we just saw, by trivializing the remedial dimensions of a lawsuit, and also by reducing the social function of the lawsuit to one of resolving private disputes. In that story, settlement appears to achieve exactly the same purpose as judgment – peace between the parties – but at considerably less expense to society. The two quarreling neighbors turn to a court in order to resolve their dispute, and society makes courts available because it wants to aid in the achievement of their private ends or to secure the peace.

In my view, however, the purpose of adjudication should be understood in broader terms. Adjudication uses public resources, and employs not strangers chosen by the parties but public officials chosen by a process in which the public participates. These officials, like members of the legislative and executive branches, possess a power that has been defined and conferred not by public law, but by private agreement. Their job is not to maximize the ends of private parties, nor simply to secure the peace, but to explicate and give force to the values embodied in authoritative texts such as the Constitution and statutes: to interpret those values and to bring reality into accord with them. This duty is not discharged when the parties settle.

In our political system, courts are reactive institutions. They do not search out interpretive occasions, but instead wait for others to bring matters to their attention. They also rely for the most part on others to investigate and present the law and facts. A settlement will thereby deprive a court of the occasion, and perhaps even the ability, to render an interpretation. A court cannot proceed (or not proceed very far) in the face of a settlement. To be against settlement is not to urge that parties be 'forced' to litigate, since that would interfere with their autonomy and distort the adjudicative process; the parties will be inclined to make the court believe that their bargain is justice. To be against settlement is only to suggest that when the parties settle, society gets less than what appears, and for a price it does not know it is paying. Parties might settle while leaving justice undone. The settlement of a school suit might secure the peace, but not racial equality. Although the parties are prepared to live under the terms they bargained for, and although such peaceful coexistence may be a necessary precondition of justice, and itself a state of affairs to be valued, it is not justice itself. To settle for something means to accept less than some ideal.

I recognize that judges often announce settlements not with a sense of frustration or disappointment, as my account of adjudication might suggest, but with a sigh of relief. But this sigh should be seen for precisely what it is. It is not a recognition that a job is done, nor an acknowledgment that a job need not be done because justice has been secured. It is instead based on another sentiment altogether, namely, that another case has been 'moved along,' which is true whether or not justice has been done or even needs to be done. Or the sigh might be based on the fact that the agony of judgment has been avoided.

Extract 3:9
A W McThenia and T L Shaffer: 'For Reconciliation' (1985) 94 *Yale Law Journal* 1660, pp 1662–1665

Fiss's description of traditional dispute resolution is a story of two neighbors 'in a state of nature' who each claim a single piece of property and who, when they cannot agree, turn to 'a stranger' to resolve their dispute. He asserts that traditional dispute resolution depicts a sociologically impoverished universe, operates in a state of nature where there are no public values or goals except a supposed 'natural harmony' of the status quo, and calls on the exercise of power by a stranger. That was never Fuller's position. Nor do we find much support in the literature or in reality for such a view of traditional adjudication. If there ever was such a world we expect it was 'nasty, brutish and short.' However, we don't really believe that traditional adjudication ever bore much resemblance to that story. Yet this is the view of the world that Fiss attributes to the advocates of ADR; his attack on ADR is premised on that notion.

Models are, of course, human creations. The good ones contain elements of the creator's perception of the world and of the reality he seeks to perceive. They are designed to invite conversation and to appeal to the reader in a search for understanding. They are abstractions; but to be effective, they must have some connection either with the creator's view of reality or with what he wants the world to be like. Fiss's model of structural reform is, in this way, an effective model. While it may not depict the world that many of us observe, it does reflect his view of the world he wishes he could find. It reflects, we suspect, more his hope than his actual belief. We honor that. The model is rich. It leads to conversation and debate.

But Fiss's model of traditional dispute resolution is flat; it is only an abstraction, and is therefore also a caricature. It has no relation to the world as it is; it does not appeal to the reader as a convincing way to understand adjudication or its alternatives. It does not permit one to express hope in alternatives to adjudication.

In any event, after setting up his 'state of nature' model of dispute resolution, Fiss attributes that view of the world to the advocates of ADR. He understands pleas to consider alternatives to current means of resolving disputes as turning on the inefficiency of traditional adjudication (his negative model), and popular dissatisfaction with it. He equates the ADR movement with those who urge settlement more than judgment and who seek a 'truce more than a true reconciliation.' He argues that settlement is 'a capitulation to the conditions of mass society,' a capitulation that 'should be neither encouraged nor praised.' He assumes that the ADR movement is one that wants peace at any price and treats settlement as 'the anticipation of the outcome of trial,' that is, trial in his stranger-judge, negative model of adjudication.

Fiss is against settlement because he views the matters that come before courts in America, and that are inappropriate for ADR, as including cases in which: (1) there are distributional inequities; (2) securing authoritative consent or settlement is difficult; (3) continued supervision following judgment is necessary; and (4) there is a genuine need for an authoritative interpretation of law. Fiss characterizes disputes in this limited way – as arguments between two neighbors, one of whom has vastly superior bargaining power over the other. It is then easy for him to prefer litigation to settlement, because litigation is a way to equalize bargaining power.

The soundest and deepest part of the ADR movement does not rest on Fiss's two-neighbors model. It rests on values – of religion, community, and work place – that are more vigorous than Fiss thinks. In many, in fact most, of the cultural traditions that argue for ADR, settlement is neither an avoidance mechanism nor a truce. Settlement is a process of reconciliation in which the anger of broken relationships is to be confronted rather than avoided, and in which healing demands not a truce but confrontation. Instead of 'trivializing the remedial process,' settlement exalts that process. Instead of 'reducing the social function to one of resolving private disputes,' settlement calls on substantive community values. Settlement is sometimes a beginning, and is sometimes a postscript, but it is not the essence of the enterprise of dispute resolution. The essence of the enterprise is more like the structural injunction, about which Fiss has written so eloquently, than like an alternative to the resolution-by-stranger described by his negative model.

The 'real divide' between us and Fiss may not be our differing views of the sorts of cases that now wind their way into American courts, but, more fundamentally, it may be our different views of justice. Fiss comes close to equating justice with law. He includes among the cases unsuited for settlement 'those in which justice needs to be done, or to put it more modestly, where there is a genuine social need for an authoritative interpretation of law.' We do not believe that law and justice are synonymous. We see the deepest and soundest of ADR arguments as in agreement with us. Justice is not usually something people get from the government. And courts (which are not, in any case, strangers) are not the only or even the most important places that dispense justice.

Fiss comes back:

Extract 3:10

O M Fiss: 'Out of Eden' (1985) 94 *Yale Law Journal* 1669

Religion can inspire. It can also distort, and this is precisely what it does for Professors McThenia and Shaffer. It leads them to mistake the periphery for the center.

In my earlier article I tried to come to terms with a movement that seeks alternatives to litigation. Known as ADR ('Alternative Dispute Resolution'), this movement is headed by Chief Justice Burger and is now sweeping the bar. It recently received the endorsement of the President of Harvard, Derek Bok, and the Advisory Committee on the Federal Rules of Civil Procedure. In 1983, the Advisory Committee managed to revise Rule 16 to strengthen the hand of the trial judge in brokering settlements, and for the last two years the Committee has been engaged in a determined campaign to amend Rule 68 to create additional pressure for settlement. The party who rejects an offer of settlement would, if the Advisory Committee has its way, stand in jeopardy of paying the attorney's fees of the other side.

Professors McThenia and Shaffer now lend their voices to this movement, but in an unusual way. They add a religious dimension. They emphasize reconciliation rather than settlement, and appear to be moved by a conception of social organization that takes the insular religious community as its model: 'Justice is what we discover – you and I, Socrates said – when we walk together, listen together, and even love one another in our curiosity about what justice is and where justice comes from.' McThenia and Shaffer speak out on behalf of social mechanisms that might restore or preserve loving relationships and, not surprisingly, they find the judicial judgment a rather inept instrument for that purpose.

I have no special interest in countering their plea: I am as much for love as the next person. What McThenia and Shaffer say is not wrong, just beside the point. Their reasons for seeking alternatives to litigation are not those of the movement. Chief Justice Burger is not moved by love, or by a desire to find new ways to restore or preserve loving relationships, but rather by concerns of efficiency and politics. He seeks alternatives to litigation in order to reduce the caseload of the judiciary or, even more plausibly, to insulate the status quo from reform by the judiciary. Of course, McThenia and Shaffer are entitled to their own reasons for supporting a social and political movement, but they should not delude themselves that they have given a general account of ADR or explained its saliency and sway within the bar today.

McThenia and Shaffer should also understand that their plea for reconciliation does not respond to the primary social situation to which ADR is addressed. In their search for alternatives to litigation, the advocates of ADR focus on social situations in which interpersonal relationships have been so thoroughly disrupted that there is no chance of reconciliation. People turn to courts when they are at the end of the road. That is why I focused my attention on settlement rather than reconciliation. As I said in the original article, ADR proposals like those embodied in Rule 16 and in the amendments to Rule 68 picture settlement not as a reconciliation, but as a truce. To be against settlement is not to be against reconciliation but to address another social situation altogether.

Of course, it would be nice if the blacks of Chicago, to take one example, did not have to go to court in order to obtain all that the Constitution promises, and instead were able to work things out with the school board by walking, and talking, and loving. But once they have turned to the courts, it strikes me as absurd for the legal system to create incentives or pressures that force them to settle. It is costly to litigate, as they well know, but it also is costly to settle. To ignore these costs and to disfavor litigation because you hope that social relations between the parties can be restored is like ignoring the dangers of plea bargaining and favoring it over trial because you wish the crime that gave rise to the prosecution had not occurred.

In defending their variant of ADR, Professors McThenia and Shaffer might contest my factual premise about the divided character of our communities. They might argue that the blacks of Chicago who turn to the courts are mistaken in their belief that they cannot get justice on their own. Or McThenia and Shaffer might insist that no matter how improbable, reconciliation is always a possibility, at least as a logical or formal matter, and that one should not be allowed into court unless one first has attempted reconciliation – a miracle is always possible. On this account, ADR emerges as an exhaustion requirement, and at one point McThenia and Shaffer draw on the experience of the ancient Hebrews and Christians to proffer such an idea: 'The [preferred] procedure involves, first, conversation; if that fails, it involves mediation; if mediation fails, it involves airing the dispute before representatives of the community.' Only if the claimant refuses to heed the advice of the community elders will he or she be allowed to turn to the courts, and then only at the greatest risk: Whatever you lose on earth should be considered lost in heaven.

I am sure that there is much to be learned from the ancient Hebrews and Christians. I am sure that there is much force to the plea for reconciliation when it is addressed to the insular religious communities that still dot the American landscape. But I think Professors McThenia and Shaffer, like my colleague Robert Cover, are fundamentally misguided in their effort to model law and the legal system of modern America on these religious communities. Such exercises result in a marvelous display of learning, and one cannot help being moved by the underlying religious commitments. But I must also admit that I am left with the firm impression that such efforts misunderstand the character of our social life and the role that the state and its courts must play in our search for justice today.

From the perspective of an insular religious community, distinguished by its cohesiveness and the devotion of its members to a set of shared values, there may be reason to doubt the claim of those who turn to the courts that reconciliation is not possible. There may even be reason to force the claimant to try those mechanisms that might restore the relationship, for what is at stake is not just a claim of right, but the totality of relationships known as the community. But once we stop thinking about the Anabaptists and start thinking about Chicago, once we stop thinking about the ancient Hebrews and Christians and turn to modern America, we can see that there is no reason in the world to engage such assumptions. There is no reason to assume either that the despair of blacks over getting justice on their own is unwarranted, or that they sue because they want some high class counseling. The more reasonable assumption is that they turn to the courts because they have to.

Moreover, once we change our perspective and consider the modern American community, whether it be a Chicago, or an Evanston, or a Gary, we can understand why an exhaustion requirement of the type Professors McThenia and Shaffer propose is likely only to compound the costs of justice. Society will come to have two (or more) processes where it now has one, because the claimant is not likely to be satisfied with conversation, mediation, or a lecture by the representatives of the community, and thus will eventually turn to the courts. The McThania-Shaffer proposal is likely to obstruct access to the courts without increasing the chance that the fabric of the community will be restored.

Milner Ball, referred to in the McThenia and Shaffer essay, is a scholar whose work is infused with a religious perspective, and yet he gets the point. He understands that my critique was not aimed at this religion-based strand of ADR, which plays a slight and trivial role in the professional debates of the day. He also understands the more general ADR version of the 1980s for what it is: not a vindication of community, religious or otherwise, but just another assault upon the activist state, 'another form of the deregulation movement, one that permits private actors with powerful economic interests to pursue self-interest free of community norms.' The force of Ball's observation is not lost on McThenia and Shaffer. They seem genuinely reluctant to defend this more general form of ADR, and in the closing paragraph of their essay specifically disassociate themselves from what they call the '[i]nformalism of the Chief Justice's formulation.' They do, however, have something in common with the Chief Justice, namely his distrust of the state and its courts. McThenia and Shaffer are anti-statists: 'Justice is not usually something people get from the government.' Apparently people get it from talking and listening to one another.

I believe that people should talk and listen to one another. But sometimes that is not possible, because their relationships have disintegrated, or because the community is fractionated, or because those who have power are not interested in either talking or listening to the weak and disadvantaged. Moreover, even when people are prepared to talk and listen to one another, they might not understand the norms of the community, or, as Professor Ball suggests, they might not be prepared to abide by them. Adjudication is but a response to this predicament. It is a social process that uses the power of the state to require the reluctant to talk and to listen, not just to each other, but also to judges (and sometimes juries) who must in turn listen and talk to the parties. These public officials are the trustees of the community. They are given the power to decide who is right and who is wrong and, if need be, to bring the conduct of the parties into conformity with the norms of the community. The underlying hope is that if all goes well, justice will be done.

I realize that all might not go well and that adjudication might fail. Justice is not reducible to the law or to the particular decisions of any court: It is an aspiration. The truth of the matter, however, is that all institutions – not just those of the state – stand in jeopardy of failing in this aspiration. And there is no reason whatsoever for believing that adjudication suffers this risk more than any other institution. In fact, given the inequalities and divisions that so pervade our society, and given the need for a power as great as that of the state to close the gap between our ideals and the actual conditions of our social life, adjudication is more likely to succeed in this aspiration. Adjudication is more likely to do justice than conversation, mediation, arbitration, settlement, rent-a-judge, mini-trials, community moots or any other contrivance of ADR, precisely because it vests the power of the state in officials who act as trustees for the public, who are highly visible, and who are committed to reason. What we need at the moment is not another assault on this form of public power, whether from the periphery or the center, or whether inspired by religion or politics, but a renewed appreciation of all that it promises.

These critiques all centre around questions of power. Comparing them, it is important to keep in view the different ways of conceptualising power – already marked out in classical social theory – that they adopt. Abel's discussion treats power as located at the level of structure, highlighting problems of stratification, issues of class and gender and of the domination enjoyed by large corporations. Looked at in this way 'power' may be concealed from, and unexamined by, the actors. De Sousa Santos' characterisation of power in terms of heterogeneous, ramifying networks is foretold in the work of Althusser and Foucault. At a different level, Fiss's discussion of power locates it, in Weberian terms, at the level of human agency: the capacity of the particular actors to make others do what they would not otherwise have done. But there is also a strong Durkheimian echo in his insistence on the irreducible role of cosmology in securing social order.

C: The Subsequent Trajectory of the ADR Movement

From the end of the 1970s the discussion of alternatives begun to be translated into institutional shape. In the broadest, schematic terms three things started to happen, more or less concurrently, in most common law jurisdictions:

- the emergence of new, embryonic professional groups offering institutionalised help for party negotiations away from the surveillance of the courts and legal profession;
- moves on the part of lawyers to re-model areas of legal practice, including a growing readiness to assume non-aligned facilitatory roles; and
- a redefinition of the role of civil courts under which the active sponsorship of settlement becomes a primary responsibility.

The 'New Professionals' in Dispute Resolution

The last two decades have seen the emergence of new specialised agencies offering a range of dispute management services in most common law jurisdictions. These agencies have not attempted to do the things which lawyers have traditionally done in the way of advisory and representative intervention. In offering mediation and some novel dispute management techniques they compete only indirectly with lawyers in holding out the possibility of an alternative route. This development took place earliest in the United States, where pioneering agencies included a National Institute of Dispute Resolution (NIDR) and the Society of Professionals in Dispute Resolution

(SPIDR),[1] alongside more specialised groupings (for example, the Academy of Family Mediators). This institutional growth, which shows all the signs of disciplinary specialisation and the emergence of an autonomous profession, is accompanied by an emerging regulatory framework surrounding such matters as selection, training, accreditation and standards of practice. See, for example, the National Institute of Dispute Resolution's *Interim Guidelines for Selecting Mediators*.[2]

Parallel developments can be found in Australia,[3] Canada and the United Kingdom, notably in the family, community and commercial spheres. In England, initiatives are visible both in the voluntary and the private sectors. In the former sector, the main institutional growth has been in 'family' and 'community' mediation. In the case of family mediation, the most extensive example is provided by the range of local agencies grouped together under the umbrella of National Family Mediation (NFM).[4] In the private field, NFM is matched by the smaller Family Mediators' Association (FMA). Important initiatives in the community, neighbourhood and restorative justice spheres have taken place under the co-ordination of Mediation UK. The Centre for Dispute Resolution (CEDR), founded in 1990, offers a full range of ADR procedures, predominantly catering for commercial disputes. ADR services are also offered across a broad range of disputes by a number of other agencies, most prominently by IDR (Europe) Ltd, a company established in 1989. In outlining these initiatives it is impossible to draw a firm line in institutional terms between lawyers and the new professionals in dispute resolution. IDR (Europe) Ltd is effectively a solicitor's organisation, drawing its mediators from a network of 24 member law firms; and the foundation of CEDR was co-sponsored by the CBI and several large commercial law firms.

The Re-modelling of Legal Practice

The arrival of the new professionals was certainly seen by the lawyers as a challenge to their monopoly position in dispute resolution; but a far greater threat – and stimulus to change – was presented by the courts' new determination to sponsor and police settlement. But in a direct sense, the ADR movement was also something that lawyers constructed for themselves. Its very vocabulary and conceptual shape were first sketched in by an academic lawyer, Frank Sander, in his seminal paper to the Pound Conference in 1976. Essentially, ADR has meant two things for lawyers in the common law world: first, the development of specialised client-management devices involving them in non-aligned and advisory roles (we look at these in

1   Now the Association for Conflict Resolution, claiming to represent more than 6,500 professionals in dispute resolution.
2   Reviewed in (1993) 9 *Negotiation Journal* 293; compare the quality control arrangements of the English National Family Mediation, summarised in (1994) 4 *Family Mediation* 18.
3   Fully discussed in H Astor and C Chinkin (2002).
4   Here some 60 services are providing facilitative support for parties wishing to retain control over decision-making in the period around and following family breakdown. NFM services encourage the parties to use lawyers in an advisory capacity and recognise that where mediated negotiations are unsuccessful, more extensive reliance on legal expertise will probably follow.

detail in Chapter Eight); second, the growing aspiration to mediate (in many cases claiming this new role as part of legal practice). An important outgrowth of ADR for lawyers has also been the establishment of private and voluntary sector corporations offering dispute resolution services. JAMS Endispute Inc provides an example of the former and the CPR Institute of Dispute Resolution an example of the latter.

Lawyers in England for the most part responded slowly to the developments noted in the preceding section, and their involvement was initially confined to the field of family disputes. Here their attempt to compete with the new professionals in dispute resolution can be traced back to the formation of Solicitors in Mediation in 1985. This body, initially consisting of five solicitors with practices in family law and the former Training Officer of the National Family Conciliation Council, began to offer 'mediation' in child-related and property disputes. The experiment quickly acquired official approval and was followed by the formation of the Family Mediators Association (FMA) under the wing of the Law Society in 1988. Under the scheme operated by the FMA, a solicitor may co-mediate with another professional 'with experience in marital or family work' in helping 'couples cope with the legal, financial and emotional problems of separation and divorce, as well as arrangements for children'.[5] This includes assisting parties 'to work out proposals for settlement' and reach joint decisions in the context of family breakdown.

The English Bar immediately responded to the initiative represented by Solicitors in Mediation with its own scheme for a joint consultancy role under which expert advice could be offered to both parties from a neutral standpoint. In 1985, the Family Law Bar Association announced that it was establishing a 'Conciliation Board' to administer a 'Recommendation Procedure' designed 'to give the parties the benefit of an impartial, confidential and economical recommendation how to settle their differences'. Under this procedure, barristers offer neutral opinions on financial issues submitted to them by the solicitors to the respective parties. This procedure, conceived 'in the hope that the intervention of a neutral, and experienced outsider might nudge the parties towards a settlement', has not been widely used. Those operating the scheme indicate that advisory opinions have been sought in not more than a handful of cases each year.[6]

By the end of the 1980s lawyers had begun to show an active, proprietorial inter-est in ADR across a wider field of disputes. One early sign was the formation of IDR (Europe) Ltd. This company, established in 1989, initially drew its mediators from solicitors working in a network of 24 member firms. The Centre for Dispute Reso-lution (CEDR), again, was largely a creature of some major commercial law firms.

During 1991, both the Bar and the Law Society hastened to sponsor major reports on ADR. These reports, prepared by Henry Brown for the Courts and Legal Services Committee of the Law Society and the Committee under Lord Justice Beldam for the Bar Council, heralded ADR as something new and important, and identified

---

5 See the publicity brochure of the Family Mediators Association, *Your Questions Answered.*
6 See the Family Law Bar Association brochure on their Conciliation Board.

central roles for lawyers in ADR processes. One major recommendation of the Beldam Report proposed a scheme of court-linked mediation to operate in county courts across a wide range of civil disputes. The proposal was that 'facilitatory mediation' should be offered to litigants at an early point in the court process. In mapping out a pilot scheme, the Committee argued that the role of mediator would most appropriately be filled by lawyers. The Committee offered the view that 'it may be preferable to choose the mediators from those with litigation experience who are barristers or solicitors and to arrange their supplementary training in mediation *so far as may be necessary*' (emphasis added). The report concluded: 'We would suggest that legal mediators should be chosen from lawyers with at least seven years' post-qualification experience' (p 11).[7]

By the end of the 1990s, these moves on the part of lawyers to occupy non-aligned advisory and mediatory roles had gained momentum. Increasing numbers of lawyers, in both the commercial and private client sectors, began training as mediators. By the end of 1997, the great majority of large commercial law firms had CEDR-trained mediators among their fee-earning staff; and in many cases firms had begun to advertise ADR services in their promotional literature.

These local developments coincided with the establishment of European offices in London by JAMS Endispute and the CPR Institute of Dispute Resolution, both agencies with a claimed history of success in mediating large commercial disputes in North America. These bodies provided a model for the local emergence of several specialist associations of commercial mediators, offering their services through a central contact site. These associations include The Panel of Independent Mediators,[8] and In Place of Strife.[9] The Panel claims to 'offer direct access to the most experienced and highly rated commercial mediators practising in the UK'. Members of the Panel claim to deal with 'a wide variety of commercial disputes, including multi-national, multi-party and high value disputes, and those involving complex issues of fact and law'. The International Dispute Resolution Centre (IDRC) in Fleet Street provides a home for a number of dispute resolution bodies including CEDR and Resolex.[10]

Correspondingly, on the private client side, the Solicitors Family Law Association, in response to the passage of the Family Law Act 1996, had initiated its own mediation training programme for members; and smaller groups of 'lawyer mediators', such as the British Association of Lawyer Mediators (BALM) had formed.

The Courts as Sponsors of Settlement

In trying to characterise the changes in legal culture now observable in the common law world, perhaps the first point to emphasise is that the most powerful challenge to

---

7 The Beldam plan was realised in experimental form in a London County Court Pilot Scheme. Genn (1999).

8 www.mediatorspanel.co.uk.   9 www.mediate.co.uk.

10 www.resolex.com. Resolex 'facilitators and moderators' offer 'a team approach to resolving disputes'.

the lawyers' traditional management of disputing has come from the courts, rather than from disenchanted clients or the emergent new professionals. As we will see in Chapters Seven and Eight, a general feature of common law courts has been an increasing determination to control pre-trial processes and in doing so actively sponsor settlement, effectively regulating the terms of access to judgment.

In England, this shift is first visible in spontaneous local initiatives by judges in the family courts at the beginning of the 1980s,[11] followed in the commercial courts a decade later,[12] and then generalised for the civil courts in a Practice Direction of the mid-1990s.[13] Lord Woolf endorsed these steps in his Interim Report on *Access to Justice*, denouncing the culture of late settlement with startling candour and proposing a regime of intensive judicial 'case management' (Extract 3:11.) While his proposals were received critically by some litigation lawyers and commentators, Lord Woolf held to them robustly in his Final Report (Extract 3:12).[14] We will seen below that revised Civil Procedure Rules, brought into force in 1999 following his Final Report, challenged the culture of late settlement in two ways: by putting serious pressure on parties to negotiate in the pre-litigation phases of a dispute; and by introducing rigorous case management once litigation has commenced. While we still have only anecdotal evidence as to lawyers' response to this new environment, the judicial statistics already reveal that Lord Woolf's ambition to bring about a cultural change has begun to be realised. The dramatic reduction in the number of starts in the civil courts can only mean that settlement is now in many cases reached in the pre-litigation phase.[15]

Extract 3:11

Lord Woolf: *Access to Justice: Interim Report to the Lord Chancellor on the Civil Justice System of England and Wales* (1995) HMSO, London, ch 3, paras 3–11, 30–39

An adversarial environment

3. By tradition the conduct of civil litigation in England and Wales, as in other common law jurisdictions, is adversarial. Within a framework of substantive and procedural law established by the state for the resolution of civil disputes, the main responsibility for the initiation and conduct of proceedings rests with the parties to each individual case, and it is normally the plaintiff who sets the pace. The role of the judge is to adjudicate on issues selected by the parties when they choose to present them to the court.

---

11 Parmiter (1981).
12 Commercial Court *Practice Statement* of 10 December 1993.
13 *Practice Direction* of 24 January 1995, issued jointly by the Lord Chief Justice and the Vice-Chancellor: [1995] 1 WLR 262.
14 See Chapter Five and Woolf (1995).
15 The Queen's Bench Division, which deals mainly with civil actions in contract and tort (but also hears more specialist matters such as applications for judicial review), appears to have been affected more than any other part of the High Court. In 1998, the year immediately prior to the introduction of the the new Civil Procedure Rules based on Lord Woolf's proposals for reform, total writs and originating summons in the QBD numbered 114,984. This figure was thereafter steadily brought down, so that by 2003 it was a mere 14,191 – a reduction of 800 per cent over the figure for 1998. See Lord Chancellor's Department (1999) and Department for Constitutonal Affairs (2004).

4. Without effective judicial control, however, the adversarial process is likely to encourage an adversarial culture and to degenerate into an environment in which the litigation process is too often seen as a battlefield where no rules apply. In this environment, questions of expense, delay, compromise and fairness may have only low priority. The consequence is that expense is often excessive, disproportionate and unpredictable; and delay is frequently unreasonable.

5. This situation arises precisely because the conduct, pace and extent of litigation are left almost completely to the parties. There is no effective control of their worst excesses. Indeed, the complexity of the present rules facilitates the use of adversarial tactics and is considered by many to require it. As Lord Williams, a former Chairman of the Bar Council, said in responding to the announcement of this Inquiry, the process of law has moved from being 'servant to master, due to cost, length and uncertainty'.

6. It is often said that the existing rules and practice directions contain the solution to the present problems, if only litigation were to be conducted in accordance with them. But the present system does not ensure this. Instead the rules are flouted on a vast scale. The timetables they contain are generally ignored and their other requirements are complied with when convenient to the interests of one of the parties and not otherwise.

7. The powers of the courts have fallen behind the more sophisticated and aggressive tactics of some litigators. The orders for costs which are made are an ineffective sanction applied after the damage is done. The delay in being able to obtain effective intervention by the court both encourages rule-breaking and discourages the party who would be prejudiced from applying for preventive measures.

8. It is significant that the main procedural tools for conducting litigation efficiently have each become subverted from their proper purpose. Whether through incompetence or deliberation, pleadings often fail to state the facts as the rules require. This leads to a fundamental deficiency, namely the failure to establish the issues in the case at a reasonably early stage, from which many problems result.

9. Witness statements, a sensible innovation aimed at a 'cards on the table' approach, have in a very short time begun to follow the same route as pleadings, with the draftsman's skill often used to obscure the original words of the witness.

10. The scale of discovery, at least in the larger cases, is completely out of control. The principle of full, candid disclosure in the interests of justice has been devalued because discovery is pursued without sufficient regard to economy and efficiency in terms of the usefulness of the information which is likely to be obtained from the documents disclosed.

11. The approach to expert evidence also shows the characteristic range of difficulties: instead of the expert assisting the court to resolve technical problems, delay is caused by the unreasonable insistence on going to unduly eminent members of the profession and evidence is undermined by the partisan pressure to which party experts are subjected....

Delay

30. Delay is an additional source of distress to parties who have already suffered damage. It postpones the compensation or other remedy to which they may be entitled. It interferes with the normal existence of both individuals and businesses. In personal injury cases, it can exacerbate or prolong the original injury. It can lead to the collapse of relationships and businesses. It makes it more difficult to establish the facts because memories fade and witnesses cannot be traced. It postpones settlement but may lead parties to settle for inadequate compensation because they are worn down by delay or cannot afford to continue.

31. Delay is of more benefit to legal advisers than to parties. It allows litigators to carry excessive caseloads in which the minimum possible action occurs over the maximum possible timescale. In a culture of delay it may even be in the interest of the opposing side's legal advisers to be indulgent to each other's misdemeanours. Judicial experience is that it is for the advisers' convenience that many adjournments are agreed. This is borne out by the fact that when the courts have required the client to be present to support a late application to adjourn the trial, the number of such applications has reduced dramatically.

32. Delay results in increased costs. As a recent publication produced by the National Center for State Courts in Williamsburg, Virginia, points out 'conventional wisdom and most research supports the thesis that reducing delay will also reduce litigation costs'.

33. There are four areas in which delay or a lengthy timescale is a matter for concern:

- the time taken to progress a case from the initial claim to a final hearing;
- the time taken to reach settlement;
- delay in obtaining a hearing date; and
- the time taken by the hearing itself.

Delay in progressing the case

34. It is often argued that there are good reasons for the elapse of time between claim and final resolution, for instance in waiting for medical conditions to stabilise. But even in such cases it should be possible to dispose of issues of liability, and to award interim damages. It is also said that litigants need time to adjust to the possibility of settlement. Sensitive explanation and a less combative approach by lawyers would be more helpful to litigants than reducing their expectations by the erosion of time.

35. In 1994, High Court cases on average took 163 weeks in London and 189 weeks elsewhere to progress from issue to trial. The great majority of this time was between issue and setting down: 123 weeks in London and 148 weeks elsewhere. The equivalent county court figures were around 80 weeks overall from issue to trial, with around 60 weeks elapsing before setting down. These figures are unacceptable in relation to the great generality of cases.

36. In the majority of cases the reasons for delay arise from failure to progress the case efficiently, wasting time on peripheral issues or procedural skirmishing to wear down an opponent or to excuse failure to get on with the case. This approach is too often condoned by the courts, paradoxically for fear of disadvantaging the litigant. Excessive discovery and the use of experts in heavy demand both contribute to delay. All of these factors need to be addressed if any impact is to be made on the problem.

Delay in reaching settlement

37. Settlement too often occurs at too late a stage in the proceedings. In the High Court in 1993, of those cases set down, the vast majority settled with or without an order of the court. Only 13 per cent were determined after trial and 9 per cent settled during the course of the trial or at the doors of the court. In the county court a much higher proportion, 57 per cent, are determined after trial. Twelve per cent settle during the course of the trial and 17 per cent settle but attend court for approval. The Supreme Court Taxing Office survey confirms the very high rates of settlement in personal injury cases in particular.

38. Settlements at a late stage of the proceedings involve the parties in substantial additional costs. These late settlements are, however, endemic throughout the system. A settlement at a late stage is better than no settlement at all. But if a case can be settled fairly at an earlier stage this is to the parties' and the courts' benefit and would help to avoid the situation where one party can bring pressure to bear on the other party to settle on unfavourable terms as a result of the burden of costs or the frustration caused by delay.

39. Professor Hazel Genn's research on compensation for the Law Commission indicated that the majority of cases took between four and six years to settle. Larger cases tended to take longer. The average time taken for settlement in non-fatal cases was over five years and in fatal cases four years.

Extract 3:12

Lord Woolf: *Access to Justice: Final Report to the Lord Chancellor on the Civil Justice System of England and Wales* (1996) HMSO, London, ch 1, paras 1–17

1. In chapters 6 and 8 of my interim report I described the introduction of judicial case management as crucial to the changes which are necessary in our civil justice system. Ultimate responsibility for the control of litigation must move from the litigants and their legal advisers to the court. The reaction to this key message in my interim report has been extremely supportive.

2. There are already examples of case management being developed at particular courts. In the High Court there is the management of substantial litigation, such as that involving Lloyd's, by the Commercial Court. The same is true of the Official Referees' Court. There are the procedures being adopted at county courts such as Central London, Truro and Wandsworth. The results are very encouraging. Similar developments have been taking place in Scotland, the United States, Canada, Australia and New Zealand. Experience in developing case management in other jurisdictions has indicated that not all cases require the same hands-on management but that a differential approach is needed. Research on existing systems has also shown the efficacy of timetabling. These developments show the way forward.

3. There are those who have misgivings about the need for my proposals and their ability to effect beneficial change. Concern has been expressed that my proposals for case management will undermine the adversarial nature of our civil justice system. The concerns are not justified. The responsibility of the parties and the legal profession for handling cases will remain. The legal profession will, however, be performing its traditional adversarial role in a managed environment governed by the courts and by the rules which will focus effort on the key issues rather than allowing every issue to be pursued regardless of expense and time, as at present.

4. It has also been suggested that judges are not well equipped to be managers. I do not see the active management of litigation as being outside a judge's function. It is an essential means of furthering what must be the objective of any procedural system, which is to deal with cases justly. Case management includes identifying the issues in the case; summarily disposing of some issues and deciding in which order other issues are to be resolved; fixing timetables for the parties to take particular steps in the case; and limiting disclosure and expert evidence. These are all judicial functions. They are extensions backwards in time of the role of the trial judge. It should be remembered that not all judges will be acting as procedural judges. I envisage that the function of procedural judges will usually be taken by Masters and district judges, although in more complex cases Circuit judges and High Court judges will perform the task. I see case management as an enhancement of the present role of Masters and district judges, but with clearly defined objectives. Obviously there will be a need for training for both judiciary and court staff in order to improve the necessary skills. The Judicial Studies Board recognises that a substantial training effort is needed and has already begun to consider what is required. I am conscious that some procedural judges may feel that their decisions, for example on limiting evidence or the order in which issues are to be dealt with, may be overturned by the trial judge or on appeal. In the future, I hope that the team system will make for a greater partnership between all the judges in every court and ensure consistency of approach to the handling of cases and the development of case management.

5. Another concern which has been expressed is that early consideration of cases, reading the papers in the case as well as conducting the conferences and pre-trial reviews, will add significantly to the burdens of already hard-pressed Masters and district judges. It has also been suggested that case management will mean an increase in the number of interlocutory hearings, when the objectives of reducing costs and delay would be better achieved by reducing the number of such hearings. Moreover, given that the majority of cases do not reach trial, it has been argued that time spent on management early in a case will be wasted time.

6. The concerns about workload and new ways of working are understandable. I accept that any new regime will initially impose additional burdens on those who have to operate it. But the concerns do not take sufficient account of the expectations of active case management by the court. The aim of case management conferences in multi-track cases is that fewer cases should need to come to a final trial, by encouraging the parties to settle their dispute or to resolve it outside the court system altogether, and that for those cases which do require resolution by the court the issues should be identified at an early stage so that as many of them as possible can be agreed or decided before the trial. The pre-trial review should then take further steps to ensure that the trial will be shorter and less expensive. Case management hearings will replace rather than add to the present interlocutory hearings. They should be seen as using time in order to save more time.

7. The last point is an aspect of the wider concern that what I am proposing will require far more staff and other resources. Both the Bar Council and the Law Society and many others have drawn attention to this. It is said that if the management of a case is now to be handled by the court instead of by the parties' lawyers, additional judicial and administrative capacity will be needed. There are several ways in which these concerns can be addressed.

(a) Case management will be proportionate. There will be hands-on judicial intervention only in cases which will require and repay it. Basic management, with a fixed timetable and standard procedure, will be used wherever possible, on the multi-track as well as the fast track.

(b) Case management conferences will involve a more focused and directed use of time which would otherwise be spent on interlocutory hearings. The number of interlocutory applications will in any event be reduced: the move from formal pleadings to fact-based statements of case, for example, will make applications about further and better particulars less necessary.

(c) Priorities for resources must be established and resources redeployed where necessary. Generally, this will mean making realistic provision for reading time for judges and more clerical assistance to enable judges to spend more time on judicial functions. It may involve the use of law clerks in heavy cases, which I discuss in chapter 8. Under the new system some tasks, such as taxation of what will become fast track cases, will no longer be needed. Increased use of information technology will provide substantial support for case management by offering easier access to information on the progress of cases and by providing tools to support the management of individual cases. Its use will also mean that court staff can be freed from other tasks to provide support to judges on case management. (I refer here to the important proposals on IT in chapter 21.)

(d) Two other significant aims of my recommendations need to be borne in mind: that of encouraging the resolution of disputes before they come to litigation, for example by greater use of pre-litigation disclosure and of ADR, and that of encouraging settlement, for example by introducing plaintiffs' offers to settle, and by disposing of issues so as to narrow the dispute. All these are intended to divert cases from the court system or to ensure that those cases which do go through the court system are disposed of as rapidly as possible. I share the view, expressed in the Commercial Court Practice Statement of 10 December 1993, that although the primary role of the court is as a forum for deciding cases it is right that the court should encourage the parties to consider the use of ADR as a means to resolve their disputes. I believe that the same is true of helping the parties to settle a case.

8. While I have always accepted that some additional resources will be necessary, especially for training and technology, I do believe that when all these considerations are borne in mind the additional resources required should be well within the bounds of what is possible.

9. It has been suggested that it is simplistic to attribute the problems of the system to one single cause, the uncontrolled nature of the litigation process, and that there is no research to back up this assertion. My approach has been to examine the many symptoms of that single underlying cause, and my proposals are designed to tackle each of those symptoms as well as to provide an overall and coherent framework which addresses the underlying cause itself. The final survey of Supreme Court Taxing Office taxed bills by Professor Genn, summarised in Annex 3, provides detailed information on the wide range of factors which contribute to the problem and the need to provide the system with procedural levers to tackle each of them.

10. It is argued by a minority that cost and delay in civil litigation are not excessive and no remedial action is required. The SCTO survey in fact reveals, in relation to taxed cases, a reduction in overall delay and a holding steady of cost in all case types except medical negligence where cost has been increasing by seven per cent a year. The perception of clients remains, however, that cost is excessive and in many cases disproportionate and that the overall time taken is still too long and when the facts are examined it is clear this perception is far from being without foundation.

11. The survey findings on proportionate cost bear this out. They indicate that average costs among the lowest value claims consistently represent more than 100 per cent of claim value and in cases between £12,500 and £25,000 average costs range from 40 per cent to 95 per cent of claim value. To put it another way, the present system provides higher benefits to lawyers than to their clients. It is only when the claim value is over £50,000 that the average combined costs of the parties are likely to represent less than the claim. These difficulties will be alleviated by my proposals for case management.

12. It has been argued that costs are only disproportionate if they are in excess of what the parties are prepared to pay and that this is not the case in relation to personal injury and other cases where the costs are predominantly met by insurers. I do not accept this argument for reasons which I explained in the interim report. I deal again in detail in chapter 2 of this report with why I do not accept this argument.

13. My proposals tackle not only the cost but also the time taken by cases to reach a conclusion. Although the SCTO survey showed that most cases had an overall duration of 20 to 35 months, personal injury and medical negligence cases lasted a median period of 54 and 61 months. Also of concern is the indication that this period is longer in personal injury cases if the case is simple rather than complex and if it is legally aided. My recommendations in relation to pre-issue disclosure and pre-litigation protocols are designed to achieve an improvement here. There are particular problems in relation to medical negligence cases; that is why I have devoted special attention to this area.

14. The survey found that the cases which lasted longest were the 54 per cent which settled, taking between 42 and 48 months, while those ending after judgment, a quarter of the sample, took on average 25 months. The categories of cases with the highest proportion of settlements are those with the longest duration which are medical negligence, personal injury and professional negligence. My recommendations in relation to timetabling of all cases, to plaintiffs' offers and the requirement on the court to consider and assist with settlement, are designed to improve matters here.

15. In conclusion, I remain convinced that there is a grave need to move to a managed system of dispute resolution and that my proposals accurately address that need.

16. Essential elements of my proposals for case management include:

(a) allocating each case to the track and court at which it can be dealt with most appropriately;

(b) encouraging and assisting the parties to settle cases or, at least, to agree on particular issues;

(c) encouraging the use of ADR;

(d) identifying at an early stage the key issues which need full trial;

(e) summarily disposing of weak cases and hopeless issues;

(f) achieving transparency and control of costs;

(g) increasing the client's knowledge of what the progress and costs of the case will involve;

(h) fixing and enforcing strict timetables for procedural steps leading to trial and for the trial itself.

17. The fast track will provide these on a standardised basis for straightforward cases under £10,000. My general approach, the detailed procedure and the costs regime are set out in chapters 2, 3 and 4. Chapter 5 sets out my detailed proposals for cases on the multi-track and chapter 6 in this section deals with sanctions.

D: Reiterating the Critiques of Informalism

The early critiques of informalism and the sponsorship of settlement clearly remain directly relevant to this prolific institutional growth; and they have been vigorously reiterated, notably by Laura Nader. In an earlier monograph on the Mexican Zapotec, *Harmony Ideology* (1990), she had underlined the potential of colonial local courts as the site of *both* 'hegemonic' and of 'counter-hegemonic' strategies. But, reflecting on the ADR movement in the United States at the end of the century, she seems to move to a position much closer to that of Richard Abel. She writes in 2002: 'it began to look very much as if ADR were a pacification scheme, an attempt on the part of powerful interests in law and in economics to stem litigation by the masses, disguised by the rhetoric of an imaginary litigation explosion' (2002: 144).[16]

While these overarching critiques are to some extent persuasive, they only provide us with a partial understanding of contemporary moves to institutionalise 'settlement' in the common law world. First, in pointing to a fundamental shift in the strategies of state power they arguably go too far. They tend to exaggerate the extent to which a discrete 'public' sphere, characterised by a distinctive rationality and actively shaping a subordinate 'private' sphere, had ever historically evolved.[17] So we need to be cautious about endorsing the general claim about governmental

---

16 Another of Nader's targets here was 'ADR's psychotherapy-influenced forums' (2002: 144). The early Californian experiments were explicitly modeled upon Gibbs' study of the West African Kpelle dispute processes (Gibbs, 1963).

17 This point can perhaps be made particularly strongly in relation to Habermas' 'system'/'lifeworld' opposition.

change in the West. There is nothing particularly novel about those at the centre aspiring to managerial oversight of local processes. More generally, government has 'always' been ready to operate in a dual manner – by central command *and* by inducement in co-opting the local and submitting it to regulation. This was, for example, exactly the mode of government adopted in England following the Conquest in the eleventh century. More recently this was the procedure followed under nineteenth and early twentieth-century British colonial expansion, as local agencies were harnessed and brought into government under the policy of Indirect Rule.[18] Again the manifold regulatory arrangements involved in schemes of late twentieth century 'privatization' had essentially the same character.[19] In this respect, traditional conceptualisations of the 'public' and the 'private' in constitutional theory have never provided us with more than a partial handle on what is going on.

Lastly, we need to recognise a profoundly conservative side to the critique of 'informal justice'. Ironically, given its origins in the Critical Legal Studies movement, the critique seems to point us toward the recovery and celebration of 'traditional' superior court adjudication. We might on one level be happy with that, given the unease which many must feel with the hybrid shapes towards which 'courts' across the common law world seem to be moving. But we should be able to imagine 'justice' without wanting to disparage 'settlement'.

E: The Direction of ADR

This contemporary resurgence of alternative forms is distinctive in several important ways. First has been the speed with which the new groups offering institutionalised support for party negotiations away from the surveillance and control of the legal profession have themselves become professionalised. Second has been the counter-movement of recovery under which lawyers have developed alternative forms, treating ADR as the umbrella under which they have re-modelled certain areas of legal practice. Third has been the extent to which the courts themselves have embraced ADR in their (in England at least) novel enthusiasm for sponsoring settlement. This final development points to the unprecedented extent to which the ideas associated with what, at first sight, seems a revolutionary movement have been co-opted by the legal profession and the state. All of this, most notably the embrace of ADR by governments bent on cost-cutting, must renew the concerns expressed in the 1980s critique of informalism. The converging enthusiasm of the courts for settlement, and government for saving money must bring the risk of weaker litigants being coerced into accommodation.[20] Here much will depend on the quality of the emergent regulatory frameworks within which ADR providers work; and upon the extent to which the traditional roles of lawyers and judges retain their identity.

18 See, for an excellent exposition, Read and Morris (1972).   19 See Black (1996).
20 A recurrent theme in the writings of Menkel-Meadow (1997; 1999).

CHAPTER FOUR

Disputes and Dispute Processes

A: Introduction

Lawyers represent disputes as 'cases' – discrete, bounded and pathological episodes, generated by rule-breach. They are, in everyday language, 'messes' which need to be 'cleared up'. In the lawyer's view they are most appropriately cleared up in a particular way, through 'litigation'. This is a process under which, ideally, evenly matched adversaries fight it out – through their legal representatives – on the level playing field of the 'justice system'. In native legal theory, litigation culminates in a final moment of adjudication in which a neutral third party reaches an authoritative determination; although, as we have already seen, lawyers have in practice come to use litigation as the vehicle for their negotiating strategies, and in so doing 'settle' the great majority of causes before judgment.

Within this universe of meaning, disputes are affairs of 'naming, blaming and claiming' as Felstiner, Abel and Sarat put it (Extract 4:1). An individual perceives herself or himself as suffering some injurious experience, identifies this as originating in a legal wrong, blames someone for this and institutes a claim against that someone, setting in train a process that will put the matter to rights. Lawyers representing the parties then reshape the dispute into a form suitable for processing in the legal system, typically transforming it in doing so.

Clearly, the lawyer's view is a selective, culturally specific understanding of disputes even in the context where it originates. First, in making litigation the paradigm case, in presenting the instance of professional management as normal, it vastly overplays the extent to which disputes – even in this culture – get anywhere near lawyers and the courts. Second, the image of evenly matched, individual adversaries is tendentious, disregarding potential inequalities of power, the fact that many disputes occur across lines of stratification, or arise as a direct consequence of the efforts of those in power to exercise a steering role. So this image disguises the extent to which conflict resides at the level of structure. In Marxist terms, for example, conflict can be seen as originating fundamentally in the clash of opposed groups over scarce resources in a stratified society. Again, the very conceptualisation of certain kinds of issue in terms of 'dispute' perhaps has an ideological aspect. This may operate both to sanitise particular instances of conflict by separating them from a context in which structural inequalities become apparent; and to mark an event as pathological and so identify it as a suitable focus for professional intervention. In a wider context, the extent to which the lawyer's folk view of conflict privileges settlement-directed talking is also problematic. While we can say that in any group you will find institutionalised means of preventing quarrels getting in the way of the essential business of everyday life – whether this is gardening, herding, cultivating, stockbroking, or whatever – sit down talking will not necessarily be central (Extract 4:2).

This Durkheimian strand in social theory, in conceptualising disputes as pathological moments separate from the even flow of normal life and best dealt with by specialists, represents a contested position. As Simmel suggests at the beginning of his essay on conflict, 'there probably exists no social unit in which convergent and divergent currents among the members are not inseparably interwoven', and even if an absolutely harmonious group could be conceived in theory it 'could show no real life process' ([1908]; 1955: 15). Cultures also differ in the extent to which quiet harmony among the members is presented as a necessary, or even ideal, condition; loud, contentious behaviour may be admired, and quarrelling be seen as normal.[1] The presentation of disputes as discrete, bounded 'cases' is problematic in another way. In any social context, disputes are embedded in everyday life, arising from a 'past' and merging into a 'future'.

Developing a related point, the very firm line drawn in this culture between the 'legal' and the 'political', marked in the distinction between conflict associated with rule-breach (identified as pathological) and that originating in competition for resources (seen as a normal part of everyday life) is not necessarily typical. The very complex relationship between rule-breach and what may be perceived as legitimate competition is illustrated in Turner's account of the devolution of political office in *Schism and Continuity in an African Society* (1957). The headship of Ndembu communities must devolve on a male member of the senior matrilineage in the village; but no detailed rules specify which member this is to be – this is a matter of individual achievement and acceptance. So whenever an existing head shows signs of growing old and loosing his grip, younger members of the matrilineage compete among themselves for the headship. Bitter quarrels attend this competition, typically involving claims to wrongdoing, accusations of witchcraft and sorcery. It is only as the new head manages to establish his ascendancy that this all subsides and disappointed competitors either knuckle down under the new regime or leave the village and found their own communities. In this process, claims about wrong are closely interwoven with struggles for political ascendancy and competition for resources; and given the constantly negotiated nature of Ndembu life, it is not helpful to view conflict as pathological and somehow in contrast to normal life processes – it is simply part of them.

---

1 See, for example, Nader (1990: 291–308); Greenhouse (1989); and Palmer (1988).

B: Typologies of Response

A number of general typologies of dispute process were formulated in the theoretical literature that developed around the extensive ethnographic evidence of disputing which had accumulated by the 1960s (Llewellyn and Hoebel, 1941; Gluckman, 1955; Bohannan, 1957; Turner, 1957; Gulliver, 1963; Nader, 1965).[2] These emphasised several core oppositions: between fighting and talking ('war' and 'law'); between agreed outcome and imposed decision ('negotiation' and 'adjudication'); and between different kinds of third-party intervener (for example, 'partisan' or 'neutral') and modes of intervention (for example, 'advice' or 'decision'). The tentative typology of dispute processes or 'responses to trouble' put forward here draws upon and reacts to these attempts. We make no large claims for it; it is simply our shot for these particular purposes.

Avoidance

At one end of the spectrum lies *avoidance*. A universally encountered response to perceived wrong is to do nothing – to 'lump it' (Felstiner, 1974; Galanter, 1974; Felstiner, 1975). We have all, again and again, encountered situations where it has made sense to 'let it go into the net' rather than to respond – perhaps because the issue was too small, or because the overall cost of trouble would have been too great having regard to the value of the relationship concerned. In the same vein, but requiring an active step, is the decision to disengage and avoid, staying away from the person one is in disagreement with. This widely recognised way of dealing with trouble has a range of important consequences: it enables parties to 'cool it'; it signals unambiguously how unwelcome actions have been received; it may put pressure on recalcitrants to step back into line. Obviously, in many situations, total avoidance will be an impossibly costly response; but there are here almost infinite possibilities of fine tuning, allowing extensive variation in scale and severity. Subtle forms of partial withdrawal and of reduction in co-operation are often available – such as stinginess in exchange – which are enough to convey the necessary message about future conduct. The ultimate form of this response is ostracism, where members of a group temporarily discontinue all co-operation with a wrongdoer, or even expel him, leaving him to manage on his own or seek admission to another group (Extract 4:3).

Self-help

At the other end of the spectrum is *self-help*. A different, potentially costly way of dealing with conflict is to make a direct physical attack on the other party in an attempt to eliminate competition, respond to a wrong or subdue them into compliance with your wishes. On one level this can be presented as an antithesis of

---

2 And which continued thereafter – see Abel (1973); Koch (1974); and Gulliver (1971; 1979).

avoidance or talking; but a bald fighting/talking, law/war dichotomy is misleading. In any society where fighting is an accepted means of reaching an outcome, it may be expected to take on a conventionalised, restricted, even ritual form. This can be illustrated in the European 'duel', or in any number of reports of New Guinea societies where fighting takes on a heavily rule-governed form. Fighting is reduced to a virtually ceremonial procedure in Eskimo head butting and battering contests; and in the *nith* songs where violence is channelled into a song exchange. Some anthropologists have gone much further than this and treat a whole range of formalised conduct as somehow 'representing' fighting – for example, where ceremonial, competitive presentations of goods are interpreted as replacements for fighting (Extract 4:4).

Talk: Public Decision-making

Dominant strands of legal theory in the West start out with a distinctive idea of the 'public' sphere in decision-making. This is a sphere represented as created and shaped by government, by definition dominated by governmental interventions (for a powerful recent statement of this position, see Loughlin, 2003). Within it, decision-making is overwhelmingly characterised by the mode of command and differentiated in such a manner that 'everyday' decisions and decisions in the context of 'dispute' are self-consciously separated. The limitations of this view, in a world where the now obtrusive – if embattled – nation state actually appeared rather late on the scene, need to be recognised before a broader panorama can be attempted.

Starting again, we begin with a recognition that the public sphere is 'always' present in the social world, before government and independent of emergent hierarchies, whatever degree of co-option by those aspiring to power may subsequently take place. Drawing in the contents of this space, we try to elaborate both the range of forms which 'intervention' may take and the varied shapes of hierarchy when this is present. Where the public sphere is colonised by government, the mode of 'command' must even then be relocated in a wider spectrum of interventions.

The Legacy of Command

A primary linkage of decision-making to 'government' gets us off to an uncertain start when thinking about the general shapes of the social world. For as long as we lawyers can remember, our thinking about decision-making has been shaped in broad, schematic terms by images of 'the King' (or some other kind of ruler) and his surrogate 'the Judge'. Laying the very foundations of modern legal theory, Austin ([1832]; 1955) built upon the centrality of command. In Maine's mid-century panorama, *Ancient Law*, legal history is solidified as the story of adjudication (1861). For Maine there were no structural changes in the process of dispute settlement process over what he saw as the fundamental stages of societal development. From the primal ascendancy of the senior male agnate onwards, disputes were resolved by decision, handed down by a third party; there was no suggestion of negotiatory modes of settlement giving way to processes of third-party adjudication. Second, the presence of a normative basis for decision-making was the key attribute of law for Maine, and the emergence of this feature heralded the transition from the pre-legal to the legal world. Third, there was the later development of specialisation as legal rules became separated off from other rules operating in society. So for Maine, social life is the product of 'government', law develops in the course of that process, and the fundamental way in which kingly power is revealed is through adjudication. Subsequently, from this emergence of specifically legal theory, attempts to theorise adjudication have dominated jurisprudence.[3] Even today, the courts remain legal theory's central preoccupation (see, for example, Dworkin, *Law's Empire*, 1986).

This way of thinking about decision-making is not peculiar to lawyers but draws on a long dominant strand of socio-political theory. Its foundations are visible in Hobbes' *Leviathan* (1651), a fundamental justification of kingship, where compliance by the subject with 'laws' commanded upon him by the sovereign is offered as the only alternative to brutish and ultimately hopeless conflict. While a less grim view of the pre-state world underlies Locke's *Two Treatises on Civil Government*, political society is still defined in terms of 'a common establish'd Law and Judicature to appeal to, with Authority to decide Controversies between them' (1690 [1924]: 87).

Much later, the centrality of a steering role in society was still taken for granted by Weber in *Economy and Society* (1917). In its essentials, Weber's view of the social world was based irreducibly on a model that assumes a leader and a following – the *leiter* and the *verband*. The leader's steering role was exercised through command, a matter of one telling others what to do. In this account a particular conception of power comes into the picture. It becomes a matter of the chances that people will comply when being told to do things they would not otherwise have done. Realisation of such arrangements is taken to require two general conditions. First, we must assume the availability of staff capable of exercising force if necessary – 'a group of men specially empowered to carry out this function'. Second, because leaders who want to be around for a sustained period cannot rely on coercive power alone, conditions must be such that at least some members of the following regard their domination as normal, even 'right'.

These parochial folk understandings of the 'modern' West, even if they depict with at least partial accuracy the particular context in which they originate, potentially distort any broader panorama. First, the central conception of 'order' as intimately linked to 'government' – in the sense of a self-consciously exercised steering role working within a separate, dominant 'public' sphere – fixes too strong an imprint on the way we see the social world. The overall picture is misleading in that it both overstates and diminishes the place of 'government'. It overstates the role of government in portraying the shapes of the social world as the skilled, intentional

---

3 Although in *The Concept of Law* (1961), Hart appeared to marginalise adjudication by identifying law as an affair of rules, MacCormick's exegesis was quick to re-present Hart's theory of law as one of adjudication (MacCormick, 1981).

achievement of those in power – making it impossible to imagine 'society' without the sovereign. It diminishes it in implying an impoverished mode of operation restricted to command.

The implications of these presuppositions for the understanding of decision-making have been far-reaching. They underlie a quite general presupposition that decision-making must be problematic in the absence of 'third parties' to secure it. For example, a widely held assumption of New Guinea anthropology was that negotiatory processes tend to be inherently unstable unless there are third parties capable of acting in a bridging position between the two sides. In commenting on his Jale ethnography in *War and Peace in Jalemo*, Klaus Koch argued that the prevalence of fighting could be put down to the fact that 'very ineffective methods exist to transform a dyadic confrontation into a triadic relationship which could secure a settlement by the intervention of the third party' (1974: 159).

Although the link between 'society' and 'government' which these understandings presuppose was challenged at an empirical level as far back as the seventeenth century, when accounts of Amerindian groups became available in the West, this knowledge was ignored, even suppressed.[4] The reality of acephalous society, of social groupings which cannot accurately be represented through the paradigmatic form of leader and following, was confirmed in the course of the subsequent encounter with small-scale, technologically simple societies that fell under imperial rule in the course of late nineteenth- and early twentieth-century colonial expansion. This reality was not easily accommodated to these dominant strands in social and political theory. Even for Malinowski 'order' was a problem: how did these acephalous societies hold together given the absence of 'codes, courts and constables' (1926: 14)? His discussion in *Crime and Custom in Savage Society* was framed as an answer to that question. There his elucidation of a complex of reciprocal economic obligations linking members of Trobriand society to each other startlingly illustrated a society with limited institutionalised leadership, let alone centralised authority or the differentiated arrangements associated with government in the contemporary West.

Not only were these societies 'without the King', but in some of them – notably those of hunter/gatherers – explicitly 'egalitarian' understandings were combined with an absence of institutionalised hierarchy, leaving disparities of strength, speed and skill to mark the boundaries of power relations. In the case of such societies accounts abound of people quickly pouring scorn and ridicule on any individual who shows signs of aspiring to personal ascendancy, of 'telling others what to do' or exploiting their labour. The Mbuti of the Ituri forests described by Turnbull (1966), the Hadza of Northern Tanzania (see Woodburn 1972) and the Amazonian Yanamamo (Clastres, 1977) provide exhaustively observed examples. In these cases – which include shifting cultivators – there is according to the accounts, no 'will

---

4 It now seems established that one of the motivations underlying Locke's *Two Treatises* was a justification of the expropriation of the Amerindians involved in European settlement, in which he was directly involved. Locke's formulation of 'political society' was shaped to provide an explicit contrast with the social organisation of Amerindian groups (Tully, 1993).

to power', no desire to acquire wealth. Production and reproduction take place and order prevails, not only in the absence of centralised authority, but also with very limited institutionalised hierarchy within the group. As Lee insists of one such society (the !Kung San hunter/gatherers of the Kalahari): 'it is not simply a question of the absence of a headman and other authority figures but also a positive insistence on the essential equality of all people and the refusal to bow to the authority of others' (Leacock and Lee, 1982: 53). As Clastres puts it of the Yanamamo: 'no one feels the quaint desire to do more, own more, or appear to be more than his neighbour' (1977: 173). Writing of the Hadza, Woodburn (1972) describes how individuals with troublesome aspirations to leadership are simply abandoned by other members of the small, mobile groups of which this society is made up.

This is not to suggest that in these societies differences of age, gender and skill will not set up diffuse power relations. While these relations are typically of fluctuating content, shifting ramification and transitory duration, to some degree such relations will be institutionalised. In the case of the Hadza, for example, Woodburn identifies a mother and her nubile daughters as constituting one enduring grouping around which a shifting population of aspirant males will congregate.

C: Reconstructing a Panorama of Decision-making

Against this background, releasing 'society' from a fundamental subordination to 'government', the overall map of public decision-making has to be re-drawn. This revision requires:

- a depiction of the 'public' sphere as an emergent feature of society rather than the achievement of government;
- a recognition of *both* the 'command' and the 'bilateral exchange' as primary modes of decision-making, cutting across any distinction between private and public spheres;
- a re-exploration of triadic forms; and
- a re-examination of hierarchy beyond command.

As we have noted, in the lawyer's 'native' view – and equally in the wider tradition of socio-political theory underpinning it – the 'public' sphere appears as something separate from and other than society, regulating (and in some versions even creating) the rest of the social world. Whatever degree of differentiation may now be present, this prioritisation of the 'public' and the very public/private opposition that this involves is misleading. The public sphere is 'always' there in the social world. It takes its primary, simplest form wherever a third party observes/becomes involved in the bilateral exchanges of everyday interaction. At the same time we can expect to find it marked out, spatially and symbolically – even in the smallest and most transitory social groups – in the central open space, in the area 'around the fire'. In that context it takes the form, variously described in numerous ethnographies, of a 'council' in which the members of a community meet together and see to their general arrangements – in Bailey's terms an 'arena council' (1969). Bloch's discussion of the Merina *fokon 'olona* (1971) provides an example. He describes meetings which deal with all the general arrangements of the group. They are not confined to some specialised area of competence or 'jurisdiction', but simply consist of the community 'doing something'. In such groups, decision-making may be by consensus, the meeting just breaking up as people disagree; alternatively, some form of decision by 'majority' may operate.

The public sphere in this form is there long before institutionalised office or government is present. So we need firmly to reverse the order as it were, so the public is seen as an emergent feature of the social, upon which differentiation or elaboration – in whatever form – may subsequently from time to time develop. We consider below the different forms of decision-making within such a public space. The whole space may be filled by two opposed groups; there may be others who are not directly involved and may intervene from a non-aligned stand point; there may be yet others who are not directly involved at all but merely have an interest in 'decisions being made' so that they can get back to the fields again. Others may just be 'there', watching, offering the tacit assurance that 'this is the way things are done . . .' The public space is obviously open to internal or external co-option, and it may well develop as the scene of hegemonic strategies; but, as Clifford Geertz warns in *Negara* (1982), we diminish it if we restrict it to the site of 'command'.

At the same time, and related to that, when we begin talking about decision-making we should make two preliminary shifts of focus. First, we need to begin by paying attention to the primary bilateral exchange as the essential springboard to more complex relations. Simmel recognised the 'dyad' as 'the simplest sociological formation, methodologically speaking . . . that which operates between two elements. It contains the scheme, germ, and material of innumerable more complex forms' ([1908]; trans 1950: 122). Restoring a primacy focus on this elementary, ubiquitous mode, under which decisions are reached by those immediately engaged, without intermediaries, through cyclical processes of information exchange and learning, should not be necessary. It is only made so by a dual historical process: the overwhelming attention given by lawyers to third-party decisions in the form of adjudication; and the parallel entrenchment of professional, partisan representation.

Second, we need to go back again and look at the 'triad', recognising the importance of this elementary form of the 'public' sphere as something that is always there in the social world. As Simmel noted, dyads 'have very special features' but 'the addition of a third person completely changes them' ([1908]; trans 1950: 138). But at the same time the triad has to be prised apart from any necessary association with hierarchy – particularly hierarchies of command – for as Geertz has warned us, and as we noted at the very beginning of Chapter One, 'impressed by command, we see little else' (Geertz, 1982: 121). The dominant, exhaustive image of the leader and following has made dyadic processes appear somehow insecure, even incomplete, and has also harmfully constrained the ways in which we think about third-party intervention.

Taking this forward, we need to explore public decision-making in four primary directions. First we need to restore the reality of stable arrangement in the absence of institutionalised triadic form, let alone the presence of command. Second, we need to re-explore the possibilities of the triad, turning away from the assumption of 'command'. Third, we need to explore command from the start, stripping away strong institutional shapes. Lastly, we need to look at institutionalised command as part of a wider complex of interventions.

The Shapes of Public Decision-making

While the 'public' sphere is always there in the social world, constituted by the presence of the triad in Simmel's sense, public decision-making need not *necessarily* be characterised by a triadic form. The public sphere may simply represent an immobile but supportive backdrop against which primary processes of decision take place. It may do no more than constitute an authentic context in which A and B negotiate a joint decision, or in which A tells B 'what to do', and thus provide the arena in which dyadic relations are played out. While both of these spare models have realised, recognisable counterparts on any social scene, we need to begin by restoring joint decision-making (negotiation and the rich variations upon it) to parity with command. It has for too long been elbowed aside by the ideology that has come to characterise the nation state.

In searching for an analytical model, the varied forms of settlement-directed communication leading to decision-making may be distinguished through a range of variables. These include: the presence or absence of third-party intervention; the form of such intervention where it takes place; and the location of power in decision-making. On the basis of these variations three basic modes of settlement-directed communication may be identified: bilateral negotiation; facilitated negotiations ('mediation'); and umpiring processes. These are sketched in here as 'models' only, cut away from context and thus achieving an analytical clarity typically absent in real-life processes.

Negotiations are represented here as the simple bilateral exchange. They are processes of communication, involving the exchange of information, potentially leading to common understanding and joint decision-making. In their simplest, bilateral form two parties in dispute approach each other without the intervention of third parties and attempt to achieve an agreed outcome through information exchange and learning. The exchange and examination of information lead to the modification or consolidation of expectations to a point at which agreement is achieved. Communication continues as long as agreement is seen by both sides as possible and advantageous. The essential feature is that control over the outcome is retained by the disputants themselves, informed by their meanings and under-standings. The simple contrast is with processes in which power is shared with, or transferred to, third parties.

The simple model of bilateral negotiations can be transformed in a number of ways. First, in the direction of multi-party negotiations, additional individuals or groups may enter the negotiations as parties. Second, partisans may be added in support of the principal disputants. The 'help' extended by such partisans may take numerous forms. At one end of the scale, assistance may be limited to tacit support, it may extend to advice, and further along the spectrum it may involve the partisan standing beside the principal as a member of a 'team'. The most extreme form of partisan intervention arises where the principal retreats into the background and is represented in negotiations by a partisan as 'champion'. The provenance of partisans is also variable, ranging from the friend or neighbour to the professional adviser or representative.

The intervention of partisans necessarily changes the shape of simple negotiations in a number of ways. First, the number or quality of partisans on one side or the other may alter existing configurations of power. Second, in so far as partisans take an active role in negotiations, rather than providing tacit support, some of the power over decision-making otherwise enjoyed by the parties alone will pass to them. Third, the universe of meaning within which negotiations proceed is necessarily extended and changed by the presence of partisans on either side; their understandings, their interpretations and their repertoire of norms will come to inform the process to a greater or lesser extent.

For the purposes of the next model, the basic structure of the decision-making process is changed by a presence of a third party who intervenes, in contrast to the partisan, from a position of at least apparent non-alignment to facilitate achievement of an outcome. The primary role of such a 'mediator' must be to facilitate communications between the parties, but the potential nature and range of involvement extends beyond that. While at first sight power in facilitated negotiations remains with the parties themselves, control necessarily passes to some extent to the intervener who may in some cases come to share power over the outcome. The nature and extent of facilitatory intervention varies greatly; the very term 'mediator' conceals a wide range of different activities and degrees of intervention, as we indicate in Chapter Six.

For the purposes of the third model, the essential change is that power over the outcome is transferred to some third-party decision-maker. Beyond this fundamental attribute, the nature and characteristics of umpiring are widely variable. Some are state-sponsored ('judges'), others are privately selected by the parties ('arbitrators'). Equally, the central role of judges can be perceived in a number of ways: as a compartment of 'government', exercising a steering role; as revising and keeping in public view central norms and understandings in society; as deciding individual disputes brought before them. Umpires differ also in the resources that they draw upon in decision-making. We explore all these questions in Chapter Seven.[5]

In the sections which follow, we illustrate the three foundational forms through vignettes taken from three African cultures. We do this with a view to distracting our

---

5 For further details see Abel's comparative essay on dispute institutions in society (1973), and Shapiro's study of courts (1979).

attention from the parochial shapes of the contemporary West. We try to draw each vignette in sufficient detail to show the context in which these processes are realised.

Negotiations

We can identify the basic elements of the bilateral exchange across widely differ-ent socio-cultural contexts. They are as visible in the unselfconscious routines of everyday life as in the formalised, set-piece exchanges of an international confer-ence. The fundamentals also remain constant whether the issue is uncontentious or a focus of extreme conflict. While the basic features of negotiation – as processes of communication, involving the exchange of information, potentially leading to common understanding and joint decision-making – hold steady across cultures, the form they take and the conventions under which they take place will be shaped by the specific cultural context.

Ethnographic examples of these bilateral and multi-party decision-making pro-cesses offer little support for that strand in political-legal theory that identifies such processes as inherently unstable in the absence of available, non-aligned, third-party intervention.[6] The reality of stable decision-making processes in a context which does not encourage non-aligned, third-party intervention is powerfully illustrated in Philip Gulliver's ethnography of the Arusha, *Social Control in an African Society* (1963):

> The Arusha are settled agriculturalists, living on the slopes of Mount Meru in North-ern Tanzania. Prior to 19th century colonial expansion they recognised no form of centralized government, but three major groupings are institutionalised in Arusha society: the lineage, the age-set and the territorial unit.
>
> All Arusha claim membership of one of a number of patrilineal descent groups, each founded by one of the male pioneer settlers in their present territory (who arrived there about 1830). But unlike the case in many societies with a strong lineage organization, lineage membership and residential grouping do not coincide. Instead, the homesteads of members of a given lineage are likely to be scattered around all over Arusha country rather than clustered together in a discrete group. As well as claiming membership of a patrilineage, each Arusha male also belongs to an age-set, into which he is admitted with others of his generation following initiation. As the members of a given set grow older, they pass through four distinct stages, each associated with particular kinds of work and responsibility within the society.
>
> Arusha do not live in well-defined villages, but in homesteads located here and there across the arable lands that they keep under cultivation. These lands are also divided up into a number of geographical units that Gulliver describes as 'parishes'. Thus any Arusha male belongs to a particular lineage, is a member of a given age-set and lives in one of the parishes into which the territory is divided. Strong ties of loyalty and mutual responsibility are meant to bind a man to other members of his lineage and to his age-mates, and although the ties between co-residents in a given parish seem

6 See Koch (1974).

less close, such residents do recognize themselves as a group to the extent of meeting together to discuss matters of common interest which arise within the parish.

Where disagreement in decision-making arises between two Arusha, each will seek to recruit a support group and once that has taken place the two groups meet for settlement-directed discussion. The three principal sub-groupings in Arusha society both define reservoirs of support for those involved in a quarrel and provide a choice of forum before which disputes can be taken. So far as the recruitment of support is concerned, the Arusha disputant can turn to members of his lineage and to his age-mates for support simply *because* they are members of his lineage or his age-mates; this is not a matter of past co-operation leading to ties of reciprocal obligation.

The organization of Arusha society similarly defines the range of fora available in decision-making. An Arusha may bring an issue before members of his parish, his lineage or his age-set. This possibility of choice is of some importance in enabling an Arusha to air his problem in the forum where he believes his support is strongest; but Arusha understandings impose limitations upon the freedom with which a forum can be chosen. According to Arusha, disagreement between members of a lineage should be kept *within* the lineage and a similar sentiment is expressed so far as age-mates are concerned. It goes with the idea of 'privacy' to the group that disputes between members of a single lineage should be taken to a meeting of the lineage, rather than to either of the other two agencies, and that quarrels between age-mates should be similarly settled within the set to which they belong. Only where two members of the same parish are in dispute who are neither age-mates nor members of the same lineage does the parish meeting constitute an approved venue for discussion.

Beyond the notion of lineage 'privacy', two further features of Arusha society determine the bilateral shape of intra-lineage decision-making. First, Arusha lineages are bifurcated in such a way that where any two members of the lineage are in disagreement the allegiance of the remaining members is automatically foretold. The two ensuing groups meet and together provide the forum within which discussion and decision takes place. Second, for Arusha a posture of non-aligned disinterest is implausible, even laughable; a person is on one 'side' or the other. So the notion and reality of the 'mediator' is not available to them. Instead, discussion takes place bilaterally between the two opposed groups aligned behind the respective 'principals'.

Leeway for decision is provided by the fact that, while Arusha normative understandings may be clear-cut and detailed, they are approached in a transactional way and become bargain counters rather than determinants in the context of disagreement. In the absence of 'mediators' pressure seems typically to come from within the opposed groups. These seldom develop into solidary 'power' groups as each will contain members of the same age sets and parishes.

The 'Third Party' in Decision-making

Where we do encounter the 'third party' in decision-making, some strong native legal stereotypes – notably those of the 'king' (or 'emperor' or some other kind of ruler) and the 'judge' – need to be recognised before triadic interventions as a whole can be reassessed. These are hierarchically positioned interveners, explicitly associated with an institutionalised role of centralised steering (and so exercising 'official' power), making imposed decisions (and so utilising the mode of 'command'). So in native legal theory, fundamental structural features of the triad, even if well marked out in sociological theory, are virtually erased. For example, the idea and the person of the 'mediator' have in many regions of the West been driven to the margins. This has resulted from a dual process: the increasing dominance of 'command' as the nation state solidified; and the emergence of lawyers as a specialist service profession. Overall we need to make the non-aligned intervener more securely theorised. In so doing we must, in particular, reverse the historical priority given to the judge and the corresponding marginalisation of 'the mediator'.

The nature of third-party intervention is inevitably closely dependent upon the socio-cultural context in which it takes place, making any attempt at generalisation hazardous. Recognising the culturally specific character of any intervention, on an analytical level we need to work along two primary planes, representing respectively:

- what interveners *do*; and
- their provenance.

Non-aligned third parties may become involved in a wide range of interventions – in constituting the means of communication (the 'go-between'), in providing advice and information, in facilitating the decisions of others (the 'mediator') and in themselves making the decisions (the 'arbitrator' and the 'judge'). Such interventions are perhaps best represented as ranged along a spectrum of progressively increasing intensity. At the minimal end is the passive observer whose mere presence sanctions bilateral decision-making. A little further along lies the 'go between' who carries messages between two poles, setting in place the communications arrangements necessary to enable decision-making to take place. At the far end lies the legislator or the judge, making decisions to which others are subject. If we seek to make a clear analytical break along this spectrum, one way of doing so is to distinguish those interventions that facilitate the decisions of others from those that constitute the decision itself. Another way of putting the same point, is to ask where 'power' over the outcome lies – drawing a line between 'the mediator' and 'the judge'.

Looking closely at the provenance of different interveners in the context of their interventions immediately forces us to take seriously the variable elements of hierarchy and institutionalisation. Many third parties are senior, through rank or office, to those in relation to whom they intervene. They may be 'elders' in terms of kinship, feudal superiors, political leaders, dominant specialists, or even rulers. They may, on the other hand, be collateral kin, friends, neighbours, bystanders or workmates. These variables obviously affect both the modes of their intervention and the manner in which that intervention will be received.

Mediatory Interventions

While 'advice' and 'mediation' may appear analytically distinct activities, in many instances it is difficult to prise them apart. First, while much advice is delivered from an openly partisan standpoint, we can recognise the reality of the non-aligned advisor, attempting to address the parties to decision in an even-handed way. Second, the label of 'mediator' seems to conceal at least two analytically distinct modes of intervention, with quite different processual shapes. One involves a primarily facilitatory role, setting in place the communications arrangements between parties which enable them to negotiate; the other a more active dominant role, associated both with the political superior and the expert consultant (the latter is a role familiar across a wide range of contemporary professions).

The role of the mediator may be as clearly recognisable in the routine, unexamined interventions of friends and kinsmen as in those of professional specialists or political superiors. Ethnographic accounts also provide numerous cases of figures who mediate in the course of a broader role – the Nuer 'leopardskin chief' (Evans-Pritchard, 1940) and the Kalinga *monkalun* (Barton, 1919), for example. But a paradigm case where leadership in decision-making is narrowly institutionalised in the shape of the mediator is described in Philip Gulliver's ethnography of the Ndendeuli of Southern Tanzania, *Neighbours and Networks* (1971):

> The Ndendeuli live in small groups of undifferentiated kinsmen within which no sharp divisions are drawn on the basis of age or particular lines of descent. They occupy woodland areas where poor soil necessitates a move to fresh fields every two or three seasons. Although they practise a very simple slash-and-burn technique of agriculture, the members of a household require the help of others if their fields are to be cleared, fenced, hoed and planted. For this purpose, the head of a household forms a clearing party, calling upon those he has himself helped in the past and will be helping in the future. Over time these arrangements develop into more generalized relationships of reciprocal obligation, involving an expectation of mutual aid outside this narrow economic sphere. This includes the expectation of help when one partner gets involved in a dispute. When a man finds himself in a quarrel, he will expect to be able to call on the support of those with whom he has cooperated most closely in the past, and in turn he will assume that he will support them in their disputes. Thus, whenever a quarrel arises in an Ndendeuli community, support groups made up of other members will be ranged behind those between whom the trouble originated.
>
> Above household level, leadership in decision-making is exercised in two principal contexts. One is where a pioneer moves away and founds a new settlement as land becomes exhausted, taking a nucleus of his undifferentiated kinsmen with him. While new communities are generally formed by men of particular skill and initiative, such people do not subsequently exercise a generalised 'governmental' role. The other opportunity to fill a leadership role arises where a member of the community attempts to intervene from a non-aligned standpoint in mediating between opposed groups in the event of a dispute. A man becomes a 'notable' through gaining a reputation as a successful mediator. But this status and its associated prestige is of a transitory nature. He remains 'big' only so long as his interventions are successful. He becomes 'small' again where his interventions fail or where he repeatedly declines the opportunity to intervene.

In the event of a dispute arising between two members of an Ndendeuli community, the approved method of dealing with it is for the disputants to meet together with their kinsmen for settlement-directed discussion. Third parties, who in the nature of these communities will inevitably be kinsmen or affines of the disputants, must in theory play one of two roles. They may join either disputant as a supporter (Gulliver describes such people as members of a disputant's 'action-set'), or seek to perform a mediatory function in a more or less impartial way by convening and facilitating meetings between the two groups. Gulliver found that the action-sets were built up of people with whom the disputants enjoyed the closest ties of material cooperation (e.g. if A has repeatedly helped B in his clearing and hoeing operations, and *vice versa*, either will expect the support of the other in the event of a dispute). Each disputant will try to secure as members of his action-set people who are influential in the community and who are listened to with respect in a meeting: sheer numbers, while important, may be matched by quality.

Mediators, on the other hand, are likely to be drawn from people with whom neither party has particularly close ties of cooperation and who stand equidistant from each in terms of kinship. Outright support in the event of a dispute strengthens the ties between the supporter and the disputant, and necessarily leads to a corresponding cooling of relations with the other party. Similarly, while successful mediation can increase prestige in the community, failure to achieve a settlement, or demonstrated partiality for one side, will be damaging. Because of this, in a small community third parties have to calculate very carefully the consequences of a particular position or alignment and judge nicely the degree of support they may extend. Each dispute leaves its mark on the community in the sense that new loyalties are established and old ones decline. Existing hostilities are similarly liable to modification.

Once a meeting has been convened, both sides outline their version of the dispute, and the competing assertions and demands will be supported by the respective action sets. As the overall picture becomes clear, those who have adopted a neutral posture hitherto may suggest possible lines of settlement, urging both parties to give ground in such a way that their respective positions converge to a point where some agreed outcome is possible. In doing so they necessarily put a given construction on events and implicitly allocate responsibility for the dispute. At this point the supporters of each disputant may themselves urge a particular compromise and outline the merits of some course of action that a mediator has proposed. In this way a solution can speedily be reached, and the meeting end successfully. But equally the meeting may break up with the rival positions hardened in deadlock. Where this happens, another meeting has to be arranged to try again. While each disputant retains a degree of independence, once the meeting begins and his action-set has been convened he is to some extent constrained by the opinions the members express and the courses of action they favour. If influential members of the set favour a particular solution by way of settlement, and advocate it strongly, there is little the disputant can do but accept this, for otherwise his group of supporters will simply melt away if the meeting ends without a conclusion. Certainly where members of the respective action-sets are as one as to the solution to be followed, there is little the principals can do but comply.

In searching for a settlement, reference may be made to socially accepted rules, to the importance of sustaining particular social ties and to the harmony of the community as a whole. While appeal to some Ndendeuli norm must underlie any claim which one party may make against the other and many form the criteria on which a settlement is urged, such norms tend to be general and ill-defined, rather than detailed and clear-cut. This lack of clarity is illustrated in the norms relating to bridewealth and to the behaviour of the son-in-law. While Ndendeuli are clear that bridewealth must be presented on marriage, and that a good son-in-law has a duty to give material help to his wife's father, the rules do not make it clear what constitutes an adequate presentation of bridewealth, what is sufficient help to a father-in-law, or where these different responsibilities begin and end in relation to each other. The uncertainty of these Ndendeuli norms thus provides ground over which argument can range if a quarrel between a man and his son-in-law should arise.

Besides any socially approved norms which may be specifically relevant to a dispute a higher appeal may also be made to the parties that they must patch up the dispute in the interests of harmony in the group. Such an appeal will run: 'We are all kinsmen, we cannot allow this quarrel to continue and disrupt our lives.' A call like this will take on particular urgency if the quarrel persists, or if it occurs at a time when its prosecution delays vital agricultural activities.

Beyond any such appeals to norms and underlying values, political undercurrents will also be present. The 'notable' is able to form a large action-set made up of the men who are influential in the community and articulate in debate, will be well-placed to achieve the more favourable settlement.

The consequences which this form of organisation has for the Ndendeuli processes of dispute settlement appear clearly in this brief account. First are the limitations imposed upon third parties where they have no authority to impose a decision on the disputants. This lack of authority is underlined in instances Gulliver cites of meetings frequently breaking up without any conclusion having been reached. Such a conclusion is only reached when the disputants themselves, however reluctantly, agree upon one. Therefore the role of third parties cannot extend beyond helping to achieve that agreement. They do this, first, by constituting a forum within which discussion may take place; second, as members of the respective action-sets, by formulating the positions of the two sides; and, third, by building the elements of a compromise out of the positions which develop. Analytically, the role of the action-set member, and that of the mediator, are distinct in this process; and in their nature will be performed by different people. But mediators are not necessarily without bias, as Gulliver's illustrations reveal. Further, members of the respective action-sets, as well as any mediator, may play a significant part in edging the respective positions closer and, finally, articulating the possible solutions implicit in the positions that have emerged. Nor should the influence of third parties in achieving a settlement be underemphasised. Although they lack any decision-making power, their assessment of what constitutes an appropriate compromise will be hard for the parties to resist, particularly if a consensus develops between the two sets, or if a preponderance of political muscle is lined up on one side or the other. No disputant can afford to hold out for a solution which his supporters do not favour, as in the short term his support will melt away and in the longer term he will put in jeopardy future valuable co-operation.

A second general point is the flavour of bargain and compromise inherent in this settlement process. As the outcome must lie in agreement, the formula will be found in the most which each party is prepared to concede and the least she or he is prepared to accept. Under such conditions norms cannot be exclusive determinants of an outcome, and considerations such as the respective economic strength and political muscle of the different parties become important. But so far as the part played by Ndendeuli norms in the process is concerned, Gulliver argues that their very lack of clarity is of vital importance. This characteristic introduces an element of flexibility that provides leeway for successful negotiation. Were the rules clear-cut, one avenue of compromise would be unavailable.

The process of settlement here is different in two major respects from that in the Arusha case described above. First, the necessary leeway for negotiation is achieved through a different means. In the Ndendeuli case, imprecision of norms provides the needed flexibility. With the Arusha there is no lack of clarity: the rules about bridewealth or that a man inherits his father's field are crisp and unambiguous. It is the fact that the norms are seen as negotiable, as resources in the process of reaching an outcome, that provides the necessary flexibility to achieve a solution. Second, the mode of settlement is different. In the Ndendeuli case, a purportedly non-aligned mediator stands between the respective groups of supporters and helps guide them to a negotiated solution. With the Arusha, the initiative towards compromise comes from *within* the opposed groups themselves. This feature is foretold in Arusha lineage organisation. These lineages are constructed in such a way that they divide into two all the way down, with the result that in the event of conflict arising within the lineage, each member knows on which side his support is due (Gulliver, 1963: 134–140). Obviously he has discretion to exert himself strongly or remain in the background; but the 'side' he is on in any conflict within the lineage is decided for him in the principles of lineage organisation. Thus, within the lineage there is no one who *can* stand in an intermediate position and behave as a neutral mediator. Further, as we noted, there is the principle of privacy to the group that operates strongly in lineage affairs. So there are strong cultural inhibitions against someone from *outside* the lineage being drawn in to mediate.

Third-Party Decisions: The Attribute of Command

While the distinction between the mediator, who facilitates a decision, and a third party who makes one may be clear-cut on an analytic level, these two shade into one another in practice. Here the language of communication may provide only a limited guide. Particularly where those involved are in relations of hierarchy, decisions may well be couched in the form of 'advice', even tentative 'suggestion'. The key variable here is the presence or absence of leeway to accept or reject the solution identified.

Where a 'command' mode of decision-making is present in the public sphere, the degree to which this is institutionalised is variable. A paradigm case of the instantly recognisable but minimally institutionalised commander is the 'big man' who repeatedly appears in Melanesian ethnography. In the earlier literature, the 'big man' was presented in sharp contrast to 'the African chief', whose incumbency was determined by 'descent' and whose relationship with his people had a prescribed character, governed by a definite repertoire of understandings.

Big men were depicted as healthy, intelligent, energetic individuals who managed to build up followings through personal ability, by manipulating wealth in the form of pigs and other valuables. Such a following would fluctuate in size in accordance with contemporary success (rather than with kinship), falling away as vigour, luck or skill deserted him; the big man would not necessarily pass on a following to his son. No following would last longer than the big man remained able to coerce his subordinates or they continued to see advantages in continued association. In much of this ethnography, coercion was central; the big man was depicted as a commander, a transitory despot, who 'told members what to do' and would in the last resort deal with them physically, in person, when faced with opposition.

On the whole, this early picture of the Melanesian big man has survived in contemporary anthropology; he is still an 'emergent individual' rather than a member of an 'ascribed category'. It is now clear, however, that these power relations varied in character from place to place, both in expression (varying from command to advice) and in degrees of consolidation, especially in the degree to which 'family' was important (in some groups it was certainly the ambition for big men to assemble followings for their sons, who were placed in advantage by their family associations – in such cases 'descent' should be seen as one variable in the make up of success, and was certainly not absent altogether). There is also now a clearer picture of the 'syndrome' of which bigmanship forms a part: accumulation and circulation of valuables; some men marrying several wives, others none at all; sexual segregation in both work and social life.

The nature of the 'big man's' ascendancy is revealed in accounts of his part in decision-making. These suggest no clear distinction between occasions directly linked to a big man's attempts to secure his domination over another member of the group, incidents arising out of efforts to maintain and discipline a following, and cases where a big man seeks to 'resolve' quarrels between two members of that following. Moreover, responses of particular big men to quarrels have an unsystematic quality and depend upon personal style and contemporary standing; they range from direct inter-personal violence to subtle or oblique diversion. Pospisil (1958) describes big men as variously clubbing recalcitrant members with billets of wood, weeping and throwing tantrums and quietly tendering fatherly advice. Each situation is confronted as it arises; issues are dealt with ad hoc. But it is important to note that the modes of power associated with 'government' – in terms of violence and persuasion are already there before institutionalised hierarchy, even though the 'caging resources' may be much more limited in scale.

Except in the extent that some big men seek to assemble followings for their sons (at which point one encounters perhaps an elementary form of institutionalisation), these relations, grounded in the person of the possessor of economic or symbolic capital, do not involve an element of transmissibility. There is no 'position' distinct from the person; 'power' cannot be thought, even primordially, as a 'possession' or 'thing', itself, independently of economic or symbolic capital, transmissible from person to person, in life or in death.

Command Institutionalised: Towards 'The State'

If in overall human history 'government' arrived late on the scene, it has now been around a long time across many regions and the forms of ascendancy associated with the pretension to exercise a generalised steering role have been extremely varied. These transformations have taken place within the public sphere, which those aspiring to ascendancy progressively co-opt, presenting themselves to be its source as they do so.

While it may be relatively straightforward to distinguish the transitory 'big man' from the 'elder' claiming to exercise leadership on the basis of genealogical seniority, pinning down 'kingship' and 'the state' is problematic. Analytically, within the spectrum of leadership roles, a clear break seems to arise with the junction of 'rank' and 'office'. This junction is realised with the emergence of an actor having authority to make decisions concerning the general arrangements of the group, holding an office with identified responsibilities which devolves from one incumbent to another in accordance with socially accepted rules. Three elements need to be explored here: the complex relationship between 'kinship' and 'kingship'; the nature of emergent 'steering' roles; and the growth of a notion of 'legality'.

First, the transition between institutions founded in kinship and those transcending kinship, although presented by scholars like Fried (1967) as the pivotal moment in state formation, is complex and uncertain. While it is common for people like kings to appeal to genealogy and use the idiom of fatherhood, the link may be more than metaphorical. In some African kingdoms, for example, the ruler *is* the genealogical senior member of a dominant patrilineage, and speaks of his activities in parental terms. We take here the example of the Tswana rulers encountered by European explorers, traders and missionaries arriving in Bechuanaland towards the end of the eighteenth century. Each Tswana ruler (*kgosi*) claimed to be the genealogically senior member of the cluster of patrilineages of which his 'tribe' (*morafe*) was made up.

> The Kgatla occupy a territory of what is today about 2,800 square miles of South East Botswana. A majority of Kgatla have a permanent home in the ruler's capital, Mochudi; the remainder live in the smaller villages outside or in isolated hamlets in the fields. Although they live in a relatively well-watered part of Botswana when one remembers that a large part of the country is made up of the Kalahari desert, by most standards the terrain is very dry. But in most years there is good grazing for cattle, and in perhaps one

in three when rain falls in sufficient quantities at the right time, good crops of maize and sorghum may be grown. The Kgatla would certainly see themselves as cattle-keepers first and arable farmers second.

The Kgatla polity is governed by an hereditary ruler (*kgosi*),[7] who may turn to three different groupings for advice and help in decision-making. First he is surrounded by a small informal council drawn by him from among his immediate senior relations (his father's and his own younger brothers, his male cousins, his maternal uncles), together with any other men who enjoy special positions of influence and trust. Secondly, he may call together all the headmen of the wards (the name conventionally given to the major administrative divisions into which the society is divided up). Finally, there may be a meeting to which all the adult male members of the society are summoned. Most everyday decisions are taken within the first of these groupings and any decision that is reached is then transmitted to the headman of each ward, who himself passes it on down the administrative hierarchy. If more serious matters have to be discussed, all the headmen are summoned; and in matters of the greatest importance all the adult males of the society may be assembled.

The procedure in a meeting at any one of these levels is very flexible, and the actual location of authority is hard to pin down. Typically, the chief raises a matter which he wishes to take action on and speaks about it for a while. Then other people present give their views. Often when a clear view emerges quickly, the chief will summarize it and propose action along that line; there will be chorused assent, and the matter is concluded. The Kgatla would say, though, that it is for the chief to decide; and not for the people at the meeting, whatever level this may be at. In one sense this may be true, but no chief would last long unless he enjoyed general acceptance and this would be swiftly eroded if he constantly tried to push through measures for which there was no support.

Many of the major decisions which are taken in these councils require action by large groups if they are to be carried out: in the past, if war was to be made, or the state organized for defence; today, if the cattle are to be rounded up, or if major water-works are to be dug. Where anything like this has to be done, the age-sets will be called to do it. A new age-set is formed every five years or so when the young males of the society then approaching physical manhood are gathered together and submitted to initiation procedures (including circumcision). All those initiated together form the new set; and as the new sets are successively formed over the years, those above rise in seniority. The physically hardest work, such as major building projects and (formerly) making war, are left to the members of the more junior sets.

The link between the chief and the senior man in each ward is ideally a genealogical one, for the office of chief should devolve from father to eldest son, while the younger sons of each ruler go off to form their own wards, assuming administrative control of these new sub-divisions of the main group. The Kgatla believe that their society was founded by Kgafela in the late seventeenth or early eighteenth century, and most

---

7 The state of affairs described here is that which existed in the last years of the nineteenth century, before the Kgatla state was absorbed in the Bechuanaland Protectorate. The Setswana term *kgosi* has conventionally been translated as 'chief', a usage which will be followed here.

of the forty-eight wards in the central village of Mochudi today are headed by men claiming descent from younger brothers of chiefs descended from Kgafela. A few wards whose members do not claim descent from younger brothers of former chiefs have been founded by men of groupings previously conquered by the Kgatla, or who have asked for permission to join them for defence against a common enemy. But apart from these exceptions, ward heads are senior members of the junior branches of the chief's lineage.

This system of administration is reflected at ground level in the residential organization of the main village. At the centre is a group of homesteads occupied by men of the chief's immediate agnatic segment, and ranged around this are fortyseven other groups of homesteads, each presided over by a ward head. Thus, the ward in this sense constitutes a geographical area; and each headman ideally lives with those over whom he has administrative control and responsibility.

Within each ward there may be anything from 200 to 600 people, and the majority of the members again claim to be related in the male line to the headman. Two further sub-divisions are also generally found inside a ward. First, all the males claiming descent from a common grandfather tend to be grouped together, and within such a sub-group a minimal unit is made up of an adult married male, occupying a homestead with his wife (or wives) and children. In many wards also, there have been incorporated individuals from other tribes who have come over time to form their own descent groups under the administrative control of the headman who is a member of the major segment.

Thus, if the group is looked at from the bottom up there is first the married male heading his own household, then the group consisting of his closest male agnates, then an aggregate of such groups forming a ward, and lastly the wards together forming the total society. Kgatla society can thus be seen as an ever-growing and deepening pyramid, the base of which is extended as more males are born and rear their own families; while in its simplest form the political and administrative organization is imposed on the lineage system like a cloak.

The Kgatla see the regularities of their everyday lives as governed by a corpus of rules which they describe as *mekgwa le melao ya Sekgatla*, a phrase which has generally been translated as 'Kgatla law and custom'. However, this translation is misleading in two ways. First, the terms *melao* and *mekgwa* are not sharply distinguished in the way that this translation would suggest. Secondly, 'Kgatla law and custom' cannot be seen as a body of rules corresponding directly to our rules of law, because the term embraces a whole repertoire of norms of different kinds, ranging from rules of polite behaviour and etiquette, through moral imperatives and rules taken very seriously in the context of dispute, and even includes examples of what we would call legislation. Everyone, even the chief, is expected to comply with these rules in their everyday behaviour, and there is a Tswana saying: 'Molao sefofu, obile otle oje mong waone' – 'The law is blind, it eats even its owner.' But there is not the distinct category of 'legal' rules which so clearly characterized our system. Norms governing social behaviour on a visit to someone else's homestead fall just as clearly within the overall classification as those prescribing what must be done when one man's cattle destroy another man's field of corn.

The origin of some of these rules is seen by the Kgatla to lie in long-established and adhered-to patterns of approved behaviour, others as arising out of decisions made by a chief in handling a dispute, yet others out of direct announcements made by him in what we would see as statutory form. The Kgatla would distinguish among such announcements those which simply restate and emphasize something which already forms part of 'Kgatla law and custom'; but which has perhaps become forgotten or carelessly observed. The occasion of any meeting in the chief's *kgotla* may provide an opportunity for such a reminder. On the other hand, an announcement which either expressly changes some existing rule, or which provides a new regulation to deal with some special contingency, has to be introduced with more careful preparation. The Kgatla say that when a chief wishes to make a change of this kind, he should call together the tribesmen so that the matter can be discussed. Only when he has done this, and following discussion in the *kgotla* announces a new rule, does such a rule become part of 'Kgatla law and custom'.

Although the Kgatla would say that it is for the ruler to announce a new law, most would agree that he *should not* do so unless the proposal he has already put to the *kgotla* meeting meets with approval. Where such a proposal does not attract support few would say that this prohibits a ruler from going ahead with his announcement, for there is a saying to the effect that 'The chief is law' (*'Lentswe lakgosi kemolao'*), but the chances of such a rule being generally complied with are greatly lessened.

Rules which Kgatla and other Tswana chiefs have announced in this way extend over a very broad field of subjects, including family life (e.g., how many wives a man may marry; what he must give by way of bridewealth; the age of a woman at marriage; the number of cattle payable as compensation when one man impregnates someone else's daughter); land tenure (regulations relating to the fencing of fields and the settling of uncleared land); public hygiene; and traffic regulations (e.g. to the effect that wagons must be fitted with proper brakes for going downhill).[8]

The extent to which one of these legislative announcements gets complied with depends upon the degree of social acceptance which it achieves and upon the capacity of the chief to enforce it. Some chiefs do not announce a measure until they feel that it will enjoy widespread acceptance, and in such a case enforcement presents few difficulties. Where a rule does not enjoy social approval, or where it is burdensome to comply with, much depends on the energy of the chief. If it involves such a matter as the fencing of the fields or the branding of stock, the matter can be handled through rigorous inspections and the punishment of those who fail to comply. On the other hand, chiefs who have tried to regulate family life have found this much harder to achieve.

As well as providing signposts for proper social behaviour, *mekgwa le melao ya Sekgatla* are also seen as furnishing the criteria according to which disputes should be settled where these arise. All Kgatla talk freely about these rules, and consider that they know them; there is no sense in which they are the special preserve of some particular sub-group within the society. In the context of a dispute these rules may be expressly

8 See Schapera (1943); and Comaroff and Roberts (1977).

invoked, or more frequently referred to by implication through the way in which the details of a particular claim are presented. People are taken to know the rules, and the mere claim that 'Molefe's son has impregnated my daughter' or 'Lesoka's cattle have trampled my corn' is sufficient to invoke by implication the body of rules which everyone knows to be associated with damage to crops by cattle and the impregnation of unmarried women.

As in most societies, *mekgwa le melao* differ considerably in their degrees of generality, and it is possible for them to be adduced in the context of a dispute in such a way as to conflict. Where, for example, two brothers are in dispute over who should inherit the mother's homestead, the one may invoke a general rule to the effect that close agnates should live peacefully together, whereas the other may rely on the much more detailed prescription to the effect that the youngest son should inherit the dwelling. It is where conflicting rules are relied on like this that it becomes necessary to talk about rules explicitly. Where both disputants agree as to the rules, but argue about the interpretation of facts in relation to an agreed rule, explicit reference is unnecessary.

Settlement directed discussion is seen under all circumstances as the most appropriate way to handle a dispute. While retaliatory violence and forceable re-taking of property are tolerated within narrow limits, these never enjoy social approval. Similarly, while it is recognized that supernatural agencies may be invoked in order to establish responsibility for harm or misfortune that has been suffered, further resort to these agencies when a human is identified as responsible is strongly discouraged. Such methods are recognized as likely to exacerbate a dispute in the event of their discovery by the other party.

The agencies for handling a dispute are located in the institutional hierarchy we have already considered. Where a quarrel breaks out between two people, the Kgatla see it as their own responsibility to try and settle it between themselves through bilateral discussion; but because they realize that such negotiations may fail, and that the help of third parties may be necessary, they each keep their senior kinsmen in touch with what is going on from a very early stage. Relatively simple and recurring problems, like the destruction of crops by cattle, are typically resolved at this level; but where the matter is more serious, or where there has been a history of bad relations between the parties, the trouble may be taken directly to senior kinsmen. Under such circumstances, with tempers running high, attempts at bilateral negotiation may be avoided entirely through fear that a fight will break out.

Where bilateral attempts at settlement fail, or where they are not made through fear that they will lead to violence and a heightening of the trouble, the disputants call on their immediate kin to resolve the matter. Although the Kgatla rely heavily on their close agnates for help in disputes, trouble is seldom contained as closely within the lineage as we saw it to be in the case of the Arusha, and close maternal kinsmen are likely to be drawn in from the beginning. These approaches may culminate in private negotiations or a formal meeting at the homestead of a senior member of the lineage to which either disputant belongs. The mode of settlement attempted at this level depends upon relationship of the parties. Where they are not close kinsmen, the respective disputants typically meet with their kin in support, and then the two groups try to feel their way towards a settlement by negotiation, without anyone seeking to mediate from a bridging position. Where they are related, a senior kinsman who can claim equally close relationship to both may try to mediate from a neutral standpoint. At this level no-one is in a position to impose a decision, and if a compromise cannot be reached through negotiation, the matter has to be taken to the headman within whose ward the earlier meetings have been held.

The headman has a range of options available to him in dealing with the dispute. He may attempt to mediate directly by suggesting solutions which may possibly be acceptable to both parties; or he may send them away for further discussion with their close kinsmen if he feels that the possibilities of that avenue have not been exhausted. However, although the headman may act as a mediator if he wishes, it is also recognized that he may attempt to resolve the matter by imposing a decision. Where he does so, the parties have the choice of accepting and complying with his decision, or taking the dispute to the chief. Where the matter is taken to the chief, he hears the report of the headman who dealt with the dispute earlier and the accounts of the disputants and their respective senior kinsmen. Then, like the headman, he may attempt to mediate, or proceed directly to resolve the matter by decision. Once a decision has been given, the chief has the capacity to enforce it if necessary. Disobedience will be met with corporal punishment, the confiscation of stock or the withdrawal of land allocations. The age-set organization provides the necessary machinery for enforcement: members of one of the more junior sets can be sent out to bring a recalcitrant individual before the chief or collect together his stock prior to confiscation (Roberts, 1979).

So, in this Kgatla example settlement-directed talk enjoys pre-eminence as a mode of handling disputes, while such means as violent self-help and sorcery are strongly disapproved. In the settlement of disputes, as in the ordering of everyday life, people are expected to follow *mekgwa le melao*; but this repertoire of norms, ranging from the general to the particular, offers the Kgatla considerable flexibility in managing their lives and in dealing with disputes. Nor can it be accurately seen as a discrete corpus of legal rules, ranging as it does from norms of polite behaviour to mandatory statutory injunctions. Further, it does not constitute a monolithic system, as variations in content and in interpretation can be found both in different geographical areas, and at different levels in the polity's organisation.

Thus, the hierarchical organisation of the Kgatla polity is also matched in the institutionalisation of disputing, as attempts at resolution should move from the disputants themselves, to the descent group, to the ward, and finally to the *kgosi*. Further, while negotiatory and mediatory means of settlement may be attempted at all levels, these give way in the last resort to a judicial mode before a headman or the *kgosi*, while the latter has access to organised force in ensuring compliance with any decision if this should prove to be necessary.

In looking at dispute institutions in a centralised polity, we have taken a third African example. We could just as well have looked further afield as these forms have developed again and again in different geographical locations in widely different historical periods. For example, in China too, authoritative third-party decision-making was deeply embedded in the hierarchical structure of the imperial state. The creation of a unified state was achieved – as we noted in Chapter Two – by the ruler of the state of Qin, who thereby installed himself as the first Chinese emperor. He brought with him a philosophy of Legalism, and although in due course this was abandoned as the official ideology, it nevertheless bequeathed China a system of formal legal institutions of considerable sophistication. But, despite the technical sophistication of the imperial legal system, parties were expected wherever possible to deal with their differences outside the purview of the courts. The fundamental cultural preference was for 'lumping' grievances – that is, simply ignoring the problem – and making concessions or *rang* in order to facilitate 'resolution'. Negotiations or '*tanpan*' were embedded in concerns with 'face' or social prestige, with building networks of favours through gift giving to make the negotiation of particular issues easier. Central was the belief that individual interests and rights should not be paramount but, rather, that parties in disagreement should compromise and thereby promote social stability. Fundamental too was a cultural preference for third-party intervention in the form of mediation – not only for disputes, but also for transactions. The 'middle person' has always had an important role to play. Often such mediators were local leaders – lineage or guild heads – and by the nineteenth century at least, elaborate systems had developed within the local political structure that enabled parties from different local communities to take their complaints to higher tribunals (Palmer, 1987: 79).

But parties did on occasion take their civil disputes to court, sometimes even in violation of lineage rules expressly forbidding recourse to the local magistrate, who combined executive and judicial roles and who, like the emperor himself, was seen in parental terms – he was the 'father and mother official' (*fumu guan*). Although inclined to 'mediate' the dispute before him, or send it back to the local community for leaders to attempt to mediate again, he would if necessary impose an authoritative decision on the parties, and records of appeal and review cases show that Chinese magistrates and their judicial and administrative superiors did provide or impose outcomes in many civil disputes by the application of statutory rules, local customary norms, and a sense of justice and fairness, as well as a felt need to secure compromise if at all possible:

> The case records . . . demonstrate that magistrates were in fact guided closely by the code in adjudging civil disputes. To be sure, they preferred to defer to extrajudicial/kin mediation whenever possible, in accordance with official ideology. But when confronted in a formal court session with suits not resolved by extrajudicial mediation, they almost always adjudicated forthwith by the code. They acted, in other words, as judges and not as mediators. Indeed, the standard magistrate handbooks . . . directed magistrates to study the code closely and adjudicate accordingly. Examining actual magisterial judgments in civil cases brings into focus some of the most frequently used substatutes of the code, often buried under misleading statutes. . . .
>
> Of the triad of principles – law, commonsense right and wrong, and peacemaking – that guided informal justice, compromise was the most important. But that is not to say

that state law did not matter. The fact that imperial state sought in its representations to deny, or at least to trivialize, civil law [did not mean that] the informal justice system . . . [was] . . . unaffected by official law. . . . All parties knew . . . that if and when community state failed, resort to the courts of the state might follow. . . .

[Thus, there was an] intermediate realm between formal and informal parts of the justice system. The majority of civil cases were settled without a formal court session, by a process that combined the workings of informal community mediation and magisterial opinion. Once a case entered the court system with the filing of a plaint, efforts at community mediation would be intensified. At the same time, expressions of magisterial opinion in the form of comments on the plaints and counterplaints, generally available to the litigants, provided a preliminary indication of the likely verdict of a formal court session. Informal mediations were generally worked out under the influence of such magisterial opinion (Huang, 1996: 12–13).[9]

We have used these vignettes to shift our understanding of three primary modes of decision – bilateral negotiation, mediation, umpiring – away from the parochial context of decision-making in the West. The arguably tedious ethnographic detail is necessary in our view to locate the possibility and reality of these foundational forms in a wider cultural context. Over the next four chapters we look in more detail at these three forms, and then the hybrids into which they may evolve in real life processes.

Extract 4:1

W Felstiner, R Abel and A Sarat: 'The Emergence and Transformation of Disputes: Naming, Blaming, Claiming . . .' (1980–81) 15 *Law and Society Review* 631, pp 634–637

An injurious experience is any experience that is disvalued by the person to whom it occurs. For the most part, people agree on what is disvalued. But such feelings are never universal. Where people do differ, these differences, in fact, generate some of the most important research questions: why do people who perceive experience similarly *value* it differently, why do they *perceive* similarly valued experience differently, and what is the relation between valuation and perception? From a practical perspective, the lack of consensus about the meaning of experiences does not interfere with any of these tasks, since their purpose is to map covariation among interpretation, perception, and external factors. But if, on the other hand, the research objective is to provide a census of injurious experiences, then the lack of an agreed-upon definition is more serious. In a census, the researcher must either impose a definition upon subjects and run the risk that the definition will fail to capture all injurious experience or permit subjects to define injurious experience as they wish and run the risk that different subjects will define the same experience differently and may include experiences the researcher does not find injurious.

---

9 And see, more generally, Galanter and Cahill (1994).

The methodological obstacle is the difficulty of establishing who in a given population has experienced an unPIE ['perceived injurious experience']. Assume that we want to know why some shipyard workers perceive they have asbestosis and others do not. In order to correlate perception with other variables, it is necessary to distinguish the sick workers who do not know they are sick from those who actually are not sick. But the very process of investigating perception and illness by inquiring about symptoms is likely to influence both. These social scientific equivalents of the uncertainty principle in physics and psychosomatic disease in medicine will create even more acute problems where the subject of inquiry is purely psychological: a personal slight rather than a somatically based illness.

Sometimes it is possible to collect the base data for the study of unPIEs by means of direct observation. For instance, house buyers injured by unfair loan contracts could be identified from inspection of loan documents. On other occasions hypotheses about the transformation of unPIE to PIE could be tested directly by inference from aggregate data. Assume that 30 percent of a population exposed to a given level of radiation will develop cancer. We study such a group and find that only ten percent know they are sick. We hypothesize that years of formal schooling are positively associated with cancer *perception*. This hypothesis can be tested by comparing the educational level of the known ten percent with that of the balance of the population. For as long as schooling is not associated with developing cancer, the mean number of school years of the former should be higher than that of the latter. Nevertheless, in many cases it will be difficult to identify and explain transformations from unPIE to PIE. This first transformation – saying to oneself that a particular experience has been injurious – we call *naming*. Though hard to study empirically, naming may be the critical transformation, the level and kind of disputing in a society may turn more on what is initially perceived as an injury than on any later decision. For instance, asbestosis only became an acknowledged 'disease' *and* the basis of a claim for compensation when shipyard workers stopped taking for granted that they would have trouble breathing after ten years of installing insulation and came to view their condition as a problem.

The next step is the transformation of a perceived injurious experience into a grievance. This occurs when a person attributes an injury to the fault of another individual or social entity. By including fault within the definition of grievance, we limit the concept to injuries viewed both as violations of norms and as remediable. The definition takes the grievant's perspective: the injured person must feel wronged and believe that something might be done in response to the injury, however politically or sociologically improbable such a response might be. A grievance must be distinguished from a complaint against no one in particular (about the weather, or perhaps inflation) and from a mere wish unaccompanied by a sense of injury for which another is held responsible (I might like to be more attractive). We call the transformation from perceived injurious experience to grievance *blaming*: our diseased shipyard worker makes this transformation when he holds his employer or the manufacturer of asbestos insulation responsible for his asbestosis.

The third transformation occurs when someone with a grievance voices it to the person or entity believed to be responsible and asks for some remedy. We call this communication *claiming*. A claim is transformed into a dispute when it is rejected in whole or in part. Rejection need not be expressed by words. Delay that the claimant construes as resistance is just as much a rejection as is a compromise offer (partial rejection) or an outright refusal.

The sociology of law should pay more attention to the early stages of disputes and to the factors that determine whether naming, blaming and claiming will occur. Learning more about the existence, absence, or reversal of these basic transformations will increase our understanding of the disputing process and our ability to evaluate dispute processing institutions. We know that only a small fraction of injurious experiences ever mature into disputes. Furthermore, we know that most of the attrition occurs at the early stages: experiences are not perceived as injurious; perceptions do not ripen into grievances; grievances are voiced to intimates but not to the person deemed responsible. A theory of disputing that looked only at institutions mobilized by disputants and the strategies pursued within them would be seriously deficient. It would be like constructing a theory of politics entirely on the basis of voting patterns when we know that most people do not vote in most elections. Recognizing the bias that would result, political scientists have devoted considerable effort to describing and explaining political apathy. Sociologists of law need to explore the analogous phenomenon – grievance apathy.

The early stages of naming, blaming, and claiming are significant, not only because of the high attrition they reflect, but also because the range of behaviour they encompass is greater than that involved in the later stages of disputes, where institutional patterns restrict the options open to disputants. Examination of this behavior will help us identify the social structure of disputing. Transformations reflect social structural variables, as well as personality traits. People do – or do not – perceive an experience as an injury, blame someone else, claim redress, or get their claims accepted because of their *social position* as well as their individual characteristics. The transformation perspective points as much to the study of social stratification as to the exploration of social psychology.

Finally, attention to naming, blaming, and claiming permits a more critical look at recent efforts to improve 'access to justice.' The public commitment to formal legal equality, required by the prevailing ideology of liberal legalism, has resulted in substantial efforts to equalize access at the later stages of disputing, where inequality becomes more visible and implicates official institutions; examples include the waiver of court costs, the creation of small claims courts, the movement toward informalism, and the provision of legal services. Access to justice is supposed to reduce the unequal distribution of advantages in society; paradoxically it may amplify these inequalities. The ostensible goal of these reforms is to eliminate bias in the ultimate transformation: disputes into lawsuits. If, however, as we suspect, these very unequal distributions have skewed the earlier stages by which injurious experiences become disputes, then current access to justice efforts will only give additional advantages to those who have already transformed their experiences into disputes. That is, these efforts may accentuate the effects of inequality at the earlier, less visible stages, where it is harder to detect, diagnose, and correct.

Extract 4:2

P Gulliver: *Disputes and Negotiations: A Cross Cultural Perspective* (1979) Academic Press, New York, London, pp 1–3

In all societies, regardless of their location in time and space, there is a wide variety of modes by which disputes are handled and resolution sought. In general terms, the range of these procedures and their variation can be comprehended within a few broad categories.

One such category is the duel: the institutionalized, organized contest or fight between disputants, or their supporters or champions, in which the winner supposedly proves the rightness or superiority of his case. The contest may be fought with physical violence or by stylized competition (eg, wrestling matches) or by verbal confrontations (eg, Eskimo song contests). A second category is violent self-help. This has been widely reported by anthropologists, particularly from noncentralized, acephalous societies where there are no obvious means for the peaceful resolution of those disputes that occur beyond the limits of fairly small groups. Where such groups are well organized and integrated, self-help may develop into feuding. This suggests that the groups involved can manage, at least for a time, without other peaceful and useful interaction between them. However, where such groups are more dependent on each other, where their individual members have valuable, persisting relationships with each other (eg, through marriage, kinship, or economic exchange), and especially where members of the groups are residentially intermingled, hostilities cannot long be tolerated. In such situations, the resort to violent self-help may be a regular means not only to express the strength of dissatisfaction and determination but also to precipitate a crisis so that other procedures can be initiated or resumed. Thus there are, for example, the raid on the opponent's home, the seizure or spoliation of property, and the industrial strike. All lead to efforts for peacemaking.

Third, there is avoidance: the more or less deliberate curtailing or limiting of further relations with the other person, letting the matter rest, accepting the status quo (at least temporarily), seeking no specific decision on the dispute, and endeavoring to prevent the continuation or escalation of conflict because of the perceived difficulties that would result. In societies where residential mobility is fairly easy one party may move away so as to evade the possible consequences of his actions or to avoid further trouble. Later, the importance of the dispute and its attendant emotions may wane and it may be possible to deal with it more easily. Alternatively, the offender may improve his behavior so that his former actions can be forgotten. However, in some circumstances disputes may not be resolvable without unacceptable repercussions and so, in avoidance, they are allowed to lapse.

Fourth, when effective, practical means are unavailable or unavailing, or where their use might bring about intolerable complications or threaten social relations, a dispute may be transformed and redefined in symbolic and supernatural terms – witchcraft accusations, performance in the ancestral cult or some other religious system, but also perhaps sporting contests or getting to the moon first. As with avoidance, the dispute is not so much resolved as deflected. Yet burying the dispute in the symbolic process may be effective. In the opinions of the people involved, the renewal of relationships and the reemphasis of group unity – potentially important features of dispute resolution – can be accomplished.

Finally, despite the prevalence of the foregoing modes of treating disputes – procedures that are not at all confined to so-called 'primitive' or simpler societies – there are two other modes that are far more common, indeed virtually universal. These are negotiation and adjudication. Although each of these two terms refers to a considerable range of behavioral patterns and cultural forms, each is characterized by certain fundamental features of process and interaction that are valid cross-culturally. Although this present study is concerned only with negotiation, this mode of treating disputes can be usefully introduced and initially identified through a discriminating contrast with adjudication. The conceptual distinction is not new and indeed it has sometimes been too much taken for granted. On the other hand, it is not one that has acquired universal acceptance.

Extract 4:3

W L F Felstiner: 'Influences of Social Organization on Dispute Processing' (1974–75) 9 *Law and Society Review* 63, pp 79–80

The frequency of avoidance as a form of dispute processing in a TSPS [technologically simple poor society] should be affected by its high costs. These costs would be incurred whether avoidance takes place within the kin group, within a non-family multiplex relationship, or in economic activities. Within the family if disputants terminate or decrease their contacts, relations between groups, which may have political and economic as well as social connotations, are jeopardized as well. Where marriages are arranged, decisions about who marries whom are generally made on prudential grounds, in a corporate process and under the influence of past social relations. As a result, disputes which are processed by avoidance will cast a long shadow, interfering with the future marriage prospects of many group members. Use of avoidance as a technique where the disputants, such as parent and grown child or siblings or affines, live and work and conduct other important activities together, is logistically difficult and psychologically dangerous – the repressed hostility felt toward the other disputant is likely to be shifted to someone or something else. Even worse, the failure to express or act upon predictable hostility will in many societies lead to accusations of witchcraft against the person who hides his antagonisms. Yet physical separation, by moving residence or work, may be socially infeasible, economically disastrous and emotionally traumatic. Since many relationships beyond the family are multiplex, avoidance as a reaction to dispute impairs not only the interest out of which the dispute arose, but all other interests shared by the disputants. As Moore points out for the Chagga, 'the continuing control exercised by the lineage neighborhood nexus over its members is illustrated by every dispute it settles. No man can hope to keep his head above water if he does not have the approval and support of his neighbors and kinsmen.' This analysis should not be construed to imply that avoidance would never or rarely occur in small communities in technologically simple societies. In fact, in nomadic tribes, where avoidance by physical separation is easy, dispute processing by such tactics is commonplace. The point is rather that avoidance has high costs in a TSPS and one would as a result expect significant use of other forms of dispute processing which are more likely to aid the maintenance of threatened, but important, social relationships.

Extract 4:4

R A Rappaport: *Pigs for the Ancestors: Ritual in the Ecology of a New Guinea People* (1967) Yale University Press, New Haven and London, pp 119, 121–123, 138–139

Most fights have two stages, which are distinguished by the weapons employed and the rituals performed.

The first of the two stages is referred to as the 'nothing fight' (*ura auere*), or 'small fight' (*bamp acîmp*). A local population that has suffered injury calls out to the enemy to prepare for an encounter on a designated fight ground. One or two days' notice is usually given, providing ample time for both sides to mobilize their allies and to clear the fight ground of underbrush. This task falls equally upon both antagonists but encounters between the bush-clearing details of the hostile groups are avoided. Informants say that if members of one of the groups arrive at the fight ground to find their opponents already at work they will withdraw for some distance until their opponents retire, after which they will enter the fight ground and finish the clearing. . . . In the small fight only bows and arrows, and perhaps throwing spears, are used. Some informants say that hand-to-hand weapons such as axes and jabbing spears are not even brought to the fight ground.

The antagonistic groups line up on the fight ground within easy bow shot of each other, according to informants, who also say that allies and principal combatants are intermingled in the formations. The shields, which are very large, averaging 2.5 by 5 feet, are propped up, permitting bowmen to dart out from behind them to take shots and leap back again. To demonstrate their bravery, men also emerge from behind the shields to draw enemy fire. Casualties are not numerous and deaths infrequent, for the unfletched arrows of the Maring seldom kill.

It may be that the 'small' or 'nothing' fight is less a serious battle than a device for ending a quarrel before more lethal fighting, with its attendant ritual constraints, develops. The relative harmlessness of a bow and arrow engagement from stationary positions with cover well provided by shields itself suggests such a possibility, but there are even more cogent reasons for seeing the small fight in such a light.

First, small fights are protracted. Accounts of engagements in the past indicate that in some instances there were four or five days of such fighting before escalation took place. Such a period might allow tempers to cool while satisfying the bellicose imperatives of manhood.

Second, while there are no third parties with either the power or authority to adjudicate disputes, the formations of the antagonists include allies, men less committed to the quarrel than the principal combatants. These men often have a considerable interest in seeing the quarrel settled before it goes any further, for they themselves have no direct grievance and may have close relatives in the enemy formation. When the Tuguma fought the Tsevent, for example, some Tsembaga went to the assistance of both of the antagonists. In one instance, this split two full brothers who had sisters married into each of the opposing groups. Although they take their places in the military formations of the antagonists, such men may serve to dampen the martial ardor of the principal combatants by obliquely counseling moderation. Allies seem to have behaved in this way during at least one confrontation between antagonists who had previously been friendly. During the Tuguma-Tsevent fight, informants say, some of the Tsembaga allies of both antagonists, instead of hurling insults at their opponents, lamented loudly and continually about the evil of brothers fighting. Their laments in this instance were unheeded, perhaps because two or three Tuguma are reported to have been killed by arrows during the little fight. If there had been no fatalities, or if only one Tuguma had been killed in reciprocation for the homicide that had led to the fight, the preachings of the Tsembaga may have had more effect.

Third, the small fight affords an opportunity for nonallied neutrals to attempt to intervene between antagonists who have previously been friendly. Reference has already been made to the fight between the Dimbagai-Yimyagai and the Merkai clan of the Tsembaga. At the initial engagement neutrals stood on a knoll, informants say, overlooking the fight ground, admonishing both sides that it is wrong for brothers to fight, demanding that the combatants quit the field and throwing rocks at both formations. Their efforts were unavailing, it must be reported, and the fight escalated.

Finally, the 'small fight' brings the antagonists within the range of each others' voices while keeping them out of the range of each others' deadlier weapons. Informants say that this opportunity for communication was used mainly to hurl insults at each other, but there is some evidence to indicate that in some fights, at least, the opportunity was used to resolve the quarrel. Information on this aspect of the small fight is ambiguous. There are several reported instances of small fights being terminated by shouted negotiations after one side had sustained a fatality that the other side could regard as full reciprocation for a homicide it had sustained and which had set off the fight. In such instances the termination of the conflict should be attributed to the fulfilment of revenge requirements, rather than to the negotiations, but the small fight at least provided an opportunity to fulfill the revenge requirements without recourse to deadlier fighting, which would have been more likely to compound grievances than to cancel them. . . .

In contrast to the weapons of 'small' or 'nothing' fight, both axes and two types of jabbing spear are employed in the 'ax' fight. The point of one type is armed with a sharpened beak of a hornbill, which remains in the wound when the weapon is withdrawn. The other is barbed for half of its seven-to-nine-foot length. Below the barbs three or four prongs project forward and outward at an angle to the shaft. Such a weapon seems designed for defense against headlong charges, which informants say were not a regular feature of Maring warfare.

On the fight ground formations were mixed; both principal combatants and allies stood side by side, it is reported. The taboo man remained in the rear, heavily protected by the men closest to him. The slightest wound sustained by a taboo man supposedly portended the inevitable death of one of the men of his group, and if he were killed it meant that his side would be routed. Such a belief could operate, of course, to mitigate the severity of fighting if both sides spent their energy in trying to shoot the taboo man of their opponents and if his men fled when he was killed. There is no suggestion from any informant, however, that ax fights degenerated into attempts to shoot the enemy taboo man while others of the enemy were being ignored.

There is little information concerning leadership on the fight ground. It is quite clear, however, that discipline was not tight nor control close. Formations were several ranks deep, and the men in the front row were relieved by those behind them from time to time. While the opposing men in the front ranks were fighting a series of duels from behind their enormous shields, bowmen in the ranks farther to the rear gave support to the men in the first rank and shot at those who exposed themselves. Fatalities generally occurred when a man in the front rank was brought down by an arrow. His opponent, supported by nearby comrades, would then rush in to finish him off with axes. The fallen man's comrades would also rush to his defense, protecting him with their shields if possible.

Informants' accounts give the impression that this static positional fight was most common. In most engagements the opposing forces stood toe-to-toe behind their shields with no tactical or strategic movement taking place. A series of such engagements frequently continued sporadically for weeks, with neither side suffering more than light casualties. The antagonists, it seems, were waiting for the day when their enemies would arrive on the fight ground without the support of their allies. On the day that a group found itself with a clear numerical advantage, instead of taking up the usual static positions it would charge.

CHAPTER FIVE

Negotiations

A: The Nature of Negotiation

Negotiation represents the primary, universal route to decision and action in the social world. The core features of negotiation are to be found in widely different contexts, ranging from the unselfconscious routines of everyday life to the formalised, set-piece exchanges of an international conference. These fundamental features remain constant whether the issue is uncontentious or a focus of extreme conflict. Thus, negotiation as a mode of decision-making spans everyday interaction and the more complex, stressful exchanges encountered in the context of disagreement and dispute.

The features of negotiation are revealed most clearly in simple, bilateral exchanges in which information flows in both directions, understanding is achieved and an outcome is reached – the lived counterpart of Habermas' theoretical construct, the 'ideal speech situation' (Habermas, 1979). So negotiation involves communication, leading to joint decision-making. It is a process over which the parties retain control; exchanges take place within a common universe of meaning; and these determine the outcome in immediate terms. Here the ultimate contrast is with acquiescence in an adjudicatory process in which power over the outcome lies with a third party (Extract 5:1).

A number of identifiable conditions have to be present if negotiation is to take place. The first involves finding some medium of communication that will allow messages to pass backwards and forwards between the parties; this may, but need not, involve finding a mutually acceptable forum. Second, the parties must formulate and successfully communicate to each other their goals, what they want to achieve in the exchange. Third, in the light of those mutually understood goals, the parties must identify and evaluate the options available to them. It will sometimes be that the greater understanding resulting from an exchange of information will reveal a convergence or compatibility of goals, resulting in an agreed outcome without shifts of position. Otherwise, if an agreed outcome is pursued, this will be an accommodation reached through further exchanges in which the respective bargaining endowments are brought to bear.

In presenting negotiations in their simplest form as a bilateral process of decision-making, achieved through information exchange and learning, we must keep in mind the inevitable embeddedness of negotiation in the surrounding social universe. Negotiation does not take place in a vacuum. Those involved at any moment find themselves as part of a going concern – when they arrive the party or dance is already in progress. Surrounded by other actors, they have been brought up in a universe of understandings, norms and interests that, by and large, they have not themselves constructed. In this context, the norms and institutions of 'law' place explicit, perceived constraints on processes of negotiation. Those involved in negotiation will entertain some picture, however erroneous, of what might happen if they resorted to other modes of decision-making instead – notably lawyer negotiations or adjudication. That picture will necessarily bear significantly on the conduct of negotiations. Mnookin and Kornhauser (1979) memorably describe negotiation as 'bargaining in the shadow of the law'. So any discussion of the nature of negotiation must show sensitivity to the environment within which negotiation takes place.

Alongside the external environment of negotiation, we need to recognise the internal complexity of many processes of negotiation. People do not necessarily negotiate over a single good with an agreed identity, like a sum of money. Honour, prestige, respect, the recognition of values or some established state of affairs may be at issue in numerous combinations. Here, what Gulliver labels the 'preference set' may differ between parties, and from one phase of negotiation to another (Extract 5:2).

A picture of negotiation in terms of a simple bilateral exchange between two poles also takes no account of complexity of another kind. While the parties to negotiations may be two 'individuals', they may also be loose groups or corporate bodies, they may be constituted of principals with attached support groups, or they may be champions acting in some representative capacity (see Sections B and F below dealing with intra- and multi-party negotiations and lawyer negotiations respectively). There may also be more than two poles with active, party involvement in negotiations – we consider these multi-party negotiations below (Section B below). The structure of negotiations is obviously further complicated by the intervention of third parties in a bridging capacity, from a 'non-aligned' standpoint – mediation is considered in the next chapter.

Extract 5:1

P Gulliver: *Disputes and Negotiations: A Cross-Cultural Perspective* (1979) Academic Press, New York and London, pp 3–7

As a first description, the picture of negotiation is one of two sets of people, the disputing parties or their representatives, facing each other across a table or from opposite sides of an open space. They exchange information and opinion, engage in argument and discussion, and sooner or later propose offers and counteroffers relating to the issues in dispute between them, seeking an outcome acceptable to both sides. The comparable picture of adjudication is that of two parties (each including one or more persons) who, separated from one another, face an adjudicator who sits in front of, apart from, and often raised above them. They address him, offering information, opinion, and argument. Each seeks to refute the other's presentation and to persuade the adjudicator to favor his own case. Eventually the adjudicator pronounces his decision on the issues, often sorting out and summing up the information given to him and explaining his judgment. Although these pictures are simplistic and merely intended to be suggestive by way of introduction, it is clear that a fundamental characteristic of negotiation is the absence of a third-party decision-maker. It is my contention that the paramount distinction between the two modes – negotiation and adjudication – comes from that fact. This is because the absence or presence of an authoritative third party produces an essential difference in the nature of the decision-making process. The locus of decision-making, together with the process leading to it and affected by it, is taken to be crucial because it is directed to the end result of dispute treatment; that is, some outcome. That outcome may be specific, conclusive, and, at least in intent, more or less permanent, or it may be quite vague and temporary, even leaving things much as they were initially. Furthermore, the outcome may be capable of practical execution or it may be no more than a matter of general intention and orientation. The range of kinds of decisions and their efficacy is, of course, enormous. Yet it is not the kind of decision-outcome that is distinctive but rather the process by which the decision is reached. Although there are a number of other characteristics that tend to be more associated with one or the other mode, I show later that these cannot form the basis for a clear distinction.

In adjudication, the decision-maker is typically a third party who is not himself directly a disputant. That third party – a single individual or a set of persons – holds the acknowledged right, that is the legitimate authority and responsibility, to reach and enunciate a decision that is the outcome of the dispute and is in some degree binding on the disputing parties. Compulsorily or voluntarily, the disputants surrender the ability to decide for themselves. They become petitioners or supplicants. Therefore, the primary concern of a disputant is to focus on the adjudicator: to present information and argument to him in the attempt to persuade him to give a decision that is favorable, or less unfavorable, to the disputant. The adjudicator is, at least for the moment, in a superior role, the disputant is in an inferior one. The disputants themselves are separated from one another as each directs himself to the adjudicator.

It is most common, of course, that disputants attempt to bring persuasion, even treat and promise, to bear on each other in the endeavor to affect each other's presentation to the adjudicator. Although important, this is a secondary matter, because in the end neither disputant himself makes the decision. Those attempts are, in intent and effect, part of the persuasion directed to the adjudicator. They are efforts to influence, alter, and diminish the presentation to him by the opposing party. The adjudicator may be quite open to persuasion on fact, interpretation, application of rules and norms, recognition of extenuating circumstances, and the like, but he may choose to disregard parts of either party's presentation. Furthermore, the adjudicator may be more or less wise and perceptive, more or less conscientious, more or less constrained by rules, values, and pragmatic considerations, more or less concerned for justice and equity, and more or less influenced by his own and others' interests. Moreover, the procedural 'rules of the game,' the sociocultural milieu, and the situtional context of the dispute and the disputants may affect the process leading up to decision-making. However, the central fact remains that the adjudicator makes the decision and that, therefore, the disputants and the process are directed toward the subject to him. To be sure, the degree of authority held and exercised by an adjudicator ranges from the virtually absolute to no more than the ephemeral, accepted ability to propose an outcome. He may represent the legitimate, stable political order – he may be the political authority and an autocrat to boot – or he may be the unchallenged holder of practical power in the situation. Alternatively, he may be no more than the exponent of opinion, the fleeting representative of neutrality or of the 'public interest.' Although the degree and nature of authority are of considerable practical and sociological importance, they do not in themselves alter the essential structuring of the process and the patterning of interaction among the participants. It is unlikely and seems not to have been demonstrated that there is any direct correlation between the degree of authority and the nature of the decision. For instance, an autocratic adjudicator, well supported by organized, coercive powers, may imperiously disregard the disputants' presentations and perhaps flout rules and values. But he may, on the other hand, for political, religious, moral, or symbolic reasons, be as much contrained as, say, the elderly villager who seeks no personal advantage but who is willing to arbitrate between quarreling neighbors. Conversely, that village arbitrator too might ignore rules and values when he is far more concerned about village interests, or those of some section of the community, than he is about the interests of the disputants or about justice. In short, differences in the authority of adjudicators are matters of degree rather than of kind.

In negotiations, by contrast, the decision is made by the disputing parties themselves. *It is a joint decision.* Each party can only obtain what the other is in the end prepared to allow. Since the two parties necessarily began with some kind of difference between them, as they perceived the situation, the process of decision-making therefore involves a convergence. At least one party, but usually both, must move toward the other. Although there may be a compromise of some sort, this is not inevitable since one party may be induced to move altogether to his opponent's position or, alternatively, there can be the joint, integrative creation of something new that is acceptable to both parties.

In the process of seeking a joint decision, the disputing parties are inherently inter-dependent if an acceptable outcome is to be obtained. Their primary concern is to influence or coerce each other. The course of negotiation therefore involves the exchange of information: alleged facts and proffered interpretation of them, argument, appeals to rules and values, threat, promise, demand, offer, counteroffer, and so on. The flow of information permits a continuous process of learning by each party about the requirements, preferences, expectations, perceptions, attitudes, feelings, strengths, and weaknesses of both the opponent and himself. A party may initially consider himself clear and well prepared, although often (and perhaps necessarily so) he is vague about his real preferences and aims and about the possibilities available. In any case, what he learns from and about the opponent, and about his own position, compels reconsideration, clarification, and adjustment of expectations. As a result of learning, that is, there are modifications (maybe including reinforcement) in preferences and demands by each party. This interaction continues. There is, and must be, a gradual willingness to coordinate and collude. Negotiators may never achieve amity, sympathy, or trust but they have to attain sufficient coordination, however reluctantly, so as to work toward and ultimately achieve a joint decision on the issues in dispute. The alternative, always an available option, is to accept the status quo or status quo ante, which is also in effect a joint decision, as preferable to anything else that appears possible.

There is no third party to determine what the outcome is or should be. The only outcome is one to which both agree, which is, therefore, in the opinion of each party, the most satisfactory (or at least satisfactory enough) that can be obtained in the circumstances. The reasons for acceptability are, of course, likely to be different for each party. Moreover, one or both may be mistaken in assessing acceptable adequacy – just as they may be mistaken about many other features of the dispute between them. One party may gain nearly all he originally desired because of overwhelmingly superior power vis-à-vis his opponent, whether that power comes from coercion, moral strength, persuasive skill, or whatever. That, however, would be an uncommon situation, if only because the various kinds of power are unlikely to be so monopolized. In any case, as Schelling has convincingly shown, even the weak or 'powerless' party may be able to turn his position into one of quite effective strength. Each party is also subject, in varying degrees, to considerations concerning the expectations, interests, and pressures of outsiders and the prospect of future relationships with them.

Third parties – mediators – are often, but certainly not always, involved in nego- tiations. They are not, however, unilateral decision-makers but rather facilitators of the process leading to the parties' joint decision. In various ways they help to increase or orient the exchange of information and to expedite the learning and adjustment process. Their presence does not deprive the disputants of the final ability, or need, to make their own individual choices and to reach an agreed decision.

The crucial distinction then, between adjudication and negotiation is that the for- mer is a process leading to unilateral decision-making by an authoritative third party, whereas the latter is a process leading to joint decision-making by the disputing par- ties themselves as the culmination of an interactive process of information exchange and learning. Let me be clear: My concern here is to emphasize that distinction. I do not wish to deny that there are also certain similarities and, in real life, sometimes an overlapping of the two processual modes.

Extract 5:2
P Gulliver: *Disputes and Negotiations: A Cross-Cultural Perspective* (1979) Academic Press, New York and London, pp 88–90

A party's preference set ideally comprises ordered evaluations of issues and conceivable outcomes. First, there is an ordering of the issues in dispute and their various attributes as a result of assessment of the expected, relative satisfactions that might be obtained from them with reference to basic objectives and requirements. This ordering allows an assessment and ordering of possible outcomes that can be contemplated as tolerable or as potentially unavoidable in view of expectations of the opponent's preferences. The preferential ordering of those conceivable outcomes is further modified by consideration of the anticipated costs of obtaining them and of the relative strengths of the two parties. Commonly, there is emphasis on three particular levels of evaluation for the issues, singly or in packages: the conceivable maxima that might be obtained, the anticipated minima below which anything is thought to be unacceptable, and the targets that are aimed for above the minima.

Three points must be made immediately about real-life conditions, although they are elaborated later. First, evaluations of preferences are often imprecise and even quite vague. Second, preferences are not necessarily altogether consistent with each other; objectives and evaluations may be established by different criteria and with varying frames of reference. Third, evaluations and preferences are not fixed and static but more or less continuously subject to change during the course of the negotiations.

Game and bargaining theorists, and other social scientists influenced by their models, have usually conceived of a fixed, limited number of finite outcomes, which is assumed to be known to the parties. In their models, the parties are able to evaluate outcomes and their costs quantitatively against a single, numerical standard. Thus comparison and ordering are fairly straightforward. When uncertainties of outcome or evaluation are fed into the model, there remains the ability to calculate and use probabilities, again in concert with quantitative measures. Moreover, as previously shown, these models have virtually ignored conditions of multiple issues and multiple criteria of evaluation.

In the desire to avoid these unrealistic simplifications and to acknowledge the much more complex conditions of real life, I am presenting a model that is closer to the messiness of reality, no more susceptible to mathematical manipulation than are the shifting, approximating assessments of actual negotiators. It is a model that accords with the general notion of negotiation as an exploratory interaction between the parties. Thus, initially, each party has some vagueness and uncertainty in his preferences. He may well be unclear about what he wants or prefers, what the possible outcomes might be and how to compare multiple, disparate issues and their attributes. In any case, the set of issues in dispute is not yet established since that, in part, depends on the ideas and aims of the opponent. It is commonplace that the issues over which dispute begins are not necessarily those that are, or become, most important for either party, that further issues are precipitated as negotiations begin and that quite new, hitherto unanticipated outcomes may become available. A party usually enters negotiations with some goals in mind that he hopes to achieve – though these are not always clearly perceived, nor are their implications fully understood at that point. Deliberately or not, he begins privately to compare and evaluate issues and possible outcomes and to clarify his aims and intentions. As information comes from the opponent, the party is able, and also compelled, to gain some better appreciation of what is probable, possible, and impossible and what the opportunity costs might be.

Thus the party refines and adjusts his preference set, and he continues to do this until the end of negotiations. It is unlikely, however, that he can reach and maintain complete clarity and certainty, for in any but the simplest of disputes the variables to be taken into account are not altogether known; for many variables only the roughest kind of evaluation is possible. Not even near the end of negotiations is such an ideal attained or attainable, nor is the preference set likely to be totally consistent. The principal sources of uncertainty and inconsistency are inherent in a range of problems that, singly and together, are not completely resolvable by the time of the culminating outcome. These are (a) the evaluation of preferences for anticipated outcomes for the various issues and the assessment of probabilities for potential outcomes and for the opponent's actions; (b) incommensurability between multiple issues and their various attributes, or between packages of them; (c) expectations about the opponent's preferences and the assessment of the strengths (and weaknesses) of each party that support (or undermine) their demands; (d) assessment of the directions and strengths of outside interests and influences; (e) the interpretation, applicability, and strength of normative rules and values; and (f) the assessment of the costs of attaining potential outcomes.

B: Intra-party and Multi-party Negotiations

We have spoken about negotiation primarily in terms of a simple bilateral exchange, and much of the existing ADR literature proceeds on the basis of this analytical simplification. However, in real life many negotiations are a good deal more com-plex than this. Some 'parties' display internal heterogeneity, and negotiations often involve more than two parties. Under these more complex conditions, we argue that the fundamental nature and processual shape of negotiation holds steady. None the less, these complexities may significantly complicate the progress of negotiation. In an intra-party context, complications are likely to arise in terms of both the cyclical and developmental dimensions of the negotiation process. In multi-party exchanges, as more parties are added the complexities progressively increase. The communication arrangements required for multi-party negotiations are necessar-ily elaborate, and at each of the processual stages identified below (Section C), the presence of more parties, with the concomitant expansion of the universe of mean-ing, complicates information exchange and decision-making. In this section, we consider the complications inherent in these two types of situation in more detail.

Intra-party Negotiations

In real life, even in two-party situations, each side to a negotiation is often a loose-knit coalition rather than a homogeneous unit. As a result, there is necessarily a good deal of consultation and manoeuvring between the constituent elements within each coalition. We must relax the assumptions ordinarily made that each party is inter-nally united, and able to conduct itself as a cohesive, coherent whole. Each side is often itself an arena within which individuals or constituent groups are intent on securing positions and outcomes that reflect their own interests and interpretations. There is a range of possibilities here: some sides will be almost as monolithic as the normal analytical models presume, but others will be heterogeneous. In some cases the heterogeneity will be deliberately created, perhaps most obviously in this context by the recruitment of lawyers and other providers of expert knowledge, in an effort to construct what Goffman has called a 'performance team' (Goffman, 1959: 79). These specially recruited partisans are intended to bolster the team's ability to analyse the position and performance of the other side and to improve its own approach to the negotiations – for example, by furnishing informed advice on substantive issues, bringing in procedural expertise, or by enhancing access to relevant sources of power and influence through personal connections. Moreover, even without the assistance of such experts, the divergence of views commonly found within a team may bring with it greater possibility of careful and effective consideration of negotiating options. Nevertheless, such heterogeneity requires some sort of 'negotiation' within or prior to the main negotiations before it can attain such benefits, and may bring with it weaknesses as well as strengths.

Thus, not all team members will have the same degree of commitment to their side's cause. Some may provide only grudging assistance because they have enrolled in or aligned themselves with the team merely because they are beholden to the leader or some other key player in the team. Others may even have chosen to give 'support' because not to do so would leave them open to accusations of disloyalty. Still others may seek to encourage cleavages and to subvert their own side's negotiating position. Their own individual interests will be enhanced, rather than undermined, by the failure of their side to negotiate a satisfactory outcome to the dispute. Such internal weaknesses may become manifest during the course of the main negotiations and be exploited by the other side.

These intra-party exchanges are, in effect, negotiations within negotiations. Perhaps because they do not arise in *direct* response to the main dispute, their precise nature is unclear. Gulliver refers to them as 'negotiations of a kind' (1979: 266) but elsewhere as 'intra-party bargaining' (1979: 267). In our view, they are a form of negotiation. They involve their own dynamic processes of information exchange and, in the case of serious disagreements between team members, they will generate an unfolding process which may lead to an agreed position, along the lines indicated by Gulliver in his developmental model (see Section C below). They are constrained by the parameters of the overt party structures and relationships and often will not involve explicit disagreement. However, for those participating in the coalition that is a party to the main dispute, these intra-party negotiations may well be as important, or more significant, than the main, inter-party negotiation. The distinctiveness of this kind of negotiation is alluded to by Goffman when he wrote: 'whether the members of a team stage similar individual performances or stage dissimilar performances which fit together into a whole, an emergent team impression arises which can be conveniently treated as a fact in its own right, as a third level of fact located between the individual performance on the one hand and the total interaction of the participants on the other' (1959: 80).

Gulliver suggests that, in general terms, internal differences and problems within a negotiating party will affect the larger negotiation process in at least three ways.

First, the repetitive exchange of information and the linked process of learning and adjustment that Gulliver characterises as the 'cyclical' model of negotiation will be significantly more complicated as a result of the internal variety in a complex team and the need to present a monolithic front. We may illustrate this by reference to the worker in an organisation who, for example, embarrasses his or her union in negotiations with management by working too hard and thereby undermining the union's definition of a hard day's work. Although such a worker can be subjected to a variety of informal, corrective sanctions, these may not necessarily alter his or her conduct, and this threat to the collective negotiating front that colleagues are attempting to promote cannot be ignored. If the workforce wishes to present a united front, it must secure an agreement with that worker in which he or she modifies his or her conduct at the workplace. Goffman has identified a number of strategies that a complex negotiating party may have to resort to in order to secure internal unanimity, or at least the appearance of unanimity (1959: 79–105). Thus, there may well be direct pressure placed on members to adhere to a unanimous line, backed by the threat of sanctions, a reduction in the role, or transfer to a primarily ceremonial role, of those who threaten the united front, controlling more effectively the setting in which the negotiations are to take place, or giving one person the right to control and direct the negotiations, and development of a collective sense of secrecy with a rule against disclosure to the other party.

Second, in the broad developmental process, the transition from one phase of the negotiations to the next is likely to be more difficult in situations in which one or both of the main negotiating parties have significant internal differences. Indeed, Raiffa has suggested that such movement may be significantly more problematic when he observes that teams with single players may 'bargain tougher' than do those with multiple players as a result of a 'tendency within teams for the members to compromise [with each other] in the direction of a tougher bargaining stance [toward the other party to the main dispute]' (Raiffa, 1982: 95). Linked to this is the possibility that the real purpose of constructing a negotiating team is not the negotiations per se but, rather, the achievement of a level of cohesion within a group of people that might otherwise be unobtainable, for example, where participation in the team mitigates structural or social cleavages within an organisation. In this fragile situation there is not only greater possibility of defection and disruption but also a need for the persons leading that party to encourage the team to adopt an aggressive stance towards the opposing party in order to promote intra-party co-operation – the possibility of internal dissent is reduced by combative posturing ostensibly adopted in the interests of dealing effectively with the opposition. The position is further complicated by the fact that unanimity is often not the only requirement in the negotiating posture for, as Goffman has indicated, 'there seems to be a general feeling that the most real and solid things in life are ones whose description individuals independently agree upon. We tend to feel that if two participants in an event decide to be as honest as they can in recounting it, then the stands they take will be acceptably similar even though they do not consult one another prior to their presentation' (1959: 88). As a result, it is often important for several members of a negotiating party to be in agreement on the positions they take and secretive about the fact that these positions were not reached independently.

This need may add to the fragile nature of the unity within the negotiating team and thereby foster an even tougher attitude toward the other side.

Third, internal dissension and efforts to cope with such dissension, may well prove singularly distracting and prevent a party from realising its actual strength in the overall negotiations. To some extent this will be because the team's negotiating goal may well be a compromise, with this fact disguised from the other side through the application of some sort of principle of collective responsibility.

In the extract that follows, Tom Colosi notes the importance of 'quasi-mediators' in securing internal consensus within a negotiating team, and the significant complications for internal cohesion that arise as a result of the process of information exchange and learning inherent in negotiating with the other party.

Extract 5:3

T Colosi: 'Negotiation in the Public and Private Sectors' (1983) 27(2) *American Behavioural Scientist* 229, pp 229–230

> Negotiations are typically depicted as involving one group sitting across a bargaining table from a second. One side presents its demands or proposals to the other, and a discussion or debate follows. Counter-proposals and compromises are offered. When the offers are eventually accepted on both sides, the dispute is settled and an agreement is signed.
>
> Within this model, all the interesting and relevant action is presumed to occur back and forth between the two sides. The model assumes that each party is monolithic, even if represented by bargaining teams. The way in which the participants are billed – labor versus management, prisoners versus guards, environmentalists versus industry – reflects the same monolithic assumption; that is, that all team members share the same set of demands, agree on a strategy for handling the opposition, and have come to the table with equal enthusiasm for the negotiating process.
>
> Unfortunately, the conventional model of negotiation obscures much of the richness and complexity of the bargaining process. In practice, bargaining teams are seldom monolithic. Team members often have conflicting goals and values; some sort of consensus must develop internally before agreement can be reached with the other side. While some students of negotiation have recognized the importance of this internal bargaining, conventional models do not explain their relationship to the functioning of the larger process.

The implications of intra-party negotiation for analysis of inter-party negotiation processes has not been given sufficient attention in the relevant literature. Existing analysis, too, has tended to focus primarily on the problems that often arise between the team leader and other members of the party coalition.[1]

---

1 Some idea of the specific difficulties that can arise in this context is provided by the comparative analysis by Bailey of team co-ordination in political contexts. Briefly stated, he suggests that much depends on the nature of the team, and he identifies four types of group, each of which, in his view, requires a different mode of internal co-ordination: unspecialised, transactional, moral and bureaucratic (see Bailey, 1969: 35–57).

Multi-party Negotiations

Multi-party disputes may be found in any context, notably in international disputes, political disputes and large-scale commercial litigation. Of course, in many multi-party negotiations coalitions will emerge that reduce the negotiating process de facto to a two-party situation – in effect, some sort of preliminary agreement is reached between several of the parties to stand together against one or more of the other parties. The dividing line between multi-party and intra-party negotiations may be especially difficult to draw in such circumstances. While the basic characteristics of negotiation that we have already identified hold good in multi-party processes, they obviously bring with them greater complexity. First, the networks of communication through which information is exchanged and learning takes place become more elaborate as the parties to the decision become more numerous. Second, as parties increase in number, the goals and interests which have to be identified, communicated and ultimately accommodated become manifold. Correspondingly, the viable options generally constrict and are subject to differential evaluation. Lastly, any bargaining stage in the negotiations becomes more important and protracted as a range of interests needs to be accommodated. The process of alliance formation through negotiations may itself be a somewhat complicated process, and the complications of a multi-party situation will affect the processes of interaction and communication between the various parties in the main negotiations and also impact on the sort of outcome to which they are able to agree.

Some of the distinctive characteristics of multi-party negotiation appear in the following extract:

Extract 5:4

T Colosi: 'Negotiation in the Public and Private Sectors' (1983) 27(2) *American Behavioural Scientist* 229, pp 241–243

> In 1973 a riot in a Rochester, New York, high school sent 16 students and teachers (8 blacks and 8 whites) to the hospital. I was one of two intervenors from the American Arbitration Association's National Center for Dispute Resolution in Washington, DC, who entered the dispute as fact-finders. In truth, we borrowed from the public sector labor-management model to characterize our roles, using the Newman model of 'mediators wearing fact-finders' hats.' The particular intervenors were teamed because one is white and the other black.
>
> About 18 different organizations, representing students, specific racial and ethnic groups, teachers, parents, and local citizens, were identified by the school board and one another as interested parties. They were invited by the American Arbitration Association to meet each other and the fact-finders. The purpose of the meeting was to determine what had caused the riot and to try to set up a process for avoiding future disruption. Once this group was assembled, one of the first questions that had to be answered was whether still other parties and organizations should be involved. Some groups already present voiced objections about inviting certain others, contending that they would ruin the process. Nevertheless, as mediator/fact-finders, we encouraged those

who were involved to invite the threatening groups to participate on the ground that any outsiders who had enough power to stymie the process would likely be important to implementing any agreement. Ultimately, the original participants did decide who would be at the table and added several parties. In effect, the negotiators defined themselves.

Once the group's composition was established, the parties had to determine how decisions would be made. Two competing models of decision-making were offered: majority vote and full consensus. Some conservative groups supported the majority vote, while the minority organizations felt better protected by full consensus; indeed, they threatened to leave the table over this issue. The intervenors kept the parties together by observing that an effective solution to the high school problem would be possible only if all the groups present were involved in the negotiations. The intervenors pointed out that a settlement unanimously endorsed by a group as broadly based as those convened would carry a great deal of clout with the school board and the public. The parties remained at the table because they had begun to believe that some common goals and solutions were possible, even though these had yet to take concrete form. Each group's attitudes on the decision-making issue was affected, in part, by its own internal structure and experience. Some groups that were accustomed to operating under an authoritarian model assumed that the mediator/fact-finders would make the decisions. Others thought that committees would be formed to discuss the issues and be given delegated powers. Majority rule, with and without minority opinion reports, were other suggestions. Before long, participants came to see how differently they all made decisions, and began to educate one another about the relative merits of each process.

The intervenors had to conduct side-bar meetings (caucuses with groups in isolation from other groups) because of one minority group's flat refusal to participate under any process except full consensus. The mediator/fact-finders created doubts in the conservative camp as to the viability of the majority rule process by asking its members if they realized how much power was available to them through the full consensus process. The intervenors pointed out that a simple veto could be exercised by any group to prevent proposals and directions that were perceived to be inappropriate or undesirable from being adopted. After many internal discussions with the conservative group, full consensus decision-making was accepted.

Continuing the process discussions, we next suggested to the group that they begin their negotiations by agreeing upon a common goal. The initial proposals were sweeping and often contradictory. Some said that the goal should be to stop busing. Others said that desegregation should be eliminated. One proposal was to abolish the school board. Even amendments to the US Constitution were put forth. It was clear that the parties were still a long way from reaching a mutually acceptable goal.

We worked patiently in a variety of process configurations and settings to try to close the many gaps. Talks took place chiefly in informal meetings. Internal discussions took place within some of the parties; there was also direct talk between the parties, both with and without the mediators. In the course of these discussions, the mediators came to realize that despite the parties' obvious differences, they shared a common attitude: fear. They feared each other, but beyond that they feared what might happen in the schools and in the community if accommodation could not be achieved. Still, they were not ready to trust each other to be reasonable or to deliver on promises.

The parties met over a six-month period with the mediators and a local coordinator. A church basement was used as the formal meeting area. There was near-perfect attendance at all the weekly and biweekly meetings; no group pulled out of the process. Ultimately, the groups agreed on a common goal: to have *safe schools*. In retrospect, the goal may seem obvious, yet the fact that it eluded the parties for so long shows that polarization and lack of trust can keep disputants from recognizing their shared interests that, under other circumstances, might be easily perceived. Once the common goal was articulated, the parties tried to formulate an overall strategy for achieving it. Their initial strategy was to continue negotiations. Trust in the negotiation process and in each other was beginning to be established, and as the parties assumed greater responsibility for tasks, the mediators of course did less.

The outside neutrals entered this polarized situation as fact-finders, worked to establish trust – first in themselves and then in the negotiation process – by showing the parties how mediation could help them. By encouraging the parties to work together on small, seemingly procedural issues, the intervenors demonstrated how people with different priorities and outlooks could work cooperatively. Once trust is established in the negotiation process and in each other, the negotiators will find that they no longer need a mediator. When this happens, the mediator should begin to leave the dispute, as his job may essentially be over. The mediator may make himself available for other process-management tasks, of course, or to resume mediation if the trust relationship breaks down for any reason.

C: The Processual Shape of Negotiation

We have conceptualised negotiation as a cyclical process of information exchange and learning but have not beyond that identified any processual shape for negotiation. In the North American writing by lawyers, process has tended to be submerged under the examination of bargaining strategies, power and an understandable pre-occupation with ethical questions. Thus bargaining, a conceptually identifiable but in many cases small, or even absent, part of the overall process, has assumed a central focus. If negotiation is to be properly theorised we have to transcend this position; but in what direction?

We have already identified conditions for negotiation, and some of the things that must happen if negotiation is to take place successfully. Negotiation demands the availability of some communication arrangements, ideally a secure forum and some ground rules. The issues need to be formulated and transmitted; differences have to be understood; possible ways forward have to be identified and evaluated; some of these ways forward may contemplate potential changes of position, so 'bargaining' may be required; a solution needs to be found and formulated – and here clarity will often be central. But can we go further than that and argue that negotiation has a conventional, or underlying shape, under which these foci of attention are linked together in any particular way, or even constitute the shape taken by successive, developmental phases in negotiations?

A number of writers have attempted to formulate a developmental process model, identifying the phases through which negotiations must pass if they are to reach an agreed outcome (for example: Douglas, 1957; 1962; Stevens, 1963; Stenelo, 1972; Gulliver, 1979). While these authors come from a variety of disciplines – labour relations, diplomacy, social anthropology – the models of processual shape they have come up with reveal striking similarity.

An early attempt by Anne Douglas, a North American writing about labour negotiations, argued that most negotiations fall into three successive phases:

- an early phase in which disagreement is emphasised and in which the outer limits of what she labels the 'negotiating range' are established;
- a middle phase in which the parties 'reconnoiter the range' and begin to focus on areas which hold some promise of agreement; and
- a final phase in which what she describes as the 'decision-making crisis' is precipitated and agreement is reached or the negotiations break up.

Douglas emphasised that the first phase tends to be characterised by turbulent, conflictual shows of strength, giving way to the calmer and more focused exchanges of the second phase. A further period of potential turbulence may follow before an outcome is reached.

Lars-Göran Stenelo, a Swede writing on international relations, also proposed a three-phase model, suggesting a very similar shape to diplomatic negotiations. He explicitly adopted Douglas' conception of a *negotiation range* in characterising the first phase. This was the phase during which an agenda and 'other procedural questions' had to be arrived at and attempts made 'to define the problem areas and basic issues with which the negotiations are to deal' (1972: 92). In this process, 'areas of disagreement . . . become more clearly delineated' and, once formulated, 'goals must be coordinated' (92, 93). Stenelo also noted, 'search strategies are used in the initial stage in order to reduce the uncertainty concerning the number of possible negotiatory outcomes' (142).

An intermediate stage then follows, labelled the *contract zone*, during which the parties identify those outcomes that they would prefer to no agreement. 'The establishment of a contract zone presupposes that the parties consider a number of alternative ways of reaching agreement' (101). At this stage, 'the parties investigate each other's propensity to make concessions . . . test the stability of each other's positions' and 'search out and identify the main obstacles to agreement' (103). At the same time, search activities 'contribute to the elimination of certain unrealistic alternatives' (143).

In a final phase, the parties use the framework established as the contract zone in trying to reach an agreement. Here the parties 'search for the final conditions required for an acceptance' (143).

So for Stenelo, negotiation is thus conceptualised as a three-phase *search* process that he summarises as follows:

- 'The initial stage of the negotiation is dominated by the parties' attempts to determine jointly the issues with which the negotiations are to deal, that is the parties attempt to establish *a negotiation range*' (92).
- 'The intermediate stage is dominated by the parties' joint attempt to establish a *contract zone*, . . . the range of outcomes the parties would prefer to no agreement' (101).
- 'In the final stage, the parties attempt to reach an *agreement* within the framework of the established contract zone by uniting on a set of solutions' (106).

A complex feature of Stenelo's formulation is that a number of analytically distinct matters are described as needing attention in the 'initial stage': issues have to be identified, an agenda formulated, areas of disagreement delineated and search activities undertaken to reduce uncertainty as to ultimate outcome. This suggests perhaps that a more elaborate model of process is called for.

In looking for such a model we turn here to the more detailed, eight-phase processual model developed by the British social anthropologist Philip Gulliver (1963; 1971; 1979) on the basis of his field research on negotiations in some small stateless societies in East Africa during the 1950s and later work he did on North American labour disputes. Gulliver expresses substantial agreement with Douglas and Stenelo, and the central phases of his model look very like the three phases they propose.

Gulliver claims that the shapes he identifies are, on an empirical level, widely observable across different cultures in the conduct of negotiations. Gulliver outlines his model briefly as follows:

> In negotiation there are two distinct though interconnected processes going on simultaneously . . . a cyclical process comprising the repetitive exchange of information between the parties, its assessment, and the resulting adjustments of expectations and preferences; there is also a developmental process involving the movement from the initiation of the dispute to its conclusion – some outcome – and its implementation.
>
> The model of the developmental process . . . comprises a series of overlapping sequences or phases, each with its peculiar emphasis and kind of interaction and each opening the way for the succeeding one in a complex progression. Summarily, these phases are (1) the search for an arena for the negotiations; (2) the formulation of an agenda and working definitions of the issues in dispute; (3) preliminary statements of demands and offers and the exploration of the dimensions and limits of the issues, with an emphasis on the differences between the parties; (4) the narrowing of differences, agreements on some issues, and the identification of the more obdurate ones; (5) preliminaries to final bargaining; (6) final bargaining; (7) ritual confirmation of the outcome; and, in many cases, (8) the implementation of the outcome or arrangements for that (1979: 82).

Something more needs to be said about the successive phases of this developmental model:

An Arena

For the process of information exchange and learning that may culminate in a joint decision to take place at all, the parties need to find sufficient common understandings to enable a conversation to take place and a medium of communication that will enable messages to pass backwards and forwards between them. The 'arena for negotiations' may, but need not, consist of a physical location within which face-to-face meetings take place. For present purposes, an arena is constituted whenever messages pass between the parties, receive attention and elicit response. The necessary arrangements can be provided even while the parties remain at a distance by the traditional 'go between', the postal services or contemporary modes of electronic communication.

Identifying the Issues and Forming an Agenda

Once communication arrangements are in place, a second phase is reached in which the parties formulate and communicate *the issues* as they respectively see them. Many negotiations conclude at this early stage as assimilation of the respective positions leads to removal of misconceptions, and growth of common definition and understanding. The parties simply come to see that there is no disagreement between them. If issues remain to be resolved, an *agenda* then has to be formed in which negotiable issues are identified, ranked and prioritised. Not all the issues initially raised by the two sides will necessarily be susceptible of negotiation. Some of what is raised may simply be to do with expression of hurt and attribution of fault.

Exploring the Limits

There then follows a phase of what Gulliver describes as 'free-roaming, antagonistic and rhetorical behaviour' (1979: 138) in which the parties explore the boundaries of the field within which negotiations may go forward. This can be a phase of open conflict and antagonism in which the sharpest differences are expressed and most extreme demands articulated on both sides.

Narrowing the Differences

Through the previous phase, the parties come to understand the dimensions of the dispute between them, and as they do so the central issues emerge as well as the potential options. Sometimes suddenly, sometimes gradually, the tone of the exchange begins to alter enabling the parties to examine in depth what they conceive as being the main issues between them and the available options. This examination may in itself reveal to the parties an outcome that is acceptable to them, or that further exchanges will be unproductive, in either case bringing the negotiations to a conclusion.

Preliminary Bargaining

If common understanding and agreement still elude the parties once the central issues have been identified, a further phase begins during which an agreed outcome is sought through further exchanges. In the course of these exchanges, adjustments of position may take place as the respective bargaining endowments of the parties are brought to bear. Gulliver suggests that 'final bargaining' is often preceded by a preliminary phase in which the stage is set by preliminaries concerned with 'the search for a viable bargaining range, the refining of persisting differences, the testing of trading possibilities, and the construction of a bargaining formula' (1979: 153). But he makes clear that these are certainly not essential pre-requisites of a successful outcome.

Final Bargaining

Gulliver defines bargaining as 'the exchange of more or less specific, substantive proposals' (1979: 160). Ensuing positional change can follow two general routes. Along the first, a 'stronger' party may continue to put his or her demands in an unrelenting and insistent way. In response, the 'weaker' party is forced into a modification of position. Along the second, the parties make linked, reciprocal concessions that enable all to recognise an acceptable outcome.

Ritual Confirmation

Negotiations may well end in impasse or breakdown, leaving the parties pursuing their dispute in other ways. But where an agreed outcome is reached, there is almost invariably a final phase in which agreement is ritually affirmed. The manner in which this is expressed will vary from one culture to another – it may involve writing, a handshake, drinking beer, the taking of oaths or participation in some ceremonial performance.

Implementation

One point widely advanced as a problem with bilateral negotiations as a mode of decision-making is the difficulty of enforcement. Gulliver, in our view rightly, suggests that this difficulty is greatly exaggerated. Consensual agreement, perceived by both parties as a better alternative to anything else available to them, generates commitment that is likely to make it self-enforcing.

Gulliver makes clear that what he is describing represents a model only, with each phase representing an 'analytically distinguishable set of interaction, exchange of information, learning and, in effect, purpose of negotiators' (1979: 172). However, in actual negotiations phases may overlap and not follow each other in a rigid chronology and, given the untidiness of actual social conduct, Gulliver 'cautions against insistence on a too neat and coherent model' (1979: 173).

We would adopt Gulliver's elegant and durable model,[2] subject to two small qualifications. First, we would prefer to treat the initial identification of issues and the subsequent formation of an agenda as analytically distinct, necessarily sequential

2 We note here that there has been an adoption and vigorous survival of Gulliver's model as the basis of practice in contemporary mediation programmes.

phases, rather than the single stage he depicts. Each party's initial formulation will have distinctive features and the quality of a performance, requiring to be heard and acknowledged. The reduction of the two or more positions involved into an accepted agenda for discussion involves a significant transformation and represents a watershed that many embryonic negotiations do not manage to traverse. Second, in Gulliver's model, the phenomenon of agreement (where that is the outcome) seems to lie uneasily between the phases of *final bargaining* and *ritual affirmation*. In many negotiations, a substantial amount of work lies between the first recognition that an agreement is 'there' and its ultimate formulation. This tricky phase needs explicit acknowledgement. That is not to deny that, in these closing moments, the instrumental and the expressive may be inextricably interwoven with final acts both marking, and conferring validity on, a newly established state of affairs.

More wide-ranging critiques of Gulliver's model question the strength of his claim to its cross-cultural applicability. Moore (1995) has questioned the specificity of this processual model to negotiations, noting that in some important respects it replicates the structure of civil litigation, thereby suggesting that Gulliver has perhaps subconsciously adapted his developmental model of negotiations from the processual phases of litigation (Moore, 1995: 16, 18). Moreover, Gulliver is characterised as assuming too easily that negotiations will come to a successful conclusion, having focused his empirical attentions on cases in which the protagonists are interdependent. We find Moore's position here hard to follow. Gulliver outlines the shape of successive phases in a bilateral process of 'information exchange and learning'. In so far as Moore is referring to lawyer negotiations that follow the path of civil process these are *negotiations* and we would have no quarrel with her. However, the processual shape of those phases of litigation which are directed towards the judge, and hence are addressed to a third party, are distinctively different. The finality of agreement that comes from negotiation is founded to a significant degree on consent, whereas the finality in adjudication comes in the form of an authoritatively imposed third-party decision.

A different critique of Gulliver's claim that the nature and processual shape of negotiation holds steady across wide social fields goes to its applicability in different cultural contexts. Sonia Shah-Kazemi (2000) argues that, cultural difference makes it difficult to delineate a universal processual shape for negotiations. There are a number of closely related questions here. First, the profound communication and power complexities in negotiations that cross lines of stratification, ethnicity and gender are undeniable. These have particular implications where negotiations are facilitated by a mediator (see Chapter Six). But, Shah-Kazemi goes further, suggesting that Gulliver's process model itself may require refinement (Extract 5:7).

Whatever view we may take of these debates, the identification of a processual shape for negotiations has two immediate consequences: it removes the exclusive, distorting preoccupation with bargaining; but at the same time identifies in a new way the central foci of strategic action – around the problem of 'moving' the negotiations from one phase to the next, the primary task of the mediator. We examine that role in the next chapter, and consider now the strategic aspects of negotiations.

Extract 5:5
Sonia Nourin Shah-Kazemi 'Cross-cultural mediation: A critical view of the dynamics of culture in family disputes' (2000) 14 *International Journal of Law, Policy and the Family*, pp 302–325

This paper offers a critique of cross-cultural mediation by exploring it from the vantage point afforded by the model of negotiations expounded by Gulliver in his watershed study Disputes and Negotiations; A Cross Cultural Perspective. He states that in order to understand mediation it is necessary to view the process as 'an integrated part of negotiation' into which the mediator enters and transforms the bilateral negotiations by becoming a party to them. My objective here is to evaluate Gulliver's model with a view to laying the foundations for a synthetic model of the processual dynamics of negotiation in the light of an analysis of cultural factors. The discussion will revolve around marital disputes as they provide a forum for debate about the forces that cultural factors inject into the negotiation process. In his conclusion, Gulliver acknowledges that he has not given enough emphasis to how 'the nature of the relationship between the disputing parties within the structure of their society affects the negotiations between them.' He then goes on to say that he has also not given enough emphasis to inter-personal disputes of all kinds and that he has presumed that his paradigm of negotiations applies to them. It is difficult to deny that the model developed by Gulliver does apply to inter-personal disputes, albeit sometimes only in a very general way. Gulliver's acknowledgement of the shortcomings in his analysis paves the way for this paper. In the first instance, it is clear that in the domain of marital disputes, the social structure, or 'social unit' within which parties find themselves has a profound impact on the negotiations between the parties to an extent not fully expounded by Gulliver; and moreover, the very assumption about the joint decision-making to take place between the negotiating parties, upon which Gulliver's model is predicated, has to be critically evaluated in the light of an understanding of the cultural factors that impose themselves upon relationships.

Arguably more than in any other domain, it is in the sphere of marital disputes that the social structure impinges upon the negotiations, because the marital relationship, and its attendant values, is the cornerstone of any particular social structure. If, as Gulliver stresses: 'the very definition of a relationship – the pattern of behavioural interaction, interests, rights, obligations, and affective content, and the extent of tolerable leeways in all these – depends on such accepted standards, more or less clearly understood by the members of the social unit', this is even more the case with the marital relationship. It is within the parameters of this intimate relationship that the individual is motivated to define his/her identity in socio-cultural terms and to practise his/her normative ethics. This is the case no matter what the cultural background of the individual; the existential reality referred to by the term 'social identity' appears to be one from which there is no escape. However, in the case of minority communities, the standards which the 'social unit' apply to define the marital relationship are often circumscribed by the very dynamic of maintaining (or rejecting) a minority identity within the larger social matrix. The fluidity of social reality however cannot be explored in sufficient depth here; suffice it to say that with the development of social structures, the complexities governing relationships multiply. To be more precise: negotiations within the domain of marital disputes assume a very particular complexity as the dynamics of both gender and identity-defining normative ethics shape the setting in which the negotiations take place, to an extent that Gulliver has not sufficiently explored. The assumption made by Gulliver in the preface to his book, about negotiations being 'a set of social processes leading to interdependent, joint decision-making by the negotiators through their dynamic interaction with one another' upon which his whole model is predicated, has to be analysed within the context of the dynamics of cultural identity. This notion of joint decision-making cannot simply be stated and left unexamined. The question of who the relevant parties in the dispute are needs to be addressed, and the particular framework of the decision-making process needs to be articulated. On the universal plane, the reality of how much choice the individual has, in terms of taking decisions regarding the dispute management process, is subject to tremendous fluctuation. There can be no doubt that the degree to which one perceives any choice in pursuing a particular course of action varies significantly. In the realm of differing cultural practices there is also no doubt that the choices which are available in any given situation vary significantly according to some of the most salient factors that make up cultural identity: ethnicity, gender, socio-economic status, religion. This understanding of variation in practices and social mores has to be applied in depth to Gulliver's model to attain a truly cross-cultural perspective.

Mindful of Gulliver's protestations that his model should not be criticized simply for not applying to specific empirical cases, in the sphere of marital disputes, where the socio-cultural context in which the dispute takes place cannot be ignored, the model does require reevaluation.

D: Power in Negotiation

So far we have represented negotiation primarily in terms of agency, or interacting individuals, and have not drawn in structural considerations. One of the central points that De Sousa Santos is making in the passage quoted in Chapter Three (pp 51–53 above) is that negotiations are not simply interactions between free, interest-pursuing 'individuals'. Participants are necessarily enmeshed in a partially perceived, but largely unexamined framework of constraint over which they have very limited control. This condition is variously represented in different traditions of social theory: in terms of structural constraint (for Marx); in terms of diffuse ('recursive'), multi-faceted networks of power running in different directions and multiple levels (for Foucault); and as 'systems' and 'sub-systems' experiencing 'turbulence' from the environment (for Luhmann). Power in these senses is always 'there'; but we frame the present discussion in straightforward Weberian terms. So 'power' for our immediate purposes is the capability of one human actor, or group of actors, to make others do things they would not otherwise have done.

One of the central implications of a bilateral mode of decision-making is that control over the outcome lies with the parties themselves, and that any outcome will necessarily be informed by the respective resources available to the parties, rather than those available to other people. This feature has encouraged much of the literature on negotiations to present them as 'power' struggles, bargaining processes, and therefore to concentrate on the strategic aspects of negotiation. While it is important to recognise this aspect of negotiations, that they need not be characterised by harmony and consensual decision-making, and that it is inherent in them that in the context of imbalances of power, the 'stronger' may dominate the weaker, two general points need to be emphasised in this context. First, negotiation is not just about 'bargaining'. It is primarily a process of information exchange and learning. Accordingly, an outcome in agreement may well flow simply from better understanding of the respective positions of the parties, as a result of information exchange, without either side's perceived interests being modified at all. The outcome may be that there is no 'issue', whatever perceptions may have been before negotiation commenced. Second, while respective sources of power inform the outcome of negotiations, power sources are multiple and imponderable. Money, love, truth and personality may all be at play. What constitute the power resources in a particular context are unlikely to be straightforward, and these are certainly not limited to material and normative resources.

Despite the complex, multiple nature of power resources in almost all negotiations, we need to distinguish some qualitatively different situations. The power imbalances that characterise differences of rank, and those that arise in the context of stratification, make negotiations across these divides particularly problematic. So, decision-making between sovereign and subject, between employer and employee, or between corporate suppliers of goods and services and individual consumers, present particular difficulty. As a general rule, we would argue that disputes crossing lines of stratification, and more generally those which involve gross imbalances of power, will seldom be well resolved through negotiation.

E: Strategy in Negotiation

We have noted already the narrowly circumscribed view of negotiation that is taken in much of the ADR literature, where negotiation is largely presented as bargaining. The most important question is identification of the best, that is, the most effective, bargaining strategies. This concern is closely followed by another, related issue – the manner in which various 'distortions' affect the pursuit of 'pure' or 'ideal' strategic behaviour, in particular, the impact of power differentials on the bargaining process and the constraints placed on negotiating conduct by ethical considerations. Much of this discussion is informed by neo-classical economics, by the idea of perfect competition, and of distortions to the perfect competition of bargaining. A great deal of this writing also has a narrow focus on the actor, and assumes that those involved in negotiations are rational, calculating beings with clearly defined goals. We would not want to diminish the importance of this attention to strategic questions, so long as such discussion takes place within an overall understanding of the processual shape of negotiations.

Contrasting views of bargaining strategy inform much of existing writing in this area, expressed in terms of 'competitive' and 'co-operative' orientations (Menkel-Meadow, 1993). These are sometimes characterised in other binary terms: distributive–integrative, adversarial–problem solving, positional–principled, claiming value–creating value, demand–exchange, non-stabilising–stabilising and so on. We consider these two approaches below, relying on the dichotomy most commonly employed, namely, the competitive and co-operative models.

The Competitive Approach

The competitive orientation is usually grounded upon several basic assumptions about what happens in negotiations. First, it assumes that in negotiations most people tend to take a competitive and self-interested view of the proceedings – each side must win as much as it can and, certainly, win more than the other side. Second, it assumes that the negotiating situation propels people towards behaviour that is not only competitive but also, potentially at least, antagonistic. Third, it presumes that in most cases, the negotiations will be focused on a limited resource. Accordingly, the negotiation problem is about distribution – what one party gains, the other side loses, because this is a zero sum game. And, fourth, because people tend to take a narrow view of the negotiation process, the conduct of negotiations today will not materially affect negotiations at some future date. As a result, the competitive orientation encourages strategies that are inherently confrontational.

Typical, recognisable patterns of behaviour of the competitive negotiator are designed to maximise gains in the immediate negotiating situation. The competitive negotiator tends to make high opening demands and to be slow to make concessions. Similarly, this type of negotiator relies on confrontation, threats and forceful arguments, and manipulates both people and process, in particular, trying to uncover as much as possible about the position of the other party and, at the same time, to mislead the other side about that negotiator's own situation. Additionally, the negotiator with a competitive orientation is not open to persuasion on substantive issues. He or she has a fixed goal and that goal is to be achieved. Moreover, the goal is viewed in quantitative and competitive terms; in particular, the concern is to maximise financial rewards. This approach is sometimes seen as *the* paradigm for negotiation, and there is evidence to suggest that in some parts of the world a significant number of parties do approach negotiations in this manner. But, of course, it does not really constitute an analysis of negotiation. Rather, it is essentially a characterisation of one type of tactical approach to negotiation. Even as a 'tactical model', however, there are widely differing views on its efficacy (see, for example, Genn, 1987; Williams, 1983; Lowenthal, 1982).

Problem-solving Orientations

Other writers, notably Fisher and Ury (1981),[3] see the competitive approach as seriously deficient in a number of ways. In their view, it is based on a false set of assumptions about the negotiating world and, as a result, is unnecessarily limiting. The co-operative approach therefore recommends a radically different view of the nature of negotiations or, at least, of what should take place in negotiations. This approach sees people negotiating in terms of self-interest, but this is an enlightened self-interest. People should, and often do, look for a better outcome for both sides by working together on the problems they face.

The co-operative approach stresses that the negotiating parties are likely to share common interests, may well be dependent on each other (especially if they are involved in a long-term relationship in which 'generalised reciprocity' rather than 'immediate returns', or specific reciprocity, is called for)[4] and will often be negotiating about limited resources (and therefore need to be flexible in their goals). Moreover, outcomes that are mutually agreeable, fair to all parties and good for the community, are more likely to be implemented and to endure. As a result, the parties, while trying to maximise their individual returns, should look for joint gains and focus on their common interests. In particular, the negotiators should try to increase the number of issues over which they might reach an agreement – that is, to 'expand the pie', before dividing it. The negotiator, instead of being argumentative, should try to understand the merits of the other party's position as objectively as possible. Accordingly, differences should be explored by non-confrontational debate rather than manipulation and coercion. Moreover, the parties should be willing to be flexible, open to persuasion on substantive issues. They should always be aware of their 'best alternative to a negotiated outcome' (BATNA).[5] For the co-operative approach is, ultimately, concerned with qualitative goals – the construction, through efficient and rational negotiation, of an agreement that is fair, wise and durable.[6]

Negative characterisations of the collaborative approach outlined above view it as 'naive' and 'romantic' and as therefore dangerously misleading because it encourages parties to be too ready to make concessions. Moreover, empirical research also indicates that even where co-operative solutions are theoretically available, other variables, such as the manner in which legal services are organised, may restrict access to such solutions (Galanter and Cahill, 1994: 1376). Further, the virtues of

---

3 See also Carrie Menkel-Meadow's essay, 'Towards Another View of Legal Negotiation' (1984).
4 See M Sahlins (1965).
5 For further details on the use of BATNA in the negotiation process see, in particular, Fisher, Ury and Patton (1991: 97–106). Briefly stated, the negotiator is advised that BATNA is the most appropriate measure with which to assess settlement offers. An offer should only be accepted if it is better than the negotiator's best alternative to a settlement.
6 For an examination of negotiation strategies based on detailed empirical research, see Menkel-Meadow (1993).

co-operative or 'win–win' solutions may be complicated by the varied interests of the actors who make up a negotiating team, so that while both sides across a table may appear to win, 'within each team . . . there are [those] who may view themselves as definite losers in the process' (Colosi, 1983: 234). As a result, just as the emphasis on competitive bargaining found in the 1970s and early 1980s was supplanted by a late 1980s concern with the virtues of the co-operative and collaborative, so the co-operative model has now been somewhat superseded by empirically more complex understandings of negotiation (see, for example, Kritzer 1991: 112–129).

Nevertheless, the competitive and co-operative dichotomy continues to define many approaches to negotiating (Menkel-Meadow, 1993: 363–366). The two basic models undoubtedly have their merits. Empirical studies do suggest that many people often approach negotiation in one of these ways, although such work also suggests that parties do not necessarily pursue such strategies once they have become repeat players (Menkel-Meadow, 1993: 376–377). The basic problem with the dichotomy, in our view, is that it is both too general and too specific. It is *too general* because in a sense it is a manifestation in the 'negotiation' context of basic debates about human nature. The *competitive* position takes a Hobbesian, *conservative* view of the social world – only the fittest will survive in our ever-competitive social environment, and the truth about negotiation is that it is the toughest, smartest bargainer who survives. In contrast, the *co-operative* approach is concerned to stress the *social* or communal nature of human life, highlighting the need to stand together, to restrain competitiveness and give full reign to co-operative instincts, in order to survive. Thus, just beneath the surface of the two models are important assumptions about the nature of society. The competitive–co-operative dichotomy is but another variant on this basic theme. On the other hand, these approaches are too narrow because they focus on the conduct of negotiators rather than the process of negotiating. As a result, we often appear to be in the world of cookbooks. These orientations are guides to the construction of a successful negotiation dish. Add a little coercion here (for example, only make one's offer after the other party has made its offer), a dash of 'deceit' there (for example, by making false statements in regard to one's 'bottom line'), or identify a rich set of agreeable ingredients (thereby expanding the negotiable pie), and a good negotiation outcome is created. But these instrumental approaches ultimately fail because they do not enhance significantly our understanding of the overall shape of the processes of negotiation.

The literature is now increasingly sensitive to the view that the binary characterisations examined above, so long dominant in ADR negotiating theory, are inadequate. Greater explanatory value is to be found in approaches that acknowledge that most negotiators are likely to combine both orientations in their actual bargaining behaviour, or that there exists a continuum of negotiating orientations. This 'intermediary' approach can be located in some of the early work of Lowenthal and Gifford (Extracts 5.6 and 5.7).

Extract 5:6

G T Lowenthal: 'A General Theory of Negotiation Process, Strategy, and Behaviour' (1982–83) 31 *Kansas Law Review* 69, pp 74–75, 112–114

[N]egotiation strategies may be categorized according to whether they call for a negotiator to compete with, or collaborate with, the other participant or participants in the negotiation. Competitive negotiators view their counterparts as 'opponents' or 'adversaries' and seek settlements that maximize their own gain at the opponent's expense. The competitive bargaining model requires negotiators to commit themselves to rigid positions and to communicate to the opposition that settlement can occur only at or near those firmly committed positions. Competitive negotiators attempt to conceal the true extent of their authority to make compromises, while learning as much as possible about the limits of an opponent's bargaining range. They seek to persuade, rather than discuss, and to create the impression that arguments directed at them fall on deaf ears. Collaborative strategy is, in many respects, the opposite of the competitive model. Collaborators attempt to remain flexible, rather than committing themselves stubbornly to stated positions. They search for solutions that do not require one party to 'lose' in proportion to what the other 'wins.' Collaborators disclose to one another the extent of their authority to compromise, and they listen to other negotiators' opinions and arguments with an open mind. Moreover, maximizing individual gain is not necessarily the primary objective of a collaborative negotiator. Other values, such as the establishment or improvement of an ongoing relationship with another party or negotiator, may be more important to a collaborator than the size of the payoff in the immediate negotiation. The competition–collaboration dichotomy is not intended as a comprehensive description of all strategy choices in negotiation. Often negotiators must choose between totally competitive alternatives – or between totally collaborative courses of action. Sometimes each course of action combines competitive and collaborative strategies. Consider, for example, the size of the initial demand by a plaintiff who is seeking a $50,000 settlement in a damage action. Should the plaintiff's lawyer demand only $52,000 and firmly indicate to defense counsel that there is little or no room for compromise, or should she make a $75,000 demand, in anticipation of a $25,000 offer by the defendant, allowing the parties to 'split the difference'? Both alternatives involve an element of competitive strategy, since the lawyer must make the opening demand seem credible to the defense attorney by communicating commitment to the sum demanded and by arguing why it is the appropriate settlement figure for that case. The second alternative, however, also requires skill in seeking collaborative solutions, since the lawyer anticipates a trading process in which each party will compromise her opening position in return for a matching compromise by the other side.

Indeed, in most negotiations, a combination of competitive and collaborative strategies is both appropriate and essential. A negotiator, for example, may wish both to disclose some previously confidential information as an act of good faith and to conceal other information. Adherence to the extreme or pure form of each of the two models is of limited practical applicability. When both sides are playing competitive 'hard ball' bargaining, each negotiator must be able to trust at least some of the representations made by the other side if the parties are to reach a lasting settlement. Likewise, there are obvious limits to a solely problem solving approach when the interests of the parties are unalterably in conflict, especially when one considers the organized bar's requirement of zealous representation in seeking the lawful objectives of a client. With these limitations in mind, however, it is important to examine the fundamental differences between the extreme forms of competitive and collaborative strategy, since each is inappropriate in many circumstances. . . . Although in certain situations . . . a single factor may compel negotiators to choose either a competitive or a collaborative approach; normally a negotiator must weigh [a variety of factors] during prenegotiation planning. When the subject matter of a negotiation, normative constraints, relationship concerns, and personality factors each suggest the same course of action, strategy decisions are easily made and one can predict with confidence the nature of the interaction between negotiators. When . . . factors . . . point in different directions, however, strategy decisions obviously are more complicated, and it is extremely difficult to determine the extent to which the two modes of negotiation can be combined in a single bargaining interaction.

In such situations, analysis of preliminary communications between the negotiators is crucial for the planning of strategy on subsequent issues, since the extent to which one party opts for either of the two negotiation models must influence the other party's choice of strategies. This follows from the principle that collaborative negotiation requires the cooperation of each of the participants. In other words, if *A* chooses a competitive approach, *B* must do so also, unless *B* can convince *A* to abandon *A*'s adversarial strategies. Therefore, if *B* is unsure before the negotiation whether the parties ultimately will be competing or collaborating, *B* can engage in 'discovery' by monitoring *A*'s flexibility and argumentation on such matters as establishing an agenda, setting deadlines, and choosing an appropriate setting for negotiations. The extent of *A*'s objectivity, candor, and fairness in discussing the facts underlying a transaction also may provide clues concerning *A*'s willingness to engage in problem solving. *B* must 'test the waters' before becoming committed to either a competitive or collaborative approach.

Sometimes negotiators engage in competitive bargaining, with distrustful and unfriendly relations, even though one or more of the parties recognizes a potential for increasing mutual gain through a collaborative process. Shifting from a competitive model to a collaborative posture may be extremely difficult to accomplish during *ongoing* negotiations because a competitor cannot easily abandon a rigidly committed position without suffering harm to her credibility, or at least without perceiving such harm. Skilled negotiators nevertheless must understand the value of collaborative strategies to break impasses when neither side of a negotiation is prepared to capitulate to the other and both recognize that compromise is more desirable than deadlock. The parties in such situations must make a bilateral decision to shift from one model to the other, since a decision by one side alone cannot accomplish collaborative negotiation. Shifting can occur, however, if each party perceives an impending deadlock, an unwillingness of both sides to end, and a preference for settlement over stalemate.

When only one side of a competitive negotiation recognizes the value of shifting to a collaborative process, several strategies may be followed to assist the remaining party or parties to adopt a problem solving approach. Some commentators have suggested that in such situations a negotiator should attempt to develop more mutual trust, respect, and good will as a necessary first step toward collaboration. To accomplish this, a negotiator may: (1) reassure an opponent that her values are legitimate; (2) avoid appearing judgmental or superior; (3) decline to exploit an opponent's weaknesses or force her to make maximum concessions; (4) perform favors for an opponent that appear to be above and beyond the call of duty; or (5) convey to an opponent that she has been heard, by repeating her arguments and stating which portions of them are acceptable.

One group of researchers spent several years, conducting 30 experiments involving more than 1,000 participants, to identify conditions that are effective in bringing about collaboration between previously competitive or warring groups. The research team developed a four-step process to bring about such change. First, the parties must examine the consequences of their ongoing competition and compare those consequences with the potential consequences of collaboration. Second, the negotiators might discuss their respective doubts and reservations concerning the success of problem solving. Third, they can seek the intervention of an appropriate behavioral scientist to reduce conflict and recast disagreements in a more favorable light. Finally, they might discuss their underlying attitudes and feelings that have resulted in distrust and discord.

A negotiator using these or other strategies to turn a competitive process into a collaborative effort faces the dilemma that most of the gestures of good will, openness, and reassurance suggested in the literature may be interpreted by a competitive opponent as a sign of weakness or a willingness to make concessions. As a result, the opponent may attempt to gain a competitive advantage by exploiting the suggestions of the party urging collaboration. To minimize this risk, the negotiator suggesting a shift to problem solving might rely on a third party to intervene and advise a change of course. Whatever the method of breaking the impasse, it is important for *each* negotiator to recognize that problem solving is an alternative mode for reaching accord, and that collaboration requires unanimous support to succeed.

Extract 5:7
D Gifford: 'A Context-Based Theory of Selection Strategy in Legal Negotiations' (1985) 46 *Ohio State Law Journal* 41, pp 54–58

The Integrative Strategy
Both the competitive and cooperative strategies focus on the opposing positions of the negotiators – each negotiator attempts to achieve as many concessions from the other as possible. These concessions move the negotiations closer to an outcome favorable to the negotiator; however, each concession diminishes the opponent's satisfaction with the potential agreement. Integrative bargaining, on the other hand, attempts to reconcile the parties' interests and thus provides high benefits to both. Integrative bargaining is usually associated with a situation in which the parties' interests are not directly opposed and the benefit of one widget for one party does not necessarily result in the loss of one widget for the opponent. Instead, the parties use a problem-solving approach to invent a solution which satisfies the interests of both parties.

Integrative bargaining recently has received widespread attention as the result of the publication of Professors Roger Fisher and William Ury's popular text, Getting to Yes: Negotiating Agreement Without Giving In. Professors Fisher and Ury's negotiation strategy is largely based on integrative bargaining theory, although it goes beyond integrative theory in important ways. The authors call their strategy principled negotiation and identify four basic points to this approach:

People: Separate the people from the problem.
Interests: Focus on interests, not positions.
Options: Generate a variety of possibilities before deciding what to do.
Criteria: Insist that the result be based on some objective standard.

The first point distinguishes integrative bargaining from both cooperative bargaining and competitive bargaining, according to Professors Fisher and Ury. The competitive bargainer believes that his relationship with the opponent is important, because he seeks to change the opponent's position through sheer willpower. The cooperative negotiator builds trust in order to reach a fair agreement. In contrast, Professors Fisher and Ury's principled negotiator attempts to separate the interpersonal relationship between the negotiators from the merits of the problem or conflict.

Professors Fisher and Ury's second and third points are the standard components of integrative bargaining theory. The negotiation dance of concession matching or positioning, which is a part of both competitive and cooperative behavior, often obscures the parties' real interests. A major component of integrative bargaining is the free exchange of information between the negotiators so that each party's motives, goals, and values are understood and appreciated.

Integrative bargaining attempts to locate a solution that satisfies both parties' respective interests. Professor Dean Pruitt, a social psychologist, identifies several types of integrative agreements. The most dramatic integrative solution emerges when the parties 'brainstorm' and develop a new option that satisfies the significant needs of both parties. The second type of integrative bargaining is often referred to as 'logrolling.' In logrolling, each negotiator agrees to make concessions on some issues while his counterpart concedes on other issues; the agreement reconciles the parties' interests to the extent that the parties have different priorities on the issues. For example, a plea bargaining agreement might provide that the defendant will plead guilty to a felony, and the prosecutor will recommend that the defendant receive probation. Defendants are often most concerned with the possibility of imprisonment; the prosecutor, in a particular case, may care more about securing a felony conviction than she does about the defendant's sentence.

Another form of integrative bargaining is described by Professor Pruitt as 'cost cutting.' A negotiator, in order to reach an agreement, may find ways to diminish the tangible or intangible costs to the opponent when the opponent accepts an agreement that satisfies the negotiator. For example, a management attorney who agrees to the wage demands of a certain type of worker might be concerned that in the future the union will expect similarly generous agreements for other workers. The union negotiator may reassure management that she understands that this wage agreement for certain employees stems from special circumstances, such as historical inequities, and that similar wage concessions should not be expected for other employees.

Several procedures facilitate reaching an integrative agreement. The free exchange of information and brainstorming efforts to invent options for mutual gains were discussed previously. In addition, the possibility of logrolling suggests that disputed issues should be considered simultaneously rather than sequentially. The negotiator should also develop a set of goals and other requirements in order to generate and screen alternative proposals. To the extent that the parties exchange negotiating proposals, the integrative negotiator should try to incorporate into his proposal some element of an opponent's previously suggested solution. Finally, the negotiator should continually alter his own proposal incrementally so he only gradually reduces the level of benefit to be realized by his client. This behavior is referred to by Professor Pruitt as 'heuristic trial and error.'

Traditional integrative bargaining strategy does not have universal applicability. The strategy is utilized most easily when the parties share a problem-solving orientation, and either an identifiable mutual gain option is available or multiple issues which can be traded off against one another exist. It is less useful when the parties disagree on only a single issue and the parties' interests are inherently opposed. Examples of situations that present direct conflicts include personal injury litigation and plea bargaining.

Professors Fisher and Ury urge the 'principled negotiator' to insist upon a result based on objective criteria when the parties' interests seem to directly conflict and no mutually advantageous solution appears to be available. In this situation, they recommend the following steps:

1. Frame each issue as a joint search for objective criteria.
2. Reason and be open to reason as to which standards are most appropriate and how they should be applied.
3. Never yield to pressure, only to principle.

By stressing the desirability of reaching a fair decision, Professors Fisher and Ury appear to be borrowing from the principles of the cooperative strategists, especially from Professor Otomar Bartos. With this addition to traditional integrative bargaining, Professors Fisher and Ury claim to have found an 'all-purpose strategy' that can be used in any negotiation regardless of the number of issues, the nature of the issues, or the orientation of the opposing party.

The Strategic Choice Model

The three negotiation strategies outlined above are not mutually exclusive; frequently a negotiator will use more than one strategy in a single negotiation. Some issues in a negotiation may lend themselves to an integrative approach, while others must be resolved through competitive or co-operative bargaining. Furthermore, most negotiations that begin with competitive approaches will culminate prior to agreement with either co-operative or integrative bargaining. Social psychologist Professor Dean Pruitt, in his strategic choice model of negotiation, recognises that various negotiation strategies will be used in the same negotiation. The strategic choice model suggests that the negotiator must choose between engaging in competitive behavior, making a unilateral concession, and suggesting an integrative proposal at every point in the negotiation process. These alternative tactics correspond closely with the competitive, co-operative, and integrative strategies previously outlined.

Professor Pruitt further suggests that negotiations frequently will progress from a competitive stage to what he refers to as a co-ordinative stage. During the competitive stage, the negotiator tries to persuade the opponent to move toward the negotiator's position and to convince the opponent that the negotiator's own position is firm. Eventually, however, if the parties are to agree, they must engage in either co-operative or integrative bargaining. The competitive antagonism between the parties diminishes as each negotiator's own goals and expectations are tempered by realism; trust is engendered as the negotiators recognise that the opponent's expectations have also been lowered. At this point, the parties are psychologically ready to trade concessions or engage in problem-solving in order to resolve the conflict.

Often, competitive behavior and co-operative behavior alternate within a single negotiation or even occur simultaneously; different issues will be at varying stages of resolution, and agreements resulting from co-operative or integrative bargaining will often produce new issues to be resolved by the parties. Negotiators, however, cannot easily shift between competitive tactics and co-operative or integrative tactics in all instances. Successful competitive tactics, which attack the opponent and his case, jeopardise the positive working relationships necessary for the co-operative and integrative strategies. The combination of competitive strategies and co-operative or integrative strategies will typically occur only at different phases of a negotiation process or on easily separable and distinct issues.

F: Representative Negotiations

Although traditionally prepared in their legal education for determination of dispute outcomes through knowledge of relevant areas of law, trial and appeal, in reality lawyers in many jurisdictions are involved in dispute resolution primarily as negotiators. They spend much of their time negotiating on behalf of a client with a view to securing a compromise outcome. This process takes place without reference to an umpire responsible for determining whether either the negotiating process, or the compromise outcome, is acceptable in wider terms of legal and moral standards and the public good. It is difficult, however, to generalise about this important activity of lawyer negotiations because even within a particular jurisdiction there is likely to be a wide range of possible processal shapes arising out of variables such as the nature of the dispute, the make-up of the parties, the negotiating 'style' of the lawyers involved, and the type of practice in which the lawyer is normally engaged. These variables have an impact on both the manner in which the lawyer approaches the dispute and its management, and the particular outcomes that he or she finds acceptable. Nevertheless, certain features of lawyer negotiations can be identified.

The first point to note about lawyer negotiations is that they are representative negotiations, in which the parties have delegated the conduct of negotiations to champions. Thus, they are both intra-party negotiations and inter-party negotiations. This necessarily increases the complexity of the processes of negotiation, requiring lines of communication along at least two planes: between each party and his or her professional representative; and between the two representatives themselves.

The picture may be even more complex than this if the principals remain in communication themselves, or if one or both seek to communicate direct with the other's legal representative. Lawyers manage this complexity by insisting that they control communications, generally discouraging direct inter-party contact. They also seek to achieve control by regulating the flow of information to their principals. Their goal is often, in fact, 'total' management of the negotiation process, their assertions regarding the need to have such control normally being buttressed by the claim that lawyers are trustworthy partisans who will promote fully their client's interests. Popular images of lawyers – for example, as untrustworthy, self-interested predators – may not accord with this claim, but the claim is made vigorously none the less.

A second general point to make about lawyer negotiations relates to the distinctive way in which lawyers choose to conduct them, utilising the arena of 'litigation'. In the common law world lawyers set out at an early stage along the path towards the court, utilising civil procedure as the framework of their negotiations (see Roberts, 1997). This strategy, in itself, imposes a distinctive shape on lawyer negotiations and often has very important implications for the progress of the dispute, especially as the emphasis in any trial that might eventually take place will be on evidence and proof, and on a binary win–lose resolution of an essentially financial character, rather than an outcome that suits both parties.

Third, with the transfer of responsibility to the lawyer, a fundamental translation takes place in the course of which the dispute is typically carried over into another universe of meaning constituted by the specialised discourse of the law – as Mnookin and Kornhauser put it in their seminal essay, lawyers bargain 'in the shadow of the law' (1979). Within this universe, an important element of understanding will be the likely outcome in the event of the dispute proceeding to expert determination by a judge. The recasting of the predominant negotiating language to 'the law' means that the lawyer's control over his or her client is significantly enhanced, for it is the lawyer who is skilled at the legal abstractions and nuances, and the processual formalities that underpin this discourse.[7] Notwithstanding this, empirical research into the realities of lawyer negotiations in the Anglo-American legal world suggests

---

7 As Sarat and Felstiner conclude: 'by limiting interpretative activity to their area of expertise, lawyers are able to explain the social world through the lenses of the legal process. They are able to structure conversation to fit their rational-purposive ideology and to limit the impact of their clients' egocentric views of social life' (1998).

that the deals that are actually cut between the parties' lawyers are not informed by legal principles at all but, rather, are very often simple compromises (see, for example, Menkel-Meadow, 1993; Genn, 1987; Condlin, 1985).

Extract 5:8

Robert H Mnookin and Ronald J Gibson (1994) 'Disputing through Agents: Co-operation and Conflict Between Lawyers in Litigation,' 94 *Columbia Law Review* 509, pp 541–546

> If lawyers are to have the potential to credibly commit their clients to cooperate, there must be gains from cooperation (and the risk of loss if the other party defects). Put in context, divorce litigation must be more than a zero-sum game in which the couple's property and children are simply divided.
>
> Divorce bargaining is sometimes seen as a purely distributive (zero-sum) game in which any benefit to the wife necessarily comes at the husband's expense, and vice versa. Both the money issues and the custody issues do have distributive elements with zero-sum characteristics. When a divorcing couple divides $2,000 in a checking account, a $100-larger share to the wife necessarily results in a $100-smaller share to the husband. Similarly, if a father must transfer more of his paycheck to the mother's household by way of support, there are fewer funds available to spend on himself. Division of the child's time also displays this distributive feature. When a child spends more time in one household, this necessarily reduces the time potentially spent in the other.
>
> But divorce bargaining is hardly a zero-sum game in its entirety: in many circumstances, cooperation can 'create value' and improve the outcome from each party's point of view. First, and most fundamentally, not all of the father and mother's interests are at odds. Parents often share a fundamental interest in the well-being of their child. If the child does well, both parents are better off. Therefore, devising an arrangement that benefits the child potentially creates joint gains for both parents. Parental cooperation in co-parenting may improve opportunities for the children, and thus both parents may benefit. Even if childless, a divorcing couple may have other shared interests as well. Reducing the costs of divorce – financial and emotional – once again may benefit both parties. To the extent that the parties can reduce the transaction costs of divorce, they obviously increase the financial and emotional resources available to build new lives. In addition to other interests the divorcing spouses may share, there are potential gains realizable from the parties' preferences and the differences in relative values that they may attach to different assets or activities. This means that there can be gains – and value created – through trades. Cooperation allows divisions to be based upon the parties' personal preferences, rather than the impersonal relative valuations of the market or a court.
>
> While it is obvious that divorcing parents can sometimes themselves devise arrangements that benefit both themselves and their children, a number of potential barriers to cooperation make the divorce lawyer's role critical. For one thing, the strong emotions attending divorce may pose a formidable barrier to collaborative rational problem-solving.
>
>> Joint problem-solving and negotiation work best with clear communication and good listening skills. Many couples lacked these skills during the marriage itself,

and divorce is obviously an extremely difficult time to develop them. Indeed, many couples may replay in the divorce process old and dysfunctional patterns of dealing with each other during the marriage, and these patterns may make cooperation difficult or impossible.

When inexperience, inability, or a soured relationship prevent divorcing spouses from cooperating themselves. . . . Cooperative divorce lawyers may therefore provide an escape: by credibly committing their clients to cooperate, the lawyers as intermediaries may be able to create gains that the spouses could not realize alone.

The potential for the sucker's payoff is also present. In the divorce process, cooperative moves by one side – if not reciprocated by the other side – may lead to exploitation. Opportunities for strategic behavior likewise exist because the parties often will not know with certainty (1) the other side's true preferences regarding the allocation of assets; (2) the other spouse's preferences or attitudes toward risk; and (3) the likely outcome in court if they do not settle their disputes. Some matrimonial lawyers are known as 'bombers,' or Rambo types who will defect in a variety of ways: by contesting custody on behalf of a client who is really interested in simply paying less support; by vigorously resisting the disclosure of relevant financial information; and by generally using discovery requests and responses, depositions, and motions to wear down the other side in what amounts to a war of attrition. . . .

[However,] family law practice tends to be both localized and specialized. A divorcing husband and wife usually hire attorneys in the same legal community. Increasingly, some lawyers have tended to specialize in family practice, especially in metropolitan areas. Typically, over a period of time, these local specialists repeatedly deal with one another. Through this repeated exposure lawyers can develop and sustain their reputations. . . .

Some lawyers cultivate reputations as cooperative problem solvers, while others are viewed as more adversarial, both by themselves and others; and that, as suggested by our pre-litigation game, there is a substantial amount of self-selection both by clients and attorneys. . . .

The lawyers interviewed suggested that most Northern California members of the [American Academy of Matrimonial Lawyers] have a problem-solving orientation, at least when involved in a case in which opposing counsel was also an Academy member. However, the members consistently described a smaller number of members as being more adversarial.

All of the cooperative problem-solvers whom we interviewed reported that over half of their practice (as measured in terms of income) involved cases in which an Academy member also represented the other spouse. With the exception of cases involving known gladiators, members of the Academy typically voluntarily exchanged information and documents reciprocally and informally. Because opposing counsel knew and trusted each other, they rarely insisted on interrogatories, depositions, or engaged in protracted formal discovery.

Not surprisingly, the interviews suggested that cooperative problem-solvers much preferred dealing with lawyers who shared their orientation. A great deal of sorting and self-selection appears to occur based on reputation. Lawyers who saw themselves as cooperative said they would describe their problem-solving orientation during initial meetings with clients. They reported that their clients often were seeking lawyers with a particular orientation. Several cooperative lawyers reported that they regularly turned away clients who sought highly adversarial representation. As one stated, 'If a client is hell bent upon hiring an advocate to disembowel the adverse party, I direct them elsewhere.' They also suggested that such clients rarely approached them in the first place. 'Clients tend to preselect their lawyers, and for whatever reason, if one spouse has chosen Attorney F, the other spouse is unlikely to seek me out.' Attorney F and Attorney D, known gladiators, were said to be chosen typically by clients who shared their outlook. When these attorneys are hired, lawyers on the other side are very aware of the ramification for their clients and the dispute resolution process.

The cooperative problem-solvers did report that they sometimes represented a spouse when a bomber was representing the other spouse. They typically did not enjoy the process.

> Every time you have a case with Attorney F, you're going to court and it's going to be big bucks. . . . She has a manner of presenting her arguments which is very off-putting. It's ugly, contentious, constantly picking at the other lawyer – 'why didn't you do this; you said you were going to do something; once again you haven't done what you said you were going to do' – repetitive nagging.

A cooperative attorney described another gladiator, Attorney D, as 'miserable to have a case with' because he insists on litigating everything. 'He really doesn't care about the answer, he cares about the process and the process goes from start to finish and doesn't stop; . . . he works every nook and cranny.' This same gladiator was described by another interviewee as constantly taking 'unreasonable stances; . . . he goes to court much too much, and overtries a case.' Interestingly, Attorney D described himself in our interview in very similar terms, although without the uncharitable spin. 'I like to try cases, and I love to dream up new legal arguments, and then have the judge decide.'

A final feature of matrimonial practice may also facilitate cooperation. Unlike a commercial litigator, a family law specialist is usually not unduly dependent upon a single client for his or her livelihood. This should make it easier for a cooperative problem solver to resist client pressure to defect after the case is underway.

We do not mean for our analysis of family law practice to suggest that matrimonial practice is exclusively or even predominantly cooperative. Instead, we use matrimonial practice to illustrate that reputational markets presently exist that permit clients to commit to cooperative strategies in circumstances in which the clients themselves might have great difficulty doing so. Our informal survey of San Francisco matrimonial specialists strongly suggests that the relationship between lawyers known to each other to have cooperative, problem-solving orientations facilitates dispute resolution.

G: Ethical Issues in Negotiation

Negotiations anywhere will be informed by the ethical understandings current in the milieu within which they take place. In many cultures, abstract notions of 'fairness' and 'honesty' take on a different meaning in the context of negotiations. Perhaps because to the onlooker, the wider audience, what often impresses is outcome rather than process, images of the 'good negotiator' seem to stress cleverness, skill and effectiveness rather than probity. It is an expected part of the negotiation process in many cultures that the parties (or their partisan representatives) misrepresent to a greater or lesser degree their real attitudes, their particular circumstances and needs, and their bottom line. Misrepresentation is often built into the negotiation process as a tolerated, perhaps even legitimate, required practice. The line between honesty and dishonesty, between fairness and unfairness, is often difficult to draw. Moreover, drawing that line objectively is also complicated by the likelihood that the parties will view borderline conduct in differing ways – one person's 'puff' is another person's 'misrepresentation'.

On the other hand, trust and credibility are important factors in negotiating relationships, especially continuing relationships, so that a reputation for honesty and fairness is also valuable. An additional complication comes with the use of professional partisans or agents, that is, lawyers, for purposes of negotiation. The professional body – the association or associations of lawyers – then has an interest in the reputation of its members and will construct rules designed to give lawyers' conduct an acceptable face, even while often encouraging lawyers to maximise returns on behalf of their clients.[8] There seems to be a number of basic issues that face such attempts to impose codes of negotiating conduct by an external authority. A seminal essay in this area is that first published in the *American Bar Foundation Journal* in 1980 by James White, 'Machiavelli and the Bar: Ethical Limitations on Lying in Negotiation'. White highlights very effectively some of the difficulties that surround any attempt to control through rules truthfulness in negotiating.

Extract 5:9

J J White: 'Machiavelli and the Bar: Ethical Limitations on Lying in Negotiation' (1980) *American Bar Foundation Research Journal* 926, pp 928–931

> The obligation to behave truthfully in negotiation is embodied in the requirement of Rule 4.2(a) that directs the lawyer to 'be fair in dealing with other participants.' Presumably the direction to be fair speaks to a variety of acts in addition to truthfulness and also different from it. At a minimum it has something to say about the threats a negotiator may use, about the favors he may offer, and possibly about the extraneous factors other than threats and favors which can appropriately be used in negotiating. As I have suggested elsewhere, each of these issues has important ramifications, and each merits independent consideration by the drafters of the Model Rules and by lawyers. In this paper I ignore those questions and limit my consideration to the question of truth telling.
>
> The comment on fairness under Rule 4.2 makes explicit what is implicit in the rule itself by the following sentence: 'Fairness in negotiation implies that representations by

---

8 Thus, for example, the American Bar Association Model Rules of Professional Conduct as last amended in 2002 require at Rule 8.4(c) that a lawyer shall not 'engage in conduct involving dishonesty, fraud, deceit or misrepresentation'.

or on behalf of one party to the other party be truthful.' Standing alone that statement is too broad. Even the Comments contemplate activities such as puffing which, in the broadest sense, are untruthful. It seems quite unlikely that the drafters intend or can realistically hope to outlaw a variety of other nontruthful behavior in negotiations. Below we will consider some examples, but for the time being we will consider the complexity of the task. Pious and generalized assertions that the negotiator must be 'honest' or that the lawyer must use 'candor' are not helpful. They are at too high a level of generality, and they fail to appreciate the fact that truth and truthful behavior at one time in one set of circumstances with one set of negotiators may be untruthful in another circumstance with other negotiators. There is no general principle waiting somewhere to be discovered as Judge Alvin B Rubin seems to suggest in his article on lawyer's ethics. Rather, mostly we are doing what he says we are not doing, namely, hunting for the rules of the game as the game is played in that particular circumstance.

The definition of truth is in part a function of the substance of the negotiation. Because of the policies that lie behind the securities and exchange laws and the demands that Congress has made that information be provided to those who buy and sell, one suspects that lawyers engaged in SEC work have a higher standard of truthfulness than do those whose agreements and negotiations will not affect public buying and selling of assets. Conversely, where the thing to be bought and sold is in fact a lawsuit in which two professional traders conclude the deal, truth means something else. Here truth and candor call for a smaller amount of disclosure, permit greater distortion, and allow the other professional to suffer from his own ignorance and sloth in a way that would not be acceptable in the SEC case. In his article Rubin recognizes that there are such different perceptions among members of the bar engaged in different kinds of practice, and he suggests that there should not be such differences. Why not? Why is it so clear that one's responsibility for truth ought not to be a function of the policy, the consequences, and the skill and expectations of the opponent?

Apart from the kinds of differences in truthfulness and candor which arise from the subject matter of the negotiation, one suspects that there are other differences attributable to regional and ethnic differences among negotiators. Although I have only anecdotal data to support this idea, it seems plausible that one's expectation concerning truth and candor might be different in a small, homogeneous community from what it would be in a large, heterogeneous community of lawyers. For one thing, all of the lawyers in the small and homogeneous community will share a common ethnic and environmental background. Each will have been subjected to the same kind of training about what kinds of lies are appropriate and what are not appropriate.

Moreover, the costs of conformity to ethical norms are less in a small community. Because the community is small, it will be easy to know those who do not conform to the standards and to protect oneself against the small number. Conversely, in the large and heterogeneous community, one will not have confidence either about the norms that have been learned by the opposing negotiator or about his conformance to those norms.

The differences that may result in perceptions about 'truth and candor' often come to the surface in my negotiations seminar at the Michigan Law School, where there will be students from all parts of the country, from large and small cities, and from a variety of ethnic backgrounds. One such seminar involved a discussion between two students who had engaged in a mock negotiation that had been heated and had resulted in an unsatisfactory outcome for both. Each student had grown up in Manhattan; one was black, the other was Jewish. Their discussion in the seminar about their personal reactions to negotiation, about their experience as children and young adults in the art of negotiation, and about their personal reactions to it was illuminating. The Jewish student, one of the best in the class, was more at ease with the negotiation process, more comfortable with the ambiguity it produced, and more experienced as a negotiator. The black student, also a good student, reported that an extended negotiation without some event to relieve the tension caused him tremendous anxiety. He reported that his youthful negotiations were short and often concluded in explosive behavior. For example, if there were an argument about where two groups would play baseball (on my lot or yours), the typical negotiation would last a few minutes and, if it were not quickly resolved, would be concluded by a fight. At the conclusion of that fight the game would be played on the winner's lot. Although the anecdote does not show systematic ethical differences between the two students, it does reveal systematically different attitudes about the negotiation process as a whole, and there is no reason to believe that there are not similar and systematic differences about the appropriate level of candor and honesty among the various ethnic and regional subgroups in our society. That is not to say that one norm is correct, only that the rules of the game played by one group are not the same as the rules played by another.

If the Comments or the body of the Model Rules are to refer to truthfulness, they should be understood to mean not an absolute but a relative truth as it is defined in context. That context in turn should be determined by the subject matter of the negotiation and, to a lesser extent, by the region and the background of the negotiators. Of course, such a flexible standard does not resolve the difficulties that arise when negotiators of different experience meet one another. I despair of solving that problem by the promulgation of rules, for to do so would require the drafters of these rules to do something that they obviously could not wish to do. That is, unless they wish to rely on the norms in the various subcultures in the bar to flesh out the rules, they will have to draft an extensive and complex body of rules.

One problem is that negotiation is typically not a *public* process. As a result, there is often little or no possibility of questioning effectively the truthfulness of assertions made during the course of negotiations. Since there is only a small likelihood of discovery and punishment, ethical norms can perhaps be violated more easily than they would in more public arenas. And once there is a general recognition of this fact in a particular sphere of activity then, and this is a special problem with representative negotiation, in acting truthfully and fairly one may be foregoing advantages that would otherwise be maintained or created by acting in a dishonest (but socially tolerated) fashion. In other words, the dilemma for the representative is, should his or her loyalty be to the wider corpus of ethical norms, which invariably call for honesty and fairness, or to the immediate and particular needs of the party being represented.

An additional difficulty is the need for a professional body to develop a code of conduct that will regulate effectively all types of negotiating. Negotiations cover an almost infinite variety of substantive issues, from war to terrorism to family disputes to contractual disagreements, and so on. In such circumstances, it is necessary to frame rules in very broad language, for example, the American Bar Association requirements that lawyers negotiate honestly and truthfully, and this will inevitably lead to problems of interpretation and enforcement.

A third problematic area, as we have already noted, is constituted by the contradictory pressures apparently inherent in many negotiations. Even if one of the parties wants to be perfectly fair and truthful, if the aim of engaging in the negotiating is to secure a favourable outcome – better than one would have achieved without a negotiated agreement – there is a basic negotiating hope that the other party will overestimate the strength of one's negotiating position. In negotiating, as a result, concealment and misrepresentation are very often seen as 'natural', and there are many ways in which they may be almost effortlessly effected: for example, the use of silence to create a false impression, verbal diversions to divert attention away from a weak point, and feigned interest in certain items on the agenda in order to increase their trading value.

A further complication arises when continuing professional relationships between negotiating specialists are present. The basic problem here is the tension between the need to represent the interests of the client in the particular case, and the need to adopt strategies that enhance one's overall effectiveness and reputation. Rules of professional conduct usually prescribe the sacrifice of clients' interests for the sake of long-term considerations. But the problem remains, especially in certain kinds of conduct, for example, plea bargaining. Patterns of reciprocity develop between repeat negotiators whose relationship is *inherently* long term and which encourage concessions in the instant case for the sake of the 'generalised reciprocity'.[9]

A fifth difficulty is to be found in the judgments that might have to be made about whether a particular outcome is or is not 'fair'. Of course, it could be argued that outcome is irrelevant – all that a professional body or some other 'significant onlooker' can or should be concerned with is fairness of the negotiating process. But what are called 'distributional issues' lurk in the background, and therefore may pose something of a dilemma for a partisan or some other third party. Indeed, one trenchant criticism of ADR is that it does not achieve its aim to produce fairer outcomes; rather, because negotiations are a social rather than legal process, outcomes inevitably reflect disparities of wealth, status and power. They do so in part because standards of truthfulness and fairness are not so high in negotiations as they are claimed to be for adjudication. An additional complication is that in any social relationship views on fairness are likely to differ, each party will have its own view of what is an equitable outcome, and this may make an objective assessment of a fair result more difficult to assess.

---

9 On generalised reciprocity, see Sahlins (1965).

Finally, we should bear in mind the view of Fiss that private, non-official processes of dispute resolution are not suitable for disputes involving important public concerns. If courts are excluded from the dispute resolution process, how is the public interest to be secured? If the dispute involves matters of substantial public policy – race relations, environmental degradation, and so on – should a body such as the court be required to review thoroughly any settlement worked out privately by the parties?

So what seems to be most at issue is that the promotion of negotiation and settlement as preferred means of dispute resolution in any system necessarily raises questions of quality of process and outcome, and regulation of those who represent others in negotiations. And the imperatives of 'effective negotiation' will continually create tensions in both these areas.

CHAPTER SIX

Mediation

A: Introduction – The Nature of Mediation

With the gradual re-institutionalisation of mediation in the West across the last years of the twentieth century, quite a strong stereotype seems in the process of emerging. This is one of the disinterested professional, deliberately attempting 'to advance the interests of the disputants' (Princen, 1992: 48) by taking responsibility for *process*, thus assisting embattled parties to reach decisions on the *substance* of the issues between them. But as we saw in Chapter Four the image of the professional mediator, self-consciously facilitating other people's decision-making on matters in which she or he has no direct stake, conveys only a partial sense of a very complex constellation of interventions, arguably universally visible in one form or another across the social world.

While the mediator receives quite limited attention in classical social theory, a defining analysis was provided early in the twentieth century by the German sociologist Georg Simmel. In some almost poetic passages of his great *Soziologie* (1908 [1950]), Simmel pointed to the fact that the mediator is always present in the social world even though she may not be named as such and her role may remain unexamined. The constellation yielding the mediator, he argued, is a structural feature, generally observable across cultures in all groups of more than two elements. Reflecting upon the nature of bilateral relations and upon the fundamental ways in which these are transformed by the presence of a third party, he noted: 'dyads ... have very specific features . . . the addition of a third person completely changes them' (1908 [1950]: 138). He went on, in a few deft paragraphs, to delineate the mediator as non-aligned facilitator, distinguished from the partisan supporter on the one hand and the arbitrator with determinative authority on the other (Extract 6.1).

Although Simmel thus firmly fixes 'the third' in a *non-aligned, non-determinative* role, mediation still represents an elusive, fugitive label, presently resorted to all too easily and with little precision in the context of contemporary transformations in the management of disputing. While a contrast with the partisan supporter, on the one hand, and the arbitrator, on the other, helps to provide an identity for the mediator in rough and ready terms, 'mediation' is a label claimed by interveners of widely different rank and ambition. Mediation may be attempted by anyone from the hesitant neighbour to an authoritative professional, and, as Simmel's primary analytic distinction indicates, 'help' may range from minimal assistance with communications to an extensive and expert advisory role.

Three general dimensions need to be explored here. First, the idea of the disinterested intermediary: mediators often – perhaps typically – have their own interests, even in the substance of a dispute. Second, wide areas of apparently mediatory intervention go far beyond the parsimonious role of facilitating decision by taking care of process. Third, professional qualification as an intervener covers a small area, capturing only a little about the provenance and standing of the mediator.

The Idea of a Non-aligned Intermediary

The image of the 'neutral' third party, purposively intervening in the affairs of others – whether out of altruistic goodwill, social responsibility or professional calling – is a very powerful one. Yet almost any third-party intermediary has *some* interest in a matter in which he or she intervenes. The bystander, the neighbour, the kinsman, the co-worker, the employer and the political leader all have a stake in things 'getting back to normal', even if this is no more than an interest in everyday life 'going on' without the dislocation of a quarrel among some of those adjacent to them.

Simmel approaches this problem of what is involved in non-alignment by contrasting the position of the mediator with that of the partisan (1908 [1950]: 149–150). For him, a defining characteristic of the mediator is that he or she is not a partisan: either because the mediator stands outside the interests of the parties; or because, although engaged, he or she stands in a structurally intermediate position. As an example of the latter situation, he offers the situation of the bishop acting as an intermediary between the secular government of the state within which his diocese is situated and the Pope in Rome (Extract 6.2).

Gulliver's discussion below (Extract 6.3) sets any claim to 'neutrality' in perspective. He shows that mediators often lean towards one or other of the parties, or may have a significant interest in the resolution of a dispute, so that the 'truly disinterested, impartial mediator is rather rare' (Gulliver, 1979: 214). In circumstances in which the process of mediation is intended to play a wider, socially transformative role, there may be a strong expectation that the mediator place communal interests before the parties' needs. Michael Palmer illustrates this clearly in the extract on China below (Extract 6:4).

With a specific focus on international disputes, Thomas Princen draws a distinction between what he labels the 'principal mediator' and the 'neutral mediator' (1992: 19 et seq). The former may well have *indirect* interests in the issue in dispute, such as securing peace in the region where the dispute in question arises; whereas the latter have no interests in the issues between the parties. That does not mean that they have *no* interest in the dispute. 'They may want to see agreement reached, peace realized, of efficiencies gained. They may want to improve their self-images or burnish their reputations as peacemakers or elder statesmen. They may have religious or philosophical reasons for involving themselves. They may be just looking for something to do. Whatever the case, neutral mediators have interests, but they lie outside the issues in dispute and, therefore, are not subject to bargaining with the disputants' (1992: 49–50). Princen also suggests that this opposition suggests two fundamentally different kinds of intervention (1992: 29).

The Ambition and Scope of the Mediator's Intervention

Mediators vary very greatly in the planned scope and ambition of their interventions. So mediation may range from a minimal intervention that aspires to do no more than set in place or improve the quality of communications between the parties – passing messages between the parties; facilitating information exchange – to an active, direct intervention encompassing the provision of specialist evaluation and advice. Here Simmel argues that the mediator functions in one of two analytically distinctive ways: either by simply providing the linkage through which negotiation may take place; or by actively seeking to eliminate differences (1950: 146–147). An extensive role may involve the mediator in seeking to inform the way in which the parties see their relations, feeding in advice and information from outside, evaluating options, proposing and pressing for favoured outcomes. In these respects, the nature of the mediator's role and the range of her interventions will closely depend both on the mediator's rank and upon the stage of the negotiations at which a particular intervention takes place. With such variations will shift the degree to which the mediator comes to share control/power over the outcome with the parties. Philip Gulliver indicates the range of possibilities here at Extracts 6:5 and 6:6 below.

A number of now classical accounts present mediation as an intervention auxiliary to decision-making processes in which the parties themselves are engaged, and so link mediation definitively to negotiations. Under such analyses the mediator's primary role involves facilitating other people's negotiations; the mediator initiates, sustains or revives negotiation. Without first imagining negotiations, it is difficult to imagine the mediator; and any understanding of the mediator's role is dependent on a primary understanding of negotiations (Stevens, 1963: 123; Gulliver, 1979: 213).[1]

While we agree with this position, it is possible to delineate mediation much more expansively than this. But we argue that in doing so two analytically distinct forms of intervention, with quite different processual shapes, become concealed beneath the conventional label of mediation. One involves a primarily facilitatory role, setting in place the communications arrangements between parties that will enable them to negotiate; the other contemplates a role of expert consultancy, familiar across a wide range of professions that prioritises skills in information retrieval, expert diagnosis and prescription (see the two 'models' at pp 157–158 below).

---

1 It is possible to identify certain forms of mediatory intervention – matchmaking and its modern variant, the dating agency come to mind as examples – in which the negotiating element may only be minimal, but these are not the norm.

Our preference would be to confine the label mediation to interventions corresponding broadly to the first of these models, contrasting those with the primarily 'advisory' interventions contemplated under the second. To be sure, modes of practice corresponding to *both* these processual models are already clearly visible within the emergent 'mediation' profession. On the whole they are treated lightly as embodying variant 'facilitatory' and 'evaluative' strands (see p 181 below) of a process that embraces all forms of intervention falling short of a decision being made *for* the parties. But this inclusive approach papers over an important analytic distinction between what we would label 'advisory' and 'facilitatory' interventions. This apparent community also conceals a huge philosophic divide between those who see mediation as fundamentally an intervention supportive of party negotiation and those who see it as another expert intervention akin to those which have long developed within, say, engineering, law and medicine.

If mediation is conceptualised as a matter of facilitating joint decision-making, the appearance of the mediator none the less transforms the simple bilateral process of negotiation. The presence of the mediator, however sensitive and unobtrusive, must necessarily extend the universe of meaning within which negotiation goes forward. The mediator's understandings must inevitably inform the subsequent course of negotiations, and some degree of control passes to the mediator, whether we describe this in terms of control over 'process' or over 'outcome'. Inevitably too, power relations between the parties may be subtly, even grossly, transformed by the arrival of the mediator. So while negotiations may be realised by the mediator, they are also changed.

In the context of the re-institutionalisation of mediation in the West during the latter part of the twentieth century, emphasis was initially placed on the relatively modest objective of *repair*, facilitating joint decision-making in the turbulent context generated by a dispute. But more ambitious, even grandiose, objectives subsequently began to emerge. First, as a logical extension of the dispute resolution role, the potential of the non-aligned facilitator in assisting with the construction and management of transactions is being developed. This form of intervention now extends to the continuous monitoring of complex transactions with a view to pre-empting the cost and delay of disputes had these been allowed to arise. Most ambitious, perhaps, has been the strand of theory and practice represented by 'transformative' mediation. Here conflicts are not viewed as problems to be resolved but rather as opportunities for personal, moral growth and transformation – occasions on which mediators can 'change people' (Bush and Folger, 1994: 81 et seq). These developments are examined further in Section C below.

The Provenance and Legitimacy of the Mediator

When we begin to think about 'mediation', we identify a relation that is always there in the social world whenever more than two people are involved. As Simmel carefully insisted, 'the triad' is almost invariably present in some form: 'the constellation thus characterized constantly emerges in all groups of more than two elements'

(1950: 148). But when we speak of 'the mediator', we are probably thinking of some-one who self-consciously assumes this relation towards others, deliberately putting its elements to use, whether in everyday life or in forwarding the business of rule.

When we ask where mediators come from, and start to inquire about the attributes that give them the standing to intervene, the answers are extremely var-ied and closely dependent on socio-cultural context. Ethnographic accounts vividly reveal this diverse provenance for the mediator. While the non-aligned 'third' may often be a kinsman or neighbour, the mediator may equally well appear as a tran-sitory 'big man' (such as the Ndendeuli 'notables' reported by Gulliver, 1971; see Chapter Four), or as religious or political superiors, holders of rank and office. In other societies mediators are drawn from among 'outsiders', marginal figures like holy men and women who live on the edge of a community (such as the Pathan 'saints' described by Barth, 1959). Under mediation's contemporary re-institutionalisation in the West, of course, mediators appear as specialists, authorita-tive professionals who have been taught how to do it, have certificates of competence and subscribe to codes of practice.

A rough typology of mediator provenance might begin in the following terms:

- The 'superior' in terms of kinship, economics or politics.
- 'Being there': the adjacent friend, neighbour or workmate.
- The 'outsider': whose very 'distance' and transparent lack of any 'stake' gives legitimacy to her interventions.
- The 'professional' mediator.

Mediation and its Neighbours

Delineating mediation as we have in this introduction draws a clear analytic line between mediation and three immediate neighbours: the partisan; the adviser; and the arbitrator. Clearly, in real life, these interventions may shade into one another. Particularly in multi-party negotiations, parties may move in and out of an intermediary role as they try to move negotiations forward; and as the Arusha example (see Chapter Four) vividly illustrates, partisans on either side may nudge their principals towards agreement. In the same way, a line between the active, directive mediator and the adviser/consultant may in practice be difficult to draw. The purpose for which an intervener activates the flow of information provides a key here. Where information is elicited primarily as the basis for expert diagnosis and prescription, this is no longer mediation. Two abstract 'models' can be used to mark out the difference involved here.

Under the first model, the intervener:

- establishes communication between the parties;
- ensures that the issues are identified and communicated;
- sees to it that options are identified and evaluated;
- encourages any necessary positional change; and
- helps with the formulation of any ensuing agreement.

Under the second model, the intervener:

- establishes communication with each of the parties;
- obtains information about the nature of the dispute;
- evaluates this information to reach a diagnosis;
- issues a prescription on the basis of expert knowledge; and
- attempts to persuade the parties to accept this solution.

Again, the line between the mediator and the arbitrator is equally clear cut in analytic terms, as Simmel insists (Extract 6:7). Whereas the arbitrator assumes power to make decisions for the parties to a dispute, no such power is surrendered to the mediator; ultimate control over the outcome remains with the parties themselves. But this line may be obscured in real-life processes, particularly where the rank or posture of the intervener may make the nature of the intervention, and hence the location of power over an outcome, appear uncertain.

Extract 6:1

G Simmel: *The Sociology of Georg Simmel*, edited by K Wolff (1950, originally 1908) Free Press, Glencoe, Ill, pp 148–149

> It is important for the analysis of social life to realize clearly that the constellation thus characterized constantly emerges in all groups of more than two elements. To be sure, the mediator may not be specifically chosen, nor be known or designated as such. But the triad here serves merely as a type or scheme; ultimately all cases of mediation can be reduced to this form. From the conversation among three persons that lasts only an hour, to the permanent family of three, there is no triad in which a dissent between any two elements does not occur from time to time – a dissent of a more harmless or more pointed, more momentary or more lasting, more theoretical or more practical nature – and in which the third member does not play a mediating role. This happens innumerable times in a very rudimentary and inarticulate manner, mixed with other actions and interactions, from which the purely mediating function cannot be isolated. Such mediations do not even have to be performed by means of words. A gesture, a way of listening, the mood that radiates from a particular person, are enough to change the difference between two individuals so that they can seek understanding, are enough to make them feel their essential commonness which is concealed under their acutely differing opinions, and to bring this divergence into the shape in which it can be ironed out the most easily. The situation does not have to involve a real conflict or fight. It is rather the thousand insignificant differences of opinion, the allusions to an antagonism of personalities, the emergence of quite momentary contrasts of interest or feeling, which continuously color the fluctuating forms of all living together; and this social life is constantly determined in its course by the presence of the third person, who almost inevitably exercises the function of mediation. This function makes the round among the three elements, since the ebb and flow of social life realizes the form of conflict in every possible combination of two members.

Extract 6:2

G Simmel: *The Sociology of Georg Simmel*, edited by K Wolff (1950, originally 1908) Free Press, Glencoe, Ill, pp 149–150

The non-partisanship that is required for mediation has one of two presuppositions. The third element is non-partisan either if he stands above the contrasting interests and opinions and is actually not concerned with them, or if he is equally concerned with both. The first case is the simpler of the two and involves fewest complications. In conflicts between English laborers and entrepreneurs, for instance, the non-partisan called in could be neither a laborer nor an entrepreneur. It is notable how decisively the separation of objective from personal elements in the conflict . . . is realized here. The idea is that the non-partisan is not attached by personal interest to the objective aspects of either party position. Rather, both come to be weighed by him as by a pure, impersonal intellect; without touching the subjective sphere. But the mediator must be subjectively interested in the persons or groups themselves who exemplify the contents of the quarrel which to him are merely theoretical, since otherwise he would not take over his function. It is, therefore, as if subjective interest set in motion a purely objective mechanism. It is the fusion of personal distance from the objective significance of the quarrel with personal interest in its subjective significance which characterizes the non-partisan position. This position is the more perfect, the more distinctly each of these two elements is developed and the more harmoniously, in its very differentiation, each cooperates with the other.

The situation becomes more complicated when the non-partisan owes his position, not to his neutrality, but to his equal participation in the interests in conflict. This case is frequent when a given individual belongs to two different interest groups, one local, and the other objective, especially occupational. In earlier times, bishops could sometimes intervene between the secular ruler of their diocese and the pope. The administrator who is thoroughly familiar with the special interests of his district, will be the most suitable mediator in the case of a collision between these special interests and the general interests of the state which employs him. The measure of the combination between impartiality and interest which is favorable to the mediation between two locally separate groups, is often found in persons that come from one of these groups but live with the other. The difficulty of positions of this kind in which the mediator may find himself, usually derives from the fact that his equal interests in both parties, that is, his inner equilibrium, cannot be definitely ascertained and is, in fact, doubted often enough by both parties.

Extract 6:3

P Gulliver: *Disputes and Negotiations: A Cross-Cultural Perspective* (1979) Academic Press, New York and London, pp 214–217

What a mediator can do, what he chooses to do, and what he is permitted to do by the disputing parties are all much affected by who he is in the particular context and why he is there at all. His relationship to the parties and to the issues in dispute and his position in the enveloping community are crucial variables in the triad. Some of the more common and generally significant statuses of mediators are briefly described subsequently. Concrete actuality may be more complex and less specific than the apparent clarity of the analytical types depicted. Therefore, they are not proposed as a watertight set of categories, nor are they altogether mutually exclusive. Rather, the intention is to emphasize particular characteristics that have a significant bearing on a mediator's participation. Some casual references are made to ethnographic examples for purposes of illustration.

The status of the mediator can initially be examined according to whether he is supposedly disinterested or acknowledged to be an interested party. By *disinterested* (or, alternatively, impartial) is meant that a mediator is not directly related to either disputing party and his own interests are not directly touched by the dispute or by possible outcomes. A disinterested status may derive from an institutionalized role in a society, such as the Nuer leopard-skin chief, a Pathan saint, or a professional agent of an established board of mediation on conciliation, as in some American states. Part of the person's role is an obligation and readiness to act as mediator as a result of his social and cultural distinction from disputants, their supporters, and interests. Alternatively, the disinterested status may derive from the context of the dispute and therefore, in a sense, it may be casual and transitory. Disputants may choose or be willing to accept someone of acknowledged prestige or ability who is not directly concerned with the issues and the potential outcome. He might be a distinguished elder, a socially eminent person, or one of recognized sagacity. The choice might, however, be some person who stands outside the structure of the society in some way – the 'stranger' whose interests are separate from the principal groups, categories, and relationships that constitute the community. Such a person has little or no extrinsic prestige or influence and by definition he is supposedly disinterested in the outcome. Moreover, he can perhaps be blamed by the parties for any disadvantages contained in the outcome. A fourth kind of avowedly disinterested mediator is the expert who can bring some sort of special knowledge and training to the negotiations: a lawyer, a technical specialist, a priest, or a genealogical expert.

In contrast, mediators may be quite clearly interested parties when their own interests make them concerned with the resolution of particular issues in dispute and with the disputants themselves. For example, the man who holds land adjacent to some disputed farmland may wish to know who his neighbor is to be, and with some urgency. He may have to coordinate with him over mutual access paths or a common irrigation channel. A tenant may wish to know to whom he should pay rent and from whom he can claim certain rights. Uncertainty can be disadvantageous or even downright harmful, so that such a person wants an early outcome so that he can get on with his own activities. He may not care much, if at all, what the outcome is so long as there is one; therefore he is acceptable as a mediator. Similarly, in international affairs, a country that might be affected if its neighbors were to go to war over their dispute might therefore act as mediator in order to prevent hostilities dangerous to it.

It can happen that a third party is not only interested in encouraging the resolution of a dispute but he is positively partial to one of the parties. Despite or even because of his known partiality, he may be acceptable as a mediator, though this may be as a last resort when negotiations appear to be heading for a breakdown or when it proves necessary to get them going at all. Elsewhere I have described an Ndendueli case with a partial mediator and a comparable case has been recorded in a Jordanian Arab village. Sometimes such a mediator emerges from among the members of one of the disputing parties as he perceives possibilities and needs for compromise that his principal is not yet willing to accept. He does not renounce his partiality altogether, but he is able to exert control over the communication and bargaining. An interesting example of obvious partiality comes from San Francisco. There the Labor Council and its Executive Committee – an association of local trade unions and clearly a pro-labor body – was able successfully to act as mediator of last resort when industrial negotiations were nearing breakdown and a strike was threatened. This intervention was institutionalized in practice with the approval of the local employers. Sometimes anyone is better than no one at all.

Another type of mediator may emerge in situations where the two disputing parties are involved in some network of relations so that there are people who are structurally intermediate between them; that is, more or less equally linked to both. For instance, there is the man who is kinsman to both, or a political or economic ally of both, or a member of a lineage collateral with the lineages of the disputants. The rationale here is that, being connected to both parties, such persons have divided loyalties and obligations and may therefore be tolerably acceptable to both. From the individual's point of view, he agrees to mediate because his interests are likely to be affected by the dispute and he seeks to protect them. He wishes to maintain his advantageous relations with both parties, and also with others in the same network, but this he finds difficult so long as they are in unresolved conflict. He therefore seeks to encourage and facilitate active negotiations and a speedy conclusion to the dispute. He also desires an outcome that damages as little as possible his own interests and his valued association with each disputant. But he may seize the opportunity to try to gain credit, prestige, and leadership and to improve his status with the parties.

However, the mediator can be in some sense a representative of a community to which both disputing parties belong: lineage, village, association, political or religious group. In that case, he is most likely to be a person of prestige, even a recognized leader, in that community, such as a member of the upper class or the headman in a traditional Chinese village. He may be a local politician, an administrative officer, a police officer, a lineage head. He acts as mediator in order to assist his fellow members of the community but also in order to influence and pressure them so as to restore peace and adequate working relations. He may take the opportunity to impress, both on the disputants and other members, the moral norms of the community and its common interests and needs. Although he can be helpful to the disputants, he commonly has the interests of the community, and perhaps his own particular interests in it, very much in mind. He may well be inclined to put those before the interests of the two parties. For instance, a quick settlement is often sought by such a mediator in the interests of the group or of its leading members. This can be at the expense of one or both parties if speed is given preference over a more genuine resolution of some important dispute. Apart from such intention, the mediator can take the opportunity to seek prestige or public attention by his efforts. He can use his temporary role to win advantage and reputation as against his competitors for influence in the group, as Ndendeuli big men sometimes did. There may be the opportunity to gain the indebtedness of one or both parties as a result of his services. In all this, the parties do not necessarily suffer. Often, however, their interests and preference are in some way distorted or disregarded, depending on the strength of the mediator's influence and manipulation and his own perceived interests at the time. Indeed, it might be that such a mediator chooses a divide-and-rule strategy. He could attempt to lead the disputants to an outcome that leaves the dispute essentially unsettled, thus weakening their relations with each other, dissipating their resources and enhancing his position, or that of his subgroup, within the community.

One way or another, then, it is highly probable that a person can and does gain advantages from taking the role of mediator. I suspect that the truly disinterested, impartial mediator is in fact rather rare. He may perhaps be quite impartial toward the two parties but be quite partial toward his own interests, sometimes at the expense of one or both disputants. We should maintain a healthy cynicism here and inquire what is in it for the man in the middle. Even the professional mediator who claims impartiality likes to gain a reputation for his ability and success as that is judged by his superiors; he may get an increase in salary, a promotion, or more interesting cases in the future. It seems evident that a Pathan saint, the conventional mediator between chiefs in Swat society in Pakistan, could gain prestige, land, and followers as the result of his successful mediation. An Ifugao go-between in the Philippines, and probably a Nuer leopard-skin chief, could acquire wealth and supporters in much the same way. Structural intermediaries, such as the kinsmen of both parties, have obvious interests to protect and foster.

Extract 6:4

M Palmer: 'The Revival of Mediation in the People's Republic of China: Extra-Judicial Mediation', in W E Butler (ed) *Yearbook on Socialist Legal Systems 1987* (1988) Transnational Books, New York, Dobbs Ferry, pp 244–252

In particular, mediation is generally expected to improve social stability and unity. Mediators are supposed not only to resolve disputes but also to prevent their occurrence. Mediators in contemporary China are important figures of social control who should be fully conversant with the detailed characteristics of local households in order that 'trouble situations' (*gehe*) may be 'nipped in the bud' and, as noted earlier, serious problems such as murder and suicide avoided. Mediators are expected to be able to get to the 'roots of a problem,' to 'formulate a medicine with which to treat the disease,' and to 'improve interpersonal relations' at their most fundamental level'. It is claimed, for example, that the revival of mediation has made significant inroads into the age-old problem of conflict between mother-in-law and daughter-in-law and that the collapse of mediation work during the Cultural Revolution had greatly exacerbated the tensions inherent in this relationship – although in this connection it should be pointed out that other reports indicate that additional factors may have been at work in smoothing this often tense social tie, for in some urban areas increased matrilocal residence is said to have significantly diminished mother-in-law – daughter-in-law conflicts.

It is in the context of dispute prevention too that the symbiotic nature of relations between the mediation committees and the local people's courts is especially stressed. In return for offering guidance to the mediation committees the people's courts benefit from the work of mediators both in reducing the number of cases that reach the courts in general and in skilfully dealing with intra-family and other often-intractable disputes in particular. For example, when the Chengde County Court in Hebei Province was revived in 1973, it was so overwhelmed with cases that the judges had to demand a similar revival in mediation work in order to stem the flood of litigation. The traditional aphorisms of 'family disputes are too difficult even for upright officials to handle,' 'one lawsuit means many years of hatred,' and so on are once more relied on in order to encourage disputants and local officials to allow quarrels to be handled by mediation committees rather than by the local courts. The emphasis on close links between courts and committees is now regarded as so crucial in some parts of China that a specific slogan 'adjudication and mediation are jointly stressed' has been coined in order to impress upon local residents and officials the value of combining both approaches. This link is more generally viewed as one element in an overall system of sociopolitical control at the local level, characterized as *zonghezhili* or 'comprehensive control,' in which mediation committees are expected to play their part in strengthening local administration by maintaining close links and cooperating closely with other important local institutions, such as public security, the police, and so on.

An additional but related function of mediation which is explicitly emphasized in the Chinese legal press is promotion of the recent revolution in China's rural economy. In the early 1980s the PRC commenced a substantial reorganization of agriculture in which the collective management of land and working of fields were replaced by a system of individual household responsibility for farm management. The new approach has also involved much greater tolerance of inequalities of wealth, as indicated by the coining of the slogan '*rang yixie nongmin xian fuqilai*' (permit some farmers to become wealthy first). Although this policy has been manifestly successful in expanding output, it has at the same time introduced a number of novel problems. Mediation is expected significantly to reduce them, not only by helping to ensure continuity of production and undertaking certain tasks of legal administration but also by protecting the rights and interests of specialized and contract households. In particular, mediators are regarded as being crucial in preventing in the countryside the spread of 'envy' (*hongyanbing*: literally, 'red-eye disease'). With the rapid expansion of market forces in rural areas some households – in particular, the specialized households – have been able to earn a great deal more than the majority and the resulting inequalities have generated discontent among those who remain committed to a more collectivist economy, such as cadres still influenced by the 'leftist' ideals of the Cultural Revolution and those who have not been able to find success under the new system. In other words, mediators function to promote general 'understanding' and acceptance of rich rural households, thereby promoting class harmony – the very activity for which mediation was criticized during the Cultural Revolution.

In this context it is interesting to note that Vice-Premier Wan Li is one of the strongest advocates of both greater commercialization of the economy and rapid expansion of mediation work – as well as local pacts, of which more will be said later. The protection of wealthy households is also an aspect of the broader duty of mediators generally to safeguard the constitutional rights of citizens. Mediation work should protect the basic principles of legal equality and linkage of rights and duties now enshrined in Article 33 of the 1982 Constitution which affirms that 'all citizens of the PRC are equal before the law. Every citizen enjoys the rights and at the same time must perform the duties prescribed by the Constitution and the law.' As we saw in Example 3, in which factory worker Li refused to support his ageing father on the ground that this constituted fatherly exploitation of the son, one of the important constitutional rights is that of elderly parents to be given care and financial support by their children in return for the gifts of life and nurture into adulthood.

The Chinese attempt to develop mediation in the post-Mao era is also informed by a desire to utilize mediators as disseminators of legal knowledge. In most socialist systems the legal institutions are typically assigned important didactic functions. Moreover, as we have already noted, a crucial feature of the mediation of disputes in the PRC is the 'education' of disputants in order that they may understand better the relevant areas of law and policy and thereby improve their future conduct. At the same time, the current leadership regards ignorance of the law as such a serious problem in post-Mao China that mediators must help to alleviate the situation by acting as 'propaganda officers' and promoting campaigns such as the current drive to 'popularize the law' (*pufa yundong*).

Ignorance of the law is seen as emanating not only from low levels of literacy and the traditional antipathy towards law and government but also from the adverse impact of radical 'leftist' policies of earlier periods which led to 'law blindness' (*famang*) among, in particular, rural cadres. The work of mediators in promoting legal knowledge is also intended to assist with juvenile delinquency. The Cultural Revolution and the interregnum that followed left many young people with a very limited appreciation of the law and, as a result, they have become 'juvenile delinquents' (*shizu qingnian*). In addition, certain households referred to as *gehehu* (literally, estranged households) or *changnaohu* (literally, noisy households) need their comprehension of law and policy improved in order to reform themselves.

More generally, mediators are expected to play an important role in improving social morality by strengthening 'spiritual civilization.' Improving spiritual civilization is regarded as being closely linked to the general policy of combining mediation and prevention and involves a wide variety of devices designed to encourage social conformity. For example, in many areas both local and factory mediation committees are responsible for encouraging the 'five-good families' among local residents and factory personnel so that more families live in harmony, enjoy friendly relations with their neighbors, practise family planning, properly socialize their children, and maintain their residences in good sanitary order. Mediators are also responsible for combatting the twin influences of feudal superstition and bourgeois values. Examples of the former include such unfortunate practices as 'child betrothals' and adoption of heirs; examples of the latter include the actions of spouses who recklessly seek divorces.

Another significant element in this area of mediation work is the promotion of local pacts (*xianggui minyue; gongyue*), the importance of which Deng Xiaoping first stressed at the CCP's Eighth Party Congress in 1956. These pacts are operated in both urban and rural areas although greater emphasis is placed on the latter. This aspect of mediation work will be considered more fully later in this chapter. Suffice it to say here that reliance on these pacts for purposes of local social control is considered to be a significant aspect of the legal system that further demonstrates the cultural distinctiveness of post-Mao legal developments in socialist China – broadly similar institutions can be identified in late Qing times.

These pacts constitute a limited form of delegated law-making and administration, and this reflects another important feature of people's mediation work in post-Mao China, namely, the role of mediation organizations as democratic institutions. Mediation committees are 'mass organizations' intended to enable local people to exercise 'self-management' (*renmin ziji quanli*) – that is, to handle disputes themselves and by means of the pacts to introduce a framework of local rules. In a number of contexts these rights are described as *minzhu* or democratic. Some element of representation in this democratic system is provided by Article 5 of the General Rules on Mediation which explicitly provides for the election of mediators: in practice, the often unpaid or poorly-remunerated position of mediator is not greatly sought after. Thus 'elections' to mediation committees in many case appears to consist of little more than requests by the chairman of local residents' and village committees to mediators to continue with their good work. Accordingly, a more important democratic aspect of mediation is to be found in the actual processes of dispute resolution, that is, the emphasis on the voluntary nature of mediation. This is specifically referred to as a democratic right and is characterized in terms of the willingness of the parties to participate in mediation, mediators' reliance on methods of persuasion rather than force and coercion, the rule that extra-judicial mediation agreements are not binding on the disputants, and the provision that parties must not be prevented from bringing their cases to court on the ground that they have not allowed their dispute to be mediated.

This characterization of the democratic functions of mediation must, however, be qualified in a number of respects. We have already noted that elections tend to be perfunctory. In addition, it must be remembered that local mediation committees operate not only under the guidance of the courts but also the leadership of the Party. People's mediation work is intended to lighten the work of both courts and Party officials. The lack of autonomy of mediation *vis-à-vis* the Party is also suggested by a number of factors: the Party has often been instrumental in establishing mediation committees; many mediators are Party members; close links are maintained between local cadres and Party functionaries on the one hand and mediation committees on the other; the expectation that mediation committees serve as channels of information for the Party; and the requirement that mediation committees uphold and promote not only the law but also Party policies.

In this context the official 'democratic' model is clearly in need of refinement. As emphasized elsewhere, in the operation of family law in the PRC many traditional patriarchal values continue to hold sway. In general, the Party does not approve of divorce, and in urban areas especially marital instability forms a very significant portion of the disputes handled by the local mediation committees. However, participation in extra-judicial mediation is in law not a condition precedent for bringing a divorce petition nor for court acceptance of such a petition. Moreover, in this context it is important to recall that the provisions of Article 6 in the Code of Civil Procedure specify merely that in civil cases 'mediation should be stressed,' and that this wording was introduced because it was felt the alternative guideline 'give priority to mediation' overemphasized the value of mediation. Nevertheless, in extra-judicial mediation of cases of marital instability mediators are *still* urged to 'give priority to mediation' in accordance with the Party's policies on marriage. Handbooks on family law continue to advise mediators to regard with suspicion 'bourgeois liberal values' as manifested in irresponsible conduct in marriage and to impress upon unhappy couples the virtues of reconciliation. In addition, the general impression given by the relevant literature is that in practice it is exceedingly difficult for unhappy spouses to avoid the attentions of extra-judicial mediators, especially as the latter are urged by the leadership to make prevention of conflict and quarrelling an important feature of their work. For example, in the municipality of Beijing a number of factory mediation committees have adopted a policy of the 'five necessary visits' in cases where domestic problems are affecting work performance, and this includes compulsory visits in instances of marital and other family disputes.

The ability of mediators to achieve reconciliation of the partners to unhappy marriages is remarkable. In one county in Liaoning Province a female mediator-cum-Party member has in recent years apparently proved so skillful in her handling of such problems that she has successfully resolved no fewer than twenty-two of the twenty-four cases of serious marital discord that have come to her attention. Similarly, there are reports of mediation committees achieving very high rates of success in their handling of cases of this nature: the mediation committee of the Inner Mongolian State-owned Second Machinery Plant, for example, reconciled no less than ninety-five couples in a total of 117 divorce disputes. In addition there are numerous cases reported in the legal press which indicate the great lengths to which mediation committees may go in order to prevent divorce. Thus:

Example 6: 'Soldier Jiang and his wife are reconciled.'
A young couple from Xiamen in Fujian Province were having trouble with their marriage. Jiang, the husband, served in the PLA elsewhere in China while the wife, Huang, stayed at home to look after the children. On the last two occasions that Jiang had returned on leave he found that his wife had moved back to live with her parents. She refused to return to the conjugal home and requested a divorce. Although members of the relevant units and the two parties were all agreed on a divorce, matters were not allowed to proceed. Questions of divorce are not just questions for the parties alone but also constitute a serious social problem. If divorce is treated too lightly it will bring utmost regret in later life and have deleterious consequences for both the parties and society. As a result, the mediators decided to approach the dispute very carefully in order to ascertain whether or not the couple's feelings for one another had really been bankrupted . . . they arranged for

a mediator who had hitherto not dealt with the case to talk to the couple in the mediation offices. The husband seemed very sad. The unhappy spouses were given tickets to see a film and a mediator also went along to the cinema in order to observe their interaction. The couple's behavior showed that they still retained a great deal of mutual affection, and the mediators therefore investigated the matter further. Among the real problems underlying the case were squabbling between the couple's parents, accommodation shortage, and the husband's absence when serving in the army. The parents were therefore counselled, a new room containing new furniture was made available for the couple in Jiang's household, and arrangements made for a mediator to visit Huang when her husband was away from home in order to help her overcome problems of loneliness.

As a result, the marriage was saved. In this case, like many other mediated marriage disputes reported in the legal press, the local committee worked together as a team in order to bring the couple together. It is my general impression that difficult marital disputes are rather more likely than other types of cases to be handled by mediation committees or groups than left in the hands of individual mediators, so that maximum pressure is placed on unhappy couples in order to get them to rethink their divorce proposals.

Thus the general policy seems quite clear. One of the most important goals of mediation work in post-Mao China, especially in urban areas, is direct intervention in the conjugal relations of unhappy spouses. Mediation is a highly effective method of resisting divorce and its disruptive effects. The education and ideological work sessions in the mediation of troubled marriages are clearly designed to reduce antagonisms between spouses and to ensure reconciliation. In practice, the emphasis is not on the parties' rights of voluntary participation and freedom from coercion but rather on restoring domestic harmony. This may be seen as reflecting a more general tension in mediation policies between the aim of promoting social stability on the one hand and service as a democratic institution on the other. When the two tendencies conflict, however, democratic principles such as voluntary participation are subordinated to the political priority of maintaining order and discipline. Although mediators are generally encouraged to handle disputes in a prompt and speedy fashion, in divorce cases procrastination leading to imposed reconciliation often seems to be the effective rule.

Extract 6:5

P Gulliver: *Disputes and Negotiations: A Cross-Cultural Perspective* (1979) Academic Press, New York and London, p 227

A special case occurs when the mediator acts as *go-between*, with the parties physically separated and not in direct communication. A go-between may be no more than a straight messenger, although this tends to be unlikely because of his obvious opportunities to control and add to or detract from the information he carries. In conveying messages to and fro, he can change their content, emphasis, and strength. He can usually add his own interpretation, with or without informing the recipient. He can add new messages and he can offer his opinion. Each party is highly dependent on him and often has little means of knowing just how far the go-between is manipulating the information. A go-between may be passive, a chairman, or an enunciator, but he tends to become a prompter or leader, especially if negotiations are going poorly or if, for his own reasons, he wishes deliberately to affect the outcome.

Extract 6:6

P Gulliver: *Disputes and Negotiations: A Cross-Cultural Perspective* (1979) Academic Press, New York and London, pp 200–225

For the purposes of exposition and clarification, mediators' roles can conveniently be described on a continuum representing the range of strengths of intervention. This continuum runs something like this: from virtual passivity, to 'chairman,' to 'enunciator,' to 'prompter,' to 'leader,' to virtual arbitrator. These terms are not proposed as principally typological but rather as useful indices along that continuum. Actual roles and associated strategies can be displayed as more or less resembling, more or less near to, one or other of these indices. This, of course, states nothing about the effectiveness of the strategies. In the following brief survey some examples are given as illustrations. Comprehensiveness is not possible and would in any case be excessively tedious. Rather, the intention is to indicate something of the range of strategic roles of mediators.

By his very presence, a quite *passive mediator* can encourage more positive communication and interaction between the parties, stimulating the continuation or the renewal of the exchange of information:

> A wise mediator once said that the mere presence of an outsider in collective bargaining negotiations, regardless of anything he says or does, brings about a change in the behavior of the parties at the bargaining table. This is true enough, and where the parties are hopelessly deadlocked any change in behavior is presumably for the better.

Because he is there, the parties are often constrained to observe minimal courtesy to each other, to reduce personal invective, and to listen and respond with some relevance. A party may feel it necessary to explain and justify his case, directly or indirectly, to the mediator because he is there at all or perhaps because he is perceived in some sense as a 'generalized other.' Thus the parties restate their arguments, perhaps rethinking them, and they may find the opportunity of starting or restarting to learn.

Deliberate passivity has been an effective strategy on occasion, for example, for some American industrial mediators. They attend a meeting between the two parties, sit and say nothing and seek to show no particular reaction to what is said and done. One mediator related that he silently made voluminous notes on the proceedings while offering no comments whatever. Another has told how he chain smoked, slumped in his chair, with his eyes carefully kept away from the negotiators. I have witnessed a similar performance by an Ndendeuli mediator, although in that instance passivity seemed to come from a disinclination to become involved and committed rather than from a deliberate strategy to encourage more positive interaction between the parties. Yet the effect was much the same. Deliberately or not, the strategy can be effective when an impasse arises because positive information is not being exchanged or evident possibilities explored as a result. One major reason for each impasse is interpersonal hostility between members of the two parties, accompanied perhaps by an intentional policy of ad hominem abuse. Sometimes a party attempts to frustrate negotiations by such behavior and by refusal to give information and engage in exchange. The mediator's presence may prevent continuation of these kinds of actions. However, a mediator is not always a free agent who is able to choose his own strategy; he can be more or less forced into some line of action by the disputing parties. Thus passivity may be partly the result of the parties effectively denying the mediator active participation. This occurs, for instance, where the mediator has been thrust upon them and they seek to ignore him in their intensive preoccupation with each other or perhaps in collusion to reject third-party interference. Yet even in such cases, the mediator's presence can still result in some change in the parties' interaction. Indeed, such collusion or the recognition of at least some common interest may provide a new starting point.

A more active participation by a mediator produces a role something like that of *chairman*. That is, in addition to the possible influence of his mere presence, he keeps order and tends to direct procedure. His actions are tolerated and accepted because he can give suggestions for order and coherence that engender coordination. At a minimum, this may help to prevent a threatening breakdown of communication and movement. Schelling has illustrated this vividly:

> When there is no apparent focal point for agreement . . . [a mediator] can create one by his own power to make a dramatic suggestion. The bystander who jumps into an intersection and begins to direct traffic at an impromptu traffic jam is conceded the power to discriminate among cars by being able to offer a sufficient increase in efficiency to benefit even the cars most discriminated against; his directions have only the power of suggestion, but coordination requires the common acceptance of some source of suggestion.

An additional implication here is that the mediator who is once accepted and found useful as coordinator may be more readily acceptable thereafter when further difficulties arise. He has shown his value and may be more trusted and listened to.

The chairman role can be extended beyond this. The mediator may announce and reiterate points of agreement, giving emphasis to them: for example, agreement by the parties to ignore an issue or to define it in a certain way or to settle it and remove it from further contention. More positively, the mediator may make procedural suggestions: to settle the immediate or overall agenda, to have separate caucus meetings for each party or a conclave between principals, to introduce new evidence or witnesses. He may actually take over procedural organization such as arranging the time and place of further meetings, calling for breaks in a particular session or curbing excessive interruptions, irrelevancies, and repetitiveness. He may suggest new or renewed concentration of focus where information and attention have become diffused or where there are problems of overabundant information.

In all this, the mediator may continue to be impartial to either party, seeking only to improve coordination of exchange. But this kind of strategy offers opportunities to influence the direction of negotiations and to favor one party, or to push toward the quickest outcome available more or less irrespective of merits. There are distinct possibilities for manipulation. A party may be unaware of what is being done or he may feel constrained, even relieved, to accept it rather than face deadlock or extended argument of indeterminate result.

A mediator goes beyond the role of keeping order and facilitating procedure – perhaps ignoring that kind of action – when he acts as *enunciator* of rules and norms relevant to issues in negotiation. This can take the form of clarification and emphasis of general rules and norms or the identification of particular ones relevant to the context. The intention is to remind the parties of what they have temporarily forgotten or neglected, which might provide a basis from which to move toward agreement. It reminds the parties, too, of the moral community to which both belong; and it articulates what may have been left unclear and obstructive between the parties. For example, in an Arusha inheritance dispute, a senior co-member of the disputants' lineage stated at successive times during the negotiations: 'We are all one lineage with one ancestor,' 'Brothers should not quarrel,' 'Property should be shared equally,' 'Unmarried men have more need of cattle than those who have married,' and 'irrigated land is more valuable than other land but not twice as valuable.'

The choice of norms, the particular juncture when they are expressed, the way this is done and kind of emphasis given must – often quite purposefully – affect the learning process. It may be done impartially or at least with that intent, or it may be deliberately partial and manipulative. Enunciation directs and interprets the information exchanged, influencing the perceptions, preferences, and demands of the parties and implying certain lines of coordination and agreement. The parties are not bound to accept the norms so propounded nor to adjust their expectations and demands accordingly. Yet the party who has been denying some rule is likely to be put at a disadvantage when the mediator in effect supports his opponent. In any case, the parties may welcome the clarification of some rule that offers some prospect of progress.

Sometimes a mediator is expected to act as enunciator: the respected elder, the ritual expert, the lawyer. In a sense he represents the wider community and the rules it embraces. He is mediator because he has special expertise and prestige. He is not, as such, making judgments for he still leaves it – as he has to – to the two parties to follow up the implications of the norms and their mode of application to the particular circumstances of the dispute. Of course, some of the issues in dispute may be scarcely susceptible to normative assessment: for instance, the level of wages, the degree of respect owed to a person, the division of blame between husband and wife, the weight of allegedly extenuating circumstances. On the other hand, even if the enunciated norms are fairly specific, the parties still have to reach an agreed outcome. Moreover, a party may deny the validity of the specified rule or he may intend to ignore it. Thus, enunciation of norms and rules may be sign posting, offering possibilities to the parties, or it may be more manipulative than that as a mediator carefully emphasizes certain directions and ignores others. He may favor one of the parties in this manner but he does not dictate. His role is limited. At most he is concerned with assisting in establishing some rules of the game within which the parties can seek some actual outcome.

In the role of *prompter*, a mediator makes a more positive contribution, although his suggestions remain tentative and limited. He does not seek to insist on his opinions, at least not overtly, or to take control of the negotiations. Rather, he attempts to clarify information and interpretation and to encourage coordination between the parties. For example, the mediator as prompter asks for a restatement of a party's argument or of particular demands and requests further information in support of them. He might himself restate an argument so as to bring out the principal points in order to obtain reaction. Typical prompter's statements are 'Am I right in saying that your position is thus and thus?' 'As I understand it, you are saying this and this.' He may realize that one party just does not apprehend the meaning or significance of what the other party is saying and so he attempts an interpretation. He persuades a party to respond directly to the opponent's points, trying tactfully to stem irrelevancies and to dissipate smoke screens. He seeks to encourage the parties to talk about the same thing at the same time, to follow a relevant pattern of exchange. He attempts to gain and maintain focus on what he perceives to be the chief priorities of each party so that each can be clearer about what these are and their implications for himself and his opponent. The prompter may in this way be able to discover and help reveal a viable range for some issues within which both parties would be prepared to settle. Such a viable range is often obscured by bluffing demands and denials, by inflated expectations and by the reasonable unwillingness of a party to commit himself immediately to something that he would, in the end, prefer rather than get nothing at all. Arguments can become so diffuse that concentration and perspective may have been lost. In any case, where the variety of issues, or the range for particular issues, is wide, the mediator's careful questioning and suggestions may produce some acceptable and useful focal point around which further exchange can concentrate. This suggestion of a focal point, or an area of salience, may be particularly valuable where there are no accepted standards for assessing the range – say, of honor – and when items are incommensurable – say, chalk and cheese. The prompter may be able to suggest packages of issues to be considered together where trading among them seems feasible.

The strategy of the prompter is probably most effective at the beginning of Phase 4 of negotiations, when differences are being narrowed and coordination developed, and in Phase 5, the preliminaries to final bargaining. Parties can find themselves in set positions from which it is difficult to emerge in order to make concessions to the opponent. They may be arguing past each other. They may be genuinely unable to see where there is common ground or how to proceed at all. False fronts may have been so thoroughly developed as the result of the earlier tactics that the parties have become affected by their own extreme positions and bluffs, to the point of losing perspective about their expectations. They deceive, or at least influence, themselves, as well as each other by their own rhetoric. The prompting mediator may be able to cut through the undergrowth or to indicate to the parties how this can be done. He does this not so much by offering his opinion as by orienting the parties' attention and efforts so that coordination becomes possible.

In the role of *leader*, a mediator more or less directly injects his own opinions and recommendations. He offers evaluation of the information from, and the preferences and demands of, either party. He may be able to suggest or endorse the basis for agreement on an issue or propose a package deal. Sometimes these are suggestions that the mediator believes a party would like to make, or at least have discussed, but the party himself fears to raise these suggestions lest they seem to indicate weakness or too great a readiness to concede, or because the implications are unclear. Thus a party may be relieved that the mediator says what he himself cannot. Coming from the mediator (even perhaps at the private instigation of the party) such a suggestion can be ignored or repudiated should it seem threatening as a result of the opponent's reaction to it. The party is not committed by the mediator's suggestion, as he might be were he to make it himself, but he can take advantage of it should that appear advantageous. An American mediator has called this 'trying on for size'.

Extract 6:7

G Simmel: *The Sociology of Georg Simmel*, edited by K Wolff (1950, originally 1908) Free Press, Glencoe, Ill, p 151

> This suggests the second form of accommodation by means of an impartial third ele-ment, namely, arbitration. As long as the third properly operates as a mediator, the final termination of the conflict lies exclusively in the hands of the parties themselves. But when they choose an arbitrator, they relinquish this final decision. They project, as it were, their will to conciliation, and this will becomes personified in the arbitrator. He thus gains a special impressiveness and power over the antagonistic forces. The volun-tary appeal to an arbitrator, to whom they submit from the beginning, presupposes a greater subjective confidence in the objectivity of judgment than does any other form of decision. For, even in the state tribunal, it is only the action of the complainant that results from confidence in just decision, since the complainant considers the decision that is favorable to him the just decision. The defendant, on the other hand, must enter the suit whether or not he believes in the impartiality of the judge. But arbitration results only when both parties to the conflict have this belief. This is the principle which sharply differentiates mediation from arbitration; and the more official the act of conciliation, the more punctiliously is this differentiation observed.

This passage also maps out the essential difference between the arbitrator and the judge, namely, that in arbitration *both* must agree the principle of resort to an umpire. This and other differences are dealt with in greater detail in Chapter Seven.

B: The Mediator in the Negotiation Process: The Processual Shape of Mediation

What an intervener should be doing will depend on how her or his role is con-ceptualised. Clearly, the polar models we outlined specify quite different tasks for the mediator – one prioritises the role of facilitator of communications; the other requires skills in information retrieval, and requires expert diagnosis and prescription. Henderson (1996) and Boulle (1996) propose classification of the mediator's task under three broad heads, going to communications (assisting in the conveyance of messages), procedure (structuring the session and providing norms of procedure) and substance (providing specialised information and advice). But even if we confine mediation to facilitating communication, we can see a spectrum of interventions, depending upon how active a role is attempted. Our sense is that most mediators would give some help in identifying the issues and making sure these were communicated effectively and assimilated. But there would be differences of view as to what involvement might be appropriate in identifying and reviewing options, let alone pressurising parties towards what the mediator might see as an appropriate outcome.

Beyond these generalisations, if mediation is identified as a process auxiliary to negotiation, identification of the different things the mediator may aspire to do is best examined by thinking about the processual shape of negotiations. Throughout the process of negotiation, the primary and undisputed role must be in providing help with communications, enabling the parties to engage in the process of information exchange and learning that lies at the heart of decision-making by negotiation (see Chapter Five). Here, the mediator is especially important in facilitating the potentially difficult transition from one phase of negotiations to another, however those phases might be conceptualised. Beyond those generalisations, the nature of the mediator's intervention may best be understood in the context of different phases in the negotiation process.

The Arena

For negotiations to take place, messages must be exchanged by the parties. The mediator may facilitate this communication, even make it possible, by acting as a go-between, providing a conduit for the information exchanged. In circumstances where the parties are distant from each other, or seriously at odds, there may be no face-to-face meeting at all, and communication may be achieved exclusively through the mediator. But in most cases the ambition of the mediator will be to establish a secure arena in which the parties can communicate directly with each other. In schematic terms, even where the parties are present together with the mediator, two modes of communication must be distinguished, direct and through the intervening third party:

(1)   Direct communications

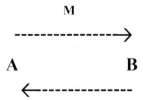

(2)   Indirect communications through the intervening third party

```
            M
            Λ
           /  \
          /    \
         /      \
        A        B
```

Obviously, these differences have implications both for the quality of the communication between the parties, and for the degree of control that the mediator exercises
over the negotiations.

While part of the mediator's role at this preliminary stage will be to provide
an arena in the physical sense, the role extends indispensably to creating a general
climate conducive to, and supportive of, negotiations. One practical way to achieve
this is by making sure some basic ground rules are acknowledged and followed. The
most rudimentary negotiations require *some* normative understandings about the
conditions of exchange. In many cases these will be shared, even taken for granted
by the parties, and require no restatement by the mediator. But in others, a central
part of the mediator's role will be the provision and guarantee of the normative
framework relating to such fundamental matters as turn-taking in communication
and physical restraint.

This dimension of mediation is captured by Fuller (1971: 325) when he identifies
'the central quality of mediation' as lying in 'its capacity to reorientate the parties
toward each other, not by imposing rules on them, but by helping them to achieve a
new and shared perception of their relationship, a perception that will redirect their
attitudes toward one another'. In bringing this about 'the primary quality of the
mediator . . . is not to propose rules to the parties and to secure their acceptance of
them, but to induce the mutual trust and understanding that will enable the parties
to work out their own rules' (1971: 326). In Extract 6.8 below, Baruch Bush (1989)
further elaborates on this central feature of the mediator's role.

The Issues as Perceived by the Parties

Once the parties are in communication, the primary task of the mediator must be
to make sure that the issues as they respectively see them are both clearly articulated
and heard by the other side. Many mediated negotiations will not proceed beyond
this stage, either because this primary exchange reveals that the 'issues' involved
are no more than misunderstandings as to respective positions, or because one
or other of the parties concludes on the basis of the information made available
that no basis for negotiation is present. But until the positions and goals of the

parties are articulated and communicated, subsequent stages in the process cannot move forward; so it is an uncontested part of the mediator's role to facilitate this.

Forming an Agenda

Once the positions and goals of the respective parties have been identified and put on the table, they have to decide which of these can be the subject of joint decision-making and then order the chosen issues into an agenda. The mediator may play a central role in this process of selection, sorting and prioritisation.

Identification and Evaluation of Options

It appears common ground among commentators on mediation (for example, Douglas, 1957; 1962; Stenelo, 1972; Gulliver, 1979) that the ensuing stage, during which the boundaries of the field are explored and central issues brought into focus, is often one of turbulence. Here the mediator plays a critical role managing this turbulence and in assisting the transition from a mood of antagonism to one in which co-operative decision-making can take place. At the same time any mediator will need to ensure that the options as the parties see them are identified and explored. At the stage where options come to be identified and evaluated, the opportunity arises for the mediator to intervene in a manner that goes beyond facilitating communication, making professional judgments and tendering advice on the substance of the dispute. Opinions will differ as to whether this more extensive role is appropriate, as to how far mediatory and advisory roles may safely be combined.

Bargaining

In the bargaining phase of negotiations, two fundamental issues as to the scope of the mediator's intervention arise. First, as in the preceding phase, there must be the question of whether it is part of the mediator's role to identify and evaluate potential components of exchange, bringing to bear outside professional expertise. Second is the question of how far it is appropriate for the mediator to go in attempting to off-set imbalances of power resources enjoyed by the respective disputants (see pp 200 et seq below).

Towards Settlement

In moving towards the stage of settlement, the question is again posed as to the extent to which an active advisory role is compatible with mediation. Is it a proper part of the mediator's role to identify the settlement that seems, in his or her professional judgment, the most appropriate to the parties' case; or should the mediator allow the parties to construct their own solution, unassisted as to what the *substance* of that solution should be?

Formulating Agreement

A further opportunity arises for an active role on the part of the mediator in formulating and arranging ritual affirmation of the outcome reached by the parties. In many instances a central element in this phase will be the skilled achievement of reducing the agreement reached to written form.

Implementation

As we noted in Chapter Five, freely agreed solutions almost by definition have something in them for all negotiating parties and should therefore be self-enforcing. But there may in some cases be a continuing role for the mediator in helping to arrange implementation, and in facilitating further negotiation where implementation proves problematic. Some contemporary mediation schemes build this element of 'monitoring' into the service that is provided.

In formulating an overall processual shape for mediation in this way, we adhere primarily to Gulliver's elegant model of negotiation introduced in Chapter Five, modified in the ways discussed there. This shape emphasises both the continuing and the changing roles of the mediator as negotiations proceed. A continuing element lies in maintaining secure communications; new roles emerge with the arrival of successive phases of the negotiations. This processual shape also emphasises another primary challenge in any successful mediation: the skilled task of moving the parties across the often difficult terrain between one processual phase and the next.

Extract 6:8

R A B Bush: 'Efficiency and Protection, or Empowerment and Recognition?: The Mediator's Role and Ethical Standards in Mediation' (1989) 41 *Florida Law Review* 253, pp 266–270

> The basis for a sounder conception of the mediator's role lies in examining what mediation *can* do that other processes cannot. In other words, what important powers or capacities are unique to mediation that are not found to the same degree, if at all, in other methods of dispute resolution? The mediator's role should then be to act in ways that fulfill these unique capacities.
>
> Thoughtful mediation theorists and practitioners have given much consideration to identifying mediation's unique powers. In their comments, two points consistently are expressed regarding the capacities of the mediation process. The first special power of mediation, and what some call '[t]he overriding feature and . . . value of mediation,' is that 'it is a consensual process that seeks self-determined resolutions.' Mediation places the substantive outcome of the dispute within the control and determination of the parties themselves; it frees them from relying on or being subjected to the opinions and standards of outside 'higher authorities,' legal or otherwise. Further, mediation not only allows the parties to set their own standards for an acceptable solution, it also requires them to search for solutions that are within their own capacity to effectuate. In other words, the parties themselves set the standards, and the parties themselves marshall the

actual resources to resolve the dispute. When agreement is reached, the parties have designed and implemented their own solution to the problem. Even when the parties do not reach an agreement, they experience the concrete possibility, to be more fully realized in other situations, that they can control their own circumstances. They discover that they need not be wholly dependent on outside institutions, legal or otherwise, to solve their problems. I call this the empowerment function of mediation: its capacity to encourage the parties to exercise autonomy, choice, and self-determination.

Some authorities explicitly recognize empowerment as a unique value of mediation, while others do so implicitly. For example, the value of empowerment certainly is one of the implied premises of Professor Stulberg's cogent argument against requiring mediators to control the 'fairness' or 'efficiency' of agreements. Concern for empowerment also underlies what could appear to be a distinct view of the special power of mediation, which stresses its capacity to 'foster unique and creative solutions that respond to the parties' needs.' While this could be seen as a separate power of mediation, I believe that its value ultimately is connected to the concern for individual empowerment. That is, self-determination and empowerment are furthered through outcomes that are designed by and for the parties, rather than outcomes designed by and (at least in part) for outsiders. Mediated outcomes empower parties by responding to them as unique individuals with particular problems, rather than as depersonalized representatives of general problems faced by classes of actors or by society as a whole.

The second special power of mediation was described classically by Professor Lon Fuller: 'The central quality of mediation [is] its capacity to reorient the parties to each other . . . by helping them to achieve a new and shared perception of their relationship, a perception that will redirect their attitudes and dispositions toward one another.' What Fuller describes here is not just a technique to produce agreements, but an inherently valuable accomplishment uniquely attainable through mediation. Fuller sees mediation as evoking in each party recognition and acknowledgement of, and some degree of understanding and empathy for, the other party's situation, even though their interests and positions may remain opposed. Of course, such mutual recognition often will help produce concrete accommodations and an ultimate agreement. But even when it does not, evoking recognition is itself an accomplishment of enormous value: the value of escaping our alienated isolation and rediscovering our common humanity, even in the midst of bitter division. Professor Riskin observes accordingly that one of the great values of mediation is that it can 'encourage the kind of dialogue that would help . . . [the disputants experience] a perspective of caring and interconnection.' Others also have stressed this special power of mediation to 'humanize' us to one another, to translate between us, and to help us recognize each other as fellows even when we are in conflict. I call this the recognition function of mediation.

C: The Late Twentieth Century Re-Institutionalisation of Mediation

Introduction

The revival of institutionalised mediation as a widely approved route to decision-making – in many respects an extraordinary and unexpected turn of events – is in an immediate sense realised through three closely linked developments. The first of these can be loosely described as the arrival of the 'new professionals' in dispute resolution. These new specialist groups have emerged over the last two decades, offering services which compete – even if only indirectly – with those provided by lawyers. The new professionals have presented mediation as promising a 'third way' between external, hierarchically imposed decision and representation by legal specialists. But the contemporary prominence of mediation – and the wider ADR movement of which the revival of mediation forms a part – is as much attributable to concurrent, independent initiatives within the courts and on the part of lawyers.

As mediators have consolidated their position as an autonomous professional group, judges in common law jurisdictions have at the same time re-presented themselves in a new primary role as sponsors of settlement, directly encouraging facilitative interventions in the vicinity of their courts and themselves acting in mediatory roles. The arrival of 'the new professionals', and the concurrent transformations in civil justice, predictably led to defensive movements of recovery on the part of the lawyers that have included laying claim to mediation as part of legal practice. These two latter strands are examined further in Chapters Seven and Eight.

Under the contemporary re-institutionalisation of mediation, emphasis has primarily been placed on the objective of *dispute resolution*, facilitating joint decision-making in the turbulent context generated by a dispute. But more ambitious objectives have subsequently begun to emerge. First, as a logical extension of the dispute resolution role, the potential of the non-aligned facilitator in assisting with the construction and management of transactions is being developed. This form of intervention now extends to the continuous monitoring of complex transactions with a view to pre-empting the cost and delay of disputes had these been allowed to arise.

More ambitious, even grandiose, has been a strand of theory and practice represented by 'transformative' mediation that claims to lead mediation beyond its primary dispute resolution role. Adherents of transformative mediation distance themselves from what they diminishingly refer to as 'the problem-solving' tradition in mediation, claiming to help bring about a paradigmatic shift from an 'individualist' to a 'relational' world-view. For the transformative mediator, 'disputes can be viewed *not* as problems at all but as opportunities for moral growth and transformation' (Bush and Folger, 1994: 81 et seq).

Extract 6:9

R A Baruch Bush and J P Folger: *The Promise of Mediation: Responding to Conflict Through Empowerment and Recognition* (1994) Jossey-Bass Publishers, San Fransisco, pp 81–85

> To construct a different approach to mediation practice, we have to begin with the underlying basis on which practice rests and reexamine our views of both what conflict is and what the ideal response to conflict should be. Rethinking the problem-solving

orientation starts by questioning the premise that conflicts need to be viewed as problems in the first place. A different premise would suggest that disputes can be viewed not as problems at all but as opportunities for moral growth and transformation. This different view is the transformative orientation to conflict.

In this transformative orientation, a conflict is first and foremost a potential occasion for growth in two critical and interrelated dimensions of human morality. The first dimension involves strengthening the self. This occurs through realizing and strengthening one's inherent human capacity for dealing with difficulties of all kinds by engaging in conscious and deliberate reflection, choice, and action. The second dimension involves reaching beyond the self to relate to others. This occurs through realizing and strengthening one's inherent human capacity for experiencing and expressing concern and consideration for others, especially others whose situation is 'different' from one's own. Moral thinkers like Carol Gilligan (1982, 1988), among others, suggest that full moral development involves an integration of individual autonomy and concern for others, of strength and compassion. Therefore, bringing out both of these inherent capacities *together* is the essence of human moral maturity. In the transformative view, conflicts are seen as opportunities for developing and exercising both of these capacities, and thus moving toward full moral development.

A conflict confronts each party with a challenge, a difficulty or adversity to be grappled with. This challenge presents parties with the opportunity to clarify for themselves their needs and values, what causes them dissatisfaction and satisfaction. It also gives them the chance to discover and strengthen their own resources for addressing both substantive concerns and relational issues. In short, conflict affords people the opportunity to develop and exercise both self-determination and self-reliance. Moreover, the emergence of conflict confronts each party with a differently situated other who holds a contrary viewpoint. This encounter presents each party with an opportunity for acknowledging the perspectives of others. It gives the individual the chance to feel and express some degree of understanding and concern for another, despite diversity and disagreement. Conflict thus gives people the occasion to develop and exercise respect and consideration for others. In sum, conflicts embody valuable opportunities for both dimensions of moral growth, perhaps to a greater degree than most other human experiences. This may be why the Chinese have a tradition of using identical characters to depict crisis and opportunity.

In the transformative orientation, the ideal response to a conflict is not to solve 'the problem.' Instead, it is *to help transform* the individuals involved, in both dimensions of moral growth. Responding to conflicts productively means utilizing the opportunities they present to change and transform the parties as human beings. It means encouraging and helping the parties to use the conflict to realize and actualize their inherent capacities both for strength of self and for relating to others. It means bringing out the intrinsic goodness that lies within the parties as human beings. If this is done, then the response to conflict itself helps transform individuals from fearful, defensive, or self-centered beings into confident, responsive, and caring ones, ultimately transforming society as well [81–83].

Success has different meanings in the problem-solving and transformative approaches to mediation. In problem-solving mediation, success is achieved when an agreement is reached that solves the problem and satisfies all sides. At the simplest level, problem-solving mediation defines the objective as improving the parties' situation from what it was before. The transformative approach instead defines the objective as improving the parties themselves from what they were before. In transformative mediation, success is achieved when the parties as persons are changed for the better, to some degree, by what has occurred in the mediation process. More specifically, transformative mediation is successful when the parties experience growth in both dimensions of moral development mentioned earlier – developing both the capacity for strength of self and the capacity for relating to others. These are the objectives of empowerment and recognition.

In a transformative approach, empowerment and recognition are the two most important effects that mediation can produce, and achieving them is its most important objective. However, these terms need careful definition, both conceptually and practically. It is fairly easy to understand the statement that 'an agreement was reached that solved the problem and satisfied all sides,' at least conceptually speaking. But what does it mean to say that empowerment and recognition were achieved in mediation, even conceptually? In the most general terms, empowerment is achieved when disputing parties experience a strengthened awareness of their own self worth and their own ability to deal with whatever difficulties they face, regardless of external constraints. Recognition is achieved when, given some degree of empowerment, disputing parties experience an expanded willingness to acknowledge and be responsive to other parties' situations and common human qualities [84–85].

Practice Models

Evolving practice models in common law jurisdictions vary substantially as to methods of communication employed, the structure of the sessions and as to the scope of the mediator's intervention. One primary variable hinges on whether the mediator plans to bring the parties together in face-to-face negotiations or simply provide communication arrangements while they remain apart. We can imagine instances in which the parties stay at a distance throughout, with the mediator moving backwards and forwards between them: the 'shuttle' mediation associated with some forms of international diplomacy here represents the paradigm case. But this approach can be found in other contexts where space or extreme hostility make direct contact problematic. While this form of mediation may be confined to a 'go between' role, it is by no means necessarily limited to such minimal intervention as the potential power of the mediator is greatly enhanced while he or she remains the only means of communication between the parties.

Even where the mediator brings the parties physically together, practice models differ sharply as to the proportion of work done in direct communication. For some mediators it is an article of faith never to see the parties outside a joint session (for example, this was the practice of the North American mediator, John Haynes: see Haynes, 1993). In other models of mediation, notably in commercial disputes, most of the work is done through separate meetings, with the parties coming together only at the beginning of the process and for affirming an outcome at the end.

Some models involve resort to separate meetings at particular stages in the process. Marian Roberts, writing about family mediation, explains the value of separate meetings at an early stage, immediately following a joint introductory session:

> The purpose of these interviews is to give each party an opportunity to state their views, objectives and any fears to the mediator on their own. This means that they can have their say free from fear of interruption or contradiction. It gives the mediator an opportunity to gain a clearer understanding of existing or future fears about safety issues and the issues in dispute. It is the common experience of mediators that a version of the dispute with which both parties apparently agree in the introductory joint session often turns out to be perceived quite differently by one party when interviewed alone (Roberts, 1997: 110–111).

Simmel (Extract 6:10) points to a further advantage of separate early stage meetings following which the positions of the respective parties are fed back in a joint session by the mediator. Where 'the non-partisan shows each party the claims and arguments of the other' they 'lose the tone of subjective passion which usually provokes the same tone on the part of the adversary' (1950: 47). Positions reported by the mediator may be heard and recognised in a way that would have been inconceivable if directly articulated by the parties. At a later stage, separate meetings can be used by the mediator in efforts to break a deadlock. Separate meetings, sometimes described as 'caucasing', in which the parties communicate only through the mediator, rather than directly in his or her presence, necessarily increase opportunities for the mediator to extend control over the process. Gulliver summarises the position succinctly in Extract 6:5 above.

Contemporary professional mediators are quite sharply divided as to the appropriate ambition and scope of their role. Proponents of the more minimalist approach to mediation are increasingly characterised in the literature and practice of ADR as providing a 'facilitative' form of mediatory intervention. They strongly resist the idea that the mediator might provide an informed prediction of the likely outcome if the dispute is adjudicated, or even an informed evaluation of the relative merits of the parties' positions. We have seen, however, the possibility that even a minimalist mediator may influence the process of dispute resolution by characterising the issues in a certain manner, clarifying factual difficulties, encouraging the parties to consider various options and so on. Such a 'minimalist' position may be contrasted with what lawyer mediators in particular now label 'evaluative mediation'. In this evolving form of mediation, the mediator advises on the respective strengths and weaknesses of each side's position and proposes solutions including the terms of a possible agreement. In the extract that follows, Leonard Riskin considers the key features of facilitative and evaluative approaches (Extract 6:11).

Extract 6:10
G Simmel: *The Sociology of Georg Simmel*, edited by K Wolff (1950, originally 1908) Free Press, Glencoe, Ill, pp 146–147

The very great opportunity that non-partisan mediation has to produce this belief lies not only in the obvious elimination of misunderstandings or in appeals to good will, etc. It may also be analyzed as follows. The non-partisan shows each party the claims and arguments of the other; they thus lose the tone of subjective passion which usually provokes the same tone on the part of the adversary. What is so often regrettable here appears as something wholesome, namely, that the feeling which accompanies a psychological content when one individual has it, usually weakens greatly when it is transferred to a second. This fact explains why recommendations and testimonies that have to pass several mediating persons before reaching the deciding individual, are so often ineffective, even if their objective content arrives at its destination without any change. In the course of these transfers, affective imponderables get lost; and these not only supplement insufficient objective qualifications, but, in practice, they alone cause sufficient ones to be acted upon.

Extract 6.11

L L Riskin: 'Mediator Orientations, Strategies and Techniques' (1994) 12(9) *Alternatives* 111, pp 111–113

The evaluative mediator assumes that the participants want and need the mediator to provide some direction as to the appropriate grounds for settlement – based on law, industry practice or technology. She also assumes that the mediator is qualified to give such direction by virtue of her experience, training and objectivity.

The facilitative mediator assumes the parties are intelligent, able to work with their counterparts, and capable of understanding their situations better than either their lawyers or the mediator. So the parties may develop better solutions than any that the mediator might create. For these reasons, the facilitative mediator assumes that his principal mission is to enhance and clarify communications between the parties in order to help them decide what to do. The facilitative mediator believes it is inappropriate for the mediator to give his opinion, for at least two reasons. First, such opinions might impair the appearance of impartiality and thereby interfere with the mediator's ability to function. Second, the mediator might not know enough – about the details of the case or the relevant law, practices or technology – to give an informed opinion.

Each of the two principal questions – Does the mediator tend toward a narrow or broad focus? and Does the mediator favor an evaluative or facilitive role? – yield responses that fall along a continuum. Thus, a mediator's orientation will be more or less broad and more or less evaluative.

Strategies and Techniques of Each Orientation

Each orientation derives from assumptions or beliefs about the mediator's role and about the appropriate focus of a mediation. A mediator employs strategies – plans – to conduct the mediation. And he uses techniques – particular moves or behaviours – to effectuate those strategies. Here are selected strategies and techniques that typify each mediation orientation.

Evaluative-Narrow

The principal strategy of the evaluative-narrow mediator is to help the parties understand the strengths and weaknesses of their positions and the likely outcome at trial. To accomplish this, the evaluative-narrow mediator typically will first carefully study relevant documents, such as pleadings, depositions, reports and mediation briefs. Then, in the mediation, she employs evaluative techniques, such as the following, which are listed from most to least evaluative:

- Urge parties to settle or to accept a particular settlement proposal or range.
- Propose position-based compromise agreements.
- Predict court (or administrative agency) dispositions.
- Try to persuade parties to accept mediator's assessments.
- Directly assess the strengths and weaknesses of each side's case (usually in private caucuses) and perhaps try to persuade the parties to accept the mediator's analysis.

Facilitative-Narrow

Like the evaluative-narrow, the facilitative-narrow mediator plans to help the participants become 'realistic' about their litigation situations. But he employs different techniques. He does not use his own assessments, predictions or proposals. Nor does he apply pressure. Moreover, he probably will not request or study relevant documents, such as pleadings, depositions, reports, or mediation briefs. Instead, because he believes that the burden of decision should rest with the parties, the facilitative-narrow mediator might ask questions – generally in private caucuses – to help the participants understand both sides' legal positions and the consequences of non-settlement. Also in private caucuses, he helps each side assess proposals in light of the alternatives.

Here are examples of the types of questions the facilitative-narrow mediator might ask:

- What are the strengths and weakness of your case? Of the other side's case?
- What are the best, worst, and most likely outcomes of litigation? How did you make these assessments? Have you thought about (other issues)?
- How long will it take to get to trial? How long will the trial last?
- What will be the associated costs – in money, emotions, or reputation?

Evaluative-Broad

The evaluative-broad mediator also helps the parties understand their circumstances and options. However, she has a different notion of what this requires. So she emphasizes the parties' interests over their positions and proposes solutions designed to accommodate these interests. In addition, because the evaluative-broad mediator constructs the agreement, she emphasizes her own understanding of the circumstances at least as much as the parties'.

Like the evaluative-narrow mediator, the evaluative-broad mediator is likely to request and study relevant documents, such as pleadings, depositions, and mediation briefs. In addition, she tries to uncover the parties' underlying interests by such methods as:

- Explaining that the goal of mediation can include addressing underlying interests.
- Encouraging the real parties, or knowledgeable representatives (with settlement authority) of corporations or other organizations to attend and participate in the mediation. For instance, the mediator might invite such individuals to make remarks after the lawyers present their opening statements, and she might include them in most settlement discussions.
- Asking about the participants' situations, plans, needs and interests.
- Speculating about underlying interests and asking for confirmation.

The evaluative-broad mediator also provides predictions, assessments and recommendations. But she emphasizes options that address underlying interests, rather than those that propose only compromise on narrow issues. In the mediation of a contract dispute between two corporations, for instance, while the facilitative-narrow mediator might propose a strictly monetary settlement, the evaluative-broad mediator might suggest new ways for the firms to collaborate (perhaps in addition to a monetary settlement).

Facilitative-Broad

The facilitative-broad mediator seeks to help the parties define, understand and resolve the problems they wish to address. She encourages them to consider underlying interests rather than positions and helps them generate and assess proposals designed to accommodate those interests. Specifically, she might:

- Encourage the parties to discuss underlying interests in joint sessions. To bring out such interests, she might use techniques such as those employed by the evaluative-broad mediator.
- Encourage and help the parties to develop their own proposals (jointly or alone) that would respond to underlying interests of both sides.

The facilitative-broad mediator does not provide assessments, predictions or proposals. However, to help the participants better understand their legal situations, she will likely allow the parties to present and discuss their legal arguments. In addition, she might ask questions such as those listed for the facilitative-narrow mediator and focus discussion on underlying interests. In a broad mediation, however, legal argument generally occupies a lesser position than it does in a narrow one. And because he emphasizes the participants' role in defining the problems and in developing and evaluating proposals, the facilitative-broad mediator does not need to fully understand the legal posture of the case. Accordingly, he is less likely to request or study litigation documents, technical reports or mediation briefs.

However, the facilitative-broad mediator must be able to quickly grasp the legal and substantive issues and to respond to the dynamics of the situation. He needs to help the parties realistically evaluate proposals to determine whether they address the parties' underlying interests.

The drift towards evaluative mediation experienced in the United States – and, to a lesser extent, in other parts of the Anglo-American common law world – over the past two decades, finds parallels elsewhere in the world. The didactic style of mediation found, for example, in the People's Republic of China is also highly evaluative, but the evaluation covers not only the legal position of the parties but also the moral and political correctness of the parties' conduct, as well as perceived societal needs (Palmer, 1988). Although that broad authority to evaluate is not matched in the mediation as it has developed within the context of the Anglo-American common law world, the rise of evaluative mediation has nevertheless attracted some trenchant criticism. Thus, for example, Lela Love and Kimberlee Kovach argue, in effect that evaluative mediation is something of an oxymoron, and that an unhappy consequence of 'Riskin's Grid' is that it appears to have encouraged mediators to play a more active and judgmental role (1998). (Extract 6:12.) Instead, they argue, there should be clarity of purpose in mediation, and no confusion of roles.

Elsewhere, Lela Love explains at some length why mediators should resist the temptation to evaluate. Love argues that the debate over whether mediators should 'evaluate' revolves around confusion over the nature of the evaluation that should take place in mediation (1997: 937). An 'evaluative' mediator does not, in her view, deliver the kind of evaluation that the parties really need. Love briefly defines an 'evaluative' mediator as one who 'gives advice, makes assessments, states opinions – including opinions on the likely court outcome, proposes a fair or workable resolution to an issue or the dispute, or presses the parties to accept a particular resolution' (1997: 938). The evaluative mediator, in evaluating, assessing and deciding for the parties, is therefore not so different from other types of 'evaluators' – judges, arbitrators and other neutral third-party decision-makers (1997: 939, 940). The role of the mediator is fundamentally different, and has at its heart the crucial task of facilitating *evaluation, assessment and decision-making by the parties themselves*. The good mediator should:

> facilitate communications, promote understanding, focus the parties on their interests, and seek creative problem solving to enable the parties to reach their own agreement. Mediators push disputing parties to question their assumptions, reconsider their positions, and listen to each other's perspectives, stories, and arguments. They urge the parties to consider relevant law, weigh their own values, principles, and priorities, and develop an optimal outcome. In so doing, mediators facilitate evaluation by the parties (1997: 939).

More specifically, there are a number of identifiable complications that the evaluative mediator brings to the mediation process. First, and perhaps foremost, the role and role requirements of evaluators and facilitators are fundamentally incompatible. When a mediator engages in evaluative tasks, she or he is diverted from the clear and simple goal of facilitation – mediators cannot effectively facilitate when they are evaluating:

> These differences between evaluators and facilitators mean that each uses different skills and techniques, and each requires different competences, training norms, and ethical qualities to perform their respective functions. Further the evaluative tasks in

determining facts, applying law or custom and delivering an opinion not only divert the mediator away from facilitation, but also can compromise the mediator's neutrality – both in actuality and in the eyes of the parties – because the mediator will be favoring one side or the other in his or her judgment. . . . Mediators cannot effectively facilitate when they are evaluating (1997: 939).

Where evaluative mediation is successful, in the sense of producing a 'result', the success is in reality the result of use of a clearly identified 'mixed process' – which we discuss in Chapter Eight – rather than the assumption of different roles by the mediator in a process of 'evaluative mediation'.

An additional complication is that evaluation by the mediator tends to encourage the parties to be competitive and adversarial. Trying to do their best to secure a result from the evaluating mediator, the parties feel the need to secure a 'result' from the evaluation, and thereby fail to develop the 'respectful collaboration' necessary for the creative problem-solving dimensions of the mediatory process. Where a mediator provides an opinion which can seriously disadvantage one of the parties, that party may choose to disagree with the unfavorable opinion, and believe that the media-tor has 'sided' with the opponent, perhaps even withdrawing from the mediation. Moreover, codes of conduct such as the Model Standards for Mediators produced by the American Arbitration Association, caution neutrals against assuming additional roles. Their thrust is that the process should be kept pure. If the neutral takes on an additional role, so that the decision-making processes become 'mixed,' as when an arbitrator mediates or a mediator evaluates, then this should only be done at the request and with the informed consent of the parties. A further problem is that by making it acceptable or customary for mediators to give opinions on likely court outcomes or merits of legal claims, a restriction is in effect placed on the types of individual who may join the ranks of mediator. In some cases, only lawyers will have the necessary competence, so weakening the field of mediators. And mediation itself may be thereby dragged into the adversarial paradigm, undermining the practice of 'good mediation'. An added complication is that incorrect mediator evaluations are difficult to undo, so that there are real concerns regarding due process and the quality of justice that disputants receive when they are diverted from courts into the private, alternative mechanism of evaluative mediation. Mediators may well be shielded by a quasi-judicial immunity from the consequences of any careless evaluative opinions – in contrast, appellate processes are in place for reversing a court's erroneous decisions, and participants in arbitration consciously waive any rights of appeal as they have chosen arbitrators on the basis of their track records or expertise in a given area. In addition, ADR already provides parties with evaluative alternatives to litigation in the form of arbitration, rent-a-judge, early neutral evalu-ation, and the summary jury trial. Accordingly, a genuinely collaborative mediation paradigm, which in Love's view excludes 'mediator evaluation', satisfies the need for a genuine alternative to the adversarial disputing paradigm where parties fight and the neutral acts as assessor. Mediators must avoid the 'trash and bash' approach – evaluative mediators are tempted to 'trash' the parties' cases, predicting loss and risk if litigation is pursued, and to 'bash' settlement proposals that the other side will not accept, so that mediation becomes 'a mere adjunct of the adversarial norm' (1997: 944). Finally, evaluative mediation blurs the lines of demarcation between mediation and other processes, so that the 'disputant consumer' does not always understand what it is that she or he has opted for – if the process is to be mixed, then better to label it so, in order to enhance integrity of process, disputant satisfaction and uniformity of practice.

Extract 6:12

Kimberlee K Kovach and Lela P Love 'Mapping Mediation: The Risks of Riskin's Grid' (1998) 3 *Harvard Negotiation Law Review* 71, pp 71–75

> We use maps for orientation and guidance. . . . They create paradigms or 'boxes' within which to operate safely and efficiently. The universe a map depicts – what is put in and what is left out – must have an internal cohesion, logic, and accuracy. If not, maps misguide their users.
>
> More than a decade ago, Professor Leonard Riskin noted that lawyers and mediators use radically different standard philosophical maps. The assumptions shaping and coloring the lawyer's map are of adversarial parties and a rule-soluble dispute. The premise underlying the mediator's map is the possibility of collaborative 'win-win' outcomes, not dictated by rules of law or precedents. Recently, Riskin published a map of the mediation universe – the Riskin Grid. The Grid divides mediation into four quadrants, each defined by a mediator's orientation with respect to two continuums: evaluative-facilitative role and narrow-broad problem definition. The Grid has made a substantial contribution both by clarifying the state of mediation practice today and by sparking a vigorous debate about the direction the practice should take in the future. The question remains, however, whether users should rely on a map that characterizes one-half the mediation universe as evaluative, whether the boundaries of mediation practice should include the option of an evaluative orientation.
>
> Since its introduction, the Grid has tended to legitimize evaluative activities conducted under the banner of mediation. Trainers and teachers discuss and explore the evaluative aspect of mediation, and some focus on how better to evaluate. A self-assessment tool has been developed for mediators to aid them in determining where their orientation fits on the Grid. Neutrals who essentially perform case evaluation feel comfortable calling themselves 'mediators.' This trend should stop.
>
> An evaluative role fits a neutral serving in dispute resolution processes where the neutral assists by deciding or opining. That orientation comports with a philosophical map that instigates adversarial advocacy before a decision-maker who applies rules to 'facts' and offers an opinion either to influence or spur party decision-making and settlement (e.g., summary jury trials, early neutral evaluation, and non-binding arbitration) or to generate 'win-lose' outcomes (e.g., arbitration, private judging, and traditional litigation). However, if mediation is to remain a unique alternative to these processes, one that fosters party autonomy and decision-making, a mediator with an evaluative role could undermine those goals and align mediation with the evaluative-adjudicative processes. Consequently, we contend that the Riskin Grid, if

used as a guide to what mediation should and can be and what mediators should and can do, will lead its users astray.

To some extent, of course, 'evaluation' inheres in every aspect of human conduct, as well as many mediator tactics. For example, the arrangement of seating, the choice of questions, and the structure of the agenda all depend on the mediator's evaluation of how to further the resolution of the conflict. However, when determining how to further resolution, mediators should be oriented towards facilitating the parties' evaluation and decision-making. The mediator diligently should avoid conduct that would usurp those key tasks. The mediator ahould not 'answer' the question posed by the dispute (i.e., what is a fair, just, or likely court outcome). That job belongs to the parties.

As Riskin's Grid indicates, many mediators in practice evaluate the fair or likely court outcome when necessary to move forward on a particular issue or on the entire dispute . . . [and] . . . in certain instances 'mixed' evaluative and facilitative processes nonetheless can prove useful. Some mediators who mix mediation and case evaluation effectively help disputing parties. While functionalists would dismiss the importance of naming the process so long as it works, accurate labels, maps, and guides have significance.

The Regulation of Mediation

The contemporary institutionalisation of mediation and its incorporation in civil justice arrangements underline the need for a well-defined regulatory framework. As Marian Roberts argues, 'the very advantages of mediation over the adversarial system can also create potential risks. Conducted privately and informally, necessarily without the safeguards of due process, there exist opportunities for manipulative and oppressive behaviour, not only between the parties themselves but also by the mediator' (Roberts, 2005: 511). Safeguarding a fair process has to go beyond the trust that creates the relationship between mediator and the parties (Extract 6:13).

The National Institute for Dispute Resolution's (NIDR) *Interim Guidelines for Selecting Mediators,* published in 1993, represent an early attempt at specifying required qualities of the mediator. In England, the first serious work on the quality assurance of mediation was carried out in the not-for-profit sector by National Family Mediation during the 1990s. This covered selection, training, accreditation, supervision of practice and performance evaluation, as well as drafting policies and standards for mediation practice (*NFM Policy Manual,* 1998). Subsequently, a single regulatory body for family mediators, the UK College of Family Mediators was formed in 1996 by the main family mediation providers. The College's main objectives are: 'to set, promote, improve and maintain the highest standards of professional conduct and training for all those practising in the field of family mediation; to advance the education of the public in the skills and practice of family mediation; and to make available the details of registered mediators qualified to provide family mediation' (Roberts, 2005: 515) (Extract 6:13).

Concurrently, a statutory basis for public funding of family mediation was enacted, introducing quality assurance requirements for those providing publicly funded mediation.[2] This legislative framework required publicly funded mediators to comply with a Code of Practice and be audited by a government body, the Legal Services Commission. This body published a Quality Mark Standard for Mediation (MQM), introducing quality assurance standards for both family and community mediators. One consequence of the introduction of government funding for mediation was to encourage family lawyers, mainly solicitors, to train as mediators in very large numbers, leading the Law Society to establish its own code of practice for 'solicitor mediators' (Roberts, 2005: 520).

Two linked initiatives have brought further consolidation of the regulatory framework for mediators in England. First, mediators in the community, civil, commercial, family and industrial relations fields participated with the Law Society, during the 1990s in a government-sponsored project to create 'occupational standards' for mediation, leading to a mediation qualification. This took place under a larger government project to devise National Vocational Qualifications (NVQs). Shortly after this project had been completed, mediation organisations in the commercial, community and family fields came together in a Joint Mediation Forum to draft a common Model Code of Conduct for mediators (Roberts, 2005: 521) (Extract 6:13).

The need for an adequate regulatory framework was underlined in the Council of Europe's Recommendation to the Governments of Member States on family mediation of 1998.[3] Section 11 states unequivocally that mediation should not in principle be compulsory. More generally, 'irrespective of how mediation is organised and delivered, States should see to it that there are appropriate mechanisms to ensure the existence of procedures for the selection, training and qualification of mediators, standards to be achieved and maintained by mediators' (s 11.c.). Following a subsequent Commission of the European Communities Green Paper on Alternative Dispute Resolution in 2002, stakeholders prepared a draft Code of Conduct for Mediators.

The determination of the Law Society in England to control the activities of solicitors practising as mediators and a growing insistence that mediation is 'part of legal practice', raise important issues of regulation across professional boundaries. In the passage at Extract 6:14 below, Carrie Menkel-Meadow examines the problem of professional responsibility. Professional accountability is just one part of the broader question of the nature of ethical conduct in mediation work, and in the Anglo-American common law world, this is a particularly problematic issue in an increasingly multi-cultural society (Extract 6.15).

Extract 6:13
Marian Roberts: 'Family Mediation: The Development of the Regulatory Framework in the United Kingdom' (2005) 22 *Conflict Resolution Quarterly* 4, 509, pp 511–512; 515–516; 520–522.

2 Family Law Act 1996, Pt III; now Access to Justice Act 1999.
3 Recommendation No. R (98)1.

Mediation is one of a number of possible dispute resolution processes that may be resorted to in circumstances of family break-up. Whichever process is involved, questions of fairness and problems of power differentials arise. Furthermore, whichever process is involved, certain requirements (eg. managing not exacerbating conflict, respecting diverse needs) are necessary if the interests of all parties, that is, family members including children, are to be served.

In mediation there are additional reasons why professional regulation is so important. Indeed, the very advantages of mediation over the adversarial system can also create potential risks. Conducted privately and informally, necessarily without the safeguards of due process, there exist opportunities for manipulative and oppressive behaviour, not only between the parties themselves but also by the mediator.

In family disputes there is a special vulnerability, of the parties and of third parties, such as children and those directly affected by the outcomes of decisions, that must be addressed. The two central and inherent disparities in situations of family dissolution go to emotional inequalities (who took the decision to separate and to what extent that decision was accepted); and where the children are living. Moreover, the dynamic reality of the subject matter of family mediation, its peculiar and powerful psychological content, its difficulty, complexity, and unpredictability compound these risks – of inequalities arising from power imbalances, of the impact of domestic abuse, and of the potential that exists for mediators to exert pressure, consciously or otherwise, in particular directions and towards particular outcomes. Concerns about alternative processes of dispute resolution magnify in respect of mandated mediation where the parties, finding themselves in a forum and with a mediator not of their choosing, may be both vulnerable *and* placed under unacceptable pressure to settle.

That is why a number of additional safeguards need to be in place in order to ensure a safe and a fair process and outcome. These safeguards include strict adherence to the core principles of mediation such as voluntariness of participation, as well as procedural, structural, psychological and ethical safeguards. The necessity for pre-agreed ground rules of participation, for devising models of practice that prevent the occurrence of what Cobb and Rifkin (1991) have identified as 'negative positioning', are examples of the kind of protections needed in order to enhance the control of the parties, the weaker in particular, in the pursuit of fairness. Again, the setting and monitoring of uniform standards for professional competence as well as for organizational provision are essential requirements both for the protection of the public and for ensuring the credibility of mediation as a professional activity.

Safeguarding a fair process requires mediators to bear constantly in mind, and to address in training and practice, the vital questions raised about their authority, power and potential to exercise influence. First, how can the authority of the mediator be exercised in ways that serve the essential objectives of the process and protect its fundamental characteristics and principles? Second, when does the exercise of that authority cease to serve those objectives, becoming instead an abuse of power with the mediator exerting unacceptable pressures upon one or both of the parties who then act (or fail to act) in ways that they would not otherwise have done? That is why trust, although still remaining the cornerstone of the relationship between the mediator and the parties, is insufficient, needing to be buttressed by the objective safeguards of professional regulation. . . . [511–512].

In 1996, a single professional body, the first and only regulatory body of its kind in the country for all family mediators (whatever their profession of origin), was established by the three main family mediation providers in the country, NFM, FMA, and Family Mediation Scotland (FMS). The UK College of Family Mediators was launched with three main objectives: to set, promote, improve and maintain the highest standards of professional conduct and training for all those practising in the field of family mediation; to advance the education of the public in the skills and practice of family mediation; and to make available the details of registered mediators qualified to provide family mediation. The UK College has claimed responsibility too to ensure that mediation is accessible to *all* members of the community regardless of their culture, religion or ethnic background.

The UK College has a current membership of about 700 individual family mediators practising in both the private and the not-for-profit sectors. Both the two routes into membership of the College are based on the demonstration of professional practice competence, amongst other requirements (eg. professional practice consultation/supervision and continuing professional development). Members represent a range of professional backgrounds though the legal and the mental health professions of origin predominate. The UK College also approves independent providers ('Approved Bodies') to carry out recruitment, selection, training (including continuing professional development courses) and consultation/supervision functions according to standards set and monitored by regular audits. In this way, the requisite separation of functions, of standard – setting and monitoring on the one hand, and of selection and training and provision on the other, has been secured.

The establishment of the UK College of Family Mediators marked the formal arrival in the UK, of family mediation as a new profession. The three hallmarks characterising the achievement of professional status were now officially in place: a recognised and distinct body of knowledge; mechanisms for the transmission of that body of knowledge; and mechanisms for self-regulation and evaluation. In establishing its own disciplinary and complaints committees, the UK College officially acknowledged the necessity for addressing bad practice by means of formal and transparent procedures.

The UK College has prepared and published a range of policies and practice guidelines, for example, on domestic abuse, recording, conflicts of interest and Memoranda of Understanding, and most recently, on the consultation of children and young persons in family mediation . . . [515–516].

Two linked initiatives have occurred in respect of the development of standards relating to mediation across fields – community (including neighbour, victim/offender and schools mediation), civil, commercial, family and industrial relations. First, representatives of these fields, and the Law Society, participated in the early 1990's in a Government-sponsored project to create 'occupational standards' for mediation. The Mediation Qualification that resulted consists of six mandatory units plus three optional units chosen from a range that includes training and development, marketing, community justice and management.

This massive piece of work formed part of the larger Government project of devising National Vocational Qualifications (NVQ's) for a wide range of occupations. This enterprise is characterised by a performance-based approach to delineating competence. What the practitioner does and how s/he does it, substantiated by direct empirical evidence of actual practice with supporting testimony, is what is relevant rather than formal qualifications. In the USA, the SPIDR Commission made similar recommendations both for a performance-base approach to qualifications and about the importance, whatever the difficulties, of testing for competence in mediation – a task yet to be accomplished.

In the mid 1990's mediators from the three main participant organisations, the commercial, community and family fields, together drafted mediation practice standards common to all. As a result, the Joint Mediation Forum (JMF) was born. Richbell [has] highlighted two main reasons for the various strands uniting for this purpose; the unstructured and therefore unregulated state of mediation in North America resulting in varied and often unsatisfactory standards of practice; and government's positive policy towards alternative dispute resolution.

Another objective of the JMF was to explore the need or otherwise for an umbrella organisation for the emerging profession of mediator to act as the inclusive body for all strands of mediation. The main purposes of this body were to advance understanding of mediation; to encourage professionalism and continuing professional development of mediators; to act as a resource and to encourage collaborative working amongst member organisations; to speak as a representative voice for all mediation bodies; and to identify and develop standards of competency for the practice of mediation. Although it had not been the intention of the JMF to set up an over-arching regulatory body or to replace the regulatory functions of existing bodies, fears were expressed about back-door regulation. As a result, proposals for the over-arching kite-marking body foundered and the JMF itself suffered a critical crisis of confidence.

Notwithstanding, there has been a remarkable outcome – the integration of all the major players, representing the different fields of mediation, around a common mediation standard, the generic, performance-based, occupational standard of competence upon which the Mediation Qualification is based. Four of the mandatory units of this qualification were adopted, intact and unmodified, by government (the LAB, now the LSC) as its competence assessment method for family mediators doing publicly funded work. The UK College of Family Mediators now deploys this assessment method as its main route into membership, qualifying its mediators to do publicly funded mediation at the same time. The same standard informed the approach of the Joint Mediation Forum and, while the Law Society adopts the language of competence in its accreditation procedure, it remains unclear whether or not empirical evidence of practice, or witness testimony substantiating direct observation of practice, are required to demonstrate competence according to objective performance criteria.

Most recently, this same standard constitutes the requisite professional competence standard of the Government Quality Mark Standard for Mediation, the official quality kite-mark available for all legal services, publicly as well as privately funded, and incorporating family and community mediation providers [520–522].

Extract 6:14

C Menkel-Meadow: 'Is Mediation the Practice of Law?' (1996) 14 *Alternatives to the High Costs of Litigation* 5, pp 57, 60–61

One of the hottest questions in ADR ethics is whether mediating a case is the 'practice of law.' If it is, (and I think it is), do we require mediators to be lawyers, even if some aren't suited to the task, while excluding people who aren't lawyers but may be excellent mediators? If it isn't, what rules should govern its use? Practitioners, drafters of standards and rules, and ethics scholars have differed on this issue. Productive as the debate may be long-term, it might lead to liability issues and problems enforcing quality and standards.

When mediation was still new, regulators and liability experts seemed to ignore this dispute resolution method as a serious pursuit. Some malpractice insurance carriers wouldn't even cover it. Mediation isn't the 'practice of law,' they argued, and doesn't fall easily into another category of professional activity, like psychology, social work, or judging. Ethics codes of the various 'related' professions did not explicitly cover mediation. Nor did the lawyers' code of professional responsibility provide any guidance for a profession patterned on adversarial, zealous partisanship.

How we answer the question, 'Is mediation the practice of law?' will determine the standards by which we judge the work – whether we rely on legal ethics codes, or those of 'coordinate' professions. A variety of different organizations have promulgated rules on the subject. Some legislatures have tried to impose liability standards, while courts tend to address liability issues on a case-by-case basis.

If mediation is the practice of law (or as Geoffrey Hazard has argued, it is the 'ancillary' practice of law), we must refer to lawyers' ethics codes. Trouble is, they provide little, if any, guidance about issues like: confidentiality (among parties and with mediators), conflicts of interests, fees, and unauthorized practice (in co-mediating, for example, with a non-lawyer). The CPR Commission on Ethics and Standards is studying mediation and third-party practice and preparing an analysis of how the Model Rules of Professional Conduct for lawyers are problematic for mediation practice issues.

The risk, as with many ethical issues, is that the desired solution to one problem determines the conclusion. Most of us in the field are concerned about access to mediation – expanding the pool of capable mediators, and the choices for consumers of mediation services. Therefore, we would like to define mediation broadly, so that it doesn't involve the practice of law. To that end, we argue that mediation in its 'pure' form of facilitation does not involve law, but communication and other skills.

One example of this approach is a proposal by the District of Columbia Bar to clarify and revise the local ethics rule dealing with the unauthorized practice of law. The proposed amendment expressly exempts mediation because, 'ADR services are not given in circumstances where there is a client relationship of trust and reliance and it is common practice for providers of ADR services explicitly to advise participants that they are not providing the services of legal counsel' (Proposed Clarification and Revision of District of Columbia Court of Appeals Rule 49 Concerning the Unauthorized Practice of Law, Rule 49 Committee of the District of Columbia Bar, at page 16).

Lawyer-Client Relationship

This approach to the issue, one of the more popular ones, treats the absence of a lawyer-client relationship as the governing test. It allows a broad range of individuals to mediate, including non-lawyers and lawyers who are not members of the local or state bar.

Anther route to the same result is to simply define away the problem. A report two years ago to the Tennessee Supreme Court Commission on Dispute Resolution by the state Board of Professional Responsibility illustrates this approach. It recommends a rule of professional responsibility that says: 'A neutral shall give legal opinions to a party only in the presence of all parties, providing, however, that a prediction of litigation outcomes by a lawyer acting as a dispute resolution neutral shall not for purposes of this section constitute the provision of a legal opinion.'

Scholars have split on interpretations of current Rule 2.2 of the Model Rules of Professional Conduct (governing the provision of 'intermediary' services). One reading is that the 'lack of representation' in mediation makes the rule inapplicable. Another is that intermediary services need not turn on whether there is a formal lawyer-client relationship, especially when two parties work with the same professional – thus complicating some of the individual confidentiality protections.

For people concerned about standards and quality control in mediation, here's the problem: to the extent that mediators, especially those who work within court programs or by court referral, 'predict' court results or 'evaluate' the merits of the case (on either factual or legal grounds), they are giving legal advice.

Mediators, courts and rules may disclaim responsibility for any information mediators give out, or treat it as not given by an agent, fiduciary, or 'counsel.' But as a practical matter, parties and others may rely on what the mediator tells them, in assessing their alternatives, suggesting other options, and agreeing to settlements.

Reliance on the Mediator

Problems that I used to dream up as hypotheticals now occur daily in mediation sessions: the mediator chosen for his or her subject matter expertise makes predictive or evaluative statements about alternatives in court that one party or counsel know to be 'wrong.' What obligation does the 'favored' party (or its lawyer) have to tell its opponent that he or she may have a better case? This problem often arises when one party is represented and the other isn't – as happens in employment discrimination cases.

The current trend (which I mostly agree with) is to grant quasi-judicial immunity to at least court-based third party neutrals. See eg *Howard v Drapkin* 222 Cal App 3d 843 (1990); *Wagshall v Foster*, 28 F.3d 1249 (DC Cir. 1994); *Meyers v Contra Costa County Department of Social Services* 812 F2d 1154 (9th Cir 1987). However, that means parties have virtually no recourse against a third-party neutral when they rely on a mediator's information or advice that is unfair, unjust or just plain wrong. For this reason, some ADR groups have argued against mediator immunity (see eg, The National Standards for Court Connected Mediation Programs (Center for Dispute Settlement, 1992)).

Ideally, we should analyze the work of third-party neutrals to see what they do, and then attempt to develop the appropriate regulatory models. I disagree with the argument that mediators can give neutral, unbiased 'legal information' that is not the practice of law. See, Sandra Purnell, The Attorney as Mediator – Inherent Conflict of Interest? 32 UCLA L. Rev. 986 (1985).

Case law attempting to define the practice of law suggests that it entails applying legal principles to concrete facts. In *Dauphin County Bar Association v Mazzacaro*, 456 Pa 545 (1976), for example, a court defined law practice as skills that included 'an ability to evaluate the strengths and weaknesses of the client's case vis-à-vis that of the adversary' (that court enjoined insurance adjusters who were not lawyers from giving such legal advice).

While some ADR experts pin their analysis on 'client representation,' I prefer to look at reliance. Where, as seems to be the current trend, there is increased liability imposed on lawyers for reliance by third-party beneficiaries on legal opinions or advice given to others, the privity of the lawyer-client relationship may not be determinative.

When mediators engage in some prediction or application of legal standards to concrete facts – and especially when they draft settlement agreements, I think they are 'practicing' law. That means neutrals who are not trained as lawyers need to be wary of evaluative mediation. They still have other options as mediators: they can limit their role to facilitation, co-mediate with lawyers, or ask the parties to release them from liability for bad legal advice. Non-lawyer mediators might still be subject to the (seldom enforced) regulations against unauthorized practice of law. Lawyers can't get such a sweeping release from their malpractice liability (See Rule 1.8(h)).

Giving legal predictions and evaluations is law work, whether or not there is a lawyer-client relationship. Within these boundaries, we need rules that permit qualified people without legal training to mediate. Some observers suggest that when mediators act more like neutral judges, the proper analog is the ABA Judicial Code of Conduct. In my view, these rules also give inadequate guidance since mediators perform different functions and hear more confidential information than judges. But that is a topic for another day.

Still, there's clearly a quality control problem. Just because a mediator has a law degree – or even an up-to-date license to practice – does not mean that he or she will give accurate legal advice, prediction or evaluation.

Complex mediation these days often involves legal questions and mediator prediction or evaluation of the legal merits or 'likely outcomes' of cases. Wouldn't you want a mediator with legal expertise if you were involved in an important case?

Immunity doctrines, which protect judges, some arbitrators and other third-party neutrals from liability for giving incorrect information or damaging rulings, will continue to protect (overbroadly, in my view) many mediators. These issues become particularly troubling when either none of the parties has a lawyer or when only one does. Mediators are most likely to 'deserve' immunity when all parties to a dispute are receiving independent legal advice.

Our next inquiry: if (some) mediation involves practicing law, who should do it? How can we regulate it? And, most importantly, how can we insure quality and competence?

Extract 6:15

C Morris: 'The Trusted Mediator: Ethics and Interaction in Mediation' in Julie Macfarlane (ed) *Rethinking Disputes: The Mediation Alternative* (1997) Cavendish Publishing, London, pp 307–308

Mediators tend to consider ethics most intensely when they are in a dilemma. Where, then, can they turn for guidance? The usual and obvious answer is to look to codes of ethics created by respected mediation organisations. Both the literature and the agendas of dispute resolution organisations indicate that discussions about ethics are often framed by people preparing to set standards which they believe are needed as 'safe-practice' guidelines for practitioners, or to protect the public from unsavoury or unwise practitioners. Another setting for discussions about ethics is training. Ethics are often taught either as an addendum or in the form of handouts. Except in the presence of an actual dilemma, the topic of ethics in mediation usually takes a back seat in favour of discussions about dispute resolution qualifications, skills and models. The irony is that ethical principles are fundamental to every assumption of both dispute resolvers and disputants. Judgments of right and wrong, good and bad, are at the root of virtually every dispute and every dispute resolution process . . .

In rapidly changing societies, one can not assume homogeneous ethical values among either disputants or mediators. Most countries are affected by increasing cultural diversity as a result of immigration as well as social change. This creates challenges for mediators in particular cases, as well as for mediation organisations creating codes of ethics.

LeBaron Duryea's research demonstrated that people who immigrate to Canada do not necessarily share the perceptions of the dominant Canadian culture as to how disputes should be resolved. In particular, the individualistic approach to conflict evidenced in Western thinking is not mirrored by those from more collectivist cultures, including Aboriginal peoples in North America. The image of a fishing net may better impart the kind of 'network conflict' reported by members of some immigrant groups in North America:

> Each person is like one of the knots in a large fishing net with its intricate interlacing of innumerable knots. Each person is tied to many others. When all of the knots are firmly tied, the net is in good working condition. If any one of the knots is too loose or too tight, the whole net is skewed. Each knot, each relationship, has an effect on the whole. If there is a tear, a gap, in the net, the net is not a working one . . . Nets are to be checked frequently, knots cared for tenderly, and if tears do appear they must be repaired.

Similarly, the individualist approach to ethics dominant in Western societies is not reflected in the ethics of many non-Western societies, where ethical values may reflect loyalty to family, religious or cultural values. Codes of ethics developed for mediators in the West implicitly incorporate dominant Western views of both conflict and ethics. In pluralistic societies, this unexamined approach to the framing of mediator ethics may not be realistic in the long-term.

Working across cultures: 'Empower or Imperial?'
It is increasingly recognised that mediation must be culturally sensitive when practised in a multicultural society. In addition, more and more trainers are being asked to conduct training or facilitate the implementation of dispute resolution programmes internationally. Significant ethical issues are raised, including the issues of working with

people whose cultural and ethical frameworks may differ from those of the mediator or trainer.

Ethical concerns are being raised as commentators become concerned about imposing dominant culture standards on minority groups, or in the case of international work, neo-colonialism in the form of exportation of dispute resolution processes based on Western values.

The Issue of Impartiality

There is quite a strong Western stereotype of the mediator as impartial, even 'neutral'; an intervener carefully distanced from the interests of either party (Gulliver, 1979: 212). In the United States, the Standards of Conduct (1994) approved by the American Arbitration Association, the Society of Professionals in Dispute Resolution and the American Bar Association Section on Dispute Resolution require the mediator to 'conduct mediation in an impartial manner', and in this country, the Law Society's Code of Conduct for Mediators defines the role as one of a 'neutral facilitator of negotiations'. But such a claim is rarely advanced without qualification by mediators themselves, and in some contexts appears as a construct set up by researchers intent on knocking it down (see, for example, Dingwall and Greatbach, 1993).

The Implication of Rank and Office in Mediation

Questions of rank and tenure of office are as important as the claimed ambition of the intervener in determining the location of control over process and outcome. The intervention of an unobtrusive neighbour will inevitably be received differently from that of the authoritative professional or holder of some identified office. However modest their respective objectives may be, parties will experience a neighbour who mediates differently from a professional intervener, however tactful and unobtrusive the latter may attempt to be. There are separate, related problems here:

- Can members of other professional groups mediate safely given the public perceptions that have been generated by the exercise of their primary roles?
- Can mediation be safely combined with the delivery of other forms of specialised help?

The predicament of the lawyer or judge who attempts to mediate provides the obvious example of the first problem. Given the long-standing familiarity of the public with the partisan advisory and representative roles of the lawyer, and with the authoritative decision-making of the judge, can either avoid bringing that primary persona into the very different role of the mediator? The second problem is equally exemplified by the lawyer. Parties experiencing difficulty with joint decision-making may require both help with communications and some expert advice or information. Can these different forms of help be safely delivered by the same person?

Extract 6:16

S Roberts: 'Mediation in Family Disputes' (1983) 46 *Modern Law Review* 537, pp 555–556

The process of mediation is most intimately linked to the law where the mediators themselves are legal specialists; barristers or solicitors who have laid aside their customary partisan stance; or judges who have abandoned for the moment their jobs as umpires. Whether or not the skills exercised by lawyers in either of these capacities qualify them well to act as mediators, their identification in the minds of disputants with established legal roles must affect their performance when they attempt to mediate. If the beauty of mediation is seen to be that it leaves responsibility for decision-making in the hands of the parties themselves, this feature is inevitably diluted or lost altogether as the process is moved in ideological terms, in terms of the intrusion of specialist personnel, even in terms of space, 'nearer to the law'. The strength of the mediator lies in his identification with the values of joint decision-making, agreement and compromise, and in his neutral posture at a point adjacent to the parties themselves. To link family mediation to the world of the law will arguably sap the vitality of both.

This problem will be present whenever we approach a barrister or solicitor to mediate. We are accustomed to go to these specialists for legal advice in matters we perceive as beyond our competence, or in search of a champion. This perception of the lawyer is probably going to remain with the client, however anxious the lawyer may be to set aside his role as partisan and champion.

The same difficulty arises in an even more acute form where registrars or judges seek to mediate; where 'in court' mediation is attempted. Here the mediation is conducted on the very premises of the law, and officials of the legal system are directly involved. It is difficult to concede the 'overriding importance' which some commentators attach to the development of 'in court' mediation, or to accept that 'the values and strategies appropriate to mediation be accommodated as part of the legal process.' In this context, one of the most disappointing features of the Inter-departmental Committee on Conciliation's Report is the failure to discuss the implications of locating mediatory forms of intervention directly adjacent to the courts. In reaching the view that conciliation 'is best provided as an adjunct to the courts system,' and putting its weight behind 'in court conciliation,' the Committee does not appear to have given any thought to the consequences which this might have for the way in which mediation and adjudication will be viewed by the disputants. It remains unclear how either of these separate ways can be enhanced by this juxtaposition.

The judge who attempts to mediate enjoys, whether he likes it or not, an authority which is in no way derived from his association with the values seen to underlie mediation. Courts are places where other people tell us what to do; registrars and judges are such people. The adjudicator represents the neutral superior, seen to hand down an imposed decision, compliance with which is externally guaranteed by the state. This in itself is going to colour the way in which mediatory intervention by registrars and judges is perceived by disputants, whether the specialists themselves want this or not. This authority is inevitably going to make disputants more disposed than they might otherwise be to follow their suggestions, and be receptive to their persuasion. The registrar or judge is not in a position to discard this authority, with which his office had invested him, even if it is made clear to the disputants that there can be no question of the particular office holder trying their case should negotiations fail. Examining the position of registrars as mediators, Davis argues that 'in order to ensure that their role as mediator is not contaminated by their adjudicative powers, they must make it clear that in no circumstances will they subsequently adjudicate in that case.' But this 'contamination' is unavoidable; their office makes it so.

It may be argued that the authority which the registrar or judge brings to mediation is a valuable attribute, as it will put further, perhaps necessary, pressure on the parties to settle. Such a lesson might be drawn from the 'success' of pre-trial reviews in reducing the number of defended divorces. These procedures may speed the achievement of an outcome and avoid formal adjudication; but we must not pretend that they have much to do with joint decision-making in which the meanings and values of the disputants themselves are those which essentially inform the outcome. At a certain point, arguably reached in contemporary experiments with 'in court' mediation, mediatory intervention becomes a process auxiliary to adjudication; less an affair of joint decision-making and more a means of lubricating third-party decision. Almost inevitably, 'conciliation' will be used by legal specialists as a means of improving their own procedures and of making these more attractive to their clients. In 'in court' mediation control is taken back by third parties despite any illusion that it is handed over to the parties themselves.

How can we evaluate the contemporary demand for 'conciliation' as the primary means of dealing with some aspects of family break-up, particularly the mediatory forms of intervention considered here? We cannot do so, until it is clearer what sort of people the mediators are going to be, and what they are going to do. An evaluation will only become possible as presently embryonic forms begin to establish themselves. As things are, the umbrella of mediation offers opportunities for people to intervene in family disputes in a range of different ways in respect of which no criteria have yet been established. There are certainly grounds for the fear that 'once adjudicatory forms are abandoned, consideration of individual rights and of justice between the parties can be subverted by notions of treatment and therapy.' Equally, the practice of 'in court' mediation is potentially alarming; it provides opportunities for coercion in the absence of those safeguards which even quite sceptical observers see as attending adjudication.

In my view quite a strong case can be made for keeping mediatory forms of intervention quite separate from the places and personnel of the law; for presenting them as 'other' than adjudication, something to be tried first. In that way neither mode loses potency through being confused with the other. At the same time, the primary goal of mediation should be a modest one, to provide the means of communication between the disputants and to encourage them to work out their own solutions in accordance with the ways in which they see the quarrel. Thus the mediator should seek to alter as little as possible the disputants' view of the world beyond assuring them that it is 'right'.

A further difficulty arises with the attempts to combine the roles of therapist and mediator. The arguments are laid out clearly in the exchange between Marian Roberts and John Haynes extracted in Chapter Eight (see, pp 304 et seq below).

The Management of Power Imbalances in Mediation

Whatever the complexities of 'power' in negotiation processes (see pp 132–133 above), outcomes of bilateral exchanges will inevitably reflect to some extent the bargaining endowments of the different parties. So, even if we conclude that mediatory intervention is generally inappropriate where significant imbalances of power exist between the parties, occasions will arise in mediation where one party appears significantly 'weaker' than the other, and the question is thus posed as to the extent to which the mediator can or should attempt to redress this imbalance. In some cultures the answer to this question is taken for granted;[4] in others it may assume considerable importance. Mediators themselves differ as to the extent to which such intervention is an appropriate part of their work. In North America, a variety of mediatory techniques and strategies have been evolved in order to deal with inequalities of power. Bush, with his concept of 'active impartiality', advocates a distinctive means of dealing with this problem.

Extract 6:17

R A B Bush: 'Efficiency and Protection, or Empowerment and Recognition?: The Mediator's Role and Ethical Standards in Mediation' (1989) 41 *Florida Law Review* 253, pp 281–282

> One crucial element not mentioned above is the obligation of impartiality, which is necessary to fulfill both aspects of the empowerment-and-recognition role. What I mean by impartiality, however, goes beyond the usual connotation of disclosure of conflicts and neutrality regarding outcome. In reading my description of the 'pushy' mediator's job, one might ask how mediators can do so much pushing without alienating one or both parties. Apart from my earlier caveat regarding the positive meaning of 'pushy' and 'pushing for', the answer lies in an expanded conception of the obligation of impartiality.
>
> Mediators should be visibly even-handed or two-sided in their pushing. In other words, they should direct their invitations, support, encouragements, challenges and urgings toward each party in turn, and each should see clearly that the other is receiving similar treatment. If necessary, mediators should explicitly assure the parties that they intend to behave identically toward each side, and of course they should always fulfill this assurance. Mediators whose pushing is positive in character, and who adhere to the requirement of *active* impartiality, can serve for each side as translator to the other and also serve each side as devil's advocate for the other. And they can do so without ever losing the trust and confidence of both sides that is necessary to fulfilling both aspects of the mediator's role. I should note, however, that this may be much easier to do if the mediator does at least some of this pushing while meeting separately with each side, a point I return to below.
>
> One other aspect of the obligation of active impartiality is also quite important in fulfilling both aspects of the empowerment-and-recognition role. The impartiality of

4 Thus, for example, in the People's Republic of China such power imbalances are often regarded as inevitable and therefore to be tolerated by the mediator and taken into account when constructing a viable solution to the disagreement between parties.

mediators means not only that they are allied with neither side, but that because of a lack of personal investment, they have more distance and perspective on the parties' discussions. This position 'above the fray' should not be a passive listening post. Rather, it should be the basis for what I call the mediator's job of narration. The mediator can impartially hear, and impartially report to the parties, many crucial parts of their own dialogue that they themselves may not have grasped fully or even heard because of their closeness to the situation. Offers, counteroffers, new options for resolution, actual agreements on issues, and statements of acknowledgment and recognition all are presented frequently in mediation sessions without one or both parties even realizing what has occurred. To fulfill both the empowerment and recognition functions, the mediator can and should be an actively impartial *narrator* who lets no relevant exchange between the parties go unheard or ignored.

While many commentators subscribe to the view that mediation is inappropriate in disputes in which there are significant power imbalances between the parties, this is not a universal view. In the extract that follows, Genevieve Chornenki argues that excessive concentration on power imbalances between the parties may well detract from mediation as an aid to joint problem-solving.

Extract 6:18

G Chornenki: 'Mediating Commercial Disputes: Exchanging "Power Over" for "Power With"' in J Macfarlane (ed) *Rethinking Disputes: The Mediation Alternative* (1997) Cavendish Publishing, London, pp 163–168

The idea of power as influence or control has been transported into the culture of mediation but not as a desirable and necessary ingredient. Rather, it is understood as a phenomenon to be controlled. The most prevalent view among mediators is that power is, primarily, a mediator's responsibility and that she ought to undertake power-balancing between or among disputants. Very often, this analysis is centred on differences between or among disputants in how much information they have or control, in how they speak and behave, in whether they exhibit more extreme behaviours such as threats, coercion, or physical or verbal abuse which may negate a party's ability to give voluntary and informed consent. Prescriptions for mediators list sources or kinds of power and identify 'power imbalances' that they can do something about, and those that they cannot alter.

Mediators frequently write and talk of 'balancing' power and the mediator is enjoined 'to either disempower the overly powerful party or empower the powerless party'. Mediators are said to 'manage' power relationships and to:

[attempt] to strike a balance between the negotiators' total power positions . . . Doing so lowers the probability the stronger negotiator will attempt to exploit the weaker and that the weaker will abandon the relationship or seek to undermine the stronger's position. To strike the balance, the mediator provides the necessary power underpinnings to the weaker negotiator – information, advice, friendship – or reduces those of the stronger. If he cannot balance the power relationship, the mediator can bargain with or use his power against the stronger negotiator to constrain the exercise of his power.

Such a view of power is entirely consistent with Anglo–Canadian jurisprudence. The concerns of both mediators and judges relate to one party having an unmatched advantage or form of dominating influence over another that is not benign. Power is 'the ability of one person to dominate the will of another, whether through manipulation, coercion, or outright but subtle abuse of power'. Protection is available in extreme cases for those who are intellectually, economically or situationally 'weaker'. However, arm's length commercial parties are almost always presumed to be of equal bargaining power, regardless of their differences, and any vulnerability is presumed to be preventable through more prudent exercise of their bargaining power.

Unfortunately, this preoccupation with power as control or influence provides commercial parties with little meaningful information about the attitudinal change that interest-based mediation requires. It suggests that mediation is but an extension of commercial norms and that if one could only do away with troublesome excesses and abuses of power, then the benefits of mediation could be enjoyed by all. In practice, interest-based mediation takes the emphasis off power as influence or control and places it on a different kind of capability, that of the 'collective'. It is the voluntary joining together of parties in the pursuit of a joint problem-solving exercise rather than their successful domination of another that is at the heart of interest-based mediation's true 'promise'. When such joint efforts take place, the parties do exercise power, but not as influence or control. Instead, they are engaged in the power of the collective, here referred to as 'power-with'.

Power-with is the power of association, or the power of the team. It is a whole-is-bigger-than-the-sum-of-its-parts phenomenon. *Power-with* is not the absence of conflict, but the focusing of individual abilities on a common goal. In the case of mediation, that goal is the creation of an agreement that meets needs on each side of the table, insofar as this is possible. Thus, *power-with* is the laser, as opposed to the dispersed light. It is the virtual corporation, the think-tank, the surgical team. It is not one disputant unilaterally compelling another to unwillingly do its bidding. When *power-with* occurs, one can observe:

> . . . the aims, processes, methods, or behaviour that create order, stability and unity of direction . . . [not] simplistic notions that [it] . . . is peace and that peace is the absence of conflict . . .

For commercial users of mediation, *power-with* is the phenomenon that must prevail in mediation for its benefits to accrue. It occurs in a mediation when the parties begin, eventually, to answer the same joint problem-solving question or to bargain in order to bring about a mutually acceptable readjustment of their interdependence. The question becomes, 'How can the problem with this software be remedied?', instead of 'Who is responsible for the fact that something went wrong?' Or, 'What price can we both agree on as being fair for the extra work?' instead of 'How can I contribute to do as little as possible?'

Power-with takes place when Worthington Savings and Loan stops insisting that Mr Desantos' claim is entirely illegitimate and when Mr Desantos stops insisting that he is entitled to 100% of an unprovable loss. It manifests itself when their joint question becomes: given that Ramero Desantos is a client of means and that the bank declined access to money that was rightfully his, what can the bank give and what will Mr Desantos accept that will restore his good will in the institution while at the same time compensating him for his loss?

Where *power-with* in mediation differs from that of the virtual corporation, the think-tank, or the surgical team, is that parties involved in those activities are interdependent by choice and generally perceive themselves as benefiting from the interdependence. Disputants in mediation, such as Eldercare and Osborne, however, are often interdependent against their will or are linked in a way that they experience as intolerable. In mediation, Eldercare and Osborne seek to terminate or restructure that interdependence and they are able to do so through their willingness to be open to each other's needs.

The most profound, and most difficult, activity that must occur at an interest-based mediation of a commercial dispute is the conversion of that dispute from an 'either/or' situation, a binary choice, to a focused, joint problem-solving exercise. It is this aspect of mediation, the voluntary participation of parties in a collective as opposed to an individual effort, which is within the unilateral control of every commercial party contemplating or engaging in mediation. A commercial party's primary willingness to do this is infinitely more important to the success of a mediation than any amount of screening for mediator aptitudes or orientation, or matching of disputes and disputants to the process, or the relative '*power over*' of the parties.

A willingness to engage in *power-with* is critical for commercial parties in mediation. It entails the conversion of a situation from one that pulls participants away from each other (the Twinnings' resolution is valid/the Twinnings' resolution is invalid) to one that moves them together, at least for the purposes of resolving a defined controversy or dispute: for example, how can the playing field for Vanity and Fontana be levelled with respect to advertising in a way that does not negate Vanity's contract with Twinnings? Bundled up in this undertaking may, and often will, be questions of who can coerce whom on what basis and for what purpose. *Power-with* does not negate or eliminate power as influence or control, but the parties' task at the mediation is so much larger and more complex than exercising or responding to conventional power.

Power-with is not something that a mediator can foster or create without the assistance of the parties and the flaw in a great deal of mediation promotion and description is that it can create the impression that the process, and/or the mediator, are able unilaterally to bring about (through technique, skill, good judgment, intuition) the kinds of conditions that will lead to elegant, economical and efficient resolutions. Nothing could be further from the truth. The mediation process requires not only a measure of cooperation with the opposite party, but at least the same measure of cooperation with the mediator and the mediation process itself. If this were more clearly understood, it would promote more appropriate case selection for mediation, for it would screen out (by self-identification) parties that are clearly unsuitable for interest-based mediation.

So how can a commercial party determine whether and to what extent the values of interest-based mediation are compatible with its own goals? The following factors are intended as a guide. The more willing each party is to participate or accept these conditions, the more likely it is that interest-based mediation will have something to offer. If these conditions prove to be unacceptable to a commercial party, no adverse judgment is intended. Mediation is not the only dispute resolution mechanism apart from litigation. Other forms, such as binding or advisory arbitration, dispute review boards, or fact-finding with recommendations, are all alternatives available to commercial parties in dispute. These often provide more controlled environments, less risk-taking disclosure, and more rule-oriented ways of proceeding. At the same time, they excuse parties from the necessity of accepting responsibility for outcomes and from surrendering their conventional approaches to power.

In an interest-based mediation, participants in commercial mediation can anticipate demands to:

- Focus individual energies on a collective problem, not an individual one. The problem may be no more elegant than 'on what basis can the plaintiff give and the defendant receive a release?' Or, it can be more complex, 'how can we foster respect and human dignity in the workplace'?
- Form a genuine commitment to examine whether and to what extent the collective problem can be solved. This need not be commitment to definitely achieve a result, but commitment to the effort entailed in constructing an outcome.
- Accept mutual influence in the sense of willingness to try and persuade others, and openness to being persuaded by others. This relates to being understood and to understanding, rather than to convincing and converting.
- Engage in overt behaviour, but not necessarily private belief, that is respectful and non-obstructionist in the sense that it does not detract from the focused energy of the group.
- Maintain a willingness to foster or at least tolerate a level of capability on the part of each individual participant in the mediation process. This involves their ability to identify and actualise goals, options, skills, resources and decision-making. While there is no requirement that the parties be equal in their abilities here, rough parity of capability is a necessary prerequisite to the kind of negotiating undertaken at an interest-based mediation.
- Sustain an ability to recognise other points of view, other interpretations, other inferences, other versions of the controversy; the ability to paddle around in the other party's canoe. Known as recognition, this is an important condition.
- From the starting point of relative self-absorption, parties achieve recognition in mediation when they voluntarily choose to become more open, attentive, sympathetic, and responsive to the situation of the other party, thereby expanding their perspective to include an appreciation for another's situation.
- The hallmark of recognition is letting go – however briefly or partially – of one's focus on self and becoming interested in the perspective of the other party as such, concerned about the situation of the other as a fellow human being, not as an instrument of fulfilling one's own need.
- As a condition of *power-with* in a commercial mediation, however, recognition need not take the form of true compassion and connection. It could merely be an expression of enlightened self-interest. What does matter is that recognition is expressed overtly in words or actions. Mere alterations in belief, while valuable, are

insufficient to bring about the active, kinetic phenomenon of *power-with* described here.

- Honesty. Engage in honest, authentic communication. If a commercial party tells the mediator that something is important to it when it is not, or advances an interest as a foil to hide what is truly important, this is counterproductive. It will busy the mediator in trying to achieve what has been stated as being important, for no useful end.

In the end result, these seven points concern the attitudes that commercial parties need to bring to the mediation process. Attitude is vital to the successful outcome of any mediation and is a factor directly within the control of any particular party. Unless a commercial party is able and willing to accept the values and attitudes that interest-based mediation requires, then it is an unlikely candidate for the process. With its emphasis on information exchange, power-with (as opposed to raw unilateral influence and control) and recognition, interest-based mediation may, in fact, require a stretch that is uncomfortable or unacceptable for many commercial parties. The truth is that it does entail some element of vulnerability and 'letting-go' in order to bring its rewards within reach. To disguise this aspect of mediation is to do a disservice to users or potential users. For commercial parties who are able and willing to suspend reliance on power as unilateral influence and control and to participate in a collective problem-solving effort, the mediation process has much to offer. It is a measured understanding of mediation's demands as opposed to its benefits that will lead them there with more realistic expectations.

Gender, Culture and Ethnicity

In the family law field, from the early 1980s, there has been a persistent feminist critique of mediation, suggesting that private, consensual processes of decision-making mask, and so perpetuate, the power inequalities suffered in particular by women in the family (Crouch, 1982; Bottomley, 1984, 1985). Under this view, women in mediation both face their former partners at a disadvantage and are subjected to the male-oriented preconceptions of the mediator. In England this critique has been renewed in the context of the passage of the Family Law Act 1996.[5] Important North American studies indicate a number of process dangers in mediation which are faced by women unless essential safeguards are maintained (Grillo, 1991) (Extract 6:19). However, recent North American and Australian research studies reveal few differences between the ways in which women and men experience the process of mediation and its outcomes (Extract 6:20).

A parallel and related critique raises questions about the conditions under which it can be safe for a member of one cultural or ethnic group to mediate in a dispute involving members of another, given the potentially diverging cultural understandings involved. In England, National Family Mediation's practice guidelines recognise

5 See, for example, Deech (1995).

this problem and propose explicit safeguards. Sonia Shah-Kazemi questions the safety of such a route (Extract 6:21).

Extract 6:19

T Grillo: 'The Mediation Alternative – Process Dangers for Woman' (1991) 100 *Yale Law Journal* 1545, pp 1605–1610

Women who have been through mandatory mediation often describe it as an experience of sexual domination, comparing mandatory mediation to rape . . . I have been struck, in the course of conversations with women who have undergone the mandatory mediation process, by how often these women have said, 'I felt as if I were raped': (I am aware that many women experience the adversary process similarly.) . . . Catharine MacKinnon's work provides a basis for explaining why, for some women, this characterization is appropriate. MacKinnon has analyzed gender as a system of power relations, evidenced primarily with respect to the control of women's sexuality. While MacKinnon recognizes the sense in which women are fundamentally connected to others, she does not celebrate it. Rather, she sees the potential for connection as invasive and intrusive. It is precisely the potential for physical connection that permits invasion into the integrity of women's bodies. It is precisely the potential for emotional connection that permits intrusion into the integrity of women's lives. . . .

Men do not experience this same fear of sexual domination, according to MacKinnon; they do not live in constant fear of having the very integrity of their lives intruded upon. . . . Because the existential and subjective experience of the world differs for men and women, it is sometimes difficult to explain, in legal language, the basis for attention to areas of law that are of particular interest to women such as rape, sexual harassment, and reproductive freedom. For example, rape might be characterized and treated as any other crime of violence if the underlying sexual domination of women by men is not taken into account. Once institutionalized sexual domination is seen as something the law should address, however, rape becomes a very particular harm unlike any other, a combination of violence and sexual domination. . . . Men may not comprehend their role in this system of sexual domination any more than women may be able to articulate the source of their feeling of disempowerment. Yet both of these dynamics are at work in the mediation setting. It may seem a large leap, from acts of physical violence and invasion to the apparently simple requirement that a woman sit in a room with her spouse working toward the resolution of an issue of mutual concern. But that which may be at stake in a court-ordered custody mediation – access to one's children – may be the main reason one has for living, as well as all one's hope for the future. And because mandatory mediation is a forced engagement, ordinarily without attorneys or even friends or supporters present, it may amount to a form of 'psychic breaking and entering' or, put another way, psychic rape.

There is always the potential for violence in the legal system: 'A judge articulates her understanding of a text, and as a result, somebody loses his freedom, his property, his children, even his life. . . . When interpreters have finished their work, they frequently leave behind victims whose lives have been torn apart by these organized, social practices of violence.'

The reality of this background of judicial violence cannot be discounted when measuring the potential trauma of the mandatory mediation setting. Although the mediation system is purportedly designed in part to help participants avoid contact with the violence that must come from judicial decisions, in significant ways the violence of the contact is more direct. Since the parties are obliged to speak for themselves in a setting to which the culture has not introduced them and in which the rules are not clear (and in fact vary from mediator to mediator), the potential violence of the legal result, combined with the invasiveness of the setting, may indeed end up feeling to the unwilling participant very much like a kind of rape. Moreover, in judging, it is understood that the critical view of the quarrel is that of the judge, the professional third party. Mediation is described as a form of intervention that reflects the disputants' view of the quarrel. But having the mediation take place on court premises with a mediator who might or might not inject her prejudices into the process may make it unlikely that the disputants' view will control. Thus, a further sense of violation may arise from having another person's view of the dispute characterized and treated as one's own?

That many reportedly find mediation helpful does not mean everyone does. Consensual sex may take place in a certain setting in one instance but that does not make all sex in that setting consensual; sometimes it is rape. And sometimes it may only seem to be consensual because forced sex is considered par for the course – that is, it is all we know or can imagine.

When I have suggested to mediators that even being forced to sit across the table and negotiate, unassisted, with a spouse might be traumatic, their reaction has been almost uniformly dismissive. Some mediators have denied that this could possibly be the case. Even mediators who acknowledge the possibility of trauma have said, in effect, 'So what?' A few hours of discomfort seems not so much to ask in return for a system that, to their mind, serves the courts and the children much better than the alternative. But a few hours of discomfort may not be all that is at stake; the trauma inflicted upon a vulnerable party during mediation can be as great as that which occurs in other psychologically violent confrontations. As such, it should not be minimized. People frequently take months or years to recover from physical or mental abuse, rape, and other traumatic events. Given the psychological vulnerability of people at the time of a divorce, it is likely that some people may be similarly debilitated by a mandatory mediation process.

Moreover, because the mandatory mediation system is more problematic for women than for men, forcing unwilling women to take part in a process which involves much personal exposure sends a powerful social message: it is permissible to discount the real experience of women in the service of someone else's idea of what will be good for them, good for their children, or good for the system.

ALTERNATIVES TO MANDATORY MEDIATION

It has been said that '[d]isputes are cultural events, evolving within a framework of rules about what is worth fighting for, what is the normal or moral way to fight, what kinds of wrongs warrant action, and what kinds of remedies are acceptable.' The process by which a society resolves conflict is closely related to its social structure. Implicit in this choice is a message about what is respectable to do or want or say, what the obligations are of being a member of the society or of a particular group within it, and what it takes to be thought of as a good person leading a virtuous life. In the adversary system, it is acceptable to want to win. It is not only acceptable, but expected, that one will rely on a lawyer and advocate for oneself without looking out for the adversary. The judge, a third party obligated to be neutral and bound by certain formalities, bears the ultimate responsibility for deciding the outcome. To the extent that women are more likely than men to believe in communication as a mode of conflict resolution and to appreciate the importance of an adversary's interests, this system does not always suit their needs.

On the other hand, under a scheme of mediation, the standards of acceptable behavior and desires change fundamentally. Parties are to meet with each other, generally without their lawyers. They are encouraged to look at each other's needs and to reach a cooperative resolution based on compromise. Although there are few restrictions on her role in the process, the mediator bears no ultimate, formal responsibility for the outcome of the mediation. In sum, when mediation is the prototype for dispute resolution, the societal message is that a good person – a person following the rules – cooperates, communicates, and compromises.

The glories of cooperation, however, are easily exaggerated. If one party appreciates cooperation more than the other, the parties might compromise unequally. Moreover, the self-disclosure that cooperation requires, when imposed and not sought by the parties, may feel and be invasive. Thus, rather than representing a change in the system to accommodate the 'feminine voice,' in actuality, mandatory mediation overrides real women's voices saying that cooperation might, at least for the time being, be detrimental to their lives and the lives of their children. Under a system of forced mediation, women are made to feel selfish for wanting to assert their own interests based on their need to survive.

There are, then, many good reasons why a party might choose not to mediate. While some argue that mediation should be required because potential participants lack the information about the process which would convince them to engage in it voluntarily, this is not a sufficient justification for requiring mediation. If the state were committed only to making sure that disputants become familiar with mediation, something less than mandatory mediation – such as viewing a videotaped mediation or attending an orientation program – could be required, and mediators would certainly not be permitted to make recommendations to the court . . . Molly Knowles, Director of the Family Referral Conciliation Service in Kingston, Ontario, Canada, has suggested that the legal system should never play an initiating role in the process of mediation. Rather, mediation services should be available to all divorcing couples at the beginning of the separation process before they go to court. She further argues that the clients alone should decide which issues should be addressed by mediation . . . That more than the simple receipt of information is required under a statutory mediation scheme demonstrates a profound disrespect for the parties' ability to determine the course of their own lives. Perhaps intrusion on the parties' lives might be justified if, in fact, children were demonstrably better off as a result of the process. There is no credible evidence, however, that this is so . . . While mediation does seem to serve the courts, there is no evidence that it serves children. Research shows that children whose parents reach a settlement in mediation are no better adjusted following the divorce than children whose parents did not use mediation . . . The legislative choice to make mediation mandatory has been a mistake.

The choice presented today in California and in some other states is between an adversary process with totally powerful legal actors, in which clients never speak for themselves (and often do not know what is going on), and a mediation process in which they are entirely on their own and unprotected. The adversary system admittedly works poorly for child custody cases in many respects. There are, however, some ways to avoid damaging custody battles under an adversary system, such as enacting presumptions that make outcomes reasonably clear in advance . . . (the primary caretaker presumption would in most circumstances result in custody to the parent who has performed the day-to-day care of the child. This rule would maintain the child's bond to the parent more directly involved in her care and make it evident that parenting during marriage, by either parent, is to be valued and rewarded) . . . court-sponsored lectures on settlement, and joint negotiation sessions with lawyers and clients present. When in court, lawyers could be held to higher standards with respect to communicating with their clients, and judges could refrain from speaking to lawyers when their clients are not present. (It is difficult to imagine how a client can know whether to trust his lawyer when significant parts of the proceedings take place out of earshot.)

The only reason to prefer mediation to other, more obvious alternatives is that the parties may, through the mediation process, ultimately benefit themselves and their children by learning how to communicate and work together. Whether this will happen in the context of a particular mediation is something only the parties can judge.

Any reform proposals, of the adversarial system or of a mediation alternative, should be rejected if they result in further disempowerment of the disempowered. Reform must operate on two simultaneous levels: first, by changing the institutions and rules that govern custody mediation, and second, by encouraging the respect of each mediator for the struggles and lives of the individuals involved in mediation. Any reforms should evince a concern for the personhood of the mediation clients, a concern that is lacking under current mediation practices.

With respect to institutional changes, an adequate mediation scheme should not only be voluntary rather than mandatory, but should also allow people's emotions to be part of the process, allow their values and principles to matter in the discussion, allow parties' attorneys to participate if requested by the parties, allow parties to choose a mediator and the location for the mediation, allow parties to choose the issues to mediate, and require that divorcing couples be educated about the availability and logistics of mediation so as to enable them to make an intelligent choice as to whether to engage in it.

The second aspect of reform represents more of a personal dynamic, one which is harder to institutionalize or to regulate. But the mediator must learn to respect each client's struggles, including her timing, anger, and resistance to having certain issues mediated, and also must learn to refrain, to the extent he is capable, from imposing his own substantive agenda on the mediation.

CONCLUSION

Although mediation can be useful and empowering, it presents some serious process dangers that need to be addressed, rather than ignored. When mediation is imposed rather than voluntarily engaged in, its virtues are lost. More than lost: mediation becomes a wolf in sheep's clothing. It relies on force and disregards the context of the dispute, while masquerading as a gentler, more empowering alternative to adversarial litigation. Sadly, when mediation is mandatory it becomes like the patriarchal paradigm of law it is supposed to supplant. Seen in this light, mandatory mediation is especially harmful: its messages disproportionately affect those who are already subordinated in our society, those to whom society has already given the message, in far too many ways, that they are not leading proper lives.

Of course, subordinated people can go to court and lose; in fact, they usually do. But if mediation is to be introduced into the court system, it should provide a better alternative. It is not enough to say that the adversary system is so flawed that even a misguided, intrusive, and disempowering system of mediation should be embraced. If mediation as currently instituted constitutes a fundamentally flawed process in the way I have described, it is more, not less, disempowering than the adversary system – for it is then a process in which people are told they are being empowered, but in fact are being forced to acquiesce in their own oppression.

Extract 6:20
J B Kelly and M A Duyree: 'Women's and Men's Views of Mediation in Voluntary and Mandatory Mediation Settings' (1995) 30 *Family and Conciliation Courts Review* 1, pp 37, 41–42, 45

This article focuses on gender differences and similarities found in two different Northern California settings offering mediation services for the resolution of custody and divorce disputes and issues. A smaller segment of data, gathered during the course of two separate, larger studies conducted independently in each setting, are compared with respect to men and women's views of the mediators' functioning and qualities, satisfaction with the process, including ability to express one's viewpoint and perceived influence over the process and agreement, and satisfaction with the outcomes. This report is unique in that the responses of disputants in the court and in the private sector are compared using the same objective measure, thus providing not only the opportunity to compare gender differences across settings but to compare perceptions of mediation clients in a voluntary and a mandatory mediation service. . . .

In the combined group of Family Court Service and NCMC respondents ($n = 184$), there were no gender differences with respect to perceptions of the mediator along a number of dimensions. Both men and women rated their mediators fairly highly on the mediators' warmth and on sensitivity to client feelings, with no significant sex difference on either measure. Further, men and women were just as likely to report that their mediators were mostly helpful in proposing options for resolving disputes and in identifying useful ways to arrange custody and visitation.

With respect to respondents' views of the impartiality and/or neutrality of the mediator, neither the women or men believed that the mediators had imposed their own viewpoints on them. Nor was there a gender difference with respect to whether men and women perceived that the mediators favored their spouse: The majority of men and women disagreed with the statement that the mediators favored their spouses in the mediation process.

There were two mediator dimensions along which there were significant gender differences. While both men and women rated fairly positively the mediators' skill, women were significantly more likely to agree that the mediators were skilful. Similarly, women rated the mediators' ability to keep the mediation focused on important issues in the session significantly more highly than did the men. . . .

The findings of research in two different settings addressing custody and divorce disputes and issues indicated that there were few significant differences between the men and women in their perceptions of the mediators' functioning, the process of mediation, and the outcomes of the mediation process. Where significant gender differences appeared, the women rated the mediation experience more favorably than did the men.

These data suggest some of the reasons why women find the mediation process a satisfactory process. First, an important element of the mediation process is the opportunity to express one's views – a place in which women have a voice. Critics of mediation have condemned the process because they believe that women's voices are not heard and integrated into the final resolutions. However, empirical data obtained from women in two very different mediation settings contradict that theoretical position.

It would appear as well that the mediation process may have benefit for women beyond being given the opportunity to have a voice. Women in both settings reported that they gained confidence in their ability to stand up to their spouse as a result of the mediation. Women not only found a voice but appeared to feel that their voices were heard and legitimated enough to provide them with greater strength or resolve in relation to their former spouse. This greater sense of empowerment may be related to the structure of mediation, which insists that the interests and views of each disputant be articulated and treated with respect. Given the concerns raised that mandatory mediation inherently disempowers people, it was an important finding that women in both voluntary and mandatory mediation settings reported this increased confidence.

Further, women appeared to place value on the opportunity that mediation provided for them to set aside (even if temporarily) some of their anger at their spouse and focus on their children's needs. This experience in mediation is in contrast to the experience of litigating custody and visiting issues, which encourages and consolidates angry parental perceptions and positions, even those which may not be reality-based nor in the children's best interests. In other ways as well, the data do not support the notion that women feel disadvantaged in the mediation process. Women, including those who did not reach full agreement, still believe in the process and would recommend it to their friends. They prefer it to litigation.

Extract 6:21

Sonia Nourin Shah-Kazemi: 'Cross-Cultural Mediation: A Critical View of the Dynamics of Culture in Family Disputes' (2000) 14 *International Journal of Law Policy and the Family* 302, pp 319–320

It is possible to perceive the benefits of exploring the different models of mediation where, for example, community members approve the third party as authorized to perform the tasks of mediation. However, if minority community members are deemed not to have the requisite neutrality required and neutral professionals are chosen instead, the principle of autonomy that community or cross-cultural mediation is predicated upon is then compromised. The initiative to mediate comes then from a source that does not really 'belong'. Contrary to the more commonly held view that it is the mediator who needs to identify with their client, advice and involvement can only be efficacious and acceptable when there is that 'identification' with the mediator by the client. Where a community is a minority, an outsider remains just that, no matter how sympathetic, so much so that even a member of the community who has rejected some of its normative ethics is considered an outsider. All of this follows as a consequence of the heightened salience accorded to the normative framework in any minority community, whose abiding identity as such is founded in large part on this framework. Whilst conducting research into the Hispanic community in America, Taylor and Sanchez argue persuasively for training to be accessible to the 'natural helpers' within the community:

> those who already command respect because of their personal attributes or their position within the community, such as the priest, the formal godparent (compadre), the social workers who are already in agencies specific to the community, and even the mother, who often informally mediates as part of her role to keep the family together. It is unrealistic to think that members of this community will seek out mediation services in little white boxes when there is no anticipation that those providing it will understand the needs and language, let alone the cultural themes and dynamics or the nuances.

The ideal, then, is for mediators to be of the same cultural background as the parties, since no form of training can, *a priori*, impart a fully comprehensive understanding of the 'universe of meaning' that shapes our responses to the whole gamut of situations that arise in the course of life. However, this does not absolve all mediators from the need to acquire training into the dynamics of culture, because to be effective mediators it is necessary to recognize problems involved in bridging the gaps – often unconscious – between the psychological responses differentiated, precisely, by divergent cultural attitudes. Only in light of this awareness can there be any question of appreciating the impact that cultural values have upon the dynamics of a dispute and its resolution.

Confidentiality in Mediation

The fact that mediation typically takes place in the context of other decision-making processes, as is the case in mediation that occurs in the context of legal proceedings, raises issues relating to the use of information disclosed and knowledge acquired in the course of mediation. Unless the substance of discussions taking place in mediation is protected against subsequent revelations, the process of mediation is likely to be affected. In particular, the exchange of information between the parties will be influenced, the independent position of the mediator may be undermined (especially if he or she is later required to report on the mediation), and third parties may be left in an exposed position. Moreover, in some systems, one of the perceived advantages of mediation is that it is often a private process, and this privacy needs to be protected. As a result, in certain parts of the United States, there are now very rigorous confidentiality rules governing information disclosed in the course of mediations.

In the passage that follows, Marian Roberts considers the need for confidentiality in the context of mediation in matrimonial disputes.

Extract 6:22

M Roberts: *Mediation in Family Disputes: Principles of Practice*, 2nd edn. (1997) Arena, Aldershot, pp 133–135

Confidentiality is integral to the relationship between the mediator and the parties . . . is one of the four fundamental and universal characteristics of mediation. It is the cornerstone of the relationship of trust that must exist between the mediator and the parties, and of the free and frank disclosure that is necessary if obstacles to settlement are to be overcome. It is crucial to the voluntariness of participation of the parties, and to the impartiality of the mediator. The parties must not feel that they might be disadvantaged by any disclosure that may be used in legal proceedings, or in any other way. They need to know they have nothing to lose by resorting to mediation.

Confidentiality between the mediator and the parties

Mediators have a duty to make clear to the parties at the outset that communications between them and the mediator are made in confidence, and that the mediator must not disclose any statements made or information received (to the court, solicitors, court welfare officers, social workers, doctors or anyone else) without their joint and express consent or an order of the court (NFM and FMA, 1993).

The risk of child abuse highlights the need to define the limits of confidentiality in mediation. Confidentiality is, of course, not absolute, as it is always subject to the requirement that the law of the land shall be complied with (*Parry-Jones v Law Society* 1968). The limits are those pertaining in all confidential or professional communications, whether between doctor and patient, priest and penitent, or journalist and informant. Therefore, the promise of confidentiality does not prevent the mediator from disclosing information in the exceptional circumstances where there is substantial risk to the life, health or safety of the parties, their children or anyone else.

Mediators, when outlining the limits to confidentiality, refer specifically to dangers to children. There may be other equally applicable life or health-threatening risks associated with situations of great stress, such as suicide or physical violence between adults.

The problem for mediators is not whether confidentiality is absolute, nor whether its limits – implied, as they generally are, in the confidential relationships described above – should be spelt out. The question that arises is *how* this should be done without at the same time stigmatizing decision-making processes with inappropriate criminal/pathological overtones, or damaging the wholehearted commitment of the mediator to the principle of confidentiality by hedging it about with too many restrictions and reservations.

National Family Mediation sets out guidelines on what courses of action to adopt when a child protection issue arises in mediation (Child Protection Guidance and Procedure, 1996), where it appears that there is 'substantial danger, particularly to a child'. In the first instance, it advises that the parties themselves should be encouraged to seek help from an appropriate agency. The mediator should take action in accordance with local child protection guidelines, and should only report the matter to both solicitors or to the social services department or the court welfare service, if already involved, where neither party is willing to do this, and normally, after discussion with both parents.

Confidential information vouchsafed to the mediator by each of the parties is also problematic. Some mediators overcome this by stating in advance that all information disclosed separately must be able to be shared in the joint session. This is intended to prevent alliances being formed between the mediator and one party. Other mediators do allow separate confidential communication, on the basis that free and frank disclosure is necessary for constructive exchanges. Often, such confidential disclosures have little immediate bearing on the matter at hand, in which case there is no problem. There is a problem, however, when information imparted in confidence to the mediator by one party is central to subsequent joint discussion of the dispute. If that party cannot be persuaded to make the necessary disclosure to the other party, then it may be necessary to end the mediation session. This may be preferable to negotiations taking place fettered by the concealment of vital information, unbeknown to the mediator and one of the parties, which might occur if separate confidential communications were not allowed in the first place.

All communications made in the course of mediation – whether between the parties themselves, or between the parties and the mediator(s), or between mediators or the parties' solicitors – are confidential, subject to certain exceptions, and will not be disclosed. In addition to the child protection exceptions already referred to, another exception relates to factual disclosures made in the course of mediation on financial or property issues. Factual data of this kind may be disclosed in any subsequent legal proceedings.

Confidentiality of communications between the parties and third parties outside the process
While confidentiality can be promised by the mediator, confidentiality belongs to the parties, and it is a matter of their own discretion and their decision what information they impart to their solicitors or anyone else. These matters should all be clearly stated at the outset, as should the fact that the court will be very reluctant to allow confidential exchanges between the parties to be used as evidence in any subsequent proceedings (see below).

Confidentiality in relation to legal proceedings (privilege)
Mediation as an alternative to litigation nevertheless occurs within a legal framework. Legal proceedings may follow mediation or take place concurrently over other disputes (for example, finance). Agreements may break down, and litigation may be resorted to subsequently. Variation proceedings may follow changes of circumstance. Details of proposed arrangements for children must be provided before a decree absolute may be granted by the court (Matrimonial Causes Act 1973, s 41).

Public policy has always favoured the settlement of disputes – it is in the public interest that disputes be settled and litigation reduced to the minimum. The privilege of 'without prejudice' negotiation (that is, without prejudice to the legal rights of the maker of the statement) has long been a principle of English law. It attaches to statements and offers of compromise made by the parties and their legal advisers in negotiations for settling disputes. These disclosures may not be used in subsequent legal proceedings without the consent of both parties. The policy of the law has also been in favour of enlarging the cloak under which negotiations may be conducted without prejudice.

Mediation Agreements

In many legal systems one of the virtues claimed for mediation is that agreements that are successfully concluded through this process are likely to be stable and to reduce problems of enforcement. Where the outcome has been reached through a consensual process, and the parties have themselves constructed the agreement with the assistance of the good services of a mediator, they are likely to comply with the terms of the deal that they have struck. However, mediation agreements are not always the conclusive stage in the dispute resolution process, and where execution of agreements becomes problematic this may have an adverse impact on the mediation process itself. The parties are not confident that any agreement reached will be final and effective.

The argument that mediation agreements are likely to secure greater compliance than adjudicated outcomes was significantly advanced in seminal essays by McEwan and Maiman on small claims courts.

Extract 6:23

C A McEwen and R J Maiman: 'Small Claims Mediation in Maine: An Empirical Assessment' (1981) 33 *Maine Law Review* 237, pp 260–264

> Prominent among the weaknesses attributed to small claims courts is the relatively low rate of compliance with their judgments. In part this occurs because a great many small claims cases are uncontested and result in default. Judgments against a 'phantom' opponent are notoriously difficult to collect. However, even among contested small claims cases, payment rates are quite low. Mediation is sometimes asserted to have a greater capacity than adjudication to secure compliance with the terms of settlement. This argument has two dimensions, the first of which is a practical one: mediators can, and often do, encourage defendants to make payment, or at least partial payment, immediately after the agreement is reached. Alternatively, mediators can help disputants set up an explicit time-payment plan as part of their agreement. The data reported earlier show that Maine small claims mediators are indeed more likely than judges to address the question of payment at the time of the settlement.
>
> The second aspect of this assertion of mediation's superiority relates to the mediation process itself: a person who has participated in the fashioning of an agreement is more likely to comply with its terms than an individual who has had a judgment imposed

Table 6.1. *Percentage of Defendants Paying Settlement or Judgment*
Against Them by Hearing Type

	Mediated Cases	Adjudicated Cases	Unsuccessfully Mediated Cases
Paid in Full	70.6	33.8	52.8
Paid in Part	16.5	21.1	13.9
No Payment	12.8	45.1	33.3

99.9 (n = 109) 100.0 (n = 139) 100.0 (n = 36)
chi square = 37.79 with 4 degrees of freedom; p < .01

upon him. Our data corroborate the premise underlying this claim, which is that mediation respondents view their dispute resolution process as more satisfactory and its outcome as fairer than do adjudication respondents.

Our data strongly support the hypothesis that mediation is more likely than adjudication to lead to compliance with the resolution. As Table 6.1 shows, 70.6% of the mediation agreements with a monetary settlement were reported to be paid in full, compared to 33.8% of the adjudications.

Another 16.5% of the mediated settlements, and 21.1% of the adjudicated judgments, were partially paid. In other words, it was more than three times as likely after an adjudicated case as after a mediated case that *no* payment had been made by the defendant. In addition, of the cases that were tried after mediation failed, 52.8% were fully paid and 13.9% were partially paid after judgment. This pattern of findings suggests that there is something about both the mediation process and the kinds of settlements it achieves that leads to higher compliance rates.

In order to understand better the effect of mediation on compliance rates, we tried to separate in our analysis the effects of participating in the mediation process from the effects of the special character of mediation settlements. Our data have shown that mediation settlements included arrangements for immediate payment much more frequently than did judgments. Immediate payment assures compliance. But does this difference between settlements and judgments alone account for mediation's higher compliance rate?

To answer this question, we focused our attention on just those cases in which no immediate payment had been arranged at trial or mediation. If immediate payment alone accounted for the observed disparity in compliance rates between mediation and adjudication, we would expect to find no significant differences in compliance for these cases. In fact, 51.6% of these mediated cases had been fully paid and 28.1% partially paid compared to 30.7% of adjudicated cases fully paid and 22.8% partially paid. This leaves only 20.3% of mediated cases unpaid compared to 46.5% of adjudicated cases. It is clear, then, that even among cases in which no immediate payment was made, mediation produced greater compliance than adjudication.

These data support the inference that there is something about the mediation process itself – as distinguished from the sort of agreements and arrangements for implementation that it tends to produce – that leads mediation defendants to be more likely than adjudication defendants to pay their debts. Some mediation advocates would attribute this to the responses which the process elicits from those who take part in it. In this regard, our data show that mediation leads more often than adjudication to settlements that litigants, defendants especially, perceive to be fair. But does this sense of fairness relate to actual implementation of agreements? In adjudicated cases it relates quite strongly to the likelihood of full or partial payment. Adjudication defendants who perceive the judgment in their case to be fair were considerably more likely to make full or partial payment (74.4%) than were those who considered the court's judgment unfair (49.3%). However, that correlation does not exist in mediated cases, where 86.1% of defendants perceiving an *unfair* settlement and 88.7% perceiving a *fair* settlement had paid the settlement in full or in part. Thus, while the greater sense of fairness in mediation than in adjudication accounts for some of the difference in compliance rates, it alone cannot explain the disparity. One must look more closely then at the feelings and perceptions of participants in mediation and adjudication to explain the differences between payment rates in the two kinds of cases.

Each interview included several questions on the subject of 'intention to pay.' Of the mediation defendants who had not yet paid their debt in full, 82% reported that they intended to pay it. In contrast, only 19% of similarly situated adjudication defendants replied that they intended to pay their unpaid judgment. When these respondents were asked whether they felt a legal obligation to pay, 73% of the mediation defendants reported feeling 'strong' or 'some' such obligation, compared with only 31% of the adjudication defendants. In these same groups, 64% from mediation, and only 12% from adjudication, reported feeling 'strong' or 'some' moral obligation to pay. In sum, mediation defendants are much more likely than adjudication defendants to come away from the process with a feeling of responsibility for their debt. Interestingly, there is a corresponding difference in the way mediation and adjudication *plaintiffs* regard the debt. Plaintiffs who had not yet received full payment from the defendant were asked whether they had taken or intended to take steps to collect the debt. Eighty-two per-cent of the mediation plaintiffs, compared with 69% of the adjudication plaintiffs, answered affirmatively.

These data suggest that the higher compliance rates found in mediated cases probably result in large part from the experience of entering into – literally, signing – an agreement to end the dispute on certain specified terms. This appears to affect both plaintiffs' and defendants' perceptions of the debt. People are more likely to feel bound by an obligation they have undertaken voluntarily and more or less publicly than one imposed upon them in a court of law. It also seems highly likely that the mediator contributes to the disputant's sense that this obligation should be taken seriously – a marked contrast to the message of pessimism or, perhaps even worse, indifference about collection of the debt which was communicated by some of the judges. Finally, the fact that defendants who took part in *unsuccessful* mediations had a substantially better compliance record than those who had not participated in mediation at all suggests that the negotiation process itself – independent of its outcome – helps to inculcate a sense of responsibility about payment. Perhaps merely facing one's opponent for a time, having the opportunity to speak with and to hear him or her, humanizes and personalizes the process enough to affect the defendant's attitude toward payment.

Of course, in many circumstances party dissatisfaction with a mediation agreement may lead to further negotiation and mediation of the dispute. Nevertheless, a key question is the extent to which a legal system or society should allow the parties to resort to the courts in their efforts to secure enforcement. The need for mediation agreements to be legally enforceable, and the ways in which this might be done, are discussed in the following observations on contemporary China.

Extract 6:24
M Palmer: 'The Revival of Mediation in the People's Republic of China: Extra-Judicial Mediation', in W E Butler (ed) *Yearbook on Socialist Legal Systems 1987* (1988) Transnational Books, New York, Dobbs Ferry, pp 270–271

An important aspect of the status of people's mediator concerns the efficacy of the agreements which they persuade the disputants to conclude. A corollary of the emphasis on the voluntary character of people's mediation and the 'mass' nature of mediation committees is the rule that – in contrast to 'in-court mediation agreements', arbitration, and adjudication – people's mediation agreements are not legally binding on the parties. The difficulty which this may create for people's mediators is illustrated by a letter to the legal press from a mediation committee in Shaanxi, central China, in which the writer observes that many local people are bypassing the committee and taking their cases straight to court. It is unlikely that such a letter would have been written had not the committee been faced with a substantial number of such cases.

In order to counteract difficulties of this nature both academic writers and the authorities have highlighted important aspects of this area of mediation work that enhance the status accorded to people's mediation agreements. Ordinarily the agreements give rise only to contractual relations between the parties, and in this connection their limited efficacy is sometimes used to illustrate the differences between extra-judicial mediation and court hearings. Nevertheless, Chinese sources stress that extra-judicial mediation agreements do have a 'constraining force' on the parties, which would seem to imply that the parties are generally expected to honor the obligations assumed in the agreement. Moreover, if the parties affirm their consent to the written instrument by having the document stamped by a 'responsible government department' within one year from the date on which the disputant's rights were infringed, then the agreement does have legal effect. In addition, it is stressed that the parties may benefit from 'administrative' implementation of their agreement in certain circumstances, such as those in which the chairman of a local village committee also serves as chairman of the mediation committee – presumably various kinds of informal sanctions would be applied if one of the parties renounced the mediated agreement.

The status of the people's mediation agreement as a civil contract has recently been confirmed by the Chinese Ministry of Justice in Article 5 of its 'Several Rules for the Work of People's Mediation Committees' (Renmin Tiaojie Gongzuo Ruogan Guiding) 2002:

> Article 5
> According to the 'Several Rules of the Supreme People's Court on Hearing Civil Cases Involving a People's Mediation Agreement', there is nature of civil contract in mediation agreements reached by means of mediation by a people's mediation committee with civil rights and obligations and signed or sealed by both parties to the dispute. All parties shall perform their obligations according to the agreement and shall not alter or dissolve the agreement without the other party's consent.

Other articles in the same set of Rules attempt to strengthen the status of the agreement. Thus, Article 36 authorises the mediation committee to conduct checks in order to ascertain if the obligations entered into in the agreement are being met. Article 37 allows a people's mediation committee to call on governmental or judicial assistance implementing an agreement in which one party (or both parties) is failing to fulfil her or his obligations, and Article 38 requires the committee to assist the court in the matter if judicial proceedings are relied on:

> Article38:
> For a civil case in which any party refuses to fulfil the agreement or goes back on her or his word after the execution of the mediation agreement is filed with the people's court, the people's mediation committee in charge of the dispute case shall assist the people's court in a trial.

D: Conclusion

Thus, a range of questions surrounds the scope and ambition of mediatory intervention:

- Should the mediator's role be confined to improving the communication arrangements between the parties, or should a more extensive role be attempted?
- Beyond providing a structural framework for the process of negotiation, how far should the mediator seek to inform, or further to control, the outcome?
- Has the mediator responsibility for the nature and quality of the outcome? Is the outcome simply a matter for the parties; or can we see the mediator as accountable?
- If the mediator is seen as responsible for the outcome, does this extend to:

  (a) handling imbalances of power in support of the weaker party?
  (b) seeking to ensure the protection of third parties who may be affected by the outcome?

A number of these concerns manifest themselves in the question of the provision of legal advice in the course of mediation.

CHAPTER SEVEN

Umpiring

A: Introduction

Once we start to imagine the range of third-party interventions in dispute processes –
forms of 'the triad' – the line between 'mediation', considered in Chapter Six, and
'umpiring' marks the essential internal boundary in analytic terms. It is a move
from *facilitation*, on the one hand, to *determination*, on the other; the power of
decision is surrendered to a third party.

The simplest case we might imagine is that where two parties in dispute agree
to approach a non-aligned third – the 'neutral stranger' – and ask her to make a
determination for them. A whole range of attributes might give the decision-maker
legitimacy in a particular case. The parties might trust her: because she has no stake
in the issue; because of her reputation as a wise and fair decision-maker; because of
her professional background and training. Simmel underlined, in Extract 6:7, the
defining quality of this simple case: it lies in the consensual nature of the reference –
the disputing parties *agree* to the determination of their issues by someone else.
As he observed: 'the voluntary appeal to an arbitrator . . . presupposes a greater
subjective confidence in the objectivity of judgement than does any other form of
decision' ([1908] 1950: 151).

Another instance of third-party determination arises where the *rank* of the third
party approached – a parent, employer, religious or political superior – gives that
person authority to decide the matter on request of one disputing party alone,
irrespective of the wishes of the other. Such situations of institutionalised hierar-
chy/seniority obviously involve quite different kinds of legitimacy claims to those
applicable in the earlier case.

The native categories of Western legal theory broadly recognise this difference
in drawing a primary distinction between agents providing private *arbitration* and
state-sponsored *courts*. A defining characteristic of the court is its link to the state.
Courts, in exercising their powers of adjudication, have almost invariably been
seen as part of government, sponsored by those at the centre who claim to exercise
a steering rule. This association with government distinguishes the court from
umpiring processes in which the choice of intervener is left to the parties themselves.
The latter processes have been conceptualised in native legal theory under the

broad heading of *arbitration* (see pp 264–275 below). Arbitration shares the basic procedural features of adjudication, namely the submission of proofs and arguments to a third party with authority to impose a binding outcome; but the basis of the arbitrator's intervention is different, lying in the joint invitation of the parties.

In this chapter, we begin by considering the relationship between government and dispute institutions, examining the implications for disputing of the processes of centralisation historically associated with state formation. We then look at the ways in which different forms of umpire acquire legitimacy. Turning specifically to state-sponsored 'courts', we consider the range of roles these can be seen as performing. While it may be a defining characteristic of a court that, by virtue of state sponsorship, it has the *capacity* to make a third-party determination, delivery of judgment is not necessarily its primary responsibility or the reason for parties to resort to it. We conclude by looking at arbitration in its principal institutional contexts.

B: Government and Dispute Institutions

We can now never hope to chart the historical emergence of umpiring institutions in more than a conjectural way; and anyway this trajectory may well have followed a different sequence from one culture to another. While anthropologists have rarely reported institutions of third-party decision-making in acephalous societies, leading texts on arbitration conventionally claim that state-sponsored adjudication developed historically out of arbitral proceedings (Mustill, 1989; Redfern and Hunter, 2004). But whether we imagine the origin in private institutions under which disputants agreed to place their differences before a trusted third party, or in the co-option of mediatory arrangements by those in power as centralisation developed, is ultimately neither here nor there. Whatever view we take of the general origins of umpiring institutions – as being present before centralised government developed and then co-opted, or as evolving with government – those in power seem invariably to have provided dispute institutions for their subjects. Further, 'courts' have historically played a central part in projects of colonial expansion. As Shapiro notes, 'the origin of judicial systems in many parts of the world is to be found in conquest' (1982: 220).

Historically, wherever we find processes of centralisation taking place, courts seem to have appeared and come to represent a central means through which 'government' has revealed itself. This was recognised long ago by Maine in his *Dissertations on Early Law and Custom* (1883: 160) where he noted the intimate link between rulership and adjudication. Subsequently others have underlined this connection (see, for example, Fuller, 1978). We can find examples of this conjunction as far apart as Imperial China (Bodde and Morris, 1967) and (much later) in the Tswana kingdoms of the Kalahari (Schapera, 1956). The extract from Shapiro's study of courts (Extract 7:1) emphasises the generality of the close relationship between government and the courts. In Europe, since medieval times, we can say for certain that courts, as final authoritative agencies of third-party decision-making, have played a central role in government. This close link between the development of courts and the extension of central government power in the common law world is firmly characterised in the account below by Van Caenegem (Extract 7:2).

This truth that courts are ultimately creatures of government has important implications. However plausibly in a modern polity they may present themselves as dispassionate neutrals – there to 'help' people by arriving at disinterested decisions in accordance with general, known criteria – they also exercise a steering role. Historically, rulers never established and underwrote judicial institutions simply for the purpose of settling disputes among their subjects. Central was the ambition to remain in power; and certainly in much of the medieval European world, for example, the principal means available to monarchs for controlling their subjects was the judge.

Extract 7:1

M Shapiro: *Courts: A Comparative and Political Analysis* (1981) University of Chicago Press, Chicago and London, pp 20, 22–24

The congruence of administering and judging must be specially noted. Indeed, the observer who did not so firmly believe in the independence of judging might take judging for a special facet of administering. Both the judge and administrator apply general rules to particular situations on a case-by-case basis. Both tend to rely heavily on precedent, fixed decisional procedures, written records, and legalized defense of their decisions. Both are supplementary lawmakers engaged in filling in the details of more general rules. Both are front-line social controllers for more distant governing authorities. And in a startling number of instances both are the same person, and a person who draws little or no distinction between administering and judging. . . .

Perhaps the most important factor in explaining the historical congruence of judging and administering is to be found in a far broader aspect of the administrator's responsibility for social control. The origin of judicial systems in many parts of the world is to be found in conquest. This is obviously true for imperial judicial systems such as those of Rome, China, and the black empires of central Africa such as the Barotse. As we shall see in chapter 2, it is also clearly true for the common law courts imposed over the old moot and hundred folk courts by the Norman conquerors. Conquest created the British courts of colonial India and Africa as well as many other colonial court systems. The Supreme Court of the United States and the lower federal courts insofar as they operate on the old Confederacy are courts of conquerors. Even where courts are not directly imposed by force of arms, they will often be identified with the political regime or with distant rather than local authority.

Conquerors use courts as one of their many instruments for holding and controlling conquered territories. And more generally, governing authorities seek to maintain or increase their legitimacy through the courts. Thus a major function of courts in many societies is a particular form of social control, the recruiting of support for the regime.

Extract 7:2

R C Van Caenegem: *The Birth of the English Common Law* (1988) Cambridge University Press, Cambridge, pp 18–23

English writers of the century of Henry I and Henry II are full of awe for the majesty of kings. The monarch is 'the likeness on earth of the divine majesty', the 'image of divinity'. The *Leges Henrici Primi* talks of the 'tremendum regie maiestatis imperium' and it is with the words *Regiam potestatem* that Glanvill opens his treatise, in a Prologue reminiscent of the Preface of Justinian's Institutes. The author of the Dialogue of the Exchequer was equally insistent on the eminent position of his master. Here too the opening words, *Ordinatis a Deo*, at once indicate in what key the work is composed. 'It is necessary', says the royal treasurer, 'to be subject and obedient to the powers ordained of God with all fear, for all power is from the Lord God'. He then argues that it therefore cannot be wrong for ecclesiastics to serve kings, 'especially' – note the word – 'in those affairs which involve neither falsehood nor dishonour'. And even if the wealth of kings is not theirs 'by strict process of law', and proceeds 'from their mere arbitrary power', 'their subjects have no right to question or condemn their actions'; they stand or fall by God's judgment and not man's. *Vis et voluntas*, force and willpower were not lacking in the English kings of the time and they were always ready to show it. The successors of the Conqueror had lost nothing of his iron determination: Henry I, the Lion of Justice, destroyed the false moneyers and Henry II ordered the Inquest of Sheriffs and did not hesitate to dismiss them wholesale. The king's word or his writ was to be obeyed by everyone as a matter of course and if this was not done at once, a second writ would express royal amazement and displeasure, impatiently enquire what caused the delay and tell the addressee to mend his ways at once: contempt of a royal writ was a plea of the crown.

The outcome of it all, to which we now turn our attention, was the rise to absolute predominance of the central royal courts under Henry II, as the free man's courts of first instance for all the more important and frequent complaints connected with land-holding throughout the country. There was a dual phenomenon here, centralization and specialization. Centralization meant that an enormous amount of litigation, that would in earlier times have originated in the local courts and stayed there, now came up before a central body of royal judges. The transfer of pleas from local courts through writs of *pone* and *tolt* was easily obtained and local courts were under constant central supervision through the rule *nemo tenetur respondere*, the writ of prohibition and the *writ de falso judicio*. Under Henry I the enforcement of new royal enactments was left to the local courts. Henry II entrusted this to his own justices in eyre. For a man who had unjustly lost his free tenement to appear in the *curia regis* was exceptional in AD 1100, but common by AD 1200. With centralization came professional specialization. The common nucleus of the central courts, ie of the justices in eyre, the Common Bench at Westminster, the Exchequer and the Bench *coram rege*, was the old feudal *curia regis*, something like the primeval amoeba in biology. In this undifferentiated body business of all sorts, political, fiscal and judicial, was transacted on non-professional, casual lines. Under pressure of work a division of labour developed. The barons of the Exchequer formed an institution, distinct, if not always separated from the king's justices; among the latter some were justices itinerant, on eyre in the counties, others, of higher rank, resided at Westminster, still others, the Bench *coram rege* travelled with the king and could consult him if necessary. Initially these men had been temporarily borrowed from their other occupations. Later their work as royal justices became their main task. Their professional outlook and expertise improved correspondingly. They all formed one cohesive group, applied one common law and one set of procedures which was so conveniently expounded in Glanvill.

We are well informed about the rise of the body of central justices. It really began under Henry I when from the *curia regis* some *curiales* were sent on occasional eyres (= *itinera*, journeys) through a certain number of counties to hold pleas – mainly crown and forest pleas – and to supervise and supplement the work of the local courts. The country was not divided into circuits so as to be completely encompassed in these missions (unlike the later system of general eyres), and the itinerant justices were few – about a dozen for the reign of Henry I, with no more than about six at work at any one time – but the essentials of the general eyre were there: a broad scope *ratione materiae* and officials sent *a latere regis* to *inter alia* judicial work on an eyre through several counties. There is nothing unique or amazing about this institution. The Carolingians had sent their *missi dominici* out, the Church knew episcopal visitations, the *curia regis* was itself constantly travelling around and doing judicial business, and even before Henry I's time the king had occasionally sent home trusted men to do justice in important causes in the country, although there had been no judicial eyres *ad omnia placita*. From the Pipe Roll of 1130 where we find such itinerant justices as Ralf Basset, Miles of Gloucester, Pain fitz John, Robert Arundel, Geoffrey de Clinton, Walter Espec, Euctace fitz John, Richard Basset, William d'Albini Brito and Aubrey de Vere we learn most of the system. The practice was obviously well established. It went under during the 'Anarchy', but was one of Henry I's experiments revived by Henry II, who was so keen to restore everything 'sicut fuit tempore avi mei' (as he often put it in his charters and writs). The revival did not come at once. The first years of the reign saw an occasional baron sent out on an eyre – Henry of Essex in southern England, Robert of Leicester in Buckinghamshire – but the general eyre reappeared in 1166, an important year in more than one respect, and from then onwards it developed far beyond anything known under Henry I. The general eyres which started again in 1166 were linked with the repression of felonies – the Assize of Clarendon – and measures to protect the possession of land – the (lost) Assize on Disseisin – beside the traditional forest pleas. While Alan de Neville was holding the latter in Worcestershire, Herefordshire, Staffordshire and Devon, Earl Geoffrey de Mandeville and Richard de Lucy were sweeping through numerous counties from the south-east to the north in quick tempo: by October this eyre was over. The year 1167 brought a pause. Geoffrey de Mandeville had died in October 1166, but Alan de Neville continued on his forest eyre and we can follow him in the pipe roll. In 1168 the general eyres started again: this year saw the beginning of the systematic visitation of the whole country, a permanent feature of English justice for centuries to come. Activity – notably the enforcement of the Assize of Clarendon – went on undiminished in 1169 and 1170 and its geographical scope approximated to the comprehensive circuits covering the whole country, which we find in 1176. Then, quite abruptly, the Inquest of Sheriffs of 1170 brought everything to a halt. Various political circumstances intervened (rebellion and tallage in 1173–4) to interrupt the course of the general eyres till 1175. In that year they were back in full force, with two circuits, one under Ranulf de Glanvill and Hugh de Cressi in the north, and another under William de Lanvalei and Thomas Basset in the south, while the king himself and several judges went on their own *iter*. The years 1176 and 1177 witnessed important general eyres, connected with the enforcement of the Assize of Northampton. We find six groups, each counting three justices, who for the first time were called *justicie errantes*. The eyre was clearly becoming a regular machine for effecting a circuit of all the English counties, although their composition still varied from eyre to eyre. In 1178 the eyres were going on when the king came back from Normandy in July and heard complaints about the excessive zeal of his itinerant justices in enforcing the Assize of Northampton of 1176. He dismissed them and appointed instead five men to hear complaints; they were to travel with him and to refer to him personally if need be. This measure seems to have been temporary and can hardly be seen as the foundation of the Bench *coram rege*. In the year 1179 after Easter there was a great council at Windsor and the justices were sent out on eyres again, this time in four groups, three of which were headed by bishops (not a very canonical arrangement!); one of the four groups of justices travelled with the king himself on the northern circuit. About this time the old, eminent barons disappeared from the eyres and were replaced by lesser men. In the 1180s the system worked regularly. On average we find some twenty justices on eyre in the provinces; in 1189 they were thirty-five, a considerable number that illustrates the progress since the eyres of Henry I.

In those years too the Bench of Common Pleas, a group of permanent royal justices sitting at Westminster, came into being. We do not know exactly when, but they were there when Glanvill wrote and their fixed seat at Westminster was one of the stipulations of Magna Carta. At Westminster the barons of the Exchequer where judicial business was sometimes done also sat. Above them all the king himself could intervene: when he was always absent, like Richard I, no regular court could develop before him, but when he was chiefly in the country, conditions were present for a Bench *coram rege*, ie a court of royal justices travelling with the king though not as a rule hearing cases in his presence. Thus the thirteenth-century Common Law courts had taken shape. The early years of the century saw the court *coram rege* become a permanent professional branch of the *curia regis*. Its competence vis-à-vis the Common Bench at Westminster is not easily defined, but it certainly included pleas that touched the king himself; much also depended on the fortuitous presence of the king in a given part of the country. Both these courts ranked higher than the itinerant justices, although they all formed one body of 'justices of the lord king' applying one, common law. The general eyres remained important until the fourteenth century. Their business was twofold. They first dealt with pleas of the crown, on the basis of a list of questions known as 'the articles of the eyre', a miscellaneous collection of criminal and feudal affairs, and such questions as market control, treasure trove and the misconduct of officials. Then they also dealt with common pleas, ordinary litigation between ordinary parties, frequently under the possessory assizes and by royal writ – they take up most of the common pleas section of the eyre rolls – but not necessarily so. As these same cases could also be brought in Westminster, the question may be asked what or who decided which cases were to go where. The answer is that cases pending in the Common Pleas from the county affected were transferred to the eyre; in fact the Common Pleas started as an exceptional means of catering for those who would not wait for the next eyre. At a further stage the judicial function of the eyre was transferred to the Court of Common Pleas on the one hand, and to itinerant justices with restricted competence on the other (to hear possessory assizes, to deliver jails and, under *nisi prius*, to take from local juries verdicts in cases pending before the central courts). The general eyre fell into disuse.

We know a good deal about Henry II's justices. What bound them together was the king's service. Some were powerful barons, but as time went on, men of simpler rank joined them. The former were rich in their own right, the latter became so by serving the king. Initially the king's household provided most of the justices, later other men with experience in royal service who had been sheriff, or had sat at the Exchequer or been keeper of a royal castle or bailiff of a royal manor were drawn in. For many this judicial work was only occasional. There were a considerable number of clerics, from bishops to simple clerks. Some were men with an academic background, enjoying the title of master, but they were a minority of about a dozen, not even ten per cent of the total force of justices between 1166 and 1189. Some had studied law in the universities, other justices had gained some acquaintance with Roman and Canon Law in a less extensive way: in general the training of a royal justice was very much a practical one. From service in the royal administration they worked their way up, learned the law and saw how justice was done. Initially they had to watch and listen. If they were lucky they found an older man who explained things at length, like the *magister* to the *discipulus* in the Dialogue of the Exchequer; at a later stage they had their law-books, where they could read it all. They belonged in one way or another to the Norman upper class and French was for many centuries the technical language of the Common Law. Rooted as they were in the feudal world of this class it is not surprising that feudal land law has been the core of the Common Law for centuries. These men, high powered professionals, were very different from the provincial suitors, lawmen and aldermen of the traditional local courts.

C: The Legitimation of Third-party Decision-making

In the simple case where two parties agree to put their dispute to a 'neutral stranger' for decision, the problem of legitimation does not really arise. Their very agreement confers legitimacy on the chosen process. So the primary legitimacy claim of the arbitrator lies simply in consent, the fact that the parties have chosen him or her to decide.[1]

---

1 Even so, the progressive steps taken in modernity to tie the enforcement of arbitral proceedings to courts at national level in itself underwrites the legitimacy of international arbitration.

In the first instance, a court's claim to legitimacy lies in its link to government. The authority of the courts to intervene is founded in their incorporation in the official hierarchy. That said, there is at first sight a paradox in the fact that courts in some cultures make a feature of their independence from the legislature and the executive. The native claim to the 'independence of the judiciary' and the doctrine of 'separation of powers' is a central part of legal ideology in the common law world. But this self-conscious claim to autonomy from other branches of government does not in any sense represent a repudiation of the courts' status as part of the apparatus of the nation state.

Concurrent claims to legitimacy are sustained by long-established processual conventions, associated with the general rubric of the 'rule of law'. The publicity of court processes, their explicit commitment to a common repertoire of rules, and the established procedural understandings determining access to them, all go to build up authority, as well as helping to engender a consistent approach to decision-making.

Another means of providing legitimacy for the outcomes of state-sponsored adjudication lies in the hierarchical appellate structure of most judicial systems. Perhaps more commonly, provision may be made for appellate and similar processes that give the losing party access to an alternative outcome. Of course, an unfavourable conclusion may be anticipated by one of the parties and efforts may be made to select a particular arena likely to confer a better result – a strategy often referred to as 'forum shopping', but it is primarily through appellate processes that the parties seek to alter a concrete outcome. The right to appeal is acknowledged in most legal systems and plays an important role not only in encouraging losing parties to accept unfavourable adjudicatory outcomes, but also in facilitating governmental control of the judicial system and, more generally, in promoting the political interests of the ruler (Extract 7:3).

The manner in which this legitimating element of hierarchical review is built into a judicial process varies from one culture to another. Common law jurisdictions are characterised by an appellate structure primarily activated by an aggrieved disputant, whereas in civilian jurisdictions this element is subordinated to an automatic revision process under which an outcome passes for review before successively senior figures in the judicial hierarchy. This striking contrast between common law and civilian traditions is examined below by Mirjan Damaska (Extract 7:4).

The role of lawyers also provides an important element in promoting acceptance of courts as authoritative third-party decision-makers. The close link that exists in the Anglo-American common law world between courts and lawyers underlines this significance. The role of the lawyer in the adjudication process has been viewed as an indispensable feature of that process, and one that promotes the legitimacy of the adversarial system itself. Fuller, for example, has argued that the involvement of the lawyer as an advocate is necessary for the good functioning of adjudication on two principal grounds. First, the slow unfolding of a case and, in particular, the presentation of evidence and arguments and challenges made by the advocate lawyer on behalf of his or her client encourages the judge to reach his or her decision in a reasoned and deliberate manner, avoiding in particular the pitfall of forming too hasty a view of the needs of each party's case. Second, the use of the lawyer as a representative enables the judge to maintain the role of neutral umpire, thereby concentrating on making a 'wise and informed decision of the case' (Fuller and Randall, 1958: 1159–1161; see also Fuller, 1978).

In most common law jurisdictions, the element of 'distance' from government is also underlined in the provenance of the higher judiciary, recruited as they are from the legal profession. The judiciary in common law countries has never been a career path within the civil service, as it has been in the civilian world; rather judicial appointment represents the ultimate career stage of the successful barrister. Judges remain on as Benchers of their Inns, and their names remain associated with the Chambers they belonged to before appointment.

In the evolving civilian tradition, however, the concern from very early on was to develop the judicial role as a professional career. And this career was located in an increasingly rigid and hierarchical bureaucracy, with the judges accorded only limited discretionary powers of decision-making. In the extract that follows, Damaska characterises this development in succinct terms (Extract 7:5).

Extract 7:3

M Shapiro: *Courts: A Comparative and Political Analysis* (1981) University of Chicago Press, Chicago and London, pp 49–52

As we noted earlier, one of the principal virtues of a trial is that it provides an official termination to conflict, relieving the disputants of the necessity of further reciprocal assertions or retributions. But too much finality may be disturbing to the losing member of the triad. One of the functions of a 'right of appeal' may be to provide a psychological outlet and a social cover for the loser at trial. For appeal allows the loser to continue to assert his rightness in the abstract without attacking the legitimacy of the legal system or refusing to obey the trial court. Indeed the loser's displeasure is funnelled into a further assertion of the legitimacy of the legal system. Appealing to a higher court entails the acknowledgment of its legitimacy.

We also noted earlier that the principal problem of the triadic form of conflict resolution was keeping the loser from perceiving the final situation as 'two against one.' Appeals mechanisms are devices for telling the loser that if he believes that it did turn out two against one, he may try another triadic figure. Perhaps just as important, the availability of appeal allows the loser to accept his loss without having to acknowledge it publicly. The purpose of a trial is to effect a termination of conflict. But too abrupt a termination may be counterproductive of true conflict resolution. Appeal, whether actually exercised, threatened, or only held in reserve, avoids adding insult to injury. The loser can leave the courtroom with his head high talking of appeal and then accept his loss, slowly, privately, and passively by failing to make an appeal. We often see appeal principally as a mode of ensuring against the venality, prejudice, and/or ignorance of trial court judges and of soothing the ruffled feelings of the loser. Appeal does indeed serve their functions, but it does so by the imposition of hierarchical controls on trial court behavior. A great deal of interest to political scientists lurks in that hierarchical element.

We have already noted that in a predominant share of the governing systems that have existed in the world, judging is either a facet of administration, or is closely aligned with it. It is a commonplace of administrative lore that no matter what the theory, Weberian hierarchies do not give the top or center adequate control over rank and file administrators in the field. Such control will not occur unless a number of alternative channels of information are available that can be cross-checked at or near the top. The best-known modern example is obviously the Soviet Union, with its trade union, government, party, control commission, and police hierarchies imposed on one another. When administrators hold courts, appeal becomes such a mechanism out of control. A 'right' of appeal is a mechanism providing an independent flow of information to the top on the field performance of administrative subordinates.

It is not only an independent flow, but one highly complementary to the normal administrative reporting. Such reporting usually takes the form of summarization. Each field administrator handles hundreds of thousands of bits of information about local affairs and his own performance. Let us suppose that each passed everything he knew along to his superiors. Each superior supervises a number of subordinates. Each would be flooded with millions of bits of information – far more than he could handle. So normally each field administrator passes to his superior only a summary of the information he has developed. And each superior passes on only a summary of those summaries to his superior. In the process much information is necessarily lost. And not unnaturally, what tend to get lost most easily are those instances in which the subordinate has done badly. The superior never sees the full details of any specific things his subordinates have done. The summaries he sees tend to emphasize his subordinates' successes and leave out the failures. ('Last year this office handled over three thousand claims of which 91 percent were settled within forty-eight hours.')

The appeals process cuts across this summarization because the unit of appeal is a single case, in all its details, rather than a summary of overall performance. It is not a single instance chosen by an administrator to illustrate his success, but an instance chosen by a consumer of administration who feels that the administrator has failed. Finally, not only is the appeals case a detailed sample of administrative work product, but it is a partially random sample. The distribution of cases appealed is not determined by either the goals of the administrative subordinate or his superior but by the nonadministrative motivations of individual litigants. Let us suppose that a chief engineer wishes to check the performance of his auto assembly line. His normal mechanism is to check the statistics reported by his foreman on the number of engines mounted, doors attached, and so on, including the final figures on cars produced. Or alternatively, he could look at every hundredth car. Appeal would allow him to check in yet another way. The customer who got the 'lemon' would bring the car in and insist that the chief engineer take it all apart to see exactly what things had been done wrong on the line.

Thus, on the one hand, while appeal is a partially random sample, it is one loaded toward administrative failure. It will not be every fifth car or every green car that is sampled, but some of the worst cars and very, very few of the best. On the other hand, the administrative superior may impose some patterning by making it known what kinds of appeal are most likely to be successful. We have already seen that English appeal courts at one time said they would listen to appeals on questions of law but not of fact. Thus they got to see cases in which trial courts had made mistakes of law, but not those where the court had done bad fact-finding. Field administrators can also partially control the pattern of appeals. In chapter 4 we shall see that a Chinese local magistrate who did not wish his superiors to know about his performance in a particular dispute could pressure the parties to settle by mediation. A mediated settlement could not be appealed.

At the opposite extreme, it is possible to run an appeals system that takes 100 percent or at least a very full sample. In Tokagawa Japan, every opinion of a trial court was prepared as only a draft of an opinion by the higher authorities. Each draft went forward and came into legal force only after the higher authorities had approved it. In this system, then, all cases are appealed. Most American states provide one appeal in criminal cases as a matter of right. The common practice of the defense bar in many of those states is to file an appeal for every losing defendant. Some states have mandatory first appeals for all cases in which the punishment is severe. These state systems approach 100 percent appeal. Whenever a central government seems to be attempting 100 percent sampling, however, the reality will usually turn out to be otherwise. Thus in states where a first appeal is routine, the intermediate appellate court that hears such appeals will usually deny 90 percent of them in one-line orders that show that they were given only a cursory glance. The appellate court will decide the other 10 percent. And of those only a very few will move on to a further appeal to the state supreme court.

Of course, where there is a separate judicial hierarchy, appeal is typically the central mode of supervision by higher courts over lower, and reversal on appeal a central form of administrative sanction. In such instances the need for multiple channels of information and controls leads the top to demand other institutions in addition to appeal, such as judicial conferences, centralized personnel systems, and administrative reporting, to increase their control over their subordinates.

The insistence, so frequently encountered, that the chain of appeal eventually arrive at the chief, the king, or the capital, instead of stopping at some intermediate level, is difficult to explain except in terms of centralized political control. If the only function of appeal were to ensure against corruptness or arbitrariness on the part of the trial judge, then appeal to anyone even a single step higher in the scale of authority would be sufficient. In the American states we have just discussed, for instance, appeals could all stop at intermediate appellate courts. Why should any go on to a state supreme court? Its justices are really no more capable of righting the injustices done to the loser in the trial court than are the appeals court judges who first heard the appeal. The top insists on being the ultimate level of appeal because it serves its purposes, not those of a losing disputant.

Of course, just as one of the functions of any appeal may be to reduce the psychic shock to losers, so the right to 'take the case all the way to the Supreme Court' provides even greater catharsis for the loser whether he employs it only rhetorically or actually does it. Yet even at this personal level, and quite apart from the question of hierarchical control, the top is likely to see the advantages in preserving a right of ultimate appeal.

Earlier we noted that the extension of judicial services outward and downward is a device for wedding the countryside to the regime. So the preservation of appeal to the chief-king-emperor-capital is a device for keeping the strings of legitimacy tied directly between the ruled and the person of the ruler or the highest institutions of government. In the imperial Chinese legal system . . . , cases involving capital punishment were automatically appealed from local courts through intermediate appeals courts and ultimately to the emperor himself. The accused was shipped along with his appeal up the appeals ladder. When the death sentence was ultimately commuted, the commutation was ceremonially delivered to the prisoner in the capital and depicted as the personal mercy of the emperor. When the death penalty was confirmed, the prisoner was shipped back down the appeals ladder. He was dispatched on the local execution ground of the trial court that had convicted him initially. No clearer declaration of the political purpose of appeal could be made.

Conversely, the ability to reach down occasionally into the most particular affairs of the countryside provides an important means of reminding the rank and file that the rulers are everywhere, that no one may use his insignificance or his embeddedness in the mass to hide from central authority. Thus the personal ruler, be he Zulu war chief or medieval monarch, rarely totally gives up his personal participation in appeals. Nor do modern central governments often provide that there be only a single appeal from trial court to regional appeals court without any opportunity to go on to a central appeals court.

Thus appellate institutions are more fundamentally related to the political purposes of central regimes than to the doing of individual justice. That this is true is evidenced by the nearly universal existence of appellate mechanisms in politically developed societies, even those whose governments place little or no value on individual rights. . . . [W]e shall examine the absence of appeal in Islamic law as a test of this hypothesis about the relation of appeal to centralization of political authority.

Even if judges did nothing but conflict resolution, appeal would be an important political mechanism both for increasing the level of central control over administrative subordinates and for ensuring the authority and legitimacy of rulers. When we enter the realms of social control and law-making, the multiple functions of appeal are even more apparent. When trial courts or first-instance judging by administrators is used as a mode of social control, appeal is a mechanism for central coordination of local control. The 'questions of law' passed on to the appeals courts are in reality requests for uniform rules of social conduct and indicators of what range of case-by-case deviation from those rules is permissible by first-line controllers.

Extract 7:4

M R Damaska: *The Faces of Justice and State Authority* (1986) Yale University Press, New Haven and London, pp 48–50, 58–60

Here I shall look more closely at various ramifications of regular superior audits: not only do they reveal characteristic aspects of the hierarchical style, but they also prevent us from mistakenly extrapolating, from identical verbal formulae, true hierarchical review from its apocryphal forms, such as can be found in predominantly coordinate judicial organizations. This confusion is endemic to discourse between Continental and common lawyers, although it often passes unnoticed.

The first important point to recognize is that the reviewing stage is conceived not as an extraordinary event but as a sequel to original adjudication to be expected in the normal run of events. In well-integrated judicial hierarchies, such as the Soviet, supervision by higher-ups need not be conditioned – as it is in classical Continental systems – upon an appeal by a disaffected party; it can also take place as part of the official duty of higher judicial authorities. Far Eastern systems have been known to go even further: original decisions were treated as mere drafts of judgments that could be announced in definitive form only by superiors. Observe that where review is routine, it is also normal to postpone enforcement of the original decision until the highest authority has spoken. Thus, in contrast to the situation in coordinate systems, where the initial decision is presumptively final, there is no need expressly to ask the primary adjudicator to postpone (stay) the execution of his decision pending review: until hierarchical supervision has been given the chance to run its course, the decision is not yet res judicata.

Hierarchical review is not only regular, it is also comprehensive. There are few aspects of lower authority's decision making that are accorded immunity from supervision: fact, law, and logic are all fair game for scrutiny and possible correction. Where reconsideration by superiors is so pervasive, it makes sense to require lower authority to make clear exactly what it has determined and why. Perfunctory and conclusory statements of grounds, so prevalent among trial judges in common-law jurisdictions, invite rebuke and reversal in a hierarchical judicial system.

Once a lower official has spoken, the procedural episode conducted before him comes to an end (*functum officio*): corrections of his decision, if needed, can now be made only by higher-ups in the organization. Requests to reconsider addressed to the initial adjudicator are therefore misplaced; such requests will be seen to characterize the coordinate style. Simultaneous review of a judgment by different echelons of authority violates the hierarchical sense of order and rank: were such parallelism permitted, subordinates could try to conceal their mistakes or render the work of their superiors superfluous by setting their own decisions right. However, reversal or modification of a decision does not necessitate a finding that the subordinate decision maker had erred or committed a fault; even if impeccable at the time of rendition, a judgment can be changed by superiors. Thus if new evidence is discovered pending an appeal (casting doubts on the propriety of a decision, but no blame on the decision maker), it must be submitted to the reviewing authority rather than to the original adjudicator. Of course, if fault is found, hierarchical organizations have a battery of instruments at their disposal to teach the errant official a lesson. Given such great disciplinary powers, there is less need in hierarchical than in coordinate organizations to resort to the costly reversal of an otherwise proper decision in order to discourage official misconduct, but the calculation of the costs and benefits of such a reversal is not exactly alike in the two settings of authority. I shall return later to this point in several contexts.

The great significance attributed to 'quality control' by superiors in a hierarchical organization inevitably detracts from the importance of original decision making: the latter acquires an aura of provisionality. It is thus a mortal sin for a comparativist to assume that the significance of trials is identical in proceedings before an officialdom gravitating toward the hierarchical or toward the coordinate ideal. On the other hand, the importance of quality control explains why a regular and comprehensive system of appeals is typically regarded in hierarchical judicial organizations as an essential guarantee of fair and orderly administration of justice, or as an essential component of personal 'due process.' It should not be surprising, therefore, to find the right to appeal enshrined in several constitutions as one of the basic rights of citizens. . . . Legal remedies against judgments of common-law decision makers are a bizarre world for Continental lawyers to contemplate. While much of what they find is vaguely familiar, it is bathed in an atmosphere in which even easily recognizable objects assume a strange surrealist quality. Much of their enigmatic character can be dispelled if Anglo-American legal remedies are interpreted as reflecting a continuing attachment to the ideal of one-level decision making upon which bits and pieces of hierarchical quality control have been grafted. I shall now explore the principal ramifications of single-level decision making in order to convey a sense of the legal landscape into which fragments of hierarchical supervision have been introduced.

In a horizontal apparatus of justice the fact that original decisions are presumptively final does not imply that they are all vested with guillotine finality and immediately enforced. With nobody to look over his shoulder, the decision maker can decide provisionally or conditionally: he can change his mind. Hence, one possibility for altering decisions is to induce the adjudicator to take a second look at his own decision or to permit a new hearing. Motions for reconsideration, so intriguing to one accustomed to a different setting of authority, are as normal and prevalent in the coordinate apparatus of authority as are requests for superior review in hierarchical judicial organizations. Another possibility, even more curious to outsiders, is for affected parties to take advantage of the horizontal relationship among coordinate officials, and to try to frustrate the enforcement of decisions that are immune from 'direct' attack. Without waiting for proceedings to run their full course to an anticipated unfavorable outcome, these persons can institute another action, pursuing roughly the same issue before another official in the hope that the second decision, favorable to them, may lead to the nullification of the effects of the first. Observe that in an organization dominated by lay officials the notion of what issues are 'identical' to those already pending in court is not likely to be rigid. Yet another strategy is for the disaffected party to request a parallel official to block the enforcement of a decision rendered by a colleague. To a mind accustomed to hierarchical ordering of authority, such procedural moves can be taken as distressing signs of a seriously flawed judicial organization, but to a mind embracing the ideal of wide distribution of adjudicative powers, such blocking maneuvers are a small price to pay for the realization of desirable power relations.

Extract 7:5

M R Damaska: *The Faces of Justice and State Authority* (1986) Yale University Press, New Haven and London, pp 32–38

The next step in the development of the Continental judicial organization was taken by the kings of France. Starting in the thirteenth century, the Capetians began to build a stratified corps of professional officials better to assert and extend royal power. Instead of entrusting local potentates with independent authority, they chose to dispatch their own agents to perform a variety of local functions. Often of lowly origin and dependent on the king for their livelihood, these royal officers were loyal to the center and relatively immune from local pressures. Divided into ranks, they were interconnected by a system of review: appeals from *prévôts* went to the bailiffs and from the bailiffs to the central royal authority. The resulting administrative apparatus became quite popular as a model for aspiring princes in other Continental lands.

There were also significant developments in the chief court of the land, the Parlement of Paris, in which trained lawyers gradually displaced magnates of the realm as decision makers. Following the lead of ecclesiastical judicial organization, the principal task of this high court became the review of decisions rendered by inferior judicial authority, including a mosaic of seigneurial courts. But even when the Parlement exercised original jurisdiction, the judges came to be removed from activities associated with trials (such as proof taking, for example), and were deprived of the fresh scrutiny characteristic of original decision making. The material needed for decision was gathered in documentary form and neatly arranged for decision makers by a variety of specialized judicial officials. One among them, charged with safeguarding the royal interest, ultimately became the public (state) prosecutor, an office widely copied in other lands. Functional differentiation affected the decision making panel as well: one judge was assigned to sift through documents and report to his colleagues about the case. Following the rendition of the decision, based in important ways on his report, the *rapporteur* was required to draft the judgment of the court. (Incidentally, the type of the judgment became increasingly formal, calling for special initiation and training). In the course of the fourteenth century a clearly defined ranking of officials emerged within the Parlement, and with it also the possibility of internal appeals. In short, emergent processes of hierarchical bureaucratization were unmistakable.

But it was not until the strengthening of princely absolutism in the sixteenth and seventeenth centuries that centralized bureaucracies started to dominate the governmental apparatus in the influential Continental countries. Even language was now affected by pressures toward regimentation. Official discourse was to be conducted in rigidly structured speech forms, dry, Latinate, and 'abstract' in comparison with the colloquial private idiom. The idea of impersonal office was extended to the very heart of government. Despite the famous later dictum of Louis XIV, '*l'état c'est moi*,' it is in this period that the idea of the state became detachable from the personal status of the ruler and converted into an institutionalized (impersonal) locus of allegiance.

In the great majority of Continental countries judicial officials became career professionals. Lay participation in the legal process, where it survived at all, was reduced to insignificance or to a ritual. No longer were judicial functionaries, now organized into a hierarchy, perceived as unrelated to the center of state power. And unlike the judges of the church, secular adjudicators were no longer permitted to mould ordinances and other legal sources to conform to their conscience. The integrity of a powerful central authority was thought to require strict governance by rules. Highly placed judges found the resulting shrinkage of discretionary space quite acceptable: they became accustomed to deciding on the basis of orderly documents that screened out 'messy' situational and personal nuances likely to exert pressure toward leeway in decision making. As a bureaucratic maxim of the period asserted, *quod non est in actis non est in mundo* ('what is not in the file does not exist').

D: The Role of Courts

Courts can be seen as fulfilling a number of analytically distinct roles, beyond being a decision-making branch of government concerned primarily with public order and helping citizens to resolve their disputes. As one of the public faces of government, the courts have primary, exemplary roles in the cognitive and normative domains, constituting, keeping in place and justifying a particular view of how the social world is, and ought to be. Powerful ideological and ritual resources are often harnessed for these purposes. In England, the gothic splendour of the Royal Courts of Justice symbolises the historical continuity of government, representing order and continuity in the social world as the long-standing, skilled achievement of those in power. In the same way, government has blatantly co-opted the potent image of the blind goddess with her scales in presenting itself as the purveyor of 'justice'. Within the building, the authority and hierarchies of government are emphasised through formality, of space, dress and language. Dickens captured the impression that this could make on an unsympathetic onlooker in a famous passage from his account of Chancery (Extract 7:6).

In the period of late nineteenth-century European colonial expansion, courts played both a symbolic and a substantive role as expressions of the metropolitan power. In the former British African territories, for example, one early jural act under Order in Council was the establishment of a High Court. A dual system was then perfected with the subsequent recognition of 'native courts' administering 'native' (later, 'customary') law. This led in jural terms to the marginalisation of indigenous agencies, whatever the realities on the ground might have been.[2] In the extract below Richard Abel explores the more general patterns of response to the imposition of Western courts in the developing world (Extract 7:7).

The decision-making practices of the courts have a further role, beyond the simple resolution of disputes. In making decisions in accordance with 'rules', the courts keep the normative repertoire under constant review and revision. We have noted earlier (see p 59 et seq above) how Fiss, in a fundamental apology for adjudication, goes so far as to argue that the role of judges in resolving disputes is secondary to their function of restating important public values: 'adjudication is the social process by which judges give meaning to our public values' (Fiss, 1979: 2). The centrality of adjudication is reasserted by presenting judgment as the means through which the core repertoire of norms in society is publicised and refurbished.[3]

---

2 It also often led to quite informal procedures in the conduct of civil trials in the colonial courts – see, for example, Johnston's account of civil proceedings in Weihaiwei, northern China (1910: 104–108).

3 The claims made by Fiss in favour of the normative role of adjudication ignore powerful strands of argument in some cultures to the effect that courts should not be involved in norm production and

In some legal cultures this represents another primary role played by an appellate structure, as Shapiro emphasises (Extract 7:8).

The story of courts as public decision-making bodies takes a new turn with the increasingly important place that is accorded to adjudication and courts in a wide range of international legal assistance programmes. Worries about the quality of governance in Africa, Latin America and Eastern Europe in particular have encouraged many donor agencies – but perhaps most strikingly the World Bank[4] – and governments to emphasise the importance of formal legal frameworks and institutions. Accordingly, the notion has gained ground that perhaps the most important responsibility of governments in developing countries is to provide a meaningful 'rule of law', and that efforts to implement this goal should give central place to an independent judiciary in which accessible and efficient courts apply the law in an even-handed, fair minded, and predictable fashion (Extract 7:9).

Courts are also used by litigants in a range of ways that go beyond the simple request for delivery of judgment. We may go to court to publicise an already existing state of affairs, or simply to waste the resources of an enemy.[5] Perhaps most notably, litigation has come to be used in the common law world as lawyers' principal vehicle for their settlement strategies. So settlement, rather than being a 'private' process, has merged procedurally with the 'public' pursuit of judgment. Conceptualising their handling of disputes from the outset as 'litigation', and setting out on the path towards the court at an early stage, lawyers aim to 'settle' disputes, typically a very long way down the avenue to trial, rather than allow them to go all the way to judgment. We noted in an earlier chapter (see p 3 above) how a particular syndrome has developed under which late settlement is achieved by using the procedural framework prescribed for bringing a dispute to trial and judgment.

Extract 7:6
C Dickens: *Bleak House* (1994, originally 1852–53) Penguin Books, Harmondsworth, Middlesex, pp 2–3

> The raw afternoon is rawest, and the dense fog is densest, and the muddy streets are muddiest, near that leaden-headed old obstruction, appropriate ornament for the threshold of a leaden-headed old corporation: Temple Bar. And hard by Temple Bar, in Lincoln's Inn Hall, at the very heart of the fog, sits the Lord High Chancellor in his High Court of Chancery.

renovation. Politically, the role of courts in rule-creating has often been regarded with suspicion, and civilian systems have traditionally allowed little scope for judicial law-making in the process of creating new legal norms – a legacy of the revolutionary distrust of courts in eighteenth-century France as creatures of the ancien regime. Legislators, and even scholars, are represented as more appropriate sources.

4 See, for example, Shihata (1995).
5 For a case study of the cultural embeddedness of the various social and legal factors that may influence the decision to go to court, see Lowy (1978).

Never can there come fog too thick, never can there come mud and mire too deep, to assort with the groping and floundering condition which this High Court of Chancery, most pestilent of hoary sinners, holds, this day, in the sight of heaven and earth.

On such an afternoon, if ever, the Lord High Chancellor ought to be sitting here – as here he is – with a foggy glory round his head, softly fenced in with crimson cloth and curtains, addressed by a large advocate with great whiskers, a little voice, and an interminable brief, and outwardly directing his contemplation to the lantern in the roof, where he can see nothing but fog. On such an afternoon, some score of members of the High Court of Chancery bar ought to be – as here they are – mistily engaged in one of the ten thousand stages of an endless cause, tripping one another up on slippery precedents, groping knee-deep in technicalities, running their goat-hair and horse-hair warded heads against walls of words, and making a pretence of equity with serious faces, as players might. On such an afternoon, the various solicitors in the cause, some two or three of whom have inherited it from their fathers, who made a fortune by it, ought to be – as are they not? – ranged in a line, in a long matted well (but you might look in vain for Truth at the bottom of it), between the registrar's red table and the silk gowns, with bills, cross-bills, answers, rejoinders, injunctions, affidavits, issues, references to masters, masters' reports, mountains of costly nonsense, piled before them. Well may the court be dim, with wasting candles here and there; well may the fog hang heavy in it, as if it would never get out; well may the stained glass windows lose their colour, and admit no light of day into the place; well may the uninitiated from the streets, who peep in through the glass panes in the door, be deterred from entrance by its owlish aspect, and by the drawl languidly echoing to the roof from the padded dais where the Lord High Chancellor looks into the lantern that has no light in it, and where the attendant wigs are all stuck in a fog-bank! This is the Court of Chancery; which has its decaying houses and its blighted lands in every shire; which has its worn-out lunatic in every madhouse, and its dead in every churchyard; which has its ruined suitor, with his slipshod heels and threadbare dress, borrowing and begging through the round of every man's acquaintance; which gives to monied might the means abundantly of wearing out the right; which so exhausts finances, patience, courage, hope; so overthrows the brain and breaks the heart; that there is not an honourable man among its practitioners who would not give – who does not often give – the warning, 'Suffer any wrong that can be done you, rather than come here!'

Extract 7:7

R Abel: 'Western Courts in Non-western Settings: Patterns of Court Use in Colonial and Neo-colonial Africa', in S Burman and B Harrell-Bond (eds) *The Imposition of Law* (1979) Academic Press, New York and London, pp 168, 195–197

The imposition [in Africa of 'Western courts'] did not occur at a single point in time. It began at the onset of colonial rule (whose first, and for a long time only, justification was the maintenance of law and order), was elaborated throughout the colonial period as new judicial institutions were introduced and existing ones modified, and has been perpetuated, even intensified, by the elite regimes that have sought modernization and development following political independence. The consequences I will explore differ from those of the usual impact study in two ways. First, I am not asking whether these new institutions attained their 'purpose' but am rather looking for their inadvertent, unintended, unforeseen, or latent consequences. Indeed, it is doubtful whether the imposition of western courts in Africa was motivated by conscious purpose other than the desire of colonial rulers to assert their belief in the superiority of metropolitan institutions. Second, my research has not yet reached the stage where I can speak with confidence of 'social' consequences; instead, I will discuss changes in the *use* made of these institutions. Obviously, such changes in the pattern of litigation will, in turn, have consequences for society, a subject for future investigators . . .

[I] conceive of the westernization of primary courts in Africa as an instance of the imposition of law, and . . . view the consequences of that imposition from the litigant's perspective. Legal institutions, whether they are imposed or evolve organically, do not determine behavior; they constrain it, offering new alternatives at the same time that they modify the old. Within these constraints, people choose whether or not to use the westernized courts, and the strategies they will employ if they do litigate. The exercise of these choices has very significant consequences. It determines the law that will be applied and thus influences the outcome of the dispute; in this sense people make law and decide cases. It affects the future relationships of the parties and settings; people embedded in tribal social structures and therefore possessed of alternative forums for airing interpersonal disputes will increasingly shun modernized courts as those are perceived to be instruments of governmental discipline.

Despite huge gaps and flaws in the evidence, I am satisfied that the theory I proposed is basically sound. Social structure and institutional structure do interact to produce patterns of litigation. Two major trends in litigation are discernible as social and institutional variables are changed. First, tribal social structures and modern courts are incompatible; the introduction of the latter into the former leads to a decline in tribal litigation. This should be a matter of some concern, regardless of one's views concerning the relative worth of tribal and modern society. Tribal social relations can be found in all societies, irrespective of their level of technological development or mode of political organization. We are constantly rediscovering multiplex, enduring, affective relationships in economic life, in the extended family, within large institutions, in residential groupings, even between criminals and their victims. Tribal litigation is integrative; it preserves and even strengthens those relationships. If courts are modernized, one forum for tribal litigation is removed. Furthermore, the mere availability of modern courts seems to undermine tribal dispute processing elsewhere in the society. Many commentators recently have deplored the absence of tribal modes of dispute processing in contemporary western society.

The second trend complements the first. Modern social structures and modern courts are compatible; the rate of modern litigation will rise in modern courts in urban areas, and only there. And modern litigation contributes to the development and maintenance of modern social structures in much the same fashion that tribal litigation integrated tribal society. In its ideal form litigants, who are strangers to each other aside from the focus of the dispute and are equals in resources and competence, assert competing claims in terms of a law that favors neither before an impartial judge who unilaterally pronounces and enforces an all-or-nothing judgment. There have certainly been times and places when actual litigation approximated this ideal type, though it is not clear from my data that litigation in contemporary urban Africa does so, or ever will. But the predictable enforcement of contractual obligations, the predication of tort liability upon fault, the free alienation of, and development of secure interests in, property, even the greater freedom to form and dissolve family relationships – all can be found in the recent history of western legal systems. And this contribution of litigation to modern society can be valued on grounds that command a broad consensus. Modern litigation is an expression of liberal political and economic theory. The individual litigant, in seeking to maximize his self-interest under clearly defined rules, is seen by classical economics as competing in a free market and thus furthering the most efficient allocation of resources. Similarly, the modern litigant, in freeing himself from traditional social constraints and asserting his political rights, is achieving maximum self-realization of his individuality. Thus the introduction of modern courts into modernizing societies does foster liberal values.

But this chapter, like other recent analyses, also suggests that these attributes of litigation under liberal capitalism are short-lived, no more than a brief, transitional way station on the road toward patterns of litigation that offend against all the values of the rule of law. Three deviations from the ideal type of modern litigation are already visible in contemporary Africa. First, there is a decline in the accessibility of the court to individual litigants, and warning of a much more radical curtailment in the future, as primary courts are thoroughly professionalized. In modern society, where much interaction occurs between strangers who are not bound together by any relationship, individual disputants confronted with an increasingly inaccessible tribunal will simply terminate the relationship – they will 'lump it'. Second, there is growing dominance of the court by criminal prosecution, and especially by administrative offenses, which renders it less attractive to potential litigants. Third, adjudication in modern courts, whether civil or criminal, becomes increasingly superficial – a rubber-stamping of decisions reached elsewhere.

Extract 7:8

M Shapiro: *Courts: A Comparative and Political Analysis* (1981) University of Chicago Press, Chicago and London, p 54

In this context social control and lawmaking are usually intimately connected. Appeal is not simply a device for ensuring a certain uniformity in the operations of rank-and-file social controllers. It also ensures that they are following rules or laws or policies of social control acceptable to the regime. Indeed, appeal is a key mechanism in injecting centralized social control into the conflict resolution activities of courts. For appeal is the channel through which the central political authority assures itself that its rank-and-file conflict resolvers are applying legal rules that resolve conflicts in the desired directions. Earlier we noted that the substitution of legislated law for rules created by the mutual consent of the parties introduced a third set of interests into two-party litigation, whatever interests were embodied in the legislation. At least in large and complex societies, trial courts are too many and too localized to articulate this third set satisfactorily. Appellate courts are more suitable.

Extract 7:9

Boaventura de Sousa Santos: 'Law and Democracy: (Mis)trusting the Global Reform of Courts', in Jane Jenson and Boaventura de Sousa Santos (eds) *Globalizing Institutions: Case Studies in Regulation and Innovation* (2000) Ashgate, Aldershot, pp 253–255, 279–280

To say that we are entering a period of globalization – of markets and institutions as of culture – is today commonsensical. Globalization of democracy and law are also talked about in this context . . . [as there is] greater social and political visibility and protagonism of courts in several countries, and . . . global call for the rule of law and the reform of the judicial system. It is . . . hard to understand why, since the late 1980s, courts have become so prominent in the daily newspapers of many countries of Europe, Latin America, Africa and Asia; why so many projects for judicial reform have been started in different countries of the various continents; and why multilateral agencies and foundations for international aid have been giving priority to judicial reform programmes and rule of law programmes in such diverse countries as Russia, Guatemala, Colombia, Sri Lanka, the Philippines, South Africa, Mozambique, Nigeria, Uruguay, China, Argentina, Cambodia and so on.

The rule of law/judicial consensus is the fourth pillar that grounds the hegemonic consensus on the alleged erosion of deep political cleavages in our time, referred to in the Introduction to this volume. This consensus derives from the other three consensuses: the neo-liberal economic consensus; the weak state consensus; and the liberal democratic consensus. The neo-liberal development model, with its greater reliance on markets and the private sector, has changed the ground rules of both private and public institutions, calling for a new legal framework for development conducive to trade, financing, and investment. The provision of such a legal framework and the responsibility for its enforcement is the new central role of the state, which is allegedly best fulfilled in a democratic polity. The rule of law is thus quintessential in development: 'the development potential of law lies in that law is not only a reflection of the prevailing forces in society; it can also be a proactive instrument to promote change' (Shihata 1995: 13). This, however, will only be possible if the rule of law is widely accepted and effectively enforced. Only then are certainty and predictability guaranteed, transaction costs lowered, property rights clarified and protected, contractual obligations enforced, and regulations applied. To achieve all this is the crucial role of the judicial system: 'a well-functioning judiciary in which judges apply the law in a fair, even, and predictable manner, without undue delays or unaffordable costs, is part and parcel of the rule of law' (Shihata 1995: 14). The judiciary is responsible for delivering equitable, expeditious and transparent judicial services to citizens, economic agents, and the state.

But inasmuch as the role of the state has been reformed to serve the new global consensus, the judicial system must be reformed as well. Judicial reform is an essential component of the new model of development and the basis of good governance, the provision for which is the priority of the non-interventionist state. As the World Bank officials confess (and 'confess' sounds right, since they seem to be atoning for old sins), 'it has taken failures of government in Africa, the collapse of dictatorships in Latin

America and profound transformations in Central and Eastern Europe to manifest that, without a sound legal framework, without an independent and honest judiciary, economic and social development risk collapse' (Rowat et al. 1995: 2).

Of all the liberal global consensuses, the rule of law/judicial consensus is by far the most complex and ambiguous. If for no other reason than because its focus is on the institution (courts) which, better than any other, represents the national character of modern institution-building and which, on this account, one might expect to resist globalizing pressures most effectively. Notwithstanding some high profile international courts in the past, and the European Court of Justice and the European Court of Human Rights today, the judicial system remains the quintessential national institution, and it has been far more difficult to internationalize it than the police or, the armed forces . . .

One of the most striking features of the focus on the judicial system is that the attention given to courts lies sometimes in the recognition of their function as the ultimate guarantors of the rule of law, sometimes in the denunciation of their incapacity to fulfil such function. In other words, the judicial system gains social and political visibility for being simultaneously part of the solution and part of the problem of the enforcement of the rule of law. When it is viewed as part of the solution, the focus is on judicial power and judicial activism; when seen as part of the problem, the focus is on judicial crisis and the need for judicial reform. However, in the latter case, the features or conditions that are now the object of criticism and reform were previously tolerated or ignored. The critical attention they now get is a product of the new role attributed to courts as a key instrument of good governance and law-based development. . . .

The focus for the last decade on the rule of law and the judicial system across the globe is a major transnational political phenomenon of our time. Sometimes a product of internal dynamics, sometimes a product of high intensity globalization pressure, more often than not, a product of a combination of both, this trend, known as judicialization of politics, or as an expansion of judicial power, is intimately related to the construction of a new state form, which can be characterized as post-welfare (in core countries) or post-developmentalist (in semi-peripheral countries). This is an efficient weak state suited to complement the efficient regulation of social and economic life by markets and the private sector. This new model of development, seemingly enjoying a global consensus (how strong or well informed this consensus is remains an open question) is premised upon the idea that social transformation has ceased to be a political issue. The rule of law and the judicial system appear to be the ideal instruments of a depoliticized conception of social transformation.

Concomitantly, democracy has been promoted as the political regime best suited to guarantee the stability, governability and social legitimacy of an efficient weak state, as well as a depoliticized capitalist social transformation. The rule of law and the courts have been called upon to be the main pillars of such a democratic project.

This hegemonic project . . . is based on the assumption that capitalism and democracy are compatible and even interdependent. Such an assumption has been highly problematic in the past, and nothing has changed in the last decade to make it less problematic now. Nothing has changed in the recent past to eliminate or even reduce, in the framework of this democratic project, the precedence of capitalism over democracy, particularly now that capitalism is global and democracy continues to be national. It is highly improbable that, against past experience, the rule of law and courts will sustain democracy against capitalism.

The vulnerability of this democratic project is twofold. First, democratic stability is dependent upon not letting social inequalities go too far. Yet, they have actually been increasing dramatically for the past decade. It is quite an open question; mediated by many political factors, when such dramatic increase will reach the breaking point beyond which turbulence will take over democratic stability. Second, a liberal democratic public sphere presupposes the rule-based equality of all citizens and the equal accountability of the government towards them. Under the neo-liberal model of development, powerful social agents are emerging in command of such an economic and political leverage that they can easily circumvent the laws, or change them to suit their interests. The principle of equality is thereby manipulated beyond recognition. On the other hand, the same development model makes the nation states tightly accountable to global capitalist enterprises, at the same time that it forces them, or allows them, to be more and more vaguely accountable to national individual citizens. The combination of these two trends may contribute to turn capitalist democratic societies into ever shrinking islands of democratic public life in a sea of societal fascisms.

E: The Heterogeneity of Court Practice

While courts generally present themselves first and foremost as agencies of authoritative third-party decision-making, they vary markedly in the way preparation for decisions is arranged. Within continental Europe we find an active, inquisitorial role under which much of the burden of preparation and inquiry falls upon the court. In England, as in North America, the courts historically remain a potent but immobile backdrop while the parties prepare for an adversarial trial at their own pace. More recently – in England only in the last decade – the common law picture has begun to change, as the judiciary has shown a growing determination to assume control over preparations for trial and overall to adopt a more active, 'managerial', role.

Heterogeneity of court practice goes considerably beyond these narrowly procedural questions; it is even an over-simplification to suggest that delivery of judgment represents the only, even the primary, aim of court-like institutions. As Martin Shapiro argues below, in some cultures courts assume openly mediatory functions (Extract 7.10). In this respect, what appear to be large-scale changes in state management of civil disputes have become visible over at least two decades right across the common law world. At the heart of these changes lies a growing recognition of 'settlement' as an approved, privileged objective of civil justice. The courts have come to present themselves not just as agencies offering judgment but also as sponsors of negotiated agreement.

Extract 7:10

M Shapiro: *Courts: A Comparative and Political Analysis* (1981) University of Chicago Press, Chicago and London, pp 8–11

If we turn to the work of those persons and institutions to which we normally award the titles judges and courts, we shall see that in reality they are simply at one end of a spectrum rather than constituting an absolutely distinct entity. Courts are clearly the least consensual and the most coercive of triadic conflict resolving institutions. The conventional prototype of courts has concentrated so heavily on the coercive aspects of courts, however, that it has tended to isolate judging unduly from other styles of conflict resolution. It is because elements of mediation and remnants of consent are integral to most court systems that the conventional prototype of courts is often misleading. Courts share with their fellow triadic conflict resolvers along the continuum the need to elicit consent. Among other things this means that mediating is not to be seen as an antithesis to judging but rather as a component in judging. Most judicial systems retain strong elements of mediation. . . .

Indeed, it would not be difficult to move about the world's legal systems endlessly multiplying the examples of the intermingling of mediation and judging. Communist legal systems might seem to have a special penchant for 'comradely mediation' between fellow members of the working class, since communists define law as an instrument of class oppression. Indeed, both in the West and in China, we encounter comradely courts that seek to resolve family, neighborhood, and work place disputes without formal judicial proceedings. But we also discover that these bodies tend to mix mediation with imposed solutions backed by the coercive authority of the party and the state. Moreover, comradely courts are almost invariably embedded in a conventional court structure staffed by professional judges applying law, or sometimes party policy that is treated as an integral part of law. Most communist states now operate their economies on a system of supply contracts entered into between industrial enterprises. Contracting parties engaged in a dispute are confronted by a range of arbitration and judicial proceedings quite similar to those in noncommunist states. Indeed, more generally, mediation and arbitration in the context of the opportunity to go into court if the parties cannot come to agreement is a typical pattern encountered in both communist and capitalist states.

Mediated solutions are most feasible when the disputed matter is divisible or can be converted into something divisible. At first glance it would seem to be injury or trespass that would be least amenable to mediation and most subject to the rule of 'an eye for an eye.' The common law system has often been taken as the model of dichotomous resolution, since it is a 'strict' law system seeking to assign legal right to one of the parties and legal wrong to the other. Yet the insistence of the common law that the central and usually sole remedy is money damages and that no resolution is possible unless one party can show he has been damaged in a compensable way reveals another dimension. The common law consistently converts indivisible disputes, that is, disputes over injury to person and property and disputes over the fulfillment or nonfulfillment of obligations into disputes over sums of money. Even a judge who must declare that one party is legally right and the other legally wrong need not resort to winner-take-all solutions. Typically he will award money damages that amount to more than the loser wants to pay but less than the winner claims he deserves. Moreover, where the Anglo-American law has developed equity as a means of resolving conflicts through remedies other than money damages, that is, through equitable decrees ordering someone to do something, it invokes the doctrine of 'balancing of equities.' That doctrine requires an equity court to shape remedies so as not to impose costs on one of the parties that far outweigh benefits to the other. In short, below the facade of dichotomous solution presented by Anglo-American courts lies the potential for mediation.

That potential is frequently realized in the courtroom itself, for instance when judge or jury reduces the amount of a damage award because the plaintiff, while legally right, was himself partly at fault. More fundamentally, money damages are mediatory because they allow the loser to substitute a money payment for the performance of some action to which he is strongly averse or for the acceptance of some distasteful retribution like suffering the loss of an arm because he has taken off someone else's.

However, in modern Anglo-American law systems, and for that matter in Continental ones, the area of mediation often moves outside the courtrooms. The bulk of conflict resolution through legal channels occurs by negotiation between the parties and their attorneys under the compulsion of eventual court proceedings should negotiations fail. To dismiss the vast bulk of conflict resolution by law in modern societies as somehow extra-judicial would both direct the student of courts away from the central phenomenon and lead to fundamental distortions of reality. For previously announced judicial rules and anticipation by the disputants of the costs and benefits of eventually going to trial are key parameters in such negotiations. They are not free bargaining based solely on the wills and immediate resources of the parties, but legalised bargaining under the shadow supervision of an available court. Such negotiation is not purely mediatory, because the bargain struck will depend in part on the 'legal' strength of the parties, that is, predictions of how each would fare in court. Yet such negotiations aim at, and in most instances achieve, a solution sufficiently satisfactory to both parties to avoid litigation. Failed negotiations may end up in court, where their judicial resolution sets the parameters for further negotiations. Thus the principal arena of modern legalised dispute settlement intimately intermixes elements of mediation and dichotomous solution, consent and judicial imposition.

F: Contemporary Transformations in the Common Law World

A very general shift in terms of both what courts 'are' and how they do their work became visible in the last years of the twentieth century right across the common law world. In the most general terms, there has been a move to include sponsorship of *settlement* as a primary objective, to be attempted first before trial and judgment. When the role of the courts was being re-examined in the United States in the mid 1970s, Frank Sander proposed the realisation of a hypothetical, ideal court as 'a flexible and diverse panoply of dispute resolution processes' and introduced the terms 'multi-door courthouse' and 'alternative dispute resolution' (Extracts 3:3 above, and 7:11 and 7:12 below). In the United States and Canada – right across North America as a whole – this vision has been vigorously realised (Extract 7:13 below). There is a general recognition that sponsorship of settlement is a primary responsibility – and this is explicitly inscribed in the procedural rules. In many United States jurisdictions, mandated mediation is one of the engines driving this process. The result in processual terms has been a progressive hybridisation of the courts.

A similar picture has developed in the Australian courts. Commercial court judges, notably, have developed strict and sophisticated regimes of 'case management'. These include:

- a move to the 'individual docket system' under which a single judge is responsible for managing a case throughout its trajectory;
- rigid timetabling after an early stage planning appointment;
- and the power to order mediation, irrespective of the wishes of the parties.[6]

In England and Wales too there has been a gradual departure from the historical position under which English judges have allowed the parties to prepare for adversarial trial very much in their own way and at their own pace, dealing with 'interlocutory' matters only where the parties bring them to their attention. Moves in this direction first appeared as spontaneous initiatives within the judiciary in a regime of early stage meetings in divorce county courts. A Commercial Court Practice Statement of 10 December 1993 and the general Practice Direction of 24 January 1995 followed, representing an enormous shift when thought about in the context of older understandings of what courts are and what they do. Reaching out into the period before the trial, they considerably extended the involvement of the court in a domain that was never 'private', because it lay along the route to the court, but which had hitherto been occupied by the parties and their professional representatives alone. Early indications that the sponsorship of settlement would become an explicit, official objective appeared first in the Heilbron /Hodge Report (1993) and then in the Interim version of the 'Woolf' Report, *Access to Justice* (1995) (Extract 7:14). In the latter, judicial 'case management' is prescribed and its overall purpose identified as:

> to encourage settlement of disputes at the earliest appropriate stage; and, where trial is unavoidable, to ensure that cases proceed as quickly as possible to a final hearing which is itself of strictly limited duration (II.5.16).

---

6 See, for example, arrangements in the Victorian courts. There, Order 50.07 of the Supreme Court Rules provides that: 'at any stage of a proceeding the Court may with or without the consent of any party order that the proceeding or any part of the proceeding be referred to a mediator'.

New Civil Procedure Rules introduced following the Woolf Reports have two radical and novel features. First, an explicit attempt is made to construct a pre-litigation phase in which the conduct of the respective legal teams is prescribed (with a primary requirement that the parties try to 'negotiate') and potentially enforced through cost sanctions. The shape of the pre-litigation phase is laid down in *Pre-Action Protocols*. Second, in providing a strict regime of case management once litigation is initiated, 'settlement' is explicitly prioritised as the primary objective of civil justice (Rule 1).[7]

The Rules begin with a broad programatic statement. This identifies an 'overriding objective' which is 'to enable the court to deal with cases justly' (Rule 1.1.(1)). They go on to provide that 'the court must further the overriding objective by actively managing cases' (Rule 1.1.(4)). This requirement (note the imperative tone: 'the court must . . .') signals the government's determination to adopt and consolidate the intention of the senior judiciary 'to change the whole culture, the ethos, applying in the field of civil litigation.'[8]

In proposing the new regime of civil procedure, Lord Woolf strongly endorsed court sponsorship of ADR in pursuit of settlement. But he expressed the view that any such facilitatory procedures should remain voluntary (Extract 7:15). The Court of Appeal, in *Halsey v Milton Keynes General NHS Trust*,[9] has endorsed this view, making a contrast with the position in other common law jurisdictions discussed above.

So common law courts are becoming *managers of negotiated settlement*, with their ultimate determinative powers in a last-resort, fall-back role. These courts can no longer be characterised as a largely immobile backdrop in the pre-trial period, awaiting a central role in trial and judgment. We discuss some features of this transformation in the direction of hybridisation further in Chapter Eight.

While the passage from Shapiro above (Extract 7:10) is an invaluable reminder that courts are not exclusively devoted to the decision-making process of adjudication, and often in effect assume mediatory functions, it should also be borne in mind that judges may in effect impose an outcome to the dispute on the parties by virtue of some preliminary judicial ruling. Thus, for example, in an essay analysing the changing relationship between adjudication and settlement in the United States, Kritzer observes that a significant number of cases are determined by authoritative decisions other than judgment. The claim often made that 'most civil cases settle' needs to be qualified because the decision to settle may, in fact, be a direct response to a significant umpiring decision imposed on the parties prior to the definitive judicial ruling on the principal issues in dispute.[10] This point is considered in Extract 7:16.

---

7 The details of these arrangements can be found on the Department for Constitutional Affairs web pages: www.dca.gov.uk/legalsys/civilproc.htm.
8 The Lord Chief Justice, announcing the general Practice Direction of 24 January 1995: (1995) 1 WLR 262.
9 (2004) EWCA (Civ) 576.   10 See also Galanter and Cahill (1994).

Extract 7:11

F E A Sander: 'Alternative Methods of Dispute Resolution: An Overview' (1985) 37 *University of Florida Law Review* 1, pp 11–13

Dispute resolution mechanisms are dispersed throughout the social fabric. The mechanisms are either public or private, mandatory or optional. Wherever disputes arise among individuals or organizations, a complex network of possible grievance mechanisms appears to be available for the venting of the grievances. The question which naturally arises is what, if any, relationship should exist among the different types of mechanisms. . . .

One can envision a system possessing a hierarchy and structure within the formal public dispute resolution system, complemented by a vast and ill-understood network of indigenous dispute resolution mechanisms. In essence, that is our present system. Disputants might first try to utilize the array of informal mechanisms provided in the particular arena where the dispute arises. Then, as a last resort, disputants might take the controversy to the public forum, the court . . . [but in fact there is a] tendency to take the case immediately to court. The net effect is that many disputes presented to court are not appropriate for court adjudication and could be better handled by some other mechanism.

This situation led me to suggest . . . a more comprehensive and diverse mechanism known as a Dispute Resolution Centre. This Centre would provide a variety of dispute resolution processes, according to the needs of the particular dispute. This concept was later termed the 'multi-door courthouse' (MDC).

What would such an institution look like? A provisional first-step type of MDC could consist essentially of a screening and referral clerk who would seek to diagnose incoming cases and refer them to the most suitable ADRMs [Alternative Dispute Resolution Mechanisms]. Depending on the available mechanisms in the particular community, referral might be made to mediation, arbitration, court adjudication, fact-finding, malpractice screening, media actions lines or an ombudsman. Such a model would be subject to all the familiar deficiencies of a referral scheme. For example, slippage often occurs between the act of referral and the receiving agency's actual handling of the case.

A more ideal model would contain all the 'doors' under one roof, as part of an integrated dispute resolution centre. Such a mansion might feature the following doors:

(1) effective and accessible small claims adjudication;
(2) services for family, landlord/tenant, and other continuing relations cases;
(3) ombudsmen for the processing of disputes between citizens and large bureaucracies;
(4) social service agencies providing mental health counseling and treatment of alcohol and drug related problems;
(5) trial court of general jurisdiction for novelty statutory and constitutional claims, as well as major criminal cases; and
(6) compulsory arbitration for small monetary claims.

Additional dispute processing forums might include those mediating or arbitrating juvenile matters and those handling ordinance violations such as bad checks and health code and building code violations. . . .

An integrated multi-door courthouse would have a number of benefits as well as potential pitfalls. First, such a full-service MDC would provide an efficient way of availing a wide range of dispute processes. It could also serve as a major source of information and referral, transcending the particular 'doors' that are available. Secondly, bringing such diverse ADRMs under the court umbrella would solve the increasingly difficult question of how to fund alternative mechanisms. Likewise it would avoid the pro-court adjudication bias inherent in the present system where the state pays the costs of court adjudication but not those of other, more suitable, mechanisms.

Third, because of the predominant emphasis on courts in our society, most alternatives are seldom used. . . . A major difficulty appears to be popular unfamiliarity with these mechanisms. This requires additional public education, but it also argues for building ADRMs into an expanded court system.

These are some of the substantial benefits that might be derived from such an ADRMs experiment. However, major obstacles exist as well. A critical feature would be the initial screening which would require a highly skilled intake worker rather than a bureaucratic court functionary. Accordingly, a crucial question is whether ADRM specialists . . . have sufficient knowledge of the particular characteristics of various dispute processes and mechanisms. This knowledge is necessary to confidently refer particular types of case to one or another mechanism.

Extract 7:12

F E A Sander: 'Alternative Dispute Resolution in the United States: An Overview', in American Bar Association (ed) *Justice for a Generation* (1985) West Publishing Company, St Paul, Minnesota, pp 260–261

It would be inappropriate to conclude this brief survey of recent dispute resolution developments in the United States without at least summary reference to some of the critical questions that are now beginning to emerge. Detailed consideration of any of these issues would necessitate a callous disregard of the limited scope of this overview paper, and is in any event premature. But it does seem appropriate at least to take note of these questions by way of lending focus and direction to future research and inquiry relating to alternative modes of dispute resolution.

If the alternatives to adjudication have all the advantages claimed for them why are they not more widely used? Are there aspects of the legal system that deter the use of alternatives? Or does the lack of demand for alternatives reflect the fact that the alternatives movement is primarily a product of the self-interest of the alternatives providers, rather than an expression of the needs of alternatives consumers?

Is there an adequate empirical basis for the claimed advantages of the alternatives? How, for example, can one adequately measure the asserted advantages of mediation over adjudications? Is it possible to develop a sophisticated cost-benefit analysis of alternative processes?

Is there a risk that the availability of alternatives will shunt low and middle-income disputants to a form of second-class justice, consisting primarily of semi-coerced compromise settlements, while the so-called first-class justice offered by the courts becomes available only to the rich and powerful? In thinking about this question, the reader should be aware that the neighborhood justice center clientele consists primarily of low-income disputants referred by courts and prosecutors as an alternative to criminal proceedings.

Is there a danger that mediation, with its emphasis on accommodation and compromise, will deter large-scale structural changes in political and societal institutions that only court adjudication can accomplish, and that it will thus serve the interests of the powerful against the disadvantaged?

To the extent that new modes of dispute resolution call for new practitioners, with skills different from those who practise in the judicial system, what steps should be taken to ensure that these practitioners have the requisite skills? Should there be regulation of the practice of dispute resolution similar to that of the practice of law?

Can the alternatives movement survive success? If alternative dispute resolution processes become widely used, will they suffer from the woes common to other heavily-used institutions – increasing costs and delay, bureaucratization, and perfunctory performance?

In light of the prominent place of the courts in American society, and the free dispute resolution services provided by the courts, how can other forms of dispute resolution, even if more appropriate for a particular dispute, succeed in attracting users and adequate funding? Does the answer lie in integrating alternative dispute resolution processes into the public justice system? One model for public institutionalization of alternative dispute resolution is the Multidoor Courthouse. This concept calls for a multi-faceted intake center where disputes are analyzed according to their salient characteristics and referred to that process, or sequence of processes, most appropriate for their resolution. This proposal is now being tested under ABA auspices in Houston, Tulsa, and Washington, DC. The results of that experiment should help to tell us whether this idea is indeed a promising herald for more effective dispute resolution.

Extract 7:13

B E Stedman: 'Multi-option Justice at the Middlesex Multi-Door Courthouse', in R Smith (ed) *Achieving Civil Justice: Appropriate Dispute Resolution for the 1990s* (1996) Legal Action Group, London, pp 119–127, 133–135, 137–140

The Middlesex Multi-Door Courthouse (MMDC) is a court-annexed ADR programme in Massachusetts which provides a comprehensive approach to dispute resolution within the administrative structure of a trial court. It was established in 1989 with the overall goal of improving the administration of justice through more timely resolution of disputes, greater cost-effectiveness for the courts and the consumers, and increased public satisfaction with process and outcome. The programme delivers a wide variety of dispute resolution services through a single coordinating entity. . . . The original planning for the multi-door courthouse was initiated outside the court system by a small group of private citizens who developed a demonstration project and raised most of the money for its implementation. Although the impetus did not originally come from the judiciary, court leaders were encouraging and supportive. From the beginning, the multi-door courthouse was planned as a court-annexed programme and organised on the understanding that, if successful, it would be formally integrated within the Massachusetts Trial Court.

The multi-door courthouse opened its doors to cases in 1990 in the Middlesex (Cambridge) Superior Court, situated just outside Boston. The Middlesex court was selected because of its demographics and the fact that it has the most active civil case load in Massachusetts. Cases are randomly selected for screening from the court's civil case list. In addition, they can be referred by the judiciary or the parties. The programme has now provided services to more than 6,000 cases. In 1994, 1,200 cases went through individual case-screening conferences. Four per cent settled at the screening or before a follow-up. Forty per cent opted out of a referral to one of the multi-door courthouse's doors. Some of these elected to go to a private ADR provider, some that the case could be settled without additional intervention, and others that judicial intervention was unnecessary (a few of these cases also will re-enter the programme at a later date). Altogether, approximately 56 per cent of the screened cases elected to go forward with one of the multi-door courthouse's dispute resolution options. Of these, 71 per cent settled at or within 60 days. Many of the rest had partial settlements or would otherwise settle before the trial date. Follow-up reports on the cases indicate that almost all participants felt that the process had been highly beneficial, even if it did not result in immediate settlement. . . . The first step in developing an ADR programme is to determine case types and intake procedures. The multi-door courthouse handles the full spectrum of civil cases. In addition to standard tort and contract cases, it has had particular success with cases involving commercial disputes, construction matters, real estate transactions, legal and other malpractice suits, product liability, business and partnership dissolutions, employment disputes (including wrongful termination, discrimination, harassment, covenants not to compete and other related issues), land use and other equitable matters. The recent introduction by the court of a mandatory non-binding conciliation programme for motor vehicle torts has removed these from the programme unless complications require more individualised attention.

Cases are still randomly selected from the court docket. However, increasingly cases are referred by the judge or lawyers involved. This reflects the increased acceptance of ADR in general and the multi-door courthouse concept in particular. Judicial referrals generally arise from status conferences, pre-trial hearings or attempts by the parties to seek equitable relief by way of injunctions or temporary restraining orders. A few cases have been sent in the middle of trial for the purpose of resolving a discrete issue or, occasionally, the entire case. In such circumstances and if a screener is available, the case is handled on a walk-in basis. Otherwise, referral occurs by way of a mandatory screening order sent out by the court. Although cases are taken randomly off the docket, they are reviewed to determine their suitability before the actual order is sent.

Extract 7:14

Lord Woolf: *Access to Justice: Interim Report to the Lord Chancellor on the Civil Justice System of England and Wales* (1995) HMSO, London, ch 4, paras 1–4, 7–12, Ch 5 paras 2–6, 16–17

Chapter 4 – The Major Reforms

1. All of the evidence which I have received in the course of my Inquiry indicates that the present system does not conform with or support the principles which I identified at the start of this Overview. I have concluded that the unrestrained adversarial culture of the present system is to a large extent responsible for this. The primary problems are:

the excesses of and the lack of control over the system of civil litigation;

the inadequate attention which the system gives to the control of costs and delay and to the need to ensure equality between the parties;

the complexity of the present system; and

the absence of any satisfactory judicial responsibility for the effective use of resources within the civil system.

The cumulative effect of all of these factors is to restrict access to justice.

2. I believe there is now no alternative to a fundamental shift in the responsibility for the management of civil litigation from litigants and their legal advisers to the courts. Successive attempts at reform which concentrated on procedural changes alone have failed to overcome the problem. The Civil Justice Review recommended court control as part of its major package of reforms. This recommendation was not implemented and a significant opportunity for reform was lost.

3. As the Council of Her Majesty's Circuit Judges has pointed out, this total change of philosophy will mean that litigants must accept that, once they commence proceedings, they no longer have sole and unfettered control over the way in which they take the case forward.

4. A change of this nature will involve not only a change in the way cases are progressed within the system. It will require a radical change of culture for all concerned. It will place a greater responsibility on the judges and the courts for the way in which a case proceeds through the system to a final hearing and for the form of the final hearing itself. The system and the procedures themselves must change to provide a framework within which judicial and court control can be exercised effectively. I have, however, been at pains to ensure that my proposals for reform do not prejudice the undoubted strengths of our existing system of civil justice. I am confident that my proposals sustain them and even play to them: the quality and commitment of the judiciary, the quality of much of our legal profession and the virtue of an approach which (despite the necessary changes) still places much of the responsibility for making progress on the parties themselves.

Working objectives for the new system

7. Within the new approach, the following are working objectives which the new system should meet:

In so far as this is practical, the parties to a dispute should be able to obtain information and advice to enable them to resolve that dispute in an economic, expeditious and practical manner and if this is not possible to conduct satisfactorily the appropriate litigation.

The parties should:

(i) whenever it is reasonable for them to do so settle their disputes (either the whole dispute or individual issues comprised in the dispute) before resorting to the courts;

(ii) where it is not possible to resolve a dispute or an issue prior to proceedings, then they should do so at as early a stage in the proceedings as is possible.

Where there exists an appropriate alternative dispute resolution mechanism which is capable of resolving a dispute more economically and efficiently than court proceedings, then the parties should be encouraged not to commence or pursue proceedings in court until after they have made use of that mechanism.

Prior to commencing and throughout the course of proceedings the parties should be able to be, and should be, kept fully informed of the likely costs and consequences of the proceedings and any alternative means of resolving those proceedings.

Proceedings should be conducted and disposed of in a manner, at a cost and within a timescale which is appropriate, taking into account the nature of the issues involved and the means of the parties.

Whenever this is practical, proceedings and the issues in the proceedings should be disposed of summarily.

Whenever practical and to the extent possible, evidence and facts should be agreed and the issues identified between the parties prior to the hearing.

Legal proceedings and trials should be subject to pre-determined timetables.

From an early stage in any proceedings, the probable and, whenever possible, the actual date of each significant step in proceedings, including the trial, should be known and the parties should only be allowed to depart from that date for good reasons.

The maximum length of any trial should be pre-determined and that length should only be exceeded for good reason.

In considering whether there is good reason for permitting the parties to depart from the pre-determined dates, and for extending the length of trial, the courts should take into account the effect of doing so not only upon the parties involved in the proceedings but also on other proceedings awaiting a hearing and the resources of the courts.

Only such discovery should take place, and only such evidence should be before the court, as is necessary for the just and appropriate disposal of the proceedings, and the evidence should be in a form which is most appropriate in all circumstances. The court's rules of procedure should give effect in a simple, clear and non-technical manner to the preceding aims.

The court system should be provided with the resources and the judicial and administrative structure necessary to fulfil these aims.

Case management

8. The introduction of judicial case management is crucial to the programme of change which I am recommending. It is the means by which I intend to achieve many of the objectives set out above. The current system applies the same procedures to all cases regardless of financial weight, complexity or importance. My proposals will involve the allocation of cases to appropriate tracks for case management and trial by the appropriate level of judge.

9. I propose:

An expanded small claims jurisdiction extended up to £3,000.

A new fast track for straightforward cases not exceeding £10,000. This will be a strictly limited procedure designed to take cases to trial within a short but reasonable timescale. There will be fixed costs. Discovery will be limited. The hearing will be no more than half a day and there will be no oral evidence from experts.

A new multi-track, for cases above £10,000, spanning both High Court and county court cases and providing appropriate and proportionate case management. Individual hands-on case management will be concentrated on those cases which require significant attention and will most benefit from it. Other cases in the multi-track will proceed on standard or individually tailored timetables, according to standard or individual directions.

Within the multi-track there will be effective consideration of the case at at least two key stages:

(i) at a case management conference early in the case; and
(ii) at a pre-trial review, shortly before trial.

10. The most complex and important cases will be heard only by High Court judges and not by deputies. Other cases will be managed and heard by the appropriate level of judge and will be able to move flexibly within the system to ensure this.

11. The cases will be managed by procedural judges who will generally be Masters or district judges working in teams with High Court and Circuit judges. For the heavier cases, requiring full hands-on judicial control, the procedural judge may be a High Court or Circuit judge. The procedural judge will:

conduct the initial scrutiny of all cases to allocate them to the appropriate management track;
conduct the case management conference unless it is more appropriate for the trial judge to do so;
generally monitor the progress of the case and investigate if parties are failing to comply with timetables or directions; and
draw the existence of Alternative Dispute Resolution (ADR) to parties' attention where this is appropriate or desirable.

The trial judge will normally conduct the pre-trial review

12. Case management will facilitate and encourage earlier settlement through earlier identification and determination of issues and tighter timetables. Other measures to encourage settlement will include the introduction of plaintiffs' offers and a requirement to report on costs at key stages.

Chapter 5 – The Need for Case Management by the Courts

2. For the reasons explained in this chapter, I have come to the conclusion that, in order to achieve both the overall aim and the specific objectives, there is no alternative to a fundamental shift in the responsibility for the management of civil litigation in this country from litigants and their legal advisers to the courts. The subsequent chapters in this section of the report set out in more detail the system of case management which I propose, and the procedural changes which I believe are required to facilitate the effective preparation of cases. I also see a need to introduce a new judicial structure with clearly defined responsibility for civil justice, to ensure that judges are deployed as effectively as possible to meet these new responsibilities. My proposals for this are set out in the next section of this report.

The role of the courts and the parties in the conduct of civil litigation

3. The conduct of civil litigation in England and Wales, as in other common law jurisdictions, is by tradition adversarial. Within a framework of substantive and procedural law established by the state for the resolution of civil disputes, the main responsibility for the initiation and conduct of proceedings rests with the parties to each individual case, and it is normally the plaintiff who sets the pace. The role of the judge is to adjudicate on issues selected by the parties when they choose to present them to the court.

4. In civil law jurisdictions, including those in other European countries, the relationship between the court and the parties to civil litigation is different. The court has greater responsibility for investigating the facts of a case and can decide, independently of the parties, what issues it needs to determine and what evidence it should hear. The role of the parties' legal advisers, as compared with that of English lawyers, tends to be smaller, and that of the judge more dominant.

The need for court control

5. The Rules of the Supreme Court (RSC) and County Court Rules (CCR) set out in considerable detail the procedural steps to be taken by the parties to civil proceedings, and the timescales within which those steps should be taken. In the absence of any effective control by the court itself, however, the timetable is frequently ignored, and the lack of firm supervision enables the parties to exploit the rules to their own advantage. Such exploitation is endemic in the system: the complexity of civil procedure itself enables the financially stronger or more experienced party to spin out proceedings and escalate costs, by litigating on technical procedural points or peripheral issues instead of focusing on the real substance of the case. All too often, such tactics are used to intimidate the weaker party and produce a resolution of the case which is either unfair or is achieved at a grossly disproportionate cost or after unreasonable delay.

6. There is considerable evidence that individual plaintiffs in personal injury cases are often forced to settle for inadequate compensation because of the delaying tactics employed by defendants' insurance companies. In larger commercial cases, discovery is used as a tactical weapon to intimidate a financially weaker opponent or to test the opponent's seriousness in pursuing the action. Expert evidence, vital to assist the courts in adjudicating on technical issues, is another source of disproportionate cost and unnecessary delay.

What case management involves
16. Case management for the purposes of this report involves the court taking the ultimate responsibility for progressing litigation along a chosen track for a predetermined period during which it is subjected to selected procedures which culminate in an appropriate form of resolution before a suitably experienced judge. Its overall purpose is to encourage settlement of disputes at the earliest appropriate stage; and, where trial is unavoidable, to ensure that cases proceed as quickly as possible to a final hearing which is itself of strictly limited duration.

The objectives of case management
17. The specific objectives of case management, as I see it, are:

achieving an early settlement of the case or issues in the case where this is practical;
the diversion of cases to alternative methods for the resolution of the dispute where this is likely to be beneficial;
the encouragement of a spirit of co-operation between the parties and the avoidance of unnecessary combativeness which is productive of unnecessary additional expense and delay;
the identification and reduction of issues as a basis for appropriate case preparation; and
when settlement cannot be achieved by negotiation, progressing cases to trial as speedily and at as little cost as is appropriate.

Extract 7:15
Lord Woolf: *Access to Justice: Interim Report to the Lord Chancellor on the Civil Justice System in England and Wales* (1995) HMSO, London, ch 18, paras 1–4

The place of ADR in the civil justice system
1. In recent years there has been, both in this country and overseas, a growth in alternative dispute resolution (ADR) and an increasing recognition of its contribution to the fair, appropriate and effective resolution of civil disputes. The fact that litigation is not the only means of achieving this aim, and may not in all cases be the best, is my main reason for including ADR in an Inquiry whose central focus is on improving access to justice through the courts. My second reason is to increase awareness still further, among the legal profession and the general public, of what ADR has to offer. Finally, it is also desirable to consider whether the various forms of ADR have any lessons to offer the courts in terms of practices and procedures.

2. From the point of view of the Court Service, ADR has the obvious advantage of saving scarce judicial and other resources. More significantly, in my view, it offers a variety of benefits to litigants or potential litigants. ADR is usually cheaper than litigation, and often produces quicker results. In some cases the parties will want to avoid the publicity associated with court proceedings. It may also be more beneficial for them, especially if they are involved in a continuing personal or business relationship, to choose a form of dispute resolution that will enable them to work out a mutually acceptable solution rather than submit to a legally correct adjudication which at least one party would inevitably find disappointing.

3. Despite these advantages I do not propose that ADR should be compulsory either as an alternative or as a preliminary to litigation. The prevalence of compulsory ADR in some United States jurisdictions is largely due to the lack of court resources for civil trials. Fortunately the problems in the civil justice system in this country, serious as they are, are not so great as to require a wholesale compulsory reference of civil proceedings to outside resolution.

4. In any event, I do not think it would be right in principle to erode the citizen's existing entitlement to seek a remedy from the civil courts, in relation either to private rights or to the breach by a public body of its duties to the public as a whole. I do, however, believe that the courts can and should play an important part, which I shall consider in more detail later in this chapter, in providing information about the availability of ADR and encouraging its use in appropriate cases.

Extract 7:16

Herbert Kritzer: 'Adjudication to Settlement: Shading in the Grey' (1986) 70(3) *Judicature* 161, pp 161–165

It is well known to those involved in the courts, either as practitioners or as researchers, that very few cases get the full adjudicatory treatment ending with a verdict (by either judge or jury) and a judgment. The figures commonly cited range from 5 per cent to 10 per cent of cases filed ever getting to trial. In the data collected by the Civil Litigation Research Project, court records indicated that only 8 per cent of the 1,649 sampled state and federal cases went to trial (and some of those were settled before the trial was completed). A typical assumption is that cases that are not resolved by trial are not adjudicated, and are not influenced by adjudication. In fact, as I will show below, adjudication is an *explicit* factor in the outcome of many cases; I will further argue that this is only the tip of the judicial 'shadow' because I have no way of assessing the role of adjudication as an *implicit* factor in the settlement process. . . .

Adjudicatory categories

Adjudication is most often thought of in terms of a trial before a judge or a jury. As mentioned above, only 8 per cent of the 1,649 cases in the CLRP sample went to trial (and some fraction of that 8 per cent settled before the trial was completed). The common assumption is that cases not resolved by trial are simply settled. However, this is not an accurate description of what goes on in ordinary civil litigation.

There are a variety of ways between trial and settlement by which a case can be resolved.

Based on the court record, one cannot tell definitively whether a case was settled; one can, however, determine the formal mode of termination, and there are several modes other than trial that clearly involve significant actions on the part of the judge or another actor carrying out an adjudicatory function. For purposes of analysis, I have defined three categories between trial and settlement that I believe are indicative of an adjudicatory function being invoked. I have labeled these categories as *arbitrated* (limited to cases from the Pennsylvania state courts which have a mandatory arbitration rule for certain categories of cases), *decided* (cases terminated by a summary judgment or something equivalent), and *dismissed for cause* (cases terminated by a ruling on a motion that is not simply technical in nature) . . . [In addition to] the 8 per cent that went to trial . . . 15 per cent of cases terminated through arbitration, decisions, or dismissal for cause; thus almost a quarter of the cases terminated through a decision of an adjudicator (and this excludes default judgments).

But this is not the end of adjudicatory involvement. Many cases may be settled because of an adverse decision on the part of a judge. I have no way of knowing with certainty the role of specific decisions, but I can look at the frequency of rulings on motions that might lead to a decision to settle. In the court record data collected by CLRP, there is detailed information on the types of motions filed in each case. I identified one set of motions as indicative of a significant, substantive decision on the part of the judge that might be instrumental in leading to a settlement; specifically, I included all motions to dismiss where an explicit basis for dismissal was given (except for consensual dismissals, dismissals for failure to prosecute, and dismissals for insufficient service), all motions for summary judgment, motions for immediate judicial intervention (eg, for restraining orders and the like), and motions that could materially affect a party's ability to present its case (eg, motions to exclude evidence or witnesses, motions to proceed as a class action).

After selecting the motions to be examined, I looked at the frequency of rulings on those motions in the 78 per cent of cases that were not terminated by trial, arbitration, decision, or dismissal for cause. Approximately 11 per cent of the subset of cases involved such motions; this represents an additional 9 per cent of the cases in the overall sample. Recognizing that I may now be overestimating the importance of some of the motions that I have counted (and that some readers may object to the inclusion or exclusion of particular types of motions in this part of the analysis), let me add this figure to the earlier 22 per cent of cases; I now have evidence of judicial involvement in the termination of as many as 31 per cent of the cases in the CLRP sample. This is a very long way from the original 8 per cent figure. . . . The message of this discussion of adjudication is that there is more to 'it' than trials. Judicial actions can play an important role in the processing of civil cases, even in the vast majority of cases that never come to trial. In this analysis, I have looked only at cases where there was some actual judicial action; I have not dealt at all with situations where the judicial action was only anticipated. If the role of the judge is identifiable simply from the court record in almost a third of the cases, it is likely that the clearly looming visage of the judge was important in another substantial proportion of cases; and, it is equally likely that the potential of adjudication was at the least a dim specter for yet more cases.

While the argument that the law or the coercive influence of potential adjudication plays an important part in the settlement of cases in our civil courts is not new, it is important to try to grasp the breadth of this influence. Much of the rhetoric surrounding the alternative dispute resolution movement that has recently come into vogue seems to presume that it would be fairly easy to simply move cases out of the courts, and one item of evidence that seems to support this argument is the small percentage of cases that actually go to trial. Yet, focusing on the trial rate misses much of the role of adjudication in the resolution of cases brought to the civil justice system. Very simply put, the settlement of many (if not most) cases relies upon the adjudication of others; to decouple those that settle from those that are adjudicated misses the fundamental reality underlying the workings of the system.

Lawyers who work in the system on a day-in, day-out basis live with this reality, whether or not they explicitly realize it. Thus one of the fundamental aspects of the work of the lawyer is to anticipate the adjudicatory alternative. In a sense, much of the discussion of alternative dispute resolution may have the world upside down. It may not be that we need to find alternatives to litigation or adjudication, but rather that we need to understand the impact of adjudication as the alternative to settlement, whether that settlement is reached through simple negotiations, mediation, or what might be called 'pseudo-adjudication' (mini-trials, summary trials, etc.).

For the judge interested in facilitating the disposition of cases, the message of this analysis is that a lot can be accomplished by adjudicating, and particularly if that adjudication is carried out in a manner that is predictable so that, where possible, parties are able to anticipate what the decision is likely to be. This is not to say that judges should not be active in the settlement process in direct and/or creative ways. It only means that *deciding* cases, in whole or in part, helps to settle not only the *decided* cases, but other cases that may never reach the judge for decision.

For those concerned about whether settlement is good or bad, or whether courts in fact do enough adjudicating, my analysis suggests that there may be an important distinction between settlement for the *right* reasons and settlement for the *wrong* reasons. Cases that leave the courts through settlement may exit because adjudication has resolved some or all of the key questions in dispute, even if the case did not go all the way to trial. Even where no adjudication takes place, settlement may occur for the 'right' reasons (eg, the parties are able to agree upon the valuation appropriate for the case when there is no real dispute over damages). This is not to suggest that some settlements occur for the 'wrong' reasons (eg, one party can no longer afford the costs of litigation, or the delay until the trial forces a party to take a lower settlement now than could be achieved through a jury trial). Rather, one cannot presume that all settlements are wrong or that all adjudicated outcomes are wrong (ie, the world is not black and white). Thus, in order to advance the discussion of adjudication, settlement, and alternative dispute resolution, researchers and reformers must come to grips with the problem of assessing when particular modes of resolution are good and bad, and when one mode of resolution is *better* than another.

Of course, even within the same legal system judges may themselves adopt quite varying approaches to the judicial role, especially where they operate in courts in which they are allowed a good deal of discretion in their formulation and expression of the judicial role. This is demonstrated by Conley and O'Barr (1990: 106–111) in their analysis of the operation of small claims courts in various parts of the United States. The authors characterise *five* different judicial approaches to decision-making that are identified by their research findings – differing approaches that undermine the stereotype of the common law judge as an impassive umpire, at least in the context of the small claims court.

The courts of the state, in which civil judgments are rendered on behalf of the government, do not necessarily monopolise third-party decision-making in civil cases. Indeed, as with the development in the common law world of the system of Chancery courts applying rules of equity, and relying more on written procedures, as supplementary to the common law, alternative forms of adjudication may develop even within the state judicial system. This internal differentiation is today reflected in a wide range of specialised courts and tribunals, offering styles of umpiring and specialist knowledge that are claimed to be particularly suitable for the resolution of family, commercial, labour, immigration and other issues.

G: The Popular Element in Courts

The stereotype of the court is that of a dispute resolution mechanism whose powers of adjudication are exercised by professional, specialist and knowledgeable decision-makers who are also members of the ruling elite. While this characterisation widely mirrors actual practice, explicit attempts have often been made for a variety of reasons to inject lay or populist elements into this state-sponsored umpiring process. In many such cases, however, it is clear that the popular element has been inserted not as a means of making the courts more accessible to the people but, rather, as a mechanism for enhancing central, state control. Thus, although the English jury may have come to represent by the nineteenth century a form of protection against a coercive judiciary, it has been asserted that it began life as 'an oppressive exercise of the highest powers of government. The jurors were compelled to answer under oath and became subject to penalties for perjury. No preordained rules set limits to the kinds of questions that might be asked' (Dawson, 1960: 119). The equivalent of the jury in the courts of the civilian tradition is the lay assessor whose significance often lies as much in the specialised, expert knowledge that he or she brings to the court as it does in the addition of a lay element. In many other situations, a system of lay judges is relied on to supplement a centralised system of professional judiciary and administration. Perhaps the best-known example of this is the development in England of the role and status of the justice of the peace. The system, however, was in reality much less an arrangement for promoting popular participation than it was a structure for enhancing the interests of central government.[11]

---

11 See, for example, Dawson (1960: 136–144).

The emphasis on popular participation often appears in particularly dramatic form during the establishment and institutionalisation of socialist regimes. In the course of the revolution, the 'people's court' or 'tribunal' provides a popular forum in which 'people's justice' is imposed on class enemies (see, for example, Leng, 1967: 14–19). In the early years of a communist regime, too, these institutions may continue to be used as revolutionary instruments for assisting in the task of undermining the old order. These courts often have jurisdiction not only over criminal cases but also over problems relating to marriage, family and property. In the extract that follows, Sachs outlines the key features of the system of 'popular justice' that developed in Mozambique (Extract 7:17).

The history of popular courts has, however, often been one of incorporation into a more regular system of socialist legality as administered by an authoritarian communist regime. They are frequently no more courts of the 'people' than the regime is a government for the 'people' – in reality, both are dominated by the Communist Party, and operate under close Party control and scrutiny. Haydon has explored the manner in which Yugoslav labour courts functioned in the late 1970s, and shown that in reality the apparent success of these 'social courts' in providing enhanced access to justice lies in their development of some of the characteristic features of regular rather than popular courts (1968: 235–243).

In this country one of the most important mechanisms for providing greater access to formal adjudicatory justice is the tribunal. This institution, which can be traced back to the earliest years of the last century, is now found in a wide variety of settings and varies considerably in its structure and processes. The principal function of the tribunal is as an administrative appeal body, hearing cases brought by citizens against decisions made on behalf of the state by civil servants and others, although some forms deal with private sector issues as, for example, in the case of industrial tribunals. The particular origins of the tribunal in this country would appear to lie in a felt need to provide an accessible, specialised forum for resolving disputes that arose as a result of reforming social welfare legislation introduced at the end of the first decade of the last century:

> in devising the national insurance scheme . . . the Liberal Government of Lloyd George . . . drew extensively on the social insurance policies of Bismark in Germany. Still convinced that the courts were inappropriate for hearing appeals of this kind, the British Government also adopted the Bismarkian idea of the tribunal. Hence, dissatisfied unemployment insurance claimants could appeal against the decision of an insurance officer to a 'court of referees'. Although labelled 'courts', courts of referees were nothing of the sort. They comprised three members, one appointed by the Board of Trade, one member from a panel representing local employers, and the final member from a workman's panel (Sainsbury and Genn, 1995: 417).

From this small beginning the idea of the tribunal has evolved significantly and come to enjoy widespread acceptance in this country, so that there are now well over 60 different tribunals operating currently. Genn and Sainsbury have argued (1995) that the recent proposals for civil justice reform made by Lord Woolf have missed an opportunity to enhance access to civil justice by failing to give sufficient regard to the potential role of tribunals.

Extract 7:17

A Sachs: 'Changing the Terms of the Debate: A Visit to a Popular Tribunal in Mozambique' (1984) 28 *Journal of African Law* 99, pp 101–104

> It is important to determine the specific circumstances which facilitated the evolution of Popular Justice in Mozambique in order to avoid the temptation to extrapolate this experience unjustifiably to other countries with different processes of development, and in order to be aware of the limits of the achievements thus far accomplished. The basic fact is that Popular Justice was not the invention of progressive lawyers determined to renovate an out-of-date legal system, nor was it a copy of legal systems that existed in other countries that may have shared similar political philosophies. It was an integral part of a much wider process of social transformation inside Mozambique itself, that had started with the proclamation of a general insurrection against colonial domination; had included the whole long period of armed struggle for national liberation; had taken in a series of practical experiences in the Liberated Zones where the very necessities of consolidating a new type of government in areas from which both the colonial and the traditional authorities had fled had forced the rapid evolution of new types of judicial structures; and had been associated with the rapid institutional transformations experienced in all spheres and in all parts of the country immediately after independence.
>
> Of particular importance was the rapidity and profundity of the destruction of what in Mozambique was called traditional-feudal power. This was a process specific to Mozambique, where it may be said that traditional power had become so closely identified with colonial power that when the latter was destroyed the former collapsed with it. The nature of Portugese colonialism forced it to adopt a high degree of direct state compulsion in its quest for labour, and the chiefs and *indunas* were given important though junior tasks in the structure of compulsion so created. They helped in the recruitment of forced labour and imposed severe physical punishments on those they regarded as recalcitrant. They participated in the collection of taxes, the provision of information to the authorities about resistance, and in the recruitment of police and soldiers. Those chiefs who showed signs of patriotism were summarily dealt with, many ending their lives as a result of torture, starvation or execution on the prison island of Ibo, not far from the village mentioned in the introductory part of this paper. Thus to the extent that the chiefs exercised power in colonial times they lost their popular authority; even the judicial power they exercised became tainted, since it came to be regarded as a perk for the services rendered to the colonial state, handsomely rewarded in terms of the gifts necessary to 'open' the court.
>
> The fierceness of class struggle in the countryside just before and just after independence remains as yet largely unrecorded. Suffice to say that in interviews with the new judges, a strongly expressed theme that emerges is the contrast they seek to establish between their work and the venality of the justice administered in the past by the *regulos*

(chiefs); in their view, the only custom that really counted in the courts of the chiefs in the late colonial period was the custom of visiting the chief's house the night before the hearing with a gift more extravagant than that given by the opponent. It might be worth observing here that in counterpoint to the lively debate occasioned by the remark from the chair by Prof. Richard Abel to the effect that the legal profession in Africa might have had a material interest in promoting a single court system functioning on the basis of a unified and codified set of laws, a large class of chiefs and religious leaders also existed with an equally strong economic stake in maintaining separate norms of which they would remain the natural and well-paid custodians.

The destruction of the institution of traditional power was accompanied in the post-colonial period by the creation of new organs of local power, in which active parts were played by women from the Women's Organisation and by young people from the Youth Organisation. The courts were accordingly not the first institutions to break away from the gerontocratic and sexist assumptions of traditional society, imposing as it were, new values from the top; this was a period in which the working poor were asserting themselves in every sphere of society, politically, socially, culturally and legally . . . if one accepts that the Popular Justice system is in fact operative and does in large measure succeed in accomplishing its stated objectives, does this mean that the problem of having a unitary legal system in a country of great cultural diversity has been resolved?

The answer clearly must be no. To begin with, the area of operation of the system has been geographically uneven, coinciding basically with zones of greatest population concentration, and being strongest in areas where new forms of community organisa-tion are most evident. There are large parts of the country where at the local level the Popular Justice system is still remote, both in the physical and the political sense. But even in the areas where the system is operating and operating well, great difficulties remain. These are the difficulties found in any legal system anywhere in the world, but especially acute in a society of great cultural diversity undergoing rapid transformation. The undoubted successes of the Popular Justice system by no means do away with the problems of unity in diversity, they merely alter the terms of the debate.

What the debate ceases to be is whether to have 'a western legal system with customary law trimmings, or a customary law system with Western trimmings, or some fusion of them both', as Professor Allott, with the weight of his extensive experience and reflection, has argued. This is not just because the term 'western' is too limiting to a country like Mozambique, which is happy to draw on the experience of 'eastern' countries, whether socialist or not, as well as the rich and original experiences of the Latin American world. It is because the debate, however neatly expressed, is considered a false one. If aspects of traditional law are rejected, that will be because they are regarded as feudal, as impediments to the creative capacity of the Mozambican people, and not because they are African or customary. Similarly, if the objective is eventually to eliminate completely the Portuguese legal codes, this is not because they were imposed by outsiders, but because their language, content and assumptions are inconsistent with the concrete legal needs of the Mozambican people. The family contemplated in the section on Family Law in the Civil Code simply bears no relation to the Mozambican family; the whole section in the Code on property rights loses its meaning once the land is nationalised; the nature of Mozambican commercial activity has changed so much that the Commercial Code becomes increasingly unresponsive to the practical problems that arise, and so on. The debate, then, is on how to create new laws that reflect the new Mozambican personality and express the interests of the Mozambican people as a whole; secondly, on how best to involve the people in the necessary legislative process; and, thirdly, on how thereafter to ensure that the people are involved in the implementation and control of the law that emerges. These are the fundamental questions: not 'African' versus 'Western'; 'customary' versus 'modern'. Furthermore, the debate ceases to revolve around technical questions such as codification or re-statement or judicial control of customary law or no control at all, while the questions of sources and internal choice of law also become largely obsolete.

In the context of the practice of the Popular Tribunals it is difficult even to convey to Mozambican lawyers and students what the debate about internal conflict of laws is all about, let alone propose solutions; people have become quite used to the fact that in their dealings with state institutions, ethnicity is not a relevant factor, and that church and state are truly separated.

But closing one debate simply opens another. The problems of relating the unified set of norms to a population with a diverse culture still exist, but express themselves in different forms. Basically they come down to the central question of finding the correct strategies in order to relate what might be called a vast sector of informal popular justice, with all its improvisations, heterogeneity and conservatism, to the more dynamic, coherent and progressive Popular Justice system of the courts.

H: Arbitration – General

In conceptual terms arbitration realises the foundational idea of the 'neutral stranger', standing ready to decide a question which the parties have brought before him or her. So here the umpire is privately chosen, and makes a decision within a procedural environment of the parties' choosing. But the contrast with state-sponsored adjudication is no longer so crisp as this ideal picture might imply. Arbitration, as an escape from the perceived problems of adjudication, has long been institutionalised within a number of locations, most notably in the commercial sphere, to the extent that notions of privacy and procedural informality have become much less significant. In its traditional 'pure' form arbitration is essentially private and voluntary, and is dependent on the parties' agreement to be bound by the decision of the arbitration panel – a creature of contractual agreement between the parties. However, arbitration is now sometimes also a compulsory, non-consensual, form of dispute settlement – it is used by the courts in a number of jurisdictions either to assist in especially troublesome types of cases, or to manage better the flow of routine cases.

However, it is important to bear in mind that even private arbitration typically involves the central elements of a court adjudication. That is, evidence and arguments are submitted to a neutral third party. That third party has the authority to issue a binding decision based on objective standards. Of course, there are important differences between the two processes, in particular, in private umpiring the parties typically attempt to resolve their disputes by recourse to procedures much less formal than those employed by the courts. In addition, the parties have both chosen to arbitrate, and selected the arbitrator themselves, or at least specified the arbitration panel from which the arbitrator will be drawn. But, in essence, arbitration is a *private* form of 'adjudication', with the third party intervening to control exchanges between both sides and to impose a decision. It is a form of private umpiring, however, which brings with it flexibility, simplified procedures and other advantages that have endeared it, in particular, to the commercial world.

It is possible to identify a number of key features of 'arbitration' of the private, voluntary kind, that is, the 'pure' or 'ideal' type of arbitration.

First, in its purer forms the parties either agree in advance that specified types of dispute will be arbitrated, or after a dispute has arisen they enter into an ad hoc agreement to arbitrate. The parties also agree that the arbitrator's decision will be binding on them. In many jurisdictions, courts will recognise and enforce agreements to arbitrate, and very often they will not provide any extended review of the *merits* of an arbitrator's decision. They will only consider setting aside the arbitration award on grounds of public policy or procedural irregularity. Indeed, looked at from the point of the state, arbitration has many advantages as a form of umpiring – it provides important interest groups with a certain and contextualised form of dispute resolution that has little or no draining effect on the resources of the state. However, as an institutionalised form of *private* umpiring it must be subjected to two particular kinds of limitation or control. First, it must not produce substantive outcomes that are unacceptable to the state – hence the public policy requirement that is found on a fairly widespread basis. Second, the state must continue to be able to make the claim that, in some respects at least, adjudication, that is, state umpiring, is fundamentally superior simply because it is state sponsored. Accordingly, the state retains the right to resist arbitration outcomes that result from the 'inferior' procedures on which arbitration relies.

Second, the usual practice is for arbitration to be carried out as a private process, and this approach to dispute settlement can take many forms because the parties have considerable freedom to choose the particular rules by which the arbitration will be conducted. They may, and often do, design the process to be employed, and provide the substantive standards to be used by the arbitrator in making a decision, these standards often being specified in the form of a contract.

Third, even in common law systems, the arbitrators do not consider themselves bound by any doctrine of precedent. Of course, in a number of fields, such as labour or industrial relations, arbitration awards are published, and arbitrators will look to such awards for guidance. But the arbitrator generally is free to decide the outcome on the merits of each party's position in the instant case.

Fourth, in arbitration the parties themselves are able to select the umpire who will decide the outcome. Typically, they use this freedom to select a decision-maker with *expert* knowledge of the substantive facts of the dispute because he or she has personal experience of the same sort of business and therefore a good grasp of the working norms and shared understandings of the trade. Thus, there is no need to attempt to educate a judge and, where employed, a jury in the specifics of the business activities involved. This need to educate is a hurdle that may, in some circumstances, be well nigh insurmountable and, in any event, will cost time and therefore money to deal with in a court case. Indeed, we might emphasise at this point that the origins of 'modern arbitration' appear to lie in the preference of eighteenth-century English merchants to resolve their disputes in accordance with trade customs rather than by 'the laws of the state', and to rely upon their own kind rather than the state for decision-making. To this day, this aspect of arbitration remains very important. The trade-specialist arbitrator's expertise may be crucial when the dispute is founded on a problem of contract interpretation that, in turn, is based on some disagreement over the nature of the trading customers' understanding of the nature of the commodities being traded; or when the dispute concerns the belief by one party that the other party has supplied goods that fail to meet certain 'expected' standards.

Of course, over the years, and in various jurisdictions, arbitration has increasingly come to be used in a wide variety of disputing contexts. Four areas of economic activity where arbitration has for some time often been very commonly used are: labour relations, construction work, manufacturer-consumer relations and insurance. Its perceived successes in these fields have further encouraged reliance on arbitration in such areas as medical malpractice, prisoner grievances, environmental disputes, and so on. In the extract which follows, Lon Fuller examines two of the fundamental problems that can arise in one of the most significant of these specialised fields, namely labour relations.

Extract 7:18

L Fuller: 'Collective Bargaining and the Arbitrator' (1963) 18 *Wisconsin Law Review* 3, pp 3–6

One conception of the role of the arbitrator is that he is essentially a judge. His job is to do justice according to the rules imposed by the parties' contract, leaving the chips to fall where they may. He decides the controversy entirely on the basis of arguments and proofs presented to him 'in open court' with the parties confronting one another face to face. He does not attempt to mediate or conciliate, for to do so would be to compromise his role as an adjudicator. He will strictly forego any private communication with the parties after the hearing. The friends of this conception see it as casting the arbitrator in the role of a man of principle, a man who respects the institutional limits of his task, a man who conscientiously refuses to exploit his powers for ulterior purposes, however benign. The critics of this conception have a less flattering view. To them it is unrealistic, prudish, purist, legalistic, an abandonment of common sense, a chasing after false models motivated perhaps by a secret hankering for the glamour and security of judicial office.

The opposing conception expects the arbitrator to adapt his procedures to the case at hand. Indeed, in its more extreme form it rejects the notion that his powers for good should be restrained at all by procedural limitations. By this view the arbitrator has a roving commission to straighten things out, the immediate controversy marking the occasion for, but not the limits of, his intervention. If the formal submission leaves fringes of dispute unsettled, he will gladly undertake to tidy them up. If the arguments at the hearing leave him in doubt as to the actual causes of the dispute, or as to what the parties really expect of him, he will not scruple to hold private consultations for his further enlightenment. If he senses the possibility of a settlement, he will not hesitate to step down from his role as arbitrator to assume that of mediator. If despite his conciliatory skill negotiations become sticky, he will . . . 'exert the gentle pressure of a threat of decision' to induce agreement.

The critics of this view are seldom charitable in describing it. They say that arbitrators who accept it think they can 'play God,' though the actual motive of their actions is usually a base instinct to meddle in other people's affairs. The conception that encourages this intermeddling rests essentially on hypocrisy, for it enables a man who pretends to be a judge to enjoy the powers of his office without accepting its restraints. It is a Messianic conception, a patent abuse of power, a substitution of one-man rule for the rule of law. So the castigations mount. There is need for a neutral term. As the nearest approach I suggest that we describe this view as one that sees the arbitrator, not as a judge, but as a labor-relations physician.

The other major controversy is, as I have said, that which relates to the interpretation of the collective bargaining agreement. By one view a labor contract is like any other legal document and ought to be subject to the same principles of interpretation. If, as it commonly does, it states that the arbitrator shall have no power to add to or to detract from its terms, the arbitrator must accept this limitation. His object is not to do justice, but to apply the agreement. If the agreement imposes hardships, it is no business of the arbitrator to alleviate them. His powers and his duties lie wholly within the four corners of the written document.

The opposing view stresses the unique quality of the collective bargaining agreement. It is not quite like any other document ever conceived by the mind of man. It is at once a constitution and the written record of an economic trade. It is a charter of the parties' rights and a set of resolutions never really expected to be fully realized in practice. From the curiously mixed nature of the collective bargaining agreement there is derived (by a logic that is certainly not obvious) the conclusion that it must be construed freely. Unlike judges, arbitrators must eschew anything like a 'literal' interpretation. Their task is not to bend the dispute to the agreement, but to bend the agreement to the unfolding needs of industrial life.

In presenting these two controversies I have purposely thrown the contending sides into a sharper opposition than commonly exists in practice. In reality the matter is never so black and white as I have just painted it. Even those arbitrators who purport to adhere to a fairly extreme position at one end or the other of the scale seldom practise entirely what they preach.

The two controversies I have outlined are to some extent two aspects of a single dispute. One can generally predict that the arbitrator with strong instincts toward mediation will also be likely to favor free principles of contract construction. This is not necessarily so, however. There is no compelling reason why the strict constructionist should not, on occasion at least, undertake the role of mediator. Indeed, he is in an especially favorable position to coax an agreement by 'the gentle threat of a decision,' for in his case this threat may be fortified by a reputation for stiff interpretations. But with this allowance it still remains true that where one will take his position on each of the two controversies is likely to be influenced by a single disposition.

This affinity of views comes to clear expression in Mr. Justice Douglas's remarks in *United Steelworkers v Warrior & Gulf Nav Co*:

> Arbitration is a means of solving the unforeseeable by molding a system of private law for all the problems which may arise and to provide for their solution in a way which will generally accord with the variant needs and desires of the parties. . . . The labor arbitrator performs functions which are not normal to the courts. . . . The parties expect that his judgment of a particular grievance will reflect not only what the contract says but, insofar as the . . . agreement permits, such factors as the effect on productivity of a particular result, its consequence to the morale of the shop, his judgment whether tensions will be heightened or diminished.

Here by a single stroke the arbitrator-physician is largely relieved both of the restraints of judicial office and of any undue concern to find justification for what he does in the words of the agreement.

Let us briefly review the 'perceived' benefits of private arbitration. These are often claimed to be: privacy of the proceedings – if the parties wish their dispute resolution to be shielded from public scrutiny, arbitration, a private forum, is preferable to the courts, which rarely deny public access; procedural informality; expertise of the decision-maker; finality of the decision – no appeal; low cost, especially if lawyers are not used; and speed – the parties do not have to wait for a trial date to be set, but can proceed to arbitration as soon as they are ready. These successes have become something of an 'ideology' of arbitration.

However, in well-developed systems of arbitration this ideology may have little to do with the reality. Costs can escalate quickly. Established arbitrators with good reputations may charge highly for travel time and study time. There are also sometimes substantial costs for mundane matters such as hire of the meeting place or providing a transcription of the hearing and of course, in large commercial cases the parties may feel impelled to employ legal representation. A 'queue' may well develop – the arbitrator with a high reputation may take a very long time to resolve the dispute, because he or she has a heavy case load. Moreover, the parties to such disputes may themselves take a very long time to agree on the arbitrator and a hearing date.

One reason for such developments is that a process of 'institutionalisation' almost inevitably takes place even in the face of efforts to keep arbitration pure, flexible and simple – new 'procedural norms' are almost necessarily developed to deal with perceived problems, so that with the passage of time the hearings become legalistic and inflexible. In other words, arbitration has an inherent tendency to become counterproductive in terms of time, costs and formality. To this difficulty may be added the criticism that arbitration often suffers from a number of interrelated difficulties that may be thought of as reflecting the practice as opposed to the rhetoric or ideology of arbitration. These include: low quality of arbitrators, who are often perceived as being 'unsuccessful professionals'; a tendency on the part of arbitrators not to adjudicate properly but rather to try to compromise – in particular, in order to maintain good relations with an otherwise 'losing party'; linked to this tendency is the problem that anticipation of an imposed 'compromise' solution may encourage inflexibility in the disputing parties' 'negotiating' positions, and this necessitates reliance on special forms of arbitration (such as final offer arbitration) to deal with the problem.

In other words, as a result of pressures of institutionalisation and imperfect control of practice, there may be an inherent tendency for arbitration to lapse into a very second-rate version of court adjudication. This, in turn, may help to turn a particular area of arbitration into a battleground between legal specialists – the lawyers, who want greater and tighter legal control of arbitration, and the trade specialists, that is, experts in the practice and customary norms and expectations of a field of economic activity who try to resist the intrusion of lawyers. On the 'juridification' of arbitration, see Flood and Caiger (1993).

I: Arbitration – court-linked

In recent years, there have been developments, especially in the United States, in the direction of so-called 'compulsory arbitration'. For example, the parties may be required to use a system annexed to state or federal trial courts if the case involves claims for money damages below a certain amount, and the case does not fall within certain specified exceptional situations. Because the decisions made by arbitrators in these court-annexed systems are not binding – the parties have a right to trial de novo – such systems are perhaps better characterised as a mixed process. Thus, one of the main goals of court-annexed arbitration is to use non-binding arbitration to promote early settlement. However, this use does not constitute traditional arbitration; the decisions of the arbitrators are *not* binding. Nor does it merely constitute a form of negotiation because an *adjudicative* process is actively used to promote settlement. As a result, we consider this and other forms of arbitration which are used in close conjunction with other primary processes in Chapter Eight.

J: Arbitration – International

Over the past few decades, an important area of development in arbitration has been the increasing tendency for international business disputes to be resolved through the process of private arbitration. The emergence of international commercial arbitration has clearly been stimulated in part by the growing processes of globalisation of economic activity. In the extract that follows, Yves Dezalay and Bryant Garth describe the emergence of the system of private international justice, and some of the current lines of development in the world of international commercial arbitration.

Extract 7:19

Y Dezalay and B Garth: *Dealing in Virtue: International Commercial Arbitration and the Construction of a Transnational Legal Order* (1996) University of Chicago Press, Chicago and London, pp 311–317

The history of international commercial arbitration does not come to an end with the transformation of the International Chamber of Commerce into an international private justice with the characteristics of offshore litigation. It is true that, as we have seen, international commercial arbitration is now flourishing; it is the accepted method for resolving transnational commercial disputes. Certainly there are challenges within the general approach, most notably by the recent efforts to promote competing technologies such as mediation or other state-of-the-art alternatives to arbitration or litigation. But the field of international commercial arbitration continues to gain new territories and to bring new converts into this multi- and transnational legal profession; and the internationalizing process in turn transforms the landscapes of national business dispute resolution. The new converts, as we have seen, create business for and extend the reach of the key centers and central arbitrators of international commercial arbitration. International commercial arbitration has become increasingly more universal.

Our account of international commercial arbitration, however, teaches also that its characteristics and success relate to a quite specific geopolitical conjuncture. Of particular importance, we can suggest, were the cold war and the interventionism of the welfare state and of third worldism. International commercial arbitration as it developed around the ICC permitted business conflicts to be handled at a distance from cold-war politics and state interventionism. This conclusion will suggest that the specific factors that gave rise to international commercial arbitration as we know it are changing, and that therefore we may look toward the development of a new international approach to the management of business conflict. If so, the role of the ICC and international commercial arbitration may change quite substantially.

The starting point for this analysis is a recognition that the market of business disputing can be organized around two poles – the jurisdictions of the state and those of the business world. We have not had to pay very much attention to the state as such in the preceding chapters because international commercial arbitration in the past thirty years has operated with the state more or less off to one side. From a longer term perspective, however, we can recall that arbitration declined initially with the development of the New Deal in the United States and welfare states elsewhere. New regulatory regimes gained power at the expense of more private dispute resolution (eg Auerbach 1983). Only later did the new international commercial arbitration develop and help recover private justice in places like the United States.

We now ask if the construction of large regional markets – the European Community, NAFTA – or detailed mechanisms for regulating international commerce – the World Trade Organization under GATT – could also disrupt the landscape and introduce new stakes and even an 'international new deal'. The restructuring of the international market of disputes would build on emerging institutions such as the European Court of Justice, NAFTA, GATT, and even revived and transformed antitrust regulations. These institutions and approaches offer new opportunities for business. Even if it is not at first apparent, these institutions compete with the International Chamber of Commerce and private arbitration. At the same time, new approaches and institutions may facilitate the recomposition of this field of practice closer to the pole of the state. There could also be new providers of dispute resolution services, and new networks – borrowing, perhaps, from certain sectors within the existing international arbitration community.

International commercial arbitration can be transformed or even replaced because it is part of a larger international *market* of commercial or business disputes, and the market is inevitably unstable. Instability, as noted in chapter 6, comes from the fact that arbitration is constantly pulled between two contradictory poles – business and law. Competition in the products that serve this market produces innovations and changes – but only over the long term. In a market in symbolic goods, it is necessary for competitors to begin by producing their credibility – producing consumers at the same time as the producers are constructed out of sustained learned investment. It may even take generations before the fruits of this investment – if successful – are enjoyed.

The best approach to understanding the potential for particular future transformations in national and international business-disputing markets is to re-examine the political and professional landscape that permitted the ICC to succeed and to ask precisely what features are in the process of changing. In undertaking such an analysis, we focus especially on the learned and institutional dimensions, since those are the places where strategies for the long term can be played.

From this point of view, we can suggest first that the ICC represented, among other things, an alliance between the European grand professors and their disciples from countries at the periphery. It was organized around institutions like the Hague Academy of International Law and doctrines that reflect a typical academic neutrality – exemplified by the *lex mercatoria*. This learned investment served to break the stigma associated with business justice as a second-class justice, and it served also to construct the technologies necessary to equip this new forum. In both respects, as we saw in chapter 3, the very success of international commercial arbitration led to transformations of these initial conditions.

In addition to the academic prominence, the ICC approach had a second aspect that set the tone for international commercial arbitration. It studiously put aside the regulations of the nation-state. The approach employed a private institutional platform – the ICC, which is after all an organization of private businesses – that has no formal ties with states. The ICC could persuasively argue that the arbitration of disputes with third-world or Communist states was simply a matter of private, commercial arbitration. It could therefore avoid or channel elsewhere potential threats by states to the needs of multinational businesses who wished to invest or trade in new markets. Not only could the ICC argue that it was divorced from the interests of Western states, but also that international commercial arbitration was neutral. The academic world of learned law was able to provide the neutral authority through the *lex mercatoria*, and this learned doctrine was validated by the authority of the European grand professors over their disciples in the third world. This authority facilitated the putting aside of potentially threatening third-worldist legal claims.

The ICC prospered on the basis of this structural foundation, and it was able to gain credibility and prominence as an accepted institution. Imitators and competitors, as we have seen, have also proliferated. As we ask what may be emerging in the future, however, we must explore what has changed in the building blocks of the arbitration structure over the past thirty to thirty-five years. We can list a few of the more prominent changes.

First, US-style legal practice has emerged increasingly as the lingua franca of international commerce. The large law firms themselves – not only from the United States, but also from London and several other countries – have set up new international offices, and local imitators spread further the influence of this style of practice. Graduate study in US law schools is now one of the key items necessary to build a valuable resume for a non-US practitioner, and the spread of US legal concepts and practices has further gained through the symbolic imperialism of the US Agency for International Development and the many US-funded international human rights organizations. The center of gravity, as noted in many places in this book, has shifted toward the United States in legal education as well as in legal practice.

In the same way, the legal picture has been transformed by the increasing dominance of the political and economic model of Western liberal democracies. No longer do we face fundamental oppositions between communism and capitalism, or between various models of authoritarianism and relatively democratic entities. There are certainly differences, including those between Asian proponents of a 'different model' of human rights and democracy and prevailing Western viewpoints; but the legitimacy of the basic liberal governing structure for the state and the economy is largely uncontested.

Given these shared characteristics, it becomes for the first time possible to build legal regulatory structures – quasi states – that can frame large regional markets or even gain a place in the global market. The political and economic stakes associated with these structures are sufficiently high, both politically and economically, that by comparison private disputes lose some of their importance, becoming more like bargaining chips than major disputes.

States are at the same time among the key actors and the major stakes of an intensified international competition. State battles that were fought in the past around such issues as the legitimacy of expropriation are increasingly fought on the double terrain of protectionism (the legitimacy of trade barriers) and antidumping (with some new interjections of antitrust and some recurring debates about compensation – eg, Iraq, Iran). The states are major players in determining the framework and even the quite specific details of the arrangements in multilateral or bilateral investment treaties.

The states, it is true, concede certain of their prerogatives to supranational entities, such as GATT or the United Nations; or to courts, exemplified by the European Court of Justice; or quasi courts, exemplified by the NAFTA and GATT panels. In practice, however, the states have the power to control the appointments of judges to such panels – a practice exemplified already in the more state-centered arbitration institutions like the Iran-United States Claims Tribunal and the International Center for the Settlement of Investment Disputes associated with the World Bank.

These developments suggest that modern trade battles are played in the first place on the terrain of the state – and by extension on that of lawmaking – rather than on the terrain of private justice or the practice of mediation of business conflicts. This change in the hierarchy of the particular settings of business conflict and its handling upsets the relative positions of the possible producers and institutional providers (and also the consumers) of regulation and dispute resolution.

We may see, in fact, a kind of reversal of the *Mitsubishi* case described in chapter 8. In *Mitsubishi*, the US Supreme Court in effect recognized international commercial arbitration's precedence over the national enforcement of antitrust laws. The new order could involve a kind of international antitrust (and, relatedly, antidumping regulated by the World Trade Organization). It could therefore be that, while national antitrust was initially pushed out of the international business-disputing domain to make room for ICC-style arbitration, it comes back in as part of a new international legal order.

States – and among them supranational entities – and state jurisdictions intervene increasingly on the scene of economic conflicts. And the relatively new entities that intervene tend to be jealous of their authority and anxious to build up their regulatory domain. Thus, for example, Brussels and the court in Luxembourg have been cool or even hostile to the International Chamber of Commerce.

As states assume more importance, legal professionals and large enterprises tend to move, almost by definition, closer to the pole of the state, leading to a process of acceleration. Those with ties to the state – as seen in the example of the Rule of Law Committee – are more likely to play the public card in business conflicts. That is to say, their expertise and connections will lead them to channel conflicts toward the state, contributing thereby to the acceleration of the recomposition of the field of business conflicts around the state.

If this line of development continues, the field of transnational business justice will be more closely connected to states and to supranational, statelike entities than it was in the period when the ICC gained its eminence. Major business conflicts would be fought on terrain closer to the states – with the states implicated in the contests and the contestants. We cannot say at this point whether this development will take place, and whether, if so, the world constituted around the ICC and its networks will assume a secondary position. But, as suggested earlier, the history of business disputing shows that change is typically made through the creation of new models and institutions rather than simply modifications of the existing institutions.

The question of institutional 'breaks' returns us to the important theoretical distinction between the international legal field and the institutions that we find, such as the International Chamber of Commerce and the *lex mercatoria*, within that field. The field represents a space of positions and struggles that produce, render obsolete, or reinvent social institutions. The field may certainly be transformed, but in the absence of major unsettling events like wars or political upheavals, the change takes place according to a social logic and even a rhythm of generations. In contrast, the space occupied by institutions is much more susceptible to breaks and reconversions. Our research focuses on the field – exploring therefore the strategies of individuals and social groups that make up the field – because the breaks and reconversions of institutions only make sense in relation to the transformations in the field[s] that produce them.

This distinction is central to any effort to ascertain the future – and the role of international commercial arbitration in it. For example, if we take seriously the suggestion of an increasing role for states and quasi-state entities in business disputing, one reaction might be to ask what this potential role of the states means for the idea of an emerging *international* legal field or for the development of *international* legal institutions. The problem is that it is relatively easy to imagine the development of international commercial arbitration as an aspect of a growing 'international legal field' – and indeed, a growing international legal order – with its own form of private justice detached from the national justice of states. As explained in the preceding paragraph, however, the institutions themselves – what is seen as an international legal order – can change quite dramatically in response to transformations in the international legal field. The institutions can move *toward or away* from states. International does not mean a necessary decline of the role of states.

The international legal field, in sum, should not be seen simplistically (or positivistically) as a putting aside or negation of the national dimension. The relevant research question is not in fact whether the international legal field exists or not. For our purposes, it is a question of whether the tool of the international legal field is useful for examining and analyzing strategic opportunities. The international legal field, therefore, should be seen as a virtual space for battles that may vary in intensity in different places and times – and that have more or less strong echoes in national and local power relations.

Internationalization can in fact best be characterized as the opening of breaches in national spaces that are otherwise more or less closed, at times almost watertight. The opening leads potentially to a redefinition or a blurring of the boundaries established and maintained in the national settings. Internationalization allows individuals and groups to construct strategies that go beyond national space. External alliances, such as that formed between the grand old men in arbitration and the large US law firms, are made possible by internationalization. And these alliances contribute to redefining internal spaces by disrupting hierarchies of values and established alliances. In the United States, for example, the connection with the world of the ICC facilitated the valorization of private justice and then the emergence of a new domestic market in private justice.

The impacts of these strategies of internationalization are felt even more strongly as one moved toward nations on the periphery. Legal actors on the periphery may be quicker to forge international connections and apply them domestically in part because their own legal systems point them toward the center. Constructed by and for international relations of economic and symbolic dependency, the legal systems that have been established on the periphery are by definition rooted in internationalization. Nevertheless, on the periphery and elsewhere, the impact of internationalization is not automatic or determined in advance. It depends in every case on the relative power and relations between the protectionist and the internationalist groups from among legal elites.

Meanwhile, as we have seen, the same strategies that promote the recomposition of the local serve also and at the same time to construct the international (or at least delocalization). But what emerges from this process is not preconstructed or inevitable. The geopolitical center of gravity of the international field depends on the result of power struggles between different national groups who fight themselves on the terrain of the international. The international legal field could be closer to Europe or closer to the United States (or to other future competitors on the terrain of law). It could also be closer (or even limited to) the domain of finance and business law, or it could include other components, including international human rights or the protection of the environment. In short, as with respect to the national legal fields, the international legal field may be limited to an alliance with the dominant groups in power or may provide places for other political forces and other social groups.

The international legal field is after all a field of struggle, which means that different outcomes are possible. Systematic examinations of the networks, alliances, and institutions by and around which the international is constituted provide the best way to ascertain what is likely to emerge from the struggles that take place. But the outcomes are indeterminate. One of the goals of this study and others like it, which explore the ways in which the legal profession and law gain their legitimacy and change over time, is in fact to help individuals see that the hierarchies and categories that make acquiescence to economic and political power seem natural and inevitable are themselves the product of struggles.

CHAPTER EIGHT

Hybrid Forms and Processual Experimentation

A: Introduction

In identifying three primary processes of decision-making – negotiation, mediation and umpiring – we have tried to give these modes an analytical clarity that is not necessarily going to be revealed so sharply in real-life forms. At the same time we have left largely unexamined the relationships prevailing between these different processes, and the relative value attached to them, where they are found together in a particular culture. But we have already noted, in Chapter Five, how negotiations are routinely pursued through litigation in the common law world, as a result of the unwillingness of lawyers to contemplate the construction of an agreed resolution to a dispute without mobilisation of the court process. So bilateral processes may take place along the route towards the court. We also saw how judges may depart from an adjudicatory procedure, abandoning a binary, win-or-lose approach to decision-making in favour of encouraging the parties to construct their own solutions. In some jurisdictions, the role of the judge may be seen as one in which mediation is stressed, and adjudication to be relied on to secure an outcome only as a final and unwelcome last resort (see the example of contemporary China: Palmer, 1989). Moreover, as Gulliver has observed, the role of mediator in some cultures is conceptualised and practised in directive, almost 'umpire-like terms' (1979: 225–226). In any event, the accumulation of experience by a mediator may tend to encourage an active, manipulative approach, resulting in an imposed solution that, in reality, crosses the line into adjudication.

The extent to which such departures from the primary processual forms is officially accepted, or even encouraged, varies considerably from one culture to another. As Gulliver argues, it is not always easy in the real world to draw a clear line between umpiring and negotiating processes. In the passage extracted below (Extract 8:1) he illustrates practices around the borderline between umpiring and facilitated negotiation, but argues that these do not invalidate the basic analytical value of the distinction.

Even under conditions where the primary processes remain distinct, they may be found closely linked together in processual terms. There may, for example, be strong cultural imperatives requiring that negotiation, mediation and adjudication should be resorted to in sequence, with parties moving on from one process to another only where attempts to achieve an outcome through the first have been exhausted. We illustrate this point through the procedural values prevailing in the Southern African Tswana kingdoms of the Kalahari during the nineteenth century, retained at local level under the Bechuanaland Protectorate and surviving on under the Republic of Botswana. There parties are required to attempt negotiation first, resort to mediatory help where that fails and seek an adjudicated solution only in the last resort (Extract 8:2). Historically, such orderly understandings have not generally characterised the arrangements of the common law world. We have already repeatedly noted the entangled relationship of lawyer negotiations and the pursuit of adjudication in contemporary common law jurisdictions; but this 'processual anarchy' went much further than this. While judgment – subject to appeal – remained final and authoritative, there were no clear understandings as to the relative beauty of different modes of resolution or as to a fixed processual trajectory.

In the West, widely shared folk assumptions about the handling of conflict attach a high value *both* to decision-making through consensual agreement and to justice. So in this culture common understandings seem to point us in two rather different directions, evoking separate images of apparently equal purity and beauty: yet the relationship and relative value of these two approaches to handling trouble has never been entirely clear. Parties could, until very recently, resort to trial and judgment without trying any other process first.

However, in the common law world the past two decades have seen significant moves away from entrenched, historic understandings about process. In broad, schematic terms three important changes are increasingly visible. First, the old processual anarchy is under challenge to the extent of a growing recognition that a negotiated solution should always be sought first. Second, the courts are increasingly seen as having a primary responsibility to sponsor settlement; they can no longer wait impassively to fulfil a final role in trial and judgment. Third, a welter of hybrid forms has grown up around each of the primary processes. Legal professionals have played a key role in the evolution of these hybrid forms, which now represent the vanguard of ADR development. Indeed, the emergence of these new forms may be viewed as something of a co-option of the ADR movement by specialists trained in legal rules and procedures. These have in many cases been given official blessing.

This general tendency towards the emergence of hybrid forms has a number of overlapping strands, but these may be essentially characterised in terms of modifications to each of the three primary processes already discussed. First, there have been attempts to enhance lawyer negotiations through the injection of facilitatory forms that mimic adjudication so that, somewhat paradoxically, ADR in this context means some sort of reimposition of adjudicatory elements and values. Examples of these initiatives are discussed later in this chapter. In all of them, specialised forecasting procedures are inserted in the process of negotiation, and the parties are themselves drawn back into the process with the support of additional lawyers in non-aligned, advisory or consultancy roles. Alongside resort to these specialised devices for forecasting outcomes and sponsoring settlement, there have been a number of developments in the manner in which mediation is practised including, in particular, its linkage to arbitration to produce so-called 'med-arb', the annexing of mediation to the court and, in family disputes, the combination of therapy and mediation. At the same time there have been a number of attempts to refurbish adjudication by modifying or supplementing the trial process with further devices – a number of these refurbishment efforts being closely related to those developed by lawyers in support of their negotiations. These court-based initiatives include judicial settlement, early neutral evaluation, court-annexed arbitration and the summary jury trial. There have also been important developments in the field of arbitration.

Extract 8:1

P Gulliver: *Disputes and Negotiations: A Cross-Cultural Perspective* (1979) Academic Press, New York and London, pp 29–33

> Another ethnographic example is the mode of treatment of interpersonal disputes in the Mexican village of Ralu'a where a judge (*presidente*) sits in the official municipal court. It seems clear that the process was adjudicatory, yet there are close parallels with the processes described in the preceding instances. The *presidente*, in reaching his judgments, not only took careful account of the disputants' opinions but sought to be guided by what was acceptable to the disputants and allowed them to come to agreement, if possible, concerning the terms of the settlement.
>
> In one case, a woman laid a complaint before the *presidente*. She alleged that her small son had been beaten and injured by a young man while she and the boy had been working in the field of that man's grandmother. On being summoned to the court, the defendant denied the allegation and counterclaimed that the boy was a mischief maker who had called him 'miserable names; he said very ugly things.' In reply to the *presidente's* questioning, the plaintiff said that she and her son worked in that field at the request of the defendant's grandmother, not the defendant himself. The *presidente* asked the plaintiff how much she wanted from the defendant to pay the costs of her son's treatment. She demanded 30 pesos. The defendant rejected that and offered 20 pesos. The *presidente* asked the plaintiff if she would accept that amount. She did and thus the case ended. The *presidente* was the focus of proceedings and of the plaintiff's complaint. She sought a decision from him in her favor. He acted with authority in summoning the defendant and seems to have controlled the hearing. He did not overtly make a judgment of the guilt of the defendant, although such is clearly implied in his action when he asked the plaintiff what payment she wanted. The defendant did not contest that implication but, following the *presidente's* lead, also turned to the matter of the size of compensation. Yet it appears that the *presidente* wished to reach a result agreeable to both parties, quite like Nyoro and Tolai adjudicators. To this end he encouraged the disputants themselves to propose offer and counteroffer so as to reach an agreed outcome, which he approved. Thus the *presidente* administered the proceedings, exercised authority, and made a judgment, but he merely endorsed the

parties' agreement on the amount to be paid. From the rest of Nader's account, it seems clear that the *presidente* could have followed up his judgment by determining the size of compensation and he might well have done so had the disputants themselves been unable to agree. In that context of a small village, characterized by multiplex, face-to-face relations, he preferred that the disputants discover agreement. Nader's other cases exhibit more obvious judgments. In her Case 1, the *presidente* decided that a driver was responsible for damages caused by his truck, saying, 'It will be most convenient in this case if the chauffeur paid for the damage.' In Case 3, the *presidente* 'pronounced' his decision in a marital dispute: that the couple should come together, forget the past, and take joint concern for their sick child. In Case 4, the *presidente* 'dictated . . . [that] the lost coffee should be restored to the plaintiff.'

Finally, a contrasting instance is taken from the Ifugao people of the Philippines, as reported by Barton. Here there were neither courts nor neighborhood tribunals. Disputing parties sought to settle matters strictly between themselves. Argument and offers were not conducted in a face-to-face manner but through a go-between (*monkalun*), a man of acknowledged prestige who carried messages, adding his own interpretations and advice, and who met with each party separately in their own houses.

Barton described a case in which a man demanded the payment of a debt of pigs from another man. Ample notice was given of the requirement since the plaintiff needed the pigs for use in connection with his son's impending marriage. The two men disagreed as to the number of pigs resultant on the natural rate of increase of the two pigs originally loaned. The plaintiff asked for five; the defendant offered four and raised a counterdebt of a chicken (and its expected progeny), a debt left over from their grandfathers' time that, it was claimed, reduced the present debt to three pigs. In a later direct confrontation, the defendant severely insulted the plaintiff by a reference to malpractice by the plaintiff's ancestor, a great-grandfather.

The plaintiff now initiated a formal dispute by sending his demands with a prestigious go-between to the defendant's house. There the go-between emphasized the enormity of the insult and made a demand for payment of 11 pigs. After much discussion with the go-between, the defendant's brother offered 4 pigs, which were to be repayment of the original debt only. During the next few days each disputant sought the support of his own kinsfolk. Then the go-between met with the plaintiff and his kin. He emphasized the earlier, unpaid debt of the chicken and its progeny, condemned a proposal to seize a valuable gong from the defendant in lieu of payment, spoke of possible violence by the defendant's party, and pictured the defendant as a poverty-stricken youth who would find it hard to pay 5 pigs. Finally he talked of the need for harmony in the community and the need for unity against its threatening neighbors. What the plaintiff and his supporters replied to all this is not reported by Barton, but the go-between left with an offer to accept 4 pigs for the debt, 1 pig for the insult, and 1 pig for the go-between's fee, plus cancellation of the debt of the chicken. This was an 'ultimate' offer on their part.

Meeting next with the defendant and his kin, the go-between told of the large number and unified determination of the plaintiff's party, explained their offer, and advised its acceptance. After discussion, the counteroffer was four pigs, plus one for the go-between and annulment of the charge of insult. The go-between departed, saying that the offer was inadequate and promising to return when the party had reconsidered the matter.

Next day, the plaintiff's son came and took the gong (of considerable ancestral value and especially prized by the defendant's mother), leaving deliberate proof of his identity. The go-between returned to the defendant's home, declaring his anger at the seizure but demanding that the dispute be settled forthwith so as to avert further trouble. The defendant's brother demanded four pigs in compensation, but the mother declared that they should pay the debt and regain the gong. Her proposal seems to have been accepted by the defendant's party. The go-between immediately visited the plaintiff, saying that the latter must return the gong and pay four pigs indemnity. After further discussion, the go-between proposed the return of the going in return for five pigs from the defendant – three for the plaintiff and two for the go-between. The plaintiff agreed to this after some argument and the go-between took the gong to his own house. He sent a message to the defendant saying that the gong would be returned on receipt of five pigs. The defendant's party considered this proposal, agreed to it, and completed the transaction straightaway. The go-between passed on three of the pigs to the plaintiff.

Here there was clearly a bargaining process, the exchange of offer and counteroffer to the point of reaching joint agreement. The influence of the go-between was considerable in the framing of the offers and in their interpretation to the other party. Only the last offer (by the defendant) was precisely the same as his own suggestion (which included his own increased fee). The go-between could not judge the issues involved and in fact he told different stories to each party. Nor could he order what the outcome should be. He could only propose terms. He expressed his views of the parties' behavior with reference to applicable cultural rules and to his estimates of the parties' strengths. Finally he gave a kind of ultimatum to the defendant. This was not an order so much as a proposal that was calculated to succeed because of the weakness of the defendant after the loss of the gong. According to Barton, a go-between could fail altogether to bring the two parties into an agreed decision, in which event he withdrew from the case as he declared a temporary truce. Later another go-between would be invited to start fresh negotiations.

In this section I have deliberately described a few marginal cases in the light of the analytical distinction between negotiation and adjudication. Let me be clear: Purely within the context of an ethnographic analysis of these particular cases it may not much matter what we call the processes of the treatment of disputes. It might be sufficient to understand them as well as possible and to discover their significance in the ongoing life of the local community and the wider society. Nevertheless, both observation and analysis might be improved by a keener appreciation of the distinction between third-party judgments and the disputants' interdependent decision-making, and by a more perceptive regard for the locus and dynamics of decision-making. My primary concern here, however, is to make cross-cultural, sociological comparison in the search for sharper conceptual tools as a preliminary to the detailed examination of the process of negotiation. I think that it has been shown that in these marginal instances the distinction is both valid and usefully suggestive. If this is so in these instances, then it is even more so in other instances where the contrast is more marked – say, between formal, largely impersonal courts and their judges, on the one hand, and collective bargaining or unmediated negotiations among the Arusha, on the other hand.

Extract 8:2

J L Comaroff and S Roberts: *Rules and Processes* (1981) University of Chicago Press, Chicago, pp 108–110

The Tswana identify four levels at which successive attempts to resolve disputes ought to be made. First, although an individual should ideally report to senior kinsmen any incident likely to be a source of conflict, the parties themselves should strive to settle their differences before provoking the active involvement of others. Second, if their initial efforts fail, the disputants must seek the advice and help of senior agnates and matrilateral kin – fathers, brothers, and paternal and maternal uncles. If such informal intervention does not result in a successful resolution, the matter should then be taken to the headman of the ward of the person against whom the complaint has been made. Only if the dispute is not settled by the ward headman is it finally taken to the chief's *kgotla*. These agencies, then, provide a hierarchical course through which any dispute may proceed; that is, a settlement ought to be sought at each level in turn, and the matter should not be referred to a higher authority unless resolution appears impossible.

At the first of these levels, where only the two parties themselves are involved, the mode of settlement is necessarily one of negotiation. Private meetings between the disputants should be occasions of explanation and apology, at which offers of compensation ought to be accompanied by assurances of future amicability and good conduct. When such bilateral contacts fail to resolve the conflict (or, as is often the case, serve only to exacerbate it), the kinsmen who are then approached to mediate have considerable latitude in choosing a procedure to follow in seeking a settlement. Typically they begin by making informal efforts to persuade the two parties, either individually or together, to come to terms with each other before the conflict escalates into a bitter public confrontation. Alternatively, they may suggest convening a formal meeting of the agnatic segment, or segments, to which the disputants belong. A meeting of the segment must in any case occur before the dispute can be taken to a higher level. At the meeting of the segment, the mode of settlement remains one of mediation. The kinsmen who intervene between the disputants may stress the implications of the available courses of action and urge them to follow an approved solution, but they have no recognized authority to impose a decision.

If a dispute is not resolved at the lower levels, it is placed before the ward headman of the individual against whom the original complaint was made. At this level there still remains some procedural flexibility. The respective groupings may make informal appeals to the headman, or the matter may be raised directly in the formal context of the open *kgotla*. Similarly, the headman also has the option of handling the dispute in either a formal or informal manner. He may decide to mediate by suggesting a solution that he considers should be acceptable to both parties; he may even send them away for further discussion among their close kin if he feels that this means has not been sufficiently explored. However, the headman has the authority to convene a hearing and to make an order-in-settlement that the parties must recognize, whether they agree with it or not. When a headman chooses to deal with a dispute in this way, the mode of settlement is one of adjudication. In the face of such a decision, the parties may appeal against the outcome and take the case to the chief. Once this has occurred, the latter must hear the report of the headman who dealt with the matter before listening to the accounts of the respective disputants and their senior kinsmen. Like the headman, the chief (or his representative) may try to effect a mediated settlement, or he may proceed directly to make a final decision, which he can enforce if necessary. In other words, negotiation, mediation, and adjudication, as modes of conflict resolution, stand in a fixed *ideal* relationship: negotiation should first be attempted at the lowest level before resort is made successively to mediation and adjudication at the higher ones. On the other hand, in everyday dispute-settlement processes, negotiation does not automatically give way to mediation and adjudication if initial efforts at resolution have proved fruitless; it is thus an oversimplification to correlate agencies and procedural modes in any rigid fashion.

B: Settlement as Civil Justice

In looking at these still evolving processes of hybridisation, the place to begin is with the contemporary representation and practice of civil justice itself. Right across the common law world, large-scale changes in governmental understanding and management of civil disputes have become visible over at least two decades (see Chapters Three and Seven). At the heart of these changes lies a growing identification of 'settlement' as an approved, privileged objective of civil justice. The courts present themselves not just as agencies offering judgement but also as sponsors of negotiated agreement. In England these changes, which first appeared as spontaneous, piecemeal initiatives within the judiciary, are now drawn together and given official blessing through entirely re-cast Civil Procedure Rules which came into force in April 1999.

On one level this apparently striking break with the past did no more than endorse what had been long established practice – the use of 'litigation' as the vehicle for lawyer negotiations. What was different was the idea of active judicial commitment to this process. The new regime of procedure, which came into force in April 1999,[1] has two radical and novel features:

- First, an explicit attempt is made to construct a pre-litigation phase in which the conduct of the respective legal teams is prescribed and potentially enforced through cost sanctions. The shape of the pre-litigation phase is laid down in *Pre-Action Protocols*.
- Second, in providing *a strict regime of case management* once litigation is initiated, 'settlement' is explicitly prioritised as the primary objective of civil justice.

The Rules begin with a broad programatic statement. This identifies an 'overriding objective' which is 'to enable the court to deal with cases justly' (Rule 1.1.(1)). It goes on to provide that 'the court must further the overriding objective by actively managing cases' (Rule 1.1.(4)). This requirement [note the imperative tone: 'the court must . . .'] signals the government's determination to adopt and consolidate

1 The Rules are available though the Department for Constitutional Affairs web pages: www.dca.gov.uk/legalsys/civilproc.htm.

the intention of the senior judiciary 'to change the whole culture, the ethos, apply-ing in the field of civil litigation'.[2] This procedural regime thus departs from the historical position under which English judges have allowed the parties to prepare for adversarial trial very much in their own way and at their own pace, dealing with 'interlocutory' matters only where the parties bring them to their attention. The court is no longer a potent but immobile backdrop in the pre-trial period, awaiting its central role in trial and judgment.

The Pre-litigation Phase

Looking first at the attempt to police the pre-litigation phase, we see on the part of government a bold, unprecedented ambition to police an area of activity formerly treated unambiguously as in the 'private' sphere. In all types of civil dispute, parties are now expected to follow *pre-action protocols* that set out the steps parties are expected to take before issuing court proceedings. For some types of dispute, spe-cific pre-action protocols exist; in all other cases the parties are expected to follow the general *Practice Direction for Pre-action Protocols.*[3] The Direction provides spe-cific guidance: 'the court will expect the parties, in accordance with the overriding objective . . . to act reasonably in exchanging information . . . and generally in trying to avoid the necessity for the start of proceedings' (Rule 4.1). Claims have to be made in writing and such claims have to be answered promptly. Normally, this pre-action phase will include 'the parties conducting genuine and reasonable negotiations with a view to settling the claim economically and without court proceedings' (Rule 4.2).

If, when litigation is subsequently commenced, these procedures have *not* first been followed, the court has power to impose cost sanctions on the parties. The Court of Appeal, in *Halsey v Milton Keynes General NHS Trust,*[4] decided that the court does not have the power to order the parties to attempt mediation; and that the court's proper role is to encourage rather than to compel settlement. But if a party is found to act unreasonably in refusing mediation, the court has power to displace the normal rules as to the allocation of costs against a successful litigant.

Dyson LJ set out some grounds on which it would be reasonable to decline mediation:

- reasonable belief in a watertight case;
- other settlement efforts already made;
- costs of entering mediation unacceptably high; and
- damaging delay.

Prior to *Halsey*, there had been some suggestion in the courts that they had power to mandate mediation.[5] *Halsey* seems to represent the better view, endorsing the

---

2 The Lord Chief Justice, announcing the general Practice Direction of 24 January 1995: (1995) 1 WLR 262.
3 Civil Procedure: vol 1 (the While Book Service 2003) pp 1983–1987.
4 (2004) EWCA (Civ) 576.
5 See *Dunnett v Railtrack plc (Practice Note)* [2002] EWCA Civ 303; [2002] 1 WLR 2434; [2002] 2 All ER 850, CA; *R (Cowl) v Plymouth City Council (Practice Note)* [2001] EWCA Civ 1935; [2002]

value of mediation while recognising the essential element of voluntariness that must underlie fair negotiation.

The Conduct of the Litigation Process

Once litigation is commenced, the Rules spell out in general terms what 'active case management' involves. This emerges as a dual process under which the court is at once required to do everything it can to facilitate settlement, and where that is not possible, to clear the route towards judgment. The first of these contrasting imperatives is expressed as a triple mandate to the judges. First, it is a matter of 'encouraging the parties to co-operate with each other in the conduct of the proceedings' (Rule 1.4.(2)(a)). Second, active case management includes 'encouraging the parties to use an alternative dispute resolution procedure if the court considers that appropriate and facilitating their use of such procedure' (Rule 1.4.(2)(e)). Third, case management also includes 'helping the parties to settle the whole or part of the case' (Rule 1.4.(2)(f)).

The primary injunction to 'co-operate' may sound no more than ordinary common sense: but its full implications are not at all clear. A minimal understanding requires the judge to prevent those analogues of warfare, delay and ambush, which have historically been normal means of wasting an adversary by postponing trial. But perhaps the requirement goes far beyond that, making the judge responsible for seeing that legal teams come clean about the negotiatory character of litigation, treating it as a process of information exchange and learning, directed towards joint decision-making. However we read it, this injunction requires a sea change in the traditional approach of lawyers to litigation, in its very essence an antagonistic, adversarial and secretive process under which actual combat ('fighting') is simply represented in an externally monitored, heavily ritualised textual and verbal exchange.

The second part of the mandate, which gives the courts a general responsibility to encourage settlement by proposing ADR and providing a necessary space in the litigation process while this is attempted, is equally remarkable. It reveals the astonishing speed with which a rather disparate bundle of foreign novelties is now confidently identified and officially adopted as a part of the English local scene. Twenty years ago, it would hardly have been possible to find the phrase 'alternative dispute resolution' in the index of a major United States law journal. Yet by 1991, even in London, the Beldam Committee on Alternative Dispute Resolution established by the General Council of the Bar was 'convinced that the case was made out for the courts themselves to embrace the systems of alternative dispute resolution . . . We believe that ADR has much to offer in support of the judicial process.'[6]

In following Beldam and embracing 'alternative dispute resolution procedures', the Civil Procedure Rules sanction the use of quite a disparate collection of practices.

---

1 WLR 803, CA; *Shirayama Shokusan Co Ltd v Danovo Ltd* [2003] EWHC 390 (Ch); [2004] 1 WLR 2985.

6 *Report of the Committee on Alternative Dispute Resolution*, General Council of the Bar, October 1991, p 1.

But these are essentially of two types: forecasting devices that enable the parties and their legal teams to examine their positions against a predicted judicial determination; and interventions that directly facilitate negotiations. Among the forecasting devices are technical procedures like the 'mini-trial' or 'executive tribunal' and 'Early Neutral Evaluation' (see Section C below). The latter comprises mediation in its manifold forms. These categories are by no means discrete, as within the former various hybrids may be found under which forecasting procedures are directly linked to facilitatory interventions. In all this, the essential point is that through writing this array of devices into the Civil Procedure Rules, the supervisory reach and technical repertoire of the civil courts are enormously extended.

The final part of the mandate, 'helping the parties to settle', potentially represents the most fundamental change of all. Beneath the simplicity and apparent good sense of this last injunction lies a shift that is qualitatively different from anything else the new Rules involve. Going beyond the management of litigation – in the sense of making sure opportunities to settle are taken where this is appropriate and speeding the parties to trial where it is not – it proposes an active engagement on the part of the judge in the settlement process itself. In short, the Rules encourage the judge to become a mediator. All this is pretty much uncharted territory in this jurisdiction, although in North America active judicial involvement in settlement has a much longer history.

Looking at this programme as a whole, it is worth emphasising an obvious point about the strategic choice which government took. The 'dual' nature that lawyers have fashioned over the years for civil litigation receives endorsement. Litigation remains the approved vehicle for lawyer negotiations. Yet an alternative route lay available. Government *could* have devised a procedural framework with the objective of prising settlement and litigation apart. The first step towards such a goal is actually made with the pre-action protocols; but this separation is not carried through as the dual objectives still continue in the litigation phase. While settlement no longer remains invisible and submerged, lawyers are still largely free to approach practice in a distinctive way that inevitably involves progressive entanglement of settlement and trial. The essential point here is that, as lawyers have come to use litigation in pursuit of settlement, negotiatory and adjudicatory resolution are inevitably entwined.

C: Negotiation-related Innovations

The Mini-trial

One 'alternative' device invoked in aid of settlement in the course of lawyer negotiations is the 'mini-trial' (sometimes labelled the 'modified settlement conference' or 'executive tribunal') first developed in North America in the context of commercial disputes.[7] The mini-trial is essentially a predictive, forecasting device conceived by

---

7 Specifically, it was first used in 1977 to resolve a dispute concerning a patent infringement.

its sponsors as a means of informing clients about the strengths and weaknesses of their respective cases and providing an indication of the likely outcome of adjudication, thus prompting them to agree to settle. This is achieved through the respective legal teams presenting their cases to the parties themselves – senior executives in commercial cases – who are assisted in evaluating their positions by a 'neutral advisor'. The neutral adviser may feed information and advice about the law into the process and, if requested to do so, offer an opinion about the likely outcome of litigation if the matter comes to trial.

This procedure has two distinctive features when compared with conventional lawyer negotiations. First, the parties themselves are drawn back into a primary role, listening to the presentation of the respective arguments, evaluating these and then, ideally, moving on to direct, bilateral negotiations. Second, there is the introduction of an independent third party, the neutral expert, in both an advisory and a forecasting capacity (Extract 8:3).

Early Neutral Evaluation

A related device, 'early neutral evaluation' (ENE) involves the respective legal teams in putting a case, at a relatively early point, to a neutral or group of neutrals (sometimes in the United States a mock jury) to obtain for the client a forecast of the possible judicial outcome, again with a view to encouraging settlement. We further discuss this innovation in the context of its use by the court (see p 328 below).

Lawyers who advocate and use these devices say that one of the greatest obstacles to settlement is the stressed, impassioned corporate executive who will not listen to sensible professional advice in cases where a negotiated outcome is in the client's best interests. They claim that these procedures are often successful in bringing clients 'back to reality', making them agree to settle.

It is hard to know what to make of these procedures, or of the justification for them offered by those who use them. They seem to imply a huge lack of confidence in traditional lawyering practices, and necessarily involve a loss of control that is often uncomfortable for lawyers, especially those well grounded in traditional approaches to litigation. One of us has argued before (Roberts, 1993) that these devices have their most immediate application as means of damping down unrealistic expectations which the legal teams may themselves have recklessly nourished, even created, at an earlier stage in the dispute process. They are, in effect, crisis management techniques made necessary in a culture where the habit of late settlement, advantageous only to the profession, has left the client with insufficient information and advice in the early phases of a dispute.

The mini-trial and ENE were initially developed by ADR specialists to be used in support of negotiations by the parties' legal teams. They have subsequently come to be used by the courts as well, introduced at early stage meetings, in the course of efforts to generate settlement discussions (see p 324 below).

Alongside resort to these specialised devices for forecasting outcomes and sponsoring settlement, there have been general moves by lawyers to present themselves in neutral advisory and consultancy roles. While in North America lawyers have for some time acted in neutral capacities alongside the traditional partisan roles, in many common law jurisdictions this pretension to neutrality is a considerable departure from established practice, and again represents a response to perceived threats represented by developments outside the legal profession. The role of the 'neutral adviser' in the 'mini-trial', typically a lawyer, is one example of this.

In England, both the Bar and the Law Society have sanctioned experiments under which lawyers may fulfil joint consultancy roles in some categories of family dispute. Under the scheme sanctioned by the Law Society, and operated by the Family Mediators' Association (FMA), a solicitor may co-operate with another professional 'with experience in marital or family work' in helping 'couples cope with the legal, financial and emotional problems of separation and divorce, as well as arrangements for children'. This includes assisting parties 'to work out proposals for settlement' and reach joint decisions in the context of family breakdown. While the FMA has given the label of 'mediation' to this innovatory form of lawyer intervention, it does not appear to be by any means limited to facilitating the communication between parties necessary to joint decision-making. Rather, at the core it is a matter of providing expert consultancy to the parties jointly upon the arrangements regarding children, finance and property necessitated by family breakdown, and providing the parties with the framework within which to put these arrangements in place.[8]

A further form of hybrid process involves the linked, sequential use of different forms of intervention by neutral third parties. The procedure known in North America as 'med-arb' is one such process. Under this procedure a neutral is called in by the parties and authorised to mediate and then move into the role of arbitrator where mediation fails to promote settlement. We take up this process in Section D below.

Extract 8:3

J K Lieberman and J F Henry: 'Lessons from the Alternative Dispute Resolution Movement' (1986) 53 *University of Chicago Law Review* 424, pp 427–428

> The mini-trial is not in fact a trial at all, but a highly-structured settlement process. Because it is a flexible device that can be tailored to the precise needs of the parties, no single procedural model of the mini-trial has yet prevailed. But in general, the known mini-trials share many of the following characteristics:
>
> 1. The parties negotiate a set of procedural ground rules (a protocol) that will govern the nonbinding mini-trial.
> 2. The time for preparation is relatively short – between six weeks and three months – and the amount of discovery is relatively limited.
> 3. The hearing itself is sharply abbreviated – usually no more than two days.
> 4. The hearing is often conducted by a third-party neutral, typically called the 'neutral advisor'.

8 The Family Law Bar Association's 'conciliation board' procedure provides another example.

5. The case is presented to representatives of the parties with authority to settle; there is no judge or jury.
6. The lawyers present their 'best' case; they do not have time to delve into side issues.
7. Immediately after the hearing, the party representatives meet privately to negotiate a settlement.
8. If they cannot reach a settlement, the neutral advisor may render an advisory opinion on how he thinks a judge would rule if the case were to go to court.
9. The proceedings are confidential: the parties generally commit themselves to refrain from disclosing details of the proceedings to any outsider.

Several observations are in order about the trust-building capacity of the mini-trial. First, the very process of negotiating the protocol tends to foster trust. Second, by concentrating on their best possible case, the lawyers usually feel constrained to discuss the central issues. Third, the kind of lawyerly hairsplitting, name-calling, and pettifogging that might delight courtroom regulars would leave the business executives to whom mini-trials are presented singularly unamused. Finally, the presence at the hearing of a neutral advisor, to whom both parties have consented, enhances the prospect that they will credit any advisory opinion that he renders.

D: Mediation-related Innovations

Another broad area of innovation has developed around attempts to reinforce mediation by infusing or joining it with other forms of dispute management. We consider two principal forms of development: med-arb and court-annexed mediation. Similar hybridisation arises where mediation is combined with another form of profession intervention. An example is provided by the attempted combination of mediation and family therapy.

Med-arb

In the process characterised as 'med-arb', the third-party intervener is expected to attempt a mediation of the differences between the parties. In the event of failure to achieve a mediated outcome acceptable to both parties, the same third party assumes the role of arbitrator and makes a binding and final award. Although ordinarily found in the institutional context of arbitration, most schemes in effect give primacy to the mediation phase of the proceedings, and in practice are attempts to enhance the efficacy of mediation by reinforcing it with the threat of umpiring – indeed, they are sometimes referred to as 'mediating with a club'. In the common law world the origins of this approach appear to lie in the contrasting views of the most appropriate role for the arbitrator found in the United States earlier in the last century:

> in the 1930s and 1940s two views of the arbitrator's role existed. One view was that the arbitrator served primarily to further the relationship of the parties. The proponents of this view thought of the arbitrator as the impartial chairman of a joint committee and believed that he should seek through mediation to assist the parties in resolving their

grievances. To the extent that the parties could resolve their disputes, it was thought that their relationship and their capacity to resolve future disputes would be strengthened. Only if the parties could not resolve a dispute through mediation would the impartial chairman impose a decision. Furthermore, when required to decide a grievance, the impartial chairman, while remaining loyal to the contract, would attempt to do so in a fashion that was guided primarily by a desire to further the parties' relationship.

The opposing view saw the arbitrator not as an impartial chairman but as an umpire who should concern himself solely with deciding the grievance. In reaching a decision, the umpire should not consider which result would benefit the relationship of the parties, but instead should limit himself to interpreting and applying the contract in the manner that would best express the parties' intent as articulated in the contract (Goldberg, 1982: 272–273).

The author of this extract, Stephen Goldberg, concludes with the observation that, in the subsequent evolution of arbitration, the impartial chairman approach declined in favour of the umpiring view.

The case against the fusion of roles that the 'impartial chairman' approach envisaged was built up most forcefully by Fuller (1963) in his analysis of the place of the arbitrator in collective bargaining (Extract 8:4). Briefly stated, he argues that mediation and arbitration are essentially different in their purpose and morality – the morality of mediation is optimum settlement, with the parties giving up what they value less in return for what they value more, whereas the morality of arbitration is to be found in the contractual agreement to enter into arbitration. They also differ, in his view, in their processual essentials in that mediation seeks to secure adjustment to the position of the parties so that an outcome is achieved that most nearly meets their interests, whereas arbitration enables each party to present arguments and proofs in his or her favour. In particular, 'private consultations with the parties, generally wholly improper on the part of an arbitrator, are an indispensable role of mediation' (Fuller, 1963: 24). In addition, for Fuller the essential facts of a dispute differ, or, if the same, are viewed differently, in the two processes. Finally, a mediator turned arbitrator will find it difficult to hear proofs and arguments with an open mind, undermining the integrity of adjudication. Indeed, Fuller maintains that even in polycentric disputes in which the parties have agreed to arbitration, the roles of mediation and arbitration must be kept firmly apart so that the 'integrity of the adjudicative process' can be preserved (1963: 38–39). Moreover, even very skilled and experienced arbitrators are unable to overcome the inherent limitations in the fused role of mediator and arbitrator.

Nevertheless, the perceived advantages of combining mediation with arbitration have steadily led to a revival of this approach, and various procedural innovations have been designed to overcome some of the difficulties involved. From the 1970s onwards, a series of arguments has been put forward for mediation-arbitration in a variety of dispute contexts. In the extract that follows, Spencer and Zammit made proposals in 1976 which highlighted the benefits that might accrue from the linked, sequential use of mediation and arbitration in disputes over child-related matters, but asserting at the same time that:

> in no event should the mediator ever serve as arbitrator, even if requested to by the parties. The possibility that the mediator might later become the arbitrator would tend to make the parties less open and candid during mediation. In addition, the arbitrator must be impartial. His activities as a mediator in the same dispute may easily have an adverse effect on this necessary characteristic of the arbitration. For the same reasons, a mediator should never be callable as a witness, expert or otherwise, during an arbitration, nor should he submit a report of any kind to the arbitrator (Spencer and Zammit, 1976: 934, n 92; (Extract 8:5)).

Other proposals and experiments have been less concerned to keep the role of mediator and arbitrator apart in the med-arb process. Indeed, in the area of family law, the state of California introduced a form of med-arb in contested child custody cases in which the mediator has the authority to make a recommendation to the court should the mediation fail to produce an agreement (see Folberg and Taylor, 1984: 277–280). A very rigorous characterisation of the need for a fusion of mediatory and arbitral roles was put forward in the early 1980s by Goldberg in proposals which provided for the issuing of an advisory (non-binding) opinion by the mediator in which the latter predicts the likely outcome if the dispute proceeds to arbitration (Extract 8:6).

The apparent success of med-arb and its variants have encouraged its adoption in the United Kingdom, and in the extracts that follow several arbitrators assess the merits and the problems that an embrace of med-arb might entail (see Extracts 8:7 and 8:8).

Extract 8:4

L L Fuller: 'Collective Bargaining and the Arbitration' (1963) 18 *Wisconsin Law Review* 3, pp 39–42

> It is well known in arbitrational circles that combining the roles of arbitrator and mediator is a tricky business. The amateur who tries it is almost certain to get in trouble. The veteran, on the other hand, takes an understandable pride in his ability to play this difficult dual role. He would be less than human if he did not seek out occasions for a display of his special talents, even to the point of discerning a need for them in situations demanding nothing more than a patient, conscientious judge, able to put a sensible meaning on the words of the contract.
>
> In practice departures from the strict judicial role are most common in the case of the so-called permanent umpire, who may preside over disputes between the same parties for many years. In such a situation success in combining the role of arbitrator with that of mediator attests not only to the arbitrator's professional skill, but to the depth of trust imposed on him by the parties. The role of arbitrator-mediator thus becomes doubly satisfying and the temptation to assume it correspondingly greater. Furthermore, with the permanent umpire, departures from the judicial role tend to

become cumulative. As the parties discover this willingness to resolve all controversies – including those unsuited to decision within the restraints of a judicial role – they are likely to become more and more dependent upon him. He becomes in effect a kind of super-manager. In the short run this role can relieve both union and management of many inconvenient responsibilities. The cost in the long run is that the moral force of the judicial role has been forfeited. It is no longer available as a reserve for meeting an eventual crisis. Meanwhile, the parties' capacity for unaided self-government may have suffered a serious decline through disuse.

The picture just drawn may lean a little toward the dismal. At the same time it is vitally important, I believe, that the apparent successes of mediative arbitration by permanent umpires be appraised with a full understanding of the situations in which they have occurred. Was the industry in question, for example, economically sick? Sick industries may need, not judges, but physicians, though, as with individuals, a sign of returning health would be a restored capacity to dispense with medical care. Again, did the apparent successes of mediative arbitration entail hidden costs not revealed in reports that confine themselves to the disposition of disputes? In this respect it is most unfortunate that readers of Harry Shulman's famous Holmes Lecture do not have available to them a careful appraisal of the effects of the philosophy therein expounded upon the total labor relations of the Ford Motor Company. Without that appraisal any judgment is bound to be one-sided.

Sometimes judgment on the issues here under discussion is influenced by a kind of slogan to the effect that an agreed settlement is always better than an imposed one. As applied to disputes before they have gone to arbitration this slogan has some merit. When the case is in the hands of the arbitrator, however, I can see little merit in it, except in the special cases I have tried previously to analyse. After all, successful industrial self-government requires not only the capacity to reach and abide by agreements, but also the willingness to accept and conform to disliked awards. It is well that neither propensity be lost through disuse. Furthermore, there is something slightly morbid about the thought that an agreement coerced by the threat of decision is somehow more wholesome than an outright decision. It suggests a little the father who wants his children to obey him, but who, in order to still doubts that he may be too domineering, not only demands that they obey but insists that they do so with a smile. After having had his day in court, a man may with dignity bend his will to a judgment of which he disapproves. That dignity is lost if he is compelled to pretend that he agreed to it.

The *ad hoc* arbitrator, called in to decide a single case, will usually be most strongly moved to undertake mediation when it becomes apparent to him that what the parties really need is not someone to judge their dispute, but a labor relations adviser. For example, a company, inexperienced in collective bargaining and perhaps generally inept in labor relations, may be insisting on its pound of flesh – which, to be sure, it is entitled to under the contract – without being aware of the price it will pay for its victory in worsened labor relations. There is no easy way out of such a predicament for the arbitrator. In most cases he will do well to proceed with his assigned role, consoling himself with the thought that there is no better teacher than experience. He should think long and hard before employing the written opinion as an outlet for his pedagogical inclinations. Perhaps later on, after the award has been rendered, some discussion might be in order if his relationship with the party concerned seems to suggest it might be useful.

Throughout this paper I have asserted that adjudication is a *social* process of decision. This is true not only in the sense that it is a process of decision in which the affected party is afforded an institutionally guaranteed form of participation. It is also true in the sense that the success of adjudication, and the maintenance of its integrity, depend not only on the arbitrator, but on everyone connected with the process as a whole. It has been said that it is impossible for a judge to rise above the level of the bar practicing before him. So it may become virtually impossible for the arbitrator to perform his proper role if the parties – through ignorance, ineptness or selfish interest – are constantly pushing him out of that role. Unions not uncommonly come to view arbitration as a kind of general-purpose facility, ready to solve their internal problems or to lend a friendly hand winning over doubtful workers. Management, in turn, has its special techniques for bending arbitration to its own ends. A company that has never really accepted collective bargaining may, by refusing to settle anything, overload arbitration to the point of breakdown. Naturally in such a situation it will demand of the arbitrator the strictest judicial properties, a circumstance that has much embarrassed the struggle to preserve the integrity of the arbitrator's role.

A viable system of law requires that parties be willing to settle the great bulk of disputes out of court. It requires not only a willingness to settle cases that are reasonably certain to be decided against the conceding party, but also to settle at least some cases he could be quite certain of winning if they were taken to litigation. The decision of a dispute by law is not always the same thing as a wise disposition of it. People who are always demanding their 'rights' can be a menace to any society. One of the responsibilities of the parties to a collective bargaining agreement is to ease the strains on arbitration by not litigating cases where there is an obvious tension between the result demanded by the terms of the contract and that which accords with practical wisdom in labor relations.

I have just been asserting that a large part of the responsibility for maintaining the integrity of arbitration rests with the parties. I do not wish to be understood as suggesting, however, that the arbitrator is entitled to thrust on the parties the whole responsibility for his role. I emphatically reject the contention made by Harry Shulman that in appraising such practices as 'meeting with the parties separately' the 'dangers envisaged with respect to judges and other governmental personnel are not equally applicable' to the arbitrator, for, 'the parties' control of the process and their individual power to continue or terminate the services of the arbitrator are adequate safeguards against these dangers.' The democratic principle does not require us, I submit, to indulge in the fiction that whatever institutions develop in a particular situation must be viewed as approved by those affected by them. There is generally no real sense, for example, in which it can be said that the workers in a particular factory have approved either a loose or a strict interpretation of the arbitrator's role. In such a matter only a few key figures, chiefly the arbitrator himself, have that sense of alternatives which is required for intelligent choice.

It may be answered that in speaking of the consent of the 'parties' Shulman meant, not the workers or the whole management staff, but simply those few officials on either side directly concerned with arbitration. That this is hardly an adequate justification on which to rest the arbitrator's practices becomes apparent when one reflects on the implications of the 'rigged' award in all its diverse manifestations.

Extract 8:5

J M Spencer and J P Zammit: 'Mediation-Arbitration: A Proposal for Private Resolution of Disputes between Divorced or Separated Parents' (1976) *Duke Law Journal* 911, pp 932–938

Mediation. Since the basic adjustment of differences between parents on matters relating to their children will have been achieved with the help of consultation, it is reasonable to rely on a basically similar method to resolve these subsequent disputes. In order to distinguish this phase of dispute settlement from the consultation discussed earlier, we shall call it mediation.

The practice of mediation developed in the labor relations field as a preferred alternative to arbitration and legal action. Unlike these more coercive forms of dispute resolution, the objective of mediation is to get the parties to compromise their positions and thereby to reach a voluntary agreement between themselves. The process is premised on the notion that the presence of a disinterested third person, familiar with the issues involved in the dispute and skilled in promoting communication, will enable the parties to overcome their antagonism and to recognize their common interest in self-determination of the particular issue. As Professor Lon Fuller has stated, the 'central quality of mediation' is

> its capacity to reorient the parties toward each other, not by imposing rules on them, but by helping to achieve a new and shared perception of their relationship, a perception that will direct their attitudes and dispositions toward one another.

In a post-marital dispute, therefore, the function of the mediator would be to mollify the interchange between the parents and to make them aware that, if the matter is settled 'within the family,' the decision will reflect their common values. In addition, because of his expertise, the mediator will be able to focus the attention of the parties on the interests of the child. This latter role does not represent an attempt to impose an external paternalistic force; rather, it reflects the assumption that the parents will want to reach a decision which will promote the child's welfare. It must be recognized, however, that parents functioning in the emotionally charged atmosphere of a marital dispute may need assistance in distinguishing the child's best interests from their own natural possessory interest in the child.

The procedure to be used will largely be determined by the individual mediators. In general, most mediators employ a combination of joint conferences and separate consultation, each step being designed to elicit certain information. For example, the mediator might initially schedule a joint conference in order to identify the elements and scope of the disagreement. He would also be able to observe and assess the relationship between the parties. Typically, however, the antagonism between the parties will preclude any meaningful conciliation, at least in the early meetings. For this reason, the mediator might then conduct a series of private meetings with the individual parties. At these consultation sessions, he would try to ascertain the points on which each party may be willing to compromise, perhaps attempting to explain the position of the other side in a reasonable manner. Such meetings also give the mediator a chance to become acquainted with the disputants in a relaxed atmosphere. Finally, the mediator may return to joint conferences in order to propose alternative settlements.

If mediation proves successful in resolving the particular controversy, primary responsibility for the child's welfare will have been left in the hands of the parents. Moreover, because of the mediator's expertise and concern, the decision will have been reached with the best interests of the child kept in mind. The accommodations reached as a result of mediation should be incorporated into an amendment to the separation agreement. Future disputes will then be resolved in terms of the separation agreement as so modified.

Obviously, not all disputes will in fact be settled through mediation. Resort to third-party decision-making may occasionally become necessary. Even in these situations, however, the unsuccessful mediation should have narrowed and more sharply defined the issues to be resolved.

Arbitration. If mediation fails, the parties may proceed to arbitration. Selection of an arbitrator is of crucial significance since the object of this scheme is to come as close as possible to duplicating parental decision-making. Skill as a consultant-mediator does not qualify one as an arbitrator. The mediator's object is to help the parties communicate and to assist them in making their own decisions. The arbitrator, on the other hand, substitutes his judgment for that of the parents. It is of the utmost importance, therefore, that the parents select an arbitrator in who they have confidence, who they feel views the needs and problems of their children from the same general perspective as themselves, who, in short, they trust to make vital decisions affecting the lives of their children if they cannot make those decisions themselves. The selection may be accomplished in either of two ways: (1) the separation agreement can name, or the parties can at the time of arbitration jointly appoint, a particular friend, relation, clergyman or other person who is willing to act as arbitrator, or (2) the parties can agree to utilize the selection machinery provided by an organization such as the American Arbitration Association. If this second method is adopted it is essential that the biographical and background material on each potential arbitrator be sufficiently extensive to enable the parties to make a meaningful choice. Moreover, the availability of arbitrators with experience in all disciplines should be made known and the parties encouraged to specify, preferably before the proposed lists are compiled, the type of arbitrator preferred. Only in this way can the parents reasonably be expected to make selections which substantially conform to their own values and which produce arbitrators who are representative parent surrogates.

One beneficial result of the increased use of arbitration in domestic relations matters may be the creation of a group of trained professionals who would be especially concerned with the integrity of the process. As in labor arbitration, these individuals will need to be sensitive to the importance of preserving the ongoing relationship between the parties. As time goes on, they will develop reputations for their judiciousness, integrity and competence which will aid the parties in the selection process.

The separation agreement or the procedural rules incorporated by reference therein should expressly confer certain extraordinary powers on the arbitrator, such as the right to call in neutral expert witnesses and to interview the children *in camera* if he deems fit. In addition, the arbitrator should be empowered to modify the agreement and fill in the gaps. Parents of intact families are always free to change their minds or adapt their child-rearing plans to new conditions. A similar flexibility ought to be accorded to the parent surrogate embodied in the arbitrator. This flexibility should not, however, become an excuse for ignoring the express terms of an agreement which the parties have labored so mightily to formulate. The arbitrator should be instructed that the agreement represents conscious value choices by the parties with respect to their children which should be upset only in response to substantially changed circumstances. In every case, the arbitrator should be guided by the statement of the parents' objectives and values contained in the separation agreement.

Enforcement of the Arbitral Award. The proposed mechanism for the resolution of post-marital disputes has been designed to preserve to the extent practicable the autonomy of the family. Only where the parents are completely unable to resolve their differences, even with the aid of a qualified consultant, is the authority to decide matters concerning their child's welfare taken out of their hands. Even in these instances, however, the decision-maker will be someone who shares the parents' basic values. In addition, the mediation-arbitration procedure is relatively private and can be accomplished with reasonable speed.

If, however, in those situations requiring arbitration, the award made is subject to de novo review by the courts, all of those attributes will be diminished. It is submitted, therefore, that an arbitral award made pursuant to the procedures outlined herein should be treated by the courts in the same fashion as an award made in commercial or labor arbitration: the arbitrator's decision should be conclusive absent misconduct on his part or a breach of public policy. In child-related cases, public policy demands only that the award not constitute, or make possible, the neglect of the child. Application of only the current minimal neglect standard, which must be met by all parents, divorced or not, would prevent the interference with family autonomy which under the present system is predicated solely on the breakdown of the marital relationship.

Unless the courts are willing to refrain from interfering in the model of dispute resolution proposed in this Article, the value of that model may be largely negated; parents will know that if they 'lose' in arbitration they can still resort to the courts. There are also reasons not directly related to the model for the courts to relinquish their parental role. In the first place, the state's prerogative to care for minors as *parens patriae* developed at a time when those seeking divorces were considered '"sick" persons, misfits, [or] hopeless neurotics. . . .' A diluted version of this attitude was reflected in this country by the enactment of statutes which permitted divorce only as a form of punishment for marital misconduct. The modern trend, however, as evidenced by the proliferation of no-fault divorce laws, is toward a recognition that most domestic difficulties are not the product of one spouse's 'sickness' or wrongdoing and that state interference in such matters should be minimal. In support of this position, it has been further argued that 'state paternalism is inconsistent with our historical and constitutional traditions,' and that parents have a fundamental right to control their children's development.

Finally, in areas involving relatively complex issues of fact, it is not unusual for adjudicatory power to be delegated to a more specialized tribunal, at least in the first instance. Many administrative agencies are empowered to try cases and hear appeals with judicial review being limited to determinations of whether the agency has acted within its authority. While it is not suggested that the states establish regulatory agencies to deal with child custody and related questions, it is submitted that, as in the administrative law context, such issues involve concepts with which trial judges are not normally familiar; and that courts therefore should give great weight to decisions reached by a specialized arbitrator.

Nevertheless, it may be unrealistic to expect the courts to surrender their traditional *parens patriae* jurisdiction. Since the procedures proposed herein assure an alternative system that will in fact protect the best interests of the child, it is suggested that legislatures amend their arbitration statutes to expressly include domestic disputes, thereby subjecting the awards made in such cases to the less stringent review given to the arbitration of commercial and labor matters.

Extract 8:6
S B Goldberg: 'The Mediation of Grievances Under a Collective Bargaining Contract: An Alternative to Arbitration' (1982) 77 *Northwestern University Law Review* 270, pp 281–284

Under the method here proposed, the parties would have the option of resorting to mediation rather than going directly to arbitration after the final step of the internal grievance procedure. The mediation procedure would be entirely informal in nature. The relevant facts would be elicited in a narrative fashion to the extent possible, rather than through examination and cross-examination of witnesses. The rules of evidence would not apply, and no record of the proceedings would be made. All persons involved in the events giving rise to the grievance would be encouraged to participate fully in the proceedings, both by stating their views and by asking questions of the other participants in the hearing.

The primary effort of the mediator would be to assist the parties in settling the grievance in a mutually satisfactory fashion. In attempting to achieve a settlement, the mediator would be free to use all the techniques customarily associated with mediation, including private conferences with only one party. If settlement is not possible, the mediator would provide the parties with an immediate opinion, based on their collective bargaining agreement, as to how the grievance would be decided if it went to arbitration. That opinion would not be final and binding but would be advisory. It would be delivered orally and would be accompanied by a statement of the reasons for the mediator's opinion. The advisory opinion could be used as the basis for further settlement discussions or for withdrawal or granting of the grievance. If the grievance is not settled, granted, or withdrawn, the parties would be free to arbitrate. If they do, the mediator could not serve as arbitrator, and nothing said or done by the parties or the mediator during mediation could be used against a party during arbitration.

The Proposal's Advantages. If grievances can be resolved through mediation, the advantages to the parties would be significant. First, mediation would be substantially quicker and less expensive than arbitration because the mediator would settle or give an advisory decision on the same day that the grievance is considered. This would eliminate the cost and delay associated with obtaining a transcript, filing briefs, and writing a decision. Furthermore, since the proceedings would be informal, the parties may choose to proceed without attorneys, resulting in still further savings of time and money.

Those parties with a substantial number of grievances could obtain still further savings in time and money by arranging for the mediator to consider more than one grievance per day. In addition, the parties could schedule mediation on a regular basis, with a mediator selected in advance. This would eliminate the wait for a free day in a busy mediator's schedule, and could result in the final resolution of grievances in 15–30 days from the completion of the internal steps of the grievance procedure.

Employees would benefit not only from the promptness with which their grievances would be resolved, they would also benefit from the process itself. Free of the constraints imposed by the quasi-judicial procedure of eliciting facts by direct and cross-examination, employees would have the opportunity to tell their stories as they wished. Furthermore, everyone at the mediation conference, including management personnel, would have the opportunity to talk to each other, not just to an examiner, cross-examiner, or arbitrator. Under this procedure, all the participants should feel that they have been heard fully and dealt with fairly, regardless of the outcome. Mediation thus may achieve more satisfactorily than does arbitration the catharsis and employee acceptability sought by arbitration.

The mediation process also offers hope of alleviating some of the situational characteristics which contribute to a large volume of arbitration. Frequently, such a volume of arbitration results from a combative relationship in which the parties approach grievances in a highly adversarial fashion. The arbitration process is unlikely to alter this attitude because of its adjudicative mode. The mediation process, however, compels a different approach. It eliminates the concept of 'winning' a grievance, substituting the concept of negotiations leading to a mutually satisfactory resolution. To the extent that the parties focus on seeking a mutually satisfactory outcome through negotiations, they should develop a mutual understanding of each other's concerns. This mutual understanding, in turn, should lead not only to the resolution of more grievances without resort to mediation or arbitration, but also to the improvement of their entire relationship.

In order for mediation of grievances to change an adversarial relationship into a more cooperative one, the parties must agree that they are arbitrating too much and must wish to arbitrate less. They also must be incapable of achieving that goal unassisted. If those conditions exist, as they frequently do, the adoption of grievance mediation would provide the parties with a technique to accomplish their goal. If either party does not wish to arbitrate less, but wishes to use the mediation step solely to increase the cost and delay involved in grievance resolution, mediation cannot succeed. A mutual desire to resolve grievances without resort to arbitration is a *sine qua non* to the success of mediation.

In addition to potentially improving the relationship of the parties, mediation also offers the prospect of a more satisfactory substantive resolution of contractual disputes than does arbitration. It is a truism of industrial relations that the negotiators of a collective bargaining contract can never anticipate and deal with all the issues which are likely to arise during its term. Hence, some issues inevitably arise which the contract does not clearly address. An arbitrator called upon to determine the 'correct' interpretation of the contract in a grievance presenting such an issue will examine the language of the contract, its bargaining history, prior practice, and various canons of construction, and conclude that, if the negotiators had foreseen the particular problem and been able to resolve it, it is more likely that they would have resolved it in one way rather than another.

A resolution of the disputed issue through negotiation at the time the dispute arises is more likely to satisfy the parties, in light of their current interests and concerns, however, than is an arbitrator's probabilistic estimate as to how they would have resolved the dispute had they been able to do so at the time of the contract negotiations. While mediation does not guarantee that the parties will achieve a current solution to a current problem, the likelihood of attaining such a result is one of the strengths of the mediatory approach to dispute resolution. Finally, the mediation process described here, in which the mediation step is entirely separate from the final and binding arbitration step, offers substantial advantages over the impartial chairman approach, in which the roles of mediator and adjudicator are combined. The fact that the 'pure' mediator has no power to issue a binding award means that the parties need not fear that their contractual rights will be over-ridden to serve the mediator's interest in obtaining a settlement or in furthering their relationship. The separation of the mediatory function from the power to issue a final and binding decision also means that the parties need not fear that facts disclosed to the mediator in an effort to obtain a settlement will be used against them in the event no settlement is reached. This should increase their willingness to be candid with the mediator and so increase the prospects for settlement.

Extract 8:7

P Newman: 'Mediation-Arbitration (MedArb): Can it Work Legally?' (1994) 60 *Arbitration* 3, pp 174–176

One method of addressing concerns about the non-binding nature of mediation is the hybrid technique of MedArb. Its purpose is to commit the parties, usually through a clause in their contractual agreement, to continue the ADR processes in a manner that will ensure resolution of the dispute. Assume the disputants will first attempt to negotiate a settlement. If that fails they will embark upon mediation and if no agreement is reached the mediator will change roles and become an arbitrator empowered to impose a binding solution on the parties. Many doubts have been expressed, particularly by lawyers, whether MedArb inevitably compromises the neutral's capacity legally to act in an adjudicative capacity while at the same time undermining the efficacy of the initial mediation where the mediator should seek to create an atmosphere of trust and a willingness to impart confidences to him in the caucus sessions. There are other extremely practical considerations. If the parties agree, during the original contract negotiations, that they will use a form of MedArb in the resolution of any disputes that arise it is difficult to assess when the mediation phase should give way to the arbitral. Simply to place the responsibility on the mediator to advise the parties when mediation should give way to arbitration is an inadequate response.

The remainder of this paper outlines some MedArb techniques and their practical as well as legal weaknesses. The problem with any such analysis, which is difficult to overcome, is the comparative lack of experience in the United Kingdom of the use of ADR hybrid techniques. Even in the United States, with its far longer 'track record', the information is scant. In ADR a Practical Guide to Resolve Construction Disputes (American Arbitration Association, 1994) Douglas H Yarn concludes:

> For all practical purposes there have been comparatively few detailed reports of medarb applications in construction disputes. Therefore, most of the available commentary about these hybrid processes is both anecdotal and speculative.

In the event that mediation fails the mediator's subsequent appointment as arbitrator of the same dispute is superficially attractive. When played out like High Court litigation, arbitration is expensive. Most arbitrators charge an hourly rate, often with substantial cancellation fees if the arbitration settles at any stage before a full hearing. Also, once a dispute blows up into a full arbitration, cohorts of lawyers and expert witnesses appear to glide effortlessly on to the stage. Anything that may lessen ultimate costs must seem a good idea to the parties. An arbitrator, already well acquainted with the facts by reason of a recently completed, although unsuccessful, mediation, does not have the same learning curve as an appointee coming fresh to the dispute. Such a neutral will have acquired a more in depth awareness of the dispute than would a conventional arbitrator and is likely to have revealed some of his own impressions as to the weaknesses and strengths of a party's case during the caucus sessions. This might assist parties more easily to draw conclusions as to how a mediator would make a final award in arbitration and, with the issues more clearly delineated, encourage them to deploy simpler arbitration procedures than they would in a conventional arbitration where the arbitrator has to be educated in the nuances of each party's case. It may be the case that the mediation phase has resolved most, but not all, issues and it is appropriate to permit the neutral to reach a binding decision on the outstanding ones. The realisation that the mediator is subsequently authorised to adjudicate, if necessary, may make MedArb more effective at producing a negotiated settlement than mediation alone.

Merely to follow the clarion call of MedArb is too superficial a response. Mediation, unlike litigation or arbitration, succeeds because it is based on communication and trust. A mediator is not constrained to accept one party's case at the expense of rejecting the other party's. The mediation process is designed to release the parties from positional bargaining, frequently articulated as the law's promotion of the establishment of rights, and to look for solutions by a re-focus on interests. With the respect and confidence of both parties, the mediator can listen to the parties communicating confidentially their real positions in the dispute and what they honestly want to achieve. A good mediator will assist the parties in looking for and achieving solutions by identifying what a party really wants. Mediation, founded on a lack of coercion, allows the parties to agree without judicial imposition. The process straddles the law by providing flexible solutions in the form of trade-offs which the law is unable to provide. In choosing to ignore that mediation is consensual and extra-judicial, whereas arbitration is confrontational and part of the legal process, perhaps the hybrid MedArb, although well intentioned, is seriously flawed. Because of pressures on his time a busy arbitrator might coerce the parties during the mediation stage into a settlement which the parties might not desire. Again, knowing that the mediator might subsequently act as their arbitrator might encourage the parties to be less forthcoming. A lazy or inexperienced neutral might cause problems and be inclined to move prematurely to the arbitration phase whenever there was an apparent impasse in the mediation.

Influenced by the information released in the mediation, the mediator's subsequent award, when sitting as arbitrator, might owe more to the mediation knowledge than to that admitted in the arbitration phase under the rules of evidence. Regardless of any protestations to the contrary, it is difficult, if not impossible, for any neutral to disregard the parties' confidential compromise positions for settlement expressed during the mediation phase and yet then have to turn round and make a non-compromising award based upon legally assessed rights incorporated perhaps in a reasoned award. Ultimately, and subject to the legal issues set out below, the efficacy of MedArb depends in large part upon the quality of the mediators/arbitrators whom we train. The relative dearth of experience of MedArb makes all criticism and discussion of the practical difficulties hypothetical and exaggerates them to a degree unacceptable to many commercial men who view what are in the minds of lawyers imperfections, at best with a smile, and at worst with extreme frustration. Neither practical nor legal difficulties have prevented the American Society of Forensic Engineers proposing a MedArb clause in the following terms:

> Any and all disputes that arise out of or relate to this agreement, or the performance or breach thereof shall be subject first to mediation in good faith by the parties and administered by the American Arbitration Association under its Construction Industry Mediation Rules, before resorting to arbitration. Thereafter, any remaining unresolved controversy or claim arising out of or relating to this agreement, or the performance or breach thereof, shall be settled by arbitration administered by the American Arbitration Association under its Construction Industry Arbitration Rules, and judgment on the award rendered by the arbitrator may be entered in any court having jurisdiction thereof. The sole arbitrator shall be the same person as the mediator who is selected under the applicable mediation rules.

In the United States a number of modifications have sought to address the difficulties posed by MedArb in its basic form where a single neutral is used. Under the first, Med-then-Arb, the mediator and subsequent arbitrator are different individuals. The arbitrator, who is not privy to the mediation phase, will not be influenced by the discussions and materials relating to the previous unsuccessful mediation. Although it solves the problem of having the same individual, it adds time and cost to the dispute resolution process. The appointee as arbitrator has the same learning curve as any other arbitrator. In an attempt to reduce the additional cost the arbitrator may be pre-selected at the commencement of the mediation and at least sit in during the open session presentations to the mediator. The downside of even this is obviously that the parties will have to pay for the arbitrator's time spent in the mediation phase. Although the technique may have some merit where the parties are reasonably confident that not all the issues will be resolved in the mediation, ultimately it is unattractive because it may cause the mediation joint sessions to be conducted in a more adversarial manner simply to impress the arbitrator.

Another modified technique is a form of MedArb whereby during the course of the mediation one party may ask the mediator to decide the remaining issues sitting as an arbitrator, provided the other parties concur. If any party objects, arbitration is conducted before a separate neutral. Proponents suggest it encourages the natural tendency of many parties in mediation to ask the mediator to resolve the intractable issues. It is unlikely of course that a disputant who has already done badly in caucus will feel comfortable authorising the mediator to arbitrate. However, the American Society of Forensic Engineers has adopted a standard clause for this type of dispute resolution process.

Two major variants of MedArb remain to be discussed. Advisory MedArb, where the arbitration award is non-binding, obviously has all the cost and time implications of any other similar process. It may be unsatisfactory for the parties merely to be left with the neutral's opinion of a likely outcome if the unresolved issues were to be settled by means of arbitration. Under concilio-arbitration, which is a form of advisory MedArb, after attempting conciliation, the conciliator produces a draft award, setting out his opinion of the outcome if the dispute were fully litigated. Parties have an opportunity to respond, at which time they can highlight any manifest errors and present further arguments and evidence before the neutral makes a final award. If both parties accept the award, it becomes binding. If the award is rejected it has advisory status. If one party accepts the award and the matter subsequently proceeds into arbitration or litigation, the party rejecting the award may contractually be obliged to pay all the legal costs of both parties in the event that the same result is achieved in litigation.

Extract 8:8

D C Elliot: 'Med/arb: Fraught with Danger or Ripe with Opportunity' (1996) 62 *Arbitration* 3, pp 175–177

The thought of mixing mediation and arbitration, with one person playing the role of both mediator and arbitrator, sends shudders through many lawyers. Why?

A. Med/arb is a hybrid

Mediation and arbitration are such distinctly different processes, often aimed at achieving very different results, that the thought of trying to combine them is an anathema to many. The basic differences include the following:

- in mediation, the mediator will seek to surface the interests of the parties in dispute with a view to broadening the potential options for settlement. In arbitration, the last thing either party may want to expose is their underlying interests;
- in mediation, the mediator controls the process and often much of the questioning. In arbitration, the arbitrator is typically less involved in questioning, allowing the parties or their counsel to present their case. This lack of process control troubles many lawyers;

- in mediation, the parties may each privately caucus with the mediator. In most arbitrations, this would result in the decision being overturned;
- in mediation, the parties will attempt to make a settlement seeking to meet their own and the other parties' interests. This will typically involve fashioning an agreement looking to their future relationship. In arbitration, interests are submerged by rights, with each side tending to cast their own case in the best light, and their opponents' in the worst;
- there is not one mediation process but many. Which process is used will largely depend on the background and training of the mediator. Some of those with a strong labour relations background may tend to be more distinctive and assertive in mediation sessions than those schooled in the Harvard model of principled negotiation, or in western Canada, in the teachings of the British Columbia Justice or the Alberta Arbitration and Mediation Society.

B. Natural justice concerns

What causes lawyers most concern is a mediator privately caucusing with each side. Fundamental to our notion of justice is the right to know and be able to answer an opponent's case. How can this be done if one side or the other has no way of knowing what the other party is saying? It is unsettling to think of what the other side might have said, and what influence that might have on the mediator turned arbitrator.

While private caucus meetings are problematic for lawyers, they can also pose a dilemma for the mediator-turned-arbitrator. How much reliance, if any, can be placed on what is said in caucus meetings (when some very frank comments might be made and when the other side may have no opportunity to rebut what is said, or to shed other light on them, or put them in a different context)?

A med/arb process may raise questions of bias, real or perceived, in the minds of the parties. This issue is most likely to arise if the mediator is particularly assertive, or provides an advisory opinion in the course of the mediation (an 'advisory opinion' is a non-binding expression of the mediator's opinion of the most likely outcome if the case goes to arbitration, based on what the mediator has heard in mediation). Equally, as a result of private caucus sessions, the mediator may feel biased to one side or other on the basis of what he or she hears in confidence.

Natural justice concerns are most often raised in jurisdictions with a mediation process that relies heavily on private caucusing and looks to the mediator providing formal or informal advice or opinions on the relative positions of the parties. The more progressive approach to mediation relies far less on private caucusing and far more on skills designed to keep the parties at the table and looking at different approaches to tackling the dispute. This is not to say that private caucusing does not or should not occur (with its attendant natural justice concerns) but it is less prevalent than it once was.

'Natural justice' concerns can be dealt with satisfactorily in a med/arb process, but only if they are canvassed, considered and dealt with by the parties on a fully informed basis.

C. Lack of control

A client who speaks out of turn in court will soon find who is allowed to speak and when. The judge and counsel control the process and, for the most part, the conduct of their clients. Much the same applies in arbitration proceedings. In mediation, quite the reverse is true. Not only can clients speak freely, but they will be invited to do so, and people will listen! This freedom can be unnerving for some counsel confident in their control of the process and of rules of court to deal with any eventuality.

Of additional concern to some, the mediator has a direct effect on the mediation process. The questions asked by the mediator will seek to bring out the interests of the parties in order to expand the settlement possibilities. The very issues that can play a vital role in mediation may be precisely the things counsel may not want canvassed in an arbitration hearing. Once underlying interests have surfaced during a mediation, it may be unrealistic to expect a mediator-turned-arbitrator to put them aside when making an arbitration award. In fact, to put aside what is said in mediation may well lessen the quality of the decision, even if it is theoretically and practically possible to do so.

Also, the quality of the information provided during mediation may be a concern. Information is not given under oath, although with all parties present this is unlikely to be a significant practical problem. What may be of more concern is the attention the mediator pays to the information traded by the parties. In mediation, it is much less important that the mediator understands the issues than that the parties understand what the other is saying and why. If communication is going well, the mediator will not interrupt, even though he or she may not fully understand the content or its importance. On the other hand, in arbitration, the parties present their cases with a view to persuading the arbitrator to their view and will make sure the arbitrator understands the issues. And the arbitrator will certainly make sure he or she understands the issues before adjourning to make a decision.

None of these concerns are intended to suggest that the legal profession as a whole opposes med/arb. In fact, it is lawyers who have pioneered the med/arb process and, in many respects, recent innovative judicial experimentations incorporate med/arb concepts.

Mediation and Therapy

There have historically also been efforts to combine mediation with family therapy. In England this took place at the end of the 1980s as family mediation was becoming institutionalised. The debates that attempts at co-option of mediation by systemic family therapists then generated are well illustrated by Extracts 8:9 and 8:10. While the controversy at the time appeared resolved in favour of those claiming mediation as a discrete and autonomous form of intervention, it has resurfaced in the context of current debates over children in the context of family breakdown. Counsellors at 'Relate' – the largest UK provider of relationship counselling – are claiming that their backgrounds qualify them to provide 'therapeutic mediation' in disputes over children.

Extract 8:9

M Roberts: 'Systems or Selves: Some Ethical Issues in Family Mediation' (1992) 10 *Mediation Quarterly* 3, pp 4–10

> This article argues that the integrity of the mediation process is threatened by another form of control. This threat comes from the importation into mediation practice

of family systems theory via the systemic approach of most family therapists. A number of family therapists work as mediators in both court and out-of-court settings. . . .

The practitioner subscribing to the systemic view of the family recognizes two fundamental theoretical imperatives. First, the family is understood as a system of mutually interacting and interdependent parts. These 'parts' can be understood only as constituents of the whole. The system possesses properties that transcend the sum of its parts. Second, the level of intervention is the whole family system. The 'site of pathology' is not the individual but the family. Individual members have no discrete existence and their behavior has no significance independent of the system. The feelings, values, perceptions, and intentions of individuals have no independent meaning. They are useful only as pieces of 'systemic information,' as evidence of the system's characteristic mode of functioning.

According to systems thinkers, this external view of the family is unlikely to be known or learned by individual family members who, by definition, are themselves part of the system being observed and explained. Their subjective perceptions exist outside the systemic framework. To include them would undermine the logic of the framework itself, for 'it is not a framework designed to accommodate alternative definitions'.

The systemic approach makes determinist assumptions about human behavior. It constructs the ideas of the family as a functioning entity, the parts and interactions of which can be observed, identified, assessed, and explained by the intervention of an expert outsider. As Burnham notes, 'Practitioners using a systemic approach aim to identify and change the meaning and functioning of *a presenting problem* within the context of such a system'. This functionalist view of the family has three major implications. First, it facilitates the notion of the family as the problem, whose dysfunctioning is deemed to require outside intervention. All families ('normal' as well as 'pathological') are potentially problematic. Second, it is an approach that is invariably treatment-oriented. Expert intervention provides the means of improving functioning by explaining and altering the 'problem-maintaining behavior configuration'. Third, the parties' own definition of the issue is reduced to the status of 'the presenting problem.' Understanding of the 'real' underlying problem is left for the therapist/expert to discover, for the therapist's views are more valid than those of the parties themselves and therefore should prevail. . . .

It has been suggested that mediation practice can be fruitfully expanded by invoking the ideas and techniques of family systems thinking. This is a misconception because the assumptions and methods of these two modes of intervention are fundamentally incompatible. Mediation is rooted in liberal, humanist values that justify its use, both for the disputants themselves and for those who choose to become mediators. Norms of fairness, mutual respect, reciprocity, and equity of exchange inform the expectations of adult behavior that go to the heart of mediation. Decision-making capacity is what defines this standard of adulthood. The realization of the parties' authority through their own control over decision-making is what distinguishes mediation from other forms of intervention, for example, adjudication. The issue of authority and its location with the parties themselves is absolutely central to mediation. Fundamental to the relationship between the mediator and the parties is the mediator's respect for the competence of the parties and for their capacity, whatever their dispute and its difficulties, to behave as reasonable adults. The openness, understanding, and dignity with which the parties are treated by the mediator sets an example and establishes the tone for their own communication.

This approach can be compared with the applied scientific theories that characterize the systemic view of the family. The differences between these two approaches to mediation are set out below.

First, by definition, the systems approach to the family denies the paramount value of the individual's own perceptions and meanings. Because the systems conceptual framework only takes account of what is relevant systemically and therefore always denies the relevance or importance of the individual's experience of any social situation, the systems perspective takes no cognizance of what people mean and intend by their actions. As Berger and Berger note, 'it is a safe bet that those individuals do not see themselves as operating units of a social system'.

Party competence is the central tenet of mediation. While it is not denied that many common understandings are socially defined, the parties are regarded as competent both to define for themselves the issues for discussion and to arrive at their own decisions following joint negotiation. The parties' control over the definition of the issues is fundamental to their control over the decision-making process and its outcome. One of the first tasks of the mediator is to gain an understanding of the issues as they are perceived by the parties themselves. The mediator has no privileged perspective on how to view and interpret experience. The skill of the mediator lies in facilitating the crucial exchanges of accurate and constructive information that lead through adjustments of expectations and preferences to greater understanding, coordination, and order, and eventually to the settlement of the dispute. This kind of expertise, involving as it does no authority to impose an outcome or to give advice, determines the unique, even paradoxical, nature of the professional relationship of the mediator with the parties.

There is no inconsistency between the principle of party control that distinguishes mediation and the principle, enshrined in the Guardianship of Minors Act, 1971 (Section 1), of the paramount value of the welfare of the child. This latter principle is intended to guide the court in decisions regarding children. The movement toward private negotiation, of which family mediation is a part, is recognized and encouraged in developments of the substantive law, starting with the introduction of irretrievable breakdown as the sole ground for divorce and the official removal of the fault basis of divorce (Matrimonial Causes Act, 1973, Section 1). For example, where the court made an order regarding access, 'reasonable access' tended to be the rule rather than the exception. Reasonable access orders were premised on the principle of parental competence, leaving the parents responsibility for making whatever access arrangements were suitable to themselves. One of the main aims of the Children Act, 1989, is to reinforce parental responsibility for decision-making and reduce to a minimum the intervention of the court (for example, in the removal of Section 41, Declaration of Satisfaction). In any event, recent research findings, showing that the basis of what is best for the child lies in the parents reaching an agreement, resolve in practice any tensions of principle between private ordering and the welfare principle.

On the other hand, the functionalist view of the family that follows from systems thinking elevates the professional's view over that of the parents. It includes the belief that the complexities and misfortunes of family life can and ought to be assessed, prescribed for, and treated. So far as disputes over children are concerned, mediators strive to revive and sustain the decision-making processes of intact families where in most cases nobody challenges notions of parental competence and there is no professional intervention. There is a danger that the preoccupation of professionals regarding the issue 'of children's interests' can give rise to a conflict not between the interests of parents and their children, but between parents and the various professionals who claim to know and represent the best interests of the children. The fundamental issue at stake here is whether divorcing parents, like parents in intact families, should be trusted to make decisions about the future of their own children.

Second, some family therapists working in other agencies in other capacities (for example, as social workers, psychologists, or mediators) recognize that systems thinking may be incompatible with the aims and tasks of those agencies. Therefore it has to be smuggled in: 'The message is again the same to the would-be family therapist: accommodate to and exploit the system in which you work'.

Voluntary participation has always been stated to be an essential characteristic of mediation. Voluntariness depends on the parties understanding and consenting to the process on which they are embarking, a process of decision making, not of treatment. Voluntariness is crucial to the goal of reaching a freely negotiated agreement. It is crucial to establishing that authority lies with the parties who agree to enter mediation, for ultimately, whatever pressures or constraints they labor under, the parties have the right *not* to participate in mediation if they so wish. Voluntariness in relation to decision making and the reaching of consensual agreements constitutes one of the primary advantages of mediation. Mediators presuppose that agreements freely constructed by the parties themselves are far more likely to be adhered to. This activity depends on the conception of the individual as morally responsible, and therefore as deliberately intending the consequences of his or her actions. This view is incompatible with the determinist conceptions of circular causality that characterize systems thinking, an approach that, despite its use of the rhetoric of party control in its application to mediation practice, regards as false 'the idea that the deliberate actions of human agents are a large part of the exploration of what happens to them'. The moral implications of this denial lead Morton to regard systems theory as 'an abomination'.

Third, for mediation to have value, it must be just to all parties concerned. Respect for the interests and objectives of each party and for those affected by any agreement, notably children, is not easily reconciled with the systems approach that analyzes the family in terms of functional needs and services. This is what advocates of the family systems approach to conciliation have to say about fairness: 'Fairness is another of those unfortunate concepts that appears so obviously to be a "good thing" that seldom is its appropriateness in a particular context questioned. At the risk therefore of appearing to support unfairness we nevertheless wish to question this notion. . . . [Fairness] represents a (perhaps legalistic?) distortion of the way in which relationships actually work. . . . [R]elationships are not fair or unfair, they are what they are'. Such an approach confuses what is with what ought to be (which is precisely what 'fairness' reminds us about). It ignores the ethical implications of situations in which the interests and rights of individual family members may be in direct conflict or where there are significant disparities of power between the parties. Systemic leveling, through the application of techniques such as positive connotation, often 'flies in the face of common conceptions of justice'. As some systems thinkers themselves describe it, 'the positive connotation [as an intervention technique] is not related to truthfulness, but to the strategy of being therapeutic'.

Reframing techniques elevate reinterpretation over action for change. Such techniques are designed to challenge the parties' different values and not only can devalue what the parties regard as significant, but also can collude with and perpetuate injustice by denying relevance to objective circumstances such as the political, economic, or gender factors of a dispute. One of the mediator's primary ethical responsibilities is to ensure that where these factors (or others) significantly affect the respective balance of power between the parties, this imbalance is recognized explicitly and duress prevented, if necessary by ceasing mediation.

Extract 8:10

J M Haynes: 'Mediation and Therapy: An Alternative View' (1992) 10 *Mediation Quarterly* 21, pp 22–24

In therapy the claim to power is clear and the therapist makes no apology for having this power. The therapist claims power over both the process and the content. This situation is not unique to family systems therapists. Psychoanalysis, for example, is guided by the analyst who determines what to comment on or what to ignore. The response of the therapist to the client defines the content and the process of the session. If the client raises issue A, which the analyst believes to be unimportant or a cover for another more relevant issue, the therapist ignores issue A and directs the client to talk about other things until issue B or some other acceptable (to the analyst) issue is raised by the client.

The same is true of the attorney-client interview. Counsel focuses on the legal content of the dialogue while ignoring the irrelevant nonlegal items. Inherent in any professional-lay dialogue is the responsibility of the professional to direct the dialogue in a way through which the professional can be useful to the client. 'Useful' in this sense is defined as the ability of the professional to use his or her special training and expertise to help the client. In every professional-lay dialogue the professional exercises power to direct the dialogue in a way that enables her to be professional and use her professional knowledge and skills. This situation is equally true for mediation.

The therapist or the attorney thus decides what things will be handled and how they will be handled. In addition, the assumptive contract between the therapist-attorney and client is that the professional will ultimately direct the client to the answer either by sharing a legal interpretation, offering insightful comments, making behavioral prescriptions, or using family system therapy strategies.

The power relationship in mediation is less clear, and thus may be more dangerous to the client. For we actually assert power in controlling the process but deny power in relation to the content. The assumed contract in mediation is that the mediator will assist the clients to resolve specific problems *on their own terms*. In divorce, these problems include the amount and duration of child and maintenance support, the appropriate division of assets, and future parenting roles.

The professional-client relationship is inherently imbalanced because the client requests an interaction with the professional *because* the professional has more knowledge (often one of the determinants of power). As Roberts has so clearly demonstrated, the mediator's management of the negotiations, problem solving, decision making, and context knowledge is the key to successful mediation.

The mediator can divest himself or herself of some of this attributed power by defining the areas in which he or she is willing and able to exercise power. I have stated elsewhere that the mediator must control the process and the family must control the outcome. Laying this out clearly at the beginning of the mediation as part of the contract with the client sets the stage for power divestiture. The mediator should make it clear that he or she is neutral as to the outcome – the product of the content over which the family as a unit must have total control.

A safeguard against the mediator's misuse of power is that any agreement must be acceptable to both parties if it is to be formalized. Thus, the balance of power rests relatively equally between the clients in the content-outcome area because each side can veto an agreement. An agreement cannot be thrust on one party against its will. The mediator *can* influence the direction of the agreement sufficiently to make one client regret it in the future, but it is doubtful that a mediator can thrust a totally unwanted agreement on a client since if he or she attempts to do so, the alternative arena (the court) will become more attractive to the pressured client.

The mediator has power whether or not she wants it. She can limit her power by limiting her use of it. It is not family systems theory per se that creates the problem of asserted power; instead, it is the relationship of the professional to the client. In raising this question, Roberts has provided mediation with a major service by helping us to understand the dangers of power and by alerting us to the need to control that power and limit it to the content.

However, the mediator does exercise power when managing the process because true process neutrality can often benefit one side at the expense of the other. Families choose mediation because they want someone to regulate a dispute and provide an environment in which a self-determined solution can be found. The mediator cannot proclaim process neutrality. He or she cannot stand aside while one party verbally abuses the other, cannot permit secrecy, and must intervene to assure that all parties understand the issues and the data that determine the issues. He or she cannot allow one party to unilaterally define the problem: the problem definition *must* be mutual. Thus, if party A defines the issue in a way that benefits him, the mediator should not accept that definition of the problem but rather work with the parties to create a new problem definition that is mutual and the solution of which benefits both parties. The mediator's neutrality is confined to the content of the agreement. He or she is not neutral on the process; indeed, he or she continually exercises power to control the process to assure a mutual problem definition, a neutral environment, and a joint decision that is mutually acceptable.

E: Refurbishing Umpiring – Adjudication

Paradoxically, dispute processes once characterised as alternatives to adjudication have in the last decade or so been increasingly co-opted by the courts. The simple opposition of the mainstream and the 'alternative' has accordingly become less clear as a result of the incorporation of 'ADR' techniques in the process of adjudication. Notwithstanding criticisms of the kind expressed by Fiss in 'Against Settlement' (see p 58 et seq above), judges themselves have become actively involved in the promotion of settlement and this objective is increasingly endorsed in statutes and rules of court. Ordinarily, in the United States such involvement takes place in the context of a judicial settlement conference consisting of an informal exchange of views guided by the trial judge, although it may also be combined with a pre-trial conference. This involvement may be one of mediation, as one judge has acknowledged: 'we are catalysts in settlement. Our role is not that of a traditional judge. Our role at that stage is that of mediator' (quoted in Galanter, 1985: 4). This approach marks the emergence of the common law judge as an active manager of the process of litigation, even ready to assist the parties to reach settlement through mediatory intervention. The latter approach has been greatly strengthened by several amendments to Rule 16 of the Federal Rules of Civil Procedure,[9] so that where authorised by local rules and relevant statutes, judges are expected to promote settlement activity. Although some states do thus empower judges to engage in settlement discussion with the disputing parties, in others, as well as in the federal courts, judges have from time to time been regarded as having promoted settlement too rigorously.

In the extracts that follow, Galanter provides an account of the growing practice of judicial involvement[10] in the settlement of civil disputes in the United States.

Extract 8:11

M Galanter: 'The Emergence of the Judge as a Mediator in Civil Cases' (1986) 69 *Judicature* 5, pp 257, 261–262

> There have always been a lot of settlements in American civil courts. It remains unclear whether the percentage of cases terminated by settlement has increased in recent years. And, if there has been an increase, it is unclear whether it is caused by the increased intervention of judges. There has been a sea change, however, in the way judges talk about settlement and think about their roles as judges. In this article I shall trace the change in judicial views over the past half century and speculate on the causes and effects of this change.

---

9 Federal Rule of Civil Procedure 16 regulates judicial supervision of litigation in pre-trial conferences. First adopted in 1938, it has been amended several times over the years (1983, 1987, 1993) in order to facilitate promotion of settlement during pre-trial conferences.

10 In the United States a partial adoption of mediatory functions by magistrates has also taken place. See, for example, Longan (1994: 733–738, 739–745).

As we look back to examine past settlement practices, it is worth noting that 'settlement' is *our* category. As one pushes back from the 1930s to the 1920s, the term settlement virtually disappears from the literature. A case may occasionally be described as 'settled,' but 'settlement' is not a category for talking about or conducting policy. (Neither, for that matter, is 'policy.') The terms employed in the 1920s, were, 'adjustment,' 'compromise,' and 'conciliation.' The last of these three deserves special attention because it carries a heavy ideological and programmatic load.

. . . in the 1970s, whatever reticence remained among federal judges was barely perceptible. There was a forthright and ardent embrace of active participation in settlement negotiations. This was based on a warm endorsement of settlement as preferable to adjudication – not on grounds of administrative convenience, but because it produced superior results. Thus at a training session for new federal judges they were counselled by a veteran judge that:

> [o]ne of the fundamental principles of judicial administration is that, in most cases, the absolute result of a trial is not as high a quality of justice as the freely negotiated, give a little, take a little settlement.

An outline distributed to the new judges reiterated that:

> [i]n most controversies, most court cases, the highest quality of justice is not the all or nothing, black or white end result of a trial but is in the grey area – in most cases a freely negotiated settlement is a higher quality of justice which is obtainable earlier and at less cost. Approximately 90 per cent of all suits filed in federal courts are disposed of without trial.

Thus settlement is thought to permit compromise positions that are unattainable in the adjudicative mode. In the words of one thoughtful federal district judge, settlement 'produces results which are probably as close to the ideal of justice as we are capable of producing.'

If settlements are good, it is also good that the judge actively participates in bringing them about. He should do this not only by his management of the court (policies about continuances, etc.) but also by acting as a mediator. As another federal district judge told a 1977 seminar for newly appointed judges:

> . . . I urge that you see your role not only as a home plate umpire in the courtroom, calling balls and strikes. Even more important are your functions as mediator and judicial administrator.

Current perspective

Active promotion of settlements is now unmistakably the 'established' position in the federal judiciary. Judges who are activists on this matter are invited to give seminars to new judges; their views are broadcast by publication in *Federal Rules Decisions* and disseminated in booklets by the Federal Judicial Center. As Charles Renfrew observed in 1975, 'Judicial activism in the settlement process appears to have received quasi-official sanction within the judicial family.' The virtue of active judicial participation in settling civil cases is part of the received wisdom.

Two recent surveys portray contemporary patterns. In a nationwide survey of trial judges, only 21.8 per cent described their typical posture as one of non-intervention in settlement discussions. Over three-quarters did typically intervene; of these, 67.9 per cent regarded their intervention as subtle, 'through the use of cues/suggestions' and 10.3 per cent as aggressive, 'through the use of direct pressure.' In a study of federal and state courts in five localities, judges were asked about the practices they follow all or most of the time. Seventy-five per cent of federal judges and 56 per cent of state judges reported that they initiated settlement talks in jury cases; and 41 per cent of federal judges and 56 per cent of state judges reported that they suggested terms of settlement in such cases. (The figures are lower in every category for bench trials.)

This shift to judicial activism received formal ratification in 1983 when Rule 16 of the Federal Rules of Civil Procedure was amended to allow judges to 'consider and take action with respect to . . . the possibility of settlement or the use of extra-judicial procedures to resolve the dispute' during the pre-trial conference. The Advisory Committee that proposed the change recognized that 'it has become commonplace to discuss settlement at pre-trial conferences.' The committee recommended that requests for a conference indicating a willingness to talk settlement 'normally should be honored' and that 'a settlement conference is appropriate at any time. . . .'

Active participation

What do we learn from this? Certainly, there has been a change in the way that judges talk about settlements and the role they play in producing them. It also seems probable that more judges do participate actively in arranging settlements than was the case earlier, that those who do are more aggressive and inventive, and that they regard it as an integral part of their judicial work. This is not to assert that this activity produces more settlements. Research has not so far confirmed that more judicial intervention produces more settlements. But it does appear that cases that once might have been settled by negotiations between opposing counsel are now settled with the participation of the judge. We have moved from dyadic to mediated bargaining.

Extract 8:12

M Galanter: '". . . A Settlement Judge is not a Trial Judge": Judicial Mediation in the United States' (1985) 12 *Journal of Law and Society* 1, pp 12–15

The judicial embrace of settlement promotion described here should be viewed as part of a landscape in which there is a general and pervasive displacement of adjudication into negotiative processes. Changes in judicial settlement behaviour have been seen as incremental adjustments in a setting where there are powerful pressures toward settlement. Negotiated settlement has long been the modal disposition of American disputes – civil, criminal, and administrative.

The most prevalent explanation of these patterns is that they are distortions or expedients resulting from massive caseloads and resources shortages that prevent institutions from operating as they are designed and supposed to operate. Plea bargaining then is the result of the immense crush of criminal cases; settlements of civil and administrative matters are a response to overburdened forums with long queues, etc.

A series of incisive analyses have demolished the notion that non-trial dispositions in criminal cases are a recent response to pressures of caseload. Heumann has shown that the proportion of non-trial dispositions had been fairly constant in the Connecticut courts since the late years of the nineteenth century. The finding that dispositional practices are not much different in high volume and low volume courts holds up when controls for available personnel are introduced. A natural quasi-experiment on an occasion when some courts had their workload substantially reduced revealed no shift toward more trials.

An alternative perspective attributes the gravitation toward settlement to fundamental strategic considerations rather than to temporary institutional conditions. In this 'strategic' view, all of the participants, seeking to achieve their goals while avoiding unacceptable risks, find full-blown adjudication inexpedient. Lawyers find trials distasteful: they may bring little financial gain, they disrupt one's practice, they require extensive preparation, and they expose one to risks of losing or revealing lack of expertise. If trial offers parties hope of complete victory or vindication, it also involves additional cost, protracted delay and a risk of losing all. And parties may find it attractive to trade off where they assign different values to different components of the outcome.

If it is understandable that lawyers and parties often prefer that adjudication decompose into something more controllable and less risky, why should the court – whose mandate is to render and enforce an authoritative decision – concur in this shift? Yet nothing is more ordinary than for the court (or other decision-maker with binding authority) to postpone invoking its arbitral power while allowing the parties to arrange a decision that is mutually agreeable to them. What does the court get out of it? A number of reasons suggest themselves:

1. Resource Savings: imposed decisions require the decision-maker to employ elaborate procedures and to supply elaborate justifications.
2. Avoidance of Supervision: settlements are largely unreviewable and their occurrence increases the autonomy of the forum from its hierarchic superiors.
3. Minimization of Enforcement Problems: imposed decision are less likely to be complied with than decisions that are consented to.
4. Political Credibility: imposition endangers credibility since at least one party is aggrieved with the forum. Settlement enables avoidance of untoward results which would attract attacks on the forum.
5. Sense of Accomplishment: participation in settlements induces a feeling of accomplishment and control.
6. Fun: finally, participation in settlements may strike a judge as an engaging activity that enables him to employ beneficially his talents as a negotiator.

But these reasons why judges, too, find settlement preferable to imposed decision are not new. Why should judicial participation have become more widespread, more commendable? It is the received wisdom that the new respectability of judicial participation is due to the increased volume of cases congesting the courts. Judicial intervention is portrayed as a response to an ominous trend of increasing caseloads. This is a functionalist restatement of the production argument: since more settlements are needed, more judicial participation is forthcoming. But as we have seen, there is reason to doubt the claims of the production argument. Many judges perceive that the functionalist argument is valid, but that shift in judicial culture deserves a more satisfying explanation.

Space permits only the most preliminary sketch of what a 'strategic' explanation might look like. It would view the movement toward judicial participation in settlements as part of a wider search for 'alternatives' that may be seen as an attempt to adapt the American pattern of litigotiation to changes within and without the legal system.

There is more law – more legislation, more administrative regulation, more published judicial decisions. This proliferation of legal controls responds to and stimulates higher expectations of protection and redress among wider sections of the public. As the body of authoritative material becomes more massive, more complex and more refined, decision-makers (and other actors) are both constrained and supplied with resources and opportunities for legal innovation.

Adjudication has become more complex, more expensive, most protracted, more rational – and more indeterminate. It is freer of arbitrary formalities, more open to evidence of complicated states of fact, and responsive to a wider range of argument. As the cost and complexity of litigation increases, both the potential inputs as well as the possible outcome of the trial became a source of bargaining counters that can be used at other phases of the process. An enlarged right to conduct discovery or to select a 'representative' jury, for example, are not only contingencies that affect those specific stages of the proceedings. They are sources of counters and stratagems throughout the process. As the process became more costly and complex, it creates new strategic options for litigants while subjecting them to new contingencies. Litigation becomes a strategic quest for information about what the other side wants, what juries are likely to believe or award, how the judge might respond at a multiplicity of low visibility, highly discretionary choice points.

Demand for brokers who can help secure this information at low cost and risk converges with changes in judicial ideology. Judges share the widespread elevated expectations of a beneficient result at the same time that they have less faith that legal doctrine provides a single right answer; or that full-blown adjudication will produce the most appropriate outcome. Concern with outcomes is juxtaposed with the realization that outcomes are affected by the contingencies of the process – by cost, delay, uncertainty, bargaining power and so forth. Process is seen as a variable involving choices to be made on substantive as well as administrative concerns. Judicial promotion of settlements, along with interest in arbitration, mediation, and various alternatives, is a response to these concerns.

Openness to these processual variations marks a salutory shift of focus from the smaller world of adjudication, to the big world of litigotiation. It implies an acceptance by the courts of responsibility to make policy not only for the cases that are fully adjudicated, but for all the cases that arrive at the court and even for the penumbra of disputes that never arrive. It is a responsibility that encompasses the bargaining process. It takes up the challenge of the quality argument, which is really the challenge of doing substantive justice in the cases – and they are the great majority – in which the courts' presence is ghostly, intermittent and indirect rather than plenary and direct.

If the question is one of upgrading the litigation process, it is evident that judicial mediation is but one of a large number of options. Some involve displacing disputes to other forums like arbitration and mediation. Others involve changes in the quality and incentives of the bargaining process by training or certification of negotiators; development of ethical controls; malpractice remedies; peer review; or adoption of fee-shifting rules. In the United States, we are in a period of experimentation with and research about these devices and their effects. We may expect a rapid growth of our systematic knowledge about both judicial mediation and about the devices that are its companions and rivals. But such knowledge requires that we develop adequate measures of the quality of processes and outcomes.

I have tried to suggest the range of what we don't know and ought to know about the bargaining processes which constitute the larger part of the American legal system and about the role of judges in that process. I want, finally, to suggest the rich possibilities for comparative study. I have spoken here about the United States, but these issues are not confined to America. The legal systems of at least some other industrial societies are also largely systems of litigotiation, or bargaining in the shadow of the law. Judges may intervene in negotiations rarely, as in Britain, or frequently, as in Germany. In all such systems, the problems of substantive justice are in some measure the problem of assuring high quality bargains or settlements.

The Judge as Mediator

In a number of jurisdictions, as Galanter indicates above, in the Anglo-American common law world over the past two or three decades mediation has been incorporated into the judicial process, either directly or indirectly. There is a wide range of innovations here, and the developments range from mediation conducted by a judge who will try the case if no settlement is reached – a process which raises a number of the issues noted by Fuller in his critique of med-arb outlined above – to court-appointed mediators who conduct compulsory mediation prior to any trial that might eventually take place. In the case of direct judicial mediation, the activities of the judge in promoting an agreement between the parties through judicial settlement conferences and the like are in reality one dimension of a growing embrace of judicial managerialism.

One rapid development has been the growing use of court-annexed mediation in matrimonial cases. In the extract that follows, Graham provides an interesting account of compulsory court-annexed mediation in one county in the United States (Extract 8:13). Nevertheless, there are powerful criticisms of the annexation or incorporation of mediation into the judicial process and of the drive to make it compulsory. There is rigorous debate about the appropriateness of court-linked mediation, raising as it does important issues relating to consent, choice of mediator, remuneration, and court accountability for the manner in which the mediation is carried out. The reader is referred to Thornquist (1989) and Ingelby (1993).

Extract 8:13

L E Graham: 'Implementing Custody Mediation in Family Courts: Some Comments on the Jefferson County Family Court Experience' (1992–93) 81 *Kentucky Law Journal* 1107, pp 1112–1116, 1120–1124

The Jefferson Family Court's process for the mediation of disputes in child custody cases is laid out in a local rule. Mediation is mandatory in that parties to a contested custody case must participate in an initial referral to mediation, unless the requirement is waived by the court upon a showing of good cause.

The local rule places the responsibility for initiating the referral process on the parties' attorneys, who must file a form with the appropriate Family Court clerk and send a copy to the Family Court support worker for the division in which the case is being heard when it becomes apparent that a genuine custody issue exists. The form provides information that allows the support worker to contact the parties and assign them to a mediator, as well as financial information that affects the cost of mediation. An attorney must attach copies of a client's most recent federal and state tax returns and his or her three most recent paycheck stubs to the filed form.

The Family Court support worker who receives this information assigns a mediator using the next name on a rotating list. An order signed by the court notifies the parties and their counsel of the name and telephone number of the assigned mediator and instructs the client to contact the mediator within ten days. Attendance at the first mediation session is mandatory. The form requests that the parties meet with the mediator a sufficient number of times to allow the process to work, but it does not order a client to attend mediation beyond the initial referral period. Clients may use a private mediator of their own selection with the court's permission. The court order also explains the procedure for opting out of mediation and the sanctions for failure to comply with the order.

Parties ordered to mediation by the Family Court may ask to be excused from participation by completing a form that provides the court with information needed to determine whether good cause for opting out exists. Litigants are asked to explain their reasons for opting out, and the Family Court support worker who investigates the case provides information to the judge hearing the case. In the determination of good cause, the presence of domestic violence is the only definitive criterion; other parameters of the good cause doctrine will no doubt be developed as the system evolves.

The local rule also sets out sanctions for a party's failure to contact the mediator as ordered or to appear at a scheduled mediation session, including assessment of attorney fees or costs. There are no sanctions for failure to continue mediation beyond the initial appointment. When mediation is terminated without an agreement, the mediator must report that fact to the court immediately 'without any comment or recommendation.' Termination or failure to agree is without prejudice to either party.

All communications between the parties in the mediator's presence, between a party and the mediator, and between the Family Court support worker and a party are treated as confidential and privileged, with the exception that a Family Court support worker is required by statute to report child abuse. The privileged status of conduct or statements which occur during mediation means that they are inadmissible as evidence at a later proceeding.

The Jefferson Family Court's local rule requires that a mediator have a college degree and basic education or training in the behavioral sciences. Mediators must receive at least forty hours of training in a program meeting the requirements of the Academy of Family mediators, unless this requirement is waived by the court because of the mediator's experience or training.

Mediators are chosen by the court after recommendations by the Mediation Review Committee. The committee includes at least one Family Court or circuit judge and representatives of the Louisville Bar Association and the Family Court Advisory Committee, as well as other members designated by the court. The names of those who are selected as mediators are placed on a list kept by the Family Court Administrator, who supplies them to Family Court workers in rotating order. Mediators must disclose facts bearing on their qualifications, and may be disqualified voluntarily or upon motion of any party. If the court disqualifies a mediator, it must name a replacement.

Because the orientation session is the only mandatory mediation under the Jefferson Family Court's rule, the mediator's duties during this session are spelled out in detail. The mediator's duty to be impartial includes the duty to advise all parties of any circumstance that affects the mediator's ability to be impartial. The mediator must advise the parties that mediation can proceed only with their consent and that they have the right to terminate mediation without prejudice.

Mediators are compensated on the basis of a sliding scale fee rate set by the court that permits parties whose income is less than $13,000 to participate for a lower fee. A party who fails to make the required financial disclosure may be taxed at the full hourly rate, but the court has the discretion to assess either party for the cost of the mediator's compensation.

If the parties reach an agreement, the mediator must report the fact of reaching agreement and nothing more to the court. A memorandum of understanding is sent to each party's attorney setting forth all relevant statements of fact and statements of future courses of conduct as agreed upon by the parties. The parties and their attorneys file this agreement with the court, which retains final authority to accept, modify, or reject the agreement. If mediation is terminated and no agreement is reached, that fact is reported to the Family Court support worker and to counsel but does not prejudice either party. . . .

Any court that contemplates the addition of a mediation component must determine the amount of control that the court will have over the mediation process. The Jefferson Family Court's local rule balances judicial discretion with the autonomy essential to the mediation process by providing for administrative tracking of case status, mediation qualification and compensation, and judicial review of mediated agreements. The mechanism for recording and following the status of cases has already been discussed.

In establishing qualifications for mediators, the Jefferson Family Court determined that it would go beyond a minimum competency requirement. The court's control of the appointment of mediators through the Mediation Review Committee finds precedent in the appointment of guardians ad litem and custody evaluators.

A court's ability to generate a list of approved mediators may be affected by the number of experienced mediators in a particular city and provisions for mediator compensation. Jefferson County is a large urban area with a population of experienced mediators. While this experienced population gave the court latitude to set high standards in selection, it also affected the need to compensate mediators. Experienced mediators should not necessarily be expected to provide regular services without compensation, but any significant compensation of mediators raises the problem of indigent litigants. Jefferson County addressed the problem of indigent custody disputants by requiring each court-approved mediator to take a percentage of causes from a list of parties who cannot pay the full mediation fee. At this early stage of the program, inability to serve clients who are unable to pay the full fee has not yet become a concern. However, any implementation of mediation services must consider the likelihood of a large population of clients for whom payment may be a financial hardship. Some attempt at estimating the size of that population may be made by looking at a representative sample of divorce cases and assessing the range of incomes demonstrated by the sample.

Two mechanisms provide for judicial review of the outcome of a mediator's work with clients. Approval of a party's request to opt out of mediation is based on a showing of good cause as determined by the court. When mediation progresses to an agreement, the court has the authority to alter its content, as well as to accept or reject the agreement as presented by the mediator. Although litigation on issues that are being mediated is suspended during the course of mediation, the court retains authority to grant 'interim or emergency relief' upon motion of a party.

D. Mandatory Mediation of Disputed Child Custody

The Jefferson Family Court Custody Mediation Rule calls for mandatory initial referral to mediation when the parties do not resolve the issue of child custody. The decision to begin a mediation program with child custody does not mean that the Jefferson Family Court believed that other issues involved in divorce were not good candidates for mediation. Segregation of child custody from other types of disputes and implementation of a separate rule for child custody reflects significant differences between the substantive rules governing child custody disputes and those that govern other aspects of marriage dissolution.

Child custody disputes are governed by a broad, somewhat vague legal standard – the best interest of the child. Despite general agreement that the child's best interest involves an evaluation of a child's psychological and developmental needs, there is less consensus on how those needs should be worked out in individual cases. Substantive Kentucky law makes each parent entitled to equal consideration, removing the presumption that young children's custody should be awarded to their mothers. Moreover, Kentucky courts have not adopted a primary caretaker emphasis to resolve custody disputes. A growing number of courts award joint custody even when one parent objects. Thus, child custody involves considerable uncertainty for parties, even in families that adopted traditional role differentiation for fathers and mothers during the marriage. Given the lack of clear rules for determining custody and the possibility that any litigated solution will include shared responsibility, parents may find mediation an attractive alternative.

Another factor that makes child custody amenable to mediation is the acknowledged influence that psychologists and social workers have in litigated custody cases. Courts routinely order custody evaluations to be done by these professionals and their testimony carries significant weight with a court that is attempting to choose between parties who cannot agree on primary custody. Attorneys may feel more comfortable allowing these professionals and others with similar training to play a role as mediators.

Finally, child custody disputes may be amenable to mediation because many parents will be able to separate their own needs from those of their children and agree that their children's needs take primacy even in the context of divorce. One factor that may influence parental attitudes is the Jefferson Family Court's ability to deliver information about children's needs through the Families in Transition Project, a separate court program of education about divorce for families with minor children between seven and fourteen. Educating parents about the impact of divorce on children may increase the number of parents who are genuinely interested in mediation.

Despite its mandatory approach to mediation, the Jefferson Family Court rule reflects significant compromise. All parents must comply with a referral to mediation, and they are encouraged by the court to give mediation an opportunity to work. However, a close reading of the rule shows that compliance with the referral may be satisfied by filing informational forms and attending an initial orientation session. Because mediation requires the active participation of the parties, compulsion to attend sessions beyond the initial stage would appear futile. Rules keeping parties in mediation beyond that point through court compulsion may have been rejected for a number of reasons, including delay and cost. Conversely, mediation advocates argue that with proper selection of subjects for mediation, both time and money are saved, particularly because of a decrease in the incidence of post-award litigation. With time, the Jefferson Family Court should be able to compare the duration and expense of mediation and litigation for specific types of cases.

Even if mediation were slightly more costly and slower than litigation, there might be reasons to expose parents to that option. The adversarial process of divorce takes a particular toll on the children who are involved. The ability of mediation to eliminate much of the anger and anxiety involved in adversarial proceedings could make it preferable for disputes involving children. Again, comparison of mediated outcomes with litigated outcomes must await long-term use of such programs.

The Special or Settlement Master

A further novel procedure, now commonly followed in North American jurisdictions, is the appointment of a 'Settlement Master' by the court at early stage appointments. The Settlement Master will be an experienced neutral, familiar with the area of dispute concerned. Such an appointment will be made where the court considers that the possibilities of settlement have not been exhaustively explored by the parties themselves, especially in particularly complex civil cases. The role of the Master is to orchestrate this exploration, reporting back to the court with a draft agreement or a recommendation that the case proceeds on to adjudication.

A more important development, however, has been the accretion of mediation functions by the Special Masters who have for many decades been an element in the more conventional process of adjudication. However, especially in order to deal with complex civil cases, courts in the United States in recent times have increasingly appointed Special Masters with a view to handling a number of the preparatory tasks in civil suits and to assist the parties to reach their own settlement. In the account that follows, the basic features of the role are considered.

Extract 8:14

L Silberman: 'Judicial Adjuncts Revisited: The Proliferation of Ad Hoc Procedure' (1989) 137 *University of Pennsylvania Law Review* 2131, pp 2134–2137, 2143–2145, 2158–2161

. . . special masters are private lawyers, retired judges, or legal academics who are appointed to assist the judge in the handling of a particular case. No standards exist for their appointment, other than the requirement of an 'exceptional condition' that appears in Rule 53(b) of the Federal Rules of Civil Procedure. The history of special masters is a much longer one, going back to early English chancery practice, continuing in federal equity practice, and introduced into the Federal Rules in 1938: Historically, special masters were used primarily to assist judges during trial in matters of account and often to report on matters of evidence. In early federal practice before 1938 special masters participated in virtually all aspects of the case, including those aspects that occurred prior to trial, but Professor (now Magistrate) Wayne Brazil argues that the 1938 adoption of Federal Rule 53, which expressly authorized the use of special masters, did not include a pre-trial role for special masters. In addition, while the Clark Papers did indicate that the original advisory committee intended to continue 'the long tradition in equity of using special masters to perform tasks after a court had determined liability,' the wide-ranging role that remedial masters now have is unlike their historic function. Indeed, existing Federal Rule 53, which provides for the appointment of special masters on a showing of exceptional conditions and envisions a report by the master subject to a 'clearly erroneous' factual review by the district judge, does not quite fit the circumstances in which special masters are used today.

Notwithstanding the compelling historical evidence that a more limited role was intended, masters have consistently been used under Rule 53 to assist in trial, pre-trial, and post-trial phases of litigation. Masters are usually private attorneys, retired judges, or legal academics, appointed by a judge under an order of reference in an individual case to assist the judge in the handling of a case when warranted by an 'exceptional condition.' Concerns over the delay and expense often associated with the use of special masters and a fear that such references amounted to an abdication of the judicial function led the Supreme Court in *La Buy v Howes Leather Co.* to limit the circumstances under which a special master could be appointed. It should be noted that the reference in *La Buy* – for what was then a large and complicated antitrust action – to a 'special master' (a practicing attorney as was the prevailing custom) was a general reference for the master to make findings of fact and conclusions of law and, in essence, to take over the adjudicatory task of the judge.

The modern uses of special masters are often quite different from the very general reference invoked in *La Buy*. To some extent, special masters' functions are often more sharply focused: to supervise various *pre-trial* phases of litigation (particularly in the large or complicated case), to facilitate settlement under a broad charter to act as a negotiator and conciliator between the parties, or to assist in shaping, monitoring, or enforcing compliance with post-judgment relief. It should be noted that the 'exceptional condition' requirement is applicable to *all* references to masters in non-jury cases (other than magistrates), except in matters of account and damage calculation, but this lesson of *La Buy* seems to be honored more in the breach than in the observance in the recent cases in which special masters have been appointed.

Masters and magistrates have taken on burdensome discovery tasks, orchestrated settlements, and issued rulings on preliminary issues. Although both have relieved the inordinate pressures on judges' time, there are practical objections to the delegations of these tasks. Discovery disputes and other pre-trial matters are now outside of direct control by the judge. The broad discretion inherent in the system of discovery rules is exercised by persons once-removed from the judge. This trend itself is inconsistent with the recent emphasis on strong and close judicial management because the magistrate and not the judge has control of the case. The delegation of case management functions itself may create an incentive for expansion of the pre-trial phase of litigation, and an additional danger comes with layering the pre-trial phases with magistrates' and masters' decisions requiring further review by the district judge.

To the extent that cases are shaped, ad hoc procedures embraced, settlements influenced and even coerced, and law articulated, special masters may represent an even greater threat to the integrity of the process because they are private individuals who are not institutionally entrusted with judicial powers. The danger of a new cottage industry, enhanced by large fees for special masters and endangered by potential cronyism and conflicts of interest, cannot be ignored when assessing the system of special masters presently in vogue. . . .

The special master's pre-trial role is most relevant to our purposes in assessing the impact on what I sense is the retreat to an equity-based system of procedure, the failure to address troublesome procedural issues with more formalized rule-making, and the absence of specialized procedures for specialized cases. I say that notwithstanding the irony that it is precisely such 'procedural specialization' that is brought to bear in cases in which special masters are used to supervise discovery. But the technique is ad hoc, informal, discretionary and expensive.

A prime example of case management and *sui generis* procedural innovation is the Ohio asbestos litigation which involved two special masters, Professors Francis

McGovern and Eric Green. In 1983, with 80 pending asbestos cases in the Northern District of Ohio (and 34 more on the way) assigned to different judges, some having been filed years earlier, Judge Lambros appointed the two special masters to oversee pre-trial and help prepare for a possible trial of these many claims. One early pre-trial activity undertaken by McGovern and Green involved the gathering of information from the parties about past trial outcomes and settlement amounts with a dual purpose of preparing for trial and establishing settlement parameters. After interviewing the parties, the masters set up a limited discovery schedule which would enable each case to be developed sufficiently for a realistic evaluation. Then the parties were brought together to discuss possible settlement. If the initial settlement conference did not yield the desired resolution, the parties could then bear the expense of further discovery which might have greater relevance with respect to a projected trial.

In addition to equalizing the information available to the parties and promoting settlement before expensive discovery, the masters also sought to group the cases into sub-categories which would conceivably lead to rapid disposition of most or all of the cases. This 'cluster' of a representative sample from each 'disease category' would proceed through discovery, settlement negotiation, and trial in an effort to induce settlement. According to McGovern, the sample contained both weak and strong cases for each side in an effort to convince each side of the possible flaws in its own case, and the strength of the other's.

Another *sui generis* procedural innovation adopted by the special masters necessitated the involvement of others besides the masters. 'Neutral' individuals who had been trained for their data collection role completed for each plaintiff an extremely detailed protocol which then was computerized. This information was supplemented by a computerized memory, in essence, of what asbestos cases had fetched in settlement, at trial, and in summary jury trials. The costs for special masters, experts, computers, and incidental design of the innovative program ran to over $250,000. The system, by now a small bureaucracy, became even more elaborate. The computers were programmed with theories of econometrics and 'dynamic' decision-making to include legal, economic, political, and psychological permutations that could influence the process of negotiation and accord. Finally, as he had done in other cases, McGovern authored an 'expert system' to mimic the decision-making process.

In sum, special masters McGovern and Green performed their assigned task – customizing a system to process asbestos claims promoting settlement while minimizing substantive unfairness to any of the parties – with insight and imagination. Yet, like Professor Brazil, I am uneasy about the development of such an elaborate and makeshift procedure given the sobering outlay of resources. As Brazil points out, there is a nagging worry that reasonably accurate evaluations of a plaintiff's case could have been produced without resorting to a complex and specially-produced apparatus. Again, this is not meant as harshly as it might sound. The number of plaintiffs in the Ohio court may have made traditional methods of case valuation impractical and too time-consuming. But if such customized tailoring – or something like it – is desirable, perhaps there is an accumulated wisdom to be applied generically to other asbestos cases. Alternatively, perhaps the costs of such customized tailoring outweigh the benefits. . . .

One other specific use of special masters deserves comment here – the appointment of a master for settlement purposes. Functionally, of course, the role is often subtly played by the master who is technically appointed to oversee discovery. Some judges, however, have separated out the settlement task more definitively in their reference orders. For example, in the *Agent Orange* case, although Judge Weinstein substituted a magistrate for the special master on discovery matters, he then appointed three lawyers as separate 'settlement masters.' Judge Aspen in Chicago has appointed special masters as 'mediators' in both 'complex and routine' cases. Notwithstanding the success (and increasing prevalence) of some of these efforts, it should be noted that use of such judicial adjuncts technically should meet, under the present rules, the exceptional condition requirement for the appointment of a master under Rule 53(b). There is, of course, nothing to stop parties from voluntarily choosing an outside party to help settle their dispute, but it is not clear that consent to the formal appointment of a special master suspends the requirement of Rule 53(b). Quite apart from the restrictions of Rule 53(b), it might be argued that Federal Rule 16 is authority for the court to experiment with extrajudicial settlement techniques in the name of pre-trial management. Rule 16(c)(7) directs consideration of 'the possibility of settlement or the use of extrajudicial procedures to resolve the dispute' at the pre-trial conference, but there is no evidence that Rule 16 represents an invitation for increased delegation to special masters whom the parties must pay. Of course, to the extent that experience demonstrates that third party mediation and settlement functions done under court auspices are effective, statutory or rule changes can be made. The policy issue is thus the one to be addressed.

The private master as a settlement facilitator might seem, in some respect, the least intrusive or objectionable role of the ones we have examined. But unless the master comes armed with the coercive power of the judge (and possibly with disclosures as to the judge's views on some of the issues in the case, as there was in *Agent Orange*), it is unclear that the intervention of an outside party will have any real impact on settlement. To the extent cases ultimately do settle, there is little evidence that third party intervention is in fact the catalyst for settlement. Indeed, additional expense and time of the special master may add overall to the parties' litigation costs. Moreover, if the master is effective because of leverage that comes from behind the scenes contact between the master and judge, serious questions of ethics and policy are presented. Of course, where the parties consent to a master for settlement, some of these objections are less pronounced, but the danger is that the 'consent' is not always so voluntarily forthcoming.

Along with the danger of involuntary consent, I have alluded to potential conflicts of interest that may arise from using special masters who serve only for a particular case. Not only is there the traditional kind of conflict that may arise because the master may have represented or opposed parties and lawyers who come before him, but also more subtle conflicts in approaches to particular issues and views of the merits may infect decision-making by those who by definition wear dual hats. The more traditional conflict came before the Court of Appeals for the District of Columbia in *Jenkins v Sterlacci*, where the special master was contemporaneously the lawyer-adversary of a law firm also representing one of the litigants in the proceeding before the special master.

The Court of Appeals found that the ABA Code of Judicial Conduct was by its terms applicable to any officer performing judicial functions, including a special master. It also reasoned that the 'clear error' standard that insulates the special master's findings makes the special master 'functionally indistinguishable' from a trial judge, and thus the special master must be held to the same standards applicable to the conduct of judges. Although ultimately holding that the law firm had waived any objection based on the appearance of bias in the particular case, the District of Columbia Circuit went on to acknowledge the potential conflicts facing special masters:

> who may wear different hats depending upon the professional function they are performing from one day to the next. In one matter they may be required to observe the impartial decorum of a decision-maker, while in another they may be called upon to assume the perspective, and the partiality, of an advocate. This duality of roles places a burden on the special master with an active law practice, but its discharge does not require that once he has accepted an assignment as a special master, an attorney places his life as an advocate in a state of suspended animation. . . . Instead, it is sufficient and necessary, that an individual who accepts an appointment as a special master scrupulously avoid any undertaking, as an advocate or otherwise, that would tend or appear to compromise his impartiality as a decision-maker.

The Summary Jury Trial

The summary jury trial is a court-based development of the mini-trial. It is a truncated trial which affords the disputants some insight into the most probable jury reaction to their cases. The process involves summarised presentations by the parties' lawyers before an advisory jury, with a judge or magistrate presiding. Attendance by the parties and their lawyers is compulsory. The jurors, who are unaware that their verdict is non-binding and advisory, are questioned about the verdict that they have reached, and about the parties' summary presentations. In the light of the verdict and the questions and answers that follow, settlement negotiations take place. The verdict of the jury is not, however, admissible at the trial that follows from failed settlement negotiations.

The aim of this procedural innovation is to afford each disputant the opportunity to predict more accurately the outcome of the trial, and to encourage the disputants and their lawyers to reach a settlement and avoid the costs of a full trial. Nevertheless, the extent to which parties are in fact encouraged to settle by this novel procedure is unclear, and it is a process that does entail significant costs. It is therefore probably most effective in cases where a lengthy trial is in prospect or particularly difficult issues of fact or law are involved.[11] It is not clear, however, that the federal courts in the United States actually do have the authority to make participation in the summary jury trial mandatory (see Woodley, 1995).

---

11 This process also, however, offers the possibility of its strategic use in pre-trial proceedings so that it becomes a complicating element in the negotiations between the parties rather than an effective aid to settlement.

Below, the inventor and leading proponent of the summary jury trial reflects on its use and value as a mechanism for promoting settlement and reducing costs of litigation (Extract 8:15). The view of an influential critic of the summary jury trial follows (Extract 8:16).

Extract 8:15

T D Lambros: 'The Summary Trial: An Effective Aid to Settlement' (1993) 77 *Judicature* 1, pp 6–8

The summary jury trial was my response to burgeoning court dockets. My desire was to streamline these dockets so that only hardcore, durable controversies would ultimately enter the courtroom. This would also enable other cases to bypass the costly and slow-moving track to the courtroom. In accomplishing these goals, the summary jury trial links the heritage of the traditional jury trial, the crown jewel of our judicial system, to the modern methods of alternative dispute resolution.

This flexible process is very much like a conventional jury trial. With counsel and parties present, each lawyer presents a summary of the case to a jury, which then deliberates and renders a non-binding verdict. The process usually lasts less than a day because the information presented to the jury is in summary form. Normally, no actual witness testimony is given. Instead, a summary of the witness's testimony is presented. After the process is completed, counsel and the parties have an opportunity to discuss the verdict with the jury. Because every case is different, judges are encouraged to mold the process to fit the unique contours and individual needs of a particular case.

Misplaced criticisms
The summary jury trial has been in use for roughly 12 years, and, not surprisingly, it has its critics. The biggest criticisms of the summary jury trial are: (1) the lack of verifiable studies indicating whether summary jury trial verdicts would be the same as conventional jury verdicts, (2) the question of whether judges are authorized to use juries to assist in settlement, and (3) the notion that a judge cannot make participation in the process mandatory.

The focus on the lack of comprehensive studies is misplaced. The summary jury trial is not intended to supplant the traditional jury trial. Instead, it is a settlement tool that provides a rational means for resolving disputes.

Judges are indeed authorized to use juries to assist in settlement. It is important to remember that the summary jury trial is a real trial, not a mock trial. The process is informative and predictive and provides a substantial factual basis upon which important decisions to settle or to go to a binding trial are made. Although nonbinding and presented in a summarized format, it is, nonetheless, a jury trial as provided by Federal Rule 38: Title 28 USC §1861 and §1863 and Federal Rule 38 are the statutory sources for providing jurors where a jury trial is authorized by law. Summary jury trials are authorized by 28 USC §473(a) (6) (B), which provides that 'the court may make available . . . summary jury trial.'

In addition, judges have the responsibility to manage their dockets pursuant to the Federal Rules of Civil Procedure, which emphasize the imperatives of efficient pretrial management and authorize the use of extrajudicial procedures. In addition to the rules and supporting case law, the criticisms of the process were countered when Congress approved the use of summary jury trials in the Civil Justice Reform Act of 1990. The act establishes goals toward which our judicial system must strive, and it gives us marching orders to develop ways to handle court dockets efficiently and effectively.

Even before this explicit statutory authorization, Federal Rules 1, 16, and 39(c) implicitly authorized courts to conduct such trials with jurors who rendered advisory verdicts that facilitated dispute resolution. Beyond that, the Judicial Conference of the United States in 1984, before summary jury trials were implemented, 'endorse[d] an experimental use of summary jury trials as a potentially effective means of promoting the fair and equitable settlement of potentially lengthy civil jury trial cases.'

The notion that a judge cannot make participation mandatory is also misplaced. When parties do consent to the process, a judge should grant the request. But when only one party consents, if the case is suitable, the inherent power of the court to control its docket permits a judge to order the parties to participate in alternative dispute resolution.

Coming to grips with reality

The belief that the summary jury trial adds another tier to the litigation process is misguided. Because the process allows lawyers to use the discovery process and try their case before a judge and jury, it permits the parties to view a realistic playing of the case. Litigants, therefore, come to grips with the reality of the case and the reality of the dynamics under which it is tried. It creates a sobering effect on litigants who are steeped in the emotion of events leading to the suit. To the extent that this emotion and other factors are barriers to settlement, the summary jury trial tends to mitigate these barriers. The process requires little time because witnesses are usually not present, and the costs are nominal compared with what would be expended if full battle preparations had to be made for a binding jury trial.

The process also produces the same kind of tensions that are present at a traditional jury trial. The benefit of this is twofold. First, the summary jury trial acts as a dress rehearsal for the real jury trial, and second, the shadow of an approaching trial intensifies the parties' efforts toward settlement. Because the clients are required to attend the summary jury trial, the procedure is particularly effective where the legal labyrinth begins to tax the patience of the litigants before the 11th hour arrives and provides the parties with a sense of reality while there is still time to do something about it.

Contrary to some critics, the purpose of the summary jury trial is not to impose settlement negotiations on litigants, nor to force the parties to settle. Rather, the process is intended to clarify issues and inform the parties of how a jury might view the facts and law of the case in order to facilitate settlement discussions. When it is clear that the parties have no interest whatsoever in settling their differences, and only a final adjudication will ultimately resolve the case, neither the summary jury trial nor any other means of judicially sponsored mediation will induce a settlement. However, where the trial court, in its discretion, believes that there is sufficient interest in a settlement or that one of the parties' view of the facts or the law is so inconsistent with the likely findings of a jury that a summary jury trial may facilitate settlement discussions, it is properly within that court's discretion to order a summary jury trial. If negotiations fail after the summary jury trial, the case may proceed to trial.

There is no downside to summary jury trials even if some cases do not settle. The bringing together of all trial participants and their going through the process enhances the quality of advocacy by making lawyers, litigants, and judges better able to deal with problems presented in the dispute. Exposure to the courtroom with a real judge and jury provides everyone with more information on which to build a better trial. Should the case proceed to trial, parties may be able to stipulate to certain issues, and judges are better able to deal with objections.

Extract 8:16

R Posner: 'The Summary Jury Trial and Other Methods of Alternative Dispute Resolution: Some Cautionary Observations' (1986) 53 *University of Chicago Law Review* 366, pp 387–389

Supposing that with the summary jury trial a higher fraction of cases is settled (at this moment a highly uncertain prediction), is this a good thing from the standpoint of society as a whole? It benefits the parties to cases that would otherwise have been tried (at least if coerced settlement is not a serious problem), because settlement is cheaper than trial. But is it a good or a bad thing for the rest of society?

The object of policy, even narrowly conceived, is not to maximize the settlement rate; it is to minimize the total costs of the system of dispute resolution. These include costs of legal error as well as the direct costs, to the parties and the judicial system, of dispute resolution. Raising the settlement rate will reduce the direct costs, in the short run, because litigation is more costly than settlement. But in the long run the litigation rate may rise. With few suits being tried and therefore few decisions being made, parties will find it difficult to predict how courts will resolve their disputes. P_p and P_d in the formal model of settlement will increasingly diverge, and cases will be litigated that would be settled if parties had better information about how their cases would be decided if they went to trial. Raising the settlement rate may also, as suggested earlier, increase the number of cases filed, by lowering the expected cost of litigating (which includes settlement, the terminating event of most lawsuits); if so, the total costs of resolving disputes may rise even if the average cost falls because more cases are settled.

But actually the summary jury trial is unlikely to affect the settlement *rate* even if, as I have been assuming, it increases the probability of settling each and every case subjected to the device. Judges have only so much time to devote to civil trials, given the pressure of their other responsibilities, in particular the pressure that the Speedy Trial Act exerts to give priority to criminal trials. Faced as most federal district judges are with many more cases filed in a year (more than 500 in the busier districts) than they can try (perhaps 40 on average, of which almost half would be criminal cases), they must, to equilibrate supply and demand, delay trials, refer disputes to magistrates, and put pressure on the parties to settle. If the summary jury trial settles some cases that would otherwise be tried, other cases will advance in the queue; or the judge will put less pressure on the parties to those cases to settle; or fewer cases will be referred to magistrates. Whatever happens, there will be the same number of trials. The summary jury trial is a substitute not for real trials but for alternative methods of pushing the parties to settle, and it is a costly substitute.

Of course, for those who believe the federal courts are being underutilized, any procedure that has a fair chance of raising the settlement rate in these courts, thereby making room for new cases, will be welcome. That is not my view, though it would take me too far afield to show why the federal courts have too much rather than too little business; it is not the view of the advocates of summary jury trial, either. They accept, regretfully or resignedly, rather than welcome, the prospect of an ever-expanding federal caseload. They merely hope to process cases more rapidly by reducing the fraction of cases that are tried. They are like highway engineers, for whom the natural solution to highway congestion is to build more and wider highways. The advocates of more efficient machinery for expediting case flow have not shown equivalent interest in measures to reduce the overall demand for federal judicial services, as by raising the jurisdictional minimum amount in controversy in diversity cases, or raising filing fees above their present ridiculously low levels, or returning some legal responsibilities to state courts. It is in those directions, I believe, that the only lasting reforms lie. It is merely a detail that the summary jury trial, despite the enthusiasm it has generated, remains problematic even on its own rather too limited terms of reference.

Early Neutral Evaluation

As noted above (p 287 et seq), an additional area in which courts have attempted to innovate by reliance on neutral intermediaries who promote settlement between the disputing parties is early neutral evaluation ('ENE'). This procedure, which originated in the United States District Court for the Northern District of California, is intended to encourage each party to understand better its own legal position in the case by providing a forum in which the parties present their respective cases and receive an independent, neutral assessment of the likely outcome. Briefly stated, the process involves a meeting between the parties and their lawyers, chaired by a neutral evaluator, in which points of agreement and the strengths and weaknesses of each party are considered. The neutral prepares a written case evaluation that, if the parties do not settle with his or her encouragement, provides guidance in the development of a plan for subsequent management of the case. The following extracts report on the Californian programme.

Extract 8:17

W Brazil: 'Special Masters in Complex Cases: Extending the Judiciary or Reshaping Adjudication?' (1990) 53 *University of Chicago Law Review* 394, pp 407–409

> Another innovative use of special masters is evolving in the Early Neutral Evaluation program in the United States District Court for the Northern District of California. This experimental program was produced by a task force of lawyers and judges appointed by Chief Judge Robert F Peckham to seek ways to reduce the parties' costs of civil litigation. The court directs a senior, highly regarded, neutral litigator to host an evaluation session for a case in an area where the litigator has substantial expertise. The parties submit

brief statements identifying issues whose early resolution might materially affect the suit as well as the discovery that should contribute most to meaningful settlement negotiations. At the evaluation, which occurs about 150 days after the complaint is filed and which clients as well as counsel must attend, each side presents its case and answers questions from the evaluator. The evaluator then frankly assesses the strengths and weaknesses of evidence and arguments, and suggests an overall case valuation range (based on educated guesses about the probability of liability and the amount of damages). If the parties are open to exploring settlement at this juncture, the evaluator may attempt to facilitate negotiations. If no settlement is reached, the evaluator helps the parties plan for sharing information and conducting discovery on key issues, in order to generate the data needed for subsequent settlement efforts. Everything that transpires at this evaluation session remains strictly confidential. In particular, everyone is prohibited from discussing information resulting from the session with the assigned judge.

The program's designers hope that it will assist case development in three ways: by affording parties a vehicle for substantive communication, providing some inexpensive and informal discovery, and forcing counsel and litigants both to investigate early and to analyze and appraise their own situations. The evaluator's assessments should serve as a reality check, and may foster early settlement discussions. In complex cases much of the session will be devoted to planning data acquisition, in the hope that the neutral will help produce a focused, commonsense, and cost-effective discovery plan.

This program is unique in its timing: it interposes serious case evaluation early in litigation, before funds are spent wastefully on ill-focused discovery. Masters preside, instead of judges, in part because of the necessary time commitment and in part because the evaluator is expected to be more assertively probing, more frank, and more judgmental than would be appropriate for a judge, at least one who might subsequently rule on important matters. The program's designers also hope that a master can create an environment that is less formal and intimidating than the courtroom. Since the evaluator, unlike a judge, has no power over the case, the parties might be more candid about their objectives and positions.

However, some thorny difficulties also arise in this context. Finding appropriate persons to serve as masters may be difficult. An ideal candidate should possess recognized expertise in the field without being so thoroughly identified with a type of client or case that parties will distrust the master's neutrality. This problem, and the related one of avoiding conflicts of interest, can be especially acute in sub-specialities of practice (such as maritime or patent law) in which only a few law firms are involved. One partial solution to this problem is employing law professors and retired judges as evaluators.

Another possible constraint on enlisting masters might be their fear of being called to testify about the evaluation session, or being sued for actions taken or opinions offered while serving as masters. Such fears could arise in connection with virtually any special master assignment, but are likely to be more pervasive in a program that institutionalizes use of masters in a significant number of cases. One antidote to this problem is a court order making confidential everything that occurs at the session. No one can be confident, however, that other jurisdictions will honor such an order.

The possibility of suits against masters raises additional concerns. Would a special master be protected by the immunity doctrines available to judges? To what extent? Would a lawyer's malpractice insurance cover a suit for acts committed while serving as a master? If not, could private attorneys insure this risk (would carriers write such policies)? Fortunately, these issues remain merely theoretical. To my knowledge, no party has either sued a master or subpoenaed one for testimony.

Extract 8:18

J D Rosenberg and H J Folberg: 'Alternative Dispute Resolution: An Empirical Analysis' (1994) 46 *Stanford Law Review* 1487, pp 1495–1496

Our study revealed an ADR program strongly influenced by the individual assigned as the neutral for a given case. For example, when the evaluator was skilled in mediation, ENE often resembled mediation. When the evaluator was more familiar with hard-nosed settlement tactics, that approach appeared to dominate the ENE session. When the evaluator was interested primarily in discovery, there was often little settlement discussion. We found that the nature and outcome of ENE sessions depended more on variations among evaluators than on any other factor, despite the relatively clear guidelines given to evaluators about how to conduct the sessions.

The creators of ENE intended the session to take place within 150 days of filing. The timing of ENE sessions varied substantially, however, and some cases were not referred to the process until they had been pending for well over a year.

The ENE process was intended to lie somewhere between mediation, in which a third party with substantial procedural expertise facilitates communication among the parties in the interest of settling some or all of the issues in dispute, and nonbinding arbitration, in which a third party with substantial subject matter expertise reviews the case presented by the litigants and determines an appropriate outcome. As conducted, ENE ran the gamut for one extreme to the other, and sometimes bore little resemblance to any other process. Most evaluators appraised their cases in some respects, but the specificity and directness of these appraisals varied tremendously from actual predictions of jury verdicts to subtle hints about possible weaknesses of a claim or defense.

Another goal of ENE was to enable the neutral to help the parties reach stipulations and plan future discovery. Some evaluators focused entirely on discovery. Others reported that if a case did not settle, they never considered the possibility of discussing discovery in ENE. Some of the variation in ENE can be traced in part to changes in the selection of neutrals. In the early stages, many of the evaluators had been involved in the development of the ENE process and were, as a result, intimately familiar with and personally committed to the process as designed. When evaluators began to be chosen from a broader group of attorneys, variation in the conduct of ENE sessions increased.

As a result of the variation in the timing and conduct of ENE sessions, we cannot easily generalize about the process. All we can say that is universally true of ENE is that it is a confidential meeting of the parties, their attorneys, and a neutral third party who is an experienced and respected trial attorney.

Despite this variation in the ENE process, about two-thirds of the parties who participated in an ENE session believed that the session was helpful and worth their efforts. Parties and attorneys divided relatively evenly over the questions whether ENE reduced costs and whether it resulted in decreased pendency time. More significant, however, was the fact that those who believed ENE did not make a valuable contribution to their case reported that the process was, at worst, a waste of time with an average cost of about $4,000 (including attorneys' fees, preparation time, and transportation). Those satisfied with the ENE process, however, reported earlier disposition of their cases, increased understanding of their cases, and an average saving of over $40,000 per participant.

F: Refurbishing Umpiring – Arbitration

Court-annexed arbitration is ordinarily used by trial courts in various parts of the United States in order to deal with cases of relatively low monetary value which raise particularly complex or novel legal issues or where the legal issues are clearly much more important than the factual dimensions of the case. The system is mandatory but non-binding, with the parties presenting their cases in an informal, simplified hearing to a court-approved arbitrator (or arbitrators) who renders an award. This award may be rejected by either party by opting for a trial de novo – otherwise, the award becomes final after a time limit has been reached. The basic features of this system, and arguments for its wider use, are outlined in Extract 8:19. The case against the evolving system of mandatory court-annexed arbitration has been forcefully put by Eisele and Posner[12] (Extracts 8:20 and 8:21). Also associated with the development of ADR have been other innovations linking arbitration and adjudication. These include not only the med-arb arrangements noted above but also 'final offer arbitration', 'arbitration under a high-low contract' and 'rent-a-judge'. Brief accounts of these last two developments are provided below (Extracts 8:22 and 8:23).

Extract 8:19

R J Broderick: 'Court-annexed Compulsory Arbitration: It Works' (1989) 72 *Judicature* 4, pp 219–222

The first program of court-annexed compulsory arbitration in the federal court system was initiated in the United States District Court for the Eastern District of Pennsylvania in February 1978: Judge Griffin Bell, then Attorney General of the United States, requested that the US district courts in Philadelphia, San Francisco and Connecticut (3 of the 94 US district courts) experiment with programs of court-annexed compulsory arbitration. Judge Bell chaired the Follow-Up Task Force of the Pound Conference and, as chairman, recommended experimentation with court-annexed arbitration in the federal courts. In urging the Senate to enact legislation authorizing such experiments,

---

12 An empirically-based criticism is provided by Bernstein (1993).

Judge Bell, as attorney general of the United States, stated that court-annexed compulsory arbitration would 'broaden access for the American people to their justice system and . . . provide mechanisms that will permit the expeditious resolution of disputes at a reasonable cost.'

The court-annexed compulsory arbitration experiment has been operating in the US District Court for the Eastern District of Pennsylvania for more than 10 years. The program's achievements have exceeded the expectations of both the bench and the bar. Court-annexed compulsory arbitration is now considered a component part of the civil justice system in the Eastern District of Pennsylvania.

Since the program was initiated in February 1978, 17,006 of the 71,588 civil cases filed during the past 129 months were placed in the arbitration program (24 per cent of the civil case filings). Of the 17,006 civil cases placed in the arbitration program, 15,779 cases have been terminated. Only 388 of the 17,006 civil cases placed in the program over the past 129 months have required a trial *de novo*. In other words, only about 2 per cent of the 17,006 cases placed in the arbitration program over the past 129 months required the traditional court-room trial.

The success of the court-annexed arbitration program is attested to by the fact that in October 1984, the bar associations of the ten southeastern counties of Pennsylvania (comprising the Eastern District of Pennsylvania) urged the court to expand its arbitration program to include all civil cases in which money damages only were being sought in an amount not exceeding $100,000. It was generally agreed that there should be some limitation on the amount in controversy. It was conceded that in cases where money damages only are being sought, the amount in controversy should be limited to an amount which might make it economically unfeasible for litigants to demand a trial *de novo*. The saving to the litigants, as well as to the courts, is not realized whenever the amount in controversy encourages the losing party to demand a trial *de novo*. It was therefore determined to limit the amount in controversy to $75,000 in order to avoid the possibility of making the arbitration program just one more layer of litigation.

The local rule was amended, effective January 1, 1985, mandating compulsory arbitration for all civil cases in which money damages only are being sought in an amount not exceeding $75,000, excluding social security and prisoners' civil rights cases. Prior to this amendment, the arbitration program was limited to civil cases wherein money damages only of $50,000 or less were being sought, and the action was (1) for injury or death of a seaman; (2) based on a negotiable instrument or a contract; (3) for personal injury or property damage; or (4) under the Federal Employers Liability Act. Also prior to this amendment, in cases where the United States was a party, only actions brought under (1) the Federal Tort Claims Act, (2) Longshoremen and Harbor Workers Compensation Act, (3) Miller Act or (4) Federal Crime Insurance Act were required to be arbitrated. Since this expansion of the arbitration program in January, 1985, almost 30 per cent of the civil cases filed in the Eastern District of Pennsylvania are being placed in the arbitration program.

For the most part, the program is administered by the clerk of the court. When the plaintiff files his or her complaint, the local rule provides that damages are presumed to be *not* in excess of $75,000 unless counsel certifies otherwise. The court may set aside any certification by counsel if it finds that the damages are not likely to exceed $75,000.

Immediately after the answer is filed, the attorneys receive a notice from the clerk advising them of the date for the trial before the arbitrators and also notifying them that discovery must be completed within 120 days. The clerk schedules the trial before the arbitrators for a certain day, usually a date about five months after the answer is filed.

The local arbitration rule specifically provides that in the event a party files a motion for judgment on the pleadings, summary judgment or similar relief, the case may not be arbitrated until the court has ruled on the motion. The rule further provides that the filing of any such motion after the judge has signed the order appointing the arbitrators will not stay the arbitration trial unless the judge specifically so orders. Furthermore, an application for leave to join an additional party is deemed untimely unless it is filed before the court signs the order appointing the arbitrators. The court appoints the three arbitrators who will preside at the trial about 30 days prior to the date scheduled for the arbitration trial. The court's order appointing the arbitrators authorizes them to change the date of the arbitration trial provided the trial is commenced within 30 days of the scheduled date. Any continuance beyond this 30-day period must be approved by the court.

Although the Federal Rules of Evidence are designated as guides for the admissibility of evidence at the arbitration trial, copies or photographs of exhibits must be marked for identification and delivered to opposing counsel at least ten days prior to the trial. The panel must receive the exhibits in evidence without formal proof unless counsel has been notified at least five days prior to the trial that his or her opposing counsel intends to raise an objection concerning the authenticity of the exhibit. The arbitration trial is not recorded unless a party at his or her own expense arranges for the recording and transcription. All arbitration trials take place in a courtroom in the federal courthouse.

At the trial *de novo*, neither the fact that the case was tried before the arbitration panel, nor the arbitrators' award is admissible. However, testimony given at the arbitration trial may be used to impeach the credibility of a party or witness. The arbitrators' award is entered on the docket immediately after it is filed, although the award itself is not placed in the official court file. In the event that no demand for a trial *de novo* is filed, the arbitration clerk prepares a judgment for the judge's signature attached to which is the arbitrators' award. If a demand for a trial *de novo* is filed, the arbitration clerk retains the arbitrators' award in a separate file in order to make certain that the arbitrators' award is not considered at or before the traditional courtroom trial.

The arbitrators

There are approximately 1,200 lawyers certified to preside at the arbitration trial. In order to qualify for certification, the lawyer must be admitted to practice before the court, be a member of the bar for at least five years, and be determined by the chief judge of the court to be competent to preside at the trial. An application to become an arbitrator is carefully considered not only by the chief judge, but, at his request, by all the other judges of the court. Furthermore, any complaints received concerning the performance of an arbitrator are considered by all the judges. Over the past 129 months of the operation of the arbitration program, the judges have not hesitated, on occasion, to censure or remove an arbitrator for failure to adhere to the standards required for all judges. Most lawyers who have been certified as arbitrators regard their certification as evidence of their performance of a worthwhile service to the community and the judicial system, and the fact that they receive only $75 for each arbitration trial is considered by them as a recognition that it is a pro bono service.

Three arbitrators are appointed to preside at each trial. They are randomly selected by the clerk of court. At the time of certification, each arbitrator states his or her primary area of practice and the clerk endeavors to assure that each panel of three arbitrators consists of one lawyer whose practice is primarily representing plaintiffs, another whose practice is primarily representing defendants, and a third whose practice does not fit either category. The panel selected by the clerk of court is scheduled for a trial date several months in advance. However, it is not until the judge signs the order designating the arbitrators who will preside at the arbitration trial (approximately 30 days prior to the trial) that counsel learn the identity of the panel members and the panel members become aware of the cases which have been assigned to them for trial.

A panel of three arbitrators has been well-received by the litigants and the bar. It has alleviated the fear of some litigants that one arbitrator might in some way be biased against their cause. Having three arbitrators, who usually represent a cross-section of the community, provides a trial which has all of the advantages of a jury and a non-jury trial.

After the trial
Immediately after the arbitration trial, the panel makes an award, eg 'Award in favor of defendant' or 'Award in favor of plaintiff in the amount of $ against (naming one or more defendants).' The panel is instructed that it should not file findings of fact, conclusions of law, or opinions of any kind. The panel is also instructed that there is to be no indication as to whether the decision is or is not unanimous. The award becomes a final judgment unless within 30 days of the filing of the award either the plaintiff, the defendant or both demand a 'trial *de novo*.' There is no appeal.

Upon the filing of a demand for trial *de novo*, the case proceeds as if it had never been tried before the arbitration panel. After the filing of the demand for trial *de novo*, the case is placed on the trial list of the judge to whom the case had originally been assigned and every effort is made by the judges to make certain that the trial *de novo* is scheduled for the earliest possible date. The party who demands a trial *de novo* (except the United States) must pay to the clerk of the court the $75 fee paid to each member of the arbitration panel, a total of $225. However, any party may petition the court to proceed *in forma pauperis*, and in the event the court signs an *in forma pauperis* order, the $225 fee need not be paid.

The arbitration fees are deposited with the clerk of court and are returned to the party demanding the trial *de novo* only in the event that the party receives a final judgment, exclusive of interest and costs, more favorable than the arbitrators' award. In the event the party demanding the trial *de novo* does not receive a final judgment more favorable than the arbitrators' award, the arbitrators' fees deposited with the clerk of court are forfeited to the United States.

Evaluation
The experiment in the Eastern District of Pennsylvania has been evaluated periodically over the past ten years. A most comprehensive study has just been completed by Barbara

Meierhoefer, senior research associate at the Federal Judicial Center. Her report, which analyzes the first eight years of the program, concludes that it is 'considered a success, accepted by the bench and bar.' To ascertain the judges' thoughts concerning the court's arbitration program, interviews with judges were conducted in the summer of 1985, followed by a mail survey in September 1986. In responding both during the interviews and to the survey, all the judges rated the arbitration program a success. As stated in the report, 'there is essentially no dissent from the view that the program is effective for judges, lawyers and litigants. . . . All either agreed or strongly agreed that other courts would do well to introduce court-annexed arbitration.'

Confirmation of the acceptance of the arbitration program by the Philadelphia bar is found in the survey of some 600 attorneys whose cases had been assigned to the program. Ninety-three per cent of the respondents either approved or strongly approved of the arbitration program. Indeed, 61 per cent named arbitration as their preferred procedure when asked if they preferred cases 'of this type' to be decided by a judge, a jury, or arbitration. Over 60 per cent of the attorneys stated that they spent less time, and that the cost to their clients was less, when the case was referred to arbitration rather than proceeding to the traditional courtroom trial. Beyond the reported savings in time and money, more than 90 per cent of the attorneys believed that the arbitration procedures were fair and impartial. Moreover, 100 per cent of the 152 arbitrators who were surveyed stated that they either approved or strongly approved of the arbitration program. The report concludes that, 'the court-annexed arbitration program in the Eastern District of Pennsylvania continues to be extremely well-received by the vast majority of the members of the bar involved in [the arbitration program] as both counsel and arbitrators.'

The report also observes that the success of the program is attributable to the willingness of the attorneys to serve as arbitrators and the fact that the program is well-administered by the clerk's office. It also points out that it is the 'availability of this opportunity to present the facts of a case to a neutral third party – at an earlier date and without the time and expense that accompany a traditional trial – that provides the basis for believing that arbitration programs can serve to broaden access to the justice system.'

Of all the evaluations, however, the statistical summary prepared on a monthly basis by Michael Kunz, the Clerk of the Court, presents the most persuasive analysis confirming the success of the program. As noted earlier, the most convincing statistic is the fact that during the ten years and nine months of the program, only 388 of the 17,006 cases placed in the court's arbitration program have required a trial *de novo*. In other words, only about 2 per cent of the 17,006 cases placed in the arbitration program required the traditional courtroom trial. During this same period, 8 per cent of the civil cases that were *not* placed in the arbitration program required the traditional courtroom trial. The median time from the date an answer to the complaint is filed to the trial before the arbitration panel was five months in 1987, whereas the median time from the date the answer was filed to the trial for all other civil cases during 1987 was 11 months.

In the early years of the arbitration program in the Eastern District of Pennsylvania there were indications that a few attorneys might have been using the program solely for the purpose of discovery and not as an opportunity for a trial on the merits. After a decision of the court denying a defendant's demand for trial *de novo* on the ground that the defendant failed to participate in good faith at the arbitration trial, the court amended its local rule to specifically provide that if a party fails to participate in the arbitration process in a meaningful manner, the court may deny that party's demand for trial *de novo*. Since this amendment to the local rule, there has been no indication that the parties are using the arbitration trial as a discovery device.

Extract 8:20

G T Eisele: 'The Case Against Court-annexed ADR Programs' (1991) 75 *Judicature* 1, pp 35–37

The stated aims of these court-annexed arbitration programs are to reduce the cost of litigation, to facilitate the speedy disposition of claims, and to reduce the overall number of cases going to trial. Like the recently enacted Biden bill these programs are touted as cost and delay reduction measures. So, what is wrong with such programs that have such laudable objectives?

Let me start by acknowledging that an immense amount of creative energy has gone into the development of a great number of alternate dispute resolution programs over the past dozen years. And let me state again that I am not out to discourage that movement. In fact, I urge attorneys to become knowledgeable of, and familiar with, all of these alternate dispute resolution vehicles. Good attorneys always try to avoid or, if that is impossible, to settle lawsuits. Some of these ADR programs may offer opportunities to settle controversies before filing a lawsuit. Even after a lawsuit has been filed, lawyers and their clients may find it beneficial to utilize one or another of these ADR devices in an attempt to resolve the case short of trial. But I am speaking of the voluntary – out of court – participation in such programs. If the lawyers and their clients wish to avoid by such means the moment of truth inherent in a trial – wonderful! But if the decision is to file suit and go to trial, it is my view that the parties should not be forced to go through one of these procedures as a condition precedent to their right to a trial before a jury or a judge.

Judge Raymond Broderick, of the Eastern District of Pennsylvania, wrote an article in *Judicature* in 1989 defending his court's program. It is entitled, *Court annexed compulsory arbitration: it works.* His description of that program, I confess, really sets my teeth on edge. 'It is, in fact, a civil trial usually held in a courtroom in a courthouse. . . . A better name for the program might well have been "Speedy Civil Trial".'

Indeed a footnote in the April 1991 Federal Judicial Center report points out that recently the Eastern District of Pennsylvania, by an amendment to its local rule, actually changed the name of its program to 'Speedy Civil Trial.' And we also constantly hear the terms 'Mini-trials' and 'Summary Jury trials.' Now really! Do truth in advertising laws not apply to federal courts? Is there any trial judge or trial attorney out there who really believes that what happens at one of these ADR proceedings is a trial? Even if it is conducted 'in a courtroom in a courthouse'! I suggest that if you agree with Judge Broderick's description, you probably have not participated in one of these court-annexed arbitration hearings or read the rules and guidelines governing their use, or, conversely, you have not tried a case before a jury or an Article III judge. As Judge Richard Enslen acknowledges in his article in the Winter 1988 issue of the *New Mexico Law Review*, Mini-Trials and Summary Jury Trials are misnamed. To use his own words: 'The Mini-Trial is not a trial at all . . . It is a settlement device.' (18 NMLR 10), and 'The Summary Jury Trial . . . is not a trial at all. It is a settlement device. . . .' (*Id.* p. 13.)

I view the Article III federal district court as something very special – the place where real trials are conducted, the truth determined, rights vindicated, and justice obtained. 'Justice,' said Daniel Webster, 'is the great interest of man on earth.' 'Justice' – not compromise, not efficiency, not cost effectiveness, but justice. There ought to be a place where that – and that alone – controls and defines the parameters of permissible procedures – where one is not forced to submit to something less than due process, even temporarily. I argue for the continuation and retention of a stand-alone Article III federal trial court where the people of this nation may truly have – and know they may have – their day in court unencumbered by costly non-judicial diversions to which they have not consented.

I do not expect any to contend that arbitration, or mediation, or mini-trials, or any other ADR is equal to – or even approaches – the effectiveness of, or I might say the majesty of, a properly conducted jury or court trial as a fact-finding, truth-determining, justice-producing device. No, the mandatory ADR advocates acknowledge that real trials are wonderful. It is just that they are too costly and time-consuming. My response: Hogwash!

Although it is my position that litigants should be entitled to their traditional 'day in court' even if it costs more than some ADR programs, still I do not concede that the immediate costs to the court, or the overall costs of dispute resolution, are reduced by annexing these ADR programs to our federal courts. Indeed, I believe that an honest cost-benefit analysis will reveal that courts that do not utilize such programs cost less to operate than those that do employ such programs. Nor do the courts which utilize such programs have a better record of prompt disposition of their civil dockets.

The role of evidence

With all due respect, it is not fair to describe ADR programs as only different in some negligible or unimportant degree from traditional trials in federal courts. They are clearly different in kind and in basic philosophy. In real trials, the objective is to arrive at the truth, vindicate rights, and to do justice. The evidence presented at a real trial is all-important. Any experienced trial judge will tell you that it is the proof and the evidence that determines the outcome of over 95 per cent of the cases and not the eloquence or histrionic talents of the lawyers. And the procedures, rules, and the evidentiary safeguards incident to true trials ensure a high degree of reliability with respect to the results obtained. Not so with ADRs. They operate in a different atmosphere: where fault, guilt or innocence, right or wrong are not central to the process; where one-tenth of a loaf is better than none; where the debating skills of attorneys – and not their real truth-revealing, fact-establishing trial skills – are glorified; where the evidence is de-emphasized; where every claim is assumed to have some value; where true justice is considered too expensive or an unattainable abstraction.

But Judge Broderick staunchly maintains on page 6 of his article: 'Arbitration cases are commenced and litigated in essentially the same manner as other civil cases except that the arbitration rules provide for a liberalized application of the rules of evidence.'

Again, he makes it sound like there is very little, if any, difference in his court's compulsory arbitration hearing and a real trial. But his stated exception swallows his major premise. I have made the point that while the evidence is all important in a real trial, evidence is de-emphasized in an arbitration hearing. This is not just argument. Note the following language from section H(5) of local rule 30 of the Western District of Missouri:

> 5 . . . The presentation of testimony shall be kept to a minimum. Each party's presentation to the arbitrators should be primarily through the statements and arguments of counsel.

In similar vein, the 1989 New Jersey Guidelines state:

> In a general sense, the court envisions this presentation process to be somewhat similar to a combination of opening and closing arguments augmented by live testimony where necessary to aid the arbitrators' fact-finding function.

Let's hear it for the New Jersey judges. At least they do not call this a trial. They call it a 'presentation process'!

The arbitration hearing is conducted before non-judicial officers. The right of cross-examination is gone, although some arbitrators, in the exercise of administrative grace, may permit it on a limited basis. The whole objective is to dramatically shorten the proceedings. Indeed, the guidelines for participation in the program in the Western District of Missouri candidly state:

> An arbitration hearing is an opportunity to present informally the essence of a dispute. An arbitration hearing should not be conducted like a formal trial. Each party's presentation should not last more than 2 hours.

And going on:

> A party's presentation should be a combination of opening statement and closing argument supplemented by evidence. A party is not required to call any witnesses. However, a party may call witnesses, but the time allotted to that party should not be enlarged solely because witnesses were present.

Does that not give a flavor of the thing? If judges permitted trials before them to be so conducted, they would not only be summarily reversed, but they would probably be considered proper candidates for impeachment.

Coerced settlement

Let us face the truth: from the court's point of view, coerced settlement is the primary objective of these compulsory ADRs, despite protests to the contrary. The many rules requiring parties or persons with settlement authority to be present at these ADR sessions should make this obvious – particularly when one realizes that in many cases the presence of such persons would not be required at the actual trial before a judge or a jury.

But Judge Broderick insists that his program 'was not designed primarily as a settlement program . . .' I appreciate his use of the word 'primarily.' But frankly, I believe that the good judge is engaged in post hoc rationalization. Remember, these programs are constantly being sold to federal judges on the ground that they take cases off our trial dockets.

But most revealing of the purpose of this program is Judge Broderick's explanation of the reasons for the Eastern District of Pennsylvania originally setting the maximum dollar limit at $75,000. Remember that, under this earlier program, if you were legitimately seeking more than $75,000, you could not be forced into the arbitration program. With few exceptions, you were forced into the program if you sought less than $75,000. How did they arrive at that figure? Let me quote Judge Broderick:

> It was generally agreed that there should be some limitation on the amount in controversy. It was conceded that in cases where money damages only are being sought, the amount in controversy should be limited to *an amount which might make it economically unfeasible for litigants to demand a trial de novo. The Savings* to the litigants as well as to the courts *is not realized whenever the amount in controversy encourages the losing party to demand a trial de novo.* It was therefore determined to limit the amount in controversy to $75,000 *in order to avoid the possibility of making the arbitration program just one more layer of litigation.*

With apology, I must characterize that statement as quite cynical. Where 'big money' is involved, you are entitled to your traditional day in court unencumbered by this costly arbitration diversion. But if you have a relatively small claim, no. How do we draw the line? According to Judge Broderick, simply by choosing a figure that will make it 'economically unfeasible' for the party who is dissatisfied with the arbitrators' decision, to then demand a trial *de novo*. Does that not create equal protection problems? This program is designed to discourage parties, who are unsuccessful in the arbitration process, from seeking vindication and justice in a real trial. After all, by that time, they will have already paid, or become liable for, the expenses and legal fees incident to the arbitration hearing. If they go forward they have to pay their lawyer again for his trial time and the expenses of the trial *de novo*. And if they do not get a more favorable result at that trial than they did at the arbitration, they must pay the fees of the arbitrators for conducting an arbitration hearing they did not want in the first place. And if a party tries to save fees and expenses at the arbitration hearing by skimping on the case, he or she will be exposed to sanctions on the ground that that party did not 'participate in the arbitration process in a meaningful manner.' (See Local Rule 8(5)(c).) So we have a real Catch-22 situation. The rule requires you to utilize what may well be very limited resources at the arbitration hearing. This in turn will, as stated by Judge Broderick, discourage you from demanding a trial *de novo* if you lose at arbitration.

So what do we have here? We are forcefully relegating a class of litigants – not, I submit, chosen on any rational basis – to procedures that do not meet minimal constitutional standards for due process; that do not meet minimal traditional judicial standards for fairness; that result in a type of discovery that is not permitted by current discovery rules; that, in turn, may fatally prejudice that party's ability to effectively present his or her case at any subsequent trial *de novo*; and that may consume the limited resources of poorer parties to the great advantage of their more affluent opponents. I ask you, do we want this in our federal courts?

But, despite these designed-in disincentives, demands for *de novo*, that is real, trials are made in more than 60 per cent of the cases that actually go through arbitration in these 10 mandatory programs. Think of it!

On what basis can we say that lawyers and their clients are not being reasonable because they fail to settle more of their cases when we know that, without any of these programs over 90 per cent of the cases are disposed of before trial. Yes, many are disposed of by motions to dismiss or motions for summary judgment, but the bulk are disposed of by settlement – worked out voluntarily between the parties and their attorneys. Is not the system working quite well if we only have to try 7 to 10 per cent of our civil cases?

I disagree with the sentiment expressed by many who apparently believe that every trial represents a failure of the system. I believe many cases should be tried. Principle should be vindicated; rights established; extortion resisted; and justice – pure justice – done at least occasionally.

Extract 8:21

R Posner: 'The Summary Trial and Other Alternative Methods of Dispute Resolution: Some Cautionary Observations' (1986) 53 *University of Chicago Law Review* 366, pp 387–389

My analytic framework can be applied to other alternatives to the conventional trial besides summary jury trials, and I want to mention two. One is 'court-annexed arbitration,' which means forcing the parties to present their case to a private lawyer-arbitrator (sometimes a panel of arbitrators) before they can go to trial. As with the summary jury trial, the arbitrator's decision is not binding; the hope is that it will encourage settlement.

This device avoids the problems of using the jury as a settlement aid. Since arbitrators are less representative of jurors than summary jurors are, it might seem obvious that arbitrators' decisions would produce less information about likely outcomes at trial, and hence fewer settlements, than a summary jury trial would do. But depending on the variance among juries, an arbitrator who is an experienced trial lawyer may render a decision more representative of what the average jury would come up with than the decision of any single jury. And of course the device is usable in bench as well as jury trials, as the summary jury trial is not.

The biggest objections to court-annexed arbitration involve expense and legality. The expense is apt to be greater than that of the summary jury trial for two reasons. First, although arbitration is less expensive than an ordinary federal trial, it is more expensive than the average settlement negotiation. It involves a trial, albeit to an arbitrator rather than a judge or jury. This means that witnesses must be prepared and examined and that lawyers must spend time in court, for which they usually charge higher fees than for out-of-court work. The summary jury trial is also a sort of trial, but no witnesses actually testify; and it is a last-ditch effort to settle a case that seems bound for trial, rather than a required step in every case. Court-annexed arbitration is ordered in every case that meets certain requirements as to amount in controversy, even through most of those cases would have been settled without court-annexed arbitration.

The cost savings from court-annexed arbitration are speculative. An example will show how the device could actually increase the cost of resolving legal disputes – and do so even if it is much cheaper than trial and even if all cases subjected to it settle after the arbitrator's decision. Suppose that without court-annexed arbitration 90 out of 100 cases filed would settle, at an average settlement cost of $1,000 (not the amount of the settlement, but the expense of effecting settlement), and the other 10 would go to trial, at an average cost of $25,000. With court-annexed arbitration, all settle, but at an average cost (the cost of the arbitration) of $5,000. The total litigation and settlement costs without court-annexed arbitration are $340,000, while the total costs with it (all settlement costs) are $500,000. If 5 percent of the arbitrated cases are tried, which would be half the litigation rate without court-annexed arbitration, the total costs of court-annexed arbitration in my example rise from $500,000 to $625,000, which is almost twice the cost without the device. This comparison is somewhat unfair because it ignores the cases that settle before the arbitration hearing; but even if most do, the total costs of dispute resolution may not be lower with court-annexed arbitration. If, for example, 60 percent of the cases settle before the arbitration hearing (at a settlement cost of $1,000 per case), 35 percent are settled after the hearing, and 5 percent are tried, the total costs will be $385,000, which again exceeds (though by a smaller margin) the total costs without court-annexed arbitration ($340,000).

The problem of legality is twofold. First, if a party to court-annexed arbitration refuses to settle after arbitration, and then does worse at trial, he must pay the arbitrator's fee, which will usually be several hundred dollars. In effect this is a fee for demanding a trial. But Congress has set no such fee.

Second, court-annexed arbitration effectively increases the statutory minimum amount in controversy. Such arbitration usually is compulsory only for claims that do not exceed a specified monetary value, most commonly $100,000. The thinking behind the limit is that with modest claims the parties will not think it worthwhile to incur the costs of two procedures – the arbitration, and then the trial – while with larger claims the parties are unlikely to accept the arbitration as binding. Apparently the combination of having to pay the arbitrator's fee if you reject his award and of having to pay the usual trial expenses for both the arbitration and the trial is a potent disincentive to insisting on a trial of a modest claim in districts that have court-annexed arbitration.

This seems an indirect method of increasing the minimum amount in controversy requirement in the federal courts from zero for virtually all federal claims, and from $10,000 for claims founded on diversity, to wherever the cut-off point for court-annexed arbitration is fixed. This cuts against the grain of Congress's decision, wise or not, to make federal courts accessible to smaller claims.

Extract 8:22

S B Goldberg, F E A Sander and N H Rodgers (eds) *Dispute Resolution: Negotiation, Mediation and Other Processes*, 2nd edn (1992) Little, Brown & Co, Boston, Toronto and London, pp 225–226

> This is essentially adjudication (often in the context of arbitration) with the limits of recovery and loss bounded by agreement of the parties. For example, in a personal injury case in which the plaintiff's demand is for $500,000, the parties may agree in advance of trial that if the jury returns a verdict for the defendant on the issue of liability, the defendant will nonetheless pay the plaintiff a predetermined amount, say $100,000. If the jury's verdict on liability is for the plaintiff, the defendant pays a higher fixed sum, say $300,000. The jury never reaches the issue of damages. The parties retain their rights to appeal on liability issues, but, obviously, waive their appeal rights as to damages.
>
> The principal advantage of arbitration or adjudication under a high-low agreement is that it reduces the risk to both sides by converting a 'win-lose' situation into a 'partial win-partial lose' situation. The plaintiff is protected against the risk of no return; the defendant is protected against the risk of a staggering liability. A second advantage is that it minimizes the time spent on trying and preparing to try damages. Other advantages include the elimination of appeals based on damages, elimination of compromise verdicts, and the establishment of a cooperative atmosphere that may of itself lead to settlement.
>
> In a variation of this approach the damage issue is also tried, but the parties agree beforehand that if the award falls outside the high-low brackets to which they have agreed, the award will be adjusted to the high or low point. If the award is within the brackets, damages are set at that figure. The disadvantage of this approach is that the parties must try the damage issue. The advantage is that it may be easier to get agreement on the high/low figures because they are not quite as crucial: they determine only the parameters, not necessarily the amount of damages. (Some doubt has been cast on the enforceability of agreements to limit damages by a district court's decision declining to overturn an arbitrator's award that was more than double the limit agreed to by the parties. *St. Luke's Hospital v SMS Computer Systems*, US Dist Ct, ED Mich 87-CV-10198-BC.)

Extract 8:23

A S Kim: 'Rent-a-Judge and the Cost of Selling Justice' (1994) 44 *Duke Law Journal* 166, pp 166–167, 189–195, 199

> Private judging – or 'rent-a-judging' – has expanded over the past decade in California into a multimillion-dollar industry. Unlike arbitrators or mediators, rent-a-judges are officially part of the state court system, and their judgments have the same effect as judgments of any other state court. Superficially, a rent-a-judge differs from his public court colleagues in only one respect: the source of his paycheck.
>
> From its beginning, rent-a-judging has prompted worries about the propriety of privatized justice. Despite its touted efficiency, the rent-a-judge system is marred by constitutional and policy concerns. Opponents have especially decried the creation of a two-tiered system of justice – one for the wealthy and one for the poor. Rent-a-judge

justice, though speedy, is also quite expensive. The most popular, and presumably the best, rent-a-judges command $5,000 a day. Consequently, only the wealthiest litigants can afford a rent-a-judge – a result that is not only inequitable but quite possibly unconstitutional under California law.

The rent-a-judge system also has raised a number of practical considerations. Critics have condemned the secrecy of rent-a-judge proceedings and the lack of disclosure requirements or other regulations to govern the behavior of rent-a-judge and ensure their impartiality. Moreover, the California courts have yet to unravel the numerous procedural implications of rent-a-judge practice. For example, the preclusive effect of a rent-a-judge's judgment still is untested, as is its authority as precedent. Also unclear is the scope of a rent-a-judge's powers. Despite some limitations, rent-a-judges appear to have broad powers, and the line between private and public judges seems fuzzy at best. Particularly disturbing is the apparent power of rent-a-judges to call juries. . . . In some ways, the rent-a-judge system seems to be an ideal hybrid of public and private justice. It offers the speed, efficiency, and convenience of arbitration and mediation along with an enforceable, appealable state court judgment. Although individual litigants have undoubtedly benefitted from rent-a-judges, the public interest has not. Unanswered are many troubling questions about the permissible scope of a rent-a-judge's authority and the role rent-a-judges should play in the state judicial system. Also troubling are the effects that rent-a-judges have on the public courts and their potential for eroding the courts' authority. Ultimately, as this Part argues, the rent-a-judge system puts too much public power into private hands.

A. Rent-a-Judges and the Authority of the Courts

The primary purpose of a judicial system, whether public or private, is to settle disputes. The byproduct of that function is rulemaking. In private justice, rulemaking is of little concern; litigants pay arbitrators and mediators to resolve only the dispute at hand. Moreover, citizens do not look to arbitrators and mediators to formulate rules for society. In the public courts, however, rulemaking takes on far greater importance. Public courts play a pivotal role in society: 'Their job is not to maximize the ends of private parties, nor simply to secure the peace, but to explicate and give force to the values embodied in authoritative texts such as the Constitution and statutes: to interpret those values and to bring reality into accord with them.' The public courts, when they speak, speak not only for the government but for society. Thus, their decisions carry far greater social weight than the decisions of private tribunals.

The rent-a-judge system, however, blurs and devalues this distinction between public and private tribunals. Although they are nominally members of the state judiciary, rent-a-judges are chosen by the litigants, and they offer individualized, private justice, much like arbitrators and mediators. Consequently, their decisions carry less force and legitimacy in the eyes of the public than those of wholly public courts. Much of the power of the public courts to speak for society comes from their public accountability:

> Adjudication uses public resources, and employs not strangers chosen by the parties but public officials chosen by a process in which the public participates. These officials, like members of the legislative and executive branches, possess a power that has been defined and conferred by public law, not by private agreement.

Rent-a-judges, however, are chosen by private agreement, and the market is the only external check upon their behavior. The system itself imposes no quality control over the judges; consent of the litigants is the only requirement for the appointment of a rent-a-judge. California's general reference statutes state no qualifications that rent-a-judges must meet. Unlike their public court counterparts, rent-a-judges do not pass through the screening process of public election or governmental appointment. Moreover, there is no disciplining body for rent-a-judges, and unlike other public court judges, rent-a-judges apparently cannot be impeached or recalled. Thus, despite their public role, rent-a-judges are not publicly accountable. Although rent-a-judges nominally enjoy the authority of the state, this authority is undermined by the lack of a public mandate. Because rent-a-judges do not have the same institutional backing as their public court brethren, their judgments lack the public weight and authority of other state court rulings.

The element of choice also diminishes the authority of rent-a-judge judgments. The rent-a-judge system creates a buyer's market that the litigants control, and the judges must tailor their reputations and their decisionmaking to attract customers. As noted above, some California rent-a-judges have even toned down their personalities to make themselves more marketable. The rent-a-judge system upends the usual balance of power between judges and litigants. Moreover, the power of choice vested in litigants diminishes the threat of state authority, which is a chief source of power for the courts: 'Among other things, government sanction implies the direct threat of compulsion by the state [and gives judgments] a degree of clarity and forcefulness.' The ability to choose a judge, however, enables litigants to shape the ultimate judgment. And where the ultimate goal is customer satisfaction, rent-a-judges are also likely to de-emphasize their coercive powers as agents of the state. Thus by empowering litigants, the rent-a-judge system weakens the judiciary.

B. Rent-a-judges and the Rule of Law

As noted above, rulemaking is a crucial function of the public courts. It is a function, however, that rent-a-judges cannot adequately perform. A rent-a-judge's public-private split personality is again the source of problems. As members of the public court system, rent-a-judges would best serve society by pronouncing broad rules of wide applicability. As privately hired dispute resolution experts, however, rent-a-judges are more likely to decide cases on very narrow grounds. As Judge Posner and Professor Landes note,

> [A] system of voluntary adjudication [such as rent-a-judge] is strongly biased against the creation of precise rules of any sort. Any rule that clearly indicates how a judge is likely to decide a case will assure that no disputes subject to the rule are submitted to that judge since one party will know that it will lose. Judges will tend to promulgate vague standards which give each party to a dispute a fighting chance.

Thus, when shopping for a judge, litigants look for someone who is likely both to rule in their favor and to meet the approval of the opposing party. The ultimate choice will be a judge with a reputation for being impartial, though 'impartial' is more likely to mean 'accommodating.' Rent-a-judges must avoid creating a coherent set of precedents; predictability could destroy a rent-a-judge's appeal to potential customers. In fact, the market provides great incentive for rent-a-judges to be deliberately inconsistent in their rulings. This behavior by rent-a-judges is destructive in several ways. The body of law thus created is nothing more than a confusing tangle of narrow and contradictory rules, many of which have little relevance to anyone beyond the immediate litigants. Even if the rules formulated by rent-a-judges are broad enough to be useful to society at large, they are not always likely to reflect the interests of the public. After all, the public is not a paying customer.

C. Private Judges and the Public Interest

A rent-a-judge's dual, public-private nature also raises questions about the permissible depth and breadth of a rent-a-judge's decisionmaking authority. Rent-a-judges are chosen by private parties and are not accountable to the public. It is therefore troubling that they should have the authority to impose their rulings upon the whole of society. Rent-a-judges could conceivably address issues involving important civil liberties, such as gun control, school prayer, or abortion. California statutes allow rent-a-judges to hear any dispute if the parties consent. Moreover, rent-a-judge judgments are treated exactly the same as other state court judgments and thus presumably have the same effects of collateral estoppel and res judicata.

The public interest, however, demands limits on the reach of rent-a-judge rulings. There are two possible approaches to determining the types of cases suitable for rent-a-judge resolution. One approach would be to categorize cases according to the type of issue at stake; under this approach, disputes over 'public law' or 'public values,' for example, should be reserved for the public courts. Such cases would include not only those involving constitutional questions or government regulation, but also those addressing 'issues of great public concern,' such as the development of legal standards in products liability cases. Because consent of the litigants is a fundamental element of the rent-a-judge system, the second approach would focus on the number of people uninvolved in the suit who are likely to be affected by a rent-a-judge judgment. Thus, rent-a-judges would be less suited to render judgments that would otherwise have broad preclusive effects on other potential litigants. Mass tort cases would be an example. The two approaches would overlap in some areas; a suit to enjoin discriminatory practices at a factory, for example, would both involve constitutional issues and affect a large number of people uninvolved in the suit. Under either of the preceding approaches, the following types of cases would be particularly suitable for resolution by a rent-a-judge:

- *Family disputes* – Divorces are especially suitable rent-a-judge cases. Few parties are involved, and the issues at stake are very rarely of public significance.
- *Torts* – Garden-variety, single-plaintiff cases that require only the application of existing standards are most appropriate for rent-a-judges to hear. In these cases, the rent-a-judge's function would be mostly factfinding. As discussed above, however, mass tort and products liability cases may be less suited for rent-a-judge courts.
- *Complex commercial litigation* – Although large sums of money are usually at stake, these cases also involve few interests, and the issues are rarely of significant public importance. Rent-a-judges may even be better suited than public court judges to hear these cases if they have expertise in a particular area.

A number of other types of cases, however, are inappropriate for resolution by rent-a-judges. Many of these have been mentioned above, such as cases involving constitutional questions or government regulation. Agency civil enforcement actions are another example of cases that should stay out of rent-a-judge courts.

Categorizing cases for rent-a-judge resolution is simple in the abstract. But in real life, pure public law cases are harder to spot. Drafting suitable guidelines for the proper diversion of cases to rent-a-judges would be an extremely difficult task. Enforcement of such guidelines would be even more difficult and could create a whole new area of time-consuming and wasteful litigation. The concerns discussed above cast serious doubt on the utility of rent-a-judges in the public court system. Essentially, the public and private roles of a rent-a-judge cannot be reconciled. . . .

The rent-a-judge system is an unconstitutional, elitist institution that unfairly grants privileges to the wealthy. Moreover, it is the product of a misguided union of the public and private sectors. In private justice, the market is the driving force, and the product is narrow and specialized. In the public courts, broader interests prevail, and the rulings of the public courts govern not only the individual litigants but society at large. The rent-a-judge system is nominally a part of the public courts, but it is essentially market-driven. Rent-a-judging is the product of a fundamental clash in goals and values, and as such, it cannot and should not survive as a meaningful part of the justice system.

G: The Ombudsperson

The term 'ombudsman' (for which the now preferred terms are 'ombuds' or 'ombudsperson') is the appellation ordinarily used to characterise an official appointed by government to receive and examine complaints made by citizens against the administration. The work of the ombudsperson involves umpiring – making judgments about claimed abuses of public administrative conduct – but it also encompasses a concern to enhance standards of government and may involve extensive use of negotiation with the parties in dispute and mediation. The French institution of 'Médiateur' referred to in Chapter One conveys the essentially hybrid nature of the ombudsperson's approach to dispute resolution, indicating something of a concern to promote conciliation as well as to deal with maladministration.

In the common law world the ombudsperson has been in effect a transplant from the civilian tradition, as the following extract (Extract 8:24) from a seminal article by Paul Verkuil indicates. During the past three decades, the ombudsperson has been established in a wide variety of jurisdictions, as Extract 8:25 from Wiegand illustrates. The perceived effectiveness of the ombudsperson has in the United Kingdom encouraged its use in the private as well as the public sectors. The influence of the United States' experience has also been important in this regard, for in that country the idea of the ombudsperson has primarily been applied as part of the management of large organisations, both public and private. The ombudsperson serves as a neutral member of the organisation, reporting directly to the most senior executive and ordinarily positioned outside the established hierarchy of management. The ombudsperson attempts through such processes as counselling, mediation, fact-finding and making recommendations to overcome disputes in the workplace (Singer, 1991: 102). In the United Kingdom, however, the ombudsperson in the private sector has come to serve primarily as an institution for investigating and dealing with complaints made by members of the public against individuals or bodies in particular areas of commercial and professional activity – insurance, banking, conveyancing, lawyers, the media, and so on (Extract 8:26).

The evolution of the role of the ombudsperson over the past few decades has been accompanied by sometimes fairly serious criticism of the manner in which the idea of the ombudsperson is being institutionalised. Some of the problems that have been highlighted, as well as arguments that can still be made in favour of the ombudsperson at least in its classical form, are considered in the following extract by Wiegand (Extract 8:27).

Extract 8:24

P R Verkuil: 'The Ombudsman and the Limits of the Adversary System' (1975) 75 *Columbia Law Review* 845, pp 847, 851–856

> . . . the three essential features of the classical definition should be kept in mind:
>
> (1) The Ombudsman is an independent and non-partisan officer of the legislature, usually provided for in the constitution, who supervises the administration;
> (2) He deals with specific complaints from the public against administrative injustice and maladministration; and
> (3) He has the power to investigate, criticize and publicize, but not to reverse, administration action. . . .
>
> In many ways the principles underlying the ombudsman model are at war with those underlying the adversary system. The ombudsman reconciles, reinforces and legitimates community or central decisionmaking; the adversary system polarizes issues, and fosters individualism and passive decisionmaking. The ombudsman, in other words, is at home in the inquisitorial system, where control in the decisionmaker is the central characteristic. It is therefore understandable that the ombudsman has developed first and most completely in countries receptive to the inquisitorial model. This does not mean that a common law, adversary model heritage is necessarily incompatible with the ombudsman idea; certainly the status of ombudsman in America, as just reviewed, would argue the contrary. Rather, this heritage suggests that efforts to introduce the ombudsman into common law countries must reconcile the different values reflected by the adversary model with the need for, and nature of, the ombudsman's powers.
>
> The experience thus far with the British Parliamentary Commissioner and the Administrative Conference of the United States reflects some modifications upon the classical ombudsman system – namely, a scope of inquiry restricted to procedural matters and limited access to the complaining public – which ameliorate the natural repugnance between this procedural innovation and the underlying adversary tradition. Britons and Americans share a heritage which is generally suspicious of official authority; reliance upon privately initiated judicial investigations is seen as a safeguard against abuses of power. What for common law countries is at best a redundant layer

of bureaucracy, and at worst an intrusive tampering with cherished modes of conflict resolution, is for countries accustomed to the inquisitorial model an organic component, providing a necessary forum for dispute resolution. Because of the control the central decisionmaker has over the discovery and presentation of facts in inquisitorial countries, there is not the 'day in court' or right of confrontation that is seen as a basic protection of adversarial decisionmaking in common law countries. This power in the inquisitorial decisionmaker quite naturally suggests the need for system checks such as the ombudsman that are, to some extent, unnecessary in the adversary form of decisionmaking.

Although further advancement of the ombudsman idea in America does not require a full-scale reversal of the established tradition of adversary procedures and judicial oversight of administrative action, as a practical matter, the future of the classical ombudsman in America does rest largely upon a willingness to limit the scope of the adversary model in public decisionmaking. A line must be drawn beyond which the adversary model will cease to be regarded as the sole means of measuring the fairness of administrative procedures; and such line-drawing requires at least a two-pronged inquiry. First, a delineation is needed of the interests at stake in public property decisionmaking as opposed to those involved in private property dispute resolution. Second, an evaluation must be made of the unique advantages the ombudsman, or any other non-adversary model, might offer in the resolution of public property decisionmaking problems.

The adversary model is culturally as much a part of our society as our liberal political and economic heritage itself. When it comes to the resolution of traditional private property disputes, adversariness is axiomatic, fulfilling the pluralistic values of individual freedom and initiative reflected in our nineteenth century liberal traditions. In any society, the legal system can be expected to complement the larger values of society at large. In our system of private property, where competition is the most esteemed social mechanism, the adversary legal system's commitment to zealous, client-centered representation manifests the spirit of competition in the legal order. Given this nexus between the legal order and our society's commitment to private property values, any modification of the adversary system has profound implications. But if the focus is shifted from private property disputes to the concerns which underlie the growth of public property – the vast network of privileges, benefits and rights that is the business of modern government – a comparable shift in appropriate procedural systems does not pose such a formidable threat to cherished conceptions.

Our abiding belief in the virtues of the adversary model as a means of resolving private property disputes need not transcend into the public property arena. Dispute resolution in the public sector involves the advancement of quite different goals. There is little reason to assume that the adversary model, anchored as it is in matters of procedural and commutative justice, should be the mechanism most compatible with the advancement of the goals of substantive and distributive justice implicit in the management of public resources. Indeed, there is reason to question whether a procedural system inspired by the private property, free enterprise and non-interventionist values of Adam Smith should be utilized to adjudicate 'property' rights that emerge from the managed economy inspired by John Maynard Keynes. The teachings of the adversary system are those of classical liberalism; the goals of contemporary liberalism may require a new conceptual scheme.

The premise here is that differing societal goals call forth a corresponding shift in procedural goals. As a result procedures which are designed to ensure mass justice in the welfare state must of necessity focus on system quality as well as individual decision quality. A tension exists between optimal efficiency for the individual – the touchstone of the adversary model – and optimal system efficiency. Efficiency in the latter sense looks to the way the procedural mechanism allocates societal resources in accordance with societal goals. When the measuring criterion is system goal advancement, adversary procedures are usually too 'expensive.' Indeed, imposing the adversary model on the public decisionmaking process is likely to be self-defeating; it would 'eat up a large part of the available pool of benefits' and thereby undermine the goals of the system itself. The counterproductive consequences of adversariness in the public property context have spawned the pursuit for procedures better designed to implement social programs. These procedures include the use of management techniques which emphasize quality control, and, as recommended by the Administrative Conference, 'positive caseload management' in government benefit and compensation programs.

Extract 8:25

S A Wiegand: 'A Just and Lasting Peace: Supplanting Mediation with the Ombuds Model' (1996) 12 *Ohio State Journal on Dispute Resolution* 1, pp 100–102

Since Denmark's adoption of the ombuds office in 1955, countries all over the world have followed the lead of the three Scandinavian countries which first adopted this mechanism. In 1962, Norway and New Zealand established national ombuds offices, followed by Australia (one state), Austria, Canada (seven provinces), Fiji, France, Ghana, Guyana, Hong Kong, Ireland, Italy, Japan, Mauritius, Netherlands, Nigeria, Pakistan, the Philippines, Portugal, Spain, United Kingdom and others. In some countries, ombuds offices have jurisdiction only in large cities or only over certain governmental agencies. For example, in 1957 West Germany established an ombuds office for its armed forces. In Israel, a 'state comptroller' eventually adopted an ombuds role, supplementing that country's appointment of a military ombudsman and Jerusalem's city ombudsman. In Switzerland, Zurich established an ombuds office in 1969. By 1973, twenty-one countries had established ombuds offices or variations on the office. The concept also reached the United States and began to make its way into new and unforeseen areas such as nongovernmental offices and universities. The rapid and widespread growth in ombuds offices from the 1950s until the 1980s prompted some observers to note that this period represented a 'surge of ombudsmania.'

As a result of its rapid growth, the ombuds office necessarily took on different characteristics, depending upon the needs and circumstances of the place and time. As developed in Sweden, the office is legislative rather than executive. All political parties must agree on the appointment of a particular ombudsperson, who then holds the office for four years but may serve additional four-year terms. The ombudsperson reports to the legislature. However, she is an impartial investigator and is politically independent, even from the legislature, and legislators are forbidden from intervening in the ombudsperson's investigations. The office is constitutionally established. Although the ombudsperson has no power to reverse or change an official act, she has tremendous influence in Sweden by virtue of her 'objectivity, competence, superior knowledge and prestige.' The ombudsperson can begin an investigation based on citizen complaint or can act on her own initiative. In either event, the results of the investigation can be made known both to the legislature and to the press. The ombudsperson has authority to prosecute officials for illegal acts, although this power is rarely exercised.

Many citizen complaints in Sweden are resolved in this manner, including complaints from prison inmates or patients in mental hospitals. The process begins when the ombudsperson receives a letter from a complainant; in some cases, however, the ombudsperson can begin an investigation based solely upon information received from other sources, such as a story in the media. The ombuds office might find that the complaint has no merit and dismiss it. But if the complaint has merit, the ombuds office can recommend action.

When this basic process is transferred to other countries, it necessarily undergoes modification because of the differing legal systems and cultures. In the United Kingdom, a number of incidents necessitated the creation of an ombuds office, but scholars cite one incident in particular: the Crichel Down affair. This incident involved the taking of a citizen's land for military use with the proviso that, after the military use had ended, the owner would have an opportunity to regain his land. When the land was released, however, the owner was not given the promised opportunity. There were allegations of misbehavior by civil servants, and a minister eventually resigned. No laws had been broken, yet the result seemed unjust and sparked widespread outrage. The incident demonstrated procedural inadequacy and contributed significantly to the creation of the ombuds office.

Unlike the Scandinavian model, in the United Kingdom the governmental ombuds office can act only in response to an individual's complaint. Citizens cannot directly gain access to the ombuds office but must instead contact a member of Parliament. But the essential components have remained remarkably similar to the first ombuds office established in Sweden in the nineteenth century.

Extract 8:26

C Harlow and R Rawlings: *Law and Administration*, 2nd edn (1997) Butterworths, London, pp 401–404

By the 1970s, administrative lawyers had become accustomed to three types of alternative to trial-type procedure. Tribunals, accepted as 'machinery for adjudication', generally dealt with small claims but had increasingly been judicialised. Inquiries, accepted as an 'advanced and sophisticated', specifically English contribution to administrative law and practice, had also suffered increasing judicialisation, though their hybrid character was theoretically admitted. With the advent of the Ombudsmen, the net had widened to trawl 'grievances' or 'complaints' as well as disputes. Describing as 'its most surprising feature' the absence of legal staff in the PCA's office, Schwartz and Wade conceded in 1972 that the PCA dealt with 'large numbers of substantial cases with great thoroughness and fairness. The complaint that he deals only with trivialities is unjustified'. Yet they were unwilling to allocate the senior of the new arrivals more than a place on the outskirts of administrative law:

> The British public has habitually made much use of the traditional channel of complaint through members of Parliament . . . But as the territory of administration expanded, and as Parliament's power weakened relatively to the government, the old methods became inadequate . . .

Since he has no substantive legal powers, the Parliamentary Commissioner stands outside the field of administrative law. But he is closely connected with it, and his work will alter the aspect of many of its problems.

[Administrative lawyers] should also welcome him as an important ally in the campaign for administrative justice, who will work alongside an independent judiciary and legal profession and supplement the role of law with the rule of administrative good sense and even of generosity.

The angle of approach was changing marginally as lawyers began to show some interest in statutory complaints procedures but the more visible parts of this machinery were relatively formal. Authors commonly 'descended' as far as tribunals, inquiries and Ombudsmen, expensive, often time-consuming machinery which was then christened 'informal'. To put this differently, if the core concept of the Access-to-Justice movement is the idea of 'unmet need', with a consequential emphasis on the extension of legal services to new clients and new types of dispute, then administrative tribunals as 'court substitutes', debates over tribunal representation or legal aid, fit the Access-to-Justice model. The advent of the Ombudsman, with investigatorial powers and documentary procedures, was a step in the direction of ADR but acceptance of Ombudsmen, Rawlings has argued, did not demand a great change in the traditional top-down, adjudicative perspective.

A 'top-down' analysis of the complaints problem might be that adjudicatory and complaints systems easily become overloaded. The legal process contains its own filters in the shape of cost and problems of access (though courts continue to suffer problems of delay and overload). The response is to seek less expensive machinery, typically a tribunal but perhaps an administrative process. Thus, the Criminal Injuries Compensation Board whose operation is described in Chapter 18 provides an alternative to personal injury litigation. Seen as alternatives to the legal process, the sole rationale of such procedures is to process 'small claims' quickly, efficiently and cheaply.

Proponents of ADR, however, will read the landscape rather differently. Not only do Ombudsmen offer an informal and cost-free alternative to courts but they possess other advantages, including a freedom to arbitrate, negotiate and redress the balance of power between individuals and large institutions. These are not typical of adjudication. Other standard administrative law techniques can be fitted into an ADR framework. Thus, public inquiries can be treated as primarily a stage in a decision-making process.

The 'MP filter' which restricts access to the PCA serves a crucial function of keeping MPs and the House of Commons in touch with their constituents. A tribunal could not perform this additional function. Again, the provisions for conciliation – a classic form of ADR – in the police complaints system (below) are not conceived merely as a filter but operate simultaneously as a public relations exercise. The core commitment of ADR is to non-judicial fora for dispute-handling and the exploration of appropriate techniques.

Lawyers had been slow to notice that 'grievances' and 'complaints' do not necessarily demand the same treatment as fully-fledged 'disputes'. To rephrase this argument, it was easier for lawyers to accept the Ombudsman as an inquisitorial substitute in administrative justice than to view the MP, through whom all complaints to the PCA must still be referred, as machinery for redress of grievance. Thus one way to look on the MP's 'complaints service' is simply as a filter, responsible for maintaining the workload of the PCA within manageable proportions. From a different angle, the MP is a more effective complaints system. The 'large numbers' of PCA complaints to which Schwartz and Wade made reference actually amounted in the year they wrote (1972) to 573, of which 318 fell outside the PCA's jurisdiction; in contrast, MPs handle as many as 3 million constituency letters annually.

Commissioned to survey literature on 'administrative justice', Rawlings set out to redress the balance. He noted that, 'even within the parameters of institutionalised complaining most people seek informal redress'. Blaming the 'top-down' focus for ignorance of the 'unstructured, fluid and poorly publicised internal procedures which handle the great bulk of grievances ventilated by citizens against public bodies', he focused on 'bottom-up studies of how people usually behave when seeking redress'; on *non-judicial* means of dispute-resolution between citizens and administration; and on *informal* procedure for the redress of grievance.

Contributing a seminal study of the way in which government handles complaints, Birkinshaw also moved to a 'bottom-up' approach, inverting the traditional approach which begins with courts and works down. Instead, Birkinshaw set out to:

> establish what [departments] did in relation to grievances from the public affected by their administration, and to study what connections there were between these informal practices and the more formal procedures for complaint resolution or dispute settlement culiminating with Ombudsmen and Court of Law.

Radical as this may sound to lawyers, for political sociologists it does not go far enough. Criticising the predominantly legalistic approach to the study of grievances, a new research study saw even the new, 'bottom-up' research as flawed by legalism. In this narrow context, 'grievance is taken as a subcomponent of dispute and dispute behaviour and is given a legalistic and institutional interpretation'. This accounts for 'the tendency to present the notion of grievance in an adversarial setting which may not be entirely helpful in developing a sociology of complaints and complaining'. In other words, the terminology of 'dispute', 'grievance' and even 'complaint' remains relatively legalistic and adversarial. This is precisely the attitude of Mulcahy and Tritter, who describe complaint systems as low level grievance procedure, arguing that there is a need in a modern state to address the issue of how they are to be handled:

Complaints systems are important and should be recognised as needing as much attention as other systems for dispute resolution. The systems represent the mass end of a disputes market; systems which users may choose to access rather than the courts. In addition, we have an overloaded court system. Access to the courts and tribunals is severely limited by financial and procedural factors as well as those based on knowledge. As the expanding state produces more opportunities for injustice low level procedures represent a cheap, accessible and often more appropriate way to resolve disputes.

This is an argument which needs to be considered very carefully. Dispute-resolution is the lawyer's trade; it is central to his function. It is natural for lawyers to see law through the spectacles of dispute-resolution and in terms of their clients' interests. Everything else is peripheral. If this were the whole story, much of what we have seen in earlier chapters – structuring through rulemaking, or regulation – is peripheral to administrative law because it is not concerned with dispute-resolution. As an explanation of lawyers' attitudes to ADR, however, the statement is helpful. Lawyers' concern is essentially with the pathological. A system may broadly function well; a lawyer's concern is typically not with the system but to protect his client if it malfunctions. Adversarial procedure plus the right of access to a court are seen as the ultimate protections the law can bestow. This is why lawyers are so often guilty of 'squaring the circle' by re-instating them.

Extract 8:27

S A Weigand: 'A Just and Lasting Peace: Supplanting Mediation with the Ombuds Model' (1996) 12 *Ohio State Journal on Dispute Resolution* 1, pp 120–122

Much of the criticism of the ombuds office is directed not at the classical model but at the transformation that has taken place as the office has been adopted by various organizational entities. Some have proposed that these transformed models no longer warrant the title of 'ombudsmen,' but instead should be termed 'quasi-ombudsmen,' because, although they share 'many of the classical ombudsman's characteristics,' they are 'lacking at least one structural feature considered fundamental to the institution. Most commonly, their *independence* is compromised in some fashion.' For example, a number of scholars have noted the lack of autonomy in university ombuds offices. Obviously, if an ombudsperson serves at the whim of administrators, with little job security, he or she may be tempted to forego well-deserved criticism of administrative actions.

Another criticism of the ombuds office is that it is ineffective because its powers are limited. The classical model provides for investigations, recommendations and reports but not for direct enforcement. The office relies for enforcement upon its persuasive power, which results from its autonomy, expertise, neutrality and status. If any of these essential characteristics are lacking, the office's effectiveness may be diminished as well.

But criticism has also been leveled at the classical model. On the one hand, the ombuds office is an 'essential instrument in the modern administrative state to reduce the gap between the administrators and the administered . . . to protect basic human rights against possible infringements by the public bureaucracy. . . .' On the other hand, it serves as a 'public pacifier, a device to assuage public critics of government operations at minimal cost without having to change anything fundamental,' a 'conservative and counter-revolutionary force, designed to make the existing order more palatable. . . .' One scholar has suggested that by 1980 the ombuds idea had been 'oversold.' He described the ombuds model as

> [t]he fine tuner on the television. It can do nothing to change the channel. In fact, because the picture is made more bearable, we citizens may continue to stare dumbly at 'All-Star Championship Wrestling' rather than make an effort to search for more meaningful fare. Ombudsmen may serve as a means of habituating us to our usual perceptions of the world, thus allowing free citizens to forget that grand responsibility of exploring alternative realities.

He adds, 'Universities now hope that the [ombuds] office will stop students from occupying the dean's office.' Such criticism has been levelled at other informal dispute resolution processes as well.

Proponents of ombuds offices, and specifically the university ombuds office, have more faith in the institution, calling it a 'conscience on the campus' which 'helped to bind the wounds of a torn academic community' and which is capable of solving 'all of the problems which basically confront a social system.' One study of Canadian university ombuds offices revealed that many university ombudspersons 'are "agents for change," recommending modifications and improvements to rules, regulations, policies and practices which are unclear, inequitable or unfair.' They serve as 'advisors, counsellors and educators . . . informing people of their rights, explaining about existing channels for grievance and appeals, and assisting people in the use of those procedures.' They 'provide a cost-effective, quick and informal route to resolve problems and grievances' and can 'be used as a useful and powerful tool for generating debate on institutional issues and as a catalyst for institutional reform.'

Much of the confusion about the ombuds office lies in the varied ways in which it has been defined within various institutions. Clearly, the structure and goals of the organizational ombuds office of McDonald's differ from those of the legislatively established ombuds office of the state of Hawaii. The success or failure of any ombuds office depends, in part, upon how closely it follows the classical model, in what ways it differs and who holds the position of ombudsperson.

Given the differing perceptions of the effectiveness of this dispute resolution mechanism, what role should it play in ADR's future? How would it fit within a taxonomy of all dispute resolution mechanisms? Before addressing these questions, it is important to examine a closely-related dispute resolution mechanism which has currently come to occupy a substantial role in the ombuds concept – mediation. For it is because of mediation's deficiencies that the ombuds office presents itself as a viable, effective and important component of the ADR revolution.

The price paid for this method of resolution [that is, mediation] may not include disruption to the workplace, increased hostilities or loss of a good employee. Rather, the price paid may be measured in diminished justice. One party may never realize that he received less than a formal grievance might have provided, or that sexist or racist attitudes biased the result or that the other party was much more experienced in mediation techniques and thereby manipulated a more favourable result.

More importantly, even if this particular result was just, it may not have achieved an organizational benefit. In fact, the result reached may have satisfied both of the mediating parties at the expense of others in the organization. For example, a supervisor may agree that a female should have received a promotion or benefit and that the denial of the promotion or benefit was unfair. Together they agree that she will receive favourable treatment at the next opportunity. Because the agreement is confidential, other employees will never know that they are disadvantaged when competing for the promotion or benefit.

The organization suffers yet another disadvantage when mediation is the process of choice. Because of the secrecy surrounding the dispute itself, mediation addresses a particular dispute between two specific persons, but does little to attack an underlying problem which may be widespread. If the problem is a particular rule, policy or employee, others in the organization will eventually be affected and require intervention, either through mediation or through the formal grievance process.

In those situations when the formal grievance process offers too much and mediation too little, when the formal grievance process represents an overreaction and mediation an under reaction, the ombuds office may offer the optimal solution.

In fact The Ombudsman Association, formed in 1982 as the Corporate Ombudsman Association, has Standards of Practice that provide ombuds-persons 'advocate for fair processes and their fair administration', 'identify new problems' and 'provide support for responsible systems change'. The Ethical Principles for University and College Ombudspersons provide: 'An ombudsperson is guided by the following principles: objectivity, independence, accessibility, confidentiality and justice; justice is pre-eminent'.

The ombudsperson historically has not been seen as a muted, facilitating neutral sitting silently by until called into service by the parties' hostile silence, then coaxing the parties into continued communication until they reach an agreement. The office includes not only these characteristics, but also much more. Initially, classical ombudspersons listen to the complainant. Then they investigate. Then, if they find the complaint legitimate, they engage others in resolution of the dispute. They may require the production of records and witnesses from anyone in the organization, including the top administrators. Once they find the complaint legitimate, they assume their role as 'citizen defenders'.

In some respects the office resembles a grand jury or inspector general, intent on protecting positions of public trust from corruption, misconduct and mismanagement. The ombudsperson's concern is not to protect the organization's reputation; rather it is to help ensure that all of the organization's members conduct themselves in a manner neither arbitrary, dishonest, illegal, disruptive nor unethical. Unlike litigation, the role of an ombuds office is not viewed as a battle of adversaries. And unlike a mediator, ombudspersons can take sides, not in favor of the complainant and against the respondent, but in favour of honesty, integrity, legality and principle. Their client is integrity. Therefore, when the university female faculty member or teaching assistant mentioned above complains to the ombudsperson, his role will not end if he finds that the conduct does not rise to the level of a federal Title VII sexual harassment violation. If the ombudsperson finds instead that the conduct demonstrates merely poor judgment but that it nevertheless disrupts the workplace or interferes with the optimal productivity of co-workers, he can take action.

His actions may involve mediation between the two parties. They may involve individual counselling only with the respondent. They may involve conducting interviews with others or gaining access to university records. The ombudsperson may discover that the female complainant has a history of asserting unfounded allegations or that the male has had several other accusations levelled against him. The ombudsperson's role ideally is to determine whether a problem exists and to remedy it. He may end the investigation shortly after it begins, or he may launch a full-scale investigation and issue a report at its conclusion.

The ombuds office offers several advantages over the use of a narrow mediation focus. The ombudsperson will in many cases serve as a mediator. But if mediation fails or if the problem is likely to recur and involves a faulty policy or employee, the role of the ombudsperson differs from the role of mediator. Rather than serving as a communications facilitator, assisting the parties in reaching an agreement, the ombudsperson serves as an organizational watchdog, assisting not only these parties but also the efficient, effective functioning of the organization and all its parts, *including* these individuals. The ombudsperson is neither a silent neutral nor an advocate for the complainant.

> Wherever the [classical] ombudsman has functioned, he has been purely and plainly an advocate of sound administration, not an advocate of the position of the complainant . . . The ombudsman . . . is simply stationed at the margin, as it were, between the citizen and the official, and he must be concerned with seeing that justice is done to public servants as well as to the public whom they serve.

The ombudsperson can *seek out* problems before they are presented to him, at all levels of the organization, including the administrative level. The ombudsperson seeks to assure all organizational constituents that their psychological security and basic human rights have a defender. The ombudsperson focuses not so much upon past actions put upon the future of the organization and its constituents. 'Since . . . the primary purpose of the external critic [ombudsman] is to build for the future rather than to exhume the past, constructive suggestions about the avoidance of similar controversies may not be precluded by inability to reach a firm conclusion about guilt in the present instance'. The ombudsperson is accountable for his response to problems within the organization and must provide a rationale for any recommendations or actions taken. Unlike the silent, invisible mediator, the ombudsperson who follows the classical model may be proactive and public. The power of the ombuds office also differs from that of a mediator. Typically, mediation proponents

> deploy the discourse of interests and needs. They re-conceptualise the person from the carrier of rights to a subject with needs and problems, and in the process hope to move the legal field from a terrain of authoritative decision making where force is deployed to an arena of distributive bargaining and therapeutic negotiation.

Thus, mediation parties may be redefined as 'individuals with interpersonal or psychologically based problems' rather than as 'rights-bearing subjects'. An employee who suffers sexual or racial discrimination or harassment should not be expected to compromise with the harasser to reach an agreement in a mediation. The employee should be informed of her options, including her right to file a formal legal complaint; if she chooses not to do so or if the harassment or discrimination may be difficult to prove in a court of law, she should know that something will be done to stop the behaviour. An ombuds office can take action, investigating the wrongdoing and recommending action, either to the wrongdoer or, in exceptional circumstances, to the CEO, or to the organization's governing board. The ombudsperson should advise the complainant and the wrongdoer of the actions taken. The ombuds office's power to publicize wrongdoing, either within the organization or to the public at large (depending upon the type of organization and the nature of the problem) serves as the sword of Damocles, encouraging prompt action.

As with any dispute resolution mechanism that falls short of full-fledged adversarial litigation, the ombuds concept may not satisfy those who insist that litigation is the only legitimate means to resolve disputes. But it clearly addresses more of the critics' concerns than does mediation.

Rather than simply settling a dispute between two or more parties, the classical ombuds office seeks to achieve justice and integrity.

CHAPTER NINE

The Trajectory of Alternative
Dispute Resolution

A: Introduction

In earlier chapters we have charted the progress of what can only be described as a sea change in civil justice arrangements. Visible right across the common law world, there have been corresponding – if less fundamental – reverberations in civilian jurisdictions too. Over two short decades, what appeared in the 1980s as marginal novelties have become established features of the disputing scene. Alternative dispute resolution, with its objective in 'settlement' and its principal institutional realisation in 'mediation', is now a virtually unremarkable feature of disputing cultures almost anywhere we look.

Looking at these transformations in the most general terms, two preliminary points might be made about them. First, they appear to realise some of the almost apocalyptic forecasts of the early 1980s concerning 'the changing nature of state power in late capitalism' (Santos, 1987), the shifting balance between understandings of 'lifeworld' and 'system' (Habermas, 1981) and the increasing dominance of 'reflexive law' (Teubner, 1983). While civil justice has historically presented itself as being fundamentally about the availability of third-party determination, an important ideological shift away from that position has taken place. Here in England, for example, Lord Woolf in his seminal reports on *Access to Justice* (1995; 1996) characterised the primary objective of civil justice as the sponsorship of settlement, with judgment reduced to the solution of last resort. Introducing the cultural change he wanted to bring about, he spoke entirely unselfconsciously of settlement as justice, leaving behind foundational images formed in the classical world and subsequently sustained over millennia in the Judeo-Christian-Islamic traditions. Virtually without fuss or protest, the Civil Procedure Rules 1998 now realise this novel vision. So settlement is now civil justice, just as 'command' has retreated behind 'inducement'.

A second aspect of this transformation in the common law world can perhaps be best described as the replacement of an historic procedural anarchy by a new formalism. For many generations it had been up to the disputing parties which route to resolution they took, what mode of achieving an outcome they tried first. There was no need to negotiate directly or resort to the 'good offices' of a non-aligned third-party before issuing a writ; but that is now no longer the case. In England, for example, the proper procedural path is now marked with absolute clarity. The three primary processes around which this book is organised now represent a virtually obligatory sequence. Pre-Action Protocols warn potential litigants to attempt negotiation first on pain of potential costs penalties; once litigation is initiated, reference out to appropriate ADR procedures as a precondition to trial is built into the early stages of civil process (see Chapters Seven and Eight).

B: The Contemporary Scene

In looking at this still evolving scene in more detail, we have characterised contemporary transformations in the culture of disputing as representing three diverging but interconnected movements: the embryonic growth of new specialised groups – 'the new professionals in dispute resolution', 'the mediators'; responsive, defensive adjustments on the part of the legal profession; and the development of novel threshold procedures in front of the courts. Thus, as we have noted, a quite disparate complex of institutions and practices has come to share the fugitive label of 'ADR' (see pp 65–69 above).

The 'New Professionals'

The first of these three movements seems the most radical, involving as it does substantial steps towards the institutionalisation of 'mediation' and the consolidation of new professional groupings. But the emergent shapes are not entirely clear-cut. First, a significant number of mediators are also lawyers, many of them in concurrent professional practice. Second, while in some respects mediators appear in more or less direct competition with lawyers, they offer to help in an entirely different way – by supporting party negotiations, rather than competing with lawyers in offering advisory and representative services.

This points to a key feature of contemporary change – the extent to which party negotiations are achieving greater prominence and becoming subject to the attention of supporting professionals. This shift raises difficult questions:

- First, what (if any) limitation would we want to see on the development of a culture in which voluntary party negotiations are seen as a primary, preferred means of managing disputes?
- Second, what forms of professional support would institutionalised party negotiations ideally receive?

On one level, reservations about the institutionalisation of party negotiations seem unnecessary, even absurd. What we are seeing is no more than open recognition of an existing state of things – consensual settlement has always been the first option, and any movement to reclaim back further control and responsibility previously lost to lawyers and the public justice system must be a good thing. But, as we saw in Chapter Three, there have been strong currents of argument against extending the ambit of 'settlement'; and the real worry that bilateral negotiations may operate to the disadvantage of weaker parties in the numerous circumstances where significant imbalances of power may be present. So the growing fashion for party negotiations raises again the important issues around which the 1980s debate about 'informalism' developed (see p 50 ff above).

A number of points can be made about this growing institutionalisation of ADR processes, reflected in the panoply of agencies now developing in support of both party and representative negotiations. First, there are diverging views among mediators about professionalisation. Family mediators have from an early stage aspired to professional status, latterly seeking to realise this through the UK College of Family Mediators. Community and neighbourhood mediators working under the umbrella of Mediation UK have, on the whole, taken another direction, preferring the image of the caring bystander to that of the skilled professional.

At the same time, institutionalisation within these various fields has taken different forms. While core strands of community and family mediation have developed through service-based provision in the not-for-profit sector, represented by Mediation UK and National Family Mediation, commercial mediation has predictably developed primarily in the private sector. Here, alongside the pioneering provider, CEDR, small specialist groups like In Place of Strife, the Panel of Independent Mediators and Resolex have become prominent in the development and provision of ADR.

Lawyers and Alternative Dispute Resolution

These developments appear to represent an open challenge to the monopoly over dispute management hitherto claimed by lawyers acting in a representative capacity, placing direct pressure upon some deeply entrenched practices. Certainly, the arrival of the new professionals in dispute resolution has prompted some reaction from the legal profession. But, in general terms, moves on the part of the courts to assume closer control over litigation have been much more influential on lawyers, forcing them to give much more attention to their practices in pursuit of settlement. These moves, threatening the lawyer's control over client and settlement process, have prompted a reassessment of settlement practices including the now notorious culture of late-stage negotiations.

We have also noted how one specific response on the part of lawyers has been to remodel some areas of legal practice, introducing the label of 'alternative dispute resolution' as the trademark of these innovations. Some of these initiatives involve the development of specific technical procedures with the ostensible objective of drawing the client back into the decision-making process and accelerating settlement: the 'mini-trial', 'early neutral evaluation' (ENE), and 'the modified settlement conference' are some examples which we considered in Chapter Eight. We posed the question there whether these are 'real' aids to settlement or simply crisis management measures, designed to allay mounting consumer anxiety and dissatisfaction.

At the same time we noted that lawyers are moving to act as mediators, even claiming mediation as an established part of legal practice. So far this development has been primarily in the family and commercial spheres but there is every sign that it will become more widespread. These developments underline the importance of some of the general questions that we posed in Chapter Six:

- First, how far can the mediator appropriately go beyond providing a structural framework for negotiations?
- Second, can an advisory role be safely combined with impartial facilitation of negotiations?
- Third, should the mediator assume responsibility for the nature and quality of the outcome of mediated negotiations?
- Finally, can mediation safely be offered as an element of legal practice, or should it develop exclusively as an independent professional intervention with its own regulatory framework?

The Changing Nature of the Court

Parallel to the emergence of the new professionals, and the responsive action of lawyers in remodelling certain areas of professional practice, has been the progressive involvement of the judiciary in the sponsorship of settlement. While this form of judicial activity has an ancient pedigree in the civilian world, and goes back some decades in North America, it has been received and become entrenched in the rest of the common law world with astonishing speed and assurance over the last decade. As we have already noted, the cultural changes involved go beyond the process of litigation. In England, for example, the Pre-Action Protocols purport to reach out into, reshape and regulate conduct that had hitherto been seen as securely in the 'private' sphere. In the context of litigation itself, the new, concurrent aspirations to management and the sponsorship of settlement require us to understand the 'court' in entirely new terms. Historically foundational responsibilities for conduct of the trial and delivery of judgment have now receded into the background, postponed to the primary task of sponsoring and managing negotiations. We should not disguise the magnitude of the shift involved as we struggle to represent, for both ourselves and others, what a court 'is'.

- How should we respond to this growing readiness on the part of the courts to reach out into, and assume management of, what was formerly securely in the 'private' sphere?
- What has 'the court' become with this assumption of a diagnostic and managerial role, and its engagement in the active sponsorship of settlement?
- How do these new ambitions accord with sustaining the capacity to deliver authoritative third-party determinations?

C: The Future

This overall picture is presently changing too fast for any accurate forecast of what the civil justice system will look like a decade from now but some suggestive markers have already been laid down. While one strand of ADR represents a movement of escape, of resistance to lawyer domination, the historic resilience of lawyers is already revealed in the speed with which they have represented ADR as part of their own repertoire. ADR is already firmly recognised as something which lawyers do, a change reflected in the way 'ADR units' have been established in many large commercial law firms, in the widespread rebranding of litigation departments in the promotional literature and in the numbers of big city lawyers now claiming to be 'trained mediators'. Just as significant has been the welcome extended by the courts across the common law world.

While ADR's fugitive and polymorphous qualities may have ensured its ready adoption by the legal establishment, from the point of view of the commentator all of this presents a formidable task of reorientation. First, with the rediscovery of institutionalised mediation there is now a new domain clearly visible on the map of dispute processes. This field needs to be marked out and carefully explored. We have only begun to ask what kind of intervention mediation is. How is it different in its reach and ambition from established professional roles? What is going to be the relationship of this precariously established terrain occupied by the 'new professionals' to the adjacent areas of civil justice and legal representation? Second, the very identity of the lawyer is placed in question by the novel pretension to occupy non-aligned roles and to claim mediation as part of legal practice. Can those we have trusted as fierce partisans readily sustain this new hybrid persona? Beyond these reorientations, the most pressing requirement is to re-think what a court 'is'. The regime of intervention prescribed in the new Civil Procedure Rules clearly endorses and consolidates an already established trend towards court sponsorship of settlement. In encouraging judges to act as mediators, the Rules also signal a profound change in the mode of intervention historically practised by the English judiciary.

As noted above, the determination of lawyers that they are going to be mediators, and that mediation should become an established part of legal practice, has implications both for the nature of mediation and for the regulatory framework within which it develops. Here a dual future seems already foretold. The new professionals in dispute resolution seem broadly set upon developing mediation as a narrow, facilitative intervention, supportive of party decision-making. But in so far as mediation develops in parallel in the context of established legal practice, it is hard to see it retaining such confined objectives, concentrated around the support of communications between the parties. It is likely to evolve, rather, as an 'evaluative' intervention (lawyers are already using this term), more akin to specialist advisory and consultative processes.

A parallel dualism is threatened in the sphere of regulation. The Law Society and the Bar are already seeking detailed control over their members in the exercise of mediatory roles, rather than seeing this activity as something outside legal practice. This determination is already establishing a parallel regime of regulation alongside those evolving among the new professionals. This must be a serious complication as it will only be through the survival of the 'mediator' as an independent professional that distinctive practice standards and institutions of quality assurance will crystallise.

We have already argued that the novel determination of common law courts to act as sponsors of settlement represents an enormous shift when thought about in the context of existing understandings of what courts are and what they do. Reaching out as some of them do into the period before the trial, they considerably extend the involvement of the court in a domain hitherto occupied by the parties and their professional representatives alone. Old understandings about what is 'private' and what is 'public' in the sphere of dispute management have already become blurred with these developments, but the likely future evolution of processes around the courts remains uncertain. One possibility might be the gradual evolution of a new, relatively discrete phase of institutionalised settlement seeking, interposed between private negotiations and the commencement of litigation, with litigation itself becoming more narrowly focused on moving to trial and judgment. The sharp reduction in the number of starts in the civil courts since the new procedural regime was introduced perhaps in itself forecasts this outcome. Certainly, most lawyers are not comfortable for a court to be supervising their negotiations. This in itself suggests that the alternative possibility of the present hybrid process continuing in the long term is improbable. So, with the identity of the mediator, the lawyer and the court uncertain, further changes of a fundamental kind must, at least potentially, remain in prospect.

All of this is going on at a moment when the centrality of state law is itself under challenge on the wider scene. The now centuries-old dominance of the nation state is in the process of being displaced from 'above', both through the progressive entrenchment of larger political groupings (the European Union, etc) and through the overarching activities of multinational corporations. It is now widely argued that 'globalisation' brings with it the formation of new legal orders at a supra-national level (Teubner, 1997); and there is certainly a plethora of new court-like institutions appearing on the scene, uncoupled from the state and national laws. Will these new institutions mimic those at national level in their lately assumed identity as sponsors of settlement, or revert to the older tradition of authoritative determination? The fact that 'courts' continue to be constituted in this negotiated space at transnational level can be read either as a grand, imaginative leap or as a sad failure of institutional design.

Bibliography

Abel, R L (1973) 'A Comparative Theory of Dispute Institutions in Society', 8 *Law and Society Review* 2, pp 250–347.

(1979a) 'Western Courts in Non-western Settings: Patterns of Court Use in Colonial and Neo-colonial Africa', in S Burman and B Harrell-Bond (eds) *The Imposition of Law*, Academic Press, New York.

(1979b) 'Delegalization: A Critical, Review of its Ideology, Manifestations and Social Consequences', in Erhard Blankenburg et al (eds) *Alternative Rechtsformen und Alternativen zum Recht* 7, paper delivered at the Second National Conference on Critical Legal Studies, Madison, Wisconsin (1978).

(1982a) 'Introduction', in R L Abel (ed) *The Politics of Informal Justice, Volume 1: The American Experience*, Academic Press, New York.

(1982b) (ed) *The Politics of Informal Justice, Volume 1: The American Experience,* Academic Press, New York and London.

(1982c) 'The Contradictions of Informal Justice', in R L Abel (ed) *The Politics of Informal Justice, Volume 1: The American Experience*, Academic Press, New York.

(1982d) (ed) *The Politics of Informal Justice, Volume 2: Comparative Studies*, Academic Press, New York and London.

Abel-Smith, B and Stevens, R (1967) *Lawyers and the Courts*, Heinemann, London.

Astor, H and Chinkin, C (2002) *Dispute Resolution in Australia*, 2nd edn, Butterworths, Chatswood, NSW.

Auerbach, J S (1983) *Justice Without Law? Resolving Disputes Without Lawyers*, Oxford University Press, Oxford.

Austin, J (1955 [orig 1832]) *The Province of Jurisprudence Determined*, Weidenfeld and Nicolson, London.

Bailey, F G (1969) *Stratagems and Spoils*, Basil Blackwell, Oxford.

Barth, F (1959) *Political Leadership among the Swat Pathans*, The Athlone Press, London.

Barton, R F (1919) *The Kalingas: Their Institutions and Customary Law*, University of Chicago Press, Chicago.

Beldam, Lord Justice (1991) *A Report of the Committee on Alternative Dispute Resolution*, General Council of the Bar, October.

Bernstein, L (1993) 'Understanding the Limits of Court-Connected ADR: A Critique of the Federal Court-Annexed Arbitration Program', 141 *University of Pennsylvania Law Review* 6, pp 2169–2259.

Bevan, A (1992) *Alternative Dispute Resolution*, Sweet & Maxwell, London.

Black, J (1996) 'Constitutionalising Self-Regulation', 59 *Modern Law Review*, pp 24–55.

Bloch, M (1971) 'Councils Among the Merina of Madagascar', in A Richards and A Kuper (eds) *Councils in Action*, Cambridge University Press, Cambridge.

Bodde, D and Morris, C (1967) *Law in Imperial China*, Harvard University Press, Cambridge, Mass.

Bohannan, P (1957) *Justice and Judgment Among the Tiv*, Oxford University Press for the International African Institute, London.

Bok, Derek (1983) 'A Flawed System of Law and Practice Training', 33 *Journal of Legal Education*, pp 570–585.

Bottomley, A (1984) 'Resolving Family Disputes: A Critical Review', in M D A Freeman (ed) *State, Law and the Family: Critical Perspectives*, Tavistock Publications and Sweet & Maxwell, London and New York.

(1985) 'What is Happening in Family Law? A Feminist Critique of Conciliation', in J Brophy and C Smart (eds) *Women in Law*, Routledge & Kegan Paul, London.

Boulle, Laurence (1996) *Mediation: Principles, Process, Practice*, Butterworths, Sydney.

Brandt, P (1997) 'The Formation of the English Legal System, 1150–1400', in A Padoa-Schioppa (ed) *Legislation and Justice*, European Science Foundation, Clarendon Press, Oxford.

Brazil, Wayne (1986) 'Special Masters in Complex Cases: Extending the Judiciary or Reshaping Adjudication?', 53 *University of Chicago Law Review*, pp 394–423.

Broderick, Raymond J (1989) 'Court Annexed Compulsory Arbitration: It Works', 72 *Judicature* 4, pp 217–225.

Brown, H (1991) *Alternative Dispute Resolution*, a report prepared by H Brown for the Courts and Legal Services Committee, Law Society, Legal Practice Directorate, July 1991.

Brown, H J and Marriott, A L (1999) *ADR Principles and Practice*, 2nd edn, Sweet & Maxwell, London.

Burger, W E (1976) 'Agenda for 2000 AD – Need for Systematic Anticipation', 70 *Federal Rules Decisions*, pp 92–94.

(1982) 'Isn't There a Better Way', 68 *American Bar Association Journal*, pp 274–277.

Bush, R A B (1989) 'Efficiency and Protection or Empowerment and Recognition? The Mediator's Role and Ethnical Standards in Mediation', 41 *Florida Law Review*, 253–286.

Bush, R A Baruch and Folger, J P (1994) *The Promise of Mediation: Responding to Conflict Through Empowerment and Recognition*, Jossey-Bass Publishers, San Francisco.

Cappelletti, Mauro, and Garth, Bryant G (1978) *Access to Justice, Volume I: A World Survey*, Sijthoff & Noordhoff, Alphen aan den Rijn.

Castan, N (1983) 'The Arbitration of Disputes Under the "Ancien Regime"', in J Bossy (ed) *Disputes and Settlements*, Cambridge University Press, Cambridge.

Chornenki, Genevieve (1997) 'Mediating Commercial Disputes: Exchanging "power over" for "power with"', in Julie Macfarlane (ed) *Rethinking Disputes: The Mediation Alternative*, Cavendish Publishing, London.

Civil Justice on Trial – The Case for Change (1993) JUSTICE, London.

Clastres, P (1977) *Society Against the State: Essays in Political Anthropology*, R Hurley (trans), Blackwell, Oxford.

Cole, S D (1902) 'English Borough Courts', 18 *Law Quarterly Review*, pp 376–387.

Colosi, T (1983) 'Negotiation in the Public and Private Sectors', 27 *American Behavioural Scientist* 2, pp 229–253.

Comaroff, J and Roberts, S (1977) 'The Invocation of Norms in Dispute Settlement: The Tswana Case', in Ian Hamnett (ed) *Social Anthropology and Law*, Academic Press, London, New York, San Francisco.

(1981) *Rules and Processes*, University of Chicago Press, Chicago.

Condlin, R (1985) '"Cases on Both Sides": Patterns of Argument in Legal-Dispute Negotiation', 44 *Maryland Law Review*, pp 65–136.

Conley, John M and O'Barr, William M (1990) *Rules Versus Relationships: The Ethnography of Legal Discourse*, The University of Chicago Press, Chicago and London.

Crouch, R E (1989) 'The Dark Side of Mediation Still Unexplored', in American Bar Association, *Alternative Means of Family Dispute Resolution*, American Bar Association, Washington DC, p 329 et seq; also (1989) 4 *Fam Adv*, p 26 et seq.

Damaska, M R (1986) *The Faces of Justice and State Authority*, Yale University Press, New Haven and London.

Danzig, R (1973) 'Towards the Creation of a Complementary, Decentralised System of Criminal Justice', 26 *Stanford Law Review*, pp 1–26.

Davis, G (1988) *Partisans and Mediators*, Oxford University Press, Oxford.

Dawson, J P (1960) *A History of Lay Judges*, Harvard University Press, Cambridge, Mass.

Department for Constitutional Affairs (2004) *Judicial Statistics: Annual Report, 2003*, Department for Constitutional Affairs, London.

Dezalay, Yves and Garth, Bryant (1996) *Dealing in Virtue: International Commercial Arbitration and the Construction of a Transnational Legal Order*, The University of Chicago Press, Chicago and London.

Dickens, Charles (1994 (originally 1852–1853)) *Bleak House*, Penguin Books, Harmondsworth, Middlesex.

Dingwall, R and Greatbach, D (1993) 'Who is in Charge? Rhetoric and Evidence in the Study of Mediation', 15 *Journal of Social Welfare and Family Law*, pp 367–387.

Doo, Leigh-wai (1973) 'Dispute Settlement in Chinese-American Communities', 21 *American Journal of Comparative Law* 627, pp 652–654.

Douglas, A (1957) 'The Peaceful Settlement of Industrial and Inter-group Disputes', 1 *Journal of Conflict Resolution*, pp 69–81.

(1962) *Industrial Peacemaking*, Columbia University Press, New York.

Dworkin, R (1986) *Law's Empire*, Fontana, London.

Efron, Jack (1989) 'Alternatives to Litigation: Factors in Choosing', 52 *Modern Law Review*, pp 480–497.

Eidmann, D and Plett, K (1991) 'Non-judicial Dispute Processing in West Germany: the *Schiedsstellen* Contribution to the Resolution of Social Conflicts and their Interaction with the Official Legal System', in K J Mackie (ed) *A Handbook of Dispute Resolution*, Routledge and Sweet & Maxwell, London and New York.

Eisele, Thomas G (1991) 'The Case Against Court-Annexed ADR Programs', 75 *Judicature* 1, pp 34–40.

Elliott, D C (1996) 'Med/arb: Fraught with Danger or Ripe with Opportunity', 62 *Arbitration* 3, pp 175–183.

Evans-Pritchard, E (1940) *The Nuer*, Oxford University Press, Oxford.

Felstiner, W L F (1974) 'Influences of Social Organization on Dispute Processing', 9 *Law and Society Review*, pp 63–94.

(1975) 'Avoidance as Dispute Processing: an Elaboration', 9 *Law and Society Review*, pp 695–706.

Felstiner, W L F, Abel, R and Sarat, A (1980–1981) 'The Emergence and Transformation of Disputes: Naming, Blaming, Claiming etc.', 15, *Law and Society Review*, pp 631–654.

Fisher, R and Ury, W (1981) *Getting to Yes*, Houghton Mifflin, Boston, Mass.

Fisher, R, Ury, W and Patten, B (1991) *Getting to Yes*, 2nd edn, Penguin Books, New York.

Fiss, O M (1979) 'Forms of Justice: Forward, the Supreme Court 1978 Term', 92 *Harvard Law Review* 1, pp 1–58.

(1984) 'Against Settlement', 93 *Yale Law Journal*, pp 1073–1090.

(1985) 'Out of Eden', 94 *Yale Law Journal*, pp 1669–1673.

Fitzpatrick, P (1993) 'The Impossibility of Popular Justice', in S Engle Merry and N Milner (eds) *The Possibility of Popular Justice: A Case Study of Community Mediation in the United States*, University of Michigan Press, Ann Arbor.

Flood, J and Caiger, A (1993) 'Lawyers and Arbitration: the Juridification of Construction Disputes', in 'Special Issue – Dispute Resolution: Civil Justice and its Alternatives', 56 *Modern Law Review* 3 (May), pp 412–440.

Folberg, J and Taylor, A (1984) *Mediation*, Jossey-Bass, San Francisco.

Freeman, M D A (1984) 'Questioning the Delegalization Movement in Family Law: Do We Really Want a Family Court?', in J M Eekelaar and S N Katz (eds) *The Resolution of Family Conflict*, Butterworths, Toronto.

Fried, M (1967) *The Evolution of Political Society*, Random House, New York.

Fuller, L. (1963) 'Collective Bargaining and the Arbitrator', 18 *Wisconsin Law Review*, pp 3–47.

(1978) 'The Forms and Limits of Adjudication', 92 *Harvard Law Review*, pp 353–409.

Fuller, L and Randall, J D (1958) 'Professional Responsibility: Report of the Joint Conference of the ABA-AALS', 44 *American Bar Association Journal*, pp 1159–1162.

Fuller, Lon (1971) 'Mediation: its Forms and Functions', 44 *Southern California Law Review*, pp 305–339.

Galanter, M (1974) 'Why the "Haves" Come Out Ahead: Speculations on the Limits of Legal Change', 9 *Law and Society Review*, pp 95–160.

(1984) 'World of Deals: Using Negotiation to Teach Legal Process', 34 *Journal of Legal Education*, pp 268–276.

(1985) '"A Settlement Judge is not a Trial Judge": Judicial Mediation in the United States', 12 *Journal of Law and Society*, 1, pp 1–18.

(1986) 'The Emergence of the Judge as a Mediator in Civil Cases', 69 *Judicature*, pp 257–262.

(1994) 'Predators and Parasites: Lawyer Bashing and Civil Justice', 28 *Georgia Law Review* 3, pp 633–681.

Galanter, M and Cahill, M (1994) 'Most Cases Settle: Judicial Promotion and Regulation of Settlements', 46 *Stanford Law Review*, pp 1339–1391.

Garlock, J (1982) 'The Knights of Labor Courts: A Case Study of Popular Justice', in R L Abel (ed) *The Politics of Informal Justice, Volume 1: The American Experience*, Academic Press, New York.

Geertz, C (1980) *Negara: the Theatre State in Nineteenth Century Bali*, Princeton University Press, Princeton.

Genn, H G (1987) *Hard Bargaining: Out of Court Settlement in Personal Injury Actions*, Clarendon Press, Oxford.

(1999a) *Paths to Justice: What People Do and Think about Going to Law*, Hart, Oxford.

Genn, Hazel (1999b) *Mediation in Action: Resolving Civil Disputes without Trial*, Calouste Gulbenkian Foundation, London.

Gibbs, J L (1963) 'The Kpelle Moot', 33 *Africa*, pp 1–10.

Gifford, Donald (1985) 'A Context-Based Theory of Selection Strategy in Legal Negotiations', 46 *Ohio State Law Journal*, pp 41–94.

Gluckman, M (1955) *The Judicial Process Among the Barotse of Northern Rhodesia*, Manchester University Press, Manchester.

Goffman, E (1959) *The Presentation of Self in Everyday Life*, Doubelday Anchor Books, New York.

Goldberg, S B (1982) 'The Mediation of Grievances Under a Collective Bargaining Contract: An Alternative to Arbitration', 77 *Northwestern University Law Review*, pp 260–315.

Goldberg, S B, Green, E D and Sander, F E A (1985) *Dispute Resolution*, Little, Brown and Company, Boston, Mass.

Goldberg, S B, Sander, F E A and Rodgers, N H (eds) (1992) *Dispute Resolution: Negotiation, Mediation and Other Processes*, 2nd edn, Little, Brown & Co, Boston, Toronto and London.

Goldberg, S B, Sander, F E A, Rogers, N H and Cole S R (2003) *Dispute Resolution: Negotiation, Mediation, and Other Processes*, 4th edn, Aspen, New York.

Graham, Louise E (1992–1993) 'Implementing Custody Mediation in Family Courts: Some Comments on the Jefferson County Family Court Experience', *Kentucky Law Journal*, pp 1107–1131.

Greenhouse, C J (1986) *Praying for Justice: Faith, Order, and Community in an American Town*, Cornell University Press, Ithaca, New York.

Greenhouse, Carol (1989) 'Interpreting American Litigiousness', in June Starr and Jane Collier (eds), *History and Power in the Study of Law: New Directions in Legal Anthropology*, Cornell University Press, Ithaca, New York.

Greenidge, A H J (1971, orig 1901) *The Legal Procedure of Cicero's Time*, Rothman Reprints, New Jersey (orig Augustus M Kelley, New York).

Griffith, J A G (1997) *The Politics of the Judiciary*, 5th edn, Fontana, London.

Grillo, T (1991) 'The Mediation Alternative: Process Dangers for Women', 100 *Yale Law Journal*, pp 1545–1610.

Gulliver, P H (1963) *Social Control in an African Society, A Study of the Arusha, Agricultural Masai of Northern Tanganyika*, Boston University Press, Boston, Mass.

(1971) *Neighbours and Networks: The Idiom of Kinship in Social Action Among the Ndendeuli of Tanzania*, University of California Press, Berkeley, Calif.

(1979) *Disputes and Negotiations: A Cross-Cultural Perspective*, Academic Press, New York and London.

Habermas, J (1979) *Communication and the Evolution of Society*, Beacon Press, Boston, Mass.

([1981], 1987) *The Theory of Communicative Action*, Vol. 2, T McCarthy (trans), Polity Press, Cambridge.

Harlow, C and Rawlings, R (1997) *Law and Administration*, 2nd edn, Butterworths, London, pp 401–404.

Harrington, C B (1985) *Shadow Justice: the Ideology and Institutionalization of Alternatives to Court*, Greenwood Press, Westport, Conn.

(1992) 'Delegalisation Reform Movements: A Historical analysis', in Richard Abel (ed), *The Politics of Informal Justice, Volume 1: The American Experience*, Academic Press, New York.

Hart, H L A (1961) *The Concept of Law*, Clarendon Press, Oxford.

Haynes, J (1993) *The Fundamentals of Family Mediation*, Old Bailey Press, London.

Haynes, John M (1992) 'Mediation and Therapy: An Alternative View', 10 *Mediation Quarterly*, pp 21–34.

Henderson, D (1996) 'Mediation Success: An Empirical Analysis', 11 *Ohio State Journal of Dispute Resolution*, pp 105–148.

Hobbes, T (1651) *Leviathan: or, The Matter, forme and power of a common-wealth ecclesiasticall and civill*, for Andrew Crooke at the Green Dragon in St Pauls Church-Yard, London.

Hofrichter, Richard (1982) 'Neighbourhood Justice and the Social Control Problems of American Capitalism: A Perspective', in Richard L Abel (ed), *The Politics of Informal Justice, Volume 1: The American Experience*, Academic Press, New York and London.

Huang, P C C (1996) *Civil Justice in China: Representation and Practice in the Qing*, Stanford University Press, Stanford, Calif.

Ingelby, R (1993) 'Court-Sponsored Mediation: The Case Against Mandatory Participation', 56 *Modern Law Review* 3 (May), pp 441–451.

Johnston, R F (1910) *Lion and Dragon in Northern China*, John Murray, London.

Johnstone, Q (1967) *Lawyers and their Work: An Analysis of the Legal Profession in the United States and England*, Bobbs-Merrill, New York.

Kelly, J B and Duyree, M A (1995) 'Women's and Men's Views of Mediation in Voluntary and Mandatory Mediation Settings', 30 *Family and Conciliation Courts Review* 1, pp 35–49.

Kelly, J M (1966) *Roman Litigation*, Clarendon Press, Oxford.

Kim, A S (1994) 'Rent-a-Judge and the Cost of Selling Justice', 44 *Duke Law Journal*, pp 166–199.

Kirsh, H (1971) 'Conflict Resolution and the Legal Culture: A Study of the Rabbinical Court', 9 *Osgoode Hall Law Journal*, pp 335–357.

Koch, K (1974) *War and Peace in Jalemo*, Harvard University Press, Cambridge, Mass.

Kovach, K L and Love, L P (1998) 'Mapping Mediation: The Risks of Riskin's Grid', 3 *Harvard Negotiation Law Review*, pp 71–110.

Kritzer, H (1986) 'Adjudication to Settlement: Shading in the Grey', 70 *Judicature* 3, pp 161–165

(1991) *Let's Make a Deal: Understanding the Negotiation Process in Ordinary Litigation*, University of Wisconsin Press, Madison, Wisconsin.

Lambros, T D (1993) 'The Summary Trial: An Effective Aid to Settlement', 77 *Judicature* 1, 6, pp 6–8.

Leacock, E B and Lee, R B (eds) (1982) *Politics and History in Band Societies*, Cambridge University Press, Cambridge.

Leng, S C (1967) *Justice in Communist China: A Survey of the Judicial System in Communist China*, Oceana Publications, Dobbs Ferry, New York.

Lieberman, Jethro and Henry, James F (1986) 'Lessons from the Alternative Dispute Resolution Movement', 53 *University of Chicago Law Review*, pp 424–439.

Llewellyn, K and Hoebel, E A (1941) *The Cheyenne Way: Conflict and Case Law: Conflict and Case Law in Primitive Jurisprudence*, University of Oklahoma Press, Norman, Oklahoma.

Locke, J (1690) *Two Treatises of Government: in the former, the false principles and foundation of Sir Robert Filmer, and his followers, are detected and overthrown. The latter is an essay concerning the true original, extent, and end of civil-government*, printed for Awnsham Churchill, London. Version cited, Intro by W S Carpenter, Dent, London, 1924.

Longan, E (1994) 'Bureaucratic Justice Meets ADR: The Emerging Role for Magistrates as Mediators', 73 *Nebraska Law Review*, pp 712–755.

Lord Chancellor's Department (1999) *Judicial Statistics: Annual Report, 1998*, Lord Chancellor's Department, London.

Loughlin, M (2003) *The Idea of Public Law*, Oxford, University Press, Oxford.

Love, L (1997) 'The Top Ten Reasons Why Mediators Should Not Evaluate', 24 *Florida State University Law Review*, pp 937–948.

Lowenthal, G (1982) 'A General Theory of Negotiation Process', 69 *University of Kansas Law Review*, pp 69–114.

Lowy, M J (1978) 'A Good Name is Worth More than the Money: Strategies of Court Use in Urban Ghana', in L Nader and H F Todd (eds) *The Disputing Process – Law in Ten Societies*, Columbia University Press, New York.

Lubman, S (1967) 'Mao and Mediation: Politics and Dispute Resolution in Communist China', 55 *California Law Review*, pp 1284–1359.

(1973) 'Judicial Work in T'aihang', 6 *Chinese Law and Government* 3, pp 12–17.

MacCormick, N (1981) *HLA Hart*, Stanford University Press, Stanford.

Mackie, K (ed) (1991) *A Handbook of Dispute Resolution: ADR in Action*, Routledge and Sweet & Maxwell, London and New York.

(2002) *A Handbook of Dispute Resolution: ADR in Action*, 2nd edn, Routledge and Sweet & Maxwell, London and New York.

Maine, Sir H S (1861) *Ancient Law: its connection with the early history of society and its relation to modern ideas*, J Murray, London.

(1883) *Dissertations on Early Law and Custom*, John Murray, London.

Malinowski, B (1926) *Crime and Custom in Savage Society.* Kegan Paul, Trench & Trubner, London.

Markesinis, B (1990) 'Litigation-Mania in England, Germany and the USA: Are We So Very Different?', 49 *Cambridge Law Journal* 2, pp 233–276.

McEwen, Craig A and Maiman, Richard J (1981) 'Small Claims Mediation in Maine: An Empirical Assessment', 33 *Maine Law Review*, pp 237–268.

McThenia, A W and Shaffer, T L (1985) 'For Reconciliation', 94 *Yale Law Journal*, pp 1660–1668.

'Mediation Projects in London', at www.onwebsite.co.uk/on.Medn.html.

Menkel-Meadow, C (1984) 'Towards Another View of Legal Negotiation. The Structure of Problem Solving', 31 *UCLA Law Review*, pp 754–842.

(1993) 'Lawyer Negotiations: Theories and Realities – What We Learn from Mediation', in 'Special Issue – Dispute Resolution: Civil Justice and its Alternatives', 56 *Modern Law Review* 3 (May), pp 361–379.

(1996) 'Is Mediation the Practice of Law?' 14 *Alternatives to the High Costs of Litigation* 5, pp 57–61.

(1997) 'When Dispute Resolution Begets Disputes of its Own: Conflicts Among Dispute Professionals', 44 *UCLA Law Review*, pp 1871–1933.

(1999) 'Ethics and Professionalism in Non-Adversarial Lawyering', 27 *Florida State University Law Review*, pp 153–192.

(2001) 'Ethics in ADR: The Many "C"s of Professional Responsibility and Dispute Resolution', 28 *Fordham Urban Law Journal*, pp 979–990.

(2003) *Dispute Processing and Conflict Resolution: Theory, Practice and Policy*, (Aldershot: Ashgate, and Burlington: Dartmouth).

Merry, S E and Milner, N (eds) (1993) *The Possibility of Popular Justice: A Case Study of Community Mediation in the United States*, University of Michigan Press, Ann Arbor.

Merry, S Engle (1993) 'Sorting Out Popular Justice', in S Engle Merry and N Milner (eds) *The Possibility of Popular Justice: A Case Study of Community Mediation in the United States*, University of Michigan Press, Ann Arbor.

Merry, Sally Engle and Milner, Neal (1993) 'Introduction' to Sally Engle Merry and Neal Milner (eds), *The Possibility of Popular Justice: A Case Study of Community Mediation in the United States*, University of Michigan Press, Ann Arbor.

Milhauser, Marguerite (1987) 'The Unspoken Resistance to Alternative Dispute Resolution', 3 *Negotiation Journal*, pp 29–35.

Mnookin, R and Kornhauser, L (1979) 'Bargaining in the Shadow of the Law: The Case of Divorce', 88 *Yale Law Journal*, pp 950–997.

Mnookin, Robert and Gibson, Ronald (1994) 'Disputing through Agents: Co-operation and Conflict Between Lawyers in Litigation', 94 *Columbia Law Review* 509.

Moore, S F (1995) 'Imperfect Communications', in P Caplan (ed) *Understanding Disputes: The Politics of Argument*, Berg Publishers, Oxford and Providence, USA.

Morris, Catherine (1997) 'The Trusted Mediator: Ethics and Interaction in Mediation', in Julie Macfarlane (ed), *Rethinking Disputes: The Mediation Alternative*, Cavendish Publishing, London.

Murphy, W T and Roberts, S (1987) 'Introduction' to Special Issue of *Modern Law Review*, 'Legal Scholarship in the Common Law World', 50 *Modern Law Review*, pp 677–687.

Murray, D E (1961) 'Genesis and Development of Equitable Procedures and Remedies in the Anglo-Saxon Laws and in the English Local and Fair Courts and Borough Customs', 3 *Sydney Law Review*, pp 451–462.

Murray, J S, Rau, A S and Sherman, E F (1989) *Processes of Dispute Resolution: The Role of Lawyers*, Foundation Press, Westbury, New York.

(1996) *Processes of Dispute Resolution: The Role of Lawyers*, 2nd edn, Foundation Press, Westbury, New York.

Mustill, Lord (1989) 'Arbitration: History and Background', 6 *Journal of International Arbitration*, pp 43–56.

Nader, L (1965) 'The Anthropological Study of Law', Special Supplement to 67 *American Anthropologist*, pp 3–32.

(1986) 'The Recurrent Dialectic Between Legality and its Alternatives: The Limits of Binary Thinking', 136 *University of Pennsylvania Law Review*, pp 621–645.

(1990) *Harmony Ideology: Justice and Control in a Zapotec Mountain Village*, Stanford University Press, Stanford.

(2002) *The Life of the Law: Anthropological Projects*, University of California Press, Berkeley.

Newman, P (1994) 'Mediation-Arbitration (MedArb): Can it Work Legally?', 60 *Arbitration* 3, 173, pp 174–176.

Palmer, M (1987) 'The Surface-Subsoil from Divided Ownership in Late Imperial China: Some Examples from the New Territories of Hong Kong', 21 *Modern Asian Studies* 1, pp 1–119.

(1988) 'The Revival of Mediation in the People's Republic of China: (1) Extra-judicial Mediation', in W E Butler (ed) *Yearbook on Socialist Legal Systems 1987*, Transnational Books, New York, Dobbs Ferry.

(1989) 'The Revival of Mediation in the People's Republic of China: (2) Judicial Mediation', in W E Butler (ed) *Yearbook on Socialist Legal Systems 1988*, Transnational Books, New York, Dobbs Ferry.

Parmiter, G M (1981) 'Bristol In-Court Conciliation Procedure', *Law Society Gazette*, 25 February.

Posner, R (1986) 'The Summary Jury Trial and other Alternative Methods of Dispute Resolution: Some Cautionary Observations', 53 *University of Chicago Law Review* 366, pp 366–393.

Pospisil, L (1958) *Kapauku Papuans and their Law*, Yale University Press, New Haven.

Pound, Roscoe (1906) 'The Causes of Popular Dissatisfaction with the Administration of Justice', 29 *American Bar Association Report* 1, pp 395–417.

Prigoff, Michael L (1990) 'No: An Unreasonable Burden', 76 *American Bar Association Journal*, pp 51.

Princen, T (1992) *Intermediaries in International Conflict*, Princeton University Press, Princton, NJ.

Raiffa, H (1982) *The Art and Science of Negotiation*, Harvard University Press, Cambridge, Mass.

Rappaport, Roy A (1967) *Pigs for the Ancestors: Ritual in the Ecology of a New Guinea People*, Yale University Press, New Haven and London.

Rau, A S, Sherman, E F and Peppet, Scott R (2002) *Processes of Dispute Resolution: The Role of Lawyers*, 3rd edn, Foundation Press, Westbury, New York.

Read, J S and Morris, H F (1972) *Indirect Rule and the Search for Justice: Essays in East African Legal History*, Oxford University Press, Oxford.

Redfern, A and Hunter, M (2004) *Law and Practice of International Commercial Arbitration*, 4th edn, Sweet & Maxwell, London.

Report by the Independent Working Party of the Bar Council and the Law Society (the Heilbron-Hodge Report), *Civil Justice on Trial – The Case for Change*, June 1993.

Riskin, L L and Westbrook, J E (1987) *Dispute Resolution and Lawyers*, West Publishing Company, St Paul, Minn.

(1997) *Dispute Resolution and Lawyers*, 2nd edn, West Publishing Company, St Paul, Minn.

Riskin, Leonard (1994) 'Mediator Orientations, Strategies and Techniques', 12 *Alternatives*, pp 111–114.

Roberts, M (1992) 'Systems or Selves: Some Ethical Issues in Family Mediation', 10 *Mediation Quarterly*, pp 3–19.

(1997) *Mediation in Family Disputes: Principles of Practice*, 2nd edn, Arena, Aldershot.

(2005) 'Family Mediation: The Development of the Regulatory Framework in the United Kingdom', 22 *Conflict Resolution Quarterly* 4, pp 509–526.

Roberts, S (1993) 'Alternative Dispute Resolution and Civil Justice: An Unresolved Relationship', 56 *Modern Law Review*, pp 452–470.

(1994) 'Re-Exploring the Pathways to Decision Making', 12 *Law in Context*, pp 9–27.

(1997) 'The Path of Negotiations', in M D A Freeman (ed) *Current Legal Problems 1996*, Oxford University Press, Oxford.

Roberts, Simon (1983) 'Mediation in Family Disputes', 46 *Modern Law Review*, pp 337–357.

Röhl, K F (1983) *The Judge as Mediator*, Dispute Processing Research Program, Working Paper 1983–89, University of Wisconsin-Madison Law School, Madison, Wisconsin.

Rosenberg, Joshua and Folberg, H Jay (1994) 'Alternative Dispute Resolution: An Empirical Analysis', 46 *Stanford Law Review*, pp 1487–1551.

Sachs, Albie (1984) 'Changing the Terms of the Debate: A Visit to a Popular Tribunal in Mozambique', 28 *Journal of African Law* 1 and 2, pp 99–106.

Sahlins, M (1965) 'On the Sociology of Primitive Exchange', in Michael Banton (ed) *The Relevance of Models for Social Anthropology*, Association of Social Anthropologists Monograph No 1, Tavistock, London.

Sainsbury, R and Genn, H (1995) 'Access to Justice; Lessons from Tribunals', in A A S Zuckerman and R Cranston (eds) *Reform of Civil Procedure: Essays on 'Access to Justice'*, Clarendon Press, Oxford.

Sander, F E A (1976) 'Varieties of Dispute Processing', 70 *Federal Rules Decisions*, pp 111–134.

(1985) 'Alternative Methods of Dispute Resolution: An Overview', 37 *University of Florida Law Review* 1, pp 11–13.

Sander, Frank E A (1985) 'Alternative Dispute Resolution in the United States: An Overview', in American Bar Association (ed), *Justice for a Generation*, West Publishing Company, St Paul, Minnesota, pp 253–261.

Santos, B de Sousa (1980) 'Law and Community: The Changing Nature of State Power in Late Capitalism', 8 *International Journal of The Sociology of Law* 397, republished in a revised form in *The Politics of Informal Justice*.

(1982a) 'Law and Community: the Changing Nature of State Power in Late Capitalism', in R L Abel (ed) *The Politics of Informal Justice, Volume 1: The American Experience*, Academic Press, New York.

(1982b) 'Law and Revolution in Portugal Community: the Experiences of Popular Justice after the 25th of April 1974', in R L Abel (ed) *The Politics of Informal Justice, Volume 2: Comparative Studies*, Academic Press, New York.

(2000) 'Law and Democracy: (Mis)trusting the Global Reform of Courts', in Jane Jenson and Boaventura De Sousa Santos (eds), *Globalizing Institutions: Case Studies in Regulation and Innovation*, Ashgate, Aldershot.

Sarat, A and Felstiner, W L F (1988) 'Law and Social Relations: Vocabularies of Motive in Lawyer/Client Interaction', 22 *Law and Society Review*, pp 737–769.

Sarkin, J (2001) 'The Tension Between Justice and Reconciliation in Rwanda: Politics, Human Rights, Due Process and the Role of the Gacaca Courts in Dealing with Genocide', 45 *Journal of African Law* 2, pp. 143–159.

Schapera, I (1943) *Tribal Legislation among the Tswana of the Bechuanaland Protectorate*, Athlone Press, London.

(1956) *Government and Politics in Tribal Societies*, Watts, London.

Schwarz, B (1957) 'On Attitudes Toward Law in China', in M Katz (ed) *Government Under Law and the Individual*, American Council of Learned Societies, Washington, DC.

Shah-Kazemi, S N (2000) 'Cross-Cultural Mediation: A Critical View of the Dynamics of Culture in Family Disputes', 14 *International Journal of Law Policy and the Family*, pp 302–325.

Shapiro, M (1981) *Courts: A Comparative and Political Analysis,* The University of Chicago Press, Chicago and London.

Shihata, I F J (1995) 'Legal Framework for Development: The World Bank's Role in Legal and Judicial Reform', in M Rowat, W Malik and D Maria (eds) *Judicial Reform in Latin America and the Caribbean*, The World Bank, Washington.

Silberman, Linda (1989) 'Judicial Adjuncts Revisited: the Proliferation of Ad Hoc Procedure', 137 *University of Pennsylvania Law Review*, pp 2131–2178.

Simmel, G ([1908], 1955) Conflict, K H Wolff (trans), The Free Press, Glencoe, Ill.

([1908], 1950) *The Sociology of Georg Simmel*, K H Wolff (trans), Free Press, Glencoe, Ill.

Singer, R (1991) *Settling Disputes*, Westview Press, Boulder, Colo.

Smith, R (ed) (1996) *Achieving Civil Justice: Appropriate Dispute Resolution for the 1990s*, Legal Action Group, London.

Spencer, J M and Zammit, J P (1976) 'Mediation-Arbitration: A Proposal for Private Resolution of Disputes between Divorced or Separated Parents', *Duke Law Journal*, pp 911–939.

Sprenkel, S van der (1962) *Legal Institutions in Manchu China*, Athlone Press, London.

Stedman, Barbara Epstein (1996) 'Multi-option Justice at the Middlesex Multi-Door Courthouse', in Roger Smith (ed), *Achieving Civil Justice: Appropriate Dispute Resolution for the 1990s*, Legal Action Group, London.

Stein, P (1984) *Legal Institutions: the Development of Dispute Settlement*, Butterworths, London.

(1999) *Roman Law in European History*, Cambridge University Press, Cambridge.

Stenelo, L-G (1972) *Mediation in International Negotiations*, Studentlitteratur, Lund.

Stevens, C M (1963) *Strategy and Collective Bargaining Negotiations*, McGraw-Hill, New York.

Teubner, G (1983) 'Substantive and Reflexive Elements in Modern Law', 17 *Law and Society Review* 239.

(1997) *Global Law Without a State*, Dartmouth, Aldershot.

Thornquist, L J (1989) 'The Active Judge in Pretrial Settlement: Inherent Authority Gone Awry', 25 *Willamette Law Review* 4, pp 743–775.

Tully, J (1993) *An Approach to Political Philosophy: Locke in Contexts*, Cambridge University Press, Cambridge.

Turnbull, C M (1966) *Wayward Servants*, Eyre & Spottiswode, London.

Turner, V (1957) *Schism and Continuity in an African Society: A Study of Ndembu Village Life*, Manchester University Press, Manchester.

Van Caenegem, R C (1988) *The Birth of the English Common Law*, Cambridge University Press, Cambridge.

Van Wezel Stone, K (2001) 'Dispute Resolution in the Boundaryless Workplace', 16 *Ohio State Journal of Dispute Resolution*, pp. 467–471.

Verkuil, P R (1975) 'The Ombudsman and the Limits of the Adversary System', 75 *Columbia Law Review*, pp 845–856.

Wang, L H (1959) *The Traditional Chinese Clan Rules*, J J Augustin, New York.

Weber, M ([1917], 1978) *Economy and Society*, G Roth and C Wittich (eds), E Fischoff et al (trans), Bedminster Press, New York.

White, James (1980) 'Machiavelli and the Bar: Ethical Limitations on Lying in Negotiation', *American Bar Foundation Research Journal*, pp 926–938.

Wiegand, Shirley (1996) 'A Just and Lasting Peace: Supplanting Mediation with the Ombuds Model', 12 *Ohio State Journal on Dispute Resolution* 1, pp 95–144.

Williams, G R (1983) *Legal Negotiation and Settlement*, West Publishing, St Paul, Minn.

Woodburn, J (1972) 'Ecology, Nomadic Movement and the Composition of the Local Group among Hunters and Gatherers: an East African Example and its Implications', in P J Uko, R Tringham and G W Dimbleby (eds), *Man, Settlement and Urbanism*, Duckworth, London.

Woodley, A E (1995) 'Saving the Summary Jury Trial: A Proposal to Halt the Flow of Litigation and End the Uncertainties', 1995 *Journal of Dispute Resolution*, pp 213–298.

Woolf, Lord (1995) *Access to Justice: Interim Report to the Lord Chancellor on the Civil Justice System of England and Wales*, HMSO, London.

(1995) *Interim Report to the Lord Chancellor on the Civil Justice System in England and Wales*, Lord Chancellor's Department, London.

(1996) *Access to Justice: Final Report to the Lord Chancellor on the Civil Justice System of England and Wales*, HMSO, London.

Index

Lightning Source UK Ltd.
Milton Keynes UK
01 April 2011

170210UK00001B/95/P